the Unofficial Guide® to

the Best RV and Tent Campgrounds in California and the West

Arizona, California, Nevada & Utah

Other Titles in the Unofficial Guide
Best RV and Tent Campgrounds Series

Florida & the Southeast

Great Lakes States

Mid-Atlantic States

The Northeast

Northwest & Central Plains

Southwest & South Central Plains

U.S.A.

Other Unofficial Guides

the Unofficial Guide® to

the Best RV and Tent Campgrounds in California and the West

1st Edition

Arizona, California,
Nevada & Utah

Joel Grossman & Christopher Brooks

Hungry Minds™

Best-Selling Books • Digital Downloads • e-Books • Answer Networks • e-Newsletters
Branded Web Sites • e-Learning

New York, NY • Indianapolis, IN • Cleveland, OH

Please note that prices fluctuate in the course of time, and travel information changes under the impact of many factors that influence the travel industry. We therefore suggest that you write or call ahead for confirmation when making your travel plans. Every effort has been made to ensure the accuracy of information throughout this book and the contents of this publication are believed correct at the time of printing. Nevertheless, the publishers cannot accept responsibility for errors or omissions or for changes in details given in this guide or for the consequences of any reliance on the information provided by the same. Assessments of attractions and so forth are based upon the author's own experience and therefore, descriptions given in this guide necessarily contain an element of subjective opinion, which may not reflect the publisher's opinion or dictate a reader's own experience on another occasion. Readers are invited to write to the publisher with ideas, comments, and suggestions for future editions.

Your safety is important to us, so we encourage you to stay alert and be aware of your surroundings. Keep a close eye on cameras, purses, and wallets, all favorite targets of thieves and pickpockets.

Published by Hungry Minds, Inc.
909 Third Avenue
New York, NY 10022

Copyright © 2002 by Bob Sehlinger

Produced by Menasha Ridge Press
COVER DESIGN BY MICHAEL J. FREELAND
INTERIOR DESIGN BY MICHELE LASEAU

ISBN 0-7645-6256-8

ISSN 1536-9641

Manufactured in the United States of America

10 9 8 7 6 5 4 3 2

Contents

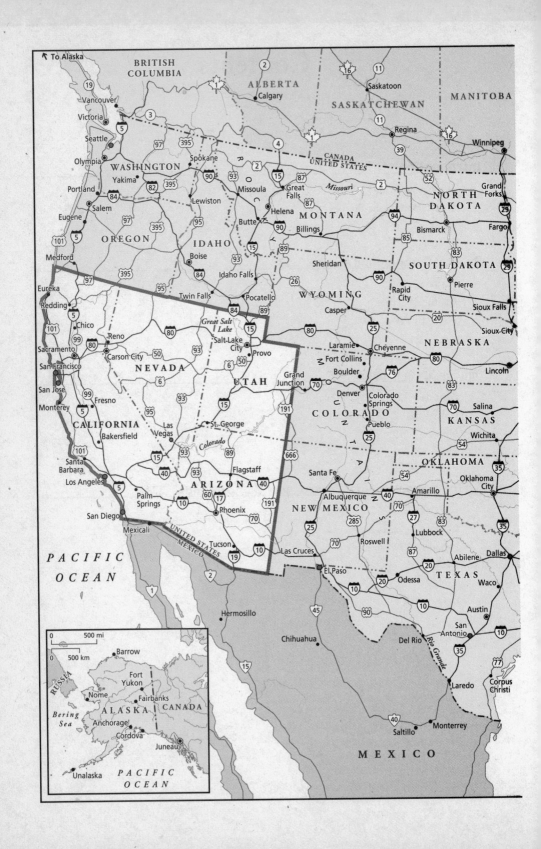

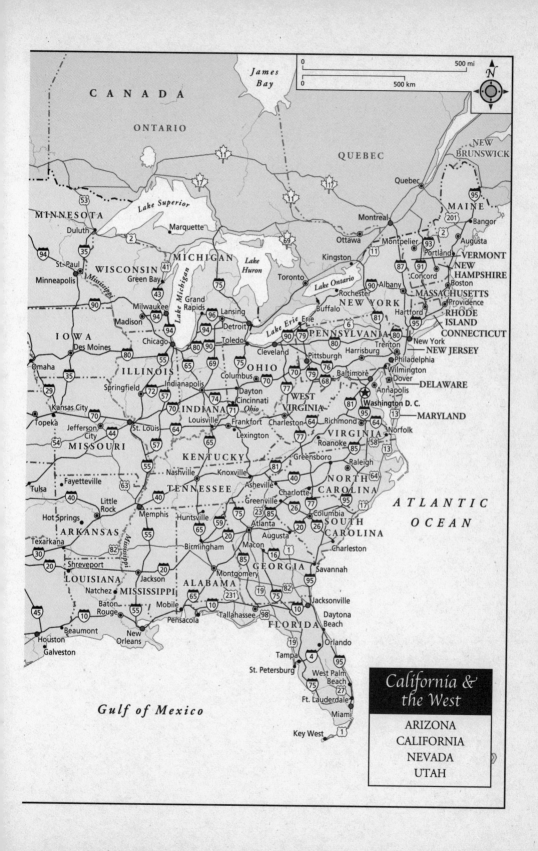

Introduction

Why Unofficial?

The material in this guide has not been edited or in any way reviewed by the campgrounds profiled. In this "unofficial" guide we represent and serve you, the consumer. By way of contrast with other campground directories, no ads were sold to campgrounds, and no campground paid to be included. Through our independence, we're able to offer you the sort of objective information necessary to select a campground efficiently and with confidence.

Why Another Guide to Campgrounds?

We developed *The Unofficial Guide to the Best RV and Tent Campgrounds in California and the West* because we recognized that campers are as discriminating about their choice of campgrounds as most travelers are about their choice of hotels. As a camper, you don't want to stay in every campground along your route. Rather, you prefer to camp only in the best. A comprehensive directory with limited information on each campground listed does little to help you narrow your choices. What you need is a reference that tells you straight out which campgrounds are the best, and that supplies detailed information, collected by independent inspectors, that differentiates those campgrounds from all of the also-rans. This is exactly what *The Unofficial Guide to the Best RV and Tent Campgrounds* delivers.

The Choice Is All Yours

Life is short, and life is about choices. You can stay in a gravel lot, elbow to elbow with other campers, with tractor-trailers roaring by just beyond the fence, or with this guide, you can spend the night in a roomy, shaded site, overlooking a sparkling blue lake. The choice is yours.

The authors of this guide have combed the Western states inspecting and comparing hundreds of campgrounds. Their objective was to create a hit parade of the very best, so that no matter where you travel, you'll never have to spend another night in a dumpy, gravel lot.

The best campgrounds in each state are described in detail in individual profiles so you'll know exactly what to expect. In addition to the fully profiled campgrounds, we provide a Supplemental Directory of Campgrounds that lists hundreds of additional properties that are quite adequate, but that didn't make the cut for the top 350 in the guide. Thus, no matter where you are, you'll have plenty of campgrounds to choose from. None of the campgrounds appearing in this guide, whether fully profiled or in the supplemental list, paid to be included. Rather, each earned its place by offering a superior product. Period.

Letters, Comments, and Questions from Readers

Many who use the Unofficial Guides write to us with questions, comments, and reports of their camping experiences. We appreciate all such input, both positive and critical. Readers' comments are frequently incorporated into revised editions of the Unofficial Guides and have contributed immeasurably to their improvement. Please write to:

The Unofficial Guide to the Best RV and Tent Campgrounds
P.O. Box 43673
Birmingham, AL 35243
UnofficialGuides@menasharidge.com

For letters sent through the mail, please put your return address on both your letter and envelope; the two sometimes become separated. Also include your phone number and email address if you are available for a possible interview.

How to Use This Guide

Using this guide is quick and easy. We begin with this introduction followed by "Campground Awards," a list of the best campgrounds for RVers, tenters, families, and more. Then we profile the best 350 campgrounds in Arizona, California, Nevada, and Utah. Next is a supplemental list of hundreds of additional campgrounds including details about prices, hookups, and more. Bringing up the rear is an alphabetical index of all campgrounds included in the guide.

Both the profiled section and the supplemental directory are ordered alphabetically, first by state and then by city. To see what campgrounds are available:

- Find the section covering the state in question.

- Within that section, look up the city alphabetically.

- Under the city, look up the campgrounds alphabetically.

You can choose and locate campgrounds in four different ways.

1. **Use the Map** If a city appears with a black, solid bullet on our map, at least one of our profiled or listed campgrounds will be located there. The converse is also the case: if the city has a hollow, outlined bullet, you can assume that we do not cover any campgrounds in that city.

2. **Check the Campground Profiles** In the section where we profile campgrounds, look up any city where you hope to find a campground. If the city isn't listed, it means we do not profile any campgrounds there.

3. **Check the Supplemental Directory of Campgrounds** Check for the same city in the supplemental listings.

4. **Use the Index** If you want to see if a specific campground is profiled or listed in the guide, look up the name of the campground in the alphabetical index at the back of the book.

When looking up campgrounds, remember that the best campgrounds are found in the profiled section; always check there first before turning to the Supplemental Directory of Campgrounds.

Understanding the Profiles

Each profile has seven important sections:

Campground Name, Address, and Contact Information   In addition to the street address, we also provide phone and fax numbers as well as website and email addresses.

Ratings   Using the familiar one- to five-star rating with five stars being best, we offer one overall rating for RV campers and a second overall rating for tent campers. The overall rating for each type of camper is based on a rough weighted average of the following eight individually rated categories:

Category	Weight
Beauty	15%
Site Privacy	10%
Site Spaciousness	10%
Quiet	15%
Security	13%
Cleanliness/upkeep	13%
Insect Control	10%
Facilities	14%

Beauty   This rates the natural setting of the campground in terms of its visual appeal. The highest ratings are reserved for campgrounds where the beauty of the campground can be enjoyed and appreciated both at individual campsites and at the campground's public areas. Views, vistas, landscaping, and foliage are likewise taken into consideration.

Site Privacy   This category rates the extent to which the campsites are set apart and/or in some way buffered (usually by trees and shrubs) from adjacent or nearby campsites. The farther campsites are from one another the better. This rating also reflects how busy the access road to the campsites is in terms of traffic. Campgrounds that arrange their sites on a number of cul-de-sacs, for example, will offer quieter sites than a campground where the sites are situated off of a busy loop or along a heavily traveled access road.

Site Spaciousness   This rates the size of the campsite. Generally, the larger the better.

Quiet   This rating indicates the relative quietness of the campground. There are three key considerations. The first is where the campground is located. Campgrounds situated along busy highways or in cities or towns are usually noisier, for example, than rural or wilderness campgrounds removed from major thoroughfares. The second consideration relates to how noise is managed at the campground. Does the campground forbid playing of radios or enforce a "quiet time" after a certain hour? Is there someone on site at night to respond to complaints about other campers being loud or unruly at a late hour? Finally, the rating considers the extent to which trees, shrubs, and the natural topography serve to muffle noise within the campground.

Security   This rating reflects the extent (if any) to which management monitors the campground during the day and night. Physical security is also included in this rating: Is the campground fenced? Is the campground gated? If so, is the gate manned? Generally, a campground located in a city or along a busy road is more exposed to thieves or vandals than a more remote campground, and should more actively supervise access.

Cleanliness   This rates the cleanliness, serviceability, and state of repair of the campground, including grounds, sites, and facilities.

Insect Control   This rating addresses questions regarding insect and pest control. Does management spray or take other steps to control the presence of mosquitoes and other insect pests? Does the campground drain efficiently following a rain? Are garbage and sewage properly collected and disposed of?

Facilities   This rates the overall variety and quality of facilities to include bath house/toilets, swimming pool, retail shops, docks, pavilions, playgrounds, etc. If the quality of respective facilities vary considerably within a given campground, inconsistencies are explained in the prose description of the campground.

Campground Description This is an informative, consumer-oriented description of the campground. It includes what makes the campground special or unique and what differentiates it from other area campgrounds. The description may additionally include the following:

- The general layout of the campground.
- Where the campground is located relative to an easily referenced city or highway.
- The general setting (wilderness, rural, or urban).
- Description of the campsites including most and least desirable sites.
- Prevailing weather considerations and best time to visit.
- Mention of any unusual, exceptional, or deficient facilities.
- Security considerations, if any (gates that are locked at night, accessibility of campground to non-campers, etc.).

Basics   Key information about the campground including:

- *Operated By* Who owns and/or operates the campground.
- *Open* Dates or seasons the campground is open.
- *Site Assignment* How sites are most commonly obtained (first-come, first served; reservations accepted; reservations only; assigned on check-in, etc. Deposit and refund policy.
- *Registration* Where the camper registers on arrival. Information on how and where to register after normal business hours (late arrival).
- *Fee* Cost of a standard campsite for one night for RV sites and tent sites respectively. Forms of payment accepted. Uses the following abbreviations for credit cards: V = VISA, AE = American Express, MC = MasterCard, D = Discover, CB = Carte Blanche, and DC = Diner's Club International.

- *Parking* Usual entry will be "At campsite" or "On road," though some campgrounds have a central parking lot from which tent campers must carry their gear to their campsite.

Facilities This is a brief data presentation that provides information on the availability of specific facilities and services.

- *Number of RV Sites* Any site where RVs are permitted.

- *Number of Tent-Only Sites* Sites set aside specifically for tent camping, including pop-up tent trailers.

- *Hookups* Possible hookups include electric, water, sewer, cable TV, phone, and Internet connection. Electrical hookups vary from campground to campground. Where electrical hookups are available, the amperage available is stated parenthetically, for example: "Hookups: Electric (20 amps), water."

- *Each Site* List of equipment such as grill, picnic table, lantern pole, fire pit, water faucet, electrical outlet, etc., provided at each campsite.

- *Dump station, laundry, pay phone, restrooms and showers, fuel, propane, RV service, general store, vending, playground* Are these items or services available on site? Their respective fields indicate the answer.

- *Internal Roads* Indicates the road type (gravel, paved, dirt), and condition.

- *Market* Location and distance of closest supermarket or large grocery store.

- *Restaurant* Location and distance of closest restaurant.

- *Swimming* Location and distance of closest pool, river, or lake.

- *Other* Boat ramp, dining pavilion, miniature golf, tennis court, lounge, etc.

- *Activities* Activities available at the campground or in the area.

- *Nearby Attractions* Can be natural or manmade.

- *Additional Information* The best sources to call for general information on area activities and attractions. Sources include local or area chambers of commerce, tourist bureaus, visitors and convention authorities, forest service, etc.

Restrictions Any restrictions that apply, including:

- *Pets* Conditions under which pets are allowed or not.

- *Fires* Campground rules for fires and fire safety.

- *Alcoholic Beverages* Campground rules regarding the consumption of alcoholic beverages.

- *Vehicle Maximum Length* Length in feet of the maximum size vehicle the campground can accommodate.

- *Other* Any other rules or restrictions, to include minimum and maximum stays; age or group size restrictions; areas off-limits to vehicular traffic; security constraints such as locking the main gate during the night; etc.

How to Get There Clear and specific directions, including mileage and landmarks, for finding the campground.

Supplemental Directory of Campgrounds

If you're looking for a campground within the territory covered in this guide and can't find a profiled campground that is close or convenient to your route, check the Supplemental Directory of Campgrounds. This directory of hundreds of additional campgrounds is organized alphabetically by state and city name. Each entry provides the campground's name, address, reservations phone, fax, website, number of sites, average fee per night, and hookups available.

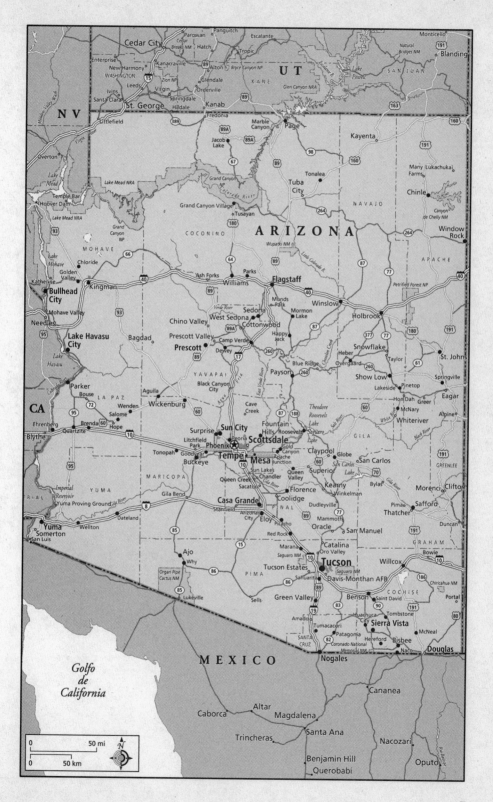

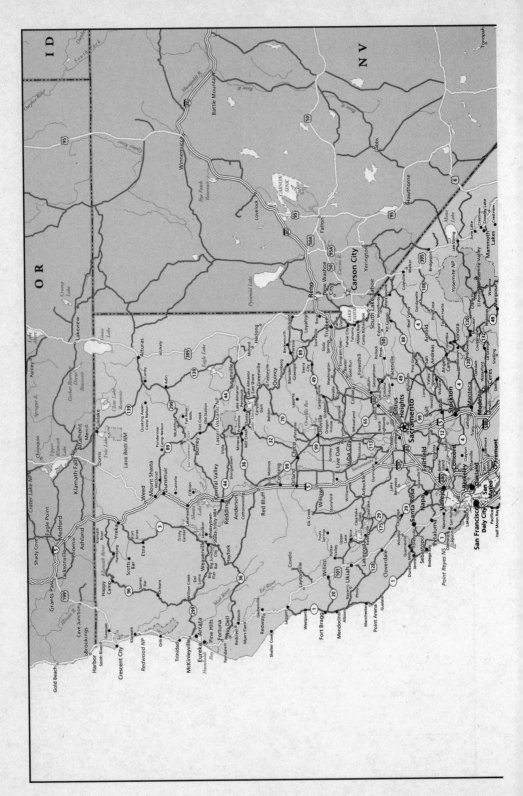

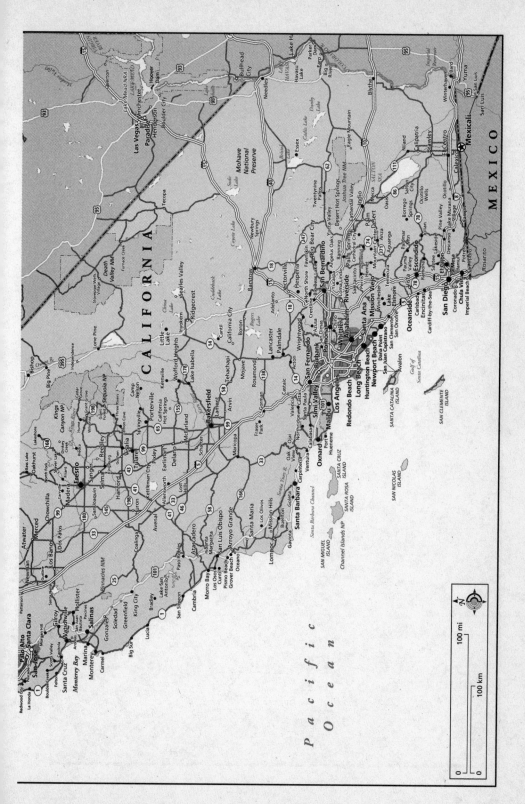

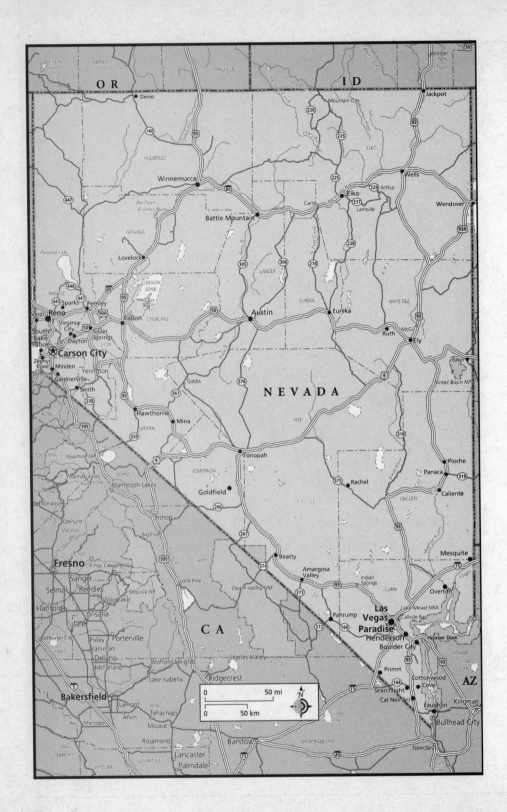

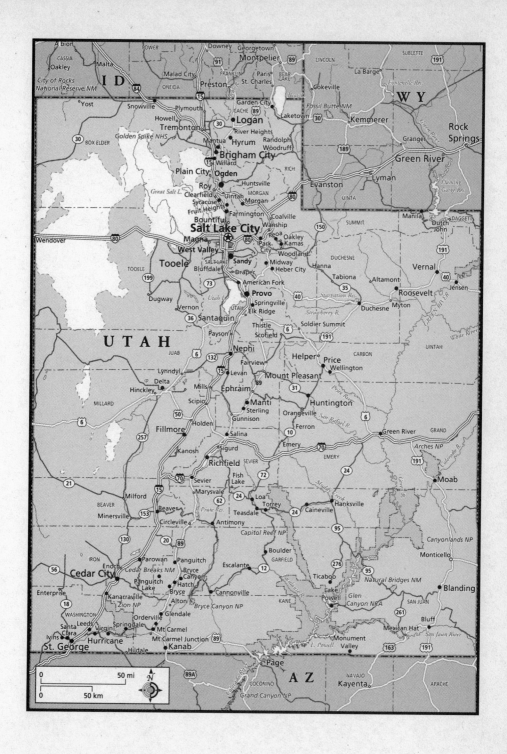

Campground Awards

ARIZONA

Best RV Camping

Fool Hollow Lake Recreation Area, Show Low

Kartchner Caverns State Park, Benson

Rancho Sonora Inn & RV Park, Florence

Usery Mountain Recreation Area, Mesa

Best Tent Camping

Catalina State Park, Tucson

Cholla Recreation Site, Roosevelt

Fool Hollow Lake Recreation Area, Show Low

Kartchner Caverns State Park, Benson

Lake Havasu State Park (Windsor Beach),
Lake Havasu City

Lost Dutchman State Park, Apache Junction

Picacho Peak State Park, Picacho Peak

Usery Mountain Recreation Area, Mesa

Most Beautiful Campgrounds

Cholla Recreation Site, Roosevelt

Hawley Lake Resort, Pinetop-Lakeside

Kartchner Caverns State Park, Benson

Lone Rock Beach, Page

Lost Dutchman State Park, Apache Junction

Organ Pipe Cactus National Monument, Lukeville

Picacho Peak State Park, Picacho Peak

Usery Mountain Recreation Area, Mesa

Most Private Campsites

Cholla Recreation Site, Roosevelt

Jacob Lake Campground, Jacob Lake

Kartchner Caverns State Park, Benson

Lake Havasu State Park (Windsor Beach), Lake
Havasu City

Lost Dutchman State Park, Apache Junction

Organ Pipe Cactus National Monument, Lukeville

Painted Rock Petroglyph Site & Campground,
Gila Bend

Picacho Peak State Park, Picacho Peak

Usery Mountain Recreation Area, Mesa

Most Spacious Campsites

Catalina State Park, Tucson

Cholla Recreation Site, Roosevelt

Gilbert Ray Campground, Tucson

Hawley Lake Resort, Pinetop-Lakeside

Jacob Lake Campground, Jacob Lake

Kartchner Caverns State Park, Benson

La Posa LTVA, Quartzsite

Lake Havasu State Park (Windsor Beach),
Lake Havasu City

Lost Dutchman State Park, Apache Junction

McDowell Mountain Regional Park, Fountain Hills

Organ Pipe Cactus National Monument, Lukeville

Painted Rock Petroglyph Site & Campground,
Gila Bend

Picacho Peak State Park, Picacho Peak

Rancho Sonora Inn & RV Park, Florence

Show Low Lake County Park, Show Low

Usery Mountain Recreation Area, Mesa

Voyager RV Resort, Tucson

ARIZONA (continued)

Quietest Campgrounds

Cholla Recreation Site, Roosevelt

Fool Hollow Lake Recreation Area, Show Low

Hawley Lake Resort, Pinetop-Lakeside

Jacob Lake Campground, Jacob Lake

Kartchner Caverns State Park, Benson

Lake Havasu State Park (Windsor Beach),
   Lake Havasu City

Lost Dutchman State Park, Apache Junction

Lyman Lake State Park, St. Johns

Morenga Palms RV Park, Wenden

Painted Rock Petroglyph Site & Campground,
   Gila Bend

Quietest Campgrounds

Rancho Sonora Inn & RV Park, Florence

Usery Mountain Recreation Area, Mesa

Wheatfields Lake, Tsaile

Most Secure Campgrounds

Branson's Motel & RV Park, Parker

Fool Hollow Lake Recreation Area, Show Low

Havasu Springs Resort, Parker

Hawley Lake Resort, Pinetop-Lakeside

Hon-Dah RV Park, Pinetop-Lakeside

Islander RV Resort, Lake Havasu City

Laguna Beach Campground, Tortilla Flat

Lake Pleasant Regional Park, Peoria

Usery Mountain Recreation Area, Mesa

Cleanest Campgrounds

Black Rock RV Park & Cafe, Brenda

Cholla Recreation Site, Roosevelt

Fool Hollow Lake Recreation Area, Show Low

Havasu Springs Resort, Parker

Hawley Lake Resort, Pinetop-Lakeside

Holbrook/Petrified Forest KOA, Holbrook

Homolovi Ruins State Park, Winslow

Hon-Dah RV Park, Pinetop-Lakeside

Islander RV Resort, Lake Havasu City

Kartchner Caverns State Park, Benson

Kingman KOA, Kingman

LaPaz County Park, Parker

Lyman Lake State Park, St. Johns

Morenga Palms RV Park, Wenden

Organ Pipe Cactus National Monument, Lukeville

Picacho Peak RV Resort, Picacho Peak

Show Low Lake County Park, Show Low

Voyager RV Resort, Tucson

Best Campground Facilities

Black Rock RV Park & Cafe, Brenda

Havasu Springs Resort, Parker

Picacho Peak RV Resort, Picacho Peak

Sandpoint Marina and RV Park, Lake Havasu City

Voyager RV Resort, Tucson

Best Rural, Farm, or Ranch Settings

Black Rock RV Park & Cafe, Brenda

Circle "S" RV Park, Huachuca City

Hon-Dah RV Park, Pinetop-Lakeside

La Posa LTVA, Quartzsite

Morenga Palms RV Park, Wenden

Mountain View RV Ranch, Tumacacori

Picacho Campground, Picacho

Picacho Peak RV Resort, Picacho Peak

Rancho Sonora Inn & RV Park, Florence

De Anza Trails RV Resort, Tumacacori

Best Urban and Suburban Settings

Black Bart's RV Park, Flagstaff

Catalina State Park, Tucson

Cochise Terrace RV Resort, Benson

Covered Wagon RV Park, Phoenix

Crazy Horse Campground & RV Park, Tucson

Davis Camp, Bullhead City

Estrella Mountain Regional Park, Goodyear

Horspitality RV Park and Boarding Stable,
   Wickenburg

Islander RV Resort, Lake Havasu City

Kingman KOA, Kingman

Krazy K RV Park, Camp Verde

Lake Havasu State Park (Windsor Beach),
   Lake Havasu City

Manzanita, Sedona

Mesa–Apache Junction KOA, Apache Junction

Ox Bow Estates RV Park, Payson

Queen Mine RV Park, Bisbee

Usery Mountain Recreation Area, Mesa

Voyager RV Resort, Tucson

ARIZONA (continued)

Welcome Home RV Park, Phoenix

Wells Fargo RV Park, Tombstone

Best Mountain Settings

Buckskin Mountain State Park, Parker

Catalina State Park, Tucson

Gilbert Ray Campground, Tucson

Hawley Lake Resort, Pinetop-Lakeside

Jacob Lake Campground, Jacob Lake

Kaibab Camper Village, Jacob Lake

Laguna Beach Campground, Tortilla Flat

Lees Ferry Campground, Marble Canyon

Lost Dutchman State Park, Apache Junction

Lyman Lake State Park, St. Johns

Manzanita, Sedona

McDowell Mountain Regional Park, Fountain Hills

Ox Bow Estates RV Park, Payson

Picacho Peak State Park, Picacho Peak

Ponderosa Forest RV Park & Campground, Parks

Sandpoint Marina and RV Park, Lake Havasu City

Usery Mountain Recreation Area, Mesa

Virgin River Canyon Recreation Area, Littlefield

Wheatfields Lake, Tsaile

Best Waterfront Settings

Alamo Lake State Park, Wenden

Branson's Motel & RV Park, Parker

Buckskin Mountain State Park, Parker

Cholla Lake County Park, Holbrook

Cholla Recreation Site, Roosevelt

Davis Camp, Bullhead City

Fool Hollow Lake Recreation Area, Show Low

Havasu Springs Resort, Parker

Hawley Lake Resort, Pinetop-Lakeside

Islander RV Resort, Lake Havasu City

Kingman KOA, Kingman

Laguna Beach Campground, Tortilla Flat

Lake Havasu State Park (Windsor Beach), Lake Havasu City

LaPaz County Park, Parker

Lone Rock Beach, Page

Lyman Lake State Park, St. Johns

Patagonia Lake State Park, Patagonia

Red Rock Resort, Parker

Sandpoint Marina and RV Park, Lake Havasu City

Show Low Lake County Park, Show Low

Trailer Village, Grand Canyon

Wahweap Campground, Page

Wahweap RV Park, Page

Wheatfields Lake, Tsaile

Windy Hill Recreation Site, Roosevelt

Most Romantic Campgrounds

Catalina State Park, Tucson

Cottonwood Campground, Chinle

Fool Hollow Lake Recreation Area, Show Low

Havasu Springs Resort, Parker

Hawley Lake Resort, Pinetop-Lakeside

Kartchner Caverns State Park, Benson

Lake Havasu State Park (Windsor Beach), Lake Havasu City

Lost Dutchman State Park, Apache Junction

Lyman Lake State Park, St. Johns

Most Family-Oriented Campgrounds

Alamo Lake State Park, Wenden

Black Bart's RV Park, Flagstaff

Buckskin Mountain State Park, Parker

Cholla Lake County Park, Holbrook

Crazy Horse Campground & RV Park, Tucson

Davis Camp, Bullhead City

Estrella Mountain Regional Park, Goodyear

Fool Hollow Lake Recreation Area, Show Low

Holbrook/Petrified Forest KOA, Holbrook

Hon-Dah RV Park, Pinetop-Lakeside

Islander RV Resort, Lake Havasu City

Kartchner Caverns State Park, Benson

Kingman KOA, Kingman

Laguna Beach Campground, Tortilla Flat

Lake Havasu State Park (Windsor Beach), Lake Havasu City

LaPaz County Park, Parker

Lone Rock Beach, Page

Lyman Lake State Park, St. Johns

McDowell Mountain Regional Park, Fountain Hills

Mesa–Apache Junction KOA, Apache Junction

Patagonia Lake State Park, Patagonia

Picacho Campground, Picacho

Picacho Peak State Park, Picacho Peak

Sandpoint Marina and RV Park, Lake Havasu City

ARIZONA (continued)

Most Family-Oriented Campgrounds

Show Low Lake County Park, Show Low

Usery Mountain Recreation Area, Mesa

Wahweap Campground, Page

Wahweap RV Park, Page

Best Swimming Pools

Covered Wagon RV Park, Phoenix

Crazy Horse Campground & RV Park, Tucson

Davis Camp, Bullhead City

De Anza Trails RV Resort, Tumacacori

Havasu Springs Resort, Parker

Holbrook/Petrified Forest KOA, Holbrook

Islander RV Resort, Lake Havasu City

Kingman KOA, Kingman

Mesa–Apache Junction KOA, Apache Junction

Mountain View RV Ranch, Tumacacori

Picacho Campground, Picacho

Picacho Peak RV Resort, Picacho Peak

Rancho Sonora Inn & RV Park, Florence

Voyager RV Resort, Tucson

Wahweap Campground, Page

Wahweap RV Park, Page

Welcome Home RV Park, Phoenix

CALIFORNIA

Best RV Camping

Antlers RV Park and Campground, Redding

Casini Ranch Family Campground, Duncan Mills

Best Tent Camping

Figueroa, Buëllton

Grandview, Big Pine

Patrick's Point State Park, Trinidad

Most Beautiful Campgrounds

Big Basin Redwoods State Park, Santa Cruz

Ellery Lake, Lee Vining

Figueroa, Buëllton

Grover Hot Springs State Park, Markleeville

Henry W. Coe State Park, Headquarters
Campground, Morgan Hill

Hidden Valley, Twentynine Palms

Red Rock Canyon State Park, Ricardo
Campground, Mojave

Twin Lakes, Mammoth Lakes

Whitney Portal, Lone Pine

Most Private Campsites

Patrick's Point State Park, Trinidad

Most Spacious Campsites

Grandview, Big Pine

Tolkan, Shelter Cove

Quietest Campgrounds

Grandview, Big Pine

Best Campground Facilities

Beaver Creek RV Park & Campground,
Middletown

Cachuma Lake Recreation Area, Santa Barbara

East Shore RV Park, Pomona

KOA Mount Shasta, Mount Shasta

Lake Skinner Recreation Area, Temecula

Malibu Beach RV Park, Malibu

Pacific Park RV Resort, San Francisco

Putah Creek Resort, Napa

Santee Lakes Regional Park & Campground,
Santee

Best Rural, Farm, or Ranch Settings

Anthony Chabot Regional Park, Oakland

Austin Creek State Recreation Area and
Armstrong Redwoods State Reserve,
Bullfrog Pond Camp, Guerneville

Casini Ranch Family Campground, Duncan Mills

Del Valle Regional Park, Livermore

Henry W. Coe State Park, Headquarters
Campground, Morgan Hill

KCL Campground, Carrizo Plain National
Monument

Montaña de Oro State Park, Morro Bay

Prado Regional Park, Pomona

CALIFORNIA (continued)

Selby Campground, Carrizo Plain National Monument

Woodson Bridge State Recreation Area, Corning

Best Urban and Suburban Settings

Anthony Chabot Regional Park, Oakland

Borrego Palm Canyon Campground, Anza-Borrego Desert State Park, Borrego Springs

Bothe–Napa Valley State Park, St. Helena

Camp Switzerland, San Bernardino

Candlestick RV Park, San Francisco

Carpinteria State Beach, Santa Barbara

Folsom Lake State Recreation Area, Beal's Point Campground, Sacramento

Pacific Park RV Resort, San Francisco

Pismo State Beach, North Beach Campground, Pismo Beach

Samuel P. Taylor State Park, San Rafael

San Onofre State Beach, San Mateo Campground, San Clemente

Santee Lakes Regional Park & Campground, Santee

South Carlsbad State Beach, Carlsbad

Spring Lake Regional Park, Santa Rosa

Yucaipa Regional Park, San Bernardino

Best Mountain Settings

Aspen Grove, Lee Vining

Azalea, Kings Canyon National Park

Big Pine Creek, Big Pine

Boulder Flat, Sonora

Butte Lake, Lassen Volcanic National Park

East Fork, Bishop

Ellery Lake, Lee Vining

Glass Creek, Mammoth Lakes

Goumaz, Susanville

Grandview, Big Pine

Grover Hot Springs State Park, Markleeville

Honeymoon Flat, Bridgeport

Ice House, Pollock Pines

Landslide, Hume

Leavitt Meadows, Dardanelle

Lundy Canyon Campground, Mono City

Mount San Jacinto State Park, Stone Creek Campground, Banning

Peppermint, Camp Nelson

Pine Cliff Resort, June Lake

Plumas-Eureka State Park, Upper Samson Creek Campground, Blairsden

Quaking Aspen, Quaking Aspen/Camp Nelson

Sonora Bridge, Coleville

Tuolumne Meadows, Yosemite National Park

Twin Lakes, Mammoth Lakes

Whitney Portal, Lone Pine

Best Waterfront Settings

Brannan Island State Recreation Area, Antioch

Buckhorn, Orland

Butte Lake, Lassen Volcanic National Park

Cachuma Lake Recreation Area, Santa Barbara

Carpinteria State Beach, Santa Barbara

Casini Ranch Family Campground, Duncan Mills

Clear Lake State Park, Lakeport

Cooper Gulch, Lewiston

D. L. Bliss State Park, South Lake Tahoe

Dixon Lake Recreation Area, Escondido

Doheny State Beach, Dana Point

El Capitan State Beach, Santa Barbara

Elam, Chester

Ellery Lake, Lee Vining

Fairview, Kernville

Fleming Meadows, La Grange

Folsom Lake State Recreation Area, Beal's Point Campground, Sacramento

Gaviota State Park, Santa Barbara

Grasshopper Flat, Portola

Holiday Harbor RV Park and Marina, Nice

Honeymoon Flat, Bridgeport

Ice House, Pollock Pines

Indian Creek, Markleeville

Kern River County Park, Kern River Campground, Bakersfield

Kirk Creek, Lucia

Ky-en, Ukiah

Lake Almanor Campground, Greenville

Lake Hemet, Banning

Lake Jennings Regional Park, El Cajon

Lake Kaweah Recreation Area, Horse Creek Campground, Visalia

Lake Morena County Park, South Shore Campground, San Diego

CALIFORNIA (continued)

Best Waterfront Settings

Lake Oroville State Recreation Area, Bidwell Canyon Campground, Oroville

Lake Perris State Recreation Area, Luiseño Campground, Riverside

Lake Skinner Recreation Area, Temecula

Logger, Truckee

Malibu Beach RV Park, Malibu

Mayflower Park, Blythe

Meeks Bay, Tahoma

Merrill, Susanville

Millerton Lake State Recreation Area, Madera

Moccasin Point, Groveland

Modesto Reservoir Regional Park, Modesto

Montaña de Oro State Park, Morro Bay

Needles Marina Park, Needles

Nelson Point, O'Brien

New Brighton State Beach, Capitola

New Hogan Lake, Acorn West and Acorn East Campgrounds, Stockton

North Pines, Yosemite National Park

Pacific Park RV Resort, San Francisco

Peninsula Recreation Area, Sunset Camp and Fashoda Camp, Pollock Pines

Pinecrest, Pinecrest

Pismo State Beach, North Beach Campground, Pismo Beach

Pit River, Fall River Mills

Pogie Point, Upper Lake

Putah Creek Resort, Napa

Salt Point State Park, Woodside and Gerstle Cove Campground, Jenner

Salton Sea State Recreation Area, Headquarters Campground, Mecca

San Clemente State Beach, San Clemente

San Luis Reservoir State Recreation Area, San Luis Creek Campground, Los Baños

Santee Lakes Regional Park & Campground, Santee

Sarah Totten, Hamburg

Shelter Cove RV Park & Campground, Garberville

Silverwood Lake State Recreation Area, Mesa Campground, San Bernardino

South Carlsbad State Beach, Carlsbad

Spring Creek, Portola

Spring Lake Regional Park, Santa Rosa

Sunset State Beach, Watsonville

Tannery Gulch, Weaverville

Tillie Creek, Wofford Heights

Tree of Heaven, Yreka

Tule Recreation Area, Porterville

Tuttletown Recreation Area, Manzanita Campground, Angels Camp

Twin Lakes, Mammoth Lakes

Wawona, Yosemite National Park

Whiskeytown National Recreation Area, Oak Bottom Campground, Whiskeytown

Wild Plum, Sierra City

Most Romantic Campgrounds

Aspen Grove, Lee Vining

Big Basin Redwoods State Park, Santa Cruz

Big Pine Creek, Big Pine

Boulder Flat, Sonora

Butano State Park, Palo Alto

Casini Ranch Family Campground, Duncan Mills

Culp Valley Primitive Camp, Anza-Borrego Desert State Park, Borrego Springs

East Fork, Bishop

Figueroa, Buëllton

Goumaz, Susanville

Grandview, Big Pine

Hidden Valley Campground, Willits

Honeymoon Flat, Bridgeport

Landslide, Hume

Lundy Canyon Campground, Mono City

Montaña de Oro State Park, Morro Bay

Owl Canyon, Barstow

Patrick's Point State Park, Trinidad

Prairie Creek Redwoods State Park, Elk Prairie Campground, Orick

Ronald W. Caspers Wilderness Park, San Juan Capistrano

Wawona, Yosemite National Park

Whitney Portal, Lone Pine

Wildrose, Death Valley

Wishon, Springville

Woodson Bridge State Recreation Area, Corning

CALIFORNIA (continued)

Most Family-Oriented Campgrounds

Antlers RV Park and Campground, Redding

Azalea, Kings Canyon National Park

Beaver Creek RV Park & Campground, Middletown

Bothe–Napa Valley State Park, St. Helena

Buckhorn, Orland

Cachuma Lake Recreation Area, Santa Barbara

Carpinteria State Beach, Santa Barbara

Casini Ranch Family Campground, Duncan Mills

Cuyamaca Rancho State Park, Paso Picacho Campground, Julian

Del Valle Regional Park, Livermore

Dixon Lake Recreation Area, Escondido

Doheny State Beach, Dana Point

Dos Picos Regional Park, Escondido

East Shore RV Park, Pomona

El Capitan State Beach, Santa Barbara

Fleming Meadows, La Grange

Hume Lake, Hume

Kern River County Park, Kern River Campground, Bakersfield

KOA Mount Shasta, Mount Shasta

Ky-en, Ukiah

Lake Hemet, Banning

Lake Jennings Regional Park, El Cajon

Lake Kaweah Recreation Area, Horse Creek Campground, Visalia

Lake Oroville State Recreation Area, Bidwell Canyon Campground, Oroville

Lake Perris State Recreation Area, Luiseño Campground, Riverside

Lake Skinner Recreation Area, Temecula

Leo Carillo State Park, Malibu

Lupine-Cedar Bluff, Bass Lake

Malibu Beach RV Park, Malibu

Mayflower Park, Blythe

Merrill, Susanville

Millerton Lake State Recreation Area, Madera

Moccasin Point, Groveland

Modesto Reservoir Regional Park, Modesto

Needles Marina Park, Needles

New Hogan Lake, Acorn West and Acorn East Campgrounds, Stockton

North Pines, Yosemite National Park

Peninsula Recreation Area, Sunset Camp and Fashoda Camp, Pollock Pines

Pfeiffer Big Sur State Park, Big Sur

Pine Cliff Resort, June Lake

Pine Flat Lake Recreation Area, Fresno

Pinecrest, Pinecrest

Pismo State Beach, North Beach Campground, Pismo Beach

Prado Regional Park, Pomona

Saddle Mountain Recreation Park and RV & Campground, Carmel

Salton Sea State Recreation Area, Headquarters Campground, Mecca

Santee Lakes Regional Park & Campground, Santee

Silverwood Lake State Recreation Area, Mesa Campground, San Bernardino

Spring Creek, Portola

Tillie Creek, Wofford Heights

Tule Recreation Area, Porterville

Tuolumne Meadows, Yosemite National Park

Tuttletown Recreation Area, Manzanita Campground, Angels Camp

William Heise County Park, Julian

Best Swimming Pools

Aspen Grove, Lee Vining

Beaver Creek RV Park & Campground, Middletown

Bothe–Napa Valley State Park, St. Helena

Cachuma Lake Recreation Area, Santa Barbara

East Shore RV Park, Pomona

Furnace Creek, Death Valley National Park

Grover Hot Springs State Park, Markleeville

KOA Mount Shasta, Mount Shasta

Lake Skinner Recreation Area, Temecula

Needles Marina Park, Needles

North Pines, Yosemite National Park

Pacific Park RV Resort, San Francisco

Rio Bend RV Resort Ranch, El Centro

Santee Lakes Regional Park & Campground, Santee

NEVADA

Best Tent Camping

Cottonwood Cove, Cottonwood Cove

Echo Bay, Lake Mead National Recreation Area

Echo Canyon State Park, Pioche

Lower & Upper Lehman Creek Campgrounds, Great Basin National Park

Spring Valley State Park, Ursine

Valley of Fire State Park, Overton

Ward Mountain Campground, Ely

Most Beautiful Campgrounds

Boulder Beach, Boulder City

Cottonwood Cove, Cottonwood Cove

Echo Canyon State Park, Pioche

Hilltop Campground, Spring Mountain National Recreation Area

Lower & Upper Lehman Creek Campgrounds, Great Basin National Park

Sportsman's Beach Recreation Site, Walker Lake

Spring Valley State Park, Ursine

Valley of Fire State Park, Overton

Ward Mountain Campground, Ely

Most Private Campsites

Berlin Ichthyosaur State Park, Gabbs

Cottonwood Cove, Cottonwood Cove

Echo Canyon State Park, Pioche

Hilltop Campground, Spring Mountain National Recreation Area

Kyle Canyon & Fletcher View Campgrounds, Spring Mountain National Recreation Area

Lower & Upper Lehman Creek Campgrounds, Great Basin National Park

McWilliams & Dolomite Campgrounds, Lee Canyon Recreation Area

Spring Valley State Park, Ursine

Valley of Fire State Park, Overton

Ward Mountain Campground, Ely

Washoe Lake State Park, Carson City

Quietest Campgrounds

Berlin Ichthyosaur State Park, Gabbs

Boulder Beach, Boulder City

Cave Lake State Park, Ely

Cottonwood Cove, Cottonwood Cove

Hilltop Campground, Spring Mountain National Recreation Area

Lower & Upper Lehman Creek Campgrounds, Great Basin National Park

McWilliams & Dolomite Campgrounds, Lee Canyon Recreation Area

Spring Valley State Park, Ursine

Valley of Fire State Park, Overton

Most Secure Campgrounds

Cottonwood Cove, Cottonwood Cove

Silverton Hotel Casino RV Park, Las Vegas

Cleanest Campgrounds

Boulder Beach, Boulder City

Cottonwood Cove, Cottonwood Cove

Las Vegas Bay Campground, Henderson

Longstreet Inn, Casino, RV Park & Golf Club, Amargosa Valley

McWilliams & Dolomite Campgrounds, Lee Canyon Recreation Area

Best Campground Facilities

The Station House, Tonopah

Cottonwood Cove, Cottonwood Cove

Longstreet Inn, Casino, RV Park & Golf Club, Amargosa Valley

Silverton Hotel Casino RV Park, Las Vegas

Best Rural, Farm, or Ranch Settings

Davis Creek Regional Park, Carson City

Echo Canyon State Park, Pioche

Fort Churchill State Historic Park, Silver Springs

Quik-Pik Mini Mart & Campground, Rachel

Valley View RV Park, Elko

Best Urban and Suburban Settings

Hi-Desert RV Park, Winnemucca

Silverton Hotel Casino RV Park, Las Vegas

Young's RV Park, Caliente

Best Mountain Settings

Berlin Ichthyosaur State Park, Gabbs

Cathedral Gorge State Park, Panaca

Cave Lake State Park, Ely

Davis Creek Regional Park, Carson City

NEVADA (continued)

Hilltop Campground, Spring Mountain National Recreation Area

Lower & Upper Lehman Creek Campgrounds, Great Basin National Park

McWilliams & Dolomite Campgrounds, Lee Canyon Recreation Area

Spring Valley State Park, Ursine

13 Mile Campground, Red Rock Canyon National Conservation Area

Valley of Fire State Park, Overton

Ward Mountain Campground, Ely

Washoe Lake State Park, Carson City

Zephyr Cove RV Park & Campground, Lake Tahoe

Best Waterfront Settings

Boulder Beach, Boulder City

Cave Lake State Park, Ely

Echo Canyon State Park, Pioche

Lahontan State Recreation Area/Silver Springs Beach, Silver Springs

Las Vegas Bay Campground, Henderson

Overton Beach Marina, Overton

Sportsman's Beach Recreation Site, Walker Lake

Spring Valley State Park, Ursine

Most Romantic Campgrounds

Berlin Ichthyosaur State Park, Gabbs

Cathedral Gorge State Park, Panaca

Hilltop Campground, Spring Mountain National Recreation Area

Lahontan State Recreation Area/Silver Springs Beach, Silver Springs

Lower & Upper Lehman Creek Campgrounds, Great Basin National Park

Valley of Fire State Park, Overton

Most Family-Oriented Campgrounds

Davis Creek Regional Park, Carson City

Hi-Desert RV Park, Winnemucca

Katherine Campground, Boulder City

Lower & Upper Lehman Creek Campgrounds, Great Basin National Park

Best Swimming Pools

Davis Creek Regional Park, Carson City

Hi-Desert RV Park, Winnemucca

Lower & Upper Lehman Creek Campgrounds, Great Basin National Park

Riverside RV Park, Laughlin

Silverton Hotel Casino RV Park, Las Vegas

UTAH

Best RV Camping

Cannonville/Bryce Valley KOA, Cannonville

Rendezvous Beach, Bear Lake State Park

Ruby's RV Park & Campground, Bryce Canyon

Shady Acres RV Park & Campground, Green River

Wasatch Mountain State Park, Midway

Best Tent Camping

Calf Creek Campground, Escalante

Cannonville/Bryce Valley KOA, Cannonville

Devil's Canyon, Blanding

Devil's Garden Campground, Arches National Park

Escalante State Park, Escalante

Goblin Valley State Park, Hanksville

Green River State Park, Green River

Kodachrome Basin State Park, Cannonville

Minersville State Park, Beaver

Mitten View Campground, Monument Valley

Natural Bridges, Natural Bridges National Monument

North Campground, Bryce Canyon

Oasis Campground, Yuba State Park

Point Supreme Campground, Cedar Breaks National Monument

Red Canyon Campground, Bryce Canyon

Ruby's RV Park & Campground, Bryce Canyon

South & Watchman Campgrounds, Zion National Park

Squaw Flat Campground, Canyonlands National Park Needles District

Sunset Campground, Bryce Canyon

Wasatch Mountain State Park, Midway

UTAH (continued)

Most Beautiful Campgrounds

Antelope Island State Park, Syracuse

Bullfrog Resort & Marina Campground/RV Park, Lake Powell

Calf Creek Campground, Escalante

Cedar Canyon Campground, Cedar City

Coral Pink Sand Dunes State Park, Kanab

Dead Horse Point State Park, Moab

Devil's Canyon, Blanding

Devil's Garden Campground, Arches National Park

Escalante State Park, Escalante

Fillmore KOA, Fillmore

Goblin Valley State Park, Hanksville

Goosenecks State Park, Mexican Hat

Kodachrome Basin State Park, Cannonville

Mitten View Campground, Monument Valley

Natural Bridges, Natural Bridges National Monument

Nephi KOA/Horseshoe Bar Ranch, Nephi

Oasis Campground, Yuba State Park

Point Supreme Campground, Cedar Breaks National Monument

Red Canyon Campground, Bryce Canyon

Red Cliffs Recreation Site, Leeds

Snow Canyon State Park, St. George

South & Watchman Campgrounds, Zion National Park

Squaw Flat Campground, Canyonlands National Park Needles District

Thousand Lakes RV Park, Torrey

Virgin River Canyon Recreation Area, Littlefield

Wasatch Mountain State Park, Midway

White Bridge Campground, Panguitch Lake

Willow Flat Campground, Canyonlands National Park Island in the Sky District

Most Private Campsites

Antelope Island State Park, Syracuse

Calf Creek Campground, Escalante

Cedar Canyon Campground, Cedar City

Coral Pink Sand Dunes State Park, Kanab

Devil's Canyon, Blanding

Devil's Garden Campground, Arches National Park

Escalante State Park, Escalante

Goblin Valley State Park, Hanksville

Green River State Park, Green River

Natural Bridges, Natural Bridges National Monument

Point Supreme Campground, Cedar Breaks National Monument

Red Canyon Campground, Bryce Canyon

Red Cliffs Recreation Site, Leeds

Squaw Flat Campground, Canyonlands National Park Needles District

Wasatch Mountain State Park, Midway

Willow Flat Campground, Canyonlands National Park Island in the Sky District

Most Spacious Campsites

Calf Creek Campground, Escalante

Coral Pink Sand Dunes State Park, Kanab

Dead Horse Point State Park, Moab

Goblin Valley State Park, Hanksville

Green River State Park, Green River

Oasis Campground, Yuba State Park

Red Canyon Campground, Bryce Canyon

Ruby's RV Park & Campground, Bryce Canyon

Shady Acres RV Park & Campground, Green River

Squaw Flat Campground, Canyonlands National Park Needles District

United Campground, Green River

Wasatch Mountain State Park, Midway

Quietest Campgrounds

Antelope Island State Park, Syracuse

Calf Creek Campground, Escalante

Goblin Valley State Park, Hanksville

Minersville State Park, Beaver

Natural Bridges, Natural Bridges National Monument

Nephi KOA/Horseshoe Bar Ranch, Nephi

Snow Canyon State Park, St. George

Squaw Flat Campground, Canyonlands National Park Needles District

White Bridge Campground, Panguitch Lake

Most Secure Campgrounds

Antelope Island State Park, Syracuse

Cadillac Ranch RV Park, Bluff

Canyonlands Campground, Moab

Coral Pink Sand Dunes State Park, Kanab

Dead Horse Point State Park, Moab

UTAH (continued)

Most Secure Campgrounds

Goulding's Monument Valley Campground, Monument Valley

Green River State Park, Green River

Moab KOA, Moab

Panguitch Big Fish KOA, Panguitch

South & Watchman Campgrounds, Zion National Park

Squaw Flat Campground, Canyonlands National Park Needles District

United Campground, Green River

Cleanest Campgrounds

Cadillac Ranch RV Park, Bluff

Canyonlands Campground, Moab

Dead Horse Point State Park, Moab

Devil's Canyon, Blanding

Devil's Garden Campground, Arches National Park

Fillmore KOA, Fillmore

Goosenecks State Park, Mexican Hat

Green River State Park, Green River

Hovenweep Campground, Hovenweep National Monument

Moab KOA, Moab

Moab Rim Campark, Moab

Natural Bridges, Natural Bridges National Monument

Nephi KOA/Horseshoe Bar Ranch, Nephi

Portal RV Park & Fishery, Moab

Squaw Flat Campground, Canyonlands National Park Needles District

Thousand Lakes RV Park, Torrey

United Campground, Green River

Willow Flat Campground, Canyonlands National Park Island in the Sky District

Wonderland RV Park, Torrey

Zion River Resort RV Park & Campground, Virgin

Best Campground Facilities

Bullfrog Resort & Marina Campground/RV Park, Lake Powell

Canyonlands Campground, Moab

Goulding's Monument Valley Campground, Monument Valley

Moab KOA, Moab

Ruby's RV Park & Campground, Bryce Canyon

Shady Acres RV Park & Campground, Green River

United Beaver Campground, Beaver

Best Rural, Farm, or Ranch Settings

Arch View Camp Park, Moab

Zion River Resort RV Park & Campground, Virgin

Brentwood RV Resort, Hurricane

Bryce/Zion KOA, Glendale

Cannonville/Bryce Valley KOA, Cannonville

Duck Creek Campground, Cedar City

Escalante State Park, Escalante

Best Rural, Farm, or Ranch Settings

Mitten View Campground, Monument Valley

Moab KOA, Moab

Moab Rim Campark, Moab

Nephi KOA/Horseshoe Bar Ranch, Nephi

Panguitch Big Fish KOA, Panguitch

Portal RV Park & Fishery, Moab

Red Rock Restaurant and Campground, Hanksville

Riverside Motel & RV Park, Hatch

Zion West RV Park, Leeds

Best Urban and Suburban Settings

Broken Bow RV Camp, Escalante

Butch Cassidy Campground, Salina

Cadillac Ranch RV Park, Bluff

Canyonlands Campground, Moab

Fillmore KOA, Fillmore

Green River KOA, Green River

Green River State Park, Green River

Shady Acres RV Park & Campground, Green River

United Beaver Campground, Beaver

United Campground, Green River

Zephyr Cove RV Park & Campground, Lake Tahoe

Best Mountain Settings

Bryce/Zion KOA, Glendale

Calf Creek Campground, Escalante

Cannonville/Bryce Valley KOA, Cannonville

Best Mountain Settings

Devil's Garden Campground, Arches National Park

Fruita Campground, Torrey

Goblin Valley State Park, Hanksville

Goulding's Monument Valley Campground, Monument Valley

Kodachrome Basin State Park, Cannonville

Mukuntweep RV Park & Campground, Zion National Park

UTAH (continued)

Nephi KOA/Horseshoe Bar Ranch, Nephi

North Campground, Bryce Canyon

Point Supreme Campground, Cedar Breaks
National Monument

Red Cliffs Recreation Site, Leeds

Snow Canyon State Park, St. George

South & Watchman Campgrounds, Zion National
Park

Squaw Flat Campground, Canyonlands National
Park Needles District

Thousand Lakes RV Park, Torrey

White Bridge Campground, Panguitch Lake

Zion Canyon Campground, Springdale

Best Waterfront Settings

Antelope Island State Park, Syracuse

Bear Paw Lakeview Resort, Panguitch Lake

Escalante State Park, Escalante

Minersville State Park, Beaver

Oasis Campground, Yuba State Park

Palisade State Park, Manti

Quail Creek State Park, St. George

Willard Bay State Park, Willard

Most Romantic Campgrounds

Antelope Island State Park, Syracuse

Calf Creek Campground, Escalante

Devil's Garden Campground, Arches National Park

Fruita Campground, Torrey

Goblin Valley State Park, Hanksville

Hovenweep Campground, Hovenweep National
Monument

Kodachrome Basin State Park, Cannonville

Mitten View Campground, Monument Valley

Nephi KOA/Horseshoe Bar Ranch, Nephi

Point Supreme Campground, Cedar Breaks
National Monument

Red Canyon Campground, Bryce Canyon

Red Cliffs Recreation Site, Leeds

Rendezvous Beach, Bear Lake State Park

Snow Canyon State Park, St. George

Wasatch Mountain State Park, Midway

Most Family-Oriented Campgrounds

Arch View Camp Park, Moab

Bear Paw Lakeview Resort, Panguitch Lake

Brentwood RV Resort, Hurricane

Bryce/Zion KOA, Glendale

Butch Cassidy Campground, Salina

Cannonville/Bryce Valley KOA, Cannonville

Coral Pink Sand Dunes State Park, Kanab

Escalante State Park, Escalante

Fillmore KOA, Fillmore

Fruita Campground, Torrey

Goulding's Monument Valley Campground,
Monument Valley

Green River KOA, Green River

Moab KOA, Moab

Nephi KOA/Horseshoe Bar Ranch, Nephi

Panguitch Big Fish KOA, Panguitch

Rendezvous Beach, Bear Lake State Park

Shady Acres RV Park & Campground, Green River

Snow Canyon State Park, St. George

United Beaver Campground, Beaver

United Campground, Green River

Wasatch Mountain State Park, Midway

Zion Canyon Campground, Springdale

Zion River Resort RV Park & Campground, Virgin

Best Swimming Pools

Arch View Camp Park, Moab

Bryce Canyon Pines, Bryce Canyon

Bryce/Zion KOA, Glendale

Butch Cassidy Campground, Salina

Cadillac Ranch RV Park, Bluff

Cannonville/Bryce Valley KOA, Cannonville

Canyonlands Campground, Moab

Fillmore KOA, Fillmore

Goulding's Monument Valley Campground,
Monument Valley

Green River KOA, Green River

Moab KOA, Moab

Nephi KOA/Horseshoe Bar Ranch, Nephi

Panguitch Big Fish KOA, Panguitch

Ruby's RV Park & Campground, Bryce Canyon

Shady Acres RV Park & Campground, Green River

Thousand Lakes RV Park, Torrey

United Beaver Campground, Beaver

United Campground, Green River

Wonderland RV Park, Torrey

Zion Canyon Campground, Springdale

Zion River Resort RV Park & Campground, Virgin

Arizona

Arizona blends a rich Native American past and present with a Wild West legacy of cowboys, cattle, and mining. Snowbirds annually flock to Arizona's deserts for the mild winter temperatures, golf and Major League Baseball's spring training Cactus League. Hundreds of RV parks with every imaginable amenity come to life to handle the winter influx, and most book full well in advance of the annual RV migration.

The desert has its own kind of beauty, and the hardiest heat lovers will brave summer temperatures soaring past 110 degrees in **Phoenix** at **Organ Pipe Cactus National Monument.** But most opt for the cooler months from fall through the spring wildflower season. **Tucson** summer temperatures are about 10 degrees cooler than those in Phoenix, though still in the 100s, and summer monsoons bring flash floods. By August, birdwatchers invade the **Upper San Pedro River Valley** southeast of Tucson, an area about 15 degrees cooler than Phoenix. History abounds in **Bisbee,** an old copper mining town with an RV Park overlooking an open pit mine. Few ghost towns rival **Tombstone's** ambiance, and **Kartchner Caverns** satisfies cravings for geological oddities.

Arizona is also a land of mountains, which means winter sports and summer campgrounds that are a refuge from the desert heat. Both deserts and mountains abound with lakes and reservoirs, and fishing and boating are a popular part of the cooling summer mix. The **Colorado River** along Arizona's western border is a water playground with a mix of private RV parks, marinas, and state and county campgrounds between Parker and Lake Havasu, home of the old **London Bridge.** Nearby **Quartzsite** becomes a giant winter flea market and gem show, attracting over a million visitors who park their RVs on Bureau of Land Management (BLM) land all over the desert.

The **Grand Canyon,** to the north, is an international attraction and gateway to the Navajo Nation. **Canyon de Chelley,** just east of the Hopi Indian mesas, is also on most international itineraries. There is no camping inside the **Painted Desert** or **Petrified Forest National Park,** but choices outside the parks, between **Winslow** and **Holbrook,** range from archaeological sites and power-plant cooling reservoirs to commercial campgrounds. South of the Petrified Forest is high mountain country, with a number of forest, lake, and reservoir campgrounds, and even a White Mountain Apache casino RV park for those wanting some Nevada style action.

The following facilities accept payment in checks or cash only:

Alamo Lake State Park, Wenden

Betatakin, Betatakin (Navajo National Monument)

Buckskin Mountain State Park, Parker

Burro Creek Recreation Site, Wikieup

Catalina State Park, Tucson

Cholla Lake County Park, Holbrook

Fool Hollow Lake Recreation Area, Show Low

Gilbert Ray Campground, Tucson

Homolovi Ruins State Park, Winslow

Horspitality RV Park and Boarding Stable, Wickenburg

Jacob Lake Campground, Jacob Lake

Kaibab Camper Village, Jacob Lake

Krazy K RV Park, Camp Verde

La Posa LTVA, Quartzsite

Lake Havasu State Park (Windsor Beach), Lake Havasu City

Lake Pleasant Regional Park, Peoria

LaPaz County Park, Parker

Lees Ferry Campground, Marble Canyon

Lone Rock Beach, Page

Lost Dutchman State Park, Apache Junction

Lyman Lake State Park, St. Johns

Manzanita, Sedona

Mather Campground, Grand Canyon

McDowell Mountain Regional Park, Fountain Hills

Organ Pipe Cactus National Monument, Lukeville

Painted Rock Petroglyph Site & Campground, Gila Bend

Patagonia Lake State Park, Patagonia

Picacho Peak State Park, Picacho Peak

Queen Mine RV Park, Bisbee

Shady Dell RV Park, Bisbee

Temple Bar, Temple Bar

Wheatfields Lake, Tsaile

The following facility features 50 sites or fewer:

Shady Dell RV Park, Bisbee

APACHE JUNCTION
Lost Dutchman State Park

6109 N. Apache Tr., Apache Junction 85219.
T: (602) 982-4485; www.pr.state.az.us.

🚐 ★★★★   ▲ ★★★★★

Beauty: ★★★★★   Site Privacy: ★★★★★
Spaciousness: ★★★★★   Quiet: ★★★★★
Security: ★★★   Cleanliness: ★★★★
Insect Control: ★★★   Facilities: ★★

The big news at Lost Dutchman State Park is the addition of showers, though being without hookups this was never the sort of place people came for RV amenities. The major attractions here are the great views of the spire-like Praying Hand rock formation backed by the tall Flatiron formation, plus many nature trails for hiking and horseback riding. The area's intriguing eroded rock formations are fronted with saguaros, palo verde cholla, and other desert vegetation tall enough to screen the campsites and add privacy. The campground's 35 sites are divided into three small loops within a larger loop, so the natural environment predominates over camping neighbors. It is these natural environment qualities, not the presence or absence of standard amenities, that causes this campground to fill up fast. The group-camping area sometimes doubles as overflow.

BASICS

Operated By: Arizona State Parks. **Open:** All year. **Site Assignment:** First come, first served. **Registration:** Office or self-pay fee station. **Fee:** $10 (cash or check only). **Parking:** At site.

FACILITIES

Number of RV Sites: 35. **Number of Tent-Only Sites:** 0. **Hookups:** None. **Each Site:** Table, grill. **Dump Station:** Yes. **Laundry:** No. **Pay Phone:** Yes. **Rest Rooms and Showers:** Yes. **Fuel:** No. **Propane:** No. **Internal Roads:** Paved & gravel, good condition. **RV Service:** No. **Market:** Apache Junction, 5 mi. **Restaurant:** Apache Junction, 3 mi. **General Store:** No. **Vending:** Yes. **Swimming:** No. **Playground:** No. **Other:** Group pavilion, amphitheater, native-plant trail near ranger station. **Activities:** Horseback riding. **Nearby Attractions:** Tortilla Flat, Phoenix. **Additional Information:** Pinal County Visitor Center, (520) 868-9433.

RESTRICTIONS

Pets: On leash. **Fires:** In grills only; ground fires strictly prohibited; no wood gathering). **Alcoholic Beverages:** Allowed. **Vehicle Maximum Length:** None. **Other:** 15-day stay limit.

TO GET THERE

From junction of US Hwy. 60 & AZ Hwy. 88 go 6 mi. northeast on Hwy. 88.

APACHE JUNCTION
Mesa-Apache Junction KOA

1520 South Tomahawk Rd., Apache Junction 85219.
T: (800) KOA-3404, (480) 982-4015; www.koa.com

🚐 ★★★★   ▲ ★★★

Beauty: ★★★   Site Privacy: ★★
Spaciousness: ★★★★   Quiet: ★★★★
Security: ★★★★   Cleanliness: ★★★★★
Insect Control: ★★★   Facilities: ★★★★

Without the age restriction of many of the megalots in the Apache Junction/Mesa area, this campground is a great family destination. The combination of decent-sized lots (50 × 25 feet on average), attractive landscaping, views of the Superstition Mountains, and full services makes this a campground worth your while to visit. Tent sites are well tucked away, but would be improved with grass instead of gravel. RV sites 116 and 177 sport a fine mature shade tree, making them the best for the money. Sites to avoid are 65, 113, 113A, 114, and 114A, as they have no tree to speak of and are located next to the rec room and an intersection in the campground road. Tent sites H–L are located next to shrubs along the border of the property, which adds to their charm. Tent sites E and F are situated closest to the playground, and worse, E has no tree whatsoever.

BASICS

Operated By: Mike & Rosemary Mortensen. **Open:** All year. **Site Assignment:** Assigned on registration. **Registration:** At office. (Late arrivals: select site from map of open sites, use drop slot in door.). **Fee:** $20–$27. **Parking:** At site.

FACILITIES

Number of RV Sites: 140. **Number of Tent-Only Sites:** 8. **Hookups:** Water, sewer, electric (30, 50 amps). **Each Site:** Picnic table, some shade trees, some trash receptacles. **Dump Station:** Yes.

Laundry: Yes. **Pay Phone:** Yes. **Rest Rooms and Showers:** Yes. **Fuel:** No. **Propane:** Yes. **Internal Roads:** Hard-packed dirt, gravel, & pavement mix; in very drivable condition. **RV Service:** No. **Market:** On site. **Restaurant:** Next door. **General Store:** Yes. **Vending:** Yes. **Swimming:** Yes. **Playground:** Yes. **Other:** Rec building, "dog relief pen." **Activities:** Shuffleboard, river tubing, TV, some fitness equipment, ping pong, basketball, horseshoes, desert Jeep tours, horseback tours, helicopter tours. **Nearby Attractions:** Mesa Southwest Museum, Champlin Fighter Museum, Superstition Springs Center, Casa Grande Ruins, Roosevelt Dam, Tonto National Monument. **Additional Information:** Apache Junction Chamber of Commerce, (602) 982-3141.

RESTRICTIONS

Pets: On leash, clean up after. **Fires:** Yes (only charcoal in grills). **Alcoholic Beverages:** At sites only. **Vehicle Maximum Length:** None. **Other:** No clotheslines, no generators, no For Sale signs.

TO GET THERE

From Hwy. 60, take Exit 197 onto Tomahawk Rd., turn north and drive for 1 mi. The entrance is on the left.

BENSON

Cochise Terrace RV Resort

1030 South Barrel Cactus Ridge, Benson 85602. T: (520) 586-0600 or (800) 495-9005; F: (520) 586-3200; www.cochise-terrace.com; rvresort@theriver.com.

 ★★★★   ▲ ★

Beauty: ★★★★	Site Privacy: ★★★★
Spaciousness: ★★★★	Quiet: ★★★★
Security: ★★★★	Cleanliness: ★★★★
Insect Control: ★★★★	Facilities: ★★★★

Far enough from the main highways so that the only external sound is the wind blowing, Cochise Terrace is like a little city with street lights. Streets have bird names like Raven Road and Quail Run, and an 80-foot-tall American flag near the front entrance office doubles as a navigation landmark. Barrel cactus, ocotillo, mesquite, and a wash are reminders that there is a desert surrounding this little oasis of paved streets. There are almost 100 annual residents of Cochise Terrace, and the 200-plus remaining RV

sites are particularly popular with snowbirds. So, if the largest 42-foot site is needed for a winter visit, call ahead and reserve it. As far as locations go, this is about as central a base for touring southeast Arizona as there is, being an easy drive to almost all the sights from Tucson and Tumacacori to Tombstone and Bisbee.

BASICS

Operated By: Art & Pat Bale. **Open:** All year. **Site Assignment:** First come, first served; winter reservations recommended. **Registration:** Office. **Fee:** $20–$23 (V, MC, AE, D). **Parking:** At site.

FACILITIES

Number of RV Sites: 223. **Number of Tent-Only Sites:** 0. **Hookups:** Electric (20, 30, 50 amp), water, sewer, cable TV, phone. **Each Site:** Table. **Dump Station:** Yes. **Laundry:** Yes. **Pay Phone:** Yes. **Rest Rooms and Showers:** Yes. **Fuel:** No. **Propane:** Yes. **Internal Roads:** Paved, excellent. **RV Service:** No. **Market:** Benson, 2 mi. **Restaurant:** Benson, 2 mi. **General Store:** No. **Vending:** Yes. **Swimming:** Pool. **Playground:** No. **Other:** Clubhouse, whirlpool, kitchen, BBQ, picnic area, basketball court, pet walk, mail service. **Activities:** Golf, horseshoes, square dancing. **Nearby Attractions:** Kartchner Caverns, Fort Huachuca, Tombstone, Bisbee, Dragoon Mountains, Cochise Stronghold, San Pedro Riparian National Conservation Area, Tucson. **Additional Information:** Benson Chamber of Commerce, (520) 586-2842, www.bensonchamberaz.com.

RESTRICTIONS

Pets: On leash and never left unattended. **Fires:** No. **Alcoholic Beverages:** Allowed. **Vehicle Maximum Length:** 42 ft. **Other:** No firearms.

TO GET THERE

From I-10 Exit 302 go south on AZ Hwy. 90 and west on S. Barrel Cactus Ridge.

BENSON

Kartchner Caverns State Park

P.O. Box 1849, Benson 85602. T: (520) 586-4100; www.pr.state.az.us.

 ★★★★★   ▲ ★★★★★

Beauty: ★★★★★	Site Privacy: ★★★★★
Spaciousness: ★★★★★	Quiet: ★★★★★
Security: ★★★★	Cleanliness: ★★★★★
Insect Control: ★★★★	Facilities: ★★★

The Caverns, which require separate admission tickets (520) 586-CAVE for cavern tour reservations), are limestone caves with pooling shelfstones, spar crystals, cave pearls, dripping stalactites, stalagmites, coral pipes, columns, and drapery. Discovered 49 miles southeast of Tucson by two cave explorers in 1974, the caverns were kept secret until purchased as a state park in 1988. The Discovery Center has an explanatory video, plus a hummingbird garden. The campsites are very large, and include 16 50-amp pullthrough sites. Thick mesquite barriers between sites provide privacy, and agave, ocotillo, and prickly pear make this campground one of the most beautiful in the desert. However, the attractive sites fill up early almost every day of the year. Since there are no campground reservations, be prepared to make this a day trip and find alternative campsites in Benson, Huachuca City, and other nearby areas.

BASICS

Operated By: Arizona State Parks. **Open:** All year. **Site Assignment:** First come, first served. **Registration:** Entrance kiosk (after hours self-pay station). **Fee:** $20 (V, MC; cash only after hours). **Parking:** At site.

FACILITIES

Number of RV Sites: 64. **Number of Tent-Only Sites:** 0. **Hookups:** Electric (30, 50 amp), water. **Each Site:** Table. **Dump Station:** Yes. **Laundry:** No. **Pay Phone:** Yes. **Rest Rooms and Showers:** Yes. **Fuel:** No. **Propane:** No. **Internal Roads:** Paved, good. **RV Service:** No. **Market:** Benson, 10 mi. **Restaurant:** Benson, 10 mi. **General Store:** No. **Vending:** Yes. **Swimming:** No. **Playground:** No. **Other:** Some grills, Discovery Center. **Activities:** Cave tours. **Nearby Attractions:** Ramsey Canyon Preserve, Patagonia Lake, Sonoita, Fort Huachuca, Tombstone. **Additional Information:** Sierra Vista Vistor Center, (800) 288-3861, www.visitsierravista.com; Sierra Vista Ranger District, (520) 378-0311.

RESTRICTIONS

Pets: On leash under owner's control. **Fires:** Yes (gas stoves only, no wood or charcoal fires). **Alcoholic Beverages:** Allowed. **Vehicle Maximum Length:** 74 ft. **Other:** 14-day stay limit.

TO GET THERE

From I-10, 1 mi. west of Benson, take Exit 302 and go 9 mi. south on AZ Hwy. 90.

BETATAKIN (NAVAJO NATIONAL MONUMENT)
Betatakin

National Park Service, Navajo National Monument, HC-71 Box 3, Tonalea 86044. T: (520) 672-2700; www.nps.gov/nava.

🚐 ★★   ⛺ ★★★★★

Beauty: ★★★★★   Site Privacy: ★★★★
Spaciousness: ★★★   Quiet: ★★★★★
Security: ★   Cleanliness: ★★★★
Insect Control: ★★★   Facilities: ★

Roughly 10 miles from the nearest highway and 30 miles to the nearest town of any size, Betatakin campsite is rustic and isolated in the extreme. Hidden amidst pinyon, juniper, sage, and a smattering of yucca, sites are far enough away from the visitor center to avoid light pollution. On a clear night, the sky comes alive with stars, and the only sounds to be heard are the chirping, fluttering, or howling of nocturnal animals. This campsite is so natural that there are even black bear warnings issued, and campers would be wise to keep their sites free of trash or food that might attract a bear. The visitor center contains a small display of artifacts, and shows informative videos upon request. Guided tours to the ruins can be reserved up to two months before your trip, but are only offered between Memorial Day and Labor Day. The canyon is still used by Navajo Indians, who herd sheep and gather herbs that can only be found in this canyon. Hopi Indians also still make a yearly pilgrimage to a sacred spot for a Sun Clan ritual.

BASICS

Operated By: National Parks Service. **Open:** All year. **Site Assignment:** First come, first served. **Registration:** None. **Fee:** None. **Parking:** At site.

FACILITIES

Number of RV Sites: 31. **Number of Tent-Only Sites:** 0. **Hookups:** None. **Each Site:** Picnic table. **Dump Station:** No. **Laundry:** No. **Pay Phone:** Yes. **Rest Rooms and Showers:** Toilets; no showers. **Fuel:** No. **Propane:** No. **Internal Roads:** Paved. **RV Service:** No. **Market:** 15 mi. in Black Mesa. **Restaurant:** 15 mi. in Black Mesa. **General Store:** No. **Vending:** Yes. **Swimming:** No. **Playground:** No. **Activities:** Hiking, seasonal tours to Betatakin & Keet Seel ruins, evening presentations at the Fire Circle. **Nearby Attractions:** Aspen Forest Overlook nature trail.

RESTRICTIONS

Pets: On leash. **Fires:** No. **Alcoholic Beverages:** None permitted on tribal land. **Vehicle Maximum Length:** 25 ft. **Other:** Hiking off trails onto tribal land is prohibited, no gathering of artifacts or natural objects.

TO GET THERE

From Kayenta, go 19 mi. west on Hwy. 160 and turn right at the sign for the Navajo National Monument at Black Mesa. Go 9.5 mi. to the visitor center. Follow the road around the center and straight into the campground.

BISBEE
Queen Mine RV Park

P.O. Box 488, Bisbee 85603. T: (520) 432-5006.

🚐 ★★★★   ▲ ★

Beauty: ★★★★   Site Privacy: ★★★★
Spaciousness: ★★★★   Quiet: ★★★★
Security: ★★★★   Cleanliness: ★★★★
Insect Control: ★★★★   Facilities: ★★★

Perched on a circular hilltop just opposite and above the Queen Mine Tour, with RVs circled around the perimeter like a wagon train, the Queen Mine RV Park looks out on orange, ochre, and gray hillside layers exposed by a deep pit copper mine known as the Lavender Pit. Some may call the pit mine a scar on the face of the Earth, but it has its beauty, particularly after a rain when the hillside colors become deeply saturated. For at least a brief moment it is possible to fantasize that a mighty river, rather than copper miners, carved out this three-quarter-mile wide, 950-foot-deep chasm filled with water at the bottom. In any event, it is just a block downhill from this clean, well-run, breezy hillside RV park to the start of Bisbee's historic old Main St. and all the shops, restaurants, hotels, galleries, theaters, and saloons.

BASICS

Operated By: Stan Dupuy. **Open:** All year. **Site Assignment:** First come, first served. **Registration:** Office. **Fee:** $19 (cash or check). **Parking:** At site.

FACILITIES

Number of RV Sites: 25. **Number of Tent-Only Sites:** 0. **Hookups:** Electric (20, 30 amp), water, sewer, cable TV. **Each Site:** Rock planter w/ small tree. **Dump Station:** Yes. **Laundry:** Yes. **Pay Phone:** Yes. **Rest Rooms and Showers:** Yes. **Fuel:** No. **Propane:** No. **Internal Roads:** Gravel, good. **RV Service:** No. **Market:** Bisbee, 2 mi. **Restaurant:** Bisbee, 2 blocks. **General Store:** No. **Vending:** No. **Swimming:** No. **Playground:** No. **Activities:** Golf, bird-watching. **Nearby Attractions:** Mine tour, museums, Tombstone, San Pedro Riparian National Conservation Area. **Additional Information:** Bisbee Chamber of Commerce, (520) 432-5421, www.bisbeearizona.com.

RESTRICTIONS

Pets: On leash under owner's control. **Fires:** Yes. **Alcoholic Beverages:** Allowed. **Vehicle Maximum Length:** None.

TO GET THERE

From AZ Hwy. 80, take downtown Bisbee Exit and follow road to Queen Mine Tour.

BISBEE
Shady Dell RV Park

1 Douglas Rd., Bisbee 85603. T: (520) 432-3567.

🚐 ★★★★   ▲ ★★

Beauty: ★★★★   Site Privacy: ★★★★
Spaciousness: ★★★★   Quiet: ★★★
Security: ★★★★   Cleanliness: ★★★★
Insect Control: ★★★★   Facilities: ★★★★

Located off a roundabout southeast of the Lavender Pit mine, Shady Dell got its start in 1927 when copper mining was going strong and Bisbee was better known than Phoenix. Getting a campsite here is tough, and late afternoon arrivals are usually of out of luck, as most of the campground is rented out to year-round campers. Even more coveted than the camping sites are the furnished aluminum travel trailer rentals, an homage to American road travel that includes a 1949 Airstream, 1950 Spartanette, 1951 Royal Mansion, and 1954 Crown, all furnished in near original blonde woods and polished aluminum with vintage radios, black-and-white TVs, phonographs, and vinyl records of early rhythm and blues and big bands.

Dot's Diner, a ten-stool 1957 art deco Valentine model, makes Shady Dell a good early breakfast stop even if not camping.

BASICS

Operated By: Ed Smith & Rita Personette. **Open:** All year. **Site Assignment:** First come, first served. **Registration:** Office. **Fee:** $10–$15 (cash or check only). **Parking:** At site.

FACILITIES

Number of RV Sites: 10. **Number of Tent-Only Sites:** 2. **Hookups:** Electric (30 amp), water, sewer, cable TV. **Each Site:** Grass & gravel. **Dump Station:** Yes. **Laundry:** Yes. **Pay Phone:** Yes. **Rest Rooms and Showers:** Yes. **Fuel:** Yes. **Propane:** Yes. **Internal Roads:** Gravel, good. **RV Service:** No. **Market:** Bisbee, 2 mi. **Restaurant:** Yes. **General Store:** No. **Vending:** No. **Swimming:** No. **Playground:** No. **Other:** Vintage travel trailer rentals. **Activities:** Golf, bird-watching, rock hunting. **Nearby Attractions:** Mine tour, museums, Tombstone, San Pedro Riparian National Conservation Area. **Additional Information:** Bisbee Chamber of Commerce, (520) 432-5421, www.bisbeearizona.com.

RESTRICTIONS

Pets: On leash. **Fires:** Yes. **Alcoholic Beverages:** Allowed. **Vehicle Maximum Length:** 24 ft.

TO GET THERE

From AZ Hwy. 80, 1.5 mi. southeast of Bisbee, follow the roundabout at the Chevron station to Douglas Rd.

BRENDA

Black Rock RV Park & Cafe

46751 East Hwy. 60, Salome 85348. T: (520) 927-4206; F: (520) 927-4210; www.blackrockrvpark.com.

🚐 ★★★★　　🅰 n/a

Beauty: ★★★★　　Site Privacy: ★★★
Spaciousness: ★★★★　　Quiet: ★★★★
Security: ★★★★　　Cleanliness: ★★★★★
Insect Control: ★★★★　Facilities: ★★★★★

A small, friendly village with a great little bakery guaranteed to defeat efforts to keep off the pounds, Black Rock is a welcome refuge from the Jan. and Feb. crowds jamming nearby Quartzsite. A few trees and cacti line gravel streets with names like Which Way, What Street, Wash Way, Fun Gully, and Easy Street. Desert amenities abound for snowbirds, and people here enjoy walking alongside the road. Winter activities include Sunday afternoon ice cream socials, bean bag baseball, line dancing, cribbage, crafts, painting classes, exercise programs, bingo, darts, pinochle, and jam sessions. The rec hall attracts entertainers like Terry Raff, the singing mountain man. The area to the north is BLM land with ATV and hiking trails, as well as 18 holes of golf and a remote control airfield for flying model planes. For some this is enough to rent a post office box and take up residence.

BASICS

Operated By: Black Rock RV Park. **Open:** All year. **Site Assignment:** First come, first served. **Registration:** Office inside cafe. **Fee:** $21 (V, MC). **Parking:** At site.

FACILITIES

Number of RV Sites: 350. **Number of Tent-Only Sites:** 0. **Hookups:** Electric (30, 50 amp), water, sewer, phone (modem), satellite TV. **Each Site:** Table. **Dump Station:** Yes. **Laundry:** Yes. **Pay Phone:** Yes. **Rest Rooms and Showers:** Yes. **Fuel:** No. **Propane:** Yes. **Internal Roads:** Gravel, good. **RV Service:** No. **Market:** Brenda, 0.5 mi. **Restaurant:** Yes. **General Store:** Yes. **Vending:** Yes. **Swimming:** No. **Playground:** No. **Other:** Soft water car/RV wash, barber, beauty shop, bakery, jeweler, post office, motel, 9-hole golf, R/C model flying field, rec hall, reverse osmosis water, oil change area. **Activities:** Golf, horseshoes. **Nearby Attractions:** Colorado River. **Additional Information:** McMullen Valley Chamber of Commerce, (520) 859-3846, www.azoutback.com.

RESTRICTIONS

Pets: On leash (quantity, size, & breed may be limited by management). **Fires:** Yes. **Alcoholic Beverages:** Allowed. **Vehicle Maximum Length:** 100 ft. **Other:** No subletting sites.

TO GET THERE

From Quartzsite go 11 mi. east on I-10 and take Exit 31 to US Hwy. 60; stay on US Hwy. 60 heading east for 4 mi.

BULLHEAD CITY
Davis Camp

P.O. Box 2078, Bullhead City 86430. T: (520) 754-4606 or (877) 757-0915 (toll free); www.daviscamp.com.

🚐 ★★★★   ▲ ★★

Beauty: ★★★★   Site Privacy: ★★★
Spaciousness: ★★★   Quiet: ★★★
Security: ★★★★   Cleanliness: ★★★★
Insect Control: ★★★★   Facilities: ★★★★

On the northern outskirts of Bullhead City, along Hwy. 68, between Davis Dam and the Laughlin Bridge, there are three clusters of camping sites with palms and eucalyptus along the banks of the Colorado River. This former federal housing area for Davis Dam workers, now a regional county park, looks across the river a mile to Laughlin, Nevada's glimmering casinos, and is the area's best combination of outdoor activities and casino proximity. Hardy outdoor types can swim, boat, jet ski, fish for world record striped bass (59 lbs., 12 oz. caught just below Davis Dam), and walk to Laughlin for food, gaming, and outlet shopping. Children have a safe, shallow swimming cove and spacious play areas with swings, slides, and basketball hoops. Dogs are commonplace, and the roar of the nearby highway and river traffic add to the noise. The most coveted sites, particularly for tents, are the 50 beachfront ramadas with tables and grills near the north beach fishing pier.

BASICS

Operated By: Mohave County Parks Dept. **Open:** All year. **Site Assignment:** First come, first served; reservations required for group area. **Registration:** At entrance kiosk. **Fee:** $10–$16 (V, MC). **Parking:** At site.

FACILITIES

Number of RV Sites: 171. **Number of Tent-Only Sites:** 0. **Hookups:** Electric (up to 50 amps), water, sewer. **Each Site:** Wide pull through. **Dump Station:** Yes. **Laundry:** Yes. **Pay Phone:** Yes. **Rest Rooms and Showers:** Yes. **Fuel:** In Bullhead City & Laughlin. **Propane:** In Bullhead City & Laughlin. **Internal Roads:** Paved, in good condition. **RV Service:** In Bullhead City & Laughlin. **Market:** In Bullhead City & Laughlin. **Restaurant:** Many in nearby Laughlin, Bullhead City. **General Store:** In Bullhead City & Laughlin. **Vending:** Yes. **Swimming:** Children's wading pool. **Playground:** Yes. **Other:** Boat ramp, dock. **Activities:** River fishing, swimming, boating. **Nearby Attractions:** Laughlin casinos & outlet shopping; Colorado River Museum, Lake Mead National Recreation Area. **Additional Information:** Bullhead Area Chamber of Commerce, (520) 754-4121.

RESTRICTIONS

Pets: Must be under handlers' control; leash laws strictly enforced. **Fires:** Grills only. **Alcoholic Beverages:** Arizona law enforced by park rangers. **Vehicle Maximum Length:** 40 ft. **Other:** No loaded firearms, 14-day stay limit for beach sites.

TO GET THERE

At junction of Bullhead Pkwy. (Laughlin Casino Bridge) and Hwy. 68.

CAMP VERDE
Krazy K RV Park

2075 Arena Del Loma, Camp Verde 86322. T: (520) 567-0565.

🚐 ★★★   ▲ ★★

Beauty: ★★   Site Privacy: ★★★
Spaciousness: ★★★   Quiet: ★★★
Security: ★★★   Cleanliness: ★★★★
Insect Control: ★★★   Facilities: ★★

Overlooked by a scrub-covered hill with exclusive houses at the crest, this campground is pretty, with well-tended landscaping. The campground is laid out in rows, half located by the entrance, and the other half or so on a terrace at the foot of the hill at the west end of the grounds. Sites are a spacious (30-feet wide), with both pull-throughs and back-ins. This campground is definitely geared more to the RVer than to tenters: tent sites are not clearly defined, and crammed in by the restrooms. The top terrace and the strip closest to the office are reserved for monthly visitors. Although the campground is close to the highway, traffic noise is not noticeable, but the proximity offers a convenient quick jaunt into town. Overall, the campground presents a very pretty face, with tasteful decorations inside the bathrooms and laundry, and landscaping using volcanic rock and local plants. Its proximity to area attractions or to destinations such as scenic Sedona are an added bonus to a charming campground.

BASICS

Operated By: Steve & Marlys Parks. **Open:** All year. **Site Assignment:** Assigned upon registration (especially when getting full). **Registration:** At office. Late arrivals go to lot #5 (Sun.–Tues.) or lot #14 (Wed.–Sat.). **Fee:** RV $18, tent $12 (no credit cards). **Parking:** At site.

FACILITIES

Number of RV Sites: 36. **Number of Tent-Only Sites:** Undesignated sites. **Hookups:** Water, sewer, electric (30, 50 amps). **Each Site:** Tree, most have tables. **Dump Station:** Yes. **Laundry:** Yes. **Pay Phone:** Yes. **Rest Rooms and Showers:** Yes. **Fuel:** No. **Propane:** Delivered. **Internal Roads:** Gravel. **RV Service:** No. **Market:** 1 mi. into town. **Restaurant:** 1 mi. into town. **General Store:** No. **Vending:** Yes. **Swimming:** Spa. **Playground:** No. **Other:** Dog walk, planned rec room w/ Internet access. **Activities:** Sightseeing, cycling, relaxing in nearby hot springs. **Nearby Attractions:** Montezuma Castle National Monument, Tuzigoot National Monument, Childs hot springs. **Additional Information:** Chamber of Commerce Visitor Center, (520) 567-9294.

RESTRICTIONS

Pets: 1 animal limit, on leash. **Fires:** No. **Alcoholic Beverages:** At sites only. **Vehicle Maximum Length:** 50 ft. **Other:** Rule sheet given upon registration.

TO GET THERE

From the intersection of Hwy. 260 and I-17, go north on I-17 for 2.5 mi., then turn right onto Middle Verde Rd. (Exit 289). Turn right and follow the road east for 1 mi. Turn right again onto Arena Del Loma, and after 1 mi., make a right turn into the gravel entrance at the sign.

CHINLE
Cottonwood Campground

P.O. Box 588, Chinle 86503. T: (520) 674-5501 or (520) 674-5510; www.nps.gov/cach.

🚐 ★★★★	🛖 ★★★★
Beauty: ★★★★	Site Privacy: ★★★★
Spaciousness: ★★★	Quiet: ★★★★
Security: ★★★★	Cleanliness: ★★★★
Insect Control: ★★★	Facilities: ★★★★

Ancient Puebloans occupied 83,000-acre Canyon de Chelly National Monument at least as long ago as 350 AD, and sites like the White House Ruins, Canyon del Muerto, and Spider Rock attract visitors from around the world. At least 20 Navajo families still seasonally graze their sheep and plant corn crops here, and four-wheel-drive and all-terrain vehicle guided tours into Canyon de Chelly are a tourist staple. Overlook views and the White House Ruins trail are free, as amazingly enough is the campground. When Cottonwood's free sites are gone, private Spider Rock RV Park (P.O. Box 2509, Chinle, AZ 86503; (520) 674-8261; no hookups) 10 miles southeast on South Rim Drive is happy to have the business. But with tall cottonwood trees providing plenty of shade and the Thunderbird Lodge Cafeteria next door staying open odd hours, this is the place to camp.

BASICS

Operated By: National Park Service. **Open:** All year. **Site Assignment:** First come, first served; group site reservations (Apr. 1–Oct. 31). **Registration:** Office. **Fee:** None. **Parking:** At site.

FACILITIES

Number of RV Sites: 96. **Number of Tent-Only Sites:** 0. **Hookups:** None. **Each Site:** Table, grill. **Dump Station:** Yes. **Laundry:** No. **Pay Phone:** Yes. **Rest Rooms and Showers:** No showers. **Fuel:** No. **Propane:** No. **Internal Roads:** Paved, good condition. **RV Service:** No. **Market:** Chinle, 1 mi. **Restaurant:** Thunderbird Lodge, adjacent. **General Store:** No. **Vending:** No. **Swimming:** No. **Playground:** No. **Other:** Museum, Visitor Center. **Activities:** Horseback riding, Canyon de Chelly guided tours, summer campfire programs & hogan talks. **Nearby Attractions:** Hubbell Trading Post, Navajo National Monument, Kayenta Burger King Navajo Code Breakers exhibit. **Additional Information:** Canyon de Chelly National Monument, (520) 674-5500, www.nps.gov/cach.

RESTRICTIONS

Pets: On leash (do not feed stray dogs, which are being live trapped). **Fires:** Yes (in grill, ground fires & wood collection prohibited). **Alcoholic Beverages:** Prohibited on Navajo reservation. **Vehicle Maximum Length:** 35 ft. **Other:** 5-day stay limit.

TO GET THERE

From junction of US Hwy. 91 and Indian Hwy. 7 in Chinle, go 4 mi. east on Hwy. 7 and then 0.25 mi. south on South Rim Dr.

FLAGSTAFF
Black Bart's RV Park

2760 East Butler Ave., Flagstaff 86004. T: (520) 774-1912.

🚐 ★★★   ▲ ★

Beauty: ★★★★	Site Privacy: ★★★
Spaciousness: ★★★	Quiet: ★★
Security: ★★	Cleanliness: ★★★
Insect Control: ★★★	Facilities: ★★★

Although the campground is sandwiched between two busy roads, one side borders woods, and there are enough trees in the park itself (most sites have several) that the camp feels more rural than its urban location should warrant. Noise is a bit of a problem, given the proximity of Hwy. 40 and the 75 trains that run daily through town. Further, since tent sites are simply RV sites that "for one reason or another" are unusable for RVs, tenters would be advised to push on to the Ponderosa Forest campground in Parks. However, RV campers don't have it nearly so bad, and there are some impressive views of Arizona's highest mountain (Humphreys Peak) from inside the park. One RVer who had stayed several nights rated the park an 8 out of 10, and the park is a reasonable, family-oriented destination.

BASICS

Operated By: Helen Kelley. **Open:** All year. **Site Assignment:** Assigned at regsitration. **Registration:** At antique store; after hours, enclose fee in envelope & slip into slot in door. **Fee:** $15–$20. **Parking:** At site.

FACILITIES

Number of RV Sites: 174. **Number of Tent-Only Sites:** 15. **Hookups:** Water, sewer, electric (50 amps; will provide converter for 30 amp vehicles). **Each Site:** Picnic table, trees. **Dump Station:** Yes. **Laundry:** Yes. **Pay Phone:** Yes. **Rest Rooms and Showers:** Yes. **Fuel:** No. **Propane:** No. **Internal Roads:** Paved but potholed. **RV Service:** No. **Market:** Yes. **Restaurant:** Yes. **General Store:** Yes. **Vending:** Yes. **Swimming:** No. **Playground:** No. **Other:** Nightly musical revue (singing waiters/waitresses) from 5:30 to close, antique store. **Activities:** Skiing, biking, hiking. **Nearby Attractions:** Coconino National Forest, Lowell Observatory, Arizona Snowbowl, volcanic crater hikes, Humphreys Peak, several museums in town. **Additional Information:** Flagstaff Visitors Bureau, (800) 842-7293.

RESTRICTIONS

Pets: On leash. **Fires:** No open fires, in summer, "prefer" no open grills due to fire hazard. **Alcoholic Beverages:** At sites only. **Vehicle Maximum Length:** None. **Other:** "Cattle rustling is punishable by hanging."

TO GET THERE

On Hwy. 40, take Exit 198 and take a quick left into the park entrance.

FLORENCE
Rancho Sonora Inn & RV Park

9160 Hwy. 79, Florence 85232. T: (520) 868-8000 or (800) 205-6817; F: (520) 868-8000; www.c2i2.com/~rancho/index.htm; rancho@c2i2.com.

🚐 ★★★★★   ▲ ★★★

Beauty: ★★★★	Site Privacy: ★★★★
Spaciousness: ★★★★★	Quiet: ★★★★★
Security: ★★★★	Cleanliness: ★★★★
Insect Control: ★★★★	Facilities: ★★★

An extremely attractive campground studded with saguaro cacti, Rancho Sonora fills with snowbirds every winter. Halfway between Tucson and Phoenix (60 miles), this extremely well-run family operation has an attractive pool area with relaxing desert views that attract visitors from as far away as Alaska. The surprising beauty found here makes it a welcome haven and escape for those visiting the neighboring state facility, as well as for those using Rancho Sonora as a tourism base to explore surrounding areas. Florence has a good Mexican restaurant and old street façades that show up in Hollywood movies and TV shows. Nearby Coolidge has major chain stores for stocking up on sundries. The extended host family is very welcoming, and does its best to help guests enjoy their stay to the maximum.

BASICS

Operated By: Brent & Linda Freeman. **Open:** All year. **Site Assignment:** Reservations needed mid-Oct. to end of Mar. (45-day cancellation, or 1 month's charge applicable to following year's space rental; $35 cancellation fee). **Registration:** Office. **Fee:** $18 tent, $22 RV (V, MC, AE). **Parking:** At site.

FACILITIES

FACILITIES

Number of RV Sites: 62. **Number of Tent-Only Sites:** 4. **Hookups:** Electric (20, 30, 50 amp), water, sewer, phone (modem). **Each Site:** Table, cement pad. **Dump Station:** Yes. **Laundry:** Yes. **Pay Phone:** Yes. **Rest Rooms and Showers:** Yes. **Fuel:** No. **Propane:** Yes. **Internal Roads:** Gravel, excellent. **RV Service:** No. **Market:** Florence, 5 mi. **Restaurant:** Florence, 5 mi. **General Store:** No. **Vending:** Yes. **Swimming:** Pool. **Playground:** No. **Other:** Putting green, whirlpool, horseshoes, BBQ, kitchen, clubhouse, pet walk, fax service, Friday night bonfire. **Activities:** Golf. **Nearby Attractions:** Casa Grande Ruins, McFarland Historical State Park, museums. **Additional Information:** Pinal County Visitor Center, (520) 868-9433.

RESTRICTIONS

Pets: On leash (not allowed in clubhouse). **Fires:** No (clubhouse fire pit only). **Alcoholic Beverages:** "Drink all you want." **Vehicle Maximum Length:** None (40 ft. width). **Other:** Children must be supervised at all times.

TO GET THERE

Go 5 mi. south of Florence on AZ Hwy. 79.

FOUNTAIN HILLS

McDowell Mountain Regional Park

P.O. Box 18415, Fountain Hills 85269. T: (602) 506-2930; F: (602) 506-4692; www.maricopa.gov/recsev; McDowellMountainPark@mail.maricopa.gov.

🚐 ★★★★   ⛺ ★★★★

Beauty: ★★★★	Site Privacy: ★★★★
Spaciousness: ★★★★★	Quiet: ★★★★
Security: ★★★★	Cleanliness: ★★★★
Insect Control: ★★	Facilities: ★★★

One of the excellent Maricopa County Parks ringing the Phoenix area, McDowell Mountain attracts many groups, individuals using the Mayo Clinic in Fountain Hills, and mountain bikers coming to race on the competitive track. With over 100 picnic tables and grills, this is also a popular day-use park, featuring 50 miles of mountain biking and horsback riding trails traversing several ecosystems with six different rattlesnake species. Even though surrounded by the Superstition, McDowell, and Four Peaks Mountains, the park is conveniently located near urban areas. An Native American casino is nearby, downtown Phoenix is just 20 miles away, and Scottsdale is within six miles for those wanting to shop and enjoy the urban amenities. The campsites at McDowell's E. I. Rowland Campground are very large and far apart. Barriers of tall desert plants like saguaro, ocotillo, and palo verde between the campsites make the privacy even more absolute.

BASICS

Operated By: Maricopa County Parks & Recreation. **Open:** All year. **Site Assignment:** First come, first served; group reservations. **Registration:** Self-pay fee station. **Fee:** $15. **Parking:** At site.

FACILITIES

Number of RV Sites: 80. **Number of Tent-Only Sites:** 0. **Hookups:** Electric (20, 30 amp), water. **Each Site:** Table, grill, fire ring. **Dump Station:** Yes. **Laundry:** No. **Pay Phone:** Yes. **Rest Rooms and Showers:** Yes. **Fuel:** No. **Propane:** No. **Internal Roads:** Gravel, good. **RV Service:** No. **Market:** Fountain Hills, 5 mi. **Restaurant:** Fountain Hills, 5 mi. **General Store:** No. **Vending:** Yes. **Swimming:** No. **Playground:** Yes. **Other:** Competitive bike track. **Activities:** Horseback riding, biking. **Nearby Attractions:** Phoenix, Scottsdale, Rio Verde. **Additional Information:** McDowell Park Assoc., (602) 837-3026; Fountain Hills Chamber of Commerce, (480) 837-1654, www.fhchamberofcommerce.org.

RESTRICTIONS

Pets: On leash under owner's control. **Fires:** Yes. **Alcoholic Beverages:** Allowed. **Vehicle Maximum Length:** None. **Other:** No glass bottles.

TO GET THERE

From Fountain Hills go 4 mi. north on Fountain Hills Blvd. to N. McDowell Mountain Rd.

GILA BEND

Painted Rock Petroglyph Site & Campground

2015 West Deer Valley Rd., Phoenix 85027. T: (602) 580-5500 or (602) 780-8090; F: (602) 581-9535.

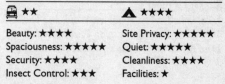

🚐 ★★   ⛺ ★★★★

Beauty: ★★★★	Site Privacy: ★★★★★
Spaciousness: ★★★★★	Quiet: ★★★★★
Security: ★★★★	Cleanliness: ★★★★
Insect Control: ★★★	Facilities: ★

Near Painted Rocks Dam and Reservoir, Painted Rock Petroglyph Site & Campground is a place for self-sufficient campers carrying their own water and firewood. It also makes a good picnic lunch stop when approaching or leaving Organ Pipe Cactus National Monument via I-8. The drive to the campground has lots of dips and flood warning signs as sculpted hills and grain and alfalfa fields teeming with birds give way to desert scrub. The one-acre rock outcropping behind the covered tables chained to the ground in the eating area is densely covered with petroglyphs depicting spirals and animals as varied as deer, lizards, snakes, coyotes, and birds. During the hot summer months of May to Oct., the campground is rarely used, and there is no fee. The only noise most nights is that of howling coyotes, though there are three huge group areas that have the potential to cause noise disturbance.

BASICS

Operated By: Bureau of Land Management. **Open:** All year. **Site Assignment:** First come, first served. **Registration:** Self-pay fee station. **Fee:** $4 (no fee May 1–Sept. 30; cash or check only). **Parking:** At site.

FACILITIES

Number of RV Sites: 40. **Number of Tent-Only Sites:** 0. **Hookups:** None. **Each Site:** Metal table, grill. **Dump Station:** No. **Laundry:** No. **Pay Phone:** No. **Rest Rooms and Showers:** No showers. **Fuel:** No. **Propane:** No. **Internal Roads:** Gravel, good. **RV Service:** No. **Market:** Gila Bend, 30 mi. **Restaurant:** Gila Bend, 30 mi. **General Store:** No. **Vending:** No. **Swimming:** No. **Playground:** No. **Other:** Picnic & group area. **Activities:** Looking at petroglyphs. **Nearby Attractions:** Organ Pipe Cactus National Monument. **Additional Information:** Gila Bend Tourist Information Center, (520) 683-7395.

RESTRICTIONS

Pets: On leash under owner's control (not allowed on petroglyph rocks). **Fires:** Yes. **Alcoholic Beverages:** Allowed. **Vehicle Maximum Length:** None. **Other:** No climbing, walking on, rubbing, or defacing petroglyph rocks.

TO GET THERE

From Gila Bend go 16 mi. west on I-8 to Exit 102, then go 15 mi. north on Painted Rocks Dam Rd. to intersection w/ Rocky Point Rd.

GOODYEAR
Estrella Mountain Regional Park

14805 West Vineyard Ave., Goodyear 85338. T: (623) 932-3811; F: (623) 932-7718; www.maricopa.gov/recsev.

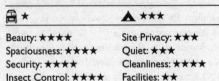

🚐 ★   ⛺ ★★★

Beauty: ★★★★   Site Privacy: ★★★
Spaciousness: ★★★★   Quiet: ★★★
Security: ★★★★   Cleanliness: ★★★★
Insect Control: ★★★★   Facilities: ★★

One of the Phoenix area's six little-known Maricopa County parks, Estrella is scenically situated 18 miles southwest of Phoenix in 19,200 acres of mountainous terrain with horse and hiking trails. Weekends during the school year, Estrella is crowded with scout and school groups, many camping in the deep mesquite shade of the Navy Area and using the park's many playgrounds. Weekdays and school vacations, with the exception of special events like dog shows and medieval pageants, Estrella is relatively empty. The six sites with RV hookups are near the amphitheater and stable area. Tent campers can camp almost anywhere on acres of flat grass, in the open or among shady mesquite groves. The mesquite tree shade can cool the area underneath by ten degrees, enough to make summer camping bearable.

BASICS

Operated By: Maricopa County Parks & Recreation Dept. **Open:** All year. **Site Assignment:** First come, first served; reservations required for group area. **Registration:** Entrance kiosk. **Fee:** $8–$15 (V, MC). **Parking:** At site.

FACILITIES

Number of RV Sites: 6. **Number of Tent-Only Sites:** 100. **Hookups:** Electric (30 amp), water, sewer. **Each Site:** Table, grill. **Dump Station:** No. **Laundry:** No. **Pay Phone:** Yes. **Rest Rooms and Showers:** No showers. **Fuel:** No. **Propane:** No. **Internal Roads:** Paved, in good condition. **RV Service:** No. **Market:** Litchfield Park, 6 mi. **Restaurant:** Litchfield Park, 6 mi. **General Store:** No. **Vending:** Yes. **Swimming:** No. **Playground:** Yes. **Other:** Amphitheater, horse, rodeo, & picnic areas, softball field, sheltered tables. **Activities:** Golf, horseback riding, archery. **Nearby Attractions:** Phoenix International Raceway, museums. **Additional Information:** Maricopa County Parks, (602) 506-2930.

RESTRICTIONS

Pets: On leash under owner's control (leash laws strictly enforced). **Fires:** Yes (grills only). **Alcoholic Beverages:** Beer in cans or kegs; no glass bottles or hard liquor. **Vehicle Maximum Length:** 20 ft.

TO GET THERE

From I-10 east of Phoenix, go south on Estrella Pkwy. (Exit 126) 5 mi. to W. Vineyard Rd.

GRAND CANYON
Mather Campground

P.O. Box 129, Grand Canyon 86023. T: Reservations, (800) 365-CAMP or Ranger, (520) 638-7953.

🚐 ★★★★   ⛺ ★★★★

Beauty: ★★★★   Site Privacy: ★★★
Spaciousness: ★★★★   Quiet: ★★
Security: ★★   Cleanliness: ★★★★
Insect Control: ★★   Facilities: ★★

One can imagine by looking at Mather Campground how the Anasazi slowly ground their way out of existence: a large number of people competing for limited resources. Campers are definitely advised to arrive early—the earlier, the better. Large numbers of people want to camp within the Grand Canyon's boundaries, and with hikers taking advantage of the maximum stay of seven nights, numerous campsites will already be taken when you arrive. By 4 p.m., it is a scramble to pick up any spot, which, naturally, leaves the slimmest picking for the late arrivals. Sites to avoid (if possible) are those closest to the restrooms, as the lights remain on all night and the doors slam with a thud that can raise the dead. In addition, try to avoid sites close to the busy roads (such as sites 53 and 54 on the Aspen Loop or 318 and 319 on the Pine Loop), with foot and car traffic that will annoy all but the soundest sleepers. Having said that, this is the Grand Canyon after all, and perhaps the greatest natural wonder of the world is only a few minutes' drive away. Further, the campground offers an extremely rugged and wild flavor. If you can abide the few annoyances inherent in a campground of this size, it is definitely worth the stay.

BASICS

Operated By: Spherics. **Open:** All year. **Site Assignment:** Reservations recommended (Apr. 1–Nov. 30); first come, first served (Dec. 1–Mar. 31). **Registration:** At kiosk at entrance. **Fee:** $15 (Apr. 1–Nov. 30); $10 (Dec. 1–Mar. 31); half price for Golden Age/Access cardholders. Cash only. **Parking:** At site.

FACILITIES

Number of RV Sites: 312. **Number of Tent-Only Sites:** 0. **Hookups:** None. **Each Site:** Picnic table, grill. **Dump Station:** Yes. **Laundry:** Yes. **Pay Phone:** Yes. **Rest Rooms and Showers:** Yes. **Fuel:** 0.5 mi. away in Market Plaza. **Propane:** No. **Internal Roads:** Paved. **RV Service:** No. **Market:** 0.5 mi. away in Market Plaza. **Restaurant:** 0.5 mi. away in Market Plaza. **General Store:** No. **Vending:** No. **Swimming:** No. **Playground:** No. **Activities:** Hiking, helicopter, plane & horseback rides through the Grand Canyon. **Nearby Attractions:** Grand Canyon National Park. **Additional Information:** North Rim park info: (520) 638-7864, South Rim park info: (520) 638-7888 or (520) 638-7770.

RESTRICTIONS

Pets: On leash, in campground only. **Fires:** Charcoal or wood in grills only. **Alcoholic Beverages:** At sites only. **Vehicle Maximum Length:** 50 ft. **Other:** 7-day stay limit; max. of 6 people or 1 family per site.

TO GET THERE

From the Grand Canyon South Entrance, take Hwy. 64 North for 2.6 mi., then turn left at the traffic light. Continue for.4 mi. and turn right onto Market Plaza Rd. Drive.9 mi., then turn right into the entrance at the sign for the campground.

GRAND CANYON
Trailer Village

1 Main St., P.O. Box 699, Grand Canyon 86023. T: (303) 29-PARKS; F: (303) 297-3175; www.amfac.com; reservations@amfac.com.

🚐 ★★★   ⛺ ★

Beauty: ★★   Site Privacy: ★★★
Spaciousness: ★★   Quiet: ★★★
Security: ★★   Cleanliness: ★★★★★
Insect Control: ★★★   Facilities: ★★★★

Imagine a department store parking lot during a Christmas tree liquidation sale. That pretty much sums up the asthetics of Trailer Village. Most lots are divided by low shrubs, and the lucky few contain trees, while some have no vegetation at all. However, as nearby Mather Campground does not offer RV hookups, those who want fuller service should consider Trailer Village—especially as there are no other full-service RV parks on the South Rim. (Some services, such as showers and laundry are shared between Mather and Trailer Village.) Arranged as a grid, the campground offers 50-foot pull-through sites spaced a scant 20 feet apart. Although tents are permitted, the mere thought of camping here in a tent seems ridiculous—unless the campgrounds are all full and you've got to stay in the Grand Canyon. Not nearly as sylvan as Mather Campground, Trailer Village is recommended to travelers who desire a less primitive experience than the campground, and don't mind taking in the sight of equal parts RV and forest while at home base.

BASICS

Operated By: AmFac Parks & Resorts. **Open:** All year. **Site Assignment:** Assigned at registration. **Registration:** At kiosk. **Fee:** $20 for 2 adults, $1.75 extra per additional adult (no Golden Access discount). **Parking:** At site & parking lot.

FACILITIES

Number of RV Sites: 84. **Number of Tent-Only Sites:** 0. **Hookups:** Water, sewer, electric (30 amps). **Each Site:** Picnic table, grill. **Dump Station:** Yes. **Laundry:** Yes (at Mather Campground). **Pay Phone:** Yes. **Rest Rooms and Showers:** Rest room on-site, showers at Mather Campground. **Fuel:** No. **Propane:** No. **Internal Roads:** Paved. **RV Service:** No. **Market:** 0.5 mi. away in Market Plaza. **Restaurant:** 0.5 mi. away in Market Plaza. **General Store:** No. **Vending:** Yes. **Swimming:** No. **Playground:** No. **Other:** Kennel for pets. **Activities:** Hiking, helicopter, plane, & horseback rides through the Grand Canyon. **Nearby Attractions:** Grand Canyon National Park. **Additional Information:** www.amfac.com.

RESTRICTIONS

Pets: On leash. **Fires:** Charcoal only in grills. **Alcoholic Beverages:** At sites only. **Vehicle Maximum Length:** 50 ft.

TO GET THERE

From the Grand Canyon South Entrance, take Hwy. 64 north for 2.6 mi., then turn left at the traffic light. Continue for 0.4 mi. and turn right onto Market Plaza Rd. Drive 1 mi., turn right at the sign for Trailer Village, and follow the road 0.2 mi. to the entrance.

HOLBROOK
Cholla Lake County Park

Navajo County Parks & Recreation Dept., Holbrook 86025. T: (520) 524-4251 or (520) 288-3717; www.parksrec@navajo.az.us; parksrec@navajo.az.us.

🚐 ★★★   ⛺ ★★★

Beauty: ★★★★   Site Privacy: ★★★★
Spaciousness: ★★★★   Quiet: ★★★★
Security: ★★★★   Cleanliness: ★★★★
Insect Control: ★★★   Facilities: ★★

Situated around a manmade cattail-ringed lake whose waters cool and generate electricity at the four adjacent coal-burning Cholla Power Plant units, rustic Cholla Lake County Park provides travelers on I-40 between Flagstaff and Gallup, New Mexico, with a convenient overnight stop or a base for exploring the Petrified Forest, Painted Desert, Mogollon Rim, and nearby Hopi and Navajo Indian Reservations. The lake, one of the largest in northeastern Arizona, can be used for boating and water sports or fished for large mouth bass, sunfish, and catfish. For some campers, the power pylons, tall cement smokestacks, and piles of coal waiting to be pulverized will seem a visual blight. Others may enjoy the educational displays explaining how scrubbers remove sulfur dioxides and particulates.

BASICS

Operated By: Navajo County Parks & Recreation Dept. **Open:** All year. **Site Assignment:** First come, first served; reservations available by email. **Registration:** Self-pay fee station. **Fee:** $8–$14 (cash or check only). **Parking:** At site.

FACILITIES

Number of RV Sites: 25. **Number of Tent-Only Sites:** 0. **Hookups:** Electric (30 amp), water. **Each Site:** Table, grill. **Dump Station:** Yes. **Laundry:** No. **Pay Phone:** Yes. **Rest Rooms and Showers:** Yes. **Fuel:** No. **Propane:** No. **Internal Roads:** Gravel, good condition. **RV Service:** No. **Market:** Holbrook, 8 mi. **Restaurant:** Holbrook, 8 mi. **General Store:** No. **Vending:** No. **Swimming:** Lake. **Playground:** Yes. **Other:** Group pavilion, water ski course, jet ski landing, fishing dock, horseshoe pits, sand volleyball court. **Activities:** Fishing, boating, bird-watching. **Nearby Attractions:** Navajo Indian Reservation, Petrified Forest, Painted Desert, Homolovi Ruins, Mongollon Rim, White Mountains. **Additional Information:** Holbrook Chamber of Commerce, (800) 524-2459.

RESTRICTIONS

Pets: On leash, crated or caged (not allowed on swimming beach or in structures). **Fires:** Yes (in grills only). **Alcoholic Beverages:** Allowed. **Vehicle Maximum Length:** 35 ft. **Other:** No glass bottles, boaters must observe no wake zone.

TO GET THERE

From Holbrook go 8 mi. west on I-40 to Exit 277 (Joseph City), then south onto park access road for 2 mi.

HOLBROOK
Holbrook/Petrified Forest KOA

102 Hermosa Dr., Holbrook 86025. T: (520) 524-6689 or (800) 562-3389; www.koa.com.

🚐 ★★★   ▲ ★★

Beauty: ★★★	Site Privacy: ★★
Spaciousness: ★★	Quiet: ★★★★
Security: ★★★★	Cleanliness: ★★★★★
Insect Control: ★★★★★	Facilities: ★★★

Flanked at the entrance by a 200-million-year-old petrified log, the Holbrook/Petrified Forest KOA has more than enough amenities for families and is an excellent location for exploring the area's geologic (Petrified Forest, Painted Desert), kitsch (teepee motel, Rte. 66), and Native American (Hopi and Navajo Indian Reservations) sights. Trees line the perimeter and a small cafe serves up pancake breakfasts and cowboy-style barbecue dinners during the peak tourist season. Fortunately, the campground is far enough from the interstate highway that truck noise is not a major problem. Though RVs are sometimes parked seemingly close enough to touch, the campground is usually relatively quiet. Pull-through sites 1–20 have cable TV ($2 extra), and sites 10, 20, 40, 50, 92, and 102 are 50 amp. Tent campers have grass sites, and pet owners are warned to keep their animals off the grass and on the pet walks.

BASICS

Operated By: KOA. **Open:** All year. **Site Assignment:** First come, first served. **Registration:**

Office. **Fee:** $18–$28 (V, MC, D). **Parking:** At site.

FACILITIES

Number of RV Sites: 109. **Number of Tent-Only Sites:** 20. **Hookups:** Electric (20, 30, 50 amp), water, sewer, cable TV, phone (modem). **Each Site:** Table, grill. **Dump Station:** Yes. **Laundry:** Yes. **Pay Phone:** Yes. **Rest Rooms and Showers:** Yes. **Fuel:** No. **Propane:** Yes. **Internal Roads:** Gravel, good. **RV Service:** No. **Market:** Holbrook, 1 mi. **Restaurant:** Holbrook, 1 mi. (small cafe on premises). **General Store:** Yes. **Vending:** Yes. **Swimming:** Pool. **Playground:** Yes. **Other:** Game room, mini-golf, pet walk, mail pickup, seasonal cowboy barbecues, cabins. **Activities:** Volleyball, basketball, tetherball, horseshoes. **Nearby Attractions:** Petrified Forest, Painted Desert, Canyon de Chelly, Second Mesa. **Additional Information:** Holbrook Chamber of Commerce, (800) 524-2459; Petrified Forest National Park, (520) 524-6228, www.nps.gov/pefo.

RESTRICTIONS

Pets: On leash & under owner's control. **Fires:** In grills only; no open fires). **Alcoholic Beverages:** Allowed. **Vehicle Maximum Length:** 50 ft. **Other:** No fireworks; tents must be removed from grass during day for watering & mowing; children & teenagers must be under parental supervision at night.

TO GET THERE

From I-40 Exit 289 to 1.5 mi. south on Navajo Blvd.

HUACHUCA CITY
Circle "S" RV Park

2224 Graham Cir., Huachuca City 85616. T: (520) 456-9801; F: (520) 456-9847; jerryrv@C212.com.

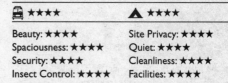

🚐 ★★★★   ▲ ★★★★

Beauty: ★★★★	Site Privacy: ★★★★
Spaciousness: ★★★★	Quiet: ★★★★
Security: ★★★★	Cleanliness: ★★★★
Insect Control: ★★★★	Facilities: ★★★★

A hardworking couple formerly in the lodging business in Florida have taken over what was formerly a combination mobile home and RV park. Jerry and Glenna Scott have been adding tent and RV sites to Circle "S," along with putting in new power, sewer, and water lines. Not to be outdone in amenities, they are also bringing in natural gas, cable TV, and phones. In contrast to the parking lot lights so common to RV parks, new light poles balancing five round bulb fixtures attractively light this campground. Large old shade trees add an attractive rural ambiance. Except for military retirees in Sierra Vista taking advantage of Fort Huachuca and bird watchers passing through to catch the Upper San Pedro River Valley migrations, few know this area. But this is a good base for exploring southeast Arizona.

BASICS

Operated By: Jerry & Glenna Scott. **Open:** All year. **Site Assignment:** First come, first served. **Registration:** Self-pay entrance fee station. **Fee:** $5 tents, $15–$18 RV. **Parking:** At site.

FACILITIES

Number of RV Sites: 25. **Number of Tent-Only Sites:** 7. **Hookups:** Electric (20, 30, 50 amp), water, sewer, cable TV, phone, natural gas. **Each Site:** Table, fireplace, cement patio. **Dump Station:** Yes. **Laundry:** Yes. **Pay Phone:** No. **Rest Rooms and Showers:** Yes. **Fuel:** No. **Propane:** No. **Internal Roads:** Gravel, good. **RV Service:** No. **Market:** Sierra Vista, 10 mi. **Restaurant:** Sierra Vista, 10 mi. **General Store:** Yes. **Vending:** No. **Swimming:** No. **Playground:** No. **Other:** Free fax & email. **Activities:** Horseback riding, bird-watching. **Nearby Attractions:** Fort Huachuca, Tombstone, Bisbee, Kartchner Caverns, San Pedro Riparian National Conservation Area. **Additional Information:** Sierra Vista Vistor Center, (800) 288-3861, www.visitsierravista.com.

RESTRICTIONS

Pets: Yes ("everybody has pets"). **Fires:** Yes. **Alcoholic Beverages:** Allowed. **Vehicle Maximum Length:** 70 ft.

TO GET THERE

1 mi. east of junction of AZ Hwys. 90 & 82.

JACOB LAKE
Jacob Lake Campground

Jacob Lake Inn, Jacob Lake 86022. T: (520) 643-7395; (520) 203-4334 (group reservations).

🚐 ★★★★	⛺ ★★★★
Beauty: ★★★★	Site Privacy: ★★★★★
Spaciousness: ★★★★★	Quiet: ★★★★★
Security: ★★★★	Cleanliness: ★★★★
Insect Control: ★★★	Facilities: ★★★★

It's camping at its best along five secluded loops in the pine forest at 7,900 feet, just an hour's drive (40 miles south via a slow, windy road) from the forested North Rim of the Grand Canyon. Widely dispersed pull-through sites provide plenty of forested privacy, yet Jacob Lake Campground is within one-quarter mile of a 24-hour gas station, general store, counter cafe, restaurant, ranger-staffed Visitor Center and motel. However, water is scarce and available only by the bucketful. In contrast to the North Rim Campground (see Appendix), which books up over a month in advance with reservations, the key to getting a spot here is a very early afternoon arrival, as Jacob Lake Campground fills up just after 4 p.m. most June, July, and Aug. afternoons. Campers wanting hookups should head to nearby Kaibab Camper Village. For a more primitive experience at a smaller campground (23 sites; 30 foot maximum) run by the same concessionaire, head south on US Hwy. 89A towards the North Rim another 23 miles to De Motte Campground (see Appendix).

BASICS

Operated By: US Forest Service/Resource Recreation Management (concessionaire). **Open:** May 15–Nov. 1. **Site Assignment:** First come, first served; group site reservations. **Registration:** Select a site, hosts collect fee later. **Fee:** $12 (cash). **Parking:** Paved loop in front of site.

FACILITIES

Number of RV Sites: 54. **Number of Tent-Only Sites:** 0. **Hookups:** None. **Each Site:** Table, fire ring. **Dump Station:** Yes. **Laundry:** No. **Pay Phone:** Yes. **Rest Rooms and Showers:** Yes. **Fuel:** No. **Propane:** No. **Internal Roads:** Paved, bumpy in spots. **RV Service:** No. **Market:** 0.3 mi. south, near Visitor Center. **Restaurant:** 0.3 mi. south, near Visitor Center. **General Store:** No. **Vending:** No. **Swimming:** No. **Playground:** No. **Activities:** Evening ranger programs, mule deer watching. **Nearby Attractions:** North Rim of Grand Canyon, Pipe Springs National Monument, Kanab, Lees Ferry. **Additional Information:** Kaibab Plateau Visitor Center, (520) 643-7298; North Kaibab Ranger District, (520) 643-7395.

RESTRICTIONS

Pets: On 6 ft leash under owner's control. **Fires:** Yes (firewood sold). **Alcoholic Beverages:** Allowed. **Vehicle Maximum Length:** 30 ft. **Other:** 14-day stay limit; wheelchair accessible site; no fireworks.

To Get There

From junction of US 89A and AZ 67, drive 0.3 mi. north on US 89A.

JACOB LAKE
Kaibab Camper Village

P.O. Box 3331, Flagstaff 86003. T: (520) 643-7804 (May 15–Oct. 15) or (800) 525-0924 (Oct. 15–May 15, outside AZ) or (520) 526-0924 (Oct. 15–May 15, inside AZ); F: (520) 527-9398; www.canyoneers.com; answers@canyoneers.com.

🚐 ★★★★   ⛺ ★★★★

Beauty: ★★★★	Site Privacy: ★★★★
Spaciousness: ★★★★	Quiet: ★★★★
Security: ★★★★	Cleanliness: ★★★★
Insect Control: ★★★	Facilities: ★★★

Tall pines, grassy meadows with picnic tables, the closest hookups to the Grand Canyon's North Rim, and wide pull-through sites make Kaibab Camper Village a top choice for quiet relaxation and North Rim excursions. Management goes to great lengths to keep the campground quiet, even banning electrical generators. Tent campers will appreciate the grassy sites separate from the RV loop. Although it feels isolated in a tall pine forest surrounded by horse pastures and tall mountain backdrops, the campground is only one mile (half via a dusty but extra wide gravel road) from a 24-hour gas station anchoring the US Forest Service's helpful Kaibab Plateau Visitor Center, a motel, an old-fashioned counter cafe, a sit-down restaurant decorated with Native American rugs, and a general store loaded with curios. All in all, it is hard to go wrong with this combination of wilderness and comforts.

BASICS

Operated By: Canyoneers (Flagstaff, AZ). **Open:** May 15–Oct. 15. **Site Assignment:** First come, first served; reservations accepted (nonrefundable prepayment of first night). **Registration:** Entrance station office. **Fee:** $12 (tents, dry sites); $22 (hookups); cash, traveler's checks, personal checks w/ 2 valid IDs. **Parking:** At site.

FACILITIES

Number of RV Sites: 67. **Number of Tent-Only Sites:** 50. **Hookups:** Electric (20, 30 amp), water, sewer. **Each Site:** Table, fire ring. **Dump Station:** Yes. **Laundry:** No. **Pay Phone:** Yes. **Rest**

Rooms and Showers: Yes. **Fuel:** No. **Propane:** No. **Internal Roads:** Gravel, good but dusty. **RV Service:** No. **Market:** 1 mi., near Visitor Center. **Restaurant:** 1 mi., near Visitor Center. **General Store:** No. **Vending:** No. **Swimming:** No. **Playground:** No. **Other:** Modem hookup at office; 30-ft.-wide pull-throughs; noon check-out. **Activities:** Horseback riding. **Nearby Attractions:** Grand Canyon North Rim (40 mi.), Bryce (115 mi.). **Additional Information:** Kaibab Plateau Visitor Center, (520) 643-7298; North Kaibab Ranger District, (520) 643-7395.

RESTRICTIONS

Pets: On 10 ft. leash & kept quiet at all times; designated dog walking area. **Fires:** Yes (only in metal firepits, firewood sold). **Alcoholic Beverages:** Allowed. **Vehicle Maximum Length:** 60 ft. **Other:** Electrical generator use not allowed, no gathering of firewood, water is scarce, & cannot be used for washing people, pets, vehicles, or clothes.

To Get There

From junction of US Hwy. 89A and AZ Hwy. 67, go 0.3 mi. south on Hwy. 67 and then 0.5 mi. west on gravel road.

KINGMAN
Kingman KOA

3820 North Roosevelt, Kingman 86401. T: (520) 757-4397 or (800) 562-3991; www.koa.com; kingkoa@citylink.net.

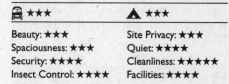

🚐 ★★★   ⛺ ★★★

Beauty: ★★★	Site Privacy: ★★★
Spaciousness: ★★★	Quiet: ★★★★
Security: ★★★★	Cleanliness: ★★★★★
Insect Control: ★★★★	Facilities: ★★★★

Kingman, a stop en route to the Grand Canyon from Las Vegas, had its heyday when local boy Andy Devine was playing Jingles in cowboy movies and Rte. 66 was still the place for getting your "kicks" when driving cross country from Chicago to Los Angeles. Downtown Kingman is just now coming out of a deep boarded-up funk, and the KOA is just about the only campground away from the noise of I-40 with a little space for campers to spread out, short of heading out of town into the Hualapai Mountains. The KOA is a little oasis with oleanders and trees between the campsites, a pleasant ambiance, free morning coffee, 50 TV channels, and newspaper machines. Tent campers have their own area, and a policy of not running generators ensures quiet.

BASICS

Operated By: KOA. **Open:** All year. **Site Assignment:** First come, first served; reservations accepted. **Registration:** Office. **Fee:** $17–$24 (V, MC, AE, D). **Parking:** At site.

FACILITIES

Number of RV Sites: 78. **Number of Tent-Only Sites:** 12. **Hookups:** Electric (30, 50 amp), water, sewer, cable TV, phone (modem). **Each Site:** Table, grill. **Dump Station:** Yes. **Laundry:** Yes. **Pay Phone:** Yes. **Rest Rooms and Showers:** Yes. **Fuel:** No. **Propane:** Yes. **Internal Roads:** Paved, good. **RV Service:** No. **Market:** Kingman, I mi. **Restaurant:** Kingman, I mi. **General Store:** Yes. **Vending:** Yes. **Swimming:** Pool. **Playground:** Yes. **Other:** Rec hall w/ kitchen & TV, video game room, mini-golf, cabins. **Activities:** Golf. **Nearby Attractions:** Rte. 66, Laughlin casinos, Colorado River recreation. **Additional Information:** Kingman Chamber of Commerce, (520) 753-6106, www.kingmanchamber.org; Powerhouse Visitor Center, www.arizonaguide.com/visitkingman.

RESTRICTIONS

Pets: On leash & under owner's control. **Fires:** Yes (only in approved grills). **Alcoholic Beverages:** Allowed. **Vehicle Maximum Length:** None. **Other:** No running of generators.

TO GET THERE

From I-40 Exits 51 & 53 take Stockton Hill Rd. or Andy Devine to intersection of Airway and Roosevelt.

LAKE HAVASU CITY
Islander RV Resort

751 Beachcomber Blvd., Lake Havasu City 86403. T: (520) 680-2000; F: (520) 855-1261; www.islanderrv.com.

🚐 ★★★★	⛺ n/a
Beauty: ★★★★	Site Privacy: ★★★
Spaciousness: ★★★★	Quiet: ★★★★
Security: ★★★★★	Cleanliness: ★★★★★
Insect Control: ★★★★	Facilities: ★★★

On the shores of Lake Havasu, Islander boasts ample amenities, including two swimming pools, boat docks, fish cleaning stations, and winter activities for snowbirds. Premium and waterfront sites have the best lake views, but inland sites have tall eucalyptus trees and some decent mountain views. Unlike Beachcomber Resort (see Appendix) down the road, which rents empty mobile home spots to RVs, Islander terminates the rental agreement of anyone showing signs of residency like enrolling kids in local schools or taking a job in town. The typical 36-foot wide space has a patio pad and enough space for parking a tow vehicle and boat. Those who like it quiet will appreciate that the park is far from noisy highways, though only a short jaunt from the London Bridge, whose 10,276 granite stones were reassembled in this planned desert city by developer Robert McCulloch.

BASICS

Operated By: Islander RV Resort. **Open:** All year. **Site Assignment:** First come, first served; reservations do not guarantee specific sites. **Registration:** Office. **Fee:** $30–$42 (waterfront sites most expensive; V, MC). **Parking:** At site.

FACILITIES

Number of RV Sites: 500. **Number of Tent-Only Sites:** 0. **Hookups:** Electric (30, 50 amp), water, sewer. **Each Site:** Patio pad, table, fire ring. **Dump Station:** Yes. **Laundry:** Yes. **Pay Phone:** Yes. **Rest Rooms and Showers:** Yes. **Fuel:** No. **Propane:** Yes. **Internal Roads:** Paved, excellent. **RV Service:** No. **Market:** Lake Havasu City, I mi. **Restaurant:** Lake Havasu City, I mi. **General Store:** Yes. **Vending:** Yes. **Swimming:** Lake, 2 pools. **Playground:** Yes. **Other:** Rec hall, billiards, shuffleboard & horseshoe areas, boat docks & launch ramp, fish cleaning station. **Activities:** Biking, golf, fishing, boating, volleyball. **Nearby Attractions:** London Bridge, Havasu National Wildlife Refuge. **Additional Information:** Lake Havasu Tourism Bureau, (520) 453-3444, (800) 242-8278.

RESTRICTIONS

Pets: Allowed (subject to separate signed agreement; aggressive breeds like pit bulls not allowed). **Fires:** In fire ring. **Alcoholic Beverages:** Excessive use prohibited. **Vehicle Maximum Length:** 50 ft. **Other:** RVIA approved self-contained RVs only; no clotheslines, firearms, or fireworks.

TO GET THERE

Get off AZ Hwy. 95 at Mesquite Ave. and go east on Lake Havasu Blvd., south to McCullough Blvd., and west across the London Bridge.

LAKE HAVASU CITY
Lake Havasu State Park
(Windsor Beach)

1801 Hwy. 95, Lake Havasu City 86406. T: (520) 855-2784; F: (520) 855-9394; www.pr.state.az.us.

🚐 ★★★★   ▲ ★★★★★

Beauty: ★★★★   Site Privacy: ★★★★★
Spaciousness: ★★★★★   Quiet: ★★★★★
Security: ★★★★   Cleanliness: ★★★★
Insect Control: ★★★   Facilities: ★★

Formed when the Colorado River was dammed near Parker to end the area's annual spring floods and provide water for Arizona and southern California, 45-mile-long Lake Havasu's boating, fishing, and bird-watching recreational possibilities can be accessed at Lake Havasu State Park's Windsor Beach Campground. The large gravel campsites at Windsor Beach combine camping in the desert scrub with a lakeside location. Plus the palo verde, mesquite, and other desert plants are lush enough here to provide each campsite with a barrier of privacy. For those desiring even more of an escape, Lake Havasu State Park also has 55 campsites accessible only by boat. For those wanting to stay closer to urban amenities, Windsor Beach has the added advantage of being only three miles from the London Bridge and Lake Havasu City's restaurants, three microbreweries, movie theaters, nightclubs, and shops.

BASICS

Operated By: Arizona State Parks. **Open:** All year. **Site Assignment:** First come, first served. **Registration:** Entrance kiosk. **Fee:** $8–$13 (cash or check only). **Parking:** At site.

FACILITIES

Number of RV Sites: 73. **Number of Tent-Only Sites:** 55. **Hookups:** None. **Each Site:** Table, grill, fire ring. **Dump Station:** Yes. **Laundry:** No. **Pay Phone:** Yes. **Rest Rooms and Showers:** Yes. **Fuel:** No. **Propane:** No. **Internal Roads:** Paved, good. **RV Service:** No. **Market:** Lake Havasu City, 3 mi. **Restaurant:** Lake Havasu City, 2 mi. **General Store:** No. **Vending:** No. **Swimming:** Lake. **Playground:** Yes. **Other:** Botanical garden, group pavilion. **Activities:** Boating, fishing, water sports, bird-watching, golf. **Nearby Attractions:** London Bridge, Havasu National Wildlife

Refuge. **Additional Information:** Lake Havasu Tourism Bureau, (520) 453-3444, (800) 242-8278.

RESTRICTIONS

Pets: On leash; water & shade must be provided. **Fires:** Yes (no fires when high winds). **Alcoholic Beverages:** Allowed (state liquor laws strictly enforced). **Vehicle Maximum Length:** None. **Other:** No glass containers on beaches or in day-use areas.

TO GET THERE

From the junction of London Bridge Rd. & AZ Hwy. 95, go 2.5 mi. west on London Bridge Rd.

LAKE HAVASU CITY
Sandpoint Marina and RV Park

P.O. Box 1469, Lake Havasu City 86405. T: (520) 855-0549; F: (520) 855-3008; www.lakehavasucity.com/sandpoint.

🚐 ★★★   ▲ ★★★

Beauty: ★★★   Site Privacy: ★★
Spaciousness: ★★★   Quiet: ★★★★
Security: ★★★★   Cleanliness: ★★★★
Insect Control: ★★★   Facilities: ★★★★★

A swimming beach, a marina with 104 boat slips, and rentals of everything from pontoons and sea doos to fishing boats and houseboats makes Sandpoint Marina a worthwhile destination on the shores of Lake Havasu. Sandpoint Marina is actually within Cattail Cove State Park, and is reached via a fork in the road at the entrance to Cattail Cove Campground (see Appendix), which makes a good alternative for large vehicles and has 40 campsites accessible only by boat. Besides the water action and karaoke in the marina cafe, the London Bridge and Lake Havasu City's three microbreweries are only a short journey away. During the winter, Sandpoint has its own newsletter and a variety of snowbird get-togethers. Monthly fishing tournaments reward the boat catching the largest stripers, catfish, carp, and bass with a trophy and up to $50 in prize money.

BASICS

Operated By: Arizona State Parks concession. **Open:** All year. **Site Assignment:** First come, first served. **Registration:** Office. **Fee:** $20–$35 (more for waterfront sites; V, MC). **Parking:** At site.

FACILITIES

Number of RV Sites: 173. **Number of Tent-Only Sites:** 0. **Hookups:** Electric (30 amp), water, sewer, satellite TV. **Each Site:** Sheltered table, grill. **Dump Station:** Yes. **Laundry:** Yes. **Pay Phone:** Yes. **Rest Rooms and Showers:** Yes. **Fuel:** Yes. **Propane:** Yes. **Internal Roads:** Paved & gravel, good. **RV Service:** No. **Market:** Lake Havasu City, 7 mi. **Restaurant:** On premises. **General Store:** Yes. **Vending:** Yes. **Swimming:** River. **Playground:** Yes. **Other:** Marina, boat rentals, dry storage, horseshoe pits, shuffleboard, rec room. **Activities:** Boating, fishing, water sports. **Nearby Attractions:** London Bridge, Buckskin Mountain State Park, Havasu National Wildlife Refuge. **Additional Information:** Lake Havasu Tourism Bureau, (520) 453-3444, (800) 242-8278.

RESTRICTIONS

Pets: On leash at all times (subject to fees; not allowed on swimming beach). **Fires:** In grills only. **Alcoholic Beverages:** Allowed (excessive or underage consumption is grounds for eviction). **Vehicle Maximum Length:** 37 ft. **Other:** No fireworks; no watercraft refueling from portable containers.

TO GET THERE

From Lake Havasu City go 12 mi. south on AZ Hwy. 95 to Cattail Cove State Park.

LUKEVILLE

Organ Pipe Cactus National Monument

Rte. 1 Box 100, Ajo 85321. T: (520) 387-6849; www.nps.gov/orpi.

🚐 ★★★   ▲ ★★★★

Beauty: ★★★★★   Site Privacy: ★★★★★
Spaciousness: ★★★★★   Quiet: ★★★
Security: ★★★★   Cleanliness: ★★★★★
Insect Control: ★★★   Facilities: ★★

Designated an International Biosphere Reserve by the United Nations in 1976, Organ Pipe Cactus National Monument showcases Sonoran Desert plants (28 cactus species) and animals adapted to extremes like summer air temperatures of 118 degrees and ground temperatures of 175 degrees. The Monument's namesake organ pipe cactus copes in part by only opening its lavender-white flowers at night. Campers cope best by coming from Oct. to Apr., when daytime temperatures are in the 60s and 70s. The campground stays open through the torrid summer, when the organ pipe and other cacti colorfully bloom and storms suddenly appear out of nowhere, triggering flash floods. Hardy tent campers can head to more primitive campgrounds, some in cooler mountains with juniper, oak, rosewood, agave, and jojoba. Lukeville has Mexican food, and plenty of hookups are available in Why and Ajo, 22 and 36 miles north, respectively.

BASICS

Operated By: National Park Service. **Open:** All year. **Site Assignment:** First come, first served. **Registration:** Visitor Center. **Fee:** $10 ($5 w/ Gold Access; cash only). **Parking:** At site.

FACILITIES

Number of RV Sites: 208. **Number of Tent-Only Sites:** 0. **Hookups:** None. **Each Site:** Table, grill, cement pad. **Dump Station:** Yes. **Laundry:** No. **Pay Phone:** Yes. **Rest Rooms and Showers:** No showers. **Fuel:** No. **Propane:** No. **Internal Roads:** Gravel, good. **RV Service:** No. **Market:** Lukeville, 5 mi. **Restaurant:** Lukeville, 5 mi. **General Store:** No. **Vending:** Yes. **Swimming:** No. **Playground:** No. **Other:** Amphitheater. **Activities:** Bird-watching. **Nearby Attractions:** Mexico, Ajo, Tohono O'odham Indian Reservation. **Additional Information:** Ajo Chamber of Commerce, (520) 387-7742.

RESTRICTIONS

Pets: On leash under owner's control. **Fires:** In grills only. **Alcoholic Beverages:** Allowed. **Vehicle Maximum Length:** 35 ft. **Other:** No wood gathering.

TO GET THERE

From Gila Bend, go 80 mi. south on AZ Hwy. 85.

MARBLE CANYON

Lees Ferry Campground

P.O. Box 1507, Page 86040. T: (520) 355-2234 or (520) 645-2471.

🚐 ★★★   ▲ ★★★★

Beauty: ★★★★   Site Privacy: ★★★★
Spaciousness: ★★★★   Quiet: ★★★★

Security: ★★★★   Cleanliness: ★★★★
Insect Control: ★★★   Facilities: ★★

The surrounding mountains have red, orange, chocolate brown, white, and green bands of sandstone that give the area its name, Marble Canyon. In the 1920s, this was an important area for crossing the Colorado River by ferry, as well as the site of Jerry Johnson's polygamous Mormon colony at Lonely Dell Ranch. Ferry service ended after a deadly accident in 1928, when the historic Navajo Bridge opened. The boat launch near Lees Ferry Campground is still one of the best places to enter the Colorado River where it flows smooth and green beneath both the old and new Navajo Bridges. The National Park Service has an interpretive center at Navajo Bridge, near where the river splits into its upper and lower basins. Only a few camp sites have trees or manmade structures for shade. Noises echo at the campground, but when the neighbors are quiet this is a peaceful spot. Few places are better for river recreation, and it's away from the hubbub of Lake Powell and Page.

BASICS

Operated By: National Park Service. **Open:** All year. **Site Assignment:** First come, first served. **Registration:** Self-pay fee station at entrance. **Fee:** $10 ($5 w/ Golden Age or Golden Access Passport; cash only). **Parking:** At site.

FACILITIES

Number of RV Sites: 50. **Number of Tent-Only Sites:** 0. **Hookups:** None. **Each Site:** Table, fire ring. **Dump Station:** Yes. **Laundry:** No. **Pay Phone:** Yes. **Rest Rooms and Showers:** No showers. **Fuel:** No. **Propane:** No. **Internal Roads:** Paved, good condition. **RV Service:** No. **Market:** 6 mi. southwest at Marble Canyon Lodge. **Restaurant:** 6 mi. southwest at Marble Canyon Lodge. **General Store:** No. **Vending:** No. **Swimming:** No. **Playground:** No. **Other:** Boat launch ramp, fish cleaning station. **Activities:** Colorado River fishing, canoeing. **Nearby Attractions:** Navajo Bridge, Lake Powell, Jacob Lake, Grand Canyon North Rim. **Additional Information:** US National Park Service, Southern AZ Group, (602) 640-5250; Marble Canyon Lodge, (520) 355-2225; Glen Canyon National Recreation Area, (520) 608-6404.

RESTRICTIONS

Pets: On 6 ft. leash under owner's control. **Fires:** In fire receptacles only, no ground fires. **Alcoholic**

Beverages: Allowed. **Vehicle Maximum Length:** 20 ft. **Other:** 14 consecutive days limit, 30 days per year max., noon checkout.

TO GET THERE

From US Hwy. 89A, go 5.7 mi. north at Marble Canyon.

MESA
Usery Mountain Recreation Area

3939 North Usery Pass Rd., Mesa 85207. T: (480) 984-0032; F: (480) 357-1542; www.maricopa.gov/recsvc/usery.

🚐 ★★★★★   ⛺ ★★★★★

Beauty: ★★★★★   Site Privacy: ★★★★★
Spaciousness: ★★★★★   Quiet: ★★★★★
Security: ★★★★★   Cleanliness: ★★★★
Insect Control: ★★★   Facilities: ★★★

Conveniently close to Mesa's urban amenities, Usery Mountain Recreation Area's Buckhorn Family Campground combines lower Sonoran Desert foreground scenery with the majestic backdrop of the Usery, Goldfield, McDowell, and Superstition Mountains. Campsites at this excellent Maricopa County campground named for King Usery, a cattle rancher who robbed stagecoaches to make ends meet, are very private thanks to intervening patches of mesquite, ocotillo, palo verde, cholla, and saguaro. During spring and fall, Mexican and Basque shepherds can be spotted with their dogs moving sheep across Usery Pass between the high country and the Salt River Valley, an area of ancient Native American village and canal ruins. Seven miles north is Saguaro Lake and Salt River tubing near Stewart Mountain Dam. Campers can also ride their horses or mountain bike park trails. During hot summer months, four covered sites are available ($110 a week in advance; 2-week limit).

BASICS

Operated By: Maricopa County Parks & Recreation Dept. **Open:** All year. **Site Assignment:** First come, first served; group reservations required. **Registration:** Host site near entrance. **Fee:** $8–$15 (V, MC). **Parking:** At site.

FACILITIES

Number of RV Sites: 73. **Number of Tent-Only Sites:** 0. **Hookups:** Electric (30, 50 amp), water. **Each Site:** Table, grill. **Dump Station:** Yes.

Laundry: No. **Pay Phone:** Yes. **Rest Rooms and Showers:** Yes. **Fuel:** No. **Propane:** No. **Internal Roads:** Paved, good. **RV Service:** No. **Market:** Mesa, 4 mi. **Restaurant:** Mesa, 4 mi. **General Store:** No. **Vending:** Yes. **Swimming:** No. **Playground:** Yes. **Other:** Horse staging area, archery range, gun range, model airplane field, flood lights for group area. **Activities:** Horseback riding, mountain biking, river tubing, golf. **Nearby Attractions:** Phoenix, colleges, museums, botanic gardens. **Additional Information:** Mesa CVB, (602) 969-1307.

RESTRICTIONS

Pets: On leash under owner's control (horses OK). **Fires:** In grills only. **Alcoholic Beverages:** Allowed (glass bottles prohibited). **Vehicle Maximum Length:** None. **Other:** 2-week stay limit; no horses in picnic areas.

TO GET THERE

From Mesa go 7.5 mi. north on US Hwy. 60 (Ellsworth/Usery Pass Rd.) to Usery Park Rd.

PAGE

Lone Rock Beach

P.O. Box 1507, Page 86040. T: (520) 608-6404; www.nps.gov/glca.

🚐 ★★   ▲ ★★

Beauty: ★★★★★	Site Privacy: ★★★
Spaciousness: ★★★★	Quiet: ★★★★
Security: ★★★★	Cleanliness: ★★★★
Insect Control: ★★	Facilities: ★★

National Park Service rangers patrol Lone Rock Beach, making this two miles of Lake Powell's 1,960 miles of shoreline among the more secure stretches of beach for camping. A large lone monolithic sandstone rock sticking out of the lake and straddling the Arizona/Utah border gives the beach its name. It seems like southern California, complete with beach bums, albeit sans surfboards and backed by the incomparable beauty of Glen Canyon sandstone. Motor homes share the hard beach sand with tents and people sleeping in the open. Off-road vehicle enthusiasts flock here for the sand dunes, and boaters sail in from Wahweap Marina for beach camping. Though a primitive beach camping experience, don't expect much privacy in July and Aug., when summer traffic jams Page and crowds flock to the beach to beat the heat. Indeed, escaping the summer crowds requires taking a boat (even houseboats are for rent) to the more remote, roadless parts of this 186-mile-long lake.

BASICS

Operated By: National Park Service. **Open:** All year. **Site Assignment:** First come, first served. **Registration:** Entrance kiosk. **Fee:** $6. **Parking:** On beach.

FACILITIES

Number of RV Sites: Unlimited (not designated sites). **Number of Tent-Only Sites:** 0. **Hookups:** None. **Each Site:** Beach sand. **Dump Station:** Yes. **Laundry:** No. **Pay Phone:** Yes. **Rest Rooms and Showers:** Yes. **Fuel:** No. **Propane:** No. **Internal Roads:** Pavement ends in hard sand. **RV Service:** No. **Market:** 9 mi. south at Wahweap. **Restaurant:** 9 mi. south at Wahweap. **General Store:** No. **Vending:** No. **Swimming:** In Lake Powell. **Playground:** No. **Other:** Boat launch. **Activities:** Beach sports, fishing, off-road vehicles on sand dunes. **Nearby Attractions:** Wahweap Marina, Glen Canyon Dam, Page, Antelope Canyon, Rainbow Bridge National Monument, Escalante Staircase National Monument. **Additional Information:** Glen Canyon National Recreation Area, (520) 608-6404.

RESTRICTIONS

Pets: On 6 ft. leash under owner's control. **Fires:** Yes. **Alcoholic Beverages:** Allowed. **Vehicle Maximum Length:** None. **Other:** Portable toilets are mandatory when camping away from restrooms; heavy fines for sewage pollution.

TO GET THERE

Go 6 mi. north from Page on US Hwy. 89, crossing AZ border into UT, then 2 mi. west down road to Lone Rock Beach.

PAGE

Wahweap Campground

P.O. Box 1597, Page 86040. T: (800) 528-6154 or (928) 645-2313; www.visitlakepowell.com.

🚐 ★★★   ▲ ★★★★

Beauty: ★★★★	Site Privacy: ★★★★
Spaciousness: ★★★★	Quiet: ★★★★
Security: ★★★★	Cleanliness: ★★★★
Insect Control: ★★★	Facilities: ★★★★

Wahweap Campground is more spacious and private in feel than Wahweap RV Park, and the

Lake Powell views are surpassed only by camping at Lone Rock Beach. However, RV campers may prefer downtown Page and the more amenity-laden Page–Lake Powell Campground (see appendix) over Wahweap Campground when Wahweap RV Park's hookups are full. Indeed, the spacious campsites and small loops are tailored to tents and small trailers, with plenty of shade trees and desert scrub separating sites from each other along smallish loops. It is slightly over a mile to the showers ($2) and Wahweap Marina amenities like pizza, a restaurant, groceries, and the Wahweap Lodge pool (open to campers). Overall, Wahweap Campground is a good tent and trailer choice, combining the feel of camping out with Lake Powell's nearby amenities.

BASICS

Operated By: Aramark. **Open:** Mar. 15–Oct. 31. **Site Assignment:** First come, first served; group reservations. **Registration:** At office/store. **Fee:** $15 (V, MC, AE, D, DC). **Parking:** At site.

FACILITIES

Number of RV Sites: 112. **Number of Tent-Only Sites:** 0. **Hookups:** None. **Each Site:** Table, grill. **Dump Station:** Yes. **Laundry:** Yes. **Pay Phone:** Yes. **Rest Rooms and Showers:** Yes. **Fuel:** No. **Propane:** No. **Internal Roads:** Paved, good condition. **RV Service:** No. **Market:** Limited groceries at office store; more at RV park. **Restaurant:** At Wahweap Marina. **General Store:** Yes. **Vending:** Yes. **Swimming:** At lodge pool; in lake. **Playground:** No. **Other:** Fine dining at Wahweap Lodge. **Activities:** Boat tours & rentals; float trips on river. **Nearby Attractions:** Rainbow Bridge, Page, Glen Canyon Dam, Antelope Canyon, Lees Ferry, Escalante Staircase National Monument. **Additional Information:** Glen Canyon National Recreation Area, (520) 608-6404; Page–Lake Powell Chamber of Commerce, 644 North Navajo Dr., Dam Plaza, P.O. Box 727, Page, AZ 86040; (888) 261-7243; www.PageLakePowell Chamber.org; info@pagelakepowellchamber.org.

RESTRICTIONS

Pets: On leash under owner's control (including barking). **Fires:** In grills only. **Alcoholic Beverages:** Allowed. **Vehicle Maximum Length:** 35 ft. **Other:** 14 consecutive days, 30 days per year camping limit; no loaded firearms, fireworks or water balloon launchers.

TO GET THERE

Take US Hwy. 198 north from Glen Canyon Dam for 4 mi., turn on Lake Shore Dr. and go to corner of Wahweap Blvd.

PAGE
Wahweap RV Park

P.O. Box 1597, Page 86040. T: (800) 528-6154 or (928) 645-2313; www.visitlakepowell.com.

🚐 ★★★★ ⛺ n/a

Beauty: ★★★   Site Privacy: ★★★
Spaciousness: ★★★   Quiet: ★★★★
Security: ★★★★   Cleanliness: ★★★★
Insect Control: ★★★   Facilities: ★★★★

Wahweap RV Park offers plenty of boat parking for nearby Wahweap Marina. An attractive grassy area with trees separates the RV Park from the road, but once inside it is more like a huge parking lot full of boats and vehicles. If hookups and amenities are of more interest than boats and the lake, downtown Page and the Page–Lake Powell Campground (see Appendix) are an attractive alternative. For a more primitive beach camping experience, head to Lone Rock Beach. The views are nothing to write home about, but the whole idea here seems to be get out on the water and play until dark. Despite the tightly-packed nature of the RV park, it stays fairly quiet. Tables on cement and shade are among the nice touches. If boating on Lake Powell plus RV amenities equal a good time, then this is the best place to be.

BASICS

Operated By: Aramark. **Open:** All year. **Site Assignment:** First come, first served; reservations (first night deposit). **Registration:** Self-pay entrance fee station. **Fee:** $17–$27 (V, MC, AE, D, DC). **Parking:** At site.

FACILITIES

Number of RV Sites: 123. **Number of Tent-Only Sites:** 0. **Hookups:** Electric (20, 30, 50 amp). **Each Site:** Table, grill. **Dump Station:** Yes. **Laundry:** Yes. **Pay Phone:** Yes. **Rest Rooms and Showers:** Yes. **Fuel:** Yes. **Propane:** Yes. **Internal Roads:** Gravel, good condition. **RV Service:** No. **Market:** Yes. **Restaurant:** At Wahweap Marina. **General Store:** Yes. **Vending:** Yes. **Swimming:** In lodge pool or lake. **Playground:** Yes. **Other:** Boat ramp & boat rentals. **Activities:** Fishing, boating, summer ranger programs, free use of lodge facilities. **Nearby Attractions:** Antelope Canyon, Glen Canyon Dam, Lees Ferry, Rainbow Bridge, Escalante Staircase National Monument. **Additional Information:** Glen Canyon National Recreation Area, (520) 608-6404; Page–Lake Powell Chamber of Commerce, 644 North Navajo Dr., Dam Plaza, P.O. Box 727, Page, AZ 86040; (888) 261-7243; www.PageLakePowellChamber.org; info@pagelakepowellchamber.org.

RESTRICTIONS

Pets: On leash under owner's control. **Fires:** Yes. **Alcoholic Beverages:** Allowed. **Vehicle Maximum Length:** 45 ft. **Other:** No tents.

TO GET THERE

From Glen Canyon Dam go 4 mi. north on US Hwy. 89, then take Lake Shore Dr. to 100 Stateline Dr.

PARKER
Branson's Motel & RV Park

7804 Riverside Dr., Parker 85344. T: (520) 667-3346; F: (520) 667-2085.

🚐 ★★★   ▲ n/a

Beauty: ★★★	Site Privacy: ★★
Spaciousness: ★★	Quiet: ★★★★
Security: ★★★★★	Cleanliness: ★★★★
Insect Control: ★★	Facilities: ★★★★

With card games, ice cream socials, and potlucks in the rec hall, Branson's caters to snowbirds in winter with its tightly packed concrete pads and grass strip RV sites. German tourists are among those flocking in summer to this hybrid mixture of marina, mobile homes, RV park, and motel units with kitchens. The motel and front row of mobile homes get the river views. But RV patrons can relax on breezy beachfront lawns under palm frond umbrellas and gaze across the lapping waters of the Colorado River to California or use the ample boat facilities for water sports. A public golf course, the top-rated Emerald Canyon, is just across the street. LaPaz County Park's abundant day-use areas and occasional swap meets are next door. After a visit to the nearby solar saloon, younger party animals will want to leave this little community to the elders and head further north on the road to Lake Havasu.

BASICS

Operated By: Branson's Resort. **Open:** All year. **Site Assignment:** First come, first served; reservations needed in winter. **Registration:** Self-pay entrance fee station. **Fee:** $21 & up (V, MC). **Parking:** At site.

FACILITIES

Number of RV Sites: 70. **Number of Tent-Only Sites:** 0. **Hookups:** Electric (30 amp), water, sewer, cable TV. **Each Site:** Table, grill. **Dump Station:** Yes. **Laundry:** Yes. **Pay Phone:** Yes. **Rest Rooms and Showers:** Yes. **Fuel:** No. **Propane:** No. **Internal Roads:** Paved, good. **RV Service:** No. **Market:** Parker, 8 mi. **Restaurant:** Parker, 2 mi. **General Store:** Yes. **Vending:** Yes. **Swimming:** River. **Playground:** No. **Other:** Boat ramps, slips & storage, horseshoe pits, volleyball court, exercise room, pool table. **Activities:** Fishing, boating, water sports, golf. **Nearby Attractions:** Nellie E. Saloon, Blythe Intaglios (CA), Quartzsite, Lake Havasu. **Additional Information:** Parker Chamber of Commerce, (520) 669-2174, www.riverinfo.com/parker.

RESTRICTIONS

Pets: Not allowed. **Fires:** Yes (when wind is not blowing). **Alcoholic Beverages:** Allowed. **Vehicle Maximum Length:** None.

TO GET THERE

From Parker go 7.5 mi. north on Riverside Dr.

PARKER
Buckskin Mountain State Park

5476 Hwy. 95, Parker 85344. T: (520) 667-3231; www.pr.state.az.us.

🚐 ★★★   ▲ ★★★

Beauty: ★★★★	Site Privacy: ★★★★
Spaciousness: ★★★★	Quiet: ★★★
Security: ★★★	Cleanliness: ★★★★
Insect Control: ★★★	Facilities: ★★

If relaxation and plenty of play space for the children are more important than partying, then Buckskin Mountain's paved sites separated by dirt and trees are a better choice than Fox's Pierpoint Landing and Tony's Road Runner. A group-use area with sheltered tables is one mile north at Buckskin Mountain State Park's River Island Unit, which has another 22 campsites and large grass play areas but no hookups on 420 acres with a boat ramp and a Colorado River swimming beach. Island Unit is closer to the highway and further from the water, but is quieter when not overrun with weekend groups. During the cooler winter months, hiking the short steep trails into the surrounding mountains for spectacular overviews of the area is a worthwhile alternative to water play. Some trails go by abandoned mines and have interpretative stops to get to better know the local ecosystems and vegetation.

BASICS

Operated By: Arizona State Parks. **Open:** All year. **Site Assignment:** First come, first served. **Registration:** Self-pay entrance fee station. **Fee:** $12–$20 (cash or check only). **Parking:** At site.

FACILITIES

Number of RV Sites: 83. **Number of Tent-Only Sites:** 0. **Hookups:** Electric (30 amp), water, sewer. **Each Site:** Table, grill. **Dump Station:** Yes. **Laundry:** No. **Pay Phone:** Yes. **Rest Rooms and Showers:** Yes. **Fuel:** No (boat fuel only). **Propane:** No. **Internal Roads:** Paved, good. **RV Service:** No. **Market:** Buckskin Market, in park. **Restaurant:** In park. **General Store:** Yes. **Vending:** Yes. **Swimming:** River. **Playground:** Yes. **Other:** Cactus garden, interpretative center, boutique, boat ramp, basketball court, volleyball, horseshoe pit. **Activities:** Boating, fishing, water sports, golf. **Nearby Attractions:** Lake Havasu. **Additional Information:** Parker Chamber of Commerce, (520) 669-2174, www.riverinfo.com/parker.

RESTRICTIONS

Pets: On leash. **Fires:** In fire grill **Alcoholic Beverages:** Allowed. **Vehicle Maximum Length:** None. **Other:** No loud nuisance noises; 15-day stay limit.

TO GET THERE

From Parker go 11 mi. north on AZ Hwy. 95.

PARKER

Havasu Springs Resort

2581 Hwy. 95, Parker 85344. T: (520) 667-3361; F: (520) 667-1098; www.havasusprings.com; havasusprings@hotmail.com.

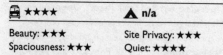

🚐 ★★★★   ⛺ n/a

Beauty: ★★★   Site Privacy: ★★★
Spaciousness: ★★★   Quiet: ★★★★

Security: ★★★★★   Cleanliness: ★★★★★
Insect Control: ★★★   Facilities: ★★★★★

A true destination resort with plenty of amenities, including an Olympic-sized pool, and enough winter activities to keep snowbirds happy, Havasu Springs Resort has over 250 boat slips, three motels, a restaurant with a bar and lounge, and everything from par 3 golf to houseboat and fishing boat rentals. In contrast to the Colorado River and Havasu partying areas, even teenagers must be under tight adult reign here. Motorcycles are also banned, which helps keep the park quiet. Gate security is also relatively tight, and visitors must obtain passes. Though the cement pads here are good, it will be a few years before the trees are large enough to provide some shade to the RV sites. But if protection from noisy Harleys and rowdy party animals is part of the Colorado River recreation game plan, then reservations here may fit the bill.

BASICS

Operated By: Havasu Springs Resort L.L.C. **Open:** All year. **Site Assignment:** First come, first served; reservations a necessity. **Registration:** Office. **Fee:** $26–$30 (V, MC, AE, D). **Parking:** At site.

FACILITIES

Number of RV Sites: 150. **Number of Tent-Only Sites:** 0. **Hookups:** Electric (30, 50 amp), water, sewer, phone, cable TV. **Each Site:** Table, grill. **Dump Station:** Yes. **Laundry:** Yes. **Pay Phone:** Yes. **Rest Rooms and Showers:** Yes. **Fuel:** Yes (boat fuel also available). **Propane:** Yes. **Internal Roads:** Paved, good. **RV Service:** No. **Market:** On premises. **Restaurant:** On premises. **General Store:** Yes. **Vending:** Yes. **Swimming:** Pool. **Playground:** No. **Other:** Marina, houseboat & fishing boat rentals, fish-cleaning stations, lighted tennis courts, 9-hole golf course, 3 motels, sporting goods store, pool tables, video games. **Activities:** Boating, fishing, golf, tennis, hunting. **Nearby Attractions:** Parker Dam, Lake Havasu. **Additional Information:** Parker Chamber of Commerce, (520) 669-2174, www.riverinfo.com/parker.

RESTRICTIONS

Pets: On leash at all times (subject to management discretion). **Fires:** Yes. **Alcoholic Beverages:** Allowed. **Vehicle Maximum Length:** None. **Other:** Only RVIA approved units w/ hard sides allowed; teenagers must be accompanied by parents; no motorcycles or go-carts.

TO GET THERE

From Parker go 17 mi. north on AZ Hwy. 95.

PARKER

LaPaz County Park

7350 Riverside Dr., Parker 85344. T: (520) 667-2069; F: (520) 667-2757; j.bennett@co.la-paz.az.us.

🚐 ★★★★   ▲ ★★★★

Beauty: ★★★★   Site Privacy: ★★★★
Spaciousness: ★★★★   Quiet: ★★★★
Security: ★★★★   Cleanliness: ★★★★★
Insect Control: ★★★   Facilities: ★★★

Though lacking ice cream socials and some of the snowbird amenities of Branson's Resort next door, LaPaz offers lots of open space and green grass. Golfers can practice on the putting green and cross the street to use the driving range or play 18 holes, and there is a baseball field, tennis court, and plenty else to do besides boating, fishing, and swimming in the Colorado River. During the winter, tent campers have a prime dirt beachfront area along the river, and designated sites are kept open for RVs. But RV sites are open to tent camping during the summer months when the snowbird migration has reversed. Tents can also be placed under trees near the group area when it does not conflict with irrigation schedules. The two-mile-long park has some big pines surrounding the inland RV sites, but beachfront RV sites 5–47 and 84–113 have the best river views.

BASICS

Operated By: LaPaz County Parks. **Open:** All year. **Site Assignment:** First come, first served. **Registration:** Self-pay entrance fee station. **Fee:** $10–$15 (cash or check only). **Parking:** At site.

FACILITIES

Number of RV Sites: 114. **Number of Tent-Only Sites:** 35. **Hookups:** Electric (30 amp), water, cable TV, phone. **Each Site:** Table, grill. **Dump Station:** Yes. **Laundry:** No. **Pay Phone:** Yes. **Rest Rooms and Showers:** Yes. **Fuel:** No. **Propane:** No. **Internal Roads:** Gravel, good. **RV Service:** No. **Market:** Parker, 8 mi. **Restaurant:** Parker, 2 mi. **General Store:** No. **Vending:** Yes. **Swimming:** River. **Playground:** Yes. **Other:** Boat ramps, putting green, tennis court, softball field, volleyball court, rec hall, horseshoe pits, some sites w/ sheltered tables. **Activities:** Boating, fishing, golf, horseshoes, volleyball, tennis. **Nearby Attrac-**tions: Nellie E. Saloon, Blythe Intaglios (CA), Quartzsite, Lake Havasu. **Additional Information:** Parker Chamber of Commerce, (520) 669-2174, www.riverinfo.com/parker.

RESTRICTIONS

Pets: On leash at all times (barking dogs not tolerated; no dogs on beachfront walkways). **Fires:** Yes. **Alcoholic Beverages:** Allowed. **Vehicle Maximum Length:** None. **Other:** No bands allowed; no firearms.

TO GET THERE

From Parker go 8 mi. north on US Hwy. 95.

PARKER

Red Rock Resort

6400 Riverside Dr., Parker 85344. T: (520) 667-3116; F: (520) 667-3116; www.redrockresort.com; redrock4@gte.net.

🚐 ★★★   ▲ ★★★

Beauty: ★★★★   Site Privacy: ★★★
Spaciousness: ★★★   Quiet: ★★★★
Security: ★★★★   Cleanliness: ★★★★
Insect Control: ★★★   Facilities: ★★

Boating, fishing, and water sports are the chief attraction at Red Rock Resort, which is notable for its waterfront cabana campsites. The large pull-through sites (41–56) and sites 64–71 near the winter overflow and RV and trailer storage areas are furthest from the Colorado River. However, site 41, a large lawn corner pull-through is closer to the water and worth the small rental premium. The best sites are right on the Colorado River, and are open only to smaller vehicles and tent camping. These waterfront cabanas, which offer the opportunity to barbecue on the banks of the Colorado River and sit in the shade, are numbered 1–40 and are difficult to score, as they are often rented for four months solid during the peak winter season. Good boat facilities, including repair, salvage, and storage, as well as RV and trailer storage, also help make this small waterfront resort with its own bar and cafe a popular destination.

BASICS

Operated By: Red Rock Resort. **Open:** All year. **Site Assignment:** First come, first served; reservations advised for peak season, holidays, weekends. **Registration:** Front desk. **Fee:** $20–$25 (V, MC). **Parking:** At site.

FACILITIES

Number of RV Sites: 90. **Number of Tent-Only Sites:** 0. **Hookups:** Electric (30, 50 amp), water, sewer, cable TV, phone. **Each Site:** Table, grill. **Dump Station:** Yes. **Laundry:** Yes. **Pay Phone:** Yes. **Rest Rooms and Showers:** Yes. **Fuel:** No. **Propane:** Yes. **Internal Roads:** Paved, good. **RV Service:** No. **Market:** Parker, 9 mi. **Restaurant:** On premises. **General Store:** Yes. **Vending:** Yes. **Swimming:** River. **Playground:** No. **Other:** Boat ramp, RV & boat storage, boat repair, game room, cafe, bar. **Activities:** Fishing, boating, water sports. **Nearby Attractions:** Parker Dam, Lake Havasu. **Additional Information:** Parker Chamber of Commerce, (520) 669-2174, www.riverinfo.com/parker.

RESTRICTIONS

Pets: On leash. **Fires:** Yes. **Alcoholic Beverages:** Allowed. **Vehicle Maximum Length:** None.

TO GET THERE

From Parker go 9 mi. north on AZ Hwy. 95.

PARKS

Ponderosa Forest RV Park & RVCampground

P.O. Box 50640, Parks 86018. T: (888) 635-0456, (520) 635-045; F: (520) 635-0659.

🚐 ★★★★★   ▲ ★★★★

Beauty: ★★★★★	Site Privacy: ★★★★
Spaciousness: ★★★★	Quiet: ★★★★★
Security: ★★★★	Cleanliness: ★★★★★
Insect Control: ★★★	Facilities: ★★★★

It is hard to imagine a more beautiful campground. Sites are spacious (average 25 feet wide) and nearly all are set into the forest. (There is a treeless strip of gravel for seven larger rigs in the middle of the park that strikes one as slightly out of place.) A gorgeous ponderosa forest surrounds the park for at least ten acres, giving this campground both a rustic feel and the clean fresh air of a mountain forest. Accommodating both pull-throughs and back-ins, Ponderosa Forest offers full amenities while giving the impression of being lost in the woods. While the tent sites could stand a little more room, the overall experience is superior to any of the campgrounds in Williams or Flagstaff. Owner Jane is extremely friendly and full of stories. Whether your destination is the Grand Canyon or Flagstaff, this campground makes a wonderful jumping-off point, and should not be missed!

BASICS

Operated By: Jane & Guren Stinson. **Open:** All year. **Site Assignment:** Assigned at registration. **Registration:** At office; late arrivals go to manager's office at back of park. **Fee:** RV $19, tent $13. **Parking:** At sites; will help park vehicles of any size.

FACILITIES

Number of RV Sites: 29. **Number of Tent-Only Sites:** 16. **Hookups:** Water, sewer, electric (30, 50). **Each Site:** Picnic table, fire ring, trash can, most have several trees. **Dump Station:** Yes. **Laundry:** Yes. **Pay Phone:** Yes. **Rest Rooms and Showers:** Yes. **Fuel:** No. **Propane:** Yes. **Internal Roads:** Packed dirt & gravel, mostly good condition. **RV Service:** No. **Market:** 0.5 mi. to Parks. **Restaurant:** 0.5 mi. **General Store:** Yes. **Vending:** Yes. **Swimming:** No. **Playground:** No. **Other:** Gift shop on premises; post office, fax, copies, hair salon, massage parlor in front of RV park. **Activities:** Hiking, fishing, hunting, 4th of July & Labor Day BBQ & potluck. **Nearby Attractions:** Kendrik Peak, historic Rte. 66. **Additional Information:** Williams–Grand Canyon Chamber of Commerce, (520) 635-4061.

RESTRICTIONS

Pets: On leash; some dog breed restrictions; do not leave unattended; no barking. **Fires:** In fire ring. **Alcoholic Beverages:** At sites. **Vehicle Maximum Length:** None. **Other:** Motorcycles & ATVs in/out use only; no generators; no clotheslines; no wood gathering.

TO GET THERE

From Hwy. 40, take Exit 178, turn north, then take immediate left and follow the road behind the shops.

PATAGONIA

Patagonia Lake State Park

P.O. Box 274, Patagonia 85624. T: (520) 287-6965; F: (520) 287-5618; www.pr.state.az.us.

🚐 ★★★★   ▲ ★★★★

Beauty: ★★★★	Site Privacy: ★★★★
Spaciousness: ★★★★	Quiet: ★★★★
Security: ★★★★	Cleanliness: ★★★★
Insect Control: ★★★	Facilities: ★★★★

Situated between Patagonia and Nogales on the Mexican border, Patagonia Lake is reached from

AZ Hwy. 82 via a curving paved road through housing developments and a hillside forest of mesquite and ocotillo. The campground is nestled in low rolling foothills amongs shady mesquite trees, yucca, and cacti. The best campsites for views of the 265-acre manmade lake are numbered 1–37, and are also nearest the swimming beach. Boaters may wish to opt for the other loops, nearer the launch ramps. There are a dozen tent-only areas scattered around the lake, but they are only accessible by boat. Besides being stocked with trout every three weeks between Nov. and late Feb., the lake offers fishing for crappie, bluegill, bass, and catfish and birding tours. Almost every Friday the campground fills early for the weekend, and peak season park closures are common.

BASICS

Operated By: Arizona State Parks. **Open:** All year. **Site Assignment:** First come, first served. **Registration:** Self-pay fee station. **Fee:** $10–$15. **Parking:** At site (except for tent areas only accessible by boat).

FACILITIES

Number of RV Sites: 106. **Number of Tent-Only Sites:** 12. **Hookups:** Water, electric (20, 30 amp). **Each Site:** Table, grill. **Dump Station:** Yes. **Laundry:** No. **Pay Phone:** Yes. **Rest Rooms and Showers:** Yes. **Fuel:** No. **Propane:** No. **Internal Roads:** Paved, good. **RV Service:** No. **Market:** Patagonia, 12 mi. **Restaurant:** Patagonia, 12 mi. **General Store:** Yes. **Vending:** Yes. **Swimming:** Lake. **Playground:** No. **Other:** Marina, boat rentals, disabled-access fishing dock, picnic area. **Activities:** Boating, fishing, bird-watching. **Nearby Attractions:** Tubac Presidio, Tumacacori National Monument, Patagonia-Sonoita Creek Preserve. **Additional Information:** Mariposa Books/Patagonia Visitors Center, (520) 394-9186; Nogales Santa Cruz County Chamber of Commerce, (520) 287-3685.

RESTRICTIONS

Pets: On 6 ft. leash under owner's control. **Fires:** In grills provided; no wood gathering. **Alcoholic Beverages:** Allowed. **Vehicle Maximum Length:** 30 ft. **Other:** 2 weeks per month max. stay; 12 people & 2 vehicles per site- no water or jet skiing or recreational device towing May 1–Oct. 1; park gate closes 10 p.m.–4 a.m.

TO GET THERE

From AZ Hwy. 82, go 4 mi. north on park access road.

PAYSON

Ox Bow Estates RV Park

HC6 Box 1050 D, Payson 85541. T: (800) 520-5239; F: (520) 474-4538.

🚐 ★★★★   ⛺ ★★

Beauty: ★★★	Site Privacy: ★★★
Spaciousness: ★★★★	Quiet: ★★★★
Security: ★★★	Cleanliness: ★★★★★
Insect Control: ★★★★	Facilities: ★★★

With its log cabin–style office and wooded lots and stream, this campground has a very woodsy atmosphere. And well it should, since it abuts Tonto National Forest on one side. (From an aerial photo in the office, you can see just how lost in the woods this campground really is.) The rest of the surrounding area is quiet residential property. Sites are laid out in a grid, with one section divided from the rest by a small creek. Most sites are shaded, including the tent sites, and average a spacious 40 × 50 feet. The campground is peaceful, laid-back, and quiet. Besides Tonto National Forest, which you can be lost in within five minutes of leaving the park, the other local attractions are a quick drive away, making this campground a relaxing yet convenient stop. Proprietors Fred and Mimi are friendly, helpful, and full of information about the region.

BASICS

Operated By: Fred & Mimi Hendrix. **Open:** All year. **Site Assignment:** Assigned at registration. **Registration:** At office; if no one is available, use courtesy phone & call number listed; late arrivals: pick a spot & use drop slot in door. **Fee:** RV $21–23, tent $19. **Parking:** At site.

FACILITIES

Number of RV Sites: 50. **Number of Tent-Only Sites:** 0. **Hookups:** Water, sewer, electric (30, 50), TV. **Each Site:** Picnic table, fire pit, charcoal grill, tree. **Dump Station:** Yes. **Laundry:** Yes. **Pay Phone:** Yes. **Rest Rooms and Showers:** Yes. **Fuel:** No. **Propane:** Yes. **Internal Roads:** Gravel, in very good condition. **RV Service:** No. **Market:** 2 miles to casino. **Restaurant:** 2 mi. to casino. **General Store:** Yes. **Vending:** Yes. **Swimming:** No. **Playground:** No. **Other:** Creek. **Activities:** Hiking, biking, fishing, summer potlucks. **Nearby Attractions:** Tonto National Forest, Tonto National Bridge Park, Tonto Cliff Dwellings. **Additional Information:** Payson Chamber of Commerce, (520) 474-4515.

RESTRICTIONS

Pets: On leash. **Fires:** In pit or grill. **Alcoholic Beverages:** Not in buildings. **Vehicle Maximum Length:** 45 ft. **Other:** No clotheslines.

TO GET THERE

From the intersection of Hwy. 260 and Hwy. 87 in Payson, go south on 87 (towards Rye) for 4.2 mi., then turn right at the sign for the campground (there is no street sign). Drive 0.8 mi. through a residential area and turn into the entrance on the right.

PEORIA
Lake Pleasant Regional Park

41835 North Castle Hot Springs Rd., Peoria 85382.
T: (520) 501-0107; F: (520) 501-1704;
www.maricopa.gov/recsev.

🚐 ★★★★	🔺 ★★★★
Beauty: ★★★★	Site Privacy: ★★★★
Spaciousness: ★★★★	Quiet: ★★★★
Security: ★★★★★	Cleanliness: ★★★★
Insect Control: ★★★	Facilities: ★★★

One of six excellent Phoenix area county parks, Lake Pleasant Regional Park contains both the Desert Tortoise and Roadrunner Campgrounds. Roadrunner's hillside sites 7–24 fill up first because of their excellent views. Desert Tortoise's tent-only and improved pull-through sites along Den and Bajada Loop Roads have coveted lake views that are also snapped up fast. On long holiday weekends it seems like all Phoenix is headed here with boats. Since there are no reservations, an early Thursday arrival is advised to ensure snagging a holiday weekend campsite. Most sites easily accommodate vehicles in the mid-30 to mid-45-foot range, though the sites tend to be narrow (e.g. the 80-foot-long site is only 13 foot wide). The native desert hillside saguaro, octotillo, and brittlebush landscape blooms with yellow, purple, and blue wildflowers after Apr. showers. Park animals include bald eagles, wild burros, javelina, and desert tortoises.

BASICS

Operated By: Maricopa County Parks & Recreation Dept. **Open:** All year. **Site Assignment:** First come, first served. **Registration:** Entrance kiosk (or camp host). **Fee:** $8–$15 (cash or check only). **Parking:** At site.

FACILITIES

Number of RV Sites: 146. **Number of Tent-Only Sites:** 4. **Hookups:** Electric (20, 30, 50 amp), water. **Each Site:** Sheltered table, grill. **Dump Station:** No. **Laundry:** No. **Pay Phone:** Yes. **Rest Rooms and Showers:** Yes. **Fuel:** No. **Propane:** No. **Internal Roads:** Paved, good. **RV Service:** No. **Market:** Peoria, 8 mi. **Restaurant:** Peoria, 8 mi. **General Store:** No. **Vending:** Yes. **Swimming:** Lake. **Playground:** Yes. **Other:** Boat ramp, dam visitor center. **Activities:** Boating, fishing, shooting range, golf. **Nearby Attractions:** Factory shops, museums, Cave Creek, Carefree. **Additional Information:** Carefree–Cave Creek Chamber of Commerce, (602) 488-3381.

RESTRICTIONS

Pets: On leash under owner's control. **Fires:** In grills only; no ground fires. **Alcoholic Beverages:** Allowed. **Vehicle Maximum Length:** 80 ft. **Other:** No wood gathering.

TO GET THERE

From I-17 north of Phoenix take Exit 223, go west on AZ Hwy. 74 (Carefree Hwy.).

PHOENIX
Covered Wagon RV Park

6540 North Black Canyon Hwy., Phoenix 85017.
T: (602) 242-2500.

🚐 ★★★	🔺 ★★
Beauty: ★★★	Site Privacy: ★★★
Spaciousness: ★★★★	Quiet: ★★
Security: ★★★★	Cleanliness: ★★★★
Insect Control: ★★★★	Facilities: ★★★

This campground is slightly less pretty than Welcome Home, due to a cement retaining wall that runs along the edge of the property from sites 34–44. In addition, while the park seems equally well insulated from highway traffic sounds, noise from a ballpark located across the street invades the entire park when games are on. Still, this is not a bad place to park your RV while you explore the humongous city of Phoenix—and it is certainly much more convenient than the several campgrounds located 30 miles out of town. There are some wonderful flowering trees, giving the grounds a city park–like feel: you know you're in the city, but removed a bit from the action. Definitely not for the tenter looking for a wilderness experience. The Covered Wagon makes a reasonable base of operations for exploring Phoenix, but one more exit on I-17 will bring you to a slightly quieter park.

BASICS

Operated By: Ted Heiser. **Open:** All year. **Site Assignment:** Assigned at registration. **Registration:** Ring bell at office. **Fee:** RV $21–$32, depending on size, tent $18. **Parking:** At site.

FACILITIES

Number of RV Sites: 47. **Number of Tent-Only Sites:** 0. **Hookups:** Water, sewer, electric (20, 30, 50 amps). **Each Site:** Mature shade trees. **Dump Station:** Yes. **Laundry:** Yes. **Pay Phone:** Yes. **Rest Rooms and Showers:** Yes. **Fuel:** No. **Propane:** No. **Internal Roads:** Paved. **RV Service:** No. **Market:** 4 blocks. **Restaurant:** 4 blocks. **General Store:** No. **Vending:** Yes. **Swimming:** Yes. **Playground:** No. **Activities:** Swimming, shopping, hiking, sightseeing. **Nearby Attractions:** Mesa Southwest Museum, Champlin Fighter Museum, Superstition Springs Center, Casa Grande Ruins, Roosevelt Dam, Tonto National Monument. **Additional Information:** Phoenix Visitors Center, (602) 254-6500.

RESTRICTIONS

Pets: On leash, clean up after. **Fires:** Only charcoal in grills. **Alcoholic Beverages:** At sites only. **Vehicle Maximum Length:** None. **Other:** No clotheslines.

TO GET THERE

From the junction of I-17 and Glendale Rd. (Exit 205), merge into the far right-hand lane. Take the frontage road 0.5 mi., turn right, then take the second right (not the immediate right) into the entrance, follow the driveway to the end and turn right. The office is the white building on the left.

PHOENIX
Welcome Home RV Park

2501 Missouri Ave., Phoenix 85017. T: (602) 249-9852.

🚐 ★★★	⛺ n/a
Beauty: ★★★	Site Privacy: ★★★★
Spaciousness: ★★★★	Quiet: ★★★★
Security: ★★★	Cleanliness: ★★★★★
Insect Control: ★★★★	Facilities: ★★

Certainly one of the closest campgrounds to downtown Phoenix, this park is being converted to accept only RVs. (It currently does not accept tents, but has a few remaining mobile homes.) The grounds are laid out on a loop, with well-shaded, comfortable lots on either side. Lots are 30 feet wide, making them spacious enough for evening outdoor activities. Although situated right next to the highway, there is very little traffic noise spillover. Located on a quiet residential street, the park presents a great little urban getaway without an overly urban feel. Downtown Phoenix is a 20-minute drive away, while the quick access to I-17 provides a convenien way to depart for further destinations.

BASICS

Operated By: Ed Little. **Open:** All year. **Site Assignment:** Assigned at registration. **Registration:** At office; if closed, go to house next door. **Fee:** $21–$24; cash preferred, no credit cards. **Parking:** At site.

FACILITIES

Number of RV Sites: 52. **Number of Tent-Only Sites:** 0. **Hookups:** Water, sewer, electric (30, 50). **Each Site:** Trees & grass, some flowering bushes. **Dump Station:** No (sewer available at all sites). **Laundry:** Yes. **Pay Phone:** No (1 block). **Rest Rooms and Showers:** No shower. **Fuel:** No (1 block). **Propane:** No. **Internal Roads:** Paved. **RV Service:** No. **Market:** 1 mi. **Restaurant:** 2 mi. **General Store:** No (1 block). **Vending:** No. **Swimming:** Yes. **Playground:** No. **Activities:** Shuffleboard, clubhouse, Christmas dinner. **Nearby Attractions:** Mesa Southwest Museum, Champlin Fighter Museum, Superstition Springs Center, Casa Grande Ruins, Roosevelt Dam, Tonto National Monument. **Additional Information:** Phoenix Visitors Center, (602) 254-6500.

RESTRICTIONS

Pets: On leash, clean up after. **Fires:** Yes (only charcoal in grills). **Alcoholic Beverages:** At sites only. **Vehicle Maximum Length:** None. **Other:** 30 ft. min. length, must be 1991 or newer RV.

TO GET THERE

From the junction of I-17 and Bethany Rd. (Exit 204), merge into the far right-hand lane heading south. Follow the frontage road 0.5 mi. to the entrance on the right.

PICACHO
Picacho Campground

P.O. Box 368, Picacho 85241. T: (520) 466-7401 or (888) 562-7453; www.pichachocampground.com.

🚐 ★★★★   🅰 ★★★★

Beauty: ★★★★   Site Privacy: ★★★
Spaciousness: ★★★★   Quiet: ★★★
Security: ★★★★   Cleanliness: ★★★★
Insect Control: ★★★★   Facilities: ★★★★

Just off I-10, 75 miles south of Phoenix and 42 miles north of Tucson, Picacho Campground is popular with horse owners because it provides corrals ($10). Children are also welcome here, though parents must keep them in sight and under control at all times, particularly around the pool. Visitors here are mostly snowbirds and overnighters. Many put out their TV antennas to pull in Phoenix and Tucson stations, which means two NBC and two CBS channels, one each from PBS and ABC and two independents. An attractive oleander perimeter mutes much of the highway truck noise, though not all of it. Cacti, eucalyptus, and an abundance of other trees shade these extra long and extra wide sites, which easily accommodate sliders. The store and office stay open from 8 a.m. to 8 p.m., adding convenience at this well-run family operation.

BASICS
Operated By: Jerry & Frankie Cross. **Open:** All year. **Site Assignment:** First come, first served; winter reservations advised. **Registration:** Office. **Fee:** $17 tent, $22–$24 RV (V, MC, D). **Parking:** At site.

FACILITIES
Number of RV Sites: 70. **Number of Tent-Only Sites:** 8. **Hookups:** Electric (30, 50 amp), water, sewer. **Each Site:** Table. **Dump Station:** Yes. **Laundry:** Yes. **Pay Phone:** Yes. **Rest Rooms and Showers:** Yes. **Fuel:** Yes. **Propane:** Yes. **Internal Roads:** Gravel, good. **RV Service:** No. **Market:** Eloy, 4 mi. **Restaurant:** Steakhouse on premises (Dec.–Mar.). **General Store:** Yes. **Vending:** Yes. **Swimming:** Pool. **Playground:** Yes. **Other:** Hot tub, shuffleboard, dog walk, cabin. **Activities:** Horseback riding, golf. **Nearby Attractions:** Picacho Peak State Park, Casa Grande Ruins, Sasco ghost town. **Additional Information:** Sunland Visitor Center, (520) 466-3007.

RESTRICTIONS
Pets: On leash under owner's control (horses welcome). **Fires:** In fire pits in tent & picnic areas only. **Alcoholic Beverages:** Allowed. **Vehicle Maximum Length:** None. **Other:** No vehicle washing or repairs.

TO GET THERE
From I-10 Picacho Exit (211A from Phoenix; 212 from Tucson), go 0.5–1 mi. on frontage road.

PICACHO PEAK
Picacho Peak RV Resort

P.O. Box 1100, Red Rock 85245. T: (520) 466-7841.

🚐 ★★★★   🅰 n/a

Beauty: ★★★   Site Privacy: ★★★
Spaciousness: ★★★★   Quiet: ★★★
Security: ★★★★   Cleanliness: ★★★★★
Insect Control: ★★★★   Facilities: ★★★★★

Often confused with Picacho Campground seven miles to the north, Picacho Peak RV Resort exudes a very different atmosphere. Though the sites are attractively landscaped with medium-sized ocotillo, cacti, and trees, Picacho Peak RV Resort feels like an upscale RV parking annex for the mobile home park sharing the rear of the property. The benefit of mixing mobile homes and RVs is sharing the clean, well-maintained mobile home amenities. The RVs are closer to the interstate highway than the mobile homes, and the sandstone-colored perimeter wall and trees do not keep out all the truck noises and nightly train sounds. Also, there is not a convenience store here with the long hours found at Picacho Campground. However, the Resort is affiliated with Adventure Outdoor Resorts, Coast to Coast Network, and Resort Parks International, and members of those groups are promised good deals here.

BASICS
Operated By: Picacho Peak Resort. **Open:** Oct.–May. **Site Assignment:** First come, first served; winter reservations advised. **Registration:** Office (hosts will come by site to collect money after hours). **Fee:** $23 (V, MC). **Parking:** At site.

FACILITIES
Number of RV Sites: 159. **Number of Tent-Only Sites:** 0. **Hookups:** Electric (30, 50 amp),

water, sewer, phone (modem). **Each Site:** Table.
Dump Station: Yes. **Laundry:** Yes. **Pay Phone:**
Yes. **Rest Rooms and Showers:** Yes. **Fuel:** No.
Propane: Yes. **Internal Roads:** Paved, excellent.
RV Service: No. **Market:** Picacho Peak, 1 mi.
Restaurant: Picacho Peak, 1 mi. **General Store:**
No. **Vending:** Yes. **Swimming:** Pool. **Playground:**
No. **Other:** Rec room, whirlpool, shuffleboard &
volleyball courts, horseshoes, planned activities.
Activities: Golf, horseback riding. **Nearby
Attractions:** Picacho Peak State Park, Casa
Grande Ruins. **Additional Information:** Sunland
Visitor Center, (520) 466-3007, Picacho State Park,
(520) 466-3183.

RESTRICTIONS

Pets: On leash under owner's control. **Fires:** Yes
(where designated). **Alcoholic Beverages:**
Allowed. **Vehicle Maximum Length:** 32 ft.

TO GET THERE

From I-10, get off at Exit 219 and go south 0.5
mi. on frontage road.

PICACHO PEAK
Picacho Peak State Park

P.O. Box 275, Picacho 85241. T: (520) 466-3183;
www.pr.state.az.us.

🚐 ★★★★　　　　🏕 ★★★★★

Beauty: ★★★★★	Site Privacy: ★★★★★
Spaciousness: ★★★★★	Quiet: ★★★★
Security: ★★★★	Cleanliness: ★★★★
Insect Control: ★★	Facilities: ★★

Picacho Peak, an ancient Hohokam Indian site,
is a colorful mixture of 22-million-year-old lava
flows and sedimentary rock strata rich in
saguaro, cacti, grasses, and cottontail rabbits.
Though it doesn't have the swimming pools and
amenities of the nearby private campgrounds,
Picacho Peak State Park is the best place to experience the raw nature of this historic area. The
three loops are far enough back from the interstate highway that noise is not a problem. The
14-site hookup loop closest to the peak and park
entrance is literally just a paved parking lot,
albeit with a spectacular view and natural surroundings. Indeed, those who end up here as
Catalina State Park overflow casualties are pleasantly surprised by the historic peak that served as

a landmark for Father Kino, the Butterfield
Overland Stage, and the forty-niners headed to
the California gold fields.

BASICS

Operated By: Arizona State Parks. **Open:** All
year. **Site Assignment:** First come, first served;
group area requires reservations. **Registration:**
Self-pay station. **Fee:** $10–$15 (cash or check only).
Parking: At site.

FACILITIES

Number of RV Sites: 109. **Number of Tent-
Only Sites:** 0. **Hookups:** Electric (30 amp), water.
Each Site: Table, grill. **Dump Station:** Yes. **Laun-
dry:** No. **Pay Phone:** Yes. **Rest Rooms and
Showers:** Yes. **Fuel:** No. **Propane:** No. **Internal
Roads:** Paved, good. **RV Service:** No. **Market:**
Picacho Peak, 1 mi. **Restaurant:** Picacho Peak, 1 mi.
General Store: No. **Vending:** No. **Swimming:**
No. **Playground:** Yes. **Other:** Small visitor center,
some sheltered tables. **Activities:** Horseback rid-
ing, golf, bird & wildlife watching. **Nearby Attrac-
tions:** Casa Grande Ruins, Catalina State Park,
Saguaro National Park West. **Additional Informa-
tion:** Sunland Visitor Center, (520) 466-3007.

RESTRICTIONS

Pets: On leash under owner's control. **Fires:** Yes
(except summer, when fire danger). **Alcoholic
Beverages:** Allowed. **Vehicle Maximum
Length:** None. **Other:** No fireworks.

TO GET THERE

From I-10, take Exit 219, Picacho Peak Rd.

PINETOP-LAKESIDE
Hawley Lake Resort

P.O. Box 448, McNary 85930. T: (520) 335-7511;
F: (520) 335-7434.

🚐 ★★★★　　　　🏕 n/a

Beauty: ★★★★★	Site Privacy: ★★★★
Spaciousness: ★★★★★	Quiet: ★★★★★
Security: ★★★★★	Cleanliness: ★★★★★
Insect Control: ★★★	Facilities: ★★★★

Created in the 1950s by impounding Trout
Creek, 300-acre Hawley Lake offers rustic waterfront camping on the lands of the White Mountain Apache. Tall ponderosa pine trees,
boulder-strewn meadows, small waterfalls, roadside fishing (requires daily White Mountain

Apache permit), and good lake views from many hillside campsites are among the attractions. Rainbow trout thrive in the lake, though Apache, brown, cutthroat, and brook trout are also caught summer and winter (ice fishing). Many prefer fall fishing when the browns come up in the shallows. Wild turkey, deer, elk, and black bear make for good wildlife viewing and attract hunters. Be prepared for cold weather here, as at 8,200 feet elevation, summer temperatures can drop below freezing at night. The last two miles into the lake are on a gravel road, and big vehicles should call ahead to make sure they can be accommodated.

BASICS

Operated By: White Mountain Apache Tribe. **Open:** All year. **Site Assignment:** First come, first served; reservations up to 1 year in advance. **Registration:** Office in store. **Fee:** $8 regular site, $25 hookups (V, MC, debit cards). **Parking:** At site.

FACILITIES

Number of RV Sites: 100. **Number of Tent-Only Sites:** 0. **Hookups:** Electric (30 amp), water, sewer. **Each Site:** Table, grill. **Dump Station:** Yes. **Laundry:** Yes. **Pay Phone:** Yes. **Rest Rooms and Showers:** Yes. **Fuel:** Yes. **Propane:** Yes. **Internal Roads:** Gravel, good (chains or 4x4 required in winter). **RV Service:** No. **Market:** Pinetop-Lakeside, 24 mi. **Restaurant:** Cafe on premises. **General Store:** Yes (summer only). **Vending:** No. **Swimming:** No. **Playground:** No. **Other:** Marina, boat rentals, lodge, cabins, summer home rentals. **Activities:** Boating, fishing, hunting, horseback riding, biking, backpacking, archery. **Nearby Attractions:** Lakes, forest, casino. **Additional Information:** White Mountain Apache Tribe Office of Tourism, (520) 338-1230, www.wmat.nsn.us.

RESTRICTIONS

Pets: On leash under owner's control. **Fires:** Yes. **Alcoholic Beverages:** Allowed (drunk driving laws strictly enforced). **Vehicle Maximum Length:** No stated limit (but check w/ tribe before bringing in big vehicles). **Other:** No tents, fireworks, ATVs, cattle rustling, or fence cutting.

TO GET THERE

From Pinetop-Lakeside, go 16 mi. southeast on AZ Hwy. 260 and 8 mi. south on AZ Hwy. 473.

PINETOP–LAKESIDE
Hon-Dah RV Park

One Hwy. 73, Pinetop 85935. T: (520) 369-7400 or (800) 929-8744+1+7400# (reservations).

🚐 ★★★★	🛖 n/a
Beauty: ★★★★	Site Privacy: ★★★
Spaciousness: ★★★★	Quiet: ★★★
Security: ★★★★★	Cleanliness: ★★★★★
Insect Control: ★★★★	Facilities: ★★★★

A popular destination requiring advance reservations, Hon-Dah RV Park is across the street from Hon-Dah Casino's 500 slot machines and offers ample amenities to those visiting the area for boating, fishing, or winter skiing at nearby (20 miles) Sunrise Park Resort. The RV Park is in a wetlands area bisected by Corduroy Creek. There are 140 RV campsites south of the creek, and 58 reached by crossing a bridge and going uphill to the north side of the creek. Though the RV Park is near enough the highway to hear the hum of passing traffic, tall pines and gravel roads make the campground feel rustic, almost like camping in the wilderness. For those who want their forests and lake country with gambling and nighttime entertainment, this is a friendly place to put down after a day of fishing or boating.

BASICS

Operated By: White Mountain Apache Tribe. **Open:** All year. **Site Assignment:** First come, first served; reservations necessary. **Registration:** Office. **Fee:** $21 (V, MC). **Parking:** At site.

FACILITIES

Number of RV Sites: 198. **Number of Tent-Only Sites:** 0. **Hookups:** Electric (20, 30, 50 amp), water, sewer, satellite TV, phone. **Each Site:** Table, grill. **Dump Station:** Yes. **Laundry:** Yes. **Pay Phone:** Yes. **Rest Rooms and Showers:** Yes. **Fuel:** Yes. **Propane:** Yes. **Internal Roads:** Gravel, well-maintained. **RV Service:** No. **Market:** Pinetop-Lakeside, 5 mi. **Restaurant:** Casino, across street. **General Store:** Yes. **Vending:** Yes. **Swimming:** No. **Playground:** Yes. **Other:** Rec hall, casino, conference center. **Activities:** Shuffleboard, horseshoes, gambling, fishing, hunting, boating, winter sports. **Nearby Attractions:** Lakes, forests. **Additional Information:** White Mountain Apache Tribe Office of Tourism, (520) 338-1230, www.wmat.nsn.us; Sunrise Park Resort, (520) 735-

7600, www.sunriseskipark.com.

RESTRICTIONS

Pets: On leash (requires prior approval; loud barking not tolerated). **Fires:** Yes. **Alcoholic Beverages:** At site only. **Vehicle Maximum Length:** None. **Other:** Pets must be walked along fence outside park perimeter; no smoking in buildings; pedestrians should carry flashlight at night; units over 10 years old must pass visual inspection (refund if turned away).

TO GET THERE

From Pinetop-Lakeside go 5 mi. east on AZ Hwy. 260 to junction w/ AZ Hwy. 73.

QUARTZSITE

La Posa LTVA

2555 Gila Ridge Rd., Yuma 85365. T: (520) 726-6300 or (520) 317-3200; www.az.blm.gov.

🚐 ★★   ⛺ ★★★

Beauty: ★★★★	Site Privacy: ★★★★
Spaciousness: ★★★★★	Quiet: ★★★★
Security: ★★★★	Cleanliness: ★★★★
Insect Control: ★★★	Facilities: ★★

Every winter Quartzsite's few thousand permanent residents are joined by 200,000 in RVs, and during the giant Gemboree (gem show/flea market) the population surges into the millions before its annual contraction back to almost nothing during the scorching summer months. Hundreds of unofficial RV parks spring up to join the official ones. Literally any patch of desert along the roadsides becomes RV habitat, though there is more security in Long-Term Visitor Areas (LTVA) like La Posa, operated by the US Department of Interior's Bureau of Land Management (BLM). Besides La Posa, BLM operates five smaller no-fee, 14-day limit camping areas (Plomosa Rd., Hi Jolly/MM112, Dome Rock Mountain, Scaddan Wash, Road Runner/MM99) around Quartzsite. Though La Posa lacks RV park amenities, it has the beauty of literally camping out in the desert wherever you choose, provided it is not too near another campsite (to reduce the danger of a fire spreading).

BASICS

Operated By: Bureau of Land Management. **Open:** All year. **Site Assignment:** First come, first served. **Registration:** Brown brick entrance contact stations. **Fee:** $20 (7-day permit; cash or check only). **Parking:** At site.

FACILITIES

Number of RV Sites: 2,000. **Number of Tent-Only Sites:** 0. **Hookups:** None. **Each Site:** At least 15 ft. distance from neighbors. **Dump Station:** Yes. **Laundry:** No. **Pay Phone:** Yes. **Rest Rooms and Showers:** No showers. **Fuel:** No. **Propane:** No. **Internal Roads:** Gravel, adequate. **RV Service:** No. **Market:** Quartzsite, 1 mi. **Restaurant:** Quartzsite, 1 mi. **General Store:** No. **Vending:** No. **Swimming:** No. **Playground:** No. **Activities:** Winter ranger presentations, gem show. **Nearby Attractions:** Colorado River. **Additional Information:** Quartzsite Chamber of Commerce, (520) 927-5600, www.quartzsitechamber.com.

RESTRICTIONS

Pets: On leash under owner's control. **Fires:** Yes (subject to posted rules). **Alcoholic Beverages:** Allowed. **Vehicle Maximum Length:** None. **Other:** No camping in desert washes.

TO GET THERE

From junction of I-10 and AZ Hwy. 95 in Quartzsite, go south 1 mi. on AZ Hwy. 95.

ROOSEVELT

Cholla Recreation Site

Tonto Basin Ranger District, HC02 Box 4800, Roosevelt 85545. T: (520) 467-3200; F: (520) 467-3239; www.fs.fed.us/r3/tonto.

🚐 ★★★   ⛺ ★★★★★

Beauty: ★★★★★	Site Privacy: ★★★★★
Spaciousness: ★★★★★	Quiet: ★★★★★
Security: ★★★★	Cleanliness: ★★★★★
Insect Control: ★★★	Facilities: ★★

The largest completely solar-powered campground in the United States, Cholla Campground and Boating Site is located on the shores of central Arizona's largest lake, Theodore Roosevelt Lake. Blue shelters make the campground look like a blue-roofed village with solar panels amidst the tall saguaro, mesquite, and palo verde providing the campsites a privacy barrier. The 13 tent-only sites furthest from the boat ramp on the steep slopes at the end of Christmas Cholla Loop and the five tent-only sites at Cane Cholla Loop on the slopes closer to the campground entrance have the best waterfront views. The gravel and sand campsites are flat, and many double sites are available for those with multiple vehicles and big boats. For those wanting a more primitive experience, head to Indian Point on the northeast side of the lake or checkout the sometimes crowded beach camping nearby at Bachelor Cove or Cholla Cove.

BASICS

Operated By: US Forest Service. **Open:** All year. **Site Assignment:** First come, first served. **Registration:** Kiosk or self-pay station. **Fee:** $11–$17 (highest for double sites; half price for Golden Age pass holders; V, MC). **Parking:** At site; separate walk-in tent site parking near restrooms.

FACILITIES

Number of RV Sites: 188. **Number of Tent-Only Sites:** 18. **Hookups:** None. **Each Site:** Sheltered table, grill, fire pit. **Dump Station:** Yes. **Laundry:** No. **Pay Phone:** No. **Rest Rooms and Showers:** Yes. **Fuel:** No. **Propane:** No. **Internal Roads:** Paved, good. **RV Service:** No. **Market:** Globe, 36 mi. **Restaurant:** Roosevelt, 5 mi. **General Store:** No. **Vending:** No. **Swimming:** Lake. **Playground:** Yes. **Other:** Boat ramp, campfire circle, fish cleaning station, barrier-free wheelchair accessibility. **Activities:** Boating, fishing. **Nearby Attractions:** Tonto National Monument, Roosevelt Dam, Globe, Payson. **Additional Information:** Salt River Project (for water level information), (602) 236-3929, www.srpnet.com; Roosevelt Lake Marina, (520) 467-2245.

RESTRICTIONS

Pets: On leash under owner's control. **Fires:** Yes. **Alcoholic Beverages:** Allowed. **Vehicle Maximum Length:** None. **Other:** No ATVs or firearms.

TO GET THERE

From Globe take AZ Hwy. 88/188 west for 36 mi.

ROOSEVELT

Windy Hill Recreation Site

HC02 Box 4800, Roosevelt 85545. T: (520) 467-3200; F: (520) 467-3239; www.fs.fed.us/r3/tonto.

 ★★★   **A ★★★★**

Beauty: ★★★★   Site Privacy: ★★★★
Spaciousness: ★★★★   Quiet: ★★★

Security: ★★★★   Cleanliness: ★★★★
Insect Control: ★★★★   Facilities: ★★

Often packed full with local boaters on summer weekends, Windy Hill feels isolated because it is two miles from the main highway and the campsites are widely dispersed among ten loops. Each loop has its own trailheads and is named after a different animal that might be seen in the area, such as javelina, desert bighorn, gray fox, and coati. However, it is the rattlesnake (which does not have a loop named after it) which has to be watched out for here and in most other Arizona campgrounds. Double sites are big enough for a small beach party, packing in up to four cars, two boats, and 20 people. The level ground is good for tenting, and abundant desert plants like palo verde, ocotillo, and mesquite between the campsites add to the feeling of isolation and privacy.

BASICS

Operated By: US Forest Service. **Open:** All year. **Site Assignment:** First come, first served; group reservations. **Registration:** Self-pay fee machines. **Fee:** $10–$11 single & tent sites, $16–$17 double sites (V, MC; no checks). **Parking:** At site.

FACILITIES

Number of RV Sites: 320. **Number of Tent-Only Sites:** 27. **Hookups:** None. **Each Site:** Sheltered table, grill. **Dump Station:** Yes (5 mi. east). **Laundry:** No. **Pay Phone:** No. **Rest Rooms and Showers:** Yes. **Fuel:** No. **Propane:** No. **Internal Roads:** Gravel, good. **RV Service:** No. **Market:** Globe, 27 mi. **Restaurant:** Roosevelt, 6 mi. **General Store:** No. **Vending:** No. **Swimming:** Lake. **Playground:** Yes. **Other:** Amphitheater, fish cleaning station, high- & low-water boat ramps, day-use picnic sites, wheelchair accessible sites. **Activities:** Boating, fishing. **Nearby Attractions:** Tonto National Monument, Roosevelt Dam, Globe. **Additional Information:** Salt River Project (for water level information), (602) 236-3929, www.srpnet.com; Roosevelt Lake Marina, (520) 467-2245.

RESTRICTIONS

Pets: On leash. **Fires:** Yes (fires prohibited when high winds). **Alcoholic Beverages:** Allowed. **Vehicle Maximum Length:** 30 ft. **Other:** No glass containers.

TO GET THERE

From Globe take AZ Hwy. 88/188 west for 25 mi., then go east for 2 mi. on Frontage Rd. 82 at Windy Hill Recreation Site entrance sign.

SEDONA
Manzanita

2323 East Greenlaw Ln., Flagstaff 86004. T: (520) 527-3600.

🚐 ★★   ⛺ ★★★★

Beauty: ★★★★★   Site Privacy: ★
Spaciousness: ★★★   Quiet: ★★★★★
Security: ★   Cleanliness: ★★★★
Insect Control: ★   Facilities: ★

Charming, gorgeous, breathtaking, revitalizing—pick any superlative, they all fit. But so does "filled quickly." This campsite is a favorite in the well-traveled Oak Creek Canyon—and for good reason. Striking red rock bursts out of the forested hills above the creek, while rocky crags jut overhead. The entire canyon is beautiful and, as one local resident put it, "plum fulla history." The campsites mostly string out along the creek, and these sites (along with 10 and 19 on the ends) are the most highly-prized. The sites to avoid are 6 and 7 situated by the outhouse and up against the road. Admittedly, this campsite is not for everyone, and the lack of services or the hairpin turn in the road that prohibits larger rigs may put off more than one. (Those who do want full hookups or don't want to negotiate that curve could press on down Hwy. 89A to the lovely Rio Verde in Cottonwood.) However, campers looking for a great base for outdoor activities or a really romantic nook should definitely try their luck at scoring one of these spots.

BASICS
Operated By: National Forest Service. **Open:** All year. **Site Assignment:** First come, first served. **Registration:** Pick a site, register w/ camp host. **Fee:** $15. **Parking:** At sites.

FACILITIES
Number of RV Sites: 18. **Number of Tent-Only Sites:** 0. **Hookups:** None. **Each Site:** Picnic table, concrete fire pit, trees. **Dump Station:** No. **Laundry:** No. **Pay Phone:** No. **Rest Rooms and Showers:** Pit toilets, no showers. **Fuel:** No. **Propane:** No. **Internal Roads:** Paved. **RV Service:** No. **Market:** 2 mi. south on Hwy. 89A. **Restaurant:** 1 mi. south on Hwy. 89A. **General Store:** No. **Vending:** No. **Swimming:** In creek. **Playground:** No. **Other:** Well water, murmur of Oak Creek. **Activities:** Hiking, fishing, swimming, mountain biking; boating & other water sports at nearby Mormon Lake. **Nearby Attractions:** Oak Creek Canyon, Mormon Lake (seasonally the largest lake in Arizona). **Additional Information:** Sedona-Oak Creek Chamber of Commerce, (800) 228-7336.

RESTRICTIONS
Pets: On leash. **Fires:** In pit or grill. **Alcoholic Beverages:** At sites only. **Vehicle Maximum Length:** Larger than 24 ft. is unfeasible, due to a hairpin bend in the road. **Other:** 7-day stay limit.

TO GET THERE
Five mi. north of "Midgely Bridgely" at the northernmost edge of town on Hwy. 89A.

SHOW LOW
Fool Hollow Lake Recreation Area

P.O. Box 288, Show Low 85901. T: (520) 537-3680; www.pr.state.az.us.

🚐 ★★★★★   ⛺ ★★★★★

Beauty: ★★★★   Site Privacy: ★★★★
Spaciousness: ★★★★   Quiet: ★★★★★
Security: ★★★★★   Cleanliness: ★★★★★
Insect Control: ★★★   Facilities: ★★★

Established in 1991 as a partnership between the city of Show Low, the US Forest Service, Arizona State Parks, and Arizona Game and Fish, Fool Hollow provides RV campers with large cement pads and hookups in four separate loops (Red Head, Mallard, Ruddy Duck, and Cinnamon Teal). Tent campers have good lake views from their three separate loops (Northern Harrier, Osprey, Bald Eagle). Pines, tall junipers, volcanic boulders, and jack rabbits contribute to the rustic feel. Show Low Creek feeds Fool Hollow Lake, which is stocked with rainbow trout by Arizona Game and Fish. There is also a good chance of catching brown trout, large and small mouth bass, black crappie, and green sunfish. Away from the water are 103 miles of hiking trails within 15 miles and golf links in the rapidly suburbanizing surrounding area.

BASICS
Operated By: Arizona State Parks. **Open:** All year. **Site Assignment:** First come, first served. **Registration:** Self-pay station. **Fee:** $10 tent, $15 RV. **Parking:** At site.

FACILITIES
Number of RV Sites: 92. **Number of Tent-Only Sites:** 31. **Hookups:** Electric (30, 50 amp), water.

Each Site: Table, grill. **Dump Station:** Yes. **Laundry:** No. **Pay Phone:** Yes. **Rest Rooms and Showers:** Yes. **Fuel:** No. **Propane:** No. **Internal Roads:** Paved, excellent. **RV Service:** No. **Market:** Show Low, 4 mi. **Restaurant:** Show Low, 4 mi. **General Store:** No. **Vending:** No. **Swimming:** Lake. **Playground:** Yes. **Other:** Boat ramps, fish cleaning station, fishing docks, covered picnic tables w/ grills, wildlife island. **Activities:** Boating, fishing, golf. **Nearby Attractions:** Lakes, forests, Mogollon Rim, Petrified Forest. **Additional Information:** Show Low Chamber of Commerce, (520) 537-2326.

RESTRICTIONS

Pets: On leash (not allowed on beaches or in buildings). **Fires:** In grills only; firewood sold. **Alcoholic Beverages:** Allowed. **Vehicle Maximum Length:** None. **Other:** Entrance gate closed 10 p.m. to 5 a.m.; no fireworks; food must be secured from bears; 8 horsepower limit on boat motors.

TO GET THERE

From junction of US Hwy. 60 and AZ Hwy. 260, go 2 mi. west on Hwy. 260 and 1.5 mi. east on Old Linden Rd. to Fool Hollow Rd.

SHOW LOW

Show Low Lake County Park

Navajo County Parks & Recreation Dept., Holbrook 86025. T: (520) 537-4126 or (520) 524-4251; www.parksrec@navajo.az.us.

🚐 ★★★	▲ ★★★★
Beauty: ★★★★	Site Privacy: ★★★★
Spaciousness: ★★★★★	Quiet: ★★★★
Security: ★★★★	Cleanliness: ★★★★★
Insect Control: ★★★	Facilities: ★★★★

Show Low Lake was formed when the Phelps Dodge Corporation built Show Low Dam as part of a water exchange agreement with the Salt River Project to supply water to its mining and metallurgical operations elsewhere in the state. Indeed, the park land is leased from Phelps Dodge. Navajo County recently issued a private vendor a special permit to run the park and take campsite reservations. At 7,000 feet elevation in the White Mountains, the area makes a relatively cool summer retreat for Phoenix and the hot desert valleys. Show Low Lake is also a popular fishing spot for trout, walleyes, bluegills, large mouth bass, and catfish. The large crushed brown volcanic gravel campsites are shaded by very tall pine trees. For electric hookups request sites 25, 26, 28, 31, 32, 33, or 35. When the need for manmade necessities strikes, the local Walmart is only a mile away.

BASICS

Operated By: Recreation Resource Management of America. **Open:** All year. **Site Assignment:** First come, first served; reservations available. **Registration:** Store (adjacent host trailer when store is closed). **Fee:** $8–$16. **Parking:** At site.

FACILITIES

Number of RV Sites: 73. **Number of Tent-Only Sites:** 0. **Hookups:** Electric (30 amp), water. **Each Site:** Table, fire pit. **Dump Station:** Yes. **Laundry:** No. **Pay Phone:** Yes. **Rest Rooms and Showers:** Yes. **Fuel:** No. **Propane:** No. **Internal Roads:** Gravel, good. **RV Service:** No. **Market:** Show Low, 1 mi. **Restaurant:** Show Low, 1 mi. **General Store:** Yes. **Vending:** Yes. **Swimming:** Lake. **Playground:** Yes. **Other:** Boat ramp, boat rental, visitor center. **Activities:** Boating, fishing. **Nearby Attractions:** Lakes, forests, Mogollon Rim, Petrified Forest. **Additional Information:** Show Low Chamber of Commerce, (520) 537-2326.

RESTRICTIONS

Pets: On leash. **Fires:** Yes (firewood sold). **Alcoholic Beverages:** Allowed. **Vehicle Maximum Length:** None. **Other:** Boats limited to one 8 horsepower motor; no firearms or woodcutting; secure food from bears.

TO GET THERE

From Show Low go 6 mi. south on AZ Hwy. 260.

ST. JOHNS

Lyman Lake State Park

P.O. Box 1428, St. Johns 85936. T: (520) 337-4441; F: (520) 337-4649; www.pr.state.az.us.

🚐 ★★★★	▲ ★★★★
Beauty: ★★★★	Site Privacy: ★★★★
Spaciousness: ★★★★	Quiet: ★★★★★
Security: ★★★★	Cleanliness: ★★★★★
Insect Control: ★★★★	Facilities: ★★★★

A favorite of local windsurfers and waterskiers because of the lake's smooth surface, boaters like 6,000-foot-elevation Lyman Lake because it doesn't have boat size and motor horsepower restrictions (though there is a no-wake area near the fishing dock). There is a self-guided petroglyph trail on Peninsula Point, as well as a ranger-guided weekend boat trip to another petroglyph trail on the opposite side of the lake. Rangers also lead a summer tour to fourteenth-century Rattlesnake Pueblo for those curious about the ancient Mogollon and Pueblo cultures formerly inhabiting this high plains area. RV campers have 38 electrical and water hookup sites attractively separated by grass and aspen and juniper trees. Tent campers can opt out of the designated sites altogether for more of a wilderness experience and camp along the shoreline beaches of this 1,500-acre reservoir.

BASICS

Operated By: Arizona State Parks. **Open:** All year. **Site Assignment:** First come, first served; group reservations. **Registration:** Office. **Fee:** $10–$15 (cash or check only). **Parking:** At site.

FACILITIES

Number of RV Sites: 61. **Number of Tent-Only Sites:** Undesignated sites. **Hookups:** Electric (30 amp), water. **Each Site:** Table, fire pit. **Dump Station:** Yes. **Laundry:** No. **Pay Phone:** Yes. **Rest Rooms and Showers:** Yes. **Fuel:** No. **Propane:** No. **Internal Roads:** Paved, good. **RV Service:** No. **Market:** St. Johns, 10 mi. **Restaurant:** St. Johns, 10 mi. **General Store:** Yes. **Vending:** Yes. **Swimming:** Lake. **Playground:** No. **Other:** Boat ramp, boat rentals, fish-cleaning station, sheltered picnic tables, tournamen-grade water ski slalom course, petroglyph trails. **Activities:** Fishing, boating, water sports, volleyball, horseshoes. **Nearby Attractions:** Sunrise Ski Area, White Mountains, Petrified Forest, Navajo Reservation. **Additional Information:** St. Johns Regional Chamber of Commerce, (520) 337-2000.

RESTRICTIONS

Pets: On leash. **Fires:** In fire pits or grills only; no wood gathering. **Alcoholic Beverages:** Allowed (provided quiet hours observed). **Vehicle Maximum Length:** 45 ft. **Other:** No harassing or removing birds.

TO GET THERE

From St. Johns go 11 mi. south on the combined US Hwy. 191/180.

TEMPLE BAR
Temple Bar

601 Nevada Hwy., Boulder City 89005. T: (702) 293-8907; F: (702) 293-8936; www.nps.gov/lame.

🚐 ★★★   ▲ ★★★★

Beauty: ★★★★   **Site Privacy:** ★★★★
Spaciousness: ★★★★   **Quiet:** ★★★★
Security: ★★★★   **Cleanliness:** ★★★★★
Insect Control: ★★★   **Facilities:** ★★★

On the Arizona side of Lake Mead, across yucca-studded desert that yields to creosote bush interspersed with brown and black chunks of lava and white hills, Temple Bar is one of the most remote designated campgrounds on Lake Mead. The Temple, a huge monolithic chunk of sandstone that glows brilliant orange at sunset, was an early landmark for Mormon settlers and the site of placer mining operations in the 1800s. The campground is a tightly packed cluster of sites beautifully landscaped with palms, oleander. and eucalyptus that provide privacy. Gravel pads make for good tent camping, and lake and mountain views are common. The campground's remoteness and isolation are part of its beauty, and like the rest of Lake Mead, the activities center around the water. There are 64 boat slips.

BASICS

Operated By: National Park Service. **Open:** All year. **Site Assignment:** First come, first served. **Registration:** Self-pay entrance fee station. **Fee:** $10. **Parking:** At site.

FACILITIES

Number of RV Sites: 166. **Number of Tent-Only Sites:** 0. **Hookups:** None. **Each Site:** Table, grill. **Dump Station:** Yes. **Laundry:** Yes. **Pay Phone:** Yes. **Rest Rooms and Showers:** Yes. **Fuel:** Yes. **Propane:** Yes. **Internal Roads:** Paved, good. **RV Service:** No. **Market:** Boulder City, 60 mi. **Restaurant:** At Temple Bar Resort. **General Store:** Yes. **Vending:** Yes. **Swimming:** In lake at own risk. **Playground:** No. **Other:** Wheelchair accessible sites, boat ramp, row boat rentals, motel, landing strip. **Activities:** Boating, fishing. **Nearby Attractions:** Lake Mead, Hoover Dam, Las Vegas. **Additional Information:** Temple Bar Resort (Seven Crowns), (800) 752-9669, (520) 767-3211.

RESTRICTIONS

Pets: On leash under owner's control. **Fires:** Yes.
Alcoholic Beverages: Allowed. **Vehicle Maximum Length:** None. **Other:** 30-night stay limit.

TO GET THERE

From Hoover Dam go 19 mi. southeast on US Hwy. 93 and turn northeast on Temple Bar Rd. for 28 mi.

TOMBSTONE

Wells Fargo RV Park

Box 1076, Tombstone 85638. T: (520) 457-3966 or (800) 269-8266; F: (520) 457-2307; si-systems.com/wellsfargorv; wellsfargorv@si-systems.com.

🚐 ★★★   ▲ ★★★

Beauty: ★★★	Site Privacy: ★★★★
Spaciousness: ★★★	Quiet: ★★★★
Security: ★★★	Cleanliness: ★★★★
Insect Control: ★★★★	Facilities: ★★★★

Though at the edge of Tombstone's historic boardwalk, Wells Fargo RV Park becomes almost as quiet as a tomb at night, as this once brawling, saloon and brothel-filled frontier mining town now shuts down at sundown. Some claim to hear ghosts at night, but usually the only commotion at this tree-lined campground is dogs in a howling frenzy as deer and javelina strolling through like they own the place. Wells Fargo's year-round residents are mostly a friendly group, and many work at local establishments like Big Nose Kate's Saloon. Next door is what locals call the best breakfast place in town, the O.K. Cafe, which also charbroils emu, ostrich, and buffalo burgers. It's "just a biscuit sling from the OK Corral," where Doc Holliday joined Wyatt and the Earp brothers for the famous shootout with the Clanton and McLaury families.

BASICS

Operated By: Joe & Buff Huntsman. **Open:** All year. **Site Assignment:** First come, first served; reservations advised Dec. 26–Memorial Day. **Registration:** Office. **Fee:** $21.50. **Parking:** At site.

FACILITIES

Number of RV Sites: 71. **Number of Tent-Only Sites:** 0. **Hookups:** Electric (20, 30 amp), water, sewer, cable TV. **Each Site:** Table, cement pad. **Dump Station:** Yes. **Laundry:** Yes. **Pay Phone:** Yes. **Rest Rooms and Showers:** Yes. **Fuel:** No. **Propane:** No. **Internal Roads:** Gravel, good. **RV Service:** No. **Market:** Bisbee, 19 mi. **Restaurant:** Tombstone, next door. **General Store:** No. **Vending:** Yes. **Swimming:** No. **Playground:** No. **Activities:** 2 p.m. daily OK Corral shootout. **Nearby Attractions:** OK Corral, Tombstone Courthouse State Park, Bird Cage Theatre, Bisbee. **Additional Information:** Tombstone Chamber of Commerce, (520) 457-9317 or (888) 457-3929, www.tombstone.org.

RESTRICTIONS

Pets: On leash under owner's control. **Fires:** No.
Alcoholic Beverages: Allowed. **Vehicle Maximum Length:** 30 ft.

TO GET THERE

From junction of US Hwy. 80 & AZ Hwy. 82, go 3 mi. south on US Hwy. 80.

TORTILLA FLAT

Laguna Beach Campground

P.O. Box 4978, Apache Junction 85278. T: (602) 944-6504 (voice option #1); F: (480) 380-9301; www.canyonlakemarinaaz.com; customer.service@canyonlakemarinaaz.com.

🚐 ★★★   ▲ ★★

Beauty: ★★★★	Site Privacy: ★★
Spaciousness: ★★★	Quiet: ★★★
Security: ★★★★★	Cleanliness: ★★★★
Insect Control: ★★★	Facilities: ★★★★

At Canyon Lake, 17 miles north of Apache Junction, a gated kiosk and steel fence encloses Laguna Beach Campground, a lakeside stretch of parking lot and grassy campsites (ten hookups) within Canyon Lake Marina. The Marina prides itself on round-the-clock security and being "a gated community with the lake as one border and steel fencing preventing land access." Campers must adhere to strict rules, like no fishing around the boat dock or restaurant without a Marina member. Jet skies, mini-bikes, boats, and trailers are among the items banned from the campground, though they can be left in the parking lot on the other side of the steel fence or stored for a fee. Getting to this maximum security campground is a scenic ordeal via a slow twisting mountain road with one-lane bridges for added adventure. If this sounds like too much of an ordeal, there is always Roosevelt Lake.

BASICS

Operated By: Canyon Lake Marina. **Open:** All year. **Site Assignment:** First come, first served; reservations recommended (no refund on cancellation of reservation made 60 days in advance or for a Friday). **Registration:** Gated entrance kiosk. **Fee:** $12–$15 tent; $15–$30 RV (V, MC, AE, DC). **Parking:** At site.

FACILITIES

Number of RV Sites: 27. **Number of Tent-Only Sites:** 19. **Hookups:** Electric (30 amp), water. **Each Site:** Table, fire ring. **Dump Station:** No. **Laundry:** No. **Pay Phone:** Yes. **Rest Rooms and Showers:** Yes. **Fuel:** No (boat fuel only). **Propane:** No. **Internal Roads:** Paved, good. **RV Service:** No. **Market:** Apache Junction, 17 mi. **Restaurant:** Marina, adjacent. **General Store:** No. **Vending:** No. **Swimming:** Lake. **Playground:** No. **Other:** Storage, boat & slip rentals. **Activities:** Boating, fishing, steamboat ride. **Nearby Attractions:** Roosevelt Lake, Tonto National Monument, parks. **Additional Information:** Apache Junction Chamber of Commerce, (800) 252-3141 or (602) 982-3141.

RESTRICTIONS

Pets: On leash. **Fires:** In fire rings only. **Alcoholic Beverages:** Allowed (glass containers prohibited; $50 bottle fine). **Vehicle Maximum Length:** 40 ft. **Other:** No gas containers; no weapons; gate closed sunset to sundown.

TO GET THERE

From Apache Junction, go northeast 17 mi. on AZ Hwy. 88 (Apache Trail).

TSAILE

Wheatfields Lake

P.O. Box 9000, Window Rock 86515. T: (520) 871-6645 or (520) 871-7307.

🚐 ★★	⛺ ★★★★
Beauty: ★★★★	Site Privacy: ★★★★
Spaciousness: ★★★★	Quiet: ★★★★★
Security: ★★★	Cleanliness: ★★
Insect Control: ★★★	Facilities: ★

Just east of Canyon de Chelly at 7,200 feet elevation, Wheatfields Lake is a relatively uncrowded

place to catch cutthroat and rainbow trout, though a fishing permit first needs to be obtained from Navajo Fish & Wildlife (call (520) 871-6451) in Window Rock. Unlike Camp Asaayi Campground at Asaayi Lake where the terrain mitigates against RVs, smaller vehicles can squeeze into Wheatfields Lake when the weather is favorable. If the beer cans left behind by those not observing the tribal prohibition on alcohol are too much of an eyesore while shoreline fishing near the roadside, the other side of the lake can be reached by vehicle, and a boat can be launched from the base of the Chuska Mountains. The campground gets plenty of shade from tall ponderosa pines, though with port-a-potties this is a primitive spot in a rural area where careful driving is advised to avoid hitting horses grazing too close to the road.

BASICS

Operated By: Navajo Nation. **Open:** All year. **Site Assignment:** First come, first served. **Registration:** Self-pay fee station. **Fee:** $5. **Parking:** At site.

FACILITIES

Number of RV Sites: 25. **Number of Tent-Only Sites:** 0. **Hookups:** None. **Each Site:** Table, grill. **Dump Station:** No. **Laundry:** No. **Pay Phone:** Yes. **Rest Rooms and Showers:** No showers. **Fuel:** No. **Propane:** No. **Internal Roads:** Dirt, bumpy. **RV Service:** No. **Market:** Window Rock, 43 mi. **Restaurant:** Tsaile, 12 mi. **General Store:** Yes (sporadically open). **Vending:** No. **Swimming:** Lake. **Playground:** No. **Activities:** Fishing, boating. **Nearby Attractions:** Canyon de Chelly, Window Rock. **Additional Information:** Navajo Nation Visitor Center, (520) 871-6436.

RESTRICTIONS

Pets: On leash under owner's control. **Fires:** Yes. **Alcoholic Beverages:** Prohibited on Navajo Reservation. **Vehicle Maximum Length:** 20 ft.

TO GET THERE

From Window Rock, go 43 mi. north on Indian Hwy. 12.

TUCSON
Catalina State Park

P.O. Box 36986, Tucson 85740. T: (520) 628-5798; www.pr.state.az.us.

🚐 ★★★★   ⛺ ★★★★★

Beauty: ★★★★   Site Privacy: ★★★★
Spaciousness: ★★★★★   Quiet: ★★★★
Security: ★★★★   Cleanliness: ★★★★
Insect Control: ★★★   Facilities: ★★

Big patches of mesquite ensure privacy at Catalina State Park, where the smallest campsite length is 55 feet and half the sites have hookups. Ten years ago this Santa Catalina Mountains desert foothill cattle ranching area was considered remote. Now Tangerine Rd. between I-10 and the park and the whole Oro Valley is filling up with subdivisions for retirees and aerospace engineers commuting to Tucson. Park roads run through a floodplain with flat ridges that provided the ancient Hohokams a home with water. When Sutherland Wash, the key floodplain drainage, becomes impossible to cross, access to hiking trails and Romero Ruins is blocked, though the campground is still reachable. From Jan. through Apr., Tucson's peak season, morning arrivals snag all the campsites by noon. Afternoon arrivals (overflow) are typically sent to either Gilbert Ray Campground or Picacho Peak State Park. Plans call for alleviating winter-use pressures by adding 75 campsites with electric hookups.

BASICS
Operated By: Arizona State Parks. **Open:** All year. **Site Assignment:** First come, first served; group reservations required. **Registration:** Self-pay station. **Fee:** $10–$15 (cash or check only). **Parking:** At site.

FACILITIES
Number of RV Sites: 48. **Number of Tent-Only Sites:** 0. **Hookups:** Electric (20, 30, 50 amp), water. **Each Site:** Table, grill. **Dump Station:** Yes. **Laundry:** No. **Pay Phone:** Yes. **Rest Rooms and Showers:** Yes. **Fuel:** No. **Propane:** No. **Internal Roads:** Paved, good condition. **RV Service:** No. **Market:** Oro Valley, 2 mi. **Restaurant:** Oro Valley, 2 mi. **General Store:** No. **Vending:** Yes. **Swimming:** Seasonal pools along hiking trails. **Playground:** No. **Other:** Romero Ruin Hohokam

Indian archaeological site. **Activities:** Horseback riding, bird-watching, golf. **Nearby Attractions:** Santa Catalina Mountains, Coronado National Forest, Biosphere 2. **Additional Information:** Santa Catalina Ranger District, (520) 749-8700.

RESTRICTIONS
Pets: On leash under owner's control. **Fires:** Yes (charcoal only; no wood fires, except 1 campfire pit in group area). **Alcoholic Beverages:** Allowed. **Vehicle Maximum Length:** 136 ft. **Other:** 14-day stay limit.

TO GET THERE
Go 9 mi. north of Tucson on AZ Hwy. 77 (Oracle Rd.) to mi. marker 81.

TUCSON
Crazy Horse Campground & RV Park

6660 South Craycroft Rd., Tucson 85706. T: (520) 574-0157 or (800) 279-6279.

🚐 ★★★★   ⛺ ★★★

Beauty: ★★★   Site Privacy: ★★★★
Spaciousness: ★★★★   Quiet: ★★★★
Security: ★★★★   Cleanliness: ★★★★
Insect Control: ★★★★   Facilities: ★★★★

Far enough back from I-10 to be quiet and near enough a truck stop to have a gas station, mini-mart, and restaurant next door, Crazy Horse is especially attractive to families with children. Thomas Jay Littletown Park, a quiet Pima County–run park two blocks north, is popular with kids and an easy walk from Crazy Horse. Most sites are pull-through, mostly 24-feet wide and accommodating vehicles up to 45 feet in length (one site accommodates a 60-foot vehicle). The attractive oleander, mesquite and agave landscaping is concentrated around the front of the campground. For more amenities and the feel of a small luxury city, the adult-oriented Voyager RV Resort a few miles down the road is a good alternative. Cochise Terrace in Benson should also be considered if the objective is establishing a base camp near Tucson for exploring places like Tombstone and Bisbee.

BASICS

Operated By: Frank & Billie Anne Weingart. **Open:** All year. **Site Assignment:** First come, first served; reservations accepted seasonally (nonrefundable fee for confirmation by mail). **Registration:** Office. **Fee:** $19–$21 (V, MC). **Parking:** At site.

FACILITIES

Number of RV Sites: 154. **Number of Tent-Only Sites:** 0. **Hookups:** Electric (20, 30, 50 amp), water, sewer, cable TV, phone. **Each Site:** Table. **Dump Station:** Yes. **Laundry:** Yes. **Pay Phone:** Yes. **Rest Rooms and Showers:** Yes. **Fuel:** Yes. **Propane:** Yes. **Internal Roads:** Paved, good. **RV Service:** No. **Market:** Tucson, 3 mi. **Restaurant:** Tucson, 1 block. **General Store:** Yes. **Vending:** Yes. **Swimming:** Pool. **Playground:** Yes. **Other:** Dog walk, rec hall. **Activities:** Golf, horseback riding. **Nearby Attractions:** Pima Air & Space Museum, Saguaro National Park East, Colossal Cave, Kartchner Caverns, museums. **Additional Information:** Tucson CVB, (800) 638-8350, www.visitTucson.org.

RESTRICTIONS

Pets: On leash under owner's control. **Fires:** In approved containers & hibachis; no open fires. **Alcoholic Beverages:** Allowed. **Vehicle Maximum Length:** 60 ft.

TO GET THERE

Take Exit 268 from I-10 and go north on S. Craycroft Rd.

TUCSON

Gilbert Ray Campground

1204 West Silverlake Rd., Tucson 85713. T: (520) 740-2690 or (520) 883-4200.

🚐 ★★★★	⛺ ★★★★
Beauty: ★★★★	Site Privacy: ★★★★
Spaciousness: ★★★★★	Quiet: ★★★★
Security: ★★★	Cleanliness: ★★★★
Insect Control: ★★★	Facilities: ★

A favorite of many for its low cost and location west of Tucson near Saguaro National Park West and the Desert Museum, Gilbert Ray's river gravel sites are a particularly convenient stopping place when driving from Ajo or Organ Pipe Cactus National Monument through the Tohono O'odham Indian Reservation en route to Tucson on Arizona Hwy. 86 (Ajo Hwy.). This large, looping Pima County campground in Tucson Mountain Park is as close as camping gets to Saguaro National Park West without backpacking. Though there are hookups, the campground has few other amenities besides newspaper machines and a large recycling area. Campers here are mostly self-sufficient types whose idea of amenities is an undeveloped landscape with saguaro-studded mountains. Kinney, Gates Pass, and McCain Loop Rds. have roller coaster–like ups and downs near Gilbert Ray, and numerous roadside pullouts double as trailheads for traversing saguaro-rich Tucson Mountain Park.

BASICS

Operated By: Pima County Parks & Recreation. **Open:** All year. **Site Assignment:** First come, first served. **Registration:** Self-pay station. **Fee:** $7 tent; $12 RV (cash or check only). **Parking:** At site.

FACILITIES

Number of RV Sites: 136. **Number of Tent-Only Sites:** 5. **Hookups:** Electric (30 amp), water, sewer. **Each Site:** Table, grill. **Dump Station:** Yes. **Laundry:** No. **Pay Phone:** No. **Rest Rooms and Showers:** No showers. **Fuel:** No. **Propane:** No. **Internal Roads:** Paved, excellent. **RV Service:** No. **Market:** Tucson Estates, 5 mi. **Restaurant:** Tucson Estates, 5 mi. **General Store:** No. **Vending:** No. **Swimming:** No. **Playground:** No. **Other:** Some sheltered tables, recycling station. **Activities:** Rifle range, archery, horseback riding, biking. **Nearby Attractions:** Old Tucson Studios, Arizona-Sonora Desert Museum, Saguaro National Park West. **Additional Information:** Friends of Saguaro National Park, (520) 622-1080, www.friendsofsaguaro.org.

RESTRICTIONS

Pets: On leash under owner's control. **Fires:** Charcoal only in grills only; no wood fires. **Alcoholic Beverages:** Allowed. **Vehicle Maximum Length:** 30 ft. **Other:** 7-day stay limit; $160 automatic noncompliance citation if site not paid for within 15 min. of occupancy.

TO GET THERE

From intersection of W. Gates Pass & Kinney Rds., go northwest to McCain Loop Rd.

TUCSON

Voyager RV Resort

8701 South Kolb Rd., Tucson 85706. T: (520) 574-5000 or (800) 424-9191; F: (520) 574-5037; www.VoyagerRV.com; info@VoyagerRV.com.

🚐 ★★★★★   ▲ n/a

Beauty: ★★★   Site Privacy: ★★★
Spaciousness: ★★★★★   Quiet: ★★★★
Security: ★★★★★   Cleanliness: ★★★★★
Insect Control: ★★★★★   Facilities: ★★★★★

Tucson's largest RV resort opened in 1984 with 37,000 square feet of enclosed recreational space, including special crafts rooms for stained glass, lapidary, ceramics, and silver. With its own bank branch, restaurant, travel desk, store, and other facilities, Voyager has the feel of a small self-contained city. Streets are numbered 1st through 18th, and then skip by tens from 20th through 50th for the pull-through area surrounding the recreational facilities. Though daily RV rentals are welcome, the orientation is adult, like many southern Arizona RV parks catering to snowbird retirees. Except during summer, when kids are welcome, families with children will do better at the more child- and family-oriented Crazy Horse Campground. Since the fees are higher here, commensurate with the myriad of recreation options, Voyager is best thought of as a destination resort. But Voyager also works well as a luxury tourism base for exploring Tucson and southeastern Arizona.

BASICS

Operated By: Ike & Blanche Issacson. **Open:** All year. **Site Assignment:** First come, first served. **Registration:** Self-pay entrance fee station. **Fee:** $24–$27 (V, MC, D). **Parking:** At site.

FACILITIES

Number of RV Sites: 1,576. **Number of Tent-Only Sites:** 0. **Hookups:** Electric (20, 30, 50 amp), water, sewer, cable TV, phone. **Each Site:** Paved, table. **Dump Station:** Yes. **Laundry:** Yes. **Pay Phone:** Yes. **Rest Rooms and Showers:** Yes. **Fuel:** Yes. **Propane:** Yes. **Internal Roads:** Paved, excellent. **RV Service:** No. **Market:** Tucson, 2 mi. **Restaurant:** On premises. **General Store:** Yes. **Vending:** Yes. **Swimming:** Pool. **Playground:** No. **Other:** Bocce, tennis, basketball & volleyball courts, mini-golf & 9-hole courses, exercise, poker, computer, & crafts rooms, ballroom, library, beautician, whirlpool, pet walk, pet grooming. **Activities:** Golf, shuffleboard, billiards. **Nearby Attractions:** Pima Air & Space Museum, Saguaro National Park East, Colossal Cave, Kartchner Caverns, museums. **Additional Information:** Tucson CVB, (800) 638-8350, www.visitTucson.org.

RESTRICTIONS

Pets: On leash under owner's control. **Fires:** Yes. **Alcoholic Beverages:** Allowed. **Vehicle Maximum Length:** 100 ft. **Other:** Children welcome May 1–day after Labor Day.

TO GET THERE

From I-10 Exit 270 go 0.5 mi. south on Kolb Rd.

TUMACACORI

De Anza Trails RV Resort

HC 65 Box 381, Tumacacori 85640. T: (520) 398-8628 or (866) 332-6022; F: 520-398-2314; www.deanzatrailsrvresort.com; DeAnzaTrailsRVResort@msn.com.

🚐 ★★★   ▲ n/a

Beauty: ★★★   Site Privacy: ★★★
Spaciousness: ★★★   Quiet: ★★★★
Security: ★★★   Cleanliness: ★★★★
Insect Control: ★★★★   Facilities: ★★★★

A collection of mundane RV parking spaces packaged with an impressive array of amenities, including an indoor pool and weight room, De Anza Trails offers 50 amp electric power, unlike Mountain View next door. However, De Anza falls short in parking convenience, as its spaces are all back-ins and require a security guard to supervise placement, in contrast to Mountain View's pull-through sites. Higher prices than the RV park next door have not helped, and on a recent summer day (admittedly the slow season this far south), De Anza had one customer while the funkier Mountain View was packed with RVs. Tents are prohibited, as are noisy trucks, cars, and motorcycles. Noise from trucks traversing the adjacent highway linking Tucson and Mexico might bother some people, but inside the clubhouse, library, and other facilities it should not be a problem.

BASICS

Operated By: De Anza Trails. **Open:** All year. **Site Assignment:** First come, first served; reservations accepted (payment in full; 30-days notice for 90% refund, otherwise "No refunds!! No exceptions!!"). **Registration:** Self-pay entrance fee station. **Fee:** $23–$28 (V, MC). **Parking:** At site.

FACILITIES

Number of RV Sites: 82. **Number of Tent-Only Sites:** 0. **Hookups:** Electric (20, 30, 50 amp), water, sewer, cable TV, phone. **Each Site:** Pole lights. **Dump Station:** Yes. **Laundry:** Yes. **Pay Phone:** Yes. **Rest Rooms and Showers:** Yes. **Fuel:** No. **Propane:** No. **Internal Roads:** Paved, excellent. **RV Service:** No. **Market:** Green Valley, 15 mi. **Restaurant:** Tumacacori, seasonal coffeeshop on premises. **General Store:** Yes. **Vending:** Yes. **Swimming:** Indoor pool. **Playground:** No. **Other:** Pet walk, jacuzzi, rec center, library, exercise/weight room, modem access. **Activities:** Cards, billiards, golf, boating, fishing. **Nearby Attractions:** Missions, Tubac Presidio, Madera Canyon, Buenos Aires Wildlife Refuge, museums, copper mine tour. **Additional Information:** Green Valley Chamber of Commerce, (520) 625-7575, (800) 858-5872, sraney@concentric.net.

RESTRICTIONS

Pets: On leash under owner's control. **Fires:** Yes (limited). **Alcoholic Beverages:** Allowed. **Vehicle Maximum Length:** 50 ft. **Other:** 1 RV & vehicle per site; no street parking; shirts & shoes required in clubhouse; swim attire permitted in swim area only; 11 a.m. checkout.

TO GET THERE

From I-19 south of Green Valley, take Exit 48 (Arivaca Junction) and go south 2 mi. on frontage road.

TUMACACORI
Mountain View RV Ranch

HRC 65 Box 380, Tumacacori 85640. T: (520) 398-9401; www.woodalls.com; Desertpark@aol.com.

🚐 ★★★   ⛺ ★★

Beauty: ★★★★   Site Privacy: ★★★
Spaciousness: ★★★★   Quiet: ★★★
Security: ★★★★   Cleanliness: ★★★
Insect Control: ★★   Facilities: ★★★★

Along the highway linking Tucson with Nogales, Mexico, a brick wall separates Mountain View RV Ranch from the newer De Anza Trails RV Resort next door. A loyal coterie of supporters keeps Mountain View humming year-round, even during the summer slow season when many other nearby RV parks look like deserted ghost towns. The virtually unlimited vehicle length and 49 40-ft. wide pull-through spaces accommodating slide-outs is one reason for Mountain View's popularity. Tent campers can choose their spot anywhere along a grass strip extending from the small rear mobile home park to near the front of the park for pool, laundry, and snack bar convenience. Sunday mornings the snack bar serves up free coffee with breakfast, and homemade soups and sandwiches top off the lunch menu. The action here includes Monday night football on a big screen TV, pot lucks, card games, Friday night bingo, and darts.

BASICS

Operated By: Esther Geisman. **Open:** All year. **Site Assignment:** First come, first served; winter reservations advised. **Registration:** In office. **Fee:** $15 tent, $17–$21 RV (V, MC, AE, D). **Parking:** At site.

FACILITIES

Number of RV Sites: 72. **Number of Tent-Only Sites:** Undesignated sites. **Hookups:** Electric (20, 30 amp), water, sewer, cable TV, phone. **Each Site:** Table. **Dump Station:** Yes. **Laundry:** Yes. **Pay Phone:** Yes. **Rest Rooms and Showers:** Yes. **Fuel:** No. **Propane:** Yes. **Internal Roads:** Gravel, good condition. **RV Service:** No. **Market:** Green Valley, 15 mi. **Restaurant:** Tumacacori, snack bar on premises. **General Store:** Yes. **Vending:** Yes. **Swimming:** Pool. **Playground:** No. **Other:** Dog walk, rental cabins. **Activities:** Shuffleboard, golf, boating, fishing. **Nearby Attractions:** Tubac Presidio, Tumacacori National Monument, Madera Canyon, Buenos Aires Wildlife Refuge, Native American casinos, museums, copper mine tour. **Additional Information:** Green Valley Chamber of Commerce, (520) 625-7575, (800) 858-5872, sraney@concentric.net.

RESTRICTIONS

Pets: On leash. **Fires:** In designated area only. **Alcoholic Beverages:** Allowed. **Vehicle Maximum Length:** None.

TO GET THERE

From I-19 south of Green Valley, take Amado Exit 48 South or 42 North.

WENDEN
Alamo Lake State Park

P.O. Box 38, Wenden 85357. T: (520) 669-2088; www.pr.state.az.us.

🚐 ★★★★   ⛺ ★★★★

Beauty: ★★★★   Site Privacy: ★★★
Spaciousness: ★★★   Quiet: ★★★★
Security: ★★★★   Cleanliness: ★★★★
Insect Control: ★★★   Facilities: ★★★★

Nestled amongst saguaros and ocotillos where wild burros roam and golden and bald eagles soar in the Bill Williams River Valley, bass-filled Alamo Lake has a collection of eight developed and primitive camping areas on widely separated loops. The section of camping area A nearest the general store, sheltered picnic tables, and ranger station has 19 coveted sites with electric and water hookups. Camping areas A and B have sites with paved pads topped with a pebble layer, and are popular for both RVs and tents. Camping area C off Cholla Rd. also has hookups, though those willing to trade hookups for maximum privacy and beauty should continue down Cholla Rd. towards the lakeshore and camping areas D and E. Though furthest from the showers, store, and other amenities, camping area E, which has portable restrooms and picnic tables because it is sometimes underwater, is best situated to enjoy beautiful lake views.

BASICS

Operated By: Arizona State Parks. **Open:** All year. **Site Assignment:** First come, first served. **Registration:** Self-pay entrance fee station. **Fee:** $8–$15 (cash or check only). **Parking:** At site.

FACILITIES

Number of RV Sites: 250. **Number of Tent-Only Sites:** 0. **Hookups:** Electric (30 amp), water. **Each Site:** Table, grill, fire ring. **Dump Station:** Yes. **Laundry:** No. **Pay Phone:** No. **Rest Rooms and Showers:** Yes. **Fuel:** No. **Propane:** No. **Internal Roads:** Paved or pebbly, good condition. **RV Service:** No. **Market:** Quartzite, 79 mi. **Restaurant:** Wenden, 38 mi. **General Store:** Yes. **Vending:** Yes. **Swimming:** Lake. **Playground:** No. **Other:** Boat ramps, fish cleaning & battery recharge station. **Activities:** Mountain biking, fishing, boating. **Nearby Attractions:** None. **Additional Information:** Alamo Lake Store (boat rental), (520) 925-0133.

RESTRICTIONS

Pets: On leash. **Fires:** In fire rings only. **Alcoholic Beverages:** Allowed. **Vehicle Maximum Length:** 30 ft. **Other:** OHV's must be street legal to operate in park.

TO GET THERE

From US Hwy. 60 in Wenden, go 38 mi. north on Alamo Dam Access Rd.

WENDEN
Morenga Palms RV Park

P.O. Box 68, Wenden 85357. T: (520) 859-3722.

🚐 ★★★★   ⛺ ★★

Beauty: ★★★★   Site Privacy: ★★★
Spaciousness: ★★★★   Quiet: ★★★★★
Security: ★★★★   Cleanliness: ★★★★★
Insect Control: ★★★   Facilities: ★★

During the five-month winter season, this small RV park is filled by regulars from around the country and Canada, some of whom have been coming here for over a decade to form part of a small community that gathers for evening cocktails while watching the sunset from the clubhouse porch before evening games commence. During the hot summer, when there is space for tent campers to plug into the electric hookups left behind by migrating snowbirds, the surrounding fields are growing cotton, cantaloupes, watermelons, and a variety of fruit and vegetables for the Delmonte cannery. Parker and the Colorado River recreation is 64 miles to the north, but Alamo Lake State Park is within about 30 miles. Wickenburg's bowling alley and many restaurants are 46 miles to the west. All in all, a small isolated gem of a stopping place for those venturing into the Arizona outback.

BASICS

Operated By: Dorothy & Bruce O'Hara. **Open:** All year. **Site Assignment:** First come, first served; winter reservations advised. **Registration:** Office. **Fee:** $16. **Parking:** At site.

FACILITIES

Number of RV Sites: 52. **Number of Tent-Only Sites:** 0. **Hookups:** Electric (30 amp), water, sewer, phone. **Each Site:** Table, bench, fire ring. **Dump Station:** Yes. **Laundry:** Yes. **Pay Phone:** Yes. **Rest Rooms and Showers:** Yes. **Fuel:** No. **Propane:** No. **Internal Roads:** Gravel, good. **RV Service:** No. **Market:** Wenden, 3 mi. **Restaurant:**

Wenden, 3 mi. **General Store:** No. **Vending:** Yes. **Swimming:** No. **Playground:** No. **Other:** Clubhouse, exercise room, picnic area w/ fire ring. **Activities:** ATVs, golf, fishing, boating. **Nearby Attractions:** Alamo Lake State Park, Quartzsite. **Additional Information:** McMullen Valley Chamber of Commerce, (520) 859-3846, www.azoutback.com.

RESTRICTIONS

Pets: On leash under owner's control. **Fires:** Yes. **Alcoholic Beverages:** Allowed. **Vehicle Maximum Length:** 40 ft. **Other:** Need own satellite dish for TV.

TO GET THERE

From Wenden go 3 mi. east on US Hwy. 60.

WICKENBURG

Horspitality RV Park and Boarding Stable

51802 Hwy. 60, Wickenburg 85390. T: (520) 684-2519.

🚐 ★★★	⛺ n/a
Beauty: ★★★	Site Privacy: ★★
Spaciousness: ★★★	Quiet: ★★★★
Security: ★★★★	Cleanliness: ★★★★
Insect Control: ★★★★	Facilities: ★★★

Founded by German immigrant Henry Wickenburg after the discovery of gold at the Vulture Mine in 1863, Wickenburg sprang into existence 60 miles northwest of Phoenix with the motto "Horses have the right of way on all Wickenburg streets." Though horses no longer wander the streets of this crossroads town of motels and restaurants, Horspitality RV Park continues the tradition of catering to horses with a boarding stable with 65 horse pens. Horspitality also borders BLM land with miles of trails for horses, hikers, and ATVs. There is no general store, but major chain stores and markets are within a mile of the RV park. Palms and deciduous trees add to the country ambiance, and some residents settle in for the winter by spreading Astroturf on their concrete porch pads. All in all, a friendly stop for those who don't want to leave their horses at home.

BASICS

Operated By: Craig & Pam Dyer. **Open:** All year. **Site Assignment:** First come, first served; reservations advised for special events. **Registration:** Office. **Fee:** $17–$20 (cash or check only). **Parking:** At site.

FACILITIES

Number of RV Sites: 109. **Number of Tent-Only Sites:** 0. **Hookups:** Electric (15, 30 amp), water, sewer. **Each Site:** Table, grill. **Dump Station:** Yes. **Laundry:** Yes. **Pay Phone:** Yes. **Rest Rooms and Showers:** Yes. **Fuel:** No. **Propane:** No. **Internal Roads:** Gravel, good. **RV Service:** No. **Market:** Wickenburg, 1 mi. **Restaurant:** Wickenburg, 1 mi. **General Store:** No. **Vending:** Yes. **Swimming:** No. **Playground:** No. **Other:** Open pens for horses, dog walk, horseshoes, adjacent BLM trails. **Activities:** Horseback riding, golf. **Nearby Attractions:** Museums, Phoenix, Prescott. **Additional Information:** Wickenburg Chamber of Commerce, (520) 684-5479.

RESTRICTIONS

Pets: On leash (horses welcome). **Fires:** Yes. **Alcoholic Beverages:** Allowed. **Vehicle Maximum Length:** None.

TO GET THERE

From junction of US Hwys. 60 & 89/93 in Wickenburg, go east 2 mi. on US Hwy. 60 to milepost 112.5.

WIKIEUP

Burro Creek Recreation Site

2475 Beverly Ave., Kingman 86401. T: (520) 692-4400.

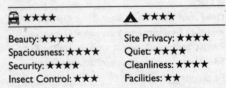

🚐 ★★★★	⛺ ★★★★
Beauty: ★★★★	Site Privacy: ★★★★
Spaciousness: ★★★★	Quiet: ★★★★
Security: ★★★★	Cleanliness: ★★★★
Insect Control: ★★★	Facilities: ★★

Nine miles north of the town of Nothing and near old copper mining towns like Bagdad, Burro Creek Recreation Site is seemingly in the middle of nowhere, though it is just off US Hwy. 93, the main artery linking Phoenix and Las Vegas, Nevada. Many regulars come back here every year because it is such a good place to just sit and relax, with little else to do besides hiking along the tree-lined creek and looking for the blue and purple agates and Apache tears that endear the area to rock hounds. Day use of the park is free, including the solar-lighted restrooms and the ample picnic area surrounded by saguaros and mesquite. The small cactus garden is a good introduction to desert botany and nesting desert pack rats. Fishing in the year-round water pools is taboo, as the Sonoran suckers and roundtail chubb are endangered. Bird watchers can spot great blue herons and bald eagles.

BASICS

Operated By: Bureau of Land Management. **Open:** All year. **Site Assignment:** First come, first served; group site reservations. **Registration:** Self-pay fee station. **Fee:** $10 (cash or check only). **Parking:** At site.

FACILITIES

Number of RV Sites: 30. **Number of Tent-Only Sites:** 0. **Hookups:** None. **Each Site:** Table, fire ring. **Dump Station:** Yes. **Laundry:** No. **Pay Phone:** No. **Rest Rooms and Showers:** No showers. **Fuel:** No. **Propane:** No. **Internal Roads:** Gravel, good. **RV Service:** No. **Market:** Wickenburg, 60 mi. **Restaurant:** Wickenburg, 60 mi. **General Store:** No. **Vending:** No. **Swimming:** No. **Playground:** No. **Other:** Some sheltered tables; 1 wheelchair-accessible site; cactus botanical garden. **Activities:** Rock collecting, birdwatching. **Nearby Attractions:** Hualapai Indian Reservation, Alamo Lake State Park. **Additional Information:** BLM Kingman Field Office, (520) 692-4400.

RESTRICTIONS

Pets: On leash under owner's control. **Fires:** Yes. **Alcoholic Beverages:** Allowed. **Vehicle Maximum Length:** None.

TO GET THERE

From Kingman go 17 mi. east on I-40, then 53 mi. south on US Hwy. 93 to signed turnoff 1 mi. south of Burro Creek Bridge and follow gravel road 1.5 mi. to campground.

WINSLOW

Homolovi Ruins State Park

HCR 63 Box 5, Winslow 86047. T: (520) 289-4106; F: (520) 289-2021; www.pr.state.az.us; homolovi@pr.state.az.us.

🚐 ★★★★   ⛺ ★★★

Beauty: ★★★★   Site Privacy: ★★★★
Spaciousness: ★★★★   Quiet: ★★★★
Security: ★★★★   Cleanliness: ★★★★★
Insect Control: ★★★   Facilities: ★★★

Mostly used as an overnight stop by travelers on I-40, Homolovi Ruins is further from the highway and not near a power plant or lake like the nearby and more rustic Cholla Lake County Park. The paved sites have small trees that should eventually grow up to provide some shade. Raised dirt pads make for comfortable tenting, though it is advisable to shake your boots for scorpions before putting them on in the morning. The name Homolovi means little hills in the Hopi language, and the area was a sacred gathering place of the clans and is still visited as a sacred place by the Hopi. The park opened in 1993, but archaeological excavations date to 1896. The over 1,000-room pueblo is the most accessible site in this park, which has good wildlife viewing areas along the Little Colorado River.

BASICS

Operated By: Arizona State Parks. **Open:** All year. **Site Assignment:** First come, first served. **Registration:** Entrance kiosk (use self-pay slot when closed). **Fee:** $10–$15 (cash or check only). **Parking:** At site.

FACILITIES

Number of RV Sites: 53. **Number of Tent-Only Sites:** 0. **Hookups:** Electric (30 amp), water. **Each Site:** Table, grill. **Dump Station:** Yes. **Laundry:** No. **Pay Phone:** Yes. **Rest Rooms and Showers:** Yes (showers May–Oct. only). **Fuel:** No. **Propane:** No. **Internal Roads:** Paved, excellent. **RV Service:** No. **Market:** Winslow, 3 mi. **Restaurant:** Winslow, 3 mi. **General Store:** No. **Vending:** Yes. **Swimming:** No. **Playground:** No. **Other:** Visitor center, museum, covered picnic tables, wildlife viewing turnouts, archaelogical sites. **Activities:** Archaeological dig tours (June, July). **Nearby Attractions:** Little Painted Desert, Second Mesa, Mogollon Rim, Meteor Crater, Walnut Canyon, Flagstaff, Petrified Forest. **Additional Information:** Winslow Chamber of Commerce Visitor Center, (520) 289-2434, www.winslow arizona.org.

RESTRICTIONS

Pets: On leash (not allowed in buildings). **Fires:** In designated areas only. **Alcoholic Beverages:** Allowed. **Vehicle Maximum Length:** None. **Other:** Gates closed from 7 p.m. to 6 a.m.

TO GET THERE

From Winslow go east 2 mi. on I-40 to Exit 257 and then north 1.5 mi. on AZ Hwy. 87.

California

California's motto, eureka, means "I have found it!" That sentiment is just as applicable to campers today as it was when it was first adopted a century and a half ago by the '49ers of the Gold Rush era. Indeed, the camping prospects are richer by far than what remains of the Golden State's mineral resources. From its 840 miles of shoreline, millions of acres of federal land, and 264 state parks (with scores more on the county level), California's scenery is a glittering reflection of all that is rare and wonderful in the natural beauty of the United States. And with its relatively mild climate, many campgrounds remain open year-round.

As one might expect in a state California's size, it is a land packed with extremes and superlatives: from **Mt. Whitney,** the highest peak in the lower 48 states, to **Badwater,** in **Death Valley,** the lowest point in the western hemisphere. Its coast redwoods are the tallest trees in the world, while the bristlecone pines of the **Inyo National Forest** are the planet's oldest living things. To the south are sun-parched deserts awash in cacti and colorfully eroded landscapes that explode with wildflowers in the spring. Up north are the **Cascade Mountains,** iced with snow, scarred by lava, laced with trout streams, alpine lakes, and thousands of miles of hiking trails. In between are snow-crusted glaciers in the **Sierra Nevada Mountains,** one crashing waterfall after another, especially in **Yosemite Valley,** more national parks and monuments than any other state in the country, and a number of historical sites honoring Native American, Spanish and Mexican explorers, and African and Chinese pioneers, among others.

Beyond its silky smooth beaches and tide pools, where passing whales and nesting seals can be observed, in addition to the superb fishing and boating in pristine lakes, rivers, and reservoirs, California's abundance of wildlife is icing on the camper's cake. Grizzly bears are long gone, but you will find Tule elk, Roosevelt elk, and fallow deer among the animals gracing the coastal preserves, big horn sheep, kangaroo rats, and desert tortoises in the arid areas, while black bears, coyotes, and black-tail deer seem to roam throughout. And one needn't be a sharp-eyed birder to enjoy the sight of condors, Canada geese, bald and golden eagles, acorn woodpeckers, hummingbirds, valley quails, and herons of various types warbling among the oaks or winging across the marshlands.

Under the Clinton presidency the Golden State gained the newly-created **Mojave National Preserve** and two national monuments, **Carrizo Plain** and **Giant Sequoia,** while the domains of **Pinnacles National Monument, Death Valley,** and **Joshua Tree National Parks** were substantially expanded. In 2000, when the state enjoyed a substantial budget surplus, it lowered its day-use and camping fees, making access to state parks one of the better deals around. Hundreds of properties within California's national forests have been revamped and are now run by concessionaires intent on keeping them clean, secure, and profitable. Dispersed camping on lands administered by the National Forest Service and Bureau of Land Management offers serious solitude-seekers and the budget-minded a less structured approach to camping.

Whatever your interests, however you like to camp, California has so much beauty and space that on pulling into a campground you may well feel like imitating the '49ers by exclaiming with exuberance, "Eureka!"

The following facilities accept payment in checks or cash only:

Afton Canyon, Barstow

Aspen Grove, Lee Vining

Azalea, Kings Canyon National Park

Bogard, Susanville

Boulder Flat, Sonora

Bow Willow Campground, Anza-Borrego
    Desert State Park, Borrego Springs

Butte Lake, Lassen Volcanic National Park

Coldbrook, Azusa

Cooper Gulch, Lewiston

Cottonwood, Twentynine Palms

Culp Valley Primitive Camp, Anza-Borrego
    Desert State Park, Borrego Springs

El Cariso North Campground, Lake Elsinore

Elam, Chester

Ellery Lake, Lee Vining

Fossil Falls, Ridgecrest

Fowlers Campground, McCloud

Gaviota State Park, Santa Barbara

Goumaz, Susanville

Hole-in-the-Ground, Mill Creek

Hole-in-the-Wall, Mojave National Preserve

Howards Gulch, Alturas

Indian Creek, Markleeville

Indian Well, Lava Beds National Monument

Kern River County Park, Kern River
    Campground, Bakersfield

Lake Almanor Campground, Greenville

Leavitt Meadows, Dardanelle

Lundy Canyon Campground, Mono City

Mesquite Spring, Death Valley

Monte Cristo, Pasadena

Owl Canyon, Barstow

Pine Cliff Resort, June Lake

Pine Flat Lake Recreation Area, Fresno

Pit River, Fall River Mills

Plumas-Eureka State Park, Upper Samson
    Creek Campground, Blairsden

Pogie Point, Upper Lake

Ponderosa, Lucia

Potwisha, Sequoia National Park

Red Rock Canyon State Park, Ricardo
    Campground, Mojave

Sarah Totten, Hamburg

Sonora Bridge, Coleville

The Pines, Groveland

Tolkan, Shelter Cove

Tuttletown Recreation Area; Manzanita
    Campground, Angels Camp

Twin Lakes, Mammoth Lakes

Upper Rush Creek, Adin

Wild Plum, Sierra City

The following facilities feature 50 sites or fewer:

Bogard, Susanville

Bow Willow Campground, Anza-Borrego
Desert State Park, Borrego Springs

Cooper Gulch, Lewiston

Culp Valley Primitive Camp, Anza-Borrego
Desert State Park, Borrego Springs

Elam, Chester

Ellery Lake, Lee Vining

Goumaz, Susanville

Hole-in-the-Ground, Mill Creek

Howards Gulch, Alturas

KCL, Carrizo Plain National Monument

Landslide, Hume

Leavitt Meadows, Dardanelle

Monte Cristo, Pasadena

Nelson Point, O'Brien

Pit River, Fall River Mills

Sarah Totten, Hamburg

Selby, Carrizo Plain National Monument

The Pines, Groveland

Tolkan, Shelter Cove

Upper Rush Creek, Adin

Campground Profiles

ADIN

Upper Rush Creek

CR 198A, Adin 96006. T: (530) 299-3215; F: (530)
299-8409; www.r5.fs.fed.us/modoc.

 ★★★   ▲ ★★★★

Beauty: ★★★★   Site Privacy: ★★★
Spaciousness: ★★★   Quiet: ★★★★
Security: ★★   Cleanliness: ★★★
Insect Control: ★★★   Facilities: ★

You will have to pass Lower Rush Creek to reach
this campground and may very well feel inclined
to stop there for the night. No problem, the two
are comparably pleasant, and Lower Rush has
several walk-in sites, hidden away beyond a small
wooden bridge, that are perfect for reclusive tenters. Upper Rush, though, is the more densely
forested, tranquil of the two and offers a better
array of sites. Conifers tower over the hilly
dominion, providing shade and—through their
fallen needles—soft padding for tents. To the
north of camp is a volcanic outcropping, while
the narrow, trickling Rush Creek sluices along its
southern boundary. Some of the real estate here
is not very level, but sites overall are very roomy
and scattered well apart. Units 3–5, nestled
above the creek, are the most picturesque. This
facility is in the Modoc National Forest, 35 miles
southwest of Alturas, off of Hwy. 299. It is nearly
a mile high in altitude, making for cold nights
early and late in the season. In winter, spigots are
capped and no potable water is available.

BASICS

Operated By: Modoc National Forest, Big Valley
Ranger District. **Open:** May–Oct. **Site Assignment:** First come, first served. **Registration:** At
entrance kiosk. **Fee:** $6, cash or check; no fee in win-
ter when water spigots are capped. **Parking:** At site.

FACILITIES

Number of RV Sites: 13. **Number of Tent-
Only Sites:** 0. **Hookups:** None. **Each Site:** Picnic
table, fire grate, barbecue grill. **Dump Station:** No.
Laundry: No. **Pay Phone:** No. **Rest Rooms and
Showers:** Vault toilets, no showers. **Fuel:** No.
Propane: No. **Internal Roads:** Dirt, good condi-
tion. **RV Service:** No. **Market:** 10 mi. south in
Adin. **Restaurant:** 10 mi. south in Adin. **General
Store:** No. **Vending:** No. **Swimming:** No. **Play-
ground:** No. **Activities:** Hiking, fishing. **Nearby
Attractions:** Lava Beds National Monument;
Modoc National Wildlife Refuge & Modoc County
Historical Museum in Alturas. **Additional Infor-
mation:** Alturas Chamber of Commerce, (530)
233-4434.

RESTRICTIONS

Pets: On leash. **Fires:** In fire grates only. **Alcoholic
Beverages:** Allowed. **Vehicle Maximum
Length:** 22 ft. **Other:** 14-day stay limit.

BANNING
Lake Hemet

56570 Hwy. 74, #4, Mountain Center 92561. T: (909) 659-2680; F: (909) 659-8509.

🚐 ★★★★   ⛺ ★★★

Beauty: ★★★   Site Privacy: ★★
Spaciousness: ★★   Quiet: ★★★★
Security: ★★★★★   Cleanliness: ★★★
Insect Control: ★★   Facilities: ★★★★

To paraphrase Dickens, Lake Hemet offers the best of campgrounds and the worst of campgrounds. It has a fine sandy beach but doesn't allow swimming in its namesake lake (wading is allowed in Hurkey Creek by the playground). The rugged, natural atmosphere radiating from the surrounding San Jacinto and Thomas mountain ranges is partly diminished by the cluttered cluster of the long-term residences. Several stands of mature ponderosa pines are scattered around the property but sites of dirt, sand, and a smattering of grass are largely exposed to the sun. And unless you like plenty of company, forget about a waterside location, especially among the RV hookups; the outlying areas without electricity are your best bet for space and seclusion. Security is one feature this facility is unequivocal about, with an entrance gate, regular patrols, and a county sheriff's office on the edge of the grounds.

BASICS
Operated By: Lake Hemet Municipal Water District. **Open:** All year. **Site Assignment:** First come, first served. **Registration:** At entrance office. **Fee:** $13, cash, V, MC. **Parking:** At site.

FACILITIES
Number of RV Sites: 275. **Number of Tent-Only Sites:** Undesignated sites. **Hookups:** Water, electric (20, 30 amps), sewer. **Each Site:** Picnic table, fire ring, some with a barbecue grill. **Dump Station:** Yes. **Laundry:** Yes. **Pay Phone:** Yes. **Rest Rooms and Showers:** Yes. **Fuel:** No. **Propane:** Yes. **Internal Roads:** Mostly paved, some dirt roads. **RV Service:** No. **Market:** 9 mi. north in Idyllwild. **Restaurant:** 9 mi. north in Idyllwild. **General Store:** Yes. **Vending:** Yes. **Swimming:** In creek. **Playground:** Yes. **Other:** Wheelchair-accessible facilities, boat launch. **Activities:** Fishing, hiking, volleyball, basketball, horseshoe pit, boat rentals. **Nearby Attractions:** Pacific Crest Trail, Gilman Historic Ranch & Wagon Museum in Banning, San

Jacinto Valley Museum. **Additional Information:** Banning Chamber of Commerce, (909) 849-4695.

RESTRICTIONS
Pets: On leash no longer than 15 ft., $1 fee. **Fires:** In fire rings only. **Alcoholic Beverages:** Allowed. **Vehicle Maximum Length:** 40 ft. **Other:** 14-day stay limit for tents, no shooting.

TO GET THERE
From Banning head south on Hwy. 243, off I-10, and drive 31 mi. Turn left on route 74 and continue for 5 mi. to the campground on the right.

BANNING
Mount San Jacinto State Park, Stone Creek Campground

25905 Hwy. 243, P.O. Box 308, Idyllwild 92549. T: (909) 659-2607 or reservations (800) 444-7275; F: (909) 659-4769; www.sanjac.statepark.org.

🚐 ★★★★   ⛺ ★★★

Beauty: ★★★★   Site Privacy: ★★★
Spaciousness: ★★★   Quiet: ★★★
Security: ★★★   Cleanliness: ★★★★
Insect Control: ★   Facilities: ★★

The scenic mountain drive along Hwy. 243 to Stone Creek is a good warm-up for your arrival at this gorgeous highland park. Set in a hilly, boulder-strewn forest of oak and incense cedar, manzanita, and ponderosa pine, the camp lies at 5,900 feet of elevation, so plan for cool evenings throughout the year. Regrettably, the somewhat wild, natural look of the place is balanced by sites that tend to be grouped a bit close together, with several lacking level tenting space. Best choices for RVers from the series of loops are sites 45, with a large pull-through slot, and 50, for privacy. Site 26 is the most secluded among the tent options. Birders will enjoy the lively community of acorn woodpeckers nesting in the vicinity and hikers should aim their boots in the direction of trails that lead into the neighboring San Jacinto Wilderness.

BASICS
Operated By: California Dept. of Parks & Recreation. **Open:** All year. **Site Assignment:** Reservations accepted w/ V, MC, D. **Registration:** At entrance kiosk. **Fee:** $7, cash or CA check. **Parking:** At site.

FACILITIES

Number of RV Sites: 23. **Number of Tent-Only Sites:** 27. **Hookups:** None. **Each Site:** Picnic table, fire grate, food storage box. **Dump Station:** No. **Laundry:** No. **Pay Phone:** Yes. **Rest Rooms and Showers:** Vault toilets, no showers. **Fuel:** No. **Propane:** No. **Internal Roads:** Paved. **RV Service:** No. **Market:** 2 mi. south in Pine Cove. **Restaurant:** 6 mi. south in Idyllwild. **General Store:** No. **Vending:** No. **Swimming:** No. **Playground:** No. **Other:** Some wheelchair-accessible facilities. **Activities:** Hiking, birding, nature programs in summer. **Nearby Attractions:** Palm Springs Aerial Tramway, Palm Springs Desert Museum, Oasis Water Park in Palm Springs, Gilman Historic Ranch & Wagon Museum in Banning. **Additional Information:** Idyllwild Chamber of Commerce, (909) 659-3259.

RESTRICTIONS

Pets: On 6 ft. leash. **Fires:** In fire grates only. **Alcoholic Beverages:** Allowed at site. **Vehicle Maximum Length:** 24 ft. **Other:** 14-day stay limit; no firearms; no wood gathering.

TO GET THERE

From I-10 in Banning exit south on Hwy. 243. Drive 20 mi. and turn left at the campground sign.

BARSTOW

Afton Canyon

Afton Canyon Rd., Barstow 92311. T: (760) 252-6000; F: (760) 252-6099; www.ca.blm.gov/caso/information.html.

🚐 ★★★	🏕 ★★★★
Beauty: ★★★★	Site Privacy: ★★★
Spaciousness: ★★★★	Quiet: ★★★
Security: ★★	Cleanliness: ★★
Insect Control: ★★★★	Facilities: ★

Your first impression of Afton Canyon may well be that it is a dusty God-forsaken over-sized sandbox where even the lowly creosote bush has difficulty putting down roots. And your second impression might echo your first, especially if a freight train should chance to rattle down the nearby tracks while you are there. But give your eyes—and your other senses—an opportunity to take in the surroundings and you may just find the low-key beauty of the place growing on you.

Some of the level, sandy sites are screened by mesquite bushes, and most are spaced well apart, while desert dunes and the russet colored namesake canyon lend texture to the setting. (So, too, does a disturbing amount of litter, but that's another story.) There's a chance you'll see the elusive desert tortoise here, though rosy boas and kangaroo rats are more likely visitors. Bring plenty of water—the source here is unreliable—and note that while the campground is less than four miles south of I-15, a hairpin curve on the dirt and gravel washboard of an access road is all but impassable for vehicles over 22 feet in length.

BASICS

Operated By: Bureau of Land Management. **Open:** All year. **Site Assignment:** First come, first served. **Registration:** At entrance kiosk. **Fee:** $6, cash or check. **Parking:** At site.

FACILITIES

Number of RV Sites: 22. **Number of Tent-Only Sites:** 0. **Hookups:** None. **Each Site:** Picnic table, fire ring; most sites have ramada & barbecue grill. **Dump Station:** No. **Laundry:** No. **Pay Phone:** No. **Rest Rooms and Showers:** Vaulted toilets, no showers. **Fuel:** No. **Propane:** No. **Internal Roads:** Packed, rocky dirt but manageable. **RV Service:** No. **Market:** 35 mi. west in Barstow. **Restaurant:** 35 mi. west in Barstow. **General Store:** No. **Vending:** No. **Swimming:** No. **Playground:** No. **Other:** Some wheelchair-accessible facilities. **Activities:** Hiking, birding, rock & mineral collecting, horseback riding, 4WD exploring. **Nearby Attractions:** Mojave National Preserve, Early Man Site, Death Valley National Park. **Additional Information:** Bureau of Land Management, Barstow Field Office, (760) 252-6091; Baker Area Chamber of Commerce, (760) 733-4469.

RESTRICTIONS

Pets: Allowed. **Fires:** In fire rings. **Alcoholic Beverages:** Allowed. **Vehicle Maximum Length:** 22 ft. **Other:** 14-day stay limit; no shooting.

TO GET THERE

From Barstow drive 40 mi. east on I-15. Exit on Afton Rd. and drive 3.5 mi south on a dirt and gravel accordion road that leads to the campground on the left.

BARSTOW
Owl Canyon

Fossil Bed Rd., Barstow 92311. T: (760) 252-6000; F: (760) 252-6099; www.ca.blm.gov/caso/information.html.

🚐 ★★★   ⛺ ★★★★

Beauty: ★★★★   Site Privacy: ★★★
Spaciousness: ★★★★   Quiet: ★★★★
Security: ★★   Cleanliness: ★★★★
Insect Control: ★★★★   Facilities: ★

Rock hounds like this area for its abundance of fossils, but they're overlooking the obvious: Owl Canyon is a diamond-in-the-rough. Conveniently located next to Rainbow Basin National Natural Landmark, just 11 miles north of Barstow, this campground is dramatically set against a colorful, eroded canyon of bentonite and limestone. Roomy, level sites are well spaced along a tri-pronged loop, with numbers 12–23 among the more private. Tableside ramadas are an essential campsite accouterment in an otherwise primitive locale that consists of just desert scrub and a few sparse Joshua trees for vegetation. Owl Canyon lies at an elevation of 2,600 feet and can be scorching hot from mid-spring through early autumn. Whenever you visit pack plenty of water, as none is available at the campground. And drive carefully, as the last time we traveled through we encountered a large, shy desert tortoise crossing the camp's dirt access road.

BASICS

Operated By: Bureau of Land Management. **Open:** All year. **Site Assignment:** First come, first served. **Registration:** At entrance kiosk. **Fee:** $6, cash or check. **Parking:** At site.

FACILITIES

Number of RV Sites: 31. **Number of Tent-Only Sites:** 0. **Hookups:** None. **Each Site:** Picnic table, fire ring, barbecue grill, ramada. **Dump Station:** No. **Laundry:** No. **Pay Phone:** No. **Rest Rooms and Showers:** Vaulted toilets, no showers. **Fuel:** No. **Propane:** No. **Internal Roads:** Gravel, decent condition. **RV Service:** No. **Market:** 10 mi. south in Barstow. **Restaurant:** 10 mi. south in Barstow. **General Store:** No. **Vending:** No. **Swimming:** No. **Playground:** No. **Other:** Some wheelchair-accessible facilities. **Activities:** Hiking,

horseback riding, scenic loop drive through canyon, birding, rock & mineral collecting. **Nearby Attractions:** Rainbow Basin National Natural Landmark, Mojave National Preserve, Afton Canyon. **Additional Information:** Bureau of Land Management, Barstow Field Office, (760) 252-6091; Barstow Area Chamber of Commerce, (760) 256-8617.

RESTRICTIONS

Pets: On leash. **Fires:** In fire rings only. **Alcoholic Beverages:** Allowed. **Vehicle Maximum Length:** None. **Other:** 14-day stay limit; no firearms; no wood gathering.

TO GET THERE

In Barstow follow the I-15 Business Loop and head north on 1st St. After 0.8 mi. turn left on Irwin Rd. and drive 6 mi., then turn left on Fossil Bed Rd. Proceed for 3 mi. and turn right. The campground is located 1.6 mi. down the road. The last 4.6 mi. are dirt w/ washboard stretches.

BASS LAKE
Lupine-Cedar Bluff

CR 222, Bass Lake 93604. T: (559) 877-2218 or reservations (877) 444-6777; F: (559) 877-3108; www.r5.fs.fed.us/sierra or www.reserveusa.com.

🚐 ★★★★   ⛺ ★★

Beauty: ★★★★   Site Privacy: ★★
Spaciousness: ★★   Quiet: ★★★
Security: ★★★   Cleanliness: ★★★
Insect Control: ★★   Facilities: ★★★

A question to ask before heading out to this campground is, how much time will you be spending at the site? Bass Lake, a pretty green mountain reservoir, is right across the street, an attractive venue for fishing, boating, and water-skiing. The surrounding national forest land and Yosemite National Park, 25 miles away, beckon to hikers. If you plan to put in most of your time soaking up the natural splendor of the environment, go ahead and book a spot at Lupine-Cedar Bluff. On second thought, make that a double. For while its hilltop setting, among an array of manzanita, oak, cedar, and pines, is superb, the exposed, grassy sites are disappointingly small and crammed right up against each other. In many cases the dimensions are so tight you won't be able to set up a tent and safely light a fire. The dozen walk-ins are a sop to tenters, as this is more of a camp for motor homes, with paved parking slips and the vast majority of its spots set aside as multiple units. There are a handful of fine single sites, but the concession that runs this property—and dares to charge $16 a night—does not permit reservations by number, only by type (single, double, on up to quadruple).

BASICS

Operated By: California Land Management, concessionaire. **Open:** All year. **Site Assignment:** Reservations recommended w/V, MC, D. **Registration:** At Forest Service office 2.7 mi. west of campground. **Fee:** $16, cash or check; up to $64 for quadruple site. **Parking:** At site or designated area for walk-ins.

FACILITIES

Number of RV Sites: 62. **Number of Tent-Only Sites:** 12. **Hookups:** None. **Each Site:** Picnic table, fire grate. **Dump Station:** No. **Laundry:** No. **Pay Phone:** No. **Rest Rooms and Showers:** Flush toilets, no showers. **Fuel:** No. **Propane:** No. **Internal Roads:** Paved. **RV Service:** No. **Market:** 10 mi. west in Oakhurst. **Restaurant:** Several options on Bass Lake. **General Store:** No. **Vending:** No. **Swimming:** In Bass Lake. **Playground:** No. **Other:** Some wheelchair-accessible facilities. **Activities:** Fishing, hiking, waterskiing, boating, eavesdropping on your neighbors. **Nearby Attractions:** Yosemite National Park; Fresno Flats Historical Site in Oakhurst; Yosemite Mountain Sugar Pine Railroad in Fish Camp. **Additional Information:** Bass Lake Chamber of Commerce, (559) 642-3676.

RESTRICTIONS

Pets: On leash. **Fires:** In fire grates only. **Alcoholic Beverages:** Allowed. **Vehicle Maximum Length:** 40 ft. **Other:** 14-day stay limit.

TO GET THERE

From Oakhurst drive 3 mi. north on Hwy. 41. Turn right on CR 222 and continue for 7 mi., bearing right at 2 consecutive forks, to the campground on the right.

BIG PINE
Big Pine Creek

Glacier Lodge Rd., Big Pine 93513. T: (760) 873-2500 or reservations (877) 444-6777; F: (760) 873-2563; www.r5.fs.fed.us/inyo or www.reserveusa.com.

�car ★★★★   🅰 ★★★★

Beauty: ★★★★	Site Privacy: ★★★
Spaciousness: ★★	Quiet: ★★★
Security: ★★★	Cleanliness: ★★★
Insect Control: ★★★	Facilities: ★★

Of the several campgrounds along Glacier Lodge Rd., Big Pine Creek, at an elevation of 7,700 feet, is preferable for its green grassy look and close proximity to the rocky jaw-line of the overhanging mountains. It is a gorgeous, natural setting, shot-through with Sierra granite, a creek running by, and an abundance of Jeffrey pines complementing its flush of aspens. There is only one blemish to all this beauty, the presence of a handful of private cabins at the center of the property. As is typical of mountain camps, many sites run toward the miniature, and seem to offer less privacy than you'd enjoy at a nudist colony. The exceptions, though, make this a winner, with the spots by the creek providing the best space and seclusion. The pick of the park are numbers 9, appealingly set in an old stone foundation, and 21–23, which are roomy and private. Showers, a snack bar, bait and tackle, and other basic supplies are available at the lodge.

BASICS

Operated By: American Land & Leisure, concessionaire. **Open:** May to mid-Oct., weather permitting. **Site Assignment:** Reservations accepted with V, MC, D. **Registration:** At entrance kiosk. **Fee:** $13, cash or check. **Parking:** At site.

FACILITIES

Number of RV Sites: 25. **Number of Tent-Only Sites:** 5. **Hookups:** None. **Each Site:** Picnic table, fire grate. **Dump Station:** No. **Laundry:** No. **Pay Phone:** No. **Rest Rooms and Showers:** Vault toilets, no showers. **Fuel:** No. **Propane:** No. **Internal Roads:** Paved, narrow & bumpy. **RV Service:** No. **Market:** 9.5 mi. east in Big Pine. **Restaurant:** 9.5 mi. east in Big Pine. **General Store:** Yes. **Vending:** No. **Swimming:** No. **Playground:** No. **Other:** Some wheelchair-accessible facilities.

Activities: Hiking, fishing, horseback riding, photography. **Nearby Attractions:** Inyo National Forest; Ancient Bristlecone Pine Forest & Laws Railroad Museum & Historic Site in Bishop; Death Valley National Park; John Muir Wilderness. **Additional Information:** Bishop Area Chamber of Commerce & Visitors Bureau, (760) 873-8405.

RESTRICTIONS

Pets: On leash. **Fires:** In fire grates only. **Alcoholic Beverages:** Allowed. **Vehicle Maximum Length:** 35 ft. **Other:** 14-day stay limit.

TO GET THERE

From Big Pine on US 395 head west on Crocker St. (which becomes Glacier Lodge Rd.). Drive 9.5 mi. to the campground entrance on the left.

BIG PINE
Grandview

White Mountain Rd., Big Pine 93513. T: (760) 873-2500; F: (760) 873-2563; www.r5.fs.fed.us/inyo.

🚐 ★★★★	⛺ ★★★★★
Beauty: ★★★★	Site Privacy: ★★★★
Spaciousness: ★★★★★	Quiet: ★★★★★
Security: ★	Cleanliness: ★★★★
Insect Control: ★★★★	Facilities: ★

Your first question on arriving at this notably primitive place will probably be, "Where's the view?" Don't despair. While none of the remarkably spacious, well-separated sites offer vistas of anything much beyond the sage-covered meadow at the center of the large loop, walk a few minutes in almost any direction and you will find rewarding panoramas of the outlying valleys and mountain ranges. The best of this national forest land, though, lies five miles farther up the road, at the Ancient Bristlecone Pine Forest, with trails leading past some of the oldest trees on the planet. (The relatively new visitor center there keeps irregular hours.) Pull-through parking slots are available at a number of sites, and most of the latter benefit at least partly from the shade cast by mature junipers, piñons, and other conifers. Weather can be scorching in late spring and early autumn, but at 8,600 feet of elevation, expect nights to be cool and quite breezy. There is no water available, and trash must be packed out.

BASICS

Operated By: Inyo National Forest, White Mountain Ranger District. **Open:** May through Oct., weather permitting. **Site Assignment:** First come, first served. **Registration:** None. **Fee:** None. **Parking:** At site.

FACILITIES

Number of RV Sites: 26. **Number of Tent-Only Sites:** 0. **Hookups:** None. **Each Site:** Picnic table, fire grate. **Dump Station:** No. **Laundry:** No. **Pay Phone:** No. **Rest Rooms and Showers:** Vault toilets, no showers. **Fuel:** No. **Propane:** No. **Internal Roads:** Packed dirt, good condition. **RV Service:** No. **Market:** 13 mi. south in Big Pine. **Restaurant:** 13 mi. south in Big Pine. **General Store:** No. **Vending:** No. **Swimming:** No. **Playground:** No. **Activities:** Hiking, photography, stargazing. **Nearby Attractions:** Inyo National Forest; Ancient Bristlecone Pine Forest & Laws Railroad Museum & Historic Site in Bishop; Death Valley National Park. **Additional Information:** Bishop Area Chamber of Commerce & Visitors Bureau, (760) 873-8405.

RESTRICTIONS

Pets: On leash. **Fires:** In fire grates only. **Alcoholic Beverages:** Allowed. **Vehicle Maximum Length:** 34 ft. **Other:** 14-day stay limit.

TO GET THERE

From Big Pine on US 395 drive 13 mi. east on Hwy. 168. Turn left on White Mountain Rd. and continue 5.5 mi. to the campground entrance on the left.

BIG SUR
Pfeiffer Big Sur State Park

47225 Hwy. 1, Big Sur 93920. T: (831) 667-2315 or reservations (800) 444-7275; F: (831) 667-2886; www.cal-parks.ca.gov or www.reserveamerica.com.

🚐 ★★★	⛺ ★★★★
Beauty: ★★★★	Site Privacy: ★★
Spaciousness: ★★	Quiet: ★★★
Security: ★★★★	Cleanliness: ★★★
Insect Control: ★	Facilities: ★★★

The redwood trees of Pfeiffer Big Sur are neither the largest nor oldest along the California coast. In fact, there is a more impressive grove just two miles south, at the privately-operated Ventana Campground. The trees are so numerous there and grow so close together that the property, with small sites priced around $40 a night, seems perpetually moist and dark. The trees at Pfeiffer, on the other hand, are big without blocking the sunlight. They compose only one part of three distinct habitats represented over the five dispersed loops, with an oak woodland and grassy meadows making up the balance. The Big Sur River parallels the campground, which consists of level sites of dirt and leaves. Those in the first two loops are a bit more spacious than elsewhere. There are some excellent hiking trails in this ever-popular park, with Buzzards Roost in particular delivering superb views of the surrounding hills. Poison oak is abundant around the campground and beggar squirrels can strip your table of food before you're even aware they've invaded.

BASICS

Operated By: California Dept. of Parks & Recreation. **Open:** All year. **Site Assignment:** Reservations recommended; V, MC, D. **Registration:** At entrance booth. **Fee:** $12, cash or CA check. **Parking:** At site.

FACILITIES

Number of RV Sites: 214. **Number of Tent-Only Sites:** 0. **Hookups:** None. **Each Site:** Picnic table, fire grate, barbecue grill. **Dump Station:** Yes. **Laundry:** Yes. **Pay Phone:** Yes. **Rest Rooms and Showers:** Yes. **Fuel:** No. **Propane:** No. **Internal Roads:** Paved. **RV Service:** No. **Market:** 1 mi. north in Big Sur. **Restaurant:** In Big Sur Lodge, within the park. **General Store:** Yes. **Vending:** Yes. **Swimming:** In Big Sur Lodge pool. **Playground:** No. **Other:** Some wheelchair-accessible facilities, Big Sur Lodge. **Activities:** Hiking, beaching, winter whale-watching, redwoods exploring, photography. **Nearby Attractions:** Several state parks in the vicinity: Julia Pfeiffer Burns, Andrew Molera, Garrapata, Limekiln State Park in Lucia, Big Sur coastal vistas. **Additional Information:** Big Sur Chamber, (831) 667-2100.

RESTRICTIONS

Pets: On 6 ft. leash. **Fires:** In fire grates only. **Alcoholic Beverages:** Allowed at site. **Vehicle Maximum Length:** 32 ft. **Other:** 14-day stay limit; no firearms; no wood gathering.

TO GET THERE

From the Big Sur Post Office on Hwy. 1, drive 1.5 mi. north and turn right into the campground.

BISHOP
East Fork

Rock Creek Rd., Toms Place 93514. T: (760) 873-2500 or reservations (877) 444-6777; F: (760) 873-2563; www.r5.fs.fed.us/inyo or www.reserveamerica.com.

🚐 ★★★★ · ⛺ ★★★

Beauty: ★★★★	Site Privacy: ★★★
Spaciousness: ★★	Quiet: ★★★
Security: ★★★	Cleanliness: ★★★
Insect Control: ★★★	Facilities: ★

East Fork is nestled in a rocky canyon with snow-capped Sierra peaks looming above, a thrilling setting very near the gorgeous Rock Creek Lake. The creek itself gurgles through the property, which consists of a hodge-podge of sites, some shaded by lodgepole pines and junipers, others screened by aspen trees, and many exposed to the sun. While most are respectably scattered apart, sites are on the small side, with some so snug there's not enough room to set up anything but a bivvy tent. Still, we find this Inyo National Forest facility infinitely preferable to that at the lake, which is basically a campers' corral in a parking lot. Creek-side site 86 is especially recessed and private, 108 is quite large, and 110–112 and 114 are very good runners-up. At 9,000 feet elevation, this high altitude camp can get hit by snow at almost any time of year, so plan your trip accordingly.

BASICS

Operated By: American Land & Leisure. **Open:** Mid-May through Oct., weather permitting. **Site Assignment:** Reservations accepted w/ MC, V, D. **Registration:** At entrance kiosk. **Fee:** $13, cash or check. **Parking:** At site.

FACILITIES

Number of RV Sites: 80. **Number of Tent-Only Sites:** 53. **Hookups:** None. **Each Site:** Picnic table, fire grate, barbecue grill. **Dump Station:** No. **Laundry:** No. **Pay Phone:** No. **Rest Rooms and Showers:** Flush toilets, no showers. **Fuel:** No. **Propane:** No. **Internal Roads:** Paved. **RV Service:** No. **Market:** 21 mi. north in Mammoth Lakes. **Restaurant:** 3 mi. northeast in Toms Place. **General Store:** No. **Vending:** No. **Swimming:** No. **Playground:** No. **Activities:** Hiking, fishing, bicycling. **Nearby Attractions:** Devil's Postpile National Monument, outlet shopping in Mammoth

Lakes, museums in Bishop, Ancient Bristlecone Pine Forest in the Inyo National Forest. **Additional Information:** Bishop Area Chamber of Commerce & Visitors Bureau, (760) 873-8405.

RESTRICTIONS

Pets: On leash. **Fires:** In fire grates only. **Alcoholic Beverages:** Allowed. **Vehicle Maximum Length:** 45 ft. **Other:** 14-day stay limit.

TO GET THERE

From Bishop head north on US 395 for 24 mi. Turn west (left) on Rock Creek Rd.; continue for 6 mi. and turn left to the campground access road.

BLAIRSDEN

Plumas-Eureka State Park, Upper Samson Creek Campground

310 Johnsville Rd., Blairsden 96103. T: (530) 836-2380; F: (530) 836-0498; www.cal-parks.ca.gov or www.ceres.ca.gov/sierradsp/plumas.html.

🚐 ★★★★	▲ ★★★★
Beauty: ★★★★	Site Privacy: ★★★
Spaciousness: ★★★	Quiet: ★★★★
Security: ★★★	Cleanliness: ★★★
Insect Control: ★★	Facilities: ★★★

"Stunning," "drop-dead gorgeous," and "breathtaking," all describe the spectacular beauty of this high altitude campground that is encircled by a series of jagged, snow-patched Sierra Nevada peaks. The rugged landscape is enhanced by its position next to Jamison Creek and the great variety of conifers, as well as willows, alders, and cottonwoods, that provide it with shade. Flourishing though the forest is, a fair degree of sunlight manages to warm the property. Most sites are roomy and set pretty well apart along a small series of loops. Eureka Peak was once known as Gold Mountain, a testimony to the extensive mining activity that went on in the Jamison area from the gold rush days through the end of the first world war. A mining history museum within the park preserves buildings and equipment from that era. Once a month, in summer, docents in period dress attempt to recreate a sense of what camp life was like in the 1890s.

BASICS

Operated By: California Dept. of Parks & Recreation. **Open:** May 15–Oct. 15, weather permitting. **Site Assignment:** First come, first served. **Registration:** At park office. **Fee:** $12, cash or CA check. **Parking:** At site.

FACILITIES

Number of RV Sites: 59. **Number of Tent-Only Sites:** 8. **Hookups:** None. **Each Site:** Picnic table, fire grate, bearproof box. **Dump Station:** Yes. **Laundry:** No. **Pay Phone:** Yes. **Rest Rooms and Showers:** Yes. **Fuel:** No. **Propane:** No. **Internal Roads:** Paved. **RV Service:** No. **Market:** 6 mi. east in Graegle. **Restaurant:** 6 mi. east in Graegle. **General Store:** No. **Vending:** No. **Swimming:** No. **Playground:** No. **Other:** Some wheelchair-accessible facilities, visitor center & museum. **Activities:** Hiking, bicycling, fishing. **Nearby Attractions:** Portola Railroad Museum; Lakes Basin Recreation Area in Graegle; Plumas County Museum in Quincy; Plumas National Forest. **Additional Information:** Plumas County Visitors Bureau, (530) 283-6345 or (800) 326-2247.

RESTRICTIONS

Pets: On 6 ft. leash. **Fires:** In fire grates only. **Alcoholic Beverages:** Allowed at site. **Vehicle Maximum Length:** 30 ft. **Other:** 14-day stay limit; no firearms; no wood gathering.

TO GET THERE

From Portola drive 10 mi. west on Hwy. 70. One mi. beyond Blairsden and after the junction w/ Hwy. 89, turn left towards Johnsville and continue for 0.6 mi. At the stop sign turn right on the Graegle-Johnsville Rd./A14. The park entrance is 4.5 mi. ahead.

BLYTHE

Mayflower Park

4980 Colorado River Rd., Blythe 92225. T: (760) 922-4665; www.riversidecountyparks.org/parks/mayflower.htm.

🚐 ★★★★	▲ ★★★
Beauty: ★★★	Site Privacy: ★★
Spaciousness: ★★	Quiet: ★★★
Security: ★★★★	Cleanliness: ★★★★
Insect Control: ★★★	Facilities: ★★★★

In the dusty desert landscape common to this part of the state, Mayflower is a welcome oasis and, situated just seven miles north of I-10, a convenient one to pilgrims sailing along the highway. Well manicured, grassy sites are partially shaded by mesquite trees, eucalyptus and cottonwoods, with the tent area—separated from two other RV loops—especially appealing. The view of the Plomosa Mountains across the state line in Arizona is superb, but it is the border itself, marked here by the Colorado River (which flows just below the campground and is accessible via an in-camp boat ramp and swimming lagoon) that is the real attraction for most visitors. Peace-and-quiet seekers take note: boating on this stretch of river during summer months—weekends especially—is more popular than a high school prom queen, so be prepared to hear the constant whine of two-stroke engines being pushed to their limits. That activity largely fades away in the off-season, but winter brings hordes of a different sort of camper, snowbirds by the RV-load.

BASICS

Operated By: Riverside County. **Open:** All Year. **Site Assignment:** First come, first served. **Registration:** At entrance office. **Fee:** $15–$16, cash, CA check or V, MC, D. **Parking:** At site.

FACILITIES

Number of RV Sites: 145. **Number of Tent-Only Sites:** 19. **Hookups:** Water, electric (30, 50 amps). **Each Site:** Picnic table, fire grate. **Dump Station:** Yes. **Laundry:** No. **Pay Phone:** Yes. **Rest Rooms and Showers:** Yes. **Fuel:** No. **Propane:** No. **Internal Roads:** Mostly paved. **RV Service:** No. **Market:** 7 mi. southwest in Blythe. **Restaurant:** 7 mi. southwest in Blythe. **General Store:** No. **Vending:** Yes. **Swimming:** In mudwallow lagoon & Colorado River. **Playground:** No. **Other:** Some wheelchair-accessible facilities, boat ramp. **Activities:** Fishing, horseshoe pits, bowling lawn, shuffleboard. **Nearby Attractions:** Colorado River, Mojave National Preserve, Cibola & Imperial National Wildlife Refuges, in Arizona. **Additional Information:** Riverside County, Regional Park & Open Space District, (909) 955-4397.

RESTRICTIONS

Pets: On leash, $2 fee. **Fires:** In fire grates only. **Alcoholic Beverages:** Allowed. **Vehicle Maximum Length:** None. **Other:** 14-day stay limit from Apr. 1–Sept. 30; no ORVs; no generators; no loaded firearms.

TO GET THERE

From I-10/US 95 drive 3.7 mi. north on Inlake Blvd. Turn right on 6th Ave. and drive 3.2 mi. into the campground.

BODEGA BAY

Sonoma Coast State Beach, Bodega Dunes Campground

Hwy. 1, Bodega Bay 94923. T: (707) 875-3483 or reservations (800) 444-7275; www.cal-parks.ca.gov or www.reserveamerica.com.

🚐 ★★★★	🏕 ★★★★
Beauty: ★★★★	Site Privacy: ★★★★
Spaciousness: ★★★	Quiet: ★★★★
Security: ★★★	Cleanliness: ★★★
Insect Control: ★★★	Facilities: ★★

This good-looking, spacious campground is right off of Hwy. 1, just a short trail's walk from the ocean. Three separate loops undulate across sandy dunes in a semi-forested environment colored by ferns, dune grass, Monterey pines, and eucalyptus. Sites of grass and sand are decently roomy and planted well apart, with a number of pull-through parking slips on hand. Of the latter, numbers 3 and 4 are very private and shaded by conifers. Similarly isolated are 24, 32, 36, 69, 86, and 88, and their nestled-in-the-dunes position is a welcome buffer against road noise and brisk coastal breezes. The steady drone of a distant foghorn is less a disturbing influence than a contributor to the pleasant seaside atmosphere. In spite of its beauty, this facility is often wonderfully under-populated. With whales routinely passing in winter months and a seal rookery located by the egress of the Russian River, you will want to pack binoculars.

BASICS

Operated By: California Dept. of Parks & Recreation. **Open:** All year. **Site Assignment:** Reservations accepted w/ V, MC, D. **Registration:** At entrance booth. **Fee:** $12, cash or CA check. **Parking:** At site.

FACILITIES

Number of RV Sites: 98. **Number of Tent-Only Sites:** 0. **Hookups:** None. **Each Site:** Picnic table, fire grate, food storage box. **Dump Station:** Yes. **Laundry:** No. **Pay Phone:** Yes. **Rest Rooms and Showers:** Yes. **Fuel:** No. **Propane:** No.

Internal Roads: Paved. **RV Service:** No. **Market:** 2 mi. south in Bodega Bay. **Restaurant:** 2 mi. south in Bodega Bay. **General Store:** No. **Vending:** No. **Swimming:** No. **Playground:** No. **Other:** Some wheelchair-accessible facilities. **Activities:** Fishing, sunning, surfing, tidepooling, beachcombing, horseback riding, bicycling, winter whale-watching at Bodega Head. **Nearby Attractions:** Santa Rosa museums & Luther Burbank Home & Memorial Gardens; Fort Ross, Kruse Rhododendron State Reserve & Salt Point State Park in Jenner. **Additional Information:** Bodega Bay Area Chamber of Commerce, (707) 875-3422.

RESTRICTIONS

Pets: On 6 ft. leash. **Fires:** In fire grates only. **Alcoholic Beverages:** Allowed at site. **Vehicle Maximum Length:** 31 ft. **Other:** 10-day stay limit from Apr. 1–Nov. 30; no firearms; no wood gathering.

TO GET THERE

From Bodega Bay drive 2 mi. north on Hwy. 1. Turn left into the park.

BORREGO SPRINGS

Borrego Palm Canyon Campground, Anza-Borrego Desert State Park

200 Palm Canyon Dr., Borrego Springs 92004. T: (760) 767-5311; F: (760) 767-3427; www.cal-parks.ca.gov, www.reserveamerica.com.

🚐 ★★★   ⛺ ★★★

Beauty: ★★★	Site Privacy: ★★★
Spaciousness: ★★★	Quiet: ★★★
Security: ★★★	Cleanliness: ★★★
Insect Control: ★★★★	Facilities: ★★★

This campground is situated in the mouth of the expansive Borrego Palm Canyon near the heart of Anza-Borrego Desert State Park. That central location insures a level of use and popularity well beyond most of the many other camps in this, the largest of state parks in the lower 48 states. A good range of facilities adds to its appeal, with drinking water, showers, full hookups, and even a few partially enclosed stone shelters (complete with fireplaces) available. Though shade is scarce, ramadas over tables provide some relief from a sun that is scorching much of the year. Tent pads are of a coarse gravel, but the overall landscape is hardly lunar, with fan palms lining one stretch of the camp road and ironwood, ocotillo, staghorn

cholla, and creosote bushes sprinkled throughout. Largely comparable sites are fairly well fanned apart, with a good number equipped with pull-through parking slots.

BASICS

Operated By: California Dept. of Parks & Recreation. **Open:** All year. **Site Assignment:** Reservations accepted w/ V, MC. **Registration:** At entrance booth. **Fee:** $10–$16, cash, CA checks or V, MC. **Parking:** At site.

FACILITIES

Number of RV Sites: 117. **Number of Tent-Only Sites:** 0. **Hookups:** Water, electric (30 amps), sewer. **Each Site:** Picnic table, fire grate, ramada (tent loop only). **Dump Station:** Yes. **Laundry:** No. **Pay Phone:** Yes. **Rest Rooms and Showers:** Yes. **Fuel:** No. **Propane:** No. **Internal Roads:** Paved. **RV Service:** No. **Market:** 2 mi. east in Borrego Springs. **Restaurant:** 2 mi. east in Borrego Springs. **General Store:** No. **Vending:** No. **Swimming:** No. **Playground:** No. **Other:** Some wheelchair-accessible facilities. **Activities:** Hiking, bicycling, seasonal nature programs. **Nearby Attractions:** Anza-Borrego Desert State Park, San Diego Wild Animal Park in Escondido. **Additional Information:** Borrego Springs Chamber of Commerce, (760) 767-5976.

RESTRICTIONS

Pets: On 6 ft. leash. **Fires:** In fire grates only. **Alcoholic Beverages:** Allowed at site. **Vehicle Maximum Length:** 35 ft. **Other:** 14-day stay limit; no firearms; no wood gathering.

TO GET THERE

From Borrego Springs drive 1 mi. west on CR S22. At the bend in the road continue straight on Palm Canyon Dr. for 0.2 mi. The campground access road is 1 mi. ahead to the right.

BORREGO SPRINGS

Bow Willow Campground, Anza-Borrego Desert State Park

CR S2, Borrego Springs 92004. T: (760) 767-5311; F: (760) 767- 3427; www.anzaborrego.statepark.org.

🚐 ★★★   ⛺ ★★★★

Beauty: ★★★★	Site Privacy: ★★★
Spaciousness: ★★★	Quiet: ★★★★
Security: ★	Cleanliness: ★★★
Insect Control: ★★★★	Facilities: ★

As the largest state park in the lower 48 states, Anza-Borrego has many attractions: a varied desert landscape, beautiful wildflowers in the spring, a mastodon site, and no shortage of fine camping options. Of these latter, Bow Willow is one of the standouts, with a pair of loops meandering along the lower contours of a rocky canyon. Sandy sites are marginally screened from each other by ocotillo, mesquite, salt bush, and cholla cacti, with numbers 1 and 16 at the periphery the most private. An easy one-and-a-half-mile trail out of camp leads to several shady groves of California fan palms, where we spotted a black hooded oriole and a fluorescent green hummingbird our last time through. No-fee overflow camping is available one mile up the road at the primitive Mountain Palm Springs.

BASICS

Operated By: California Dept. of Parks & Recreation. **Open:** All year. **Site Assignment:** First come, first served. **Registration:** At entrance kiosk. **Fee:** $7, cash or CA check. **Parking:** At site.

FACILITIES

Number of RV Sites: 16. **Number of Tent-Only Sites:** 0. **Hookups:** None. **Each Site:** Picnic table, fire grate, ramada. **Dump Station:** No. **Laundry:** No. **Pay Phone:** No. **Rest Rooms and Showers:** Pit toilets, no showers. **Fuel:** No. **Propane:** No. **Internal Roads:** Sandy washboard, decent condition. **RV Service:** No. **Market:** 44 mi. northwest in Julian. **Restaurant:** 44 mi. northwest in Julian. **General Store:** 10.5 mi. north in Agua Caliente Hot Springs. **Vending:** No. **Swimming:** No. **Playground:** No. **Activities:** Hiking, rock scrambling, birding. **Nearby Attractions:** Palm Springs Desert Museum, Agua Caliente Cultural Museum. **Additional Information:** Borrego Springs Chamber of Commerce, (800)559-5524.

RESTRICTIONS

Pets: On 6 ft. leash. **Fires:** In fire grates only. **Alcoholic Beverages:** Allowed at site. **Vehicle Maximum Length:** None. **Other:** 14-day stay limit; no firearms; no wood gathering.

TO GET THERE

Turn off I-8 at the Ocotillo Exit. Follow CR S2 north through Ocotillo, and turn left into campground after 18 mi.

BORREGO SPRINGS

Culp Valley Primitive Camp, Anza-Borrego Desert State Park

CR S22, Borrego Springs 92004. T: (760) 767-5311; F: (760) 767-3427.

🚐 ★★★★   ⛺ ★★★★

Beauty: ★★★★   Site Privacy: ★★★★
Spaciousness: ★★★★   Quiet: ★★★★
Security: ★   Cleanliness: ★★★★
Insect Control: ★★★★   Facilities: ★

To those who appreciate the low key beauty of the desert and enjoy roughing it, Culp Valley, nine miles west of Borrego Springs, is a hidden gem. Large granite boulders litter a chaparral landscape punctuated by buckwheat, cat's claw, staghorn cholla, and dwarf oak. Most sites are extraordinarily spacious, and several are shielded from view by high hedges of sugar bush, which makes for a more peaceful experience than what is possible in the more popular—and populated—developed campgrounds elsewhere in Anza-Borrego. The trade-off is that creature comforts are limited to surprisingly clean vaulted toilets; no water is available and you will have to pack out your trash. A greater nuisance though is the biting wind that tends to whistle through camp from late fall through early spring. That and an altitude of 3,400 feet will make you glad you packed a heavy sweater, should you visit in the off-season. If you come in summer, well, you'll very likely find yourself alone in the whole blazing park.

BASICS

Operated By: California Dept. of Parks & Recreation. **Open:** All year. **Site Assignment:** First come, first served. **Registration:** At entrance kiosk. **Fee:** $5, cash or CA check; no fee in winter. **Parking:** At site.

FACILITIES

Number of RV Sites: 15. **Number of Tent-Only Sites:** 0. **Hookups:** None. **Each Site:** Space & privacy. **Dump Station:** No. **Laundry:** No. **Pay Phone:** No. **Rest Rooms and Showers:** Vault toilets, no showers. **Fuel:** No. **Propane:** No. **Internal Roads:** Hard sand, some rock, some washboard, negotiable. **RV Service:** No. **Market:** 9 mi. west in Borrego Springs. **Restaurant:** 9 mi. west in Borrego Springs. **General Store:** No.

Vending: No. **Swimming:** No. **Playground:** No. **Activities:** Hiking, photography, stargazing, rock scrambling. **Nearby Attractions:** Anza-Borrego Desert State Park, San Diego Wild Animal Park in Escondido, historic Julian, scenic views. **Additional Information:** Borrego Springs Chamber of Commerce, (760) 767-5976.

RESTRICTIONS

Pets: On 6 ft. leash. **Fires:** No. **Alcoholic Beverages:** Allowed. **Vehicle Maximum Length:** None, but think twice if over 22 ft. **Other:** 14-day stay limit; no shooting.

TO GET THERE

From Borrego Springs drive 9 mi. east on CR S22. Check for a sign between mi. markers 9 and 10 on the right (north) side of the road.

BRIDGEPORT

Honeymoon Flat

Twin Lakes Rd., Bridgeport 93517. T: (760) 932-7070 or reservations (877) 444-6777; F: (760) 932-1299; www.r5.fs.fed.us/htnf/honecamp.htm or www.reserveusa.com.

🚐 ★★★★   ⛺ ★★★★

Beauty: ★★★★	Site Privacy: ★★★
Spaciousness: ★★★	Quiet: ★★★
Security: ★★★	Cleanliness: ★★★★
Insect Control: ★★	Facilities: ★

A campground sporting the name Honeymoon Flat had better be the sort of cozily romantic place you'd want to take your sweetheart. Well, go right ahead, as this idyllic spot lives up to that promise, and then some. Twin Lakes Rd. divides it into two sections, with both hugging Robinson Creek. Many of the grassy sites along the camp's series of sandy loops abut the water, allowing you to fish for trout from tent-side, or simply dandle your toes in the rippling water. Though sites are a shade small, privacy is well above average, with screening provided by a mix of pines and, especially, the luminescent leaves of quaking aspen. Site 3, very recessed and with water flowing by on three sides, might well be the envy of Diana. Number 5 is similarly romantic. There are half a dozen other campgrounds in the neighborhood, but this is the only one that hasn't been smothered by an excess of asphalt. When you are at 7,000 feet, surrounded by the high Sierras, a campground shouldn't look like a parking lot. The pit toilets are reportedly going to be replaced with new restrooms; we expect the concessionaire will raise the rates as a consequence.

BASICS

Operated By: American Land & Leisure, concessionaire. **Open:** Mid-Apr. through Oct., weather permitting. **Site Assignment:** Reservations accepted w/ V, MC, D. **Registration:** At entrance kiosk. **Fee:** $10, cash or check. **Parking:** At site.

FACILITIES

Number of RV Sites: 31. **Number of Tent-Only Sites:** 4. **Hookups:** None. **Each Site:** Picnic table, fire grate. **Dump Station:** No. **Laundry:** No. **Pay Phone:** No. **Rest Rooms and Showers:** Pit toilets, no showers. **Fuel:** No. **Propane:** No. **Internal Roads:** Sandy & somewhat bumpy. **RV Service:** No. **Market:** 8.5 mi. north in Bridgeport. **Restaurant:** 8.5 mi. north in Bridgeport. **General Store:** No. **Vending:** No. **Swimming:** No. **Playground:** No. **Activities:** Hiking, fishing, whispering sweet nothings into your sweetheart's ear. **Nearby Attractions:** Bodie State Historic Park in Bridgeport; Lower Twin Lake, Mono Lake Tufa State Reserve in Lee Vining. **Additional Information:** Eastern Sierra Interagency Visitor Center, (760) 876-6222; Bridgeport Chamber of Commerce, (760) 932-7500.

RESTRICTIONS

Pets: On leash. **Fires:** In fire grates only. **Alcoholic Beverages:** Allowed. **Vehicle Maximum Length:** 45 ft. **Other:** 14-day stay limit.

TO GET THERE

From US 395 on Bridgeport's west side, turn south onto Twin Lakes Rd. Drive 8.2 mi. to the campground entrance on both sides of the road.

BUËLLTON

Figueroa

Figueroa Mountain Rd., Los Olivos 93441. T: (805) 925-9538; F: (805) 681-2781; www.r5.fs.fed.us/lospadres.

🚐 ★★★   ⛺ ★★★★★

Beauty: ★★★★★	Site Privacy: ★★★★
Spaciousness: ★★★★	Quiet: ★★★★
Security: ★★	Cleanliness: ★★★★
Insect Control: ★★★★	Facilities: ★

As far as rustic campgrounds go, this one, set at 4,000 feet among alpine meadows and mixed tree communities high in the rugged mountains of the Los Padres National Forest, is almost perfect. It is so far out—the nearest town is more than 15 miles away—that the only sounds likely to disturb you will come from Stellar's jays, acorn woodpeckers, owls, or coyotes. Unless you happen to have particularly obnoxious neighbors. Even so, most of the dirt and pebbly sites along the double loop are regally spacious and far apart, screened by manzanita, live oak, and Coulter pines, with an accent here and there of shiny, putty colored rock outcroppings. Shade is abundant, though several units are open and sunny, and a few offer superb vistas of sunsets and the valley far below. In spring the hills are a velvety green that is a delight to behold, but be alert to changing weather as the pockmarked road leading here can be very tricky when wet. Figueroa is a pack-in, pack-out facility with an unreliable water supply.

BASICS

Operated By: Los Padres National Forest, Santa Lucia Ranger District. **Open:** All year. **Site Assignment:** First come, first served. **Registration:** No. **Fee:** No fee, but National Forest Adventure Pass ($5 per day, $30 annual pass) required. **Parking:** At site.

FACILITIES

Number of RV Sites: 33. **Number of Tent-Only Sites:** 0. **Hookups:** None. **Each Site:** Picnic table, fire grate, barbecue grill. **Dump Station:** No. **Laundry:** No. **Pay Phone:** No. **Rest Rooms and Showers:** Vault toilets, no showers. **Fuel:** No. **Propane:** No. **Internal Roads:** Paved. **RV Service:** No. **Market:** 23 mi. southwest in Buëllton. **Restaurant:** 23 mi. southwest in Buëllton. **General Store:** No. **Vending:** No. **Swimming:** No. **Playground:** No. **Other:** Some wheelchair-accessible facilities. **Activities:** Hiking, birding, stargazing. **Nearby Attractions:** Mission Santa Inés & museums in Solvang, La Purísima Mission State Historic Park in Lompoc, Lake Cachuma. **Additional Information:** Buëllton Visitors Bureau, (805) 688-7829.

RESTRICTIONS

Pets: On leash. **Fires:** In fire grates only. **Alcoholic Beverages:** Allowed. **Vehicle Maximum Length:** 22 ft. **Other:** 14-day stay limit.

TO GET THERE

In Los Olivos on Hwy. 154 head north on Figueroa Mountain Rd. Watch out for potholes on this narrow, windy road. Drive 13.8 mi. and turn right into the campground.

CAMP NELSON
Peppermint

FR 21S07A, Ponderosa/Camp Nelson 93208. T: (559) 539-2607; www.r5.fs.fed.us/sequoia.

🚐 ★★★★	▲ ★★★★
Beauty: ★★★★	Site Privacy: ★★★★
Spaciousness: ★★★★	Quiet: ★★★
Security: ★	Cleanliness: ★★
Insect Control: ★★★	Facilities: ★

The last time we stopped by this primitive camp we were surprised to find half a dozen motor homes in residence. Not that the dirt access road off of Western Divide Hwy. is bad—it isn't (though the internal lane verges on abominable in places). It's just that for ages Peppermint has been a refuge for budget-minded tenters. Word of its rustic appeal must have spread. There are about a dozen tables scattered around this rocky, forested mountain knoll, mostly downhill by Peppermint Creek. There is also a dilapidated outhouse, of a similar vintage to the one at Quaking Aspen, just up the road. If you want more in creature comforts, you best bring 'em with you or go elsewhere. Undesignated sites are well hidden among lodgepole, ponderosa and Jeffrey pines, alders and aspens, cedars and dirt. Those with tables are snapped up first, but there are many more across the hill with simply a crude ring of stones as an amenity. Bring your own drinking water, pack out trash, and, since you'll be camping at an altitude of 7,100 feet, dress warmly. Telephone, gasoline, propane, and a general store are available 1.5 miles north at Ponderosa Lodge.

BASICS

Operated By: Sequoia National Forest, Tule River Ranger District. **Open:** May through Oct., weather permitting. **Site Assignment:** First come, first served. **Registration:** None. **Fee:** None. **Parking:** No restriction.

FACILITIES

Number of RV Sites: Unspecified, dispersed camping. **Number of Tent-Only Sites:** 0. **Hookups:** None. **Each Site:** 12 scattered picnic tables, many makeshift fire rings. **Dump Station:** No. **Laundry:** No. **Pay Phone:** No. **Rest Rooms and Showers:** Vault toilets, no showers. **Fuel:** No. **Propane:** No. **Internal Roads:** Rocky forest floor. **RV Service:** No. **Market:** 45 mi. west in Porterville. **Restaurant:** 30 mi. west in Springville. **General Store:** No. **Vending:** No. **Swimming:** No. **Playground:** No. **Activities:** Hiking, fishing, whittling. **Nearby Attractions:** Sequoia National Forest; Porterville Historical Museum & Zauld House & Gardens; California Hot Springs. **Additional Information:** Springville Chamber of Commerce, (559) 539-2312; Porterville Chamber of Commerce, (559) 784-7503.

RESTRICTIONS

Pets: On leash. **Fires:** By permit, issued at the Tule River Ranger District in Springville; use fire ring. **Alcoholic Beverages:** Allowed. **Vehicle Maximum Length:** 22 ft. **Other:** 14-day stay limit.

TO GET THERE

From Porterville drive 44 mi. east on Hwy. 190 (which becomes the Western Divide Hwy.). Turn left on FR 21S07B and after 0.5 mi. turn left again on 21S07A. The campground lies straight ahead.

CAPITOLA

New Brighton State Beach

1500 Park Ave., Hwy. 1, Capitola 95010. T: (831) 464-6330 or reservations (800) 444-7275; www.cal-parks.ca.gov or www.reserveamerica.com.

🚐 ★★★★   ⛺ ★★★★

Beauty: ★★★★	Site Privacy: ★★★
Spaciousness: ★★★★	Quiet: ★★★
Security: ★★★	Cleanliness: ★★★★
Insect Control: ★★	Facilities: ★★

Tired of sweeping buckets of sand out of your tent or RV after every trip to the beach? Then you owe it to yourself to check out this splendid campground, located just five miles east of Santa Cruz off of Hwy. 1. The bluff-top real estate is lush and grassy, graced with a comforting balance of shade and sun that filters through a high canopy of pines and eucalyptus trees. Many of the refreshingly spacious spots enjoy great vistas of the crashing surf. And of those that do not, a hefty share have the edge in privacy, being buffered by dense hedges of coastal chaparral. Sites 25 and 94 are the most isolated, while 36 is the best screened of the view options. And if sand in your shelter isn't a problem, you can always bring a bucketful back from the idyllic beach, reachable via a short trail next to site 50. Poison oak thrives around the edges of this park.

BASICS

Operated By: California Dept. of Parks & Recreation. **Open:** All year. **Site Assignment:** Reservations recommended; V, MC, D. **Registration:** At entrance booth. **Fee:** $12, cash or CA check. **Parking:** At site.

FACILITIES

Number of RV Sites: 112. **Number of Tent-Only Sites:** 0. **Hookups:** None. **Each Site:** Picnic table, fire grate, food storage box. **Dump Station:** Yes. **Laundry:** No. **Pay Phone:** Yes. **Rest Rooms and Showers:** Yes. **Fuel:** No. **Propane:** No. **Internal Roads:** Paved. **RV Service:** No. **Market:** 5 mi. west in Santa Cruz. **Restaurant:** 5 mi. west in Santa Cruz. **General Store:** No. **Vending:** No. **Swimming:** In Pacific Ocean. **Playground:** No. **Other:** Some wheelchair-accessible facilities. **Activities:** Surf fishing, sunning, hiking, ranger-led programs in summer. **Nearby Attractions:** Santa Cruz Beach Boardwalk, mission, museums, Seymour Marine Discovery Center, Arboretum & Natural Bridges State Beach; Roaring Camp Railroads in Felton. **Additional Information:** Capitola Chamber of Commerce, (831) 475-6522; Santa Cruz County Conference & Visitors Council, (831) 425-1234 or (800) 833-3494.

RESTRICTIONS

Pets: On 6 ft. leash. **Fires:** In fire grates only. **Alcoholic Beverages:** Allowed at site. **Vehicle Maximum Length:** 36 ft. **Other:** 7-day stay limit from Apr. 1–Oct. 31; no firearms; no wood gathering.

TO GET THERE

From Santa Cruz drive 5 mi. south on Hwy. 1 and take the New Brighton Beach Exit. Drive 1 block west to the stop sign. Turn left on McGregor Dr. After 0.2 mi. turn right into the park.

CARLSBAD
South Carlsbad State Beach

Carlsbad Blvd./Pacific Coast Hwy. 101, Carlsbad 92008. T: (760) 438-3143; www.cal-parks.ca.gov or www.reserveamerica.com.

🚐 ★★★★   ▲ ★★

Beauty: ★★★	Site Privacy: ★★
Spaciousness: ★★★	Quiet: ★
Security: ★★★	Cleanliness: ★★
Insect Control: ★★	Facilities: ★★★★

There is much to like about South Carlsbad State Beach. Such as the pretty beach, and its convenient location just off I-5, 25 miles north of San Diego. Sites are positioned side-by-side high above the sea on a sandy bluff, and are both spacious and buffered with thick hedges that provide a certain degree of privacy. The straight-in linear layout of the camp road endows half the property with fine views of the Pacific Ocean. Of course, the narrowness of the bluff means that you are likely to have neighbors on three of your spot's four sides when the camp is busy, which is most of the year, given its near-constant use by hordes of college-age campers. At those times the flow of traffic can seem never-ending, a problem compounded by the busy external road that parallels the park's entire length. True, that constant hum of vehicles helps drown out the boisterousness of other campers and the squealing whistles of Amtrak trains that tend to pass the property on an hourly basis, but that may be of small consolation to light sleepers. At least the ocean-side sites benefit from the sonorous sound of the surf. Overall, South Carlsbad is quieter than San Elijo State Beach to the south, where the deafening roar of railroad and highway vehicles seems to be bearing down on one's tent. San Elijo does, however, offer some sites with hookups.

BASICS
Operated By: California Dept. of Parks & Recreation. **Open:** All year. **Site Assignment:** Reservations recommended; V, MC, D. **Registration:** At entrance booth. **Fee:** $12, cash, CA check or V, MC, D. **Parking:** At site.

FACILITIES
Number of RV Sites: 222. **Number of Tent-Only Sites:** 0. **Hookups:** None. **Each Site:** Picnic table, fire ring. **Dump Station:** Yes. **Laundry:** Yes.

Pay Phone: Yes. **Rest Rooms and Showers:** Yes. **Fuel:** No. **Propane:** Yes. **Internal Roads:** Paved. **RV Service:** No. **Market:** 4 mi. north in Carlsbad. **Restaurant:** 4 mi. north in Carlsbad. **General Store:** Yes. **Vending:** Yes. **Swimming:** In Pacific Ocean. **Playground:** No. **Other:** Some wheelchair-accessible facilities. **Activities:** Sunning, surfing, rock & shell hounding, surfboard & boogie board rentals. **Nearby Attractions:** Coastal air tours, outlet shopping, Museum of Making Music, Legoland. **Additional Information:** Carlsbad CVB, (760) 434-6093; San Diego CVB, (619) 232-3101.

RESTRICTIONS
Pets: On leash no longer than 6 ft.; not allowed on the beach. **Fires:** In fire rings only. **Alcoholic Beverages:** Allowed at site. **Vehicle Maximum Length:** 35 ft. **Other:** 14-day stay limit; no firearms.

TO GET THERE
From Carlsbad drive 4.5 miles south on Hwy. 101. Bear to the right into the campground, which is easy to overshoot since signs are lacking.

CARMEL
Saddle Mountain Recreation Park and RV & Campground

27625 Schulte Rd., Carmel 93923. T: (831) 624-1617; F: (831) 624-4470.

🚐 ★★★   ▲ ★★

Beauty: ★★★	Site Privacy: ★★
Spaciousness: ★★	Quiet: ★★★★
Security: ★★★	Cleanliness: ★★
Insect Control: ★★	Facilities: ★★★

Planning to be in the Monterey vicinity? If you are hauling a trailer or driving an RV you will find that Saddle Mountain has a lot going for it. Like full hookups, including cable television, a heated swimming pool (Memorial Day through Labor Day), basketball, volleyball, horseshoes, hiking, and even fishing in the nearby Carmel River. Its suburban location is a plus, too, just five miles from Carmel in the hills of Potrero Canyon, with great vistas of the surrounding mountains. Terraced clusters of sites are rather close together but shady and well-screened by cypress trees, Monterey pines, and flowering oleanders, with a pretty rock garden adding to the attractive landscaping. Tent sites, sequestered up the hill from

RVs, are similarly shaded and slightly more spacious. A latticed picnic area and deck overlook the pool. Although the moderate climate makes it possible for this privately-operated campground to remain open throughout the year, maintenance slackens somewhat in the off-season.

BASICS

Operated By: Saddle Mountain Recreation Park & RV & Campground. **Open:** All year. **Site Assignment:** Reservations accepted w/ V, MC. **Registration:** At office. **Fee:** $25–$40, cash or V, MC. **Parking:** At site.

FACILITIES

Number of RV Sites: 25. **Number of Tent-Only Sites:** 25. **Hookups:** Water, electric (20, 30 amps), sewer, cable TV. **Each Site:** Picnic table, barbecue grill. **Dump Station:** Yes. **Laundry:** No. **Pay Phone:** Yes. **Rest Rooms and Showers:** Yes. **Fuel:** No. **Propane:** No. **Internal Roads:** Paved, dirt in the tent area. **RV Service:** No. **Market:** 5 mi. west in Carmel. **Restaurant:** 5 mi. west in Carmel. **General Store:** No. **Vending:** Yes. **Swimming:** In heated pool seasonally. **Playground:** Yes. **Other:** Limited wheelchair-accessible facilities, game room. **Activities:** Hiking, volleyball, horseshoe pit, golf. **Nearby Attractions:** Mission San Carlos Borromeo del Rio Carmelo & outlet shopping in Carmel; Monterey peninsula w/ its museums & aquarium. **Additional Information:** Carmel Valley Chamber of Commerce, (831) 659-4000.

RESTRICTIONS

Pets: On leash no longer than 6 ft.; not allowed in the tent area. **Fires:** In grills only. **Alcoholic Beverages:** Allowed at site. **Vehicle Maximum Length:** 40 ft. **Other:** 14-day stay limit.

TO GET THERE

From Carmel on Hwy. 1 follow the Carmel Valley Rd. inland for 4.7 miles. Turn right on Schulte Rd. The park is one mile ahead on the windy road.

CARRIZO PLAIN NATIONAL MONUMENT
KCL Campground

Soda Lake Rd., Maricopa 93252. T: (805) 475-2131 or (661) 391-6000; www.ca.blm.gov.

🚐 ★★★   ⛺ ★★★★

Beauty: ★★★★   Site Privacy: ★★★
Spaciousness: ★★★   Quiet: ★★★★
Security: ★   Cleanliness: ★★★
Insect Control: ★★★★   Facilities: ★

Formerly the ranch of Kern County Land Company, KCL is now one of two camps in Carrizo Plain National Monument, a park established near the end of president Clinton's term in office. The monument's staff suggests upgraded facilities are coming, but for now this campground offers nil beyond a portable toilet. No water, no trash pick-up, no host, just a pretty setting alongside a photogenic barn and corral. The large sites are shaded by ancient eucalyptus trees, backed up against the base of the Caliente Mountains and with a view across the grasslands to the San Andreas fault and the Temblor Range. Ten miles to the east is Painted Rock, a pictograph-covered relic from when Native Americans still roamed the plains. Near that is Soda Lake, a glistening salt-crusted body of water that attracts migrating birds, most notably the sandhill crane, throughout the winter. The tall grass of the plains, where pronghorn antelope and black-tailed deer frequently graze, is streaked yellow with wildflowers in the spring before the scorching heat of summer turns everything brown. Note that the deeply rutted dirt camp road is impassable when wet, and the nearest telephone is at the intersection of Soda Lake Rd. and Hwy. 166, 20 miles southeast of KCL.

BASICS

Operated By: Bureau of Land Management, Bakersfield Field Office. **Open:** All year. **Site Assignment:** First come, first served. **Registration:** No. **Fee:** No fee, donations accepted. **Parking:** At site.

FACILITIES

Number of RV Sites: 8. **Number of Tent-Only Sites:** 0. **Hookups:** None. **Each Site:** Picnic table, fire ring. **Dump Station:** No. **Laundry:** No. **Pay Phone:** No. **Rest Rooms and Showers:** Pit toilet, no showers. **Fuel:** No. **Propane:** No. **Internal Roads:** Dirt, can be slick when wet. **RV Service:** No. **Market:** 35 mi. east in Taft. **Restaurant:** 35 mi. east in Taft. **General Store:** No. **Vending:** No. **Swimming:** No. **Playground:** No. **Other:** Limited wheelchair-accessible facilities. **Activities:** Hiking, birding, wildflower walks, photography, pictographs & old farm structures to explore. **Nearby Attractions:** Tule Elk State Reserve in Buttonwillow; Kern Oil Museum in Taft. **Additional Information:** Taft District Chamber of Commerce, (661) 765-2165.

RESTRICTIONS

Pets: Allowed. **Fires:** In fire rings only. **Alcoholic Beverages:** Allowed. **Vehicle Maximum Length:** None. **Other:** 14-day stay limit; no loaded firearms; no wood gathering.

TO GET THERE

From San Luis Obispo drive 8.8 mi. north on US 101. Exit on Hwy. 58 and head east for 47 mi., through Santa Margarita and California Valley. Turn right on Soda Lake Rd. and drive 26 mi. to the campground entrance on the right.

CARRIZO PLAIN NATIONAL MONUMENT
Selby Campground

Soda Lake Rd., Maricopa 93252. T: (805) 475-2131 or (661) 391-6000; www.ca.blm.gov.

🚐 ★★★   ⛺ ★★★

Beauty: ★★★★	Site Privacy: ★★★
Spaciousness: ★★★	Quiet: ★★★★
Security: ★	Cleanliness: ★★
Insect Control: ★★★★	Facilities: ★

This campground is in a park that is way the heck off the beaten track, with just a portable toilet and non-potable water for amenities. Most of the year wind howls through camp, and when it finally ceases the heat of summer feels like a blast furnace. So why bother to visit Carrizo Plain, one of the newest monuments in the national park system? For several reasons, actually, such as to see sandhill cranes—and many other water fowl—nesting during the winter by the salt-glistening shores of Soda Lake. And for ranger-led tours of Painted Rock, a 55-foot high rock decorated with Native American pic-

tographs, with some estimated to be as old as 2,000 years. There is also a trail to the San Andreas fault that showcases the awesome power of earthquakes. Spring wildflower displays, too, are sensational. Trails into a Wilderness Study Area, part of the Caliente Mountains, start at Selby and pass through hills dotted with juniper, sage and salt bush. Selby, set at the base of a slanting escarpment, features five oversize, unshaded sites with plenty of parking for even the largest of RVs. The nearest telephone is 14.5 miles away in California Valley.

BASICS

Operated By: Bureau of Land Management, Bakersfield Field Office. **Open:** All year. **Site Assignment:** First come, first served. **Registration:** No. **Fee:** No fee, donations accepted. **Parking:** At site.

FACILITIES

Number of RV Sites: 5. **Number of Tent-Only Sites:** 0. **Hookups:** None. **Each Site:** Picnic table, fire ring. **Dump Station:** No. **Laundry:** No. **Pay Phone:** No. **Rest Rooms and Showers:** Portable toilet, no showers. **Fuel:** No. **Propane:** No. **Internal Roads:** Dirt, can be slick when wet. **RV Service:** No. **Market:** 45 mi. east in Taft. **Restaurant:** 45 mi. east in Taft. **General Store:** No. **Vending:** No. **Swimming:** No. **Playground:** No. **Other:** Limited wheelchair-accessible facilities. **Activities:** Hiking, birding, wildflower walks, photography, pictographs & old farm structures to explore. **Nearby Attractions:** Tule Elk State Reserve in Buttonwillow; Kern Oil Museum in Taft. **Additional Information:** Taft District Chamber of Commerce, (661) 765-2165.

RESTRICTIONS

Pets: Allowed. **Fires:** In fire rings only. **Alcoholic Beverages:** Allowed. **Vehicle Maximum Length:** None. **Other:** 14-day stay limit; no loaded firearms; no wood gathering.

TO GET THERE

From San Luis Obispo drive 8.8 mi. north on US 101. Exit on Hwy. 58 and continue east for 47 mi., through Santa Margarita and California Valley. Turn right on Soda Lake Rd. and drive 16.5 mi. to the campground entrance on the right. Follow the windy access road for 4.7 mi. into camp.

CHESTER
Elam

Hwy. 32, Chester 96020. T: (530) 258-2141; F: (530) 258-5194; www.r5.fs.fed.us/lassen.

🚐 ★★★   ▲ ★★

Beauty: ★★★   Site Privacy: ★★
Spaciousness: ★★   Quiet: ★★★
Security: ★★   Cleanliness: ★★★
Insect Control: ★★   Facilities: ★

Elam is a small, primitive national forest facility that is about 15 miles west of Chester, to the south of Lassen Volcanic National Park. It would be quite an appealing camp if it were not over-crowded so much of the time. A bubbling creek flows by one side of its short access lane, a steep embankment parallels the other, and granite rocks and boulders litter the narrow grounds. Why is Elam so popular? The answer, in a word, is trout. The creek is regularly stocked, and unlike other bodies of water in the area, fisher-men are allowed to keep what they catch. You can spend the day trying to lure the fish onto your hook, then while away the evenings swap-ping stories with newly-made fishing buddies about the huge ones that got away. Level, dirt-surfaced sites are small and exposed—not just to each other but also to the picnic area directly across the creek—major shortcomings in such a highly trafficked property. Number 15, at the end of the lane, is the most private site, followed by 14, at the water's edge, and 11, also creekside. The altitude of 4,400 feet justifies packing a sweater, even in summer.

BASICS

Operated By: CSU Chico Research Foundation, concessionaire, & Lassen National Forest, Almanor Ranger District. **Open:** May through Oct., weather permitting. **Site Assignment:** First come, first served. **Registration:** At entrance kiosk. **Fee:** $12, cash or check. **Parking:** At site.

FACILITIES

Number of RV Sites: 15. **Number of Tent-Only Sites:** 0. **Hookups:** None. **Each Site:** Picnic table, fire grate. **Dump Station:** No. **Laundry:** No. **Pay Phone:** No. **Rest Rooms and Showers:** Vault toilets, no showers. **Fuel:** No. **Propane:** No. **Internal Roads:** Paved. **RV Service:** No. **Market:** 16 mi. east in Chester. **Restaurant:** 16 mi. east in

Chester. **General Store:** No. **Vending:** No. **Swimming:** No. **Playground:** No. **Activities:** Fishing, hiking, bicycling, bragging about the fish that got away. **Nearby Attractions:** Westwood Museum & Paul Bunyan & Babe the Blue Ox Stat-ues; Lassen National Scenic Byway (Hwys. 89-44-36); Lassen Volcanic National Park; Lake Almanor. **Additional Information:** Chester–Lake Almanor Chamber of Commerce, (530) 258-2426 or (800) 350-4838.

RESTRICTIONS

Pets: On leash. **Fires:** In fire grates only. **Alcoholic Beverages:** Allowed. **Vehicle Maximum Length:** 22 ft. **Other:** 14-day stay limit from Memorial Day through Labor Day, 21-day stay limit for the rest of the year.

TO GET THERE

From Chester on Hwy. 36 drive 13 mi. west to the junction w/ Hwy. 32. Turn left on Hwy. 32 and continue for 3.6 mi. The campground is to the right.

COLEVILLE
Sonora Bridge

Hwy. 108, Coleville 96107. T: (760) 932-7070; F: (760) 932-1299; www.r5.fs.fed.us/htnf/soncamp.htm.

🚐 ★★★★   ▲ ★★★★

Beauty: ★★★★   Site Privacy: ★★★
Spaciousness: ★★★   Quiet: ★★★★
Security: ★★★   Cleanliness: ★★★★
Insect Control: ★★★★   Facilities: ★

There is a rough-surfaced russet knob of granite on one flank of this expansive camp, a steep rocky slope on another, and all around are fabulous views of the mountains. Thick-trunked Jeffrey pines are the dominant trees in these parts, though the campground is also accented by juniper and such chaparral as salt bush and sage. Unlike Leav-itt Meadows, just up the road, there's no river flowing by this turf, but sites here are clearly supe-rior, and many offer pull-through parking. Most are roomier and largely more private, owing partly to a thick undergrowth of mountain mahogany, and partly to their wider distribution along a series of four loops. Additionally, the breathtaking views of the Sierras simply cannot be beat. Unless, that is, you strap a pack to your back and hoof it higher into the mountains, or head out to the

Walker River to fish for rainbow trout. Elevation at Sonora Bridge, which is 20 miles west of Bridgeport, is 6,800 feet; icy winds whistle through camp early and late in the year, so bring along some warm clothing.

BASICS

Operated By: American Land & Leisure, concessionaire. **Open:** Mid-May through mid-Oct., weather permitting. **Site Assignment:** First come, first served. **Registration:** At entrance kiosk. **Fee:** $10, cash or check. **Parking:** At site.

FACILITIES

Number of RV Sites: 23. **Number of Tent-Only Sites:** 0. **Hookups:** None. **Each Site:** Picnic table, fire grate. **Dump Station:** No. **Laundry:** No. **Pay Phone:** No. **Rest Rooms and Showers:** Vault toilets, no showers. **Fuel:** No. **Propane:** No. **Internal Roads:** Dirt but smooth. **RV Service:** No. **Market:** 19 mi. east in Bridgeport. **Restaurant:** 19 mi. east in Bridgeport. **General Store:** No. **Vending:** No. **Swimming:** No. **Playground:** No. **Activities:** Hiking, fishing, star-gazing. **Nearby Attractions:** Bodie State Historic Park in Bridgeport; Sonora Pass. **Additional Information:** Eastern Sierra Interagency Visitor Center, (760) 876-6222; Bridgeport Chamber of Commerce, (760) 932-7500.

RESTRICTIONS

Pets: On leash. **Fires:** In fire grates only. **Alcoholic Beverages:** Allowed. **Vehicle Maximum Length:** 30 ft. **Other:** 14-day stay limit.

TO GET THERE

From Bridgeport drive 17 mi. north on US 395. Turn west (left) onto Hwy. 108 and drive 1.5 mi. to the campground entrance on the left.

CORNING
Woodson Bridge
State Recreation Area

South Ave., Corning 96021. T: (530) 839-2112 or reservations (800) 444-7275; www.cal-parks.ca.gov or www.norcal.parks.ca.us or www.reserveamerica.com.

🚐 ★★★★	🏕 ★★★★
Beauty: ★★★★	Site Privacy: ★★★
Spaciousness: ★★★	Quiet: ★★★
Security: ★★★★	Cleanliness: ★★★★
Insect Control: ★	Facilities: ★★

The marked increase in visitation to this sweet gem of a park proves The Secret is out. No wonder, with its grounds, which overlap the Sacramento River, so fertile and grassy, and its recessed, scattered campsites framed by massive, aged valley oaks. Unbelievably, this sylvan glade is not concealed in some forested outback, but instead is located a scant six miles east of Corning and I-5, three miles west of Hwy. 99 and Vina. If fishing is your game, prepare to mark your datebook: king salmon runs are optimum from Oct. through May, the peak for shad is in July and Aug., striped bass in early fall, steelhead in Oct. and Nov., and catfish may be caught just about any time of year. If that is not enough to lure you to this appealing recreation area, perhaps its extraordinary birding will, with yellow-billed cuckoos, hummingbirds, pheasants, hawks, falcons, and many other species commonly seen. So are swarms of mosquitoes, from spring through mid-summer—plan to bring repellant. Older guidebooks list Woodson Bridge as having a dump station but fallen trees now make that inaccessible. There are no plans yet to restore it.

BASICS

Operated By: California Dept. of Parks & Recreation. **Open:** All year. **Site Assignment:** Reservations accepted w/ V, MC, D. **Registration:** At entrance booth. **Fee:** $14 from May 15–Sept. 15, $10 the rest of the year; cash or CA check. **Parking:** At site.

FACILITIES

Number of RV Sites: 37. **Number of Tent-Only Sites:** 0. **Hookups:** None. **Each Site:** Picnic table, fire grate. **Dump Station:** No, inaccessible because of fallen trees. **Laundry:** No. **Pay Phone:** Yes. **Rest Rooms and Showers:** Yes. **Fuel:** No. **Propane:** No. **Internal Roads:** Paved. **RV Service:** No. **Market:** 6 mi. west in Corning. **Restaurant:** 6 mi. west in Corning. **General Store:** No. **Vending:** No. **Swimming:** In Sacramento River. **Playground:** No. **Other:** Some wheelchair-accessible facilities. **Activities:** Fishing, hiking, birding, boating. **Nearby Attractions:** Tejama County Park in Corning; Chico museums & Bidwell Mansion State Historic Park; outlet shopping in Anderson; William B. Ide Adobe State Historic Park near Red Bluff. **Additional Information:** Corning District Chamber of Commerce, (530) 824-5550; Chico Chamber of Commerce & Visitor Bureau, (530) 891-5556 or (800) 852-8570.

RESTRICTIONS

Pets: On 6 ft. leash. **Fires:** In fire grates only. **Alcoholic Beverages:** Allowed at site. **Vehicle Maximum Length:** 31 ft. **Other:** 14-day stay limit from June through Sept., 30-day stay limit from Oct. through May; no firearms; no wood gathering.

TO GET THERE

In Corning on I-5 take the South Ave. Exit. Head east for 6.3 mi. and turn left into the campground.

CRESCENT CITY

Del Norte Coast Redwoods State Park, Mill Creek Campground

US 101 South, Crescent City 95532. T: (707) 464-6101, ext. 5102 or reservations (800) 444-7275; www.cal-parks.ca.gov or www.reserveamerica.com.

🚐 ★★★★   ⛺ ★★★★

Beauty: ★★★★	Site Privacy: ★★★★
Spaciousness: ★★★	Quiet: ★★★
Security: ★★★	Cleanliness: ★★★★
Insect Control: ★★★	Facilities: ★★

This campground is set in the heart of Mill Creek Canyon among a concentration of red alders and second-growth redwoods. It is a moist, antediluvian environment, with winter rainfall, which averages 100 inches, contributing to a fertile, mossy, jungle-like luminescence. Rhododendrons, azaleas, maples, and ferns thrive here, along with pale yellow slugs as thick as a thumb and a good deal longer. A sextet of loops features level grass and dirt sites that are smallish and rather crowded together, but fairly well-screened by the flourishing foliage and equipped with capacious car slips. One of the larger spots is 38, by the creek, and of the many walk-up units, 4, 5, and 6 offer the best privacy. A pristine stretch of beach is accessible via the challenging Damnation Creek Trail, an old Native American path that loses 1,000 feet as it descends through a grove of old-growth redwoods. Mill Creek is closed to fishing from Oct. through Apr. to protect spawning salmon.

BASICS

Operated By: California Dept. of Parks & Recreation. **Open:** Apr. through Sept. **Site Assignment:** Reservations accepted w/ V, MC, D. **Registration:** At entrance booth. **Fee:** $12, cash or CA check. **Parking:** At site.

FACILITIES

Number of RV Sites: 145. **Number of Tent-Only Sites:** 0. **Hookups:** None. **Each Site:** Picnic table, fire grate, food storage box. **Dump Station:** Yes. **Laundry:** No. **Pay Phone:** No. **Rest Rooms and Showers:** Yes. **Fuel:** No. **Propane:** No. **Internal Roads:** Paved, w/ bumps & potholes. **RV Service:** No. **Market:** 6 mi. north in Crescent City. **Restaurant:** 6 mi. north in Crescent City. **General Store:** No. **Vending:** No. **Swimming:** In Smith River. **Playground:** No. **Other:** Some wheelchair-accessible facilities. **Activities:** Hiking, bicycling, fishing. **Nearby Attractions:** Redwood National & State Parks; Battery Point Lighthouse, Ocean World & Del Norte County Historical Museum in Crescent City. **Additional Information:** Crescent City–Del Norte County Chamber of Commerce, (707) 464-3174 or (800) 343-8300.

RESTRICTIONS

Pets: On 6 ft. leash. **Fires:** In fire grates only. **Alcoholic Beverages:** Allowed at site. **Vehicle Maximum Length:** 31 ft. **Other:** 14-day stay limit from May 1–Sept. 30; no firearms; no wood gathering; no mushroom-plucking.

TO GET THERE

From Crescent City head 6 mi. south on US 101 to the marked access road for the State Park. Turn left; the park entrance is 1.5 mi. ahead.

CRESCENT CITY

Jedediah Smith Redwoods State Park

US 199 South, Crescent City 95532. T: (707) 464-6101, ext. 5112 or reservations (800) 444-7275; www.cal-parks.ca.gov or www.reserveamerica.com.

🚐 ★★★★   ⛺ ★★★★

Beauty: ★★★★	Site Privacy: ★★★
Spaciousness: ★★★★	Quiet: ★★★
Security: ★★★	Cleanliness: ★★★★
Insect Control: ★★★	Facilities: ★★★

Heading south from Oregon along Hwy. 199, Jedediah Smith Redwoods State Park is the northern-most of several redwoods-focused state parks. Named for the first white man known to cross the Coast Range of mountains, Jed Smith is a striking introduction to Sequoia sempervirens. These giant redwood trees are the tallest living things in the world, with several old-growth groves towering over the 10,000-acre preserve. The campground is less than ten miles northeast of Crescent City, set beside the emerald-green Smith River. Tan oaks, maples, and rhododendrons thrive among the red barked atavars, with moss and hanging lichen contributing to the cool, shady, rainforest atmosphere. The roomy and well-screened sites are spread decently apart over a series of loops, the most private being 68 (with a river view), 70 (a spacious end spot), and 77. 60 has pull-through parking. Years ago local American Indians gathered the green, stringy lichen that hangs from the trees and dried it to use as soft bedding material. It—and all other vegetation within the park—is now protected by the state.

BASICS

Operated By: California Dept. of Parks & Recreation. **Open:** All year. **Site Assignment:** Reservations recommended; V, MC, D. **Registration:** At entrance booth. **Fee:** $12, cash or CA check. **Parking:** At site.

FACILITIES

Number of RV Sites: 106. **Number of Tent-Only Sites:** 5. **Hookups:** None. **Each Site:** Picnic table, fire grate, food storage box. **Dump Station:** Yes. **Laundry:** No. **Pay Phone:** Yes. **Rest Rooms and Showers:** Yes. **Fuel:** No. **Propane:** No. **Internal Roads:** Paved. **RV Service:** No. **Market:** 9 mi. west in Crescent City. **Restaurant:** 9 mi. west in Crescent City. **General Store:** No. **Vending:** No. **Swimming:** No. **Playground:** No. **Other:** Some wheelchair-accessible facilities. **Activities:** Hiking, fishing, bicycling, horseback riding, canoeing, rafting. **Nearby Attractions:** Redwood National & State Parks; Battery Point Lighthouse, Ocean World & Del Norte County Historical Museum in Crescent City. **Additional Information:** Crescent City–Del Norte County Chamber of Commerce, (707) 464-3174 or (800) 343-8300.

RESTRICTIONS

Pets: On 6 ft. leash. **Fires:** In fire grates only. **Alcoholic Beverages:** Allowed at site. **Vehicle Maximum Length:** 36 ft. **Other:** 14-day stay limit from May 1–Sept. 30; no firearms; no wood gathering.

TO GET THERE

From Crescent City drive 3.5 mi. north on US 101. Exit on US 199 and head east towards Grants Pass. Continue for 5 mi. to the park entrance on the right.

DANA POINT
Doheny State Beach

25300 Dana Point Harbor Dr., Dana Point 92629. T: (949) 496-6171; www.cal-parks.ca.gov or www.reserveamerica.com.

🚐 ★★★★   ▲ ★★★

Beauty: ★★★★	Site Privacy: ★★★
Spaciousness: ★★	Quiet: ★★
Security: ★★★	Cleanliness: ★★★★
Insect Control: ★	Facilities: ★★

This state park provides sun and surf lovers access to more than a mile of beautiful beach, with the good news for campers being that a healthy number of sites are set right on the sand. Stroll from your tent to the shore in one fluid motion, or bask in a sunset radiating over the water from the comfort of your picnic table. If it is high tide, this must be "surfin' USA"! And if the water is low, grab your children and go check out the tide pools. All of these somewhat tightly packed sites benefit from the fresh breeze of the salty sea, but the ones to the rear of camp are annoyingly close to railroad tracks, and also have the dubious distinction of facing a large housing development across the interstate. Best by far are those on the beach, such as 38–43, and odd numbers from 45–59. Though swimming is ideal from late June through early autumn, solitude-seekers will enjoy camping here in winter, when daytime temperatures are still comfortable.

BASICS

Operated By: California Dept. of Parks & Recreation. **Open:** All year. **Site Assignment:** Reservations recommended; w/ V, MC, D. **Registration:** At entrance booth. **Fee:** $12, cash or CA check. **Parking:** At site.

FACILITIES

Number of RV Sites: 120. **Number of Tent-Only Sites:** 0. **Hookups:** None. **Each Site:** Picnic table, fire grate. **Dump Station:** Yes. **Laundry:** No. **Pay Phone:** Yes. **Rest Rooms and Showers:** Yes (cold beach showers). **Fuel:** No. **Propane:** No. **Internal Roads:** Paved. **RV Service:** No. **Market:** 1 mi. east in Dana Point. **Restaurant:** 1 mi. east in Dana Point. **General Store:** No. **Vending:** No. **Swimming:** In Pacific Ocean. **Playground:** No. **Other:** Some wheelchair-accessible facilities. **Activities:** Surfing, swimming, fishing, people-watching, tide pool exploring, volleyball, whale-watching. **Nearby Attractions:** San Clemente, Dana Point, Mission San Juan Capistrano. **Additional Information:** Dana Point Chamber of Commerce, Tourism & Visitors Center, (949) 496-1555.

RESTRICTIONS

Pets: On 6 ft. leash. **Fires:** In fire grates only. **Alcoholic Beverages:** Not allowed. **Vehicle Maximum Length:** 35 ft. **Other:** 7-day stay limit from June 1–Sept. 30, 14-day stay limit for the rest of the year; no firearms; no wood gathering.

TO GET THERE

From San Juan Capistrano head 3 mi. south on I-5 to the Beach Cities/Pacific Coast Hwy. Exit. Turn left onto Dana Point Harbor Dr., then left again onto Park Lantern into the park.

DARDANELLE
Leavitt Meadows

Hwy. 108, Dardanelle 95314. T: (760) 932-7070; F: (760) 932-1299; www.r5.fs.fed.us/htnf/bpcamp.htm.

🚐 ★★★   ▲ ★★★★

Beauty: ★★★★	Site Privacy: ★★★
Spaciousness: ★★	Quiet: ★★
Security: ★★★	Cleanliness: ★★★
Insect Control: ★★	Facilities: ★

If you are looking for a taste of the high Sierras without having to venture too far off the road, Leavitt Meadows, at 7,000 feet elevation and 25 miles west of Bridgeport, should be a good fit. This roadside camp, ensconced in a bend in the West Walker River, is close enough to the water that the raging current drowns out much of the noise of passing traffic. Rising across the river is a flinty outcropping, and a granite-streaked ridge looms above camp. Juniper, aspen, sage, and various conifers set the stage around the single loop, where diminutive, dirt sites are well spread apart. The handful of spots nearest the water are the most exposed, and tenters may find the waterward tilt challenging. An exception is number 9, which is well-screened and has pull-through parking. Away from the river, 15, while a touch small, is under a large pine and shielded by aspens. Drinking water is shut off early and late in the year, due to the higher risk of freezing weather. That is, nonetheless, our preferred time to visit this part of the Sierra Nevadas, when visitation is at its lightest.

BASICS

Operated By: American Land & Leisure, concessionaire. **Open:** Late Apr. to mid-Oct., weather permitting. **Site Assignment:** First come, first served. **Registration:** At entrance kiosk. **Fee:** $10, cash or check; $5 in winter when no water. **Parking:** At site.

FACILITIES

Number of RV Sites: 16. **Number of Tent-Only Sites:** 0. **Hookups:** None. **Each Site:** Picnic table, fire grate. **Dump Station:** No. **Laundry:** No. **Pay Phone:** No. **Rest Rooms and Showers:** Vault toilets, no showers. **Fuel:** No. **Propane:** No. **Internal Roads:** Dirt, somewhat bumpy. **RV Service:** No. **Market:** 25 mi. east in Bridgeport. **Restaurant:** 25 mi. east in Bridgeport. **General Store:** No. **Vending:** No. **Swimming:** No. **Playground:** No. **Activities:** Fishing, hiking, horseback riding, star-gazing. **Nearby Attractions:** Bodie State Historic Park in Bridgeport; Pinecrest Lake, Sonora Pass. **Additional Information:** Eastern Sierra Interagency Visitor Center, (760) 876-6222; Bridgeport Chamber of Commerce, (760) 932-7500.

RESTRICTIONS

Pets: On leash. **Fires:** In fire grates only. **Alcoholic Beverages:** Allowed. **Vehicle Maximum Length:** 22 ft. **Other:** 14-day stay limit.

TO GET THERE

From Bridgeport drive 17 mi. north on US 395. Turn west (left) onto Hwy. 108 and drive 7.5 mi. to the campground entrance on the left.

DEATH VALLEY
Mesquite Spring

Grapevine Rd., Death Valley 92328. T: (760) 786-23317; F: (760) 786-3283; www.nps.gov/deva.

🚐 ★★★   ▲ ★★★

Beauty: ★★★★	Site Privacy: ★★★
Spaciousness: ★★★	Quiet: ★★★
Security: ★★★★	Cleanliness: ★★★
Insect Control: ★★★★	Facilities: ★★

The vast tract of land that is Death Valley National Park is far more than a barren, stagnant desert. Give it a chance and your appreciation for the parched beauty of the scenery will likely grow as you explore the park: from the volcanic craters in the north to the salt water basins to its south, from its shifting sand dunes to the multicolored mountains that range like twin spines up its entire length. You'll be in good position at Mesquite Spring to check out Ubehebe Crater and Scotty's Castle, a lavish 1920s vacation home built in Spanish mission style. This campground is more exposed than Furnace Creek, but it benefits, after the sun goes down, from being 2,000 feet higher. It is set against a mud-colored canyon wall and a dry creek, with two low mountain ridges paralleling its double loop. Dusty, pebbly sites are on the spacious side, and they are grouped farther apart than at Furnace Creek, allowing for a greater degree of privacy. A couple of cottonwoods mark where the spring is. The nearest pay phone is at the Grapevine Ranger Station, 2.5 miles north; fuel is available at Scotty's Castle; a general store is in Stovepipe Wells, 41 miles south.

BASICS

Operated By: National Park Service. **Open:** All year. **Site Assignment:** First come, first served. **Registration:** At entrance kiosk. **Fee:** $10–$16, cash or check (in addition to the park entrance fee). **Parking:** At site.

FACILITIES

Number of RV Sites: 30. **Number of Tent-Only Sites:** 0. **Hookups:** None. **Each Site:** Picnic table, fire grate. **Dump Station:** Yes. **Laundry:** No. **Pay Phone:** No. **Rest Rooms and Showers:** Flush toilets, no showers. **Fuel:** No. **Propane:** No. **Internal Roads:** Paved. **RV Service:** No. **Market:** 53 mi. east in Beatty. **Restaurant:** 41 mi. south in Stovepipe Wells. **General Store:** No. **Vending:** No. **Swimming:** No. **Playground:** No. **Other:** Some wheelchair-accessible facilities. **Activities:** Hiking, driving tours, stargazing, photography. **Nearby Attractions:** Badwater, Scotty's Castle, Dantes View, Stovepipe Wells Village, mountains, mines & more in Death Valley National Park. **Additional Information:** Death Valley Chamber of Commerce, (760) 852-4524.

RESTRICTIONS

Pets: On leash no longer than 6 ft., not allowed on trails. **Fires:** In fire grates only. **Alcoholic Beverages:** Allowed at site. **Vehicle Maximum Length:** 50 ft. **Other:** 30-day stay limit; no loaded firearms; no wood gathering.

TO GET THERE

From Furnace Creek head north on Hwy. 190 and drive 19 mi. to Sand Dune Junction. Turn right, direction Scotty's Castle, and continue for

32 mi. Turn left onto the campground access road. Proceed for another 2 mi. into the campground.

DEATH VALLEY
Wildrose

Wildrose Canyon Rd., Death Valley National Park 92328. T: (760) 786-2331; F: (760) 786-3283; www.nps.gov/deva.

| 🚐 ★★★★ | 🔺 ★★★★ |

Beauty: ★★★★ | Site Privacy: ★★★
Spaciousness: ★★★★ | Quiet: ★★★★
Security: ★★ | Cleanliness: ★★★★
Insect Control: ★★★★ | Facilities: ★

The wonderful, oleander-shaded picnic area in the dramatically eroded Wildrose Canyon is misleading. You will find nothing so pleasant in the way of plantings at the similarly-named campground. Still, there is a Spartan beauty to this arid, primitive camp. Very Spartan. It is located in a side gully of the canyon, with rumpled hills on either side. There are no shade trees to shelter the dusty, pebbly ground, only such scrub as creosote and salt bushes. The same, of course, might also be said of most of Death Valley's other campgrounds; at least Wildrose has potable water (from late spring through early autumn). Because the campground, which is 30 miles south of Stovepipe Wells Village, is at 4,100 feet of elevation, evenings are blessedly cooler here than elsewhere in the park. Comparable spots are roomy but exposed, and dispersed in two sections (the upper one being reserved for tents). Even when Furnace Creek and Stovepipe Wells are brimming with campers, you are likely to find plenty of space and tranquility at this remote place. Use it as a base for exploring such Death Valley attractions as the beehive-shaped charcoal kilns, Ski-doo, a ghost town, and the Eureka mine.

BASICS

Operated By: National Park Service. **Open:** All year. **Site Assignment:** First come, first served. **Registration:** None. **Fee:** None (but there is a park entrance fee). **Parking:** At site.

FACILITIES

Number of RV Sites: 11. **Number of Tent-Only Sites:** 11. **Hookups:** None. **Each Site:** Picnic table, fire grate and/or barbecue grill. **Dump**

Station: No. **Laundry:** No. **Pay Phone:** No. **Rest Rooms and Showers:** Vault toilets, no showers. **Fuel:** No. **Propane:** No. **Internal Roads:** Gravel, good condition. **RV Service:** No. **Market:** 65 mi. south in Ridgecrest. **Restaurant:** 30 mi. north in Stovepipe Wells. **General Store:** No. **Vending:** No. **Swimming:** No. **Playground:** No. **Activities:** Hiking, solitudinous meditation, stargazing. **Nearby Attractions:** Ballarat Ghost Town; Trona Pinnacles. **Additional Information:** Death Valley Chamber of Commerce, (760) 852-4524.

RESTRICTIONS

Pets: On leash no longer than 6 ft., not allowed on trails. **Fires:** In fire grates only. **Alcoholic Beverages:** Allowed at site. **Vehicle Maximum Length:** 25 ft. **Other:** 30-day stay limit; no loaded firearms; no wood gathering.

TO GET THERE

From Ridgecrest drive 13 mi. east on Hwy. 178. Turn left on Trona Rd. and continue for 42 mi. to Wildrose Canyon Rd. Turn right and proceed for 9 mi. Bear right at the fork in the road; the campground is 0.25 mi. ahead on the left.

DEATH VALLEY NATIONAL PARK
Furnace Creek

Hwy. 190, Death Valley 92328. T: (760) 786-2331 or reservations (800) 365-2267; F: (760) 786-3283; www.nps.gov/deva or reservations.nps.gov.

🚐 ★★★★	🏕 ★★★
Beauty: ★★★★	Site Privacy: ★★
Spaciousness: ★★	Quiet: ★★★
Security: ★★★★	Cleanliness: ★★★
Insect Control: ★★★★	Facilities: ★★

Visit this campground between May and Sept. and you'll have a good idea of what Hades is all about; you are also likely to have most of the domain to yourself. Certainly the "furnace" half of its name seems apt, with an oppressive blanket of heat clinging to the dry terrain in much the manner that bark hugs the trunk of a tree. As to the "creek," just be thankful for water spigots. Level sites of hard clay are closely grouped around a series of loops, with a bit of shade provided by mesquite, creosote bushes, a few palms, and tamarisk trees. (These latter are non-native, and the park service intends to uproot them.)

The blistering heat seems magnified by the camp's position at 196 feet below sea level, but we prefer it to Stovepipe Wells, which is little more than a pebbly parking lot without a twig of shade. The park visitor center is next to the campground, and a number of excellent hikes and drives are in the vicinity. Laundry machines, showers, swimming pool, general store, and gasoline are available at Furnace Creek Ranch.

BASICS

Operated By: National Park Service. **Open:** All year. **Site Assignment:** Reservations recommended; V, MC, D. **Registration:** At entrance booth. **Fee:** $10–$16, cash or check (in addition to the park entrance fee). **Parking:** At site.

FACILITIES

Number of RV Sites: 101. **Number of Tent-Only Sites:** 35. **Hookups:** None. **Each Site:** Picnic table, fire grate, barbecue grill. **Dump Station:** Yes. **Laundry:** No. **Pay Phone:** Yes. **Rest Rooms and Showers:** Flush toilets, no showers. **Fuel:** No. **Propane:** No. **Internal Roads:** Paved. **RV Service:** No. **Market:** 47 mi. north in Beatty. **Restaurant:** At Furnace Creek Ranch. **General Store:** No. **Vending:** No. **Swimming:** No. **Playground:** No. **Other:** Some wheelchair-accessible facilities, visitor center, museum. **Activities:** Hiking, driving tours, ranger-led activities, photography, frying eggs on the sidewalk. **Nearby Attractions:** Badwater, Scotty's Castle, Dantes View, Stovepipe Wells Village, mountains, mines, & more in Death Valley National Park. **Additional Information:** Death Valley Chamber of Commerce, (760) 852-4524.

RESTRICTIONS

Pets: On 6 ft. leash; not allowed on trails. **Fires:** In fire grates only. **Alcoholic Beverages:** Allowed at site. **Vehicle Maximum Length:** 50 ft. **Other:** 7-day stay limit from Oct. 15 to Apr. 15, 14-day stay limit for the rest of the year; no loaded firearms; no wood gathering.

TO GET THERE

From the Furnace Creek Visitor Center drive 0.5 mi. north on Hwy. 190 to the campground entrance on the left.

DUNCAN MILLS

Casini Ranch Family Campground

22855 Moscow Rd., Duncan Mills 95430. T: (707)
865-2255 Ext. 13 or reservations (800) 451-8400;
www.caohwy.com/c/casinirf.htm.

🚐 ★★★★★   ▲ ★★★★

Beauty: ★★★★   Site Privacy: ★★★★
Spaciousness: ★★★★   Quiet: ★★★★
Security: ★★★★   Cleanliness: ★★★
Insect Control: ★★★   Facilities: ★★★★

Not too many years ago this family-operated
campground was a dairy farm and many of the
rustic buildings from that era remain, along with
miscellaneous farm implements that have been
decoratively strewn about the property. It is hard
to imagine, though, that the scene was any prettier when cows lowed through the grassy meadows and varied woodland than it is today, even
when brimming with campers. The level property sits in an oxbow bend of the Russian River, a
perfect position that blesses it not only with a
number of water-view sites but also a greater
amount of serenity than the bucolic camp's roadside counterparks. True, the full hookup area
next to a row of pollarded trees at Casini's core is
typically congested. If you don't require pull-
through parking and can get by without a sewer
connection, such pleasantly secluded spots as
88–90, 92–94, and 96–98 are infinitely more
appealing. Similarly, 36–40 are the pick of the
primitive options, where grassy sites are so spacious and well buttressed by vegetation as to satisfy even the most finicky of tent campers.

BASICS

Operated By: Casini family. **Open:** All year. **Site
Assignment:** Reservations accepted w/V, MC, D,
AE. **Registration:** At entrance booth or office.
Fee: $20–$27 plus 9% local tax, cash or V, MC, AE,
D. **Parking:** At site.

FACILITIES

Number of RV Sites: 225. **Number of Tent-
Only Sites:** 0. **Hookups:** Water, electric (30
amps), sewer, cable TV. **Each Site:** Picnic table, fire
grate. **Dump Station:** Yes. **Laundry:** Yes. **Pay
Phone:** Yes. **Rest Rooms and Showers:** Yes.
Fuel: No. **Propane:** Yes. **Internal Roads:** Packed
gravel & dirt, good condition. **RV Service:** No.

Market: 0.75 mi. away in Duncans Mills. **Restaurant:** 0.75 mi. away in Duncans Mills. **General
Store:** Yes. **Vending:** Yes. **Swimming:** In Russian
River. **Playground:** Yes. **Other:** Some wheelchair-
accessible facilities, rec hall, boat ramp. **Activities:**
Fishing, kayak & canoe rentals. **Nearby Attractions:** Fort Ross State Historic Park, Kruse Rhododendron State Reserve & Salt Point State Park in
Jenner; Austin Creek State Recreation Area & Armstrong Redwoods State Reserve in Guerneville;
winery tours. **Additional Information:** Russian
River Chamber of Commerce & Visitors Center,
(707) 869-9212 or (877) 644-9001.

RESTRICTIONS

Pets: On leash. **Fires:** In fire grates only. **Alcoholic
Beverages:** Allowed. **Vehicle Maximum
Length:** None. **Other:** 30-day stay limit; no
firearms; no wood gathering.

TO GET THERE

From Guerneville head west on Hwy. 116 and
drive 8.4 mi. to Duncans Mills. Turn left on
Moscow Rd. and continue for 0.75 mi. to the
well-signed campground entrance.

DUNSMUIR

Castle Crags State Park

Castle Creek Rd., Castella 96017. T: (530) 235-2684
or reservations (800) 444-7275; www.cal-
parks.ca.gov or www.norcal.parks.state.ca.us or
www.reserveamerica.com.

🚐 ★★★   ▲ ★★★

Beauty: ★★★★   Site Privacy: ★★
Spaciousness: ★★   Quiet: ★★
Security: ★★★   Cleanliness: ★★★
Insect Control: ★★★   Facilities: ★★

The stark, saw-toothed spires that give this small
park its name rise some 4,000 feet from the
Sacramento River to the tips of their granite
peaks. If the challenging, highly strenuous hike
up there from the campground doesn't take your
breath away, the spectacular views will. The
domain straddles I-5, with the larger part of it,
including the crags, lying west of the highway. To
the east, just beyond the railroad tracks and right
alongside the river, are 12 grassy sites that are
ideal for anglers. The main campground,
though, is across the road, higher up toward the

summit. Its three ascending loops snake through an attractively wooded hillside of oaks, cedars, and pines, with mediocre screening between closely-set, shallow sites. The most private is 11, though its rear faces a chain-link fence. Similarly recessed are 14 and 15, and both 26 and 37 have pull-through parking. The stone masonry of the fire pits dates from when the Civilian Conservation Corps was active here more than 60 years ago. The continuous roar of traffic emanating from the interstate is a jarring note to an otherwise splendid setting.

BASICS

Operated By: California Dept. of Parks & Recreation. **Open:** All year. **Site Assignment:** Reservations accepted w/ V, MC, D. **Registration:** At entrance booth. **Fee:** $12, cash or CA check. **Parking:** At site.

FACILITIES

Number of RV Sites: 76. **Number of Tent-Only Sites:** 6. **Hookups:** None. **Each Site:** Picnic table, fire grate, food storage box. **Dump Station:** No. **Laundry:** No. **Pay Phone:** Yes. **Rest Rooms and Showers:** Yes. **Fuel:** No. **Propane:** No. **Internal Roads:** Paved. **RV Service:** No. **Market:** 7 mi. north in Dunsmuir. **Restaurant:** 7 mi. north in Dunsmuir. **General Store:** No. **Vending:** No. **Swimming:** In Sacramento River. **Playground:** No. **Other:** Some wheelchair-accessible facilities. **Activities:** Hiking, fishing, canoeing, rafting, bicycling. **Nearby Attractions:** Lake Siskiyou; Mount Shasta Ski Park, Mount Shasta Hatchery & Sisson Museum; downtown Dunsmuir. **Additional Information:** Mount Shasta Chamber of Commerce & Visitors Bureau, (530) 926-4865 or (800) 926-4865; Dunsmuir Chamber of Commerce, (530) 235-2177.

RESTRICTIONS

Pets: On 6 ft. leash. **Fires:** In fire grates only. **Alcoholic Beverages:** Allowed at site. **Vehicle Maximum Length:** 27 ft. **Other:** 14-day stay limit from May 1–Sept. 30, 30-day limit the rest of the year; no firearms; no wood gathering.

TO GET THERE

From Dunsmuir on I-5 drive 6.5 mi. south to the Castella Exit. Turn west (right) and continue for 0.3 mi. Turn right into the well-signed park. The campground is 0.7 mi. beyond the entrance station.

EL CAJON
Lake Jennings Regional Park

10108 Bass Rd., Lakeside 92046. T: (858) 69403049 or reservations (858) 565-3600; www.co.san-diego.ca.us/parks.

🚐 ★★★★   ⛺ ★★★

Beauty: ★★★★   Site Privacy: ★★★★
Spaciousness: ★★★   Quiet: ★★★
Security: ★★★★   Cleanliness: ★★★
Insect Control: ★★★   Facilities: ★★★

People familiar with Lake Jennings from previous years may be excused if they fail to recognize it in its current state. The most obvious change is the spruced up landscaping, with geraniums and other annuals lending a welcome splash of color to a ridge-top setting marked by holly, acacia, prickly pear cacti, eucalyptus, pepper trees, and a variety of conifers. That's not all, as structural renovations have encompassed the restrooms and showers, as well as upgraded electrical hookups. Unaffected by these alterations, alas, are the gravel sites themselves, which are shoe-horned close together, several resting on ground so tilted that hammocks might seem preferable to tents. Thankfully, abundant vegetation yields some privacy and many units along the park's spiraling loop road enjoy excellent vistas. Numbers 20, 22, 24, 43, and 45 are among the standout tenting options, with 89–91 tops for RVs. The lake is stocked with trout in the winter and catfish summertime, but boating is only allowed on weekends.

BASICS

Operated By: County of San Diego, Dept. of Parks & Recreation. **Open:** All year. **Site Assignment:** Reservations accepted w/ V, MC, D. **Registration:** At entrance booth. **Fee:** $12–$16, cash or V, MC, D. **Parking:** At site.

FACILITIES

Number of RV Sites: 90. **Number of Tent-Only Sites:** 6. **Hookups:** Water, electric (20, 30 amps), sewer. **Each Site:** Picnic table, fire grate, barbecue grill. **Dump Station:** Yes. **Laundry:** No. **Pay Phone:** Yes. **Rest Rooms and Showers:** Yes. **Fuel:** No. **Propane:** No. **Internal Roads:** Paved. **RV Service:** No. **Market:** 2 mi west in Lakeside. **Restaurant:** 2 mi. west in Lakeside. **General Store:** No. **Vending:** Yes. **Swimming:** No. **Playground:** Yes. **Other:** Some wheelchair-accessible facilities. **Activities:** Fishing, hiking, horseshoe pit. **Nearby Attractions:** San Diego & its waterfront, museums, zoo, historic district. **Additional Information:** Lakeside Chamber of Commerce, (619) 561-1031; City of El Cajon, (619) 441-1776.

RESTRICTIONS

Pets: On 6 ft. leash; $1 fee. **Fires:** In fire grates only. **Alcoholic Beverages:** Allowed at site, not exceeding 40 proof. **Vehicle Maximum Length:** 35 ft. **Other:** 14-day stay limit; no firearms.

TO GET THERE

From I-8 in El Cajon take Hwy. 67 north and drive 4.5 mi. Turn right onto Maple View St. and drive 2.2 mi. The road changes into Lake Jennings Park Rd. The campground entrance is on the left.

EL CENTRO

Rio Bend RV Resort Ranch

1589 Drew Rd., El Centro 92243. T: (760) 352-7061; F: (760) 352-0055; www.riobendrv.com.

🚐 ★★★★   ▲ ★

Beauty: ★★	Site Privacy: ★★
Spaciousness: ★★	Quiet: ★★★
Security: ★★★	Cleanliness: ★★★★
Insect Control: ★	Facilities: ★★★★

In many ways Rio Bend is a community unto itself. RVs are parked side by side along dirt lanes attractively lined with palms, eucalyptus, and citrus trees; the central plaza is colorfully accented with flowering oleanders, a couple of Conestoga wagons, and some bales of hay; there are even a post office, swimming pool, nine-hole golf course, and two stocked fishing ponds on the premises. No wonder then that the resort is also well stocked each winter with snowbirds looking to ride out the cooler months at 50 feet below sea level. True, shade trees are scarce in the short term camping area and tents, relegated to the thick grass outside the office, are given short shrift. But with so many amenities, these small hardships are a little easier to wink at.

BASICS

Operated By: Wayne & Shirlee Miller, managers. **Open:** All year. **Site Assignment:** Reservations accepted w/ V, MC. **Registration:** In office at the end of the driveway. **Fee:** $13–$26, cash or V, MC. **Parking:** At site.

FACILITIES

Number of RV Sites: 270. **Number of Tent-Only Sites:** Undesignated sites. **Hookups:** Water, electric (50 amps), cable TV, Internet. **Each Site:** Full hookups. **Dump Station:** Yes. **Laundry:** Yes. **Pay Phone:** Yes. **Rest Rooms and Showers:** Yes. **Fuel:** No. **Propane:** No. **Internal Roads:** Paved & packed dirt. **RV Service:** No. **Market:** 8.5 mi. east in El Centro. **Restaurant:** 8.5 mi. east in El Centro. **General Store:** Yes. **Vending:** No. **Swimming:** In heated pool. **Playground:** No. **Other:** Some wheelchair-accessible facilities, post office, 2 fishing ponds. **Activities:** 9-hole golf course, pool, spa, fishing, shuffleboard, horseshoe pit. **Nearby Attractions:** Shopping in Mexicali across the Mexican border, Anza-Borrego Desert State Park, Salton Sea National Wildlife Refuge, Imperial (Algodones) Sand Dunes (east of El Centro). **Additional Information:** El Centro Chamber of Commerce & Visitors Bureau, (760) 352-3681.

RESTRICTIONS

Pets: On leash. **Fires:** No. **Alcoholic Beverages:** Allowed. **Vehicle Maximum Length:** None. **Other:** No stay limit.

TO GET THERE

From El Centro head west on I-8 for 8 mi. Take the Drew Rd. Exit and turn left (south). Drive 0.5 mi. to the resort on the right.

ESCONDIDO

Dixon Lake Recreation Area

1700 North La Honda Dr., Escondido 92027. T: (760) 741-3328 or reservations (760) 839-4680; www.dixonlake.com.

🚐 ★★★   ▲ ★★★★

Beauty: ★★★★	Site Privacy: ★★★★
Spaciousness: ★★★	Quiet: ★★★★
Security: ★★★	Cleanliness: ★★★
Insect Control: ★★	Facilities: ★★★

Dixon Lake is almost too good to be true: the camp's hilltop location lies at just over 1,000 feet elevation, with a dramatic panorama of greater Escondido on one side and the small lake on the other. This latter is actually a stocked reservoir with great fishing for trout in the fall and catfish and bass year-round. Like the fish you'll throw back, some sites may be a tad small, but they are spaced fairly well apart amid a field of granite boulders that just beg to be scrambled over, and amply shaded by an appealing potpourri of trees, including the ubiquitous eucalyptus, live oak, a variety of pines, toyon, and ceanothus, as well as a healthy accent of agave. Aside from the handful of spots near the park road, it is hard to go wrong, with numbers 8, 11, 12, and 37 particularly private and 26 and 29 yielding great city views. And when you tire of boating, fishing, and hiking, the San Diego Wild Animal Park is just a 15 minutes' drive away.

BASICS

Operated By: City of Escondido. **Open:** All year. **Site Assignment:** Reservations accepted w/ V, MC. **Registration:** At ranger office. **Fee:** $12–$16, cash or V, MC. **Parking:** At site.

FACILITIES

Number of RV Sites: 44. Number of Tent-Only Sites: 0. Hookups: Water, electric (20, 30 amps), sewer. **Each Site:** Picnic table, fire grate, trash bin. **Dump Station:** Yes. **Laundry:** No. **Pay Phone:** Yes. **Rest Rooms and Showers:** Yes. **Fuel:** No. **Propane:** No. **Internal Roads:** Paved. **RV Service:** No. **Market:** 3 mi. south in Escondido. **Restaurant:** 3 mi. south in Escondido. **General Store:** Yes. **Vending:** No. **Swimming:** No. **Playground:** Yes. **Other:** Some wheelchair-accessible facilities, snackbar, boat launch. **Activities:** Fishing, bicycling, hiking, horseshoe pit, boat rentals. **Nearby Attractions:** Heritage Walk & Museum, San Pascal Battlefield State Historic Park, Deer Park Auto Museum, San Diego Wild Animal Park. **Additional Information:** Escondido Chamber of Commerce, (760) 745-2125.

RESTRICTIONS

Pets: Not allowed. **Fires:** No. **Alcoholic Beverages:** Allowed at site, not exceeding 28 proof. **Vehicle Maximum Length:** 50 ft. **Other:** 14-day stay limit; no firearms.

TO GET THERE

From I-15 in Escondido take the El Norte Pkwy. Exit and drive 3.3 mi. north. Turn left on La Honda Dr. and continue 1.2 mi. straight into the rec area.

ESCONDIDO
Dos Picos Regional Park

17953 Dos Picos Park Rd., Ramona 92065. T: (858) 694-3049 or reservations (858) 565-3600; www.co.san-diego.ca.us/parks.

🚐 ★★★★   ⛺ ★★★

Beauty: ★★★★   Site Privacy: ★★
Spaciousness: ★★★   Quiet: ★★★
Security: ★★   Cleanliness: ★★
Insect Control: ★   Facilities: ★★★

In the "location is everything" department, Dos Picos comes up a winner. It lies in a hillside riparian forest just a half hour drive from downtown San Diego, and a little less than that from the San Diego Wild Animal Park in Escondido. The dirt and grass surfaced sites, spread out over several loops, are amply shaded by eucalyptus and live oak, with several enormous 300-year-olds among the latter. Of the many amenities here, highlights include a jogging track, soccer field, hiking trails, and a kids-only fishing pond. The park loses points, though, for its rundown lavatories, in which three of four toilets in one men's room were out of commission on a recent weekend visit, and such noise problems as many low-flying aircrafts and neighborhood dogs barking throughout the night. Drivers of long RVs should plan to reserve site 56, one of the few with pull-through parking, while 9 and 12 are the more private, roomier tent options.

BASICS

Operated By: County of San Diego, Dept. of Parks & Recreation. **Open:** All year. **Site Assignment:** Reservations accepted w/ V, MC. **Registration:** At entrance booth. **Fee:** $10–$14, cash or V, MC. **Parking:** At site.

FACILITIES

Number of RV Sites: 60. Number of Tent-Only Sites: 0. Hookups: Water, electric (20 amps). **Each Site:** Picnic table, fire grate, barbecue grill. **Dump Station:** Yes. **Laundry:** No. **Pay Phone:** Yes. **Rest Rooms and Showers:** Yes. **Fuel:** No. **Propane:** No. **Internal Roads:** Paved. **RV Service:** No. **Market:** 5.5 mi. northeast in Ramona. **Restaurant:** 5.5 mi. northeast in Ramona. **General Store:** No. **Vending:** Yes. **Swimming:**

No. **Playground:** Yes. **Other:** Limited wheelchair-accessible facilities. **Activities:** Hiking, children's fishing, horseshoe pit, jogging track, soccer field. **Nearby Attractions:** San Diego Wild Animal Park, San Pasqual Battlefield. **Additional Information:** Ramona Chamber of Commerce, (760) 789-1311.

RESTRICTIONS

Pets: On leash, $1 fee. **Fires:** In fire grates only. **Alcoholic Beverages:** Allowed at site, not exceeding 40 proof. **Vehicle Maximum Length:** 35 ft. **Other:** 14-day stay limit; no firearms.

TO GET THERE

In Escondido drive 20 mi. east on Hwy. 78 to Ramona. Turn south on Hwy. 67 and drive 3.5 mi., then turn left on Mussey Grade Rd. and drive 1.1 mi. Turn right on Dos Picos Park Rd. The entrance is less than 1 mi. ahead.

ESCONDIDO
Palomar Mountain State Park

19952 State Park Rd., Palomar Mountain 92060. T: (760) 765-0755; www.palomar.statepark.org.

🚐 ★★★	🛖 ★★★★
Beauty: ★★★★	Site Privacy: ★★★
Spaciousness: ★★★	Quiet: ★★★
Security: ★★★	Cleanliness: ★★★
Insect Control: ★★★★	Facilities: ★★

Palomar Mountain State Park is located very near an observatory that houses one of America's largest ground-based telescopes, a testimony to the clarity of the night sky in these parts. That facility is off-limits to the public, but barring an overcast sky you should be able to see plenty of stars from the privacy of your campsite. Most are pretty spacious and hug the contours of the hilly mountainside, which compensates for an overall lack of screening. Which is not to suggest that the terraced loops meander over a denuded knob (though there is a fair share of gray granite and mossy rocks scattered about the domain). On the contrary, this charming campground is well forested with cedars, live oak, Douglas firs, and Coulter pines. The restrooms and a couple of sites are wheelchair accessible, but most of the rest involve negotiating a few stone stairs, solid relics from when the Civilian Conservation Corps was working in the area 60 years ago. The best seasons to camp here are spring and fall, though at an elevation of 4,700 feet the risk of snowfall exists from Nov. through early Apr. Plan accordingly.

BASICS

Operated By: California Dept. of Parks & Recreation. **Open:** All year. **Site Assignment:** Reservations accepted w/ V, MC, D. **Registration:** At entrance kiosk. **Fee:** $12, cash or CA check. **Parking:** At site.

FACILITIES

Number of RV Sites: 12. **Number of Tent-Only Sites:** 19. **Hookups:** None. **Each Site:** Picnic table, fire grate, barbecue grill, food storage box. **Dump Station:** No. **Laundry:** No. **Pay Phone:** Yes. **Rest Rooms and Showers:** Yes. **Fuel:** No. **Propane:** No. **Internal Roads:** Paved. **RV Service:** No. **Market:** 47 mi. northwest in Temecula. **Restaurant:** 47 mi. northwest in Temecula. **General Store:** No. **Vending:** No. **Swimming:** No. **Playground:** No. **Other:** Some wheelchair-accessible facilities. **Activities:** Hiking, fishing, ranger-led activities in summer. **Nearby Attractions:** Palomar Mountain Observatory, San Diego Wild Animal Park, Mission San Antonio de Pala. **Additional Information:** Escondido Chamber of Commerce, (760) 745-2125.

RESTRICTIONS

Pets: On 6 ft. leash. **Fires:** In fire grates only. **Alcoholic Beverages:** Allowed at site. **Vehicle Maximum Length:** 27 ft. **Other:** 7-day stay limit; no firearms; no wood gathering.

TO GET THERE

From Escondido on I-15 drive 15 mi. north. Turn east on Hwy. 76 and continue for 21 mi. Turn left on CR S6 direction Palomar Mountain. Follow S6/South Grade Rd. for 7 mi., then turn left on East Grade/State Park Rd. The park entrance is 3.5 mi. ahead.

EUREKA
Humboldt Redwoods State Park, Burlington Campground

Ave. of the Giants, Weott 95571. T: (707) 946-2409 or (707) 946-2015 or reservations (800) 444-7275; F: (707) 946-2326; www.cal-parks.ca.gov or www.reserveamerica.com; hrsp@humboldtredwoods.org.

🚐 ★★★   ⛺ ★★★

Beauty: ★★★★   Site Privacy: ★★
Spaciousness: ★★★   Quiet: ★★
Security: ★★★   Cleanliness: ★★★
Insect Control: ★★★   Facilities: ★★

Unlike many of the other state-run campgrounds situated in redwood forests, this one is easy to get to on a smooth piece of road just five miles off US 101, 40 miles south of Eureka. The highly scenic Ave. of the Giants flows through the park, threading for 32 miles past several impressive groves, including the must-see Rockefeller Forest. Of the three campgrounds here, only Burlington is open year-round. Its sites are grouped fairly closely together across a convoluted double loop, with 29 one of the more spacious and 37 a roomy corner spot. There are some impressive specimens of Sequoia sempervirens within Burlington, sturdy red pillars that allow only filtered streaks of sunlight through to the dirt and pine needle-layered forest floor. There are also a handful of decaying logs and a shocking number of redwood stumps. These latter serve as sober reminders of what might well have befallen the remaining giants had it not been for the efforts of conservationists.

BASICS
Operated By: California Dept. of Parks & Recreation. **Open:** All year. **Site Assignment:** Reservations recommended; V, MC, D. **Registration:** At entrance booth. **Fee:** $12, cash or CA check. **Parking:** At site.

FACILITIES
Number of RV Sites: 57. **Number of Tent-Only Sites:** 0. **Hookups:** None. **Each Site:** Picnic table, fire grate, food storage box. **Dump Station:** No. **Laundry:** No. **Pay Phone:** Yes. **Rest Rooms and Showers:** Yes. **Fuel:** No. **Propane:** No. **Internal Roads:** Paved. **RV Service:** No. **Market:**

4 mi. south in Meyers Flat. **Restaurant:** 4 mi. south in Meyers Flat. **General Store:** No. **Vending:** No. **Swimming:** In Eel River. **Playground:** No. **Other:** Some wheelchair-accessible facilities, visitor center. **Activities:** Hiking, bicycling, horseback riding, fishing. **Nearby Attractions:** Ave. of the Giants; Richardson Grove State Park in Garberville; Pacific Lumber Company Logging Museum in Scotia, Ferndale museums. **Additional Information:** Garberville-Redway Area Chamber of Commerce, (707) 923-2613; Ferndale Chamber of Commerce, (707) 786-4477.

RESTRICTIONS
Pets: On 6 ft. leash. **Fires:** In fire grates only. **Alcoholic Beverages:** Allowed at site. **Vehicle Maximum Length:** 33 ft. **Other:** 14-day stay limit; no firearms; no wood gathering.

TO GET THERE
Exit US 101 at Meyers Flat, turning west on Ave. of the Giants. Drive 4.5 mi. to the campground entrance on the right, immediately behind the visitor center.

FALL RIVER MILLS
Pit River

Pit No. 1 Powerhouse Rd., Fall River Mills 96028. T: (530) 233-4666; F: (530) 233-5696; www.ca.blm.gov/alturas.

🚐 ★★   ⛺ ★★★★

Beauty: ★★★★   Site Privacy: ★★★
Spaciousness: ★★★   Quiet: ★★★★
Security: ★★★   Cleanliness: ★★
Insect Control: ★★   Facilities: ★

This inauspiciously-named campground, also known as Pit No. 1, is actually in a very pretty—if somewhat overgrown—forested setting abutting the Pit River. You may find it totally vacant, which is ideal since the best site, which is right on the water looking across to a tiny island, is also the most popular. Or the twin loops might be choked with vehicles, especially on weekends from late spring through summer. Most of the level, leaf-strewn sites lie in the shadow of oaks and a few pines, next to a scruffy meadow. The handful of spots by the water are crammed closely together; otherwise there is space and privacy galore. Pit lies at 3,000 feet of elevation, which is quite comfortable for this region of the Cascade Mountain range. Though not exactly an Eden, Pit River has had its share of serpents, in the form of litterers, despite the presence of plenty of trash bins. No potable water is available, nor does the Bureau of Land Management seem to supervise the land. Local police, though, occasionally patrol. The nearest telephone is in Fall River Mills.

BASICS

Operated By: Bureau of Land Management, Alturas Field Office. **Open:** All year, weather permitting. **Site Assignment:** First come, first served. **Registration:** No. **Fee:** None. **Parking:** No designated slips.

FACILITIES

Number of RV Sites: 10. **Number of Tent-Only Sites:** 0. **Hookups:** None. **Each Site:** Picnic table, fire ring. **Dump Station:** No. **Laundry:** No. **Pay Phone:** No. **Rest Rooms and Showers:** Pit toilets, no showers. **Fuel:** No. **Propane:** No. **Internal Roads:** Dirt, bumpy. **RV Service:** No. **Market:** 6 mi. east in Fall River Mills. **Restaurant:** 6 mi. east in Fall River Mills. **General Store:** No. **Vending:** No. **Swimming:** No. **Playground:** No. **Other:** Natural small boat launch. **Activities:** Fishing, hiking, canoeing, birding. **Nearby Attractions:** Lassen Volcanic National Park; Fort Crook Museum in Fall River Mills; McArthur-Burney Falls Memorial State Park in Burney; Ahjumawi Lava Springs State Park in McArthur; Hat Creek Recreation Area in Old Station. **Additional Information:** Fall River Valley Chamber of Commerce, (530) 336-5840; Burney Chamber of Commerce, (530) 335-2111.

RESTRICTIONS

Pets: Allowed. **Fires:** In fire rings only. **Alcoholic Beverages:** Allowed. **Vehicle Maximum Length:** 22 ft. is an absolute max. **Other:** 14-day stay limit.

TO GET THERE

From Fall River Mills drive 4.5 mi. west on Hwy. 299. Turn left on Pit No. 1 Powerhouse Rd. and continue 1.1 mi. to the campground, bearing right at the entrance to Pit River Lodge. The road turns to dirt here and becomes impassable when wet.

FELTON

Henry Cowell Redwoods State Park

101 North Big Trees Park Rd., Felton 95018. T: (831) 438-2396 or reservations (800) 444-7275; www.cal-parks.ca.gov or www.reserveamerica.com.

🚐 ★★★   ⛺ ★★★

Beauty: ★★★★	Site Privacy: ★★★
Spaciousness: ★★★	Quiet: ★★
Security: ★★	Cleanliness: ★★★
Insect Control: ★★★	Facilities: ★★

The first thing you may notice on pulling into the pair of double loops that comprise this campground is that despite the park's name there are precious few burly-looking redwoods in evidence. The natural forested atmosphere derives from an abundance of knob cone pines, madrone trees, and moss-covered oaks. The Cowell grove of redwoods is a 40-minute hike (or 5-minute drive) away. Such minor misrepresentations aside, this is a fine park with roomy leaf- and dirt-based sites ranging from sun-dappled to shady, from exposed to well-shielded. Unfortunately, noise carries here and can be a big problem on weekends when Bay Area residents descend in droves. The presence of a summer-time host augments an otherwise lax enforcement of quiet time. Trash tossed into fire grates is another nuisance. Be alert to poison oak and if you plan to visit in the spring pack along insect repellant.

BASICS

Operated By: California Dept. of Parks & Recreation. **Open:** Feb. 15–Nov. 30. **Site Assignment:** Reservations accepted w/ V, MC. **Registration:** At entrance booth. **Fee:** $12, cash or CA check. **Parking:** At site.

FACILITIES

Number of RV Sites: 112. **Number of Tent-Only Sites:** 0. **Hookups:** None. **Each Site:** Picnic table, fire grate, food storage box. **Dump Station:** No. **Laundry:** No. **Pay Phone:** Yes. **Rest Rooms and Showers:** Yes. **Fuel:** No. **Propane:** No. **Internal Roads:** Paved. **RV Service:** No. **Market:** 2 mi. west in Felton. **Restaurant:** 2 mi. west in Felton. **General Store:** No. **Vending:** No. **Swimming:** No. **Playground:** No. **Other:** Some wheelchair-accessible facilities. **Activities:** Hiking, bicycling, horseback riding, horseshoe pit. **Nearby**

Attractions: Santa Cruz Beach Boardwalk, mission, museums, Seymour Marine Discovery Center, Arboretum & Natural Bridges State Beach; Roaring Camp Railroads in Felton. **Additional Information:** Santa Cruz County Conference & Visitors Council, (831) 425-1234 or (800) 833-3494.

RESTRICTIONS

Pets: On 6 ft. leash. **Fires:** In fire grates only. **Alcoholic Beverages:** Allowed at site. **Vehicle Maximum Length:** 35 ft. **Other:** 7-day stay limit from Apr. 1–Oct. 31; no firearms; no wood gathering.

TO GET THERE

From Santa Cruz on Hwy. 1 take Hwy. 9 north. Drive 6.5 mi. to the stop light; bear right on Graham Hill Rd. The campground is 2.7 mi. ahead on the right.

FRESNO

Pine Flat Lake Recreation Area

Pine Flat Rd., Piedra 93649. T: (559) 488-3004; F: (559) 488-1988.

🚐 ★★★★	🏕 ★★★
Beauty: ★★★	Site Privacy: ★★
Spaciousness: ★★★	Quiet: ★★★★
Security: ★★★★	Cleanliness: ★★
Insect Control: ★★★	Facilities: ★★

One of the more pleasant aspects of this county park is that it does not get over-run by hordes of campers, unlike other lakeside camps in the area. Boaters are not in dry-dock country, though; there is good fishing in the Kings River, which flows from the Pine Flat Dam past one side of camp, and boat-ramp access to the reservoir is nearby. The level, grassy turf is attractively punctuated here and there by a great range of such shade trees as oak, sycamore, and black walnut, and encompassed by undulating hills of golden grass and traces of granite. There is a uniformity to the double-loop layout, with open sites so comparable that one is as good as another. This is an invaluable oasis during the summer, which runs in these parts from May through Sept. The grounds are raked and well maintained, though some restrooms lack taps and have a neglected air to them. There is a general store and fuel station in Piedra, three miles to the west.

BASICS

Operated By: Fresno County Parks Dept. **Open:** All year. **Site Assignment:** First come, first served. **Registration:** At entrance booth. **Fee:** $11, cash or CA check. **Parking:** At site.

FACILITIES

Number of RV Sites: 55. **Number of Tent-Only Sites:** 0. **Hookups:** None. **Each Site:** Picnic table, barbecue grill. **Dump Station:** Yes. **Laundry:** No. **Pay Phone:** Yes. **Rest Rooms and Showers:** Flush toilets, no showers. **Fuel:** No. **Propane:** No. **Internal Roads:** Paved. **RV Service:** No. **Market:** 20 mi. southwest in Sanger. **Restaurant:** 20 mi. southwest in Sanger. **General Store:** No. **Vending:** No. **Swimming:** In Kings River. **Playground:** No. **Other:** Some wheelchair-accessible facilities. **Activities:** Fishing, hiking. **Nearby Attractions:** Museums, Forestiere Underground Gardens, Chaffee Zoological Gardens, Rotary Storyland & Playland in Fresno; Sanger Depot Museum. **Additional Information:** Sanger District Chamber of Commerce, (559) 875-4575; Fresno City & County CVB, (800) 788-0836.

RESTRICTIONS

Pets: On 6 ft. leash. **Fires:** In fire grills only. **Alcoholic Beverages:** Allowed. **Vehicle Maximum Length:** None. **Other:** 14-day stay limit.

TO GET THERE

From Fresno drive 15 mi. east on Hwy. 180/ Kings Canyon Rd. to Centerville. Bear left on Trimmer Springs Rd. Continue for 10 mi., past the small town of Piedra, then turn right on Pine Flat Rd. Proceed for 2.5 mi., over the bridge, to the campground entrance on the right.

GARBERVILLE

Shelter Cove RV Park & Campground

492 Machi Rd., Shelter Cove 95589. T: (707) 986-7474; F: (707) 986-7101; www.sojourner2000.com.

🚐 ★★★	🏕 ★★
Beauty: ★★★★	Site Privacy: ★★
Spaciousness: ★★	Quiet: ★★
Security: ★★	Cleanliness: ★★
Insect Control: ★★★	Facilities: ★★★★

Shelter Cove RV Park is for the Bohemian at heart, for people who love the ocean, enjoy fishing for salmon, and don't mind stray dogs wandering through their campsite. It is also for people who live to socialize and don't require much sleep, because in peak season the entire patch of gently tilting grassland that makes up this domain can seem like one continuous block party. On summer weekends there is live music on the patio and sizzling barbecues are centered around the giant crab cooker. Sites are small and shoe-horned together, but enjoy unobstructed views of the ocean, which is a few yards off the lot. Rugged highlands loom over the inland side of Shelter Cove. A small public park—complete with a diminutive lighthouse—lies immediately to its south, and at the opposite end is a county airport. Unfortunately, the occasional plane that approaches the airstrip comes in so low you might think it's trying to land on top of your RV. Of the single lavatory located at the deli/snack bar, we've seen cleaner facilities at the end of a four-day beer festival. Your best bet is to use the toilets in the public park. This campground lies 25 tortuous miles west of Garberville across the King Range National Conservation Area, a drive that requires your vehicle's brakes to be in good working order.

BASICS

Operated By: Shelter Cove Enterprises. **Open:** All year. **Site Assignment:** Reservations recommended; V, MC, D. **Registration:** At store. **Fee:** $16–$27, cash, check or V, MC, D. **Parking:** At site.

FACILITIES

Number of RV Sites: 103. **Number of Tent-Only Sites:** 0. **Hookups:** Water, electric (30 amps), sewer, Internet. **Each Site:** Picnic table, fire grate. **Dump Station:** Yes. **Laundry:** Yes. **Pay Phone:** Yes. **Rest Rooms and Showers:** Yes. **Fuel:** No. **Propane:** Yes. **Internal Roads:** Gravel, good condition. **RV Service:** No. **Market:** 22 mi. east in Redway. **Restaurant:** 1 mi. away in Shelter Cove. **General Store:** Yes, w/ deli. **Vending:** No. **Swimming:** No. **Playground:** No. **Other:** Limited wheelchair-accessible facilities, 6-lane boat launch. **Activities:** Fishing, beachcombing, clamming, hiking, whale-watching. **Nearby Attractions:** Richardson Grove State Park in Garberville; Smithe Redwoods State Reserve & Standish Hickey State Recreation Area in Leggett; Ave. of the Giants north of Garberville; Humboldt Redwoods State Park in Weott. **Additional Information:** Shelter Cove Informa-

tion Bureau, (707) 923-1830; Garberville-Redway Area Chamber of Commerce, (707) 923-2613.

RESTRICTIONS

Pets: On leash, $1 fee. **Fires:** In fire grates only. **Alcoholic Beverages:** Allowed. **Vehicle Maximum Length:** 40 ft. **Other:** No stay limit.

TO GET THERE

Exit US 101 at Garberville and drive through the downtown, turning left on Redwood Rd. at the sign for the King Range National Conservation Area. After 2.6 mi. turn left on Briceland Rd. which becomes the meandering and steep Shelter Cove Rd. Drive 22.2 mi., turn south on Upper Pacific Rd. and continue for 0.5 mi. to the campground on the right.

GASQUET

Smith River National Recreation Area, Panther Flat Campground

10600 US 199 South, Gasquet 95543. T: (707) 457-3131 or reservations (877) 444-6777; F: (707) 457-3794; www.r5.fs.fed.us/sixrivers or www.reserveusa.com.

🚐 ★★★★	🛖 ★★★★
Beauty: ★★★★	Site Privacy: ★★★
Spaciousness: ★★★★	Quiet: ★★★
Security: ★★★	Cleanliness: ★★★★
Insect Control: ★★★	Facilities: ★★

This tidy, well-maintained campground is perched just above the Middle Fork of the Smith River, about 20 miles northeast of Crescent City along Hwy. 199. Though a rather average facility, it is a worthy alternative to Jedediah Smith Redwood State Park, just down the road, if the latter is full, or if the wild, moldering atmosphere of a moss-encrusted old-growth forest leaves you shivering. Its central location within the Smith River National Recreation Area also makes Panther Flat a suitable base camp for day hikes and fishing the several rivers in the locale. There are only a few redwoods here, of the spindly second-growth variety, and they are overshadowed by tan oaks and madrones. Level gravel sites, well-groomed and equipped with large back-in parking slips, are moderately spacious and evenly distributed around a small grassy meadow at the heart of the elongated double-oval camp lane. The nearest telephone is in Gasquet, three miles west.

BASICS

Operated By: Six Rivers National Forest, Smith River National Recreation Area. **Open:** All year. **Site Assignment:** Reservations accepted w/V, MC. **Registration:** At entrance kiosk. **Fee:** $15, cash or check. **Parking:** At site.

FACILITIES

Number of RV Sites: 39. **Number of Tent-Only Sites:** 0. **Hookups:** None. **Each Site:** Picnic table, fire grate. **Dump Station:** No. **Laundry:** No. **Pay Phone:** No. **Rest Rooms and Showers:** Yes. **Fuel:** No. **Propane:** No. **Internal Roads:** Paved. **RV Service:** No. **Market:** 2 mi. south in Gasquet. **Restaurant:** 2 mi. south in Gasquet. **General Store:** No. **Vending:** No. **Swimming:** In Smith River. **Playground:** No. **Other:** Some wheelchair-accessible facilities. **Activities:** Fishing, hiking, kayaking. **Nearby Attractions:** Redwood National & State Parks; Battery Point Lighthouse, Ocean World, & Del Norte County Historical Museum in Crescent City; Rowdy Creek Fish Hatchery in Smith River. **Additional Information:** Crescent City–Del Norte County Chamber of Commerce, (707) 464-3174 or (800) 343-8300.

RESTRICTIONS

Pets: On leash. **Fires:** In fire grates only. **Alcoholic Beverages:** Allowed. **Vehicle Maximum Length:** 40 ft. **Other:** 14-day stay limit.

TO GET THERE

From Crescent City drive 3.5 mi. north on US 101. Exit on US 199 and head east towards Grants Pass. Continue for 17 mi. to the well-marked campground entrance on the left.

GILROY
Mount Madonna County Park

Pole Line Rd., Gilroy 95020. T: (408) 358-3741 or group reservations (408) 358-3751; www.parkhere.org/prkpages/madonna.htm.

🚐 ★★★★	⛺ ★★★★
Beauty: ★★★★	Site Privacy: ★★★
Spaciousness: ★★★	Quiet: ★★★★
Security: ★★★	Cleanliness: ★★★
Insect Control: ★★★	Facilities: ★★★

Redwood trees are what this park is all about, with some groves so dense you may find yourself won-

dering whether the sun has gone into eclipse. Madrone trees and tan oaks round out a very natural, attractive hilltop forest habitat that is laced with 20 miles of hiking trails. Sites of matted leaves and grass are above average in size and distributed over four separate loops, with those in Tan Oak both more private and open to diffused sunlight. There is also a generous amount of gravel-surfaced pull-through parking slips available throughout the campground. The Civilian Conservation Corps was based here in the early 1930s; fieldstone fire pits in some sites are solid reminders of their efforts. Around the same time, William Hearst donated a pair of white fallow deer to the park. Their descendants are still present, housed in a pen near the visitor center. Black tailed deer, coyotes, foxes, and bobcats also call this part of the Santa Cruz Mountain range home.

BASICS

Operated By: County of Santa Clara, Parks & Recreation Dept. **Open:** All year. **Site Assignment:** First come, first served. **Registration:** At entrance booth. **Fee:** $15–$25, cash, CA check, V, MC. **Parking:** At site.

FACILITIES

Number of RV Sites: 117. **Number of Tent-Only Sites:** 0. **Hookups:** Water, electric (20, 30 amps). **Each Site:** Picnic table, fire grate, food storage box. **Dump Station:** Yes. **Laundry:** No. **Pay Phone:** Yes. **Rest Rooms and Showers:** Yes. **Fuel:** No. **Propane:** No. **Internal Roads:** Paved. **RV Service:** No. **Market:** 8 mi. west in Watsonville. **Restaurant:** 8 mi. west in Watsonville. **General Store:** No. **Vending:** No. **Swimming:** No. **Playground:** No. **Other:** Some wheelchair-accessible facilities, visitor center. **Activities:** Hiking, horseback riding, archery, fishing for children. **Nearby Attractions:** Mission San Juan Bautista; John Steinbeck House & Library in Salinas; outlet shopping in Gilroy; Monterey peninsula. **Additional Information:** Gilroy Visitors Bureau & Information Center, (408) 842-6436.

RESTRICTIONS

Pets: On 6 ft. leash. **Fires:** In fire grates only. **Alcoholic Beverages:** Allowed at site & picnic area. **Vehicle Maximum Length:** 35 ft. **Other:** 14-day stay limit; no firearms; no wood gathering.

TO GET THERE

From Gilroy on US 101 take the Hwy. 152 Exit and drive west for 10.5 mi. Turn right on Pole Line Rd., which leads to the park.

GRASS VALLEY

Schoolhouse

Marysville Rd., Camptonville 95922. T: (530) 288-3231 or reservations & marina (530) 692-3200; F: (530) 288-0727; www.r5.fs.fed.us/tahoe.

🚐 ★★★★   ▲ ★★★

Beauty: ★★★★   Site Privacy: ★★★
Spaciousness: ★★★   Quiet: ★★★★
Security: ★★★   Cleanliness: ★★★
Insect Control: ★★★   Facilities: ★★

Dark Day Campground, a tent-only, walk-in facility just up the road from Schoolhouse, is blessed from its bluff-top aerie with a heavenly vista of Bullards Bar Reservoir. Sites at Schoolhouse, on the other hand, enjoy no water views. Even so, it is a peaceful, engaging camp, located above the lake on a hill that is thick with conifers, madrone, toyon, and dogwood. The triple loop winds its way across an undulating terrain, where roomy sites are granted a fair degree of privacy. There is plenty of pull-through parking available, and many of the back-ins are large enough for vehicles hauling boats. The most secluded spots are 24, 37, and 40, while 26, a pull-through, is very deep. From mid-Oct. through early spring only sites 1–14 are kept open and no potable water is available. Bullards Bar Dam, constructed in 1969, is California's largest, and ranks fourth in size in the United States.

BASICS

Operated By: Tahoe National Forest, North Yuba/Downieville Ranger District & Yuba City Water Agency. **Open:** All year. **Site Assignment:** Reservations accepted w/ V, MC. **Registration:** At Emerald Cove Marina at the dam; permit required. **Fee:** $14 from Apr. 15–Oct. 15, cash, check or V, MC; no fee in winter when water spigots are capped. **Parking:** At site.

FACILITIES

Number of RV Sites: 56. **Number of Tent-Only Sites:** 0. **Hookups:** None. **Each Site:** Picnic table, fire grate. **Dump Station:** No. **Laundry:** No. **Pay Phone:** Yes. **Rest Rooms and Showers:** Flush & vault toilets, no showers. **Fuel:** No. **Propane:** No. **Internal Roads:** Paved, more potholes than pavement. **RV Service:** No. **Market:** 26 mi. east in Downieville. **Restaurant:** 26 mi. east in

Downieville. **General Store:** Yes, at marina. **Vending:** No. **Swimming:** In Bullards Bar Reservoir. **Playground:** No. **Other:** Boat ramp, marina. **Activities:** Fishing, hiking, horseback riding, mountain biking, boating. **Nearby Attractions:** Empire Mine State Historic Park in Grass Valley; Malakoff Diggins State Historic Park in Nevada City; Downieville Foundry/Museum, Gallows & County Museum. **Additional Information:** Grass Valley–Nevada County Chamber of Commerce, (530) 273-4667; Sierra County Chamber of Commerce, (530) 862-0308 or (800) 200-4949.

RESTRICTIONS

Pets: On leash. **Fires:** In fire grates only. **Alcoholic Beverages:** Allowed. **Vehicle Maximum Length:** 35 ft. **Other:** 14-day stay limit.

TO GET THERE

Exit Hwy. 70 at Marysville and drive twelve mi. east on Hwy. 20. Turn left on Marysville Rd./E21, at the sign for Bullards Bar Reservoir, and continue for 11 mi. Head right on Old Marysville Rd. and drive 17 mi., across the dam, to the campground on the left.

GREENVILLE

Lake Almanor Campground

15778 Hwy. 89, Prattville 95923. T: (916) 386-5164; www.r5.fs.fed.us/lassen.

🚐 ★★★★   ▲ ★★★★

Beauty: ★★★★   Site Privacy: ★★★
Spaciousness: ★★★   Quiet: ★★★
Security: ★★★   Cleanliness: ★★★★
Insect Control: ★★★   Facilities: ★★

Of the many level, rather spacious sites here, there is a healthy balance between those that are open and exposed and others that are flanked by incense cedars, manzanita, Douglas firs, and ponderosa pines. Shade or sun, boating and fishing versus hiking or swimming, one thing that everybody can agree on is that the sightlines are magnificent from camp to glimmering Lake Almanor and the rumpled mountains looming above. Access to the lake is easy, too, with only a gentle tilt to the ground near the water—instead of the steep embankments of many other reservoir lakes—and loops that hug the meandering contours of the shore. Arguably, the very finest site is 40, isolated on a finger of land projecting into the lake; its neighbor, 41, is a very good runner-up. Similarly situated is 50, a double site that's ideal for large groups or oversize RVs. Tent campers should angle for 12, a cedar-shaded walk-in near the shore. A "camp library" of paperbacks is located in a cabinet across from the "supervisor," an on-site employee of American Land & Leisure, which operates the property for Pacific Gas & Electric.

BASICS

Operated By: American Land & Leisure, concessionaire. **Open:** May through Oct. **Site Assignment:** First come, first served. **Registration:** At entrance kiosk. **Fee:** $15, cash or check. **Parking:** At site.

FACILITIES

Number of RV Sites: 125. **Number of Tent-Only Sites:** 6. **Hookups:** None. **Each Site:** Picnic table, fire grate, food storage box. **Dump Station:** Yes. **Laundry:** No. **Pay Phone:** Yes. **Rest Rooms and Showers:** Vault toilets, no showers. **Fuel:** No. **Propane:** No. **Internal Roads:** Paved. **RV Service:** No. **Market:** 12 mi. south in Greenville. **Restaurant:** 12 mi. south in Greenville. **General Store:** No. **Vending:** No. **Swimming:** In Lake Almanor. **Playground:** No. **Other:** Some wheelchair-accessible facilities, boat ramp. **Activities:** Fishing, boating, waterskiing, hiking, birding. **Nearby Attractions:** Westwood Museum & Paul Bunyan & Babe the Blue Ox Statues; Lassen National Scenic Byway (Hwys. 89-44-36); Lassen Volcanic National Park. **Additional Information:** Chester–Lake Almanor Chamber of Commerce, (530) 258-2426 or (800) 350-4838.

RESTRICTIONS

Pets: On leash, $1 fee. **Fires:** In fire grates only. **Alcoholic Beverages:** Allowed. **Vehicle Maximum Length:** 40 ft. **Other:** 14-day stay limit.

TO GET THERE

From Greenville drive 12 mi. north on Hwy. 89. The campground entrance is on the right.

GROVELAND
Moccasin Point

Jacksonville Rd., Moccasin 95347. T: (209) 852-2396 or marina (209) 989-2206; F: (209) 857-2780; www.donpedrolake.com.

🚐 ★★★★   ⛺ ★★★

Beauty: ★★★★	Site Privacy: ★★★
Spaciousness: ★★★	Quiet: ★★★
Security: ★★★★	Cleanliness: ★★★
Insect Control: ★★★	Facilities: ★★★★

Given a choice between camping at Moccasin Point or Fleming Meadows, just down the road, the first wins hands down. For one thing, sites at Moccasin are not wedged together quite as tightly, and they benefit from a greater concentration of such shade and privacy providers as oaks, various conifers, and manzanita. Another point in its favor is the picturesque landscape, which ranges from chaparral-covered Sierra foothills to rolling fields of wildflower-dotted golden grass. The layout consists of a figure-8 loop and a triple circuit, both of which descend toward the jade-green water over a series of tiers. The most private sites are B 6, 10, 17, C 7, 8, 15, and 16. One drawback of this fine campground is the dearth of lake views. Oddly, the best water access is available via its primitive D and E overflow loops, the latter being graced with its own lagoon. Site distribution is more concentrated there, but shade is abundant.

BASICS

Operated By: Don Pedro Recreation Agency. **Open:** All year. **Site Assignment:** Reservations accepted w/ V, MC or check. **Registration:** At entrance booth. **Fee:** $12–$22, cash or V, MC. **Parking:** At site.

FACILITIES

Number of RV Sites: 91. **Number of Tent-Only Sites:** 0. **Hookups:** Water, electric (20, 30 amps), sewer. **Each Site:** Picnic table, barbecue grill, food storage box. **Dump Station:** Yes. **Laundry:** No. **Pay Phone:** Yes. **Rest Rooms and Showers:** Yes. **Fuel:** No. **Propane:** Yes. **Internal Roads:** Paved. **RV Service:** No. **Market:** 8 mi. east in Groveland. **Restaurant:** 8 mi. east in Groveland. **General Store:** Yes. **Vending:** Yes. **Swimming:** In Don Pedro Lake. **Playground:** No. **Other:** Some wheelchair-accessible facilities, boat ramp, marina. **Activities:** Fishing, waterskiing, motorboat & houseboat rentals, sailing. **Nearby Attractions:** Northern Mariposa County History Center in Coulterville; Tuolumne County Museum & History Center in Sonora; Yosemite National Park. **Additional Information:** Coulterville Visitors Center, (209) 878-3074; Tuolumne County Visitors Bureau, (209) 533-4420 or (800) 446-1333.

RESTRICTIONS

Pets: Not allowed. **Fires:** Groundfires not allowed. **Alcoholic Beverages:** Allowed. **Vehicle Maximum Length:** None. **Other:** 14-day stay limit; no fireworks.

TO GET THERE

From Groveland on Hwy. 120 head 7 mi. west to the junction w/ Hwy. 49. Turn north (right) on Hwy. 49 and continue for 2 mi. Turn right on Jacksonville Rd., followed by another right into the campground.

GROVELAND
The Pines

Hwy. 120, Groveland 95321. T: (209) 962-7825; F: (209) 962-6406; www.r5.fs.fed.us/stanislaus.

🚐 ★★★   ⛺ ★★★

Beauty: ★★★	Site Privacy: ★★
Spaciousness: ★★★	Quiet: ★★★★
Security: ★★★	Cleanliness: ★★★
Insect Control: ★★★	Facilities: ★

No one cares to stay at The Pines very long, seldom more than one night. That is no reflection on this peaceful haven just off of Hwy. 120, nine miles east of Groveland. It's just that with the entrance to Yosemite National Park 15 miles farther on, this serves more as a brief lay-over camp than a destination in its own right. The clean, attractive campground, located behind a forest ranger station, features level, grassy sites scattered over an L-shaped access road. There are plenty of oak trees, manzanita, and cedars sprinkled in among the mature pines, yielding abundant shade to this lush sward. Even so, sites, while somewhat roomy, are rather exposed. Best of the group are a pair of walk-ins, 6 and 7, which are well-recessed amid a clutch of stumps and a small marsh. Elevation is 3,200 feet, auguring for cool-but-pleasant nights most of the year.

BASICS

Operated By: American Land & Leisure, concessionaire. **Open:** All year. **Site Assignment:** First come, first served. **Registration:** At entrance kiosk. **Fee:** $10, cash or check. **Parking:** At site.

FACILITIES

Number of RV Sites: 7. **Number of Tent-Only Sites:** 5. **Hookups:** None. **Each Site:** Picnic table, fire grate. **Dump Station:** No. **Laundry:** No. **Pay Phone:** No. **Rest Rooms and Showers:** Vault toilets, no showers. **Fuel:** No. **Propane:** No. **Internal Roads:** Paved. **RV Service:** No. **Market:** 9 mi. west in Groveland. **Restaurant:** 9 mi. west in Groveland. **General Store:** No. **Vending:** No. **Swimming:** No. **Playground:** No. **Activities:** Hiking, rafting on the Tuolumne River. **Nearby Attractions:** Yosemite National Park; Don Pedro Lake; Northern Mariposa County History Center in Coulterville. **Additional Information:** Tuolumne County Visitors Bureau, (209) 533-4420 or (800) 446-1333; Yosemite Area Traveler Information, (209) 723-3153.

RESTRICTIONS

Pets: On leash. **Fires:** In fire grates only. **Alcoholic Beverages:** Allowed. **Vehicle Maximum Length:** 22 ft. **Other:** 14-day stay limit.

TO GET THERE

From Groveland drive 8.5 mi. east on Hwy. 120. Turn right at the sign for the Groveland Ranger District Office and follow the signs to the campground, 0.6 mi. ahead.

GUERNEVILLE
Austin Creek State Recreation Area, Bullfrog Pond Campground

17000 Armstrong Woods Rd., Guerneville 95446. T: (707) 869-2015; F: (707) 869-5629; www.cal-parks.ca.gov.

🚐 ★★★   ⛺ ★★★★

Beauty: ★★★★	Site Privacy: ★★★
Spaciousness: ★★★	Quiet: ★★★★
Security: ★★★	Cleanliness: ★★★★
Insect Control: ★★	Facilities: ★★

Shortly after the end of World War II, renowned ceramist Marguerite Wildenhain of the Bauhaus school came to settle in this area. She found inspiration in the sublime beauty of her surroundings, a feeling that countless campers have shared since then. If you are able to get your vehicle up the steep, narrow, meandering access road—and that's a big if—you will find stunning mountain views and an enchanting forested atmosphere. Feral pigs, wild turkeys, bobcats, and the elusive spotted owl make their homes in these redwood- and tan oak–covered hills. You are more likely, though, to see frogs by the pond, where the camp lane ends. Fern-freckled sites are distributed fairly well apart and though they are a tad small and some are planted on slanting ground, such minor discomforts seem an acceptable tradeoff for camping in so attractive a place. The park closes when the fire risk is extreme, so be sure to call ahead in summer.

BASICS

Operated By: California Dept. of Parks & Recreation. **Open:** All year, weather & fire danger permitting. **Site Assignment:** First come, first served. **Registration:** At kiosk, 3.2 mi. beyond entrance booth. **Fee:** $12, cash or CA check. **Parking:** At site.

FACILITIES

Number of RV Sites: 23. **Number of Tent-Only Sites:** 0. **Hookups:** None. **Each Site:** Picnic table, fire grate, food storage box. **Dump Station:** No. **Laundry:** No. **Pay Phone:** Yes. **Rest Rooms and Showers:** Flush toilets, no showers. **Fuel:** No. **Propane:** No. **Internal Roads:** Paved, narrow & bumpy. **RV Service:** No. **Market:** 5.5 mi. south in Guerneville. **Restaurant:** 5.5 mi. south in Guerneville. **General Store:** No. **Vending:** No. **Swimming:** No. **Playground:** No. **Other:** Some wheelchair-accessible facilities. **Activities:** Hiking, fishing, horseback riding, birding, canoeing (in the Russian River). **Nearby Attractions:** Healdsburg Museum & Sonoma County Wine Library; Fort Ross State Historic Park, Kruse Rhododendron State Reserve & Salt Point State Park in Jenner; winery tours. **Additional Information:** Healdsburg Chamber of Commerce & Visitors Center, (707) 823-3032 or (877) 828-4748; Russian River Chamber of Commerce & Visitors Center, (707) 869-9212 or (877) 644-9001.

RESTRICTIONS

Pets: On 6 ft. leash; not allowed on trails. **Fires:** In fire grates only; not allowed when fire danger is extreme. **Alcoholic Beverages:** Allowed at site. **Vehicle Maximum Length:** 20 ft.; no trailers

allowed. **Other:** 14-day stay limit; no firearms; no wood gathering.

TO GET THERE

From downtown Guerneville on Hwy. 116, turn north on Armstrong Woods Rd. The park entrance is 2.3 mi. ahead, w/ the campground entrance is 3.2 mi. beyond that.

HAMBURG
Sarah Totten

Hwy. 96, Hamburg 96086. T: (530) 493-2243 or reservations (877) 444-6777; F: (530) 493-1796; www.r5.fs.fed.us/klamath; wrwilliams@fs.fed.us.

🚐 ★★★	🏕 ★★★★
Beauty: ★★★★	Site Privacy: ★★★★
Spaciousness: ★★★★	Quiet: ★★★
Security: ★	Cleanliness: ★★★
Insect Control: ★★★	Facilities: ★★

A popular rafting stretch of the Klamath River flows right by this pretty little campground, with easy put-in access to the water. Like Fort Goff to the west, this is a roadside facility, with a key difference being that Sarah Totten is recessed from Hwy. 96 and thus approaching autos do not seem to be bearing down on one's tent. In fact, road noise in most sites is pretty effectively muffled by the melodious churning of the Klamath. Of the two neighboring loops, the left-hand one contains five walk-in sites, with the oak-shaded number 3 the most spacious. Oak, pines, and horsetail grass also thrive in the second circuit, where peculiar mounds of river stones near the entrance are relics from the Gold Rush era, circa 1850, when extensive mining of the river occurred. Sites 6 and 7, with paved back-in parking, are tailor-made for RVs. The most private spot is 9, hidden behind an overgrown thicket of vines and weeds; it also has a water view. This is a splendid property, 40 miles east of Happy Camp, albeit somewhat neglected and overgrown.

BASICS

Operated By: Klamath National Forest. **Open:** May to Nov. **Site Assignment:** First come, first served; reservations required for group site. **Registration:** At entrance kiosk. **Fee:** $10, cash or check; no fee when in winter when spigots are capped. **Parking:** At site.

FACILITIES

Number of RV Sites: 5. **Number of Tent-Only Sites:** 12. **Hookups:** None. **Each Site:** Picnic table, barbecue grill, fire ring. **Dump Station:** No. **Laundry:** No. **Pay Phone:** No, emergency phone only. **Rest Rooms and Showers:** Vault toilets, no showers. **Fuel:** No. **Propane:** No. **Internal Roads:** Mostly paved, also dirt & rocks. **RV Service:** No. **Market:** 10 mi. east in Seiad Valley. **Restaurant:** 10 mi. east in Seiad Valley. **General Store:** No. **Vending:** No. **Swimming:** In Klamath River. **Playground:** No. **Other:** Limited wheelchair-accessible facilities. **Activities:** Fishing, hiking, rafting, kayaking, birding. **Nearby Attractions:** Klamath National Forest; Yreka National Historic District, Western Railroad, Siskiyou County Courthouse & Museum in Yreka. **Additional Information:** Siskiyou County Visitors Bureau, (530) 926-3850; Yreka Chamber of Commerce, (530) 842-1649.

RESTRICTIONS

Pets: On 6 ft. leash. **Fires:** In fire rings only. **Alcoholic Beverages:** Allowed. **Vehicle Maximum Length:** 22 ft. **Other:** 14-day stay limit.

TO GET THERE

From Happy Camp drive 30 mi. east on Hwy. 96. The campground entrance is on the left side of the road.

HAPPY CAMP

Elk Creek Camp & RV Park

921 Elk Creek Rd., Happy Camp 96039. T: (530) 493-2208; www.elkcreekcampground.com; eddiedav@sisqtel.net.

🚐 ★★★   ▲ ★★

Beauty: ★★★   Site Privacy: ★★
Spaciousness: ★★   Quiet: ★★★
Security: ★★★★   Cleanliness: ★★★★
Insect Control: ★★★   Facilities: ★★★★

Elk Creek is a privately operated campground with a rocky creek running through it, offering good fishing and swimming opportunities within easy walking distance of sites. The rustic feeling of the locale stems in part from its being thinly forested with maple, oak, madrone, and several types of pine, but also from its chaotic criss-crossing layout of lanes. Sites are level and surfaced either with grass, gravel, or dirt; the ones just above the creek are the roomiest and most secluded. While the setting is generally quite attractive, the appeal of Elk Creek is diminished by the presence of several unsightly long-term trailers, some of which sport license tags that haven't been renewed in years. A recent change in management, though, bodes well, with a rec room, equipped with ping pong and pool tables, recently installed and the genial new owners determined to turn this place around. Miniature show horses are bred on the premises.

BASICS

Operated By: Eddie & Jean Davenport, owners. **Open:** All year. **Site Assignment:** Reservations accepted w/ V, MC, D, AE. **Registration:** At the office. **Fee:** $10–$20, cash, check or V, MC, C, AE. **Parking:** At site.

FACILITIES

Number of RV Sites: 78. **Number of Tent-Only Sites:** Undesignated sites. **Hookups:** Water, electric (30, 50 amps), sewer, cable TV, Internet. **Each Site:** Picnic table, fire grate. **Dump Station:** Yes. **Laundry:** Yes. **Pay Phone:** Yes. **Rest Rooms and Showers:** Yes. **Fuel:** No. **Propane:** Yes. **Internal Roads:** Dirt & gravel, negotiable. **RV Service:** No. **Market:** 1 mi. northeast in Happy Camp. **Restaurant:** 1 mi. northeast in Happy Camp. **General Store:** No. **Vending:** Yes. **Swimming:** In Elk Creek & Klamath River. **Playground:** No. **Other:** Some wheelchair-accessible facilities, rec room. **Activities:** Hiking, fishing, kayaking, rafting. **Nearby Attractions:** Oregon Caves National Monument; Yreka National Historic District; Klamath National Forest. **Additional Information:** Siskiyou County Visitors Bureau, (530) 926-3850.

RESTRICTIONS

Pets: On leash. **Fires:** In fire grates only. **Alcoholic Beverages:** Allowed. **Vehicle Maximum Length:** None. **Other:** No stay limit; no wood gathering.

TO GET THERE

From Happy Camp drive 0.5 mi. south on Hwy. 96 to Elk Creek Rd. Turn left and drive 1 mi. to the campground entrance on the right. The unpaved access road descends steeply.

HUME

Hume Lake

Hume Lake Rd., Hume 93628. T: (599) 338-2251 or reservations (877) 444-6777; F: (559) 338-2131; www.r5.fs.fed.us/sequoia or www.reserveusa.com.

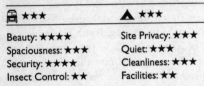

🚐 ★★★	⛺ ★★★
Beauty: ★★★★	Site Privacy: ★★★
Spaciousness: ★★★	Quiet: ★★★
Security: ★★★★	Cleanliness: ★★★
Insect Control: ★★	Facilities: ★★

Hume Lake lies just below this good-looking woodland campground. Fishing and boating are popular pastimes here, so much so that you'll need reservations on summer weekends. It is well situated as a base camp for exploring the newly-minted Giant Sequoia National Monument, of which it is a part, and launching into the neighboring Kings Canyon National Park. Manzanita, Jeffrey and ponderosa pines, oak, and cedar thrive across this hilly domain, where dirt- and pine needle–surfaced sites are spread decently apart over a convoluted series of six loops. That's the good news. The bad news is that few spots are blessed with lake vistas, and those that are, such as 63 and 64, are not specifically reservable. The concession that manages Hume Lake for the national forest service restricts reservations to "type," not site number. Thus, car campers with a tent might reserve a "type one" spot, while a motor home would require a "type two" or "type three," at a higher fee. Unfortunately, many in the first category have parking slips that are so tight you may wish you rolled in on two wheels instead of four. Gasoline and a general store are available at the Christian camp in Hume, two miles south.

BASICS

Operated By: California Land Management, concessionaire. **Open:** May through Sept., weather permitting. **Site Assignment:** Reservations accepted w/ V, MC, D. **Registration:** At entrance booth. **Fee:** $16, cash or check; $32 for a double site; add $2 per night for holiday weekends. **Parking:** At site.

FACILITIES

Number of RV Sites: 74. **Number of Tent-Only Sites:** 0. **Hookups:** None. **Each Site:** Picnic table, fire grate, some sites have bearproof box. **Dump Station:** No. **Laundry:** No. **Pay Phone:** No. **Rest Rooms and Showers:** Flush toilets, no showers. **Fuel:** No. **Propane:** No. **Internal Roads:** Paved. **RV Service:** No. **Market:** 41 mi. west in Sanger. **Restaurant:** 10 mi. southwest in Grant Grove Village. **General Store:** Yes. **Vending:** No. **Swimming:** In Hume Lake. **Playground:** No. **Other:** Boat ramp. **Activities:** Fishing, boat rentals, hiking. **Nearby Attractions:** Giant Sequoa National Monument; Kings Canyon & Sequoia National Parks; Reedley Opera House, Museum & Mennonite Quilting Center. **Additional Information:** Fresno City & County CVB, (800) 788-0836; Reedley District Chamber of Commerce & Visitors Bureau, (559) 638-3548.

RESTRICTIONS

Pets: On leash. **Fires:** In fire grates only. **Alcoholic Beverages:** Allowed. **Vehicle Maximum Length:** 30 ft. **Other:** 14-day stay limit.

TO GET THERE

From Grant Grove on Hwy. 180 in Kings Canyon National Park drive 6.2 mi. north, direction Cedar Grove. At the sign for Hume Lake make a right onto Hume Rd. and continue for 3.2 mi. to the Hume Lake campground turnoff. Make a left and proceed for 0.4 mi. to the campground straight ahead.

HUME

Landslide

Ten Mile Creek Rd., Hume 93628. T: (559) 338-2251 or reservations (877) 444-6777; F: (559) 338-2131; www.r5.fs.fed.us/sequoia or www.reserveusa.com.

🚐 ★★★	⛺ ★★★★
Beauty: ★★★★	Site Privacy: ★★★
Spaciousness: ★★★★	Quiet: ★★★
Security: ★★★	Cleanliness: ★★★
Insect Control: ★★	Facilities: ★

Located just down the road from Hume Lake (and 15 miles from Grant Grove Village in Kings Canyon National Park), this thickly-forested campground is a worthy alternative to that oft-overrun facility. It's small, and picks up traffic noise from the forest road, but the setting reflects an authentic Sierra Nevada flavor, with granite boulders highlighting the rolling turf, and several meandering streams trickling through. Sizable sites of dirt and grass are positioned well apart along the curvilinear camp lane, with abundant shade provided by incense cedars and Jeffrey pines—but no sequoias. Late spring, when neon-red snow plants push up through the ground, is a good time to visit, but at an altitude of 5,800 feet, evenings then can be downright chilly. Formerly, Landslide was a no-fee national forest camp, but now that it is part of the newly-minted Giant Sequoia National Monument, the concession that operates it has imposed a $10 fee. Gasoline and a general store are located at the Christian camp in Hume, three miles north.

BASICS

Operated By: California Land Management, concessionaire. **Open:** May 25 through Oct., weather permitting. **Site Assignment:** Reservations accepted for some sites; V, MC, D. **Registration:** At entrance kiosk. **Fee:** $10, cash or check. **Parking:** At site.

FACILITIES

Number of RV Sites: 7. **Number of Tent-Only Sites:** 2. **Hookups:** None. **Each Site:** Picnic table, fire grate. **Dump Station:** No. **Laundry:** No. **Pay Phone:** No. **Rest Rooms and Showers:** Vault toilets, no showers. **Fuel:** No. **Propane:** No. **Internal Roads:** Mostly dirt, but smooth. **RV Service:** No. **Market:** 44 mi. west in Sanger. **Restaurant:** 13 mi. southwest in Grant Grove Village. **General Store:** Yes. **Vending:** No. **Swimming:** No. **Playground:** No. **Other:** Limited wheelchair-accessible facilities. **Activities:** Fishing, boat rentals, hiking. **Nearby Attractions:** Giant Sequoia National Monument; Kings Canyon & Sequoia National Parks; Reedley Opera House, Museum & Mennonite Quilting Center. **Additional Information:** Fresno City & County CVB, (800) 788-0836; Reedley District Chamber of Commerce & Visitors Bureau, (559) 638-3548.

RESTRICTIONS

Pets: On leash. **Fires:** In fire grates only. **Alcoholic Beverages:** Allowed. **Vehicle Maximum Length:** 30 ft. **Other:** 14-day stay limit.

TO GET THERE

From Grant Grove on Hwy. 180 in Kings Canyon National Park drive 6.2 mi. north, direction Cedar Grove. At the sign for Hume Lake make a right onto Hume Rd. (which becomes Ten Mile Creek Rd.) and continue for 7.5 mi. to the campground on the right.

JENNER

Salt Point State Park, Woodside and Gerstle Cove Campground

Hwy. 1, Jenner 95450. T: (707) 865-2391 or (707) 847-3221 or reservations (800) 444-7275; F: (707) 865-2046; www.cal-parks.ca.gov or www.reserveamerica.com.

🚐 ★★★	🅰 ★★★
Beauty: ★★★	Site Privacy: ★★★
Spaciousness: ★★★★	Quiet: ★★★
Security: ★★★	Cleanliness: ★★★
Insect Control: ★★★	Facilities: ★

Hwy. 1 is a sleepy, sparsely-traveled stretch of pavement in this part of the state, which is a good thing as it cuts directly through Salt Point State Park. The campground's two loops lie on either side of the road and that quirk of geography could not result in more contrasting realms. The west-facing Gerstle Cove consists of 30 roomy sites spaced well apart around a small grassy meadow. Most of the pines at the perimeter died years ago, victims of a forest fire. As a result, their skeletal limbs have an eerie appearance, especially when veiled in the fog that frequently cloaks this section of the park. When the air is clear the camp commands a great view of the sandy cove below, one of a series of small bays and inlets in the vicinity. Inland is Woodside, where the dense concentration of mixed conifers, madrones, and ferns emerged unscathed from the fire. Sites here are no less roomy than across the road, but the forest environment contributes to better screening and thus superior privacy. Amateur mycologists will be delighted to find that king boletes and chanterelles thrive in these woods. Divers will want to explore the protected underwater reserve just off shore.

BASICS

Operated By: California Dept. of Parks & Recreation. **Open:** All year. **Site Assignment:** Reservations accepted w/ V, MC, D. **Registration:** At entrance booth. **Fee:** $12, cash or CA check. **Parking:** At site.

FACILITIES

Number of RV Sites: 109. **Number of Tent-Only Sites:** 30. **Hookups:** None. **Each Site:** Picnic table, fire grate, food storage box. **Dump**

Station: No. **Laundry:** No. **Pay Phone:** Yes. **Rest Rooms and Showers:** Flush toilets, no showers. **Fuel:** No. **Propane:** No. **Internal Roads:** Paved. **RV Service:** No. **Market:** 1 mi. south on Hwy. 1. **Restaurant:** 1 mi. south on Hwy. 1. **General Store:** No. **Vending:** No. **Swimming:** No. **Playground:** No. **Other:** Some wheelchair-accessible facilities, underwater park. **Activities:** Hiking, fishing, bicycling, horseback riding, mushroom collecting, abalone diving, tidepooling. **Nearby Attractions:** Fort Ross State Historic Park & Kruse Rhododendron State Reserve in Jenner; Armstrong Redwoods State Reserve & Austin Creek State Recreation Area in Guerneville; Sonoma County Wine Library in Healdsburg. **Additional Information:** Sebastopol Area Chamber of Commerce & Visitors Center, (707) 823-3032 or (877) 828-4748.

RESTRICTIONS

Pets: On leash no longer than 6 ft., not allowed on trails. **Fires:** In fire grates only. **Alcoholic Beverages:** Allowed at site. **Vehicle Maximum Length:** 31 ft. **Other:** 10-day stay limit; no firearms; no wood gathering.

TO GET THERE

From Guerneville drive 12.3 mi. west on Hwy. 116 to Jenner. Turn right (north) onto Hwy. 1 and continue for 20 mi. Woodside is to the right, Gerstle Cove is 2 mi. farther on Hwy. 1, to the left.

JULIAN

Cuyamaca Rancho State Park, Paso Picacho Campground

12551 Hwy. 79, Descanso 92016. T: (760) 765-0755; www.cuyamaca.statepark.org.

🚐 ★★★   ⛺ ★★★★

Beauty: ★★★★   Site Privacy: ★★★
Spaciousness: ★★★   Quiet: ★★★
Security: ★★★★   Cleanliness: ★★★
Insect Control: ★★★   Facilities: ★★

Paso Picacho is open all year but if you come in the winter plan to dress warmly and don't be surprised if there is snow on the ground. That's because at an elevation of nearly 5,000 feet this is one of the higher camps in southern California, and thus one of the more pleasant—and hugely popular—in summer. Of course its rough-hewn mountainous setting has something to do with that appeal, with roomy sites shaded by oak, manzanita, and pines, and dispersed through a series of loops that snake across the hilly contours of the park. As with many mountain camps, finding a level site can be a challenge: Best in that department (as well as for privacy and space) are numbers 3–12. Rangers report that area mountain lions have become bold, with a number of sightings, two attacks and one fatality over the last 14 years.

BASICS

Operated By: California Dept. of Parks & Recreation. **Open:** All year. **Site Assignment:** Reservations recommended; V, MC, AE. **Registration:** At entrance booth. **Fee:** $12, cash or CA check. **Parking:** At site.

FACILITIES

Number of RV Sites: 85. **Number of Tent-Only Sites:** 0. **Hookups:** None. **Each Site:** Picnic table, fire grate. **Dump Station:** Yes. **Laundry:** No. **Pay Phone:** Yes. **Rest Rooms and Showers:** Yes. **Fuel:** No. **Propane:** No. **Internal Roads:** Paved. **RV Service:** No. **Market:** 11 mi. north in Julian. **Restaurant:** 11 mi. north in Julian. **General Store:** No. **Vending:** No. **Swimming:** No. **Playground:** No. **Other:** Some wheelchair-accessible facilities. **Activities:** Hiking, horseback riding, boating & fishing in Lake Cuyamaca less than 2 mi. away, ranger-led activities in summer. **Nearby Attractions:** San Diego Wild Animal Park in Escondido, historic Julian. **Additional Information:** Julian Chamber of Commerce, (760) 765-1857.

RESTRICTIONS

Pets: On 6 ft. leash. **Fires:** In fire grates only. **Alcoholic Beverages:** Allowed at site. **Vehicle Maximum Length:** 27 ft. **Other:** 30-day stay limit; no firearms; no wood gathering.

TO GET THERE

From San Diego head east on I-8 for 43 mi. Exit on Rte. 79 north and drive 12.2 mi. The campground entrance is on the left.

JULIAN
William Heise County Park

4945 Heise Park Rd., Julian 92036. T: (858) 694-3049; www.co.san-diego.ca.us/parks.

🚐 ★★★   ⛺ ★★★

Beauty: ★★★★   Site Privacy: ★★★
Spaciousness: ★★★   Quiet: ★★★
Security: ★★★   Cleanliness: ★★★
Insect Control: ★   Facilities: ★★★

This agreeable campground mixes grassy meadows with a forest environment and comes up with a series of loops laid out in a terracing of such shade trees as live oaks, Coulter pines, and incense cedars. The largely comparable sites have coarse sand and dirt for tent pads, with 73 and 84 giving tenters the most space and 36 optimum for RVers. You're likely to hear acorn woodpeckers clowning around up in the leafy canopy, and last time we camped here a number of wild turkeys gobbled through our site. There are seven miles of hiking trails in the park, with the scenic overlook on Desert View Trail especially rewarding. Looking for more? How about heated restrooms, a nicely civilized touch of comfort. The park is just six miles from the scenic mountain town of Julian, making it a great base when the latter holds its Apple Days festival throughout Oct.

BASICS

Operated By: County of San Diego, Dept. of Parks & Recreation. **Open:** All year. **Site Assignment:** Reservations accepted w/V, MC, D. **Registration:** At entrance booth & park office. **Fee:** $12–$14, cash or V, MC, D. **Parking:** At site.

FACILITIES

Number of RV Sites: 61. **Number of Tent-Only Sites:** 43. **Hookups:** None. **Each Site:** Picnic table, fire ring, some w/ a barbecue grill. **Dump Station:** Yes. **Laundry:** Yes. **Pay Phone:** Yes. **Rest Rooms and Showers:** Yes. **Fuel:** No. **Propane:** No. **Internal Roads:** Paved. **RV Service:** No. **Market:** 5.5 mi. north in Julian. **Restaurant:** 5.5 mi. north in Julian. **General Store:** No. **Vending:** Yes. **Swimming:** No. **Playground:** Yes. **Other:** Some wheelchair-accessible facilities. **Activities:** Hiking, bicycling, horseback riding, horseshoe pit. **Nearby Attractions:** Anza-Borrego Desert State Park, historic Julian, Lake Cuyamaca. **Additional Information:** Julian Chamber of Commerce, (760) 765-1857.

RESTRICTIONS

Pets: On 6 ft. leash; $1 fee. **Fires:** In fire rings only. **Alcoholic Beverages:** Allowed at site, not exceeding 40 proof. **Vehicle Maximum Length:** 40 ft. **Other:** 14-day stay limit; no firearms.

TO GET THERE

From Julian head west on Hwy. 78 for 1 mi. Turn left on Pine Hills Rd. and drive 2.3 mi. Turn left again on Frisius Rd. and continue for 2.2 mi. to the park.

JUNE LAKE
Pine Cliff Resort

Pine Cliff Rd., June Lake 93529. T: (760) 648-7558; F: (760) 648-7428.

🚐 ★★★★   ⛺ ★★★

Beauty: ★★★★   Site Privacy: ★★
Spaciousness: ★★   Quiet: ★★★★
Security: ★★★★   Cleanliness: ★★★★
Insect Control: ★★★   Facilities: ★★★★

June Lake is a lovely body of water, encircled by wavy, golden grasslands, with the choppy, rocky eastern Sierra range looming above. Pine Cliff Resort capitalizes on this rugged setting by positioning many of its sandy, mostly level sites among large gray boulders, while others rub up against high desert chaparral. Jeffrey pines thrive throughout the tilting, mountainous domain, providing shade and highlighting its natural beauty. Despite the trees, there is little screening here, and sites, which are on the small side, are too often crowded together. For the most privacy, try to reserve such perimeter slots as 133, 135, and 136; or any of 66–72, for their dramatic location amid a rift of Sierra uplift. Management deserves credit for the competitive pricing of its fuel and basic supplies, though for "people skills," campers give it mixed reviews. Pine Cliff Resort lies at 7,600 feet altitude, less than 15 miles south of Lee Vining. The sandy access road to the beach and boat ramp is very bumpy.

BASICS

Operated By: Pine Cliff Resort. **Open:** All year. **Site Assignment:** Reservations recommended; checks only. **Registration:** At entrance booth. **Fee:** $10–$18, cash only. **Parking:** At site.

FACILITIES

Number of RV Sites: 190. **Number of Tent-Only Sites:** 60. **Hookups:** Water, electric (20, 30 amps), sewer. **Each Site:** Half-size picnic table, fire grate. **Dump Station:** No. **Laundry:** Yes. **Pay Phone:** Yes. **Rest Rooms and Showers:** Yes. **Fuel:** Yes. **Propane:** Yes. **Internal Roads:** Sandy & smooth. **RV Service:** No. **Market:** 13 mi. north in Lee Vining. **Restaurant:** 13 mi. north in Lee Vining. **General Store:** Yes. **Vending:** No. **Swimming:** In June Lake. **Playground:** Yes. **Other:** Some wheelchair-accessible facilities, boat launch, beach. **Activities:** Fishing, hiking, volleyball, basketball, horseshoe pit, boat & tackle rentals. **Nearby Attractions:** Mono Lake Tufa State Reserve in Lee Vining; Devils Postpile National Monument, Mammoth Mountain Bike Park, Mammoth Museum & outlet shopping in Mammoth Lakes. **Additional Information:** Mono County Tourism Commission, (760) 924-3699; Mammoth Lakes Visitors Bureau, (888) GO-MAMMOTH

RESTRICTIONS

Pets: On leash. **Fires:** In fire grates only & out by 10:30 p.m. **Alcoholic Beverages:** Allowed. **Vehicle Maximum Length:** None. **Other:** No stay limit.

TO GET THERE

From Lee Vining drive 11 mi. south on US 395, ignoring the 1st turnoff for Hwy. 158 north. Turn right on the 2nd turnoff, Hwy. 158 south for the June Lake Loop. Drive 1 mi. to North Shore Dr. and turn right on it. Continue for 0.6 mi., then turn left on Pine Cliff Rd. The campground entrance is 0.4 mi. ahead on the right, well-signed.

KERNVILLE
Fairview

Sierra Way, Fairview/Kernville 93238. T: (760) 376-3781 or reservations (877) 444-6777; F: (760) 376-3795; www.r5.fs.fed.us/sequoia or www.reserveusa.com.

🚐 ★★★★	▲ ★★★
Beauty: ★★★★	Site Privacy: ★★★
Spaciousness: ★★	Quiet: ★★★
Security: ★★★	Cleanliness: ★★★
Insect Control: ★★★	Facilities: ★★

The turbulent Kern River is a rafters' delight, and Fairview puts campers where the action is, right alongside that purling cascade of water. The saw-toothed Sierra range circles this rocky, mountainous setting, which is at an altitude of 3,500 feet. Very small, level sites, with equally tight parking slips, are crowded together over rocky, sandy ground. The host's spot has the best shade; elsewhere over the three loops it is sparsely provided by a few pines and cottonwoods, with Mormon tea and other chaparral making up the ground cover. Spring, when snow melt adds to the Kern's power, is the best time to visit, but bear in mind that the concession operating this national forest property charges the same fee whether you picnic, day-use, or camp. There are many maverick camps along the Kern that budget-minded campers may want to investigate. Many are sizable enough to handle small RVs and if they don't have facilities, at least they offer more seclusion and fairer river access than this and the many other developed camps in the area.

BASICS

Operated By: California Land Management, concessionaire. **Open:** Apr. through Nov. **Site Assignment:** Reservations recommended; V, MC, D. **Registration:** With campground host. **Fee:** $12, cash or check; $24 for double site; add $2 per night for holiday weekends. **Parking:** At site.

FACILITIES

Number of RV Sites: 55. **Number of Tent-Only Sites:** 0. **Hookups:** None. **Each Site:** Picnic table, fire grate, coffee can ashtray. **Dump Station:** No. **Laundry:** No. **Pay Phone:** Yes. **Rest Rooms and Showers:** Vault toilets, no showers. **Fuel:** No. **Propane:** No. **Internal Roads:** Paved & meandering. **RV Service:** No. **Market:** 17 mi. south in Kernville. **Restaurant:** 17 mi. south in Kernville. **General Store:** Yes. **Vending:** No. **Swimming:** No. **Playground:** No. **Other:** Some wheelchair-accessible facilities. **Activities:** Rafting, fishing, hiking, bicycling. **Nearby Attractions:** Sequoia National Forest; Isabella Lake; California Hot Springs; Porterville Historical Museum & Zauld House & Gardens. **Additional Information:** Porterville Chamber of Commerce, (559) 784-7503.

RESTRICTIONS

Pets: On leash. **Fires:** In fire grates only. **Alcoholic Beverages:** Allowed. **Vehicle Maximum Length:** 40 ft. **Other:** 14-day stay limit.

TO GET THERE

From Kernville drive 17 mi. north on Sierra Way. The campground entrance is on the left.

KINGS CANYON NATIONAL PARK
Azalea

Hwy. 180, Grant Grove Village, Kings Canyon
National Park 93633. T: (559) 565-3341;
www.nps.gov/seki.

🚐 ★★★★　　　　　　Δ ★★★

Beauty: ★★★★　　　　Site Privacy: ★★
Spaciousness: ★★★　　Quiet: ★★★
Security: ★★★　　　　Cleanliness: ★★★
Insect Control: ★★★　　Facilities: ★★

One of the more appealing aspects of this campground is its central location, within easy walking distance of the General Grant Grove of
massive redwood trees and the Grant Grove Visitor Center. The first thing you may notice,
though, on driving in is that many sites are considerably less than mediocre—tiny, unshaded,
and exposed, as if carved out of the pine needle–packed ground as an afterthought. Indeed,
for a rugged, hilly setting that is rich in redwoods, cedar, manzanita, madrone, and various
pines, the overall absence of privacy throughout
the many loops is hugely disappointing. Still,
spacing between sites is not that bad, and if you
persevere you'll notice a few that take advantage
of protruding boulders for a little extra cover,
with 89 and 113 in this better category. There
are also several tent-only spots, though many are
grouped closely together. If you have the time, be
sure to drive the awe-inspiring Kings Canyon
Scenic Byway (closed in winter). Sentinel, near
the road's end, is a beautiful, wooded campground laid out around a small meadow.

BASICS

Operated By: National Park Service. **Open:** All
year. **Site Assignment:** First come, first served.
Registration: At entrance kiosk. **Fee:** $14, cash or
check (in addition to the park entrance fee). **Parking:** At site.

FACILITIES

Number of RV Sites: 93. **Number of Tent-
Only Sites:** 17. **Hookups:** None. **Each Site:** Pic-
nic table, fire grate, some sites have bearproof box.
Dump Station: No. **Laundry:** No. **Pay Phone:**
Yes. **Rest Rooms and Showers:** Yes. **Fuel:** No.
Propane: No. **Internal Roads:** Paved. **RV Ser-
vice:** No. **Market:** 31 mi. west in Sanger. **Restau-
rant:** In Grant Grove Village. **General Store:** Yes.

Vending: Yes. **Swimming:** No. **Playground:** No.
Other: Some wheelchair-accessible facilities.
Activities: Hiking, horseback riding, ranger-led
activities. **Nearby Attractions:** Giant Sequoia
National Monument; Sequoia National Park; Reed-
ley Opera House, Museum & Mennonite Quilting
Center. **Additional Information:** Fresno City &
County CVB, (800) 788-0836; Reedley District
Chamber of Commerce & Visitors Bureau, (559)
638-3548.

RESTRICTIONS

Pets: On 6 ft. leash; not allowed on trails. **Fires:** In
fire grates only. **Alcoholic Beverages:** Allowed at
site. **Vehicle Maximum Length:** 32 ft. **Other:**
14-day stay limit; no firearms; no food in vehicles
(bear habitat).

TO GET THERE

From Grant Grove Village drive 0.2 mi. north
on Hwy. 180. Turn left at the sign for Azalea
and a quick left again into the campground.

LA GRANGE
Fleming Meadows

81 Bonds Flat Rd., La Grange 95329. T: (209) 852-
2396 or marina (209) 852-2369;
www.donpedrolake.com.

🚐 ★★★★　　　　　　Δ ★★★

Beauty: ★★★★　　　　Site Privacy: ★★
Spaciousness: ★★★　　Quiet: ★★★
Security: ★★★★　　　　Cleanliness: ★★★
Insect Control: ★★★　　Facilities: ★★★★

In an area where summers are long and hot, Don
Pedro Lake, 35 miles east of Modesto, is a marvelous sight. The rolling hills around its multi-
pronged arms are speckled green with oaks and
awash in golden grass. The reservoir features 160
miles of shoreline, endowing Fleming Meadows
campground with no end of water vistas. There
is a trade-off for those splendid views; many of
the dirt-surfaced sites lack privacy and space. Of
the four loops, sites in the A group are better
shaded and seem a little more spacious. The optimum are A 24 and 25, which overlook the lake
and are framed by a large oak; A 34, a comfortable unit with pull-through parking; and A 58,
59, 61, 62, and 64. Boaters may also indulge in
primitive camping along the opposite shoreline.
Not that a boat is necessary to enjoy this huge

recreation area. Facilities include a sandy swimming lagoon that is six feet deep and two acres across, a softball field, horseshoe pits, volleyball, and no end of fishing opportunities. Boat service, fuel, a snack bar, and store are available at the marina.

BASICS

Operated By: Don Pedro Recreation Agency. **Open:** All year. **Site Assignment:** Reservations accepted w/ V, MC or check. **Registration:** At entrance booth. **Fee:** $12–$22, cash or V, MC. **Parking:** At site or designated area for walk-ins.

FACILITIES

Number of RV Sites: 231. **Number of Tent-Only Sites:** 36. **Hookups:** Water, electric (20, 30 amps), sewer. **Each Site:** Picnic table, fire grate, food storage box, some sites have a ramada. **Dump Station:** Yes. **Laundry:** Yes. **Pay Phone:** Yes. **Rest Rooms and Showers:** Yes. **Fuel:** No. **Propane:** Yes. **Internal Roads:** Paved. **RV Service:** No. **Market:** 8.5 mi south in La Grange. **Restaurant:** 8.5 mi. south in La Grange. **General Store:** Yes. **Vending:** Yes. **Swimming:** In lagoon. **Playground:** No. **Other:** Some wheelchair-accessible facilities, boat ramp, marina, beach. **Activities:** Fishing, waterskiing, motorboat & houseboat rentals, sailing, horseshoe pit, volleyball, softball. **Nearby Attractions:** Northern Mariposa County History Center in Coulterville; Turlock Lake State Recreation Area; Yosemite National Park. **Additional Information:** Coulterville Visitors Center, (209) 878-3074; Tuolumne County Visitors Bureau, (209) 533-4420 or (800) 446-1333.

RESTRICTIONS

Pets: Not allowed. **Fires:** In fire grates only. **Alcoholic Beverages:** Allowed. **Vehicle Maximum Length:** 50 ft. **Other:** 14-day stay limit; no fireworks.

TO GET THERE

From La Grange on Hwy. 132 drive 5 mi. north on La Grange Rd./J59. Turn right on Bonds Flat Rd. and proceed for another 3.3 mi. to the park entrance on the left.

LA HONDA
Portola Redwoods State Park

9000 Portola State Park Rd. Box F, La Honda 94020. T: (650) 948-9098 or reservations (800) 444-7275; F: (650) 948-0137; www.cal-parks.ca.gov or www.reserveamerica.com.

🚐 ★★★   ▲ ★★★★

Beauty: ★★★★
Spaciousness: ★★★
Security: ★★
Insect Control: ★★★
Site Privacy: ★★★
Quiet: ★★★★
Cleanliness: ★★★
Facilities: ★★

As you make your way along the access road to Portola Redwoods State Park you'll enjoy some breathtaking valley views. Some may feel that is small reward for the clutch-grinding, white-knuckle drive from one hairpin curve to another. But on finally arriving at the park you may have the entire campground to yourself, especially if visiting midweek or out of season. The three small loops are deftly arranged across a hilly canyon to maximize the usable space. That is a good thing, as aside from the fallen giants that border some of the fern-dappled sites, screening is minimal. Still, this is a handsomely forested camp, with ancient moss-covered sentinels surrounded by their smaller, second-growth descendants, as well as oaks and azaleas. Site 28 overlooks a creek and is, with neighboring 29, among the better ones for privacy. Numbers 37 and 39 are attractive, too, though on the small side. Pull-through slots are available but drivers of long rigs should think twice about trying to navigate the goat-path of a road up to Portola.

BASICS

Operated By: California Dept. of Parks & Recreation. **Open:** Mar.–Nov. **Site Assignment:** Reservations accepted w/ V, MC, D. **Registration:** At entrance booth or visitor center. **Fee:** $12, cash or CA check. **Parking:** At site.

FACILITIES

Number of RV Sites: 46. **Number of Tent-Only Sites:** 14. **Hookups:** None. **Each Site:** Picnic table, fire grate, food storage box. **Dump Station:** No. **Laundry:** No. **Pay Phone:** Yes. **Rest Rooms and Showers:** Yes. **Fuel:** No. **Propane:** No. **Internal Roads:** Paved. **RV Service:** No. **Market:** 25 mi. east in Palo Alto. **Restaurant:** 25 mi. east in Palo Alto. **General Store:** No. **Vending:**

No. **Swimming:** No. **Playground:** No. **Activities:** Hiking, ranger-led activities in summer, exploring redwood forests. **Nearby Attractions:** Palo Alto museums; state beaches along the coast; Mission Santa Clara de Asis & various museums in Santa Clara; San Jose museums, architecture & zoo. **Additional Information:** Palo Alto Chamber of Commerce, (650) 324-3121; Santa Clara CVB, (408) 224-9660 or (800) 272-6822; San Jose CVB, (888) SAN-JOSE.

RESTRICTIONS

Pets: On 6 ft. leash; not allowed on trails or in creeks. **Fires:** In fire grates only. **Alcoholic Beverages:** Allowed at site. **Vehicle Maximum Length:** 24 ft. **Other:** 14-day stay limit from Apr. 1–Oct. 31; no loaded firearms; no wood gathering; no bicycling; no horseback riding; no fishing.

TO GET THERE

From Palo Alto drive south on I-280 and take the Page Mill Rd. Exit. Turn right (south) and drive 8.8 mi., straight through the stop sign, to Alpine Rd. Follow this road for 3.5 mi., then turn left on Portola State Park Rd. The park entrance is 3.1 mi. ahead.

LAKE ELSINORE
El Cariso North Campground

Hwy. 74/Ortega Hwy., Lake Elsinore 92530. T: (909) 736-1811; F: (909) 736-3002; www.r5.fs.fed.us/cleveland; mailroomr5cleveland@fs.fed.us.

🚐 ★★★	🏕 ★★★
Beauty: ★★★	Site Privacy: ★★
Spaciousness: ★★★	Quiet: ★
Security: ★★★	Cleanliness: ★★★
Insect Control: ★★	Facilities: ★

This is a small roadside campground in the Cleveland National Forest, conveniently located along Hwy. 74, just ten miles west of I-15. It is a primitive facility with a single loop passing through a grove of aged oak trees and a sprinkling of pines. Sites are well shaded and deep, largely level, and equipped with dirt tent pads. Because Hwy. 74 connects to I-5 on the coast there tends to be a good deal of traffic flowing past El Cariso, making spots 10, 14, 19, 21, and 24, positioned toward the rear of the campground, the most desirable. The meandering creek (dry most of the year) that bisects the camp

has been found to be the habitat of the endangered Southwestern Arroyo Toad. To protect it during its breeding cycle El Cariso North is closed from Apr. 1 through Sept. 30. A public telephone is available just across the street at the national forest fire station.

BASICS

Operated By: Cleveland National Forest, Trabuco Ranger District. **Open:** From Oct. 1–Mar. 31. **Site Assignment:** First come, first served. **Registration:** At entrance kiosk. **Fee:** $15, cash or CA check. **Parking:** At site.

FACILITIES

Number of RV Sites: 24. **Number of Tent-Only Sites:** 0. **Hookups:** None. **Each Site:** Picnic table, fire grate, barbecue grill. **Dump Station:** No. **Laundry:** No. **Pay Phone:** No. **Rest Rooms and Showers:** Pit toilets, no showers. **Fuel:** No. **Propane:** No. **Internal Roads:** Paved. **RV Service:** No. **Market:** 1 mi. west in El Cariso Village. **Restaurant:** 10 mi. east in Lake Elsinore. **General Store:** No. **Vending:** No. **Swimming:** No. **Playground:** No. **Activities:** Hiking, boating, fishing. **Nearby Attractions:** Lake Elsinore, Orange Empire Railway Museum in Perris, Ortega Falls. **Additional Information:** Lake Elsinore Valley Chamber of Commerce, (909) 245-8848.

RESTRICTIONS

Pets: On 6 ft. leash. **Fires:** In fire grates only. **Alcoholic Beverages:** Allowed. **Vehicle Maximum Length:** 35 ft. **Other:** 14-day stay limit.

TO GET THERE

From I-15 in Lake Elsinore drive 10 mi. west on Hwy. 74. The campground is on the right.

LAKEPORT
Clear Lake State Park

5300 Soda Bay Rd., Kelseyville 95451. T: (707) 279-4293 or reservations (800) 444-7275; www.cal-parks.ca.gov or www.reserveamerica.com.

🚐 ★★★★	🏕 ★★★★
Beauty: ★★★★	Site Privacy: ★★★
Spaciousness: ★★★	Quiet: ★★★
Security: ★★★★	Cleanliness: ★★★
Insect Control: ★★	Facilities: ★★★

Clear Lake is one of the largest freshwater lakes in California. The angling in its shimmering blue-green waters is so good, particularly for bass, bluegill, and catfish, that you just might forget for a moment the other liquids for which this wine-producing region is renowned. There is an appealingly wild, untamed air to the forested hills around the lake, and the park takes full advantage of that by dispersing its campground into four zones ranging from lake and creekside on up into the higher woodland. The prime water sites are 58–60 in the Kelsey Creek loop, where plant life is highlighted by manzanita, willow, cottonwood, and black walnut. The opposite side of that loop overlooks a creek (very buggy in spring) and numbers 29, 31, 32, 38, 39, 41, 42, 44, and 45 are gratifyingly spacious and private. Pines, oak, and sycamore are the dominant tree species at the two Bayview circuits up the road, with 110–112, shady and overlooking the lake, ideal for small RVs. Cole Creek, close and parallel to the access road near the park entrance, is the least attractive of the camping areas.

BASICS

Operated By: California Dept. of Parks & Recreation. **Open:** All year. **Site Assignment:** Reservations accepted w/ V, MC, D. **Registration:** At entrance booth. **Fee:** $12, cash or CA check. **Parking:** At site.

FACILITIES

Number of RV Sites: 145. **Number of Tent-Only Sites:** 2. **Hookups:** None. **Each Site:** Picnic table, fire grate. **Dump Station:** Yes. **Laundry:** No. **Pay Phone:** Yes. **Rest Rooms and Showers:** Yes. **Fuel:** No. **Propane:** No. **Internal Roads:** Paved. **RV Service:** No. **Market:** 4 mi. south in Kelseyville. **Restaurant:** 4 mi. south in Kelseyville. **General Store:** No. **Vending:** No. **Swimming:** In Clear Lake. **Playground:** No. **Other:** Some wheelchair-accessible facilities, boat ramp, visitor center. **Activities:** Fishing, hiking, waterskiing, birding, kayak rentals. **Nearby Attractions:** Lakeport County Museum in Lakeport; Clear Lake Queen, Outrageous Waters Water Park & Fun Center & Anderson Marsh State Historic Park in Clearlake. **Additional Information:** Lakeport Chamber of Commerce, (707) 263-5092; Clearlake Chamber of Commerce, (707) 994-3600.

RESTRICTIONS

Pets: On 6 ft. leash. **Fires:** In fire grates only. **Alcoholic Beverages:** Allowed at site. **Vehicle Maximum Length:** 35 ft. **Other:** 14-day stay limit from Apr. 1–Oct. 1; no firearms; no wood gathering.

TO GET THERE

From Lakeport head 8 mi. south on Hwy. 29 to Kelseyville. Turn left on Merritt Rd. which leads into Gaddy Ln. Drive 3.5 mi., then turn right on Soda Bay and continue for 1 mi. to the park entrance on the left.

LASSEN VOLCANIC NATIONAL PARK
Butte Lake

Butte Lake Rd., Mineral 96063. T: (530) 595-4444; F: (530) 595-3262; www.nps.gov/lavo.

🚐 ★★★★   ▲ ★★★★

Beauty: ★★★★	Site Privacy: ★★★
Spaciousness: ★★★	Quiet: ★★★
Security: ★★★★	Cleanliness: ★★★
Insect Control: ★★★	Facilities: ★

The remote location of Butte Lake campground provides a tranquil respite from the crowds of sightseers thronging to Manzanita Lake, Summit Lakes, and such main attractions of Lassen Volcanic National Park as Bumpass Hell and the Sulfur Works. While only one site, B-1, actually enjoys a view of the stunning Butte Lake, the campground's proximity to the water, to a cinder peak, and to several fine hikes, makes it a winner. Roomy sites, evenly positioned across a slightly undulating hillside, are partially shaded by lodgepole pines and a smattering of ponderosas. As is typical in national park venues, few of them offer much privacy. Of the A and B circuits, the second area has the larger sites and more pull-through parking: best bets, in addition to B-1, are B-3, which overlooks the lava flow field, and the partly screened B-55. A pay phone, gasoline, and a general store are available at Old Station, 17 miles west on Hwy. 44. Butte Creek, a national forest camp on the dirt and gravel access road to Butte Lake, is a passable alternative when the latter is full or closed.

BASICS

Operated By: National Park Service. **Open:** June 16 to Sept. 25, weather permitting. **Site Assignment:** First come, first served. **Registration:** At entrance kiosk. **Fee:** $10, cash or check (in addition to the park entrance fee). **Parking:** At site.

FACILITIES

Number of RV Sites: 42. **Number of Tent-Only Sites:** 0. **Hookups:** None. **Each Site:** Picnic table, fire grate, bearproof box. **Dump Station:** No. **Laundry:** No. **Pay Phone:** No. **Rest Rooms and Showers:** Vault toilets, no showers. **Fuel:** No. **Propane:** No. **Internal Roads:** Gravel, good condition. **RV Service:** No. **Market:** 48 mi. east in Susanville. **Restaurant:** 48 mi. east in Susanville. **General Store:** No. **Vending:** No. **Swimming:** In Butte Lake. **Playground:** No. **Other:** Some wheelchair-accessible facilities, boat launch. **Activities:** Hiking, fishing, boating (no motors), birding. **Nearby Attractions:** Hat Creek Recreation Area in Old Station; Lassen Historical Museum & Railroad Depot in Susanville. **Additional Information:** Burney Chamber of Commerce, (530) 335-2111.

RESTRICTIONS

Pets: On 6 ft. leash; not allowed on trails. **Fires:** In fire grates only. **Alcoholic Beverages:** Allowed at site. **Vehicle Maximum Length:** 35 ft. **Other:** 14-day stay limit; no loaded firearms; no wood gathering.

TO GET THERE

From Old Station at the junction of Hwys. 44 and 89 drive 11 mi. east on Hwy. 44. Turn south (right) on Butte Lake Rd. and follow this dirt road for 6.5 mi. to the campground entrance on the right.

LASSEN VOLCANIC NATIONAL PARK
Manzanita Lake

Lassen Park Rd., Mineral 96063. T: (530) 595-4444; F: (530) 595-3262; www.nps.gov/lavo.

🚐 ★★★   ⛺ ★★★

Beauty: ★★★★	Site Privacy: ★★★
Spaciousness: ★★★	Quiet: ★★
Security: ★★★	Cleanliness: ★★★
Insect Control: ★★★	Facilities: ★★★

Lassen Volcanic National Park was established as a monument in 1907, and upgraded to national park status nine years later. An astoundingly beautiful chunk of the Cascade Mountain range, the park has hundreds of miles of hiking trails, several geothermal attractions, an abundance of wildlife, and a handful of excellent campgrounds. Of those, Manzanita Lake is one of the best, with its namesake body of glimmering water abutting it and snow-capped Mt. Lassen hovering above. Just five miles from Lassen's north entrance, the camp enjoys an illusion of privacy that stems in part from its thick concentration of various conifers, as well as from the pull-through and back-in sites being well-dispersed through a series of many loops. The shade provided by those evergreens keeps things cool and on the dark side, but tenters will find comfort in the spongy layer of pine needles that has accumulated on the forest floor. Best time to visit is Sept. to mid-Oct., when the park sees fewer visitors. Just remember, at an altitude of 5,890 feet, Manzanita Lake can be chilly most anytime of year: Extra layers of clothing and rain gear are advised. And use the bearproof boxes to protect your vehicle from a furry intruder. Many sites are wheelchair accessible.

BASICS

Operated By: National Park Service. **Open:** May 25 to Sept. 25 w/ water, then without water until snow requires closure. **Site Assignment:** First come, first served. **Registration:** Self-registration at entrance kiosk. **Fee:** $14, cash or check (in addition to the park entrance fee). **Parking:** At site.

FACILITIES

Number of RV Sites: 179. **Number of Tent-Only Sites:** 0. **Hookups:** None. **Each Site:** Picnic table, fire ring, barbecue grill, bearproof box. **Dump Station:** Yes. **Laundry:** Yes. **Pay Phone:** Yes. **Rest Rooms and Showers:** Yes. **Fuel:** No. **Propane:** Yes. **Internal Roads:** Paved. **RV Service:** No. **Market:** 50 mi. west in Redding. **Restaurant:** 19 mi. west in Shingletown. **General Store:** Yes. **Vending:** Yes. **Swimming:** In Manzanita Lake. **Playground:** No. **Other:** Some wheelchair-accessible facilities, boat launch, Loomis Museum. **Activities:** Hiking, fishing, boating (no motors), bike rentals, ranger-led programs. **Nearby Attractions:** Westwood Museum & Paul Bunyan & Babe the Blue Ox Statues; Lassen National Scenic Byway (Hwys. 89-44-36); Lake Almanor; Hat Creek Recreation Area in Old Station. **Additional Information:** Burney Chamber of Commerce, (530) 335-2111.

RESTRICTIONS

Pets: On 6 ft. leash; not allowed on trails. **Fires:** In fire rings only. **Alcoholic Beverages:** Allowed at site. **Vehicle Maximum Length:** 35 ft. **Other:** 14-day stay limit; no firearms; no fireworks.

TO GET THERE

From Redding drive 48 mi. east on Hwy. 44 to the junction w/ Hwy. 89. Drive 1 mi. south on Hwy. 89 (which becomes Lassen Park Rd. once you pass the park entrance station). Turn right onto the campground access road and continue for 0.5 mi. to the campground.

LAVA BEDS NATIONAL MONUMENT

Indian Well

Lava Beds National Monument Rd., Tulelake 96134. T: (530) 667-2282, ext. 230; F: (530) 667-2737; www.nps.gov/labe.

🚐 ★★★   ⛺ ★★★

Beauty: ★★★★   Site Privacy: ★★★
Spaciousness: ★★★   Quiet: ★★★
Security: ★★★   Cleanliness: ★★★★
Insect Control: ★★★★   Facilities: ★★

At just over 46,000 acres, Lava Beds National Monument may not seem a very large preserve. It manages, though, to pack a great deal within the confines of its boundaries. Located 55 miles south of Klamath Falls, Oregon, this high desert terrain has been dramatically painted by lava runoff from the Medicine Lake volcano, and a large swath of its rugged, rocky tufa–terrain saw the final curtain drawn on the Modoc war. Most dramatically, there are over 380 lava tube caves in the park, with two dozen developed for easy— and often thrilling—exploration. Most of those are a short drive from the campground, which is divided into a pair of loops. Cinder and spatter cones mark the approach to camp, and such desert scrub as sage brush, rabbit brush, bitter brush, and mountain mahogany contribute a hint of green to the bituminous landscape. Aged, gnarly junipers scattered over the undulating lava meadow shed shade on a few fortunate sites, such as the roomy, recessed B 25 and both A 5 and A 6, the latter two also being graced with expansive valley views. At 4,770 feet of elevation, nights at Indian Well can be quite windy and cold from late Oct. through early Apr. Keep an eye out for kangaroo rats after dark.

BASICS

Operated By: National Park Service. **Open:** All year. **Site Assignment:** First come, first served. **Registration:** At entrance kiosk. **Fee:** $10, cash or check. **Parking:** At site.

FACILITIES

Number of RV Sites: 43. **Number of Tent-Only Sites:** 0. **Hookups:** None. **Each Site:** Picnic table, fire ring, barbecue grill. **Dump Station:** No. **Laundry:** No. **Pay Phone:** Yes. **Rest Rooms and Showers:** Seasonal flush toilets, vault toilets, no showers. **Fuel:** No. **Propane:** No. **Internal Roads:** Paved. **RV Service:** No. **Market:** 14 mi. south in Tionesta (basic supplies). **Restaurant:** 30 mi. north in Tulelake. **General Store:** No. **Vending:** Yes. **Swimming:** No. **Playground:** No. **Other:** Some wheelchair-accessible facilities, visitor center. **Activities:** Hiking, lava tube dwelling, birding. **Nearby Attractions:** Tule Lake & Klamath National Wildlife Refuges; Medicine Lake Recreation Area; Petroglyph Section at the northeast entrance of Lava Beds National Monument. **Additional Information:** Tulelake Chamber of Commerce, (530) 667-5312.

RESTRICTIONS

Pets: On 6 ft. leash; not allowed on trails. **Fires:** In fire rings only. **Alcoholic Beverages:** Allowed at site. **Vehicle Maximum Length:** 30 ft. **Other:** 14-day stay limit; no loaded firearms; wood gathering only in designated areas.

TO GET THERE

From Tulelake drive 26 mi. south on Hwy. 139. Turn right (west) on Tionesta Rd. and continue for 2.7 mi. Turn right again on Lava Beds National Monument Rd. and proceed for 14 mi. The campground entrance is to the right, directly across the visitor center.

LEE VINING

Aspen Grove

Hwy. 120, Lee Vining 93541. T: (760) 932-5451; F: (760) 932-5458.

🚐 ★★★   ⛺ ★★★

Beauty: ★★★★   Site Privacy: ★★★
Spaciousness: ★★★   Quiet: ★★★
Security: ★★   Cleanliness: ★★★
Insect Control: ★★★   Facilities: ★

There is an enchanting quality to the raw, mountainous beauty of Aspen Grove, particularly in spring, just after its many aspens have leafed out into a fluttering luminescence. Jeffrey pines, sage, and other high desert scrub compose the complement of vegetation at this creekside, county-operated camp, which is just five miles west of Lee Vining along the Tioga Rd. At 7,500 feet elevation, you'll find breathtaking views of the snow-laced Sierra Nevada peaks all around, with Mono Dome, at 10,622 feet, dominating the scene. Some of the dirt-packed, somewhat rocky sites are on uneven ground, others (most notably, those by the creek) are squeezed for space. The lion's share, though, are delightfully large and very recessed. Among the better choices for RVs are 22, 23, and 25, facing the creek. Great tenting spots include 54, also by the creek; 18, hidden among pines and horsetail grass; and, away from the water, 37 and 39, both being very private. Similarly rustic sites are available at Big Bend campground, half a mile east.

BASICS

Operated By: Mono County Building & Parks Dept. **Open:** May through Oct., weather permitting. **Site Assignment:** First come, first served. **Registration:** At entrance kiosk. **Fee:** $7, cash only. **Parking:** At site.

FACILITIES

Number of RV Sites: 58. **Number of Tent-Only Sites:** 0. **Hookups:** None. **Each Site:** Picnic table, makeshift fire ring. **Dump Station:** No. **Laundry:** No. **Pay Phone:** No. **Rest Rooms and Showers:** Pit & portable toilets, no showers. **Fuel:** No. **Propane:** No. **Internal Roads:** Dirt, rocky & bumpy. **RV Service:** No. **Market:** 6 mi. northeast in Lee Vining. **Restaurant:** 6 mi. northeast in Lee Vining. **General Store:** No. **Vending:** No. **Swimming:** No. **Playground:** No. **Activities:** Fishing, hiking, photography. **Nearby Attractions:** Yosemite National Park; Mono Lake Tufa State Reserve in Lee Vining; Bodie State Historic Park in Bridgeport. **Additional Information:** Lee Vining Chamber of Commerce, (760) 647-6629; Yosemite Area Traveler Information, (209) 723-3153.

RESTRICTIONS

Pets: On 10 ft. leash. **Fires:** In fire rings only. **Alcoholic Beverages:** Allowed. **Vehicle Maximum Length:** 40 ft. **Other:** No stay limit.

TO GET THERE

Just south of Lee Vining on US 395 head west on Hwy. 120. Drive 3.2 mi. and turn left onto Poole Power Plant Rd. Make a quick right onto the campground access road and continue for 1.5 mi. to the entrance on the left.

LEE VINING
Ellery Lake

Hwy. 120, Lee Vining 93541. T: (760) 873-2400 or (760) 647-3044; F: (760) 647-3046; www.r5.fs.fed.us/inyo.

🚐 ★★★★   ⛺ ★★★

Beauty: ★★★★★	Site Privacy: ★★
Spaciousness: ★★	Quiet: ★★
Security: ★★★★	Cleanliness: ★★★
Insect Control: ★	Facilities: ★

There is only one site here with a view of the camp's namesake Ellery Lake, lucky 13, a walk-in. Don't let that, or the overall lack of privacy and elbowroom, nettle you, though. This is an exquisite environment, surrounded by the jagged, snow-iced mountain peaks of Lee Vining Canyon, with a small creek gurgling by. The ground is level, parking slips paved, and a smattering of lodgepole pines and low-lying willows vie with boulders and campers for ground space. You can fish for trout in the creek or, better still, the nearby lake. The campground, which is at an altitude of 9,500 feet, is also a fine base for day trips into Yosemite National Park's high country, its east entrance being a scant three miles away. Nearly half the sites are walk-ins for tenters, with access to them cutting directly through other sites, an unfortunate sacrifice in privacy. The better spots are 9–14, shielded from Hwy. 120 in a nook behind talus rock. A general store is 0.5 miles to the west.

BASICS

Operated By: Sierra Recreation, concessionaire. **Open:** June through Oct., weather permitting. **Site Assignment:** First come, first served. **Registration:** At entrance kiosk. **Fee:** $11, cash or check. **Parking:** At site.

FACILITIES

Number of RV Sites: 6. **Number of Tent-Only Sites:** 6. **Hookups:** None. **Each Site:** Picnic table, fire grate. **Dump Station:** No. **Laundry:** No. **Pay**

Phone: No. **Rest Rooms and Showers:** Vault toilets, no showers. **Fuel:** No. **Propane:** No. **Internal Roads:** Paved. **RV Service:** No. **Market:** 11 mi. east in Lee Vining. **Restaurant:** 11 mi. east in Lee Vining. **General Store:** No. **Vending:** No. **Swimming:** No. **Playground:** No. **Other:** Some wheelchair-accessible facilities. **Activities:** Fishing, hiking, photography. **Nearby Attractions:** Yosemite National Park; Mono Lake Tufa State Reserve in Lee Vining; Bodie State Historic Park in Bridgeport. **Additional Information:** Lee Vining Chamber of Commerce, (760) 647-6629; Yosemite Area Traveler Information, (209) 723-3153.

RESTRICTIONS

Pets: On leash. **Fires:** In fire grates only. **Alcoholic Beverages:** Allowed. **Vehicle Maximum Length:** 30 ft. **Other:** 14-day stay limit.

TO GET THERE

Just south of Lee Vining on US 395, head west on Hwy. 120. Drive 10 mi. and turn left into the campground.

LEWISTON
Cooper Gulch

Trinity Dam Blvd., Lewiston 96052. T: (530) 623-2121; F: (530) 623-6010; www.r5.fs.fed.us/shastatrinity.

🚐 ★★★★   ▲ ★★★

Beauty: ★★★★	Site Privacy: ★★
Spaciousness: ★★	Quiet: ★★★
Security: ★★★★	Cleanliness: ★★★★
Insect Control: ★★★	Facilities: ★

The first thing you may notice about Cooper Gulch is the high tension wires that run directly over the campground. That impression won't linger. Not when you see how close the five level sites are to the edge of Lewiston Lake. That they are also close to each other and lack privacy is not really a problem, either, since almost everybody devotes their attention to the rippling water just a few steps away. Bring your hammock and anchor it to a couple of the pines and incense cedars that shade this charming spot. And don't forget your canoe or kayak, which can be launched from the small dirt ramp right in camp. It is hard to go wrong with any of these medium-small, pine needle–carpeted sites, but 4 is closest to the lake and 5, sheltered by oaks, is

the most private. Amazingly, a host occupies one of the five coveted slots in summer.

BASICS

Operated By: Hodge Management, concessionaire. **Open:** Apr. through Nov. **Site Assignment:** First come, first served. **Registration:** At entrance kiosk. **Fee:** $11, cash or check. **Parking:** At site.

FACILITIES

Number of RV Sites: 5. **Number of Tent-Only Sites:** 0. **Hookups:** None. **Each Site:** Picnic table, fire grate. **Dump Station:** No. **Laundry:** No. **Pay Phone:** No. **Rest Rooms and Showers:** Vault toilets, no showers. **Fuel:** No. **Propane:** No. **Internal Roads:** Paved. **RV Service:** No. **Market:** 4 mi. south in Lewiston. **Restaurant:** 4 mi. south in Lewiston. **General Store:** No. **Vending:** No. **Swimming:** No. **Playground:** No. **Other:** Some wheelchair-accessible facilities, small boat launch. **Activities:** Fishing, boating, hiking, birding. **Nearby Attractions:** Weaverville museums, National Historic District & Joss House State Historic Park; Historic Trinity River Bridge in Lewiston. **Additional Information:** Weaverville Chamber of Commerce, (530) 623-3840; Trinity County Chamber of Commerce, (530) 623-6101 or (800) 487-4648.

RESTRICTIONS

Pets: On 6 ft. leash. **Fires:** In fire grates only. **Alcoholic Beverages:** Allowed. **Vehicle Maximum Length:** 16 ft. **Other:** 14-day stay limit.

TO GET THERE

From Redding drive 26 mi. west on Hwy. 299 to Trinity Dam Blvd./Lewiston Exit. Turn right and continue for 8.6 mi. to the campground entrance on the right.

LIVERMORE
Del Valle Regional Park

7000 Del Valle Rd., Livermore 94550. T: (510) 636-1684 or reservations (510) 562-2267; www. ebparks.org.

🚐 ★★★★   ▲ ★★★★

Beauty: ★★★★	Site Privacy: ★★★
Spaciousness: ★★★	Quiet: ★★★
Security: ★★★★	Cleanliness: ★★
Insect Control: ★★★	Facilities: ★★★

Del Valle Regional Park is a quiet, unassuming place that just happens to be one of the more beautiful of the many parklands in the immediate Bay Area. A part of the Diablo Range, this rugged canyon setting consists of grassy hills, meadows punctuated by thick concentrations of oak, eucalyptus, knob cone pine, and sycamore, and at its heart a narrow reservoir lake that stretches five miles from end to end. Windsurfers and sailing enthusiasts take to the water like a child to chocolate, with motorboats restricted to a maximum speed of ten miles per hour. Fishing conditions are only average, despite regular plantings of rainbow trout. There are no views of the lake from the campground, but roomy, grass-covered sites are spaced well apart over a double loop, helping to compensate for that handicap. Birders will find pleasure in the many species that make this territory their home, including several wild turkeys and a pair of peacocks. The park loses points, though, for haphazard maintenance: during a recent tour we found sites littered with above average amounts of plastic, paper, bottle caps, and cigarette butts. The open-air restrooms are also in urgent need of an overhaul.

BASICS

Operated By: East Bay Regional Park District. **Open:** All year. **Site Assignment:** Reservations accepted w/ V, MC. **Registration:** At entrance booth. **Fee:** $15–$18, cash or V, MC. **Parking:** At site.

FACILITIES

Number of RV Sites: 150. **Number of Tent-Only Sites:** 0. **Hookups:** Water, sewer. **Each Site:** Picnic table, fire grate. **Dump Station:** Yes. **Laundry:** No. **Pay Phone:** Yes. **Rest Rooms and Showers:** Yes. **Fuel:** No. **Propane:** No. **Internal Roads:** Paved. **RV Service:** No. **Market:** 9.5 mi. north in Livermore. **Restaurant:** 9.5 mi. north in Livermore. **General Store:** Yes, in summer. **Vending:** No. **Swimming:** In designated areas of Lake Del Valle. **Playground:** No. **Other:** Some wheelchair-accessible facilities, marina, boat launch. **Activities:** Hiking, fishing, horseback riding, bicycling, boat & sailboard rentals, windsurfing, sailing, nature programs. **Nearby Attractions:** Mission San Jose & Ardenwood Historic Farm in Fremont; winery tours. **Additional Information:** Livermore Chamber of Commerce, (925) 447-1606.

RESTRICTIONS

Pets: On leash, $1 fee. **Fires:** In fire grates only. **Alcoholic Beverages:** Allowed at site & picnic

areas. **Vehicle Maximum Length:** 35 ft. **Other:** 14-day stay limit; no firearms.

TO GET THERE

From Livermore and Hwy. 84 head south on South Livermore Ave., which changes into Tesla Rd. After 2.4 mi. turn right on Mines Rd. Continue for 3.6 mi. and bear right on Del Valle Park Rd. The park entrance is 3.2 mi. ahead.

LONE PINE
Whitney Portal

Whitney Portal Rd., Lone Pine 93545. T: (760) 876-6200 or reservations (877) 444-6777; F: (760) 876-6202; www.r5.fs.fed.us/inyo or www.reserveusa.com.

🚐 ★★★★	🏕 ★★★★
Beauty: ★★★★★	Site Privacy: ★★★
Spaciousness: ★★★	Quiet: ★★★
Security: ★★★	Cleanliness: ★★★
Insect Control: ★★★	Facilities: ★★

Even if you don't plan to hike Mt. Whitney, which, at 14,495 feet, is the highest peak in the lower 48 states, this campground is a worthwhile, breathtaking retreat. From its rocky, pine-shrouded sites, up to the aspen-fringed trailhead, from the many streams noisily cascading down the mountain to the saw-toothed, jaw-like peaks that hover menacingly above, this is one spectacular, picture-perfect scene. As you lounge by your tent at 8,000 feet elevation, low-floating clouds seem close enough to reach out and grab. Boulders provide respectable privacy between closely-grouped sites, and shade is derived from Jeffrey and ponderosa pines, as well as mountain mahogany. The most secluded sites are 8 and 9, flanked by large slabs of granite. Avoid the spots just below Whitney Portal Rd., which pick up more traffic noise than the others, and try to visit on a weekday, when there are fewer mountain climbers in camp. The trailhead picnic area is an Arcadian delight.

BASICS

Operated By: American Land & Leisure, concessionaire. **Open:** Mid-May through mid-Oct., weather permitting. **Site Assignment:** Reservations accepted w/ V, MC, D. **Registration:** At entrance kiosk. **Fee:** $14, cash or check. **Parking:** At site.

FACILITIES

Number of RV Sites: 43. **Number of Tent-Only Sites:** 0. **Hookups:** None. **Each Site:** Picnic table, fire grate or barbecue grill, some sites have bearproof box. **Dump Station:** No. **Laundry:** No. **Pay Phone:** No. **Rest Rooms and Showers:** Chemical toilets, no showers. **Fuel:** No. **Propane:** No. **Internal Roads:** Paved, windy. **RV Service:** No. **Market:** 12 mi. east in Lone Pine. **Restaurant:** 12 mi. east in Lone Pine. **General Store:** Yes. **Vending:** No. **Swimming:** No. **Playground:** No. **Other:** Some wheelchair-accessible facilities, snack bar. **Activities:** Hiking, fishing, photography. **Nearby Attractions:** Manzanar National Historic Site & Eastern California Museum in Independence; Diaz Lake Recreation Area in Lone Pine; Mount Whitney. **Additional Information:** Lone Pine Chamber of Commerce, (760) 876-4444; Independence Chamber of Commerce, (760) 878-0084.

RESTRICTIONS

Pets: On leash. **Fires:** In fire grates only. **Alcoholic Beverages:** Allowed. **Vehicle Maximum Length:** 32 ft. **Other:** 7-day stay limit.

TO GET THERE

From Lone Pine on US 395 drive 12 mi. west on Whitney Portal Rd. to the campground on the left.

LOS BAÑOS

San Luis Reservoir State Recreation Area, San Luis Creek Campground

31426 Gonzaga Rd., Gustine 95322. T: (209) 826-1196 or reservations (800) 444-7275; F: (209) 826-0284; www.cal-parks.ca.gov or www.reserveamerica.com.

🚐 ★★★★	🏕 ★★★
Beauty: ★★★★	Site Privacy: ★★
Spaciousness: ★★★	Quiet: ★★★★
Security: ★★★★	Cleanliness: ★★★★
Insect Control: ★★★	Facilities: ★★★

San Luis Reservoir lies in the heart of California's valley region, just off of I-5, about 40 miles south of Modesto. Summer starts early in these parts, with the sun scorching the neighboring hills brown by Apr. Water sports are therefore the logical activity of choice and fortunately there is usu-ally enough H_2O in the reservoir to satisfy boaters and swimmers throughout the hot season. Of the three campgrounds in the park, only San Luis Creek on the O'Neill Forebay has hookups. It is a grassy, peaceful camp with many of its fairly exposed, roomy sites set close to the shore. Adding a splash of color to the setting are eucalyptus trees, pines, and sycamores. The latter are still too small to cast much shade but they are just large enough to attract larks and other song birds. The only off-key note is the presence of power lines looming above a few of the sites. Showers are available across the street at Basalt Campground.

BASICS

Operated By: California Dept. of Parks & Recreation. **Open:** All year. **Site Assignment:** Reservations accepted w/ V, MC, D. **Registration:** At entrance booth. **Fee:** $14, cash or CA check. **Parking:** At site.

FACILITIES

Number of RV Sites: 53. **Number of Tent-Only Sites:** 0. **Hookups:** Water, electric (30 amps). **Each Site:** Picnic table, fire grate. **Dump Station:** Yes. **Laundry:** No. **Pay Phone:** Yes. **Rest Rooms and Showers:** Pit toilets, no showers. **Fuel:** No. **Propane:** No. **Internal Roads:** Paved. **RV Service:** No. **Market:** 15 mi. east in Los Baños. **Restaurant:** 15 mi. east in Los Baños. **General Store:** No. **Vending:** No. **Swimming:** In the reservoir. **Playground:** No. **Other:** Some wheelchair-accessible facilities. **Activities:** Fishing, boating, birding, hiking. **Nearby Attractions:** Modesto museums; Mission San Juan Bautista; Los Baños Great Valley Grasslands State Park & Wildlife Area. **Additional Information:** Santa Nella Chamber of Commerce, (209) 826-8282; Los Baños Chamber of Commerce, (209) 826-2495.

RESTRICTIONS

Pets: On 6 ft. leash. **Fires:** In fire grates only. **Alcoholic Beverages:** Allowed at site. **Vehicle Maximum Length:** 30 ft. **Other:** 14-day stay limit from May 1– Sept. 30; no firearms; no wood gathering.

TO GET THERE

From Gilroy on US 101 follow Hwy. 152 east for 36 mi. Turn left into the park. The campground entrance is 1 mi. ahead to the left.

LUCIA
Kirk Creek

Hwy. 1, Lucia 93921. T: (831) 385-5434; F: (831) 385-0628; www.r5.fs.fed.us/lospadres.

🚐 ★★★　　　　　　　🅰 ★★★★

Beauty: ★★★★　　　　Site Privacy: ★★★
Spaciousness: ★★　　　Quiet: ★★★
Security: ★★★　　　　Cleanliness: ★★★
Insect Control: ★★　　 Facilities: ★

This is a rough-cut, wild-looking campground with a grassy, unmanicured feel to its sites. One might even say "bucolic," a quality that is entirely appropriate given its location, just off Hwy. 1 along the unspoiled Big Sur coast. Coastal chaparral and shrubs provide excellent screening for sites that are mostly small, unshaded and tend to tilt toward the ocean. That the handsome national forest land slopes steeply water-ward has an upside in the auditorium effect of projecting the roar of the surf into camp—thus drowning out the din of passing traffic—and endowing most slots with commanding views of the Pacific. Best for privacy along the figure-8 loop are 8, 9, 21, 22, and 11, with the latter located next to the beach. Be sure to avoid tiny number 1, which picks up too much road noise. The only abrasive chord is struck by the nightly fee of $16, a hefty sum given the Spartan facilities. Golden poppies color the hillside in spring.

BASICS
Operated By: Parks Management, concessionaire. **Open:** All year. **Site Assignment:** First come, first served. **Registration:** At entrance kiosk. **Fee:** $16, cash or check. **Parking:** At site.

FACILITIES
Number of RV Sites: 32. **Number of Tent-Only Sites:** 3. **Hookups:** None. **Each Site:** Picnic table, fire ring, barbecue grill. **Dump Station:** No. **Laundry:** No. **Pay Phone:** No. **Rest Rooms and Showers:** Flush toilets, no showers. **Fuel:** No. **Propane:** No. **Internal Roads:** Paved. **RV Service:** No. **Market:** 4 mi. north in Lucia. **Restaurant:** 4 mi. north in Lucia. **General Store:** No. **Vending:** No. **Swimming:** No. **Playground:** No. **Activities:** Hiking, fishing. **Nearby Attractions:** Hearst Castle & National Geographic Theater in San Simeon; Mission San Antonio de Padua in Jolon; Limekiln State Park; Big Sur coast. **Additional Information:** Big Sur Chamber, (831) 667-2100.

RESTRICTIONS
Pets: On leash. **Fires:** In fire rings only. **Alcoholic Beverages:** Allowed. **Vehicle Maximum Length:** 30 ft. **Other:** 14-day stay limit; no firearms; no wood gathering.

TO GET THERE
From Lucia on Hwy. 1 drive 4 mi. south and turn right into the campground.

LUCIA
Ponderosa

Nacimiento Fergusson Rd., Lucia 93921. T: (831) 385-5434; F: (831) 385-0628; www.r5.fs.fed.us/lospadres.

🚐 ★★★　　　　　　　🅰 ★★★★

Beauty: ★★★★　　　　Site Privacy: ★★★★
Spaciousness: ★★★★　 Quiet: ★★★★
Security: ★　　　　　　Cleanliness: ★★★
Insect Control: ★　　　 Facilities: ★

This isolated camp is located within the tree-choked Los Padres National Forest, 15 miles and an hour's drive from the coast along the windy, occasionally broken up, mountainous Nacimiento Rd. On pulling into Ponderos,a don't expect that Hoss and Little Joe will be there to greet you. In fact, there may not be anyone present at all, which is one of the virtues of this pretty property, in contrast to its overflowing counterparts along the Big Sur coast. Roomy sites of dirt and grass are well separated along the serpentine loop, with a babbling creek running by several and a handful of walk-ins especially secluded. This hilly campground lies at 1,650 feet of elevation near the crest of the Santa Lucia Mountain range and is shaded more by live oaks, oddly, than its namesake pines. We prefer this facility to Nacimiento, two miles to the west, the latter featuring exposed, shallow sites that are very close to the road.

BASICS
Operated By: Parks Management Company, concessionaire. **Open:** All year, weather permitting. **Site Assignment:** First come, first served. **Registration:** At entrance kiosk. **Fee:** $12, cash or check. **Parking:** At site.

FACILITIES

Number of RV Sites: 18. **Number of Tent-Only Sites:** 5. **Hookups:** None. **Each Site:** Picnic table, fire ring, barbecue grill. **Dump Station:** No. **Laundry:** No. **Pay Phone:** No. **Rest Rooms and Showers:** Vault toilets, no showers. **Fuel:** No. **Propane:** No. **Internal Roads:** Paved. **RV Service:** No. **Market:** 20 mi. northwest in Lucia. **Restaurant:** 20 mi. northwest in Lucia. **General Store:** No. **Vending:** No. **Swimming:** In Pacific Ocean, if you dare. **Playground:** No. **Other:** Some wheelchair-accessible facilities. **Activities:** Hiking, fishing. **Nearby Attractions:** Hearst Castle & National Geographic Theater in San Simeon; Mission San Antonio de Padua in Jolon; Limekiln State Park; Big Sur coast; Pinnacles National Monument. **Additional Information:** Big Sur Chamber, (831) 667-2100.

RESTRICTIONS

Pets: On leash. **Fires:** In fire rings only. **Alcoholic Beverages:** Allowed. **Vehicle Maximum Length:** 35 ft. **Other:** 14-day stay limit.

TO GET THERE

From Lucia on Hwy. 1 drive 4 mi. south. Turn inland (left) on Nacimiento Fergusson Rd. and follow this windy, ascending road for 14 mi. The campground entrance is to the right.

MADERA

Millerton Lake State Recreation Area

5290 Millerton Rd., Friant 93626. T: (559) 822-2332 or reservations (800) 444-7275; F: (559) 822-2319; www.cal-parks.ca.gov or www.reserveamerica.com.

🚐 ★★★★	🅰 ★★★★
Beauty: ★★★★	Site Privacy: ★★★★
Spaciousness: ★★★	Quiet: ★★★
Security: ★★★	Cleanliness: ★★★
Insect Control: ★★	Facilities: ★★★

State officials estimate that on holiday weekends as many as 25,000 people descend on Millerton Lake, an indication of its popularity, as well as when to avoid visiting. Beyond the charming setting, amid a series of wrinkly, dimpled hills, with long, golden grass and monzo-granite gleaming in the sun, the attraction is obvious, given the scorching temperatures here during summer months. But while the lake is the main show, the campground is no ugly stepchild. Its level sites of grass and dirt are very well scattered over an extended series of loops, endowing many with privacy and prime vantages of the water. Several kinds of oak grace the domain, as well as sycamores, willow, eucalyptus, and various conifers, providing a balance of shade and filtered sun. The best of many fine sites is 59, on a point of land jutting out into the lake; 6–8 are on the small side but secluded. There are also 25 boat-in spots, and a marina with a snackbar and vending machines. Be sure to visit the Millerton Courthouse, circa 1867, preserved within the park.

BASICS

Operated By: California Dept. of Parks & Recreation. **Open:** All year. **Site Assignment:** Reservations accepted w/ V, MC, D. **Registration:** At entrance booth. **Fee:** $12–$18, cash or CA check. **Parking:** At site.

FACILITIES

Number of RV Sites: 138. **Number of Tent-Only Sites:** 0. **Hookups:** Water, electric (20, 30, 50 amps), sewer. **Each Site:** Picnic table, fire grate, some sites have food storage box and/or ramada. **Dump Station:** Yes. **Laundry:** No. **Pay Phone:** Yes. **Rest Rooms and Showers:** Yes. **Fuel:** No. **Propane:** No. **Internal Roads:** Paved. **RV Service:** No. **Market:** 23 mi. west in Madera. **Restaurant:** 23 mi. west in Madera. **General Store:** No. **Vending:** No. **Swimming:** In Millerton Lake. **Playground:** No. **Other:** Some wheelchair-accessible facilities, marina, boat launch, beach when water level drops. **Activities:** Fishing, boat rentals, horseback riding, hiking, waterskiing, windsurfing. **Nearby Attractions:** Museums, Forestiere Underground Gardens, Chaffee Zoological Gardens, Rotary Storyland & Playland in Fresno; Madera County Historical Museum & Quady Winery. **Additional Information:** Fresno City & County CVB, (800) 788-0836; Madera Chamber of Commerce, (559) 673-3563.

RESTRICTIONS

Pets: On 6 ft. leash. **Fires:** In fire grates only. **Alcoholic Beverages:** Allowed at site. **Vehicle Maximum Length:** 36 ft. **Other:** 14-day stay limit from May 1–Sept. 15, 30 for the rest of the year; no firearms; no wood gathering.

TO GET THERE

From Madera drive 16 mi. east on Hwy. 145. Proceed through the intersection w/ Hwy. 41 (where Hwy. 145 becomes Millerton Rd.). Continue 3.5 mi., then bear left. After 1.3 mi. turn right. The campground is 2.2 mi. ahead.

MALIBU
Leo Carillo State Park

Pacific Coast Hwy., Malibu 90265. T: (805) 488-5223; www.cal-parks.ca.gov or www.reserveamerica.com.

🚐 ★★★★   ▲ ★★★★

Beauty: ★★★★   Site Privacy: ★★★
Spaciousness: ★★★★   Quiet: ★★★
Security: ★★★★   Cleanliness: ★★★
Insect Control: ★★   Facilities: ★★★

The campground at Leo Carillo State Park is located directly across the Pacific Coast Hwy. from a wide sandy beach. While this detached position may at first appear to be a drawback, it is in fact the best of two worlds, with easy access to the ocean via a walkway under the road and a campground free of coastal winds due to its dramatic nest by the base of the steep Santa Monica Mountains. Gnarly sycamore trees overhang grassy sites along a double loop, with most being fairly spacious and decently screened by such riparian chaparral as bay willow, buckwheat, coastal sage and black walnut. The largest and most private sites, 54, 57, 59, 61, 63, and 66, are on the west side of camp along the creek. On weekends, restrooms can be in an atrocious state, but overall the campground is surprisingly clean, given the high traffic it receives from large family groups. Reservations are highly recommended from Easter through mid-Sept. Rangers routinely patrol the grounds.

BASICS

Operated By: California Dept. of Parks & Recreation. **Open:** All year. **Site Assignment:** Reservations recommended; V, MC, D. **Registration:** At entrance booth. **Fee:** $12, cash or CA check. **Parking:** At site.

FACILITIES

Number of RV Sites: 139. **Number of Tent-Only Sites:** 1. **Hookups:** None. **Each Site:** Picnic table, fire ring. **Dump Station:** Yes. **Laundry:** No. **Pay Phone:** Yes. **Rest Rooms and Showers:** Yes. **Fuel:** No. **Propane:** No. **Internal Roads:** Paved. **RV Service:** No. **Market:** 5.5 mi. east in Malibu. **Restaurant:** 5.5 mi. east in Malibu. **General Store:** No. **Vending:** No. **Swimming:** In Pacific

Ocean. **Playground:** No. **Other:** Some wheelchair-accessible facilities. **Activities:** Surfing, fishing, beachcombing, tide pools, cave & reef exploring. **Nearby Attractions:** Hollywood's theme parks, J. P. Getty Museum, La Brea Tar Pits, Will Rogers State Historic Park, Disneyland, historic Ventura. **Additional Information:** Santa Monica Mountains District, (810) 706-1310.

RESTRICTIONS

Pets: On 6 ft. leash. **Fires:** In fire rings only. **Alcoholic Beverages:** Allowed at site. **Vehicle Maximum Length:** 36 ft. **Other:** 7-day stay limit in summer, 14-day stay limit for the rest of the year; no firearms; no wood gathering.

TO GET THERE

At the intersection of Trancas Canyon and Broad Beach in Malibu, drive 5.5 mi. west on the Pacific Coast Hwy. The park entrance is on the right (north) side of the road.

MALIBU
Malibu Beach RV Park

25801 Pacific Coast Hwy., Malibu 90265. T: (800) 622-6052 or (310) 456-6052; F: (310) 456-2532; www.malibubeachrv.com; info@maliburv.com.

🚐 ★★★★   ▲ ★★★

Beauty: ★★★★   Site Privacy: ★★
Spaciousness: ★★   Quiet: ★★★
Security: ★★★   Cleanliness: ★★★★
Insect Control: ★★★   Facilities: ★★★★★

On the surface Malibu Beach looks like just another run-of-the-mill RV facility. Caravans are wedged one next to another, with a tenting area attached to the end of the serpentine camp lane seemingly as an afterthought. Probe a bit, though, and you will find this a superior property, just six miles west of Malibu on the Pacific Coast Hwy. on the inland side of the road. Shrewd terracing stretches sites up a bluff, thus maximizing vistas of the ocean. Yes, site privacy is nearly nil, but with that ocean panorama and the beautiful sunsets, who cares! Eucalyptus, palms, pines, and sycamores decorate the landscape and while they do little to provide shade, at least they don't obstruct the view. Though they will probably be taken already, try to get any of numbers 6–33 or V1–V13. Even the dirt walk-in tenting area atop the bluff is attractive, with small sycamores providing shade. Double-wide sites and pull-throughs are available, as well as a hot tub, game room, and Internet connection.

BASICS

Operated By: Malibu Beach RV Park. **Open:** All year. **Site Assignment:** Reservations recommended; V, MC, D, AE, DC. **Registration:** At entrance office. **Fee:** $22–$48 in summer (May 1–Sept. 30); $18–$40 in winter (Oct. 1–Apr. 30). **Parking:** At site.

FACILITIES

Number of RV Sites: 115. **Number of Tent-Only Sites:** 50. **Hookups:** Water, electric (30, 50 amps), sewer, cable TV, Internet. **Each Site:** Picnic table, barbecue grill. **Dump Station:** Yes. **Laundry:** Yes. **Pay Phone:** Yes. **Rest Rooms and Showers:** Yes. **Fuel:** No. **Propane:** Yes. **Internal Roads:** Paved. **RV Service:** No. **Market:** 3 mi. east in Malibu. **Restaurant:** 3 mi. east in Malibu. **General Store:** Yes. **Vending:** Yes. **Swimming:** In Pacific Ocean. **Playground:** Yes. **Other:** Some wheelchair-accessible facilities, game room. **Activities:** Surfing, fishing, hiking, dolphin & whale-watching. **Nearby Attractions:** Hollywood's theme parks, J. P. Getty Museum, La Brea Tar Pits, Will Rogers State Historic Park, Venice Beach Boardwalk, Santa Monica Pier & museums. **Additional Information:** Malibu Chamber of Commerce, (310) 456-9025.

RESTRICTIONS

Pets: Well behaved pets in RV sites only; no rotweilers, pit bulls, German sheperds, Doberman pinschers. **Fires:** No wood fires allowed. **Alcoholic Beverages:** Allowed. **Vehicle Maximum Length:** 45 ft. **Other:** 7-month stay limit in winter.

TO GET THERE

From the Pacific Coast Hwy. in Malibu turn inland just 3 mi. west of Coral Canyon Rd. The campground is well signposted.

MALIBU
Malibu Creek State Park

1925 Las Virgenes Rd., Calabasas 91302. T: (818) 880-0367; www.cal-parks.ca.gov or www.reserveamerica.com.

🚐 ★★★   ⛺ ★★★★

Beauty: ★★★★   Site Privacy: ★★★
Spaciousness: ★★★   Quiet: ★★★

Security: ★★★★   Cleanliness: ★★★
Insect Control: ★★★   Facilities: ★★

If you managed to get a site here without a reservation it may be time to buy a lottery ticket, that's how good your luck is. "Popular" doesn't begin to describe this park, which lies just six miles north of Malibu, on the sloping side of a grassy hill in the shadow of the Santa Monica Mountains. Though a forest of live oak borders the camp, there is scant shade to be found within its single loop. A recent round of plantings holds the promise of many shade trees to come, albeit years from now. And while the tilt of the terrain and small parking slips make RV camping a challenge, most sites are large enough for tenters to scratch out a satisfactory patch of turf. Heavy visitation means that restrooms tend toward the messy, especially on weekends. Overall, though, this is a remarkably well-maintained place. There are some Hollywood sets in the park, leftover from when it was owned by Universal Studios, but most people come for the great hiking, mountain biking, and horseback riding. Try to get here in spring, while the long flowing grass is still green and wildflowers are in bloom.

BASICS

Operated By: California Dept. of Parks & Recreation. **Open:** All year. **Site Assignment:** Reservations highly recommended; V, MC, D. **Registration:** At entrance booth. **Fee:** $12, cash or CA check. **Parking:** At site.

FACILITIES

Number of RV Sites: 63. **Number of Tent-Only Sites:** 0. **Hookups:** None. **Each Site:** Picnic table, fire grate. **Dump Station:** Yes. **Laundry:** No. **Pay Phone:** Yes. **Rest Rooms and Showers:** Yes. **Fuel:** No. **Propane:** No. **Internal Roads:** Paved. **RV Service:** No. **Market:** 6 mi. south in Malibu. **Restaurant:** 6 mi. south in Malibu. **General Store:** No. **Vending:** No. **Swimming:** No. **Playground:** No. **Other:** Some wheelchair-accessible facilities. **Activities:** Hiking, mountain biking, horseback riding, birding. **Nearby Attractions:** Santa Monica Pier & museums, Venice Beach Boardwalk, Hollywood's theme parks, La Brea Tar Pits. **Additional Information:** Malibu Chamber of Commerce, (310) 456-9025.

RESTRICTIONS

Pets: On 6 ft. leash. **Fires:** In fire grates only, not allowed after the grass turns brown late spring/early summer. **Alcoholic Beverages:** Allowed at site. **Vehicle Maximum Length:** 30 ft. **Other:** 7-day stay limit June 1–Sept. 30, 14-day stay limit Oct. 1–May 31; no firearms; no wood gathering.

TO GET THERE

From the Pacific Coast Hwy. in Malibu head north on CR N1/Malibu Canyon Rd. Drive 6 mi. to the campground entrance on the left.

MAMMOTH LAKES
Glass Creek

Glass Creek Rd., Crestview 93546. T: (760) 647-3044; F: (760) 647-3046; www.r5.fs.fed.us/inyo.

🚐 ★★★★   ⛺ ★★★★

Beauty: ★★★   Site Privacy: ★★★
Spaciousness: ★★★★   Quiet: ★★★
Security: ★   Cleanliness: ★★★
Insect Control: ★★★★   Facilities: ★

It may be true that there is no such thing as a free lunch, but fortunately for budget-minded campers there are still a few no-fee campgrounds left. Glass Creek is one of those, a primitive national forest camp with no potable water, no trash pick-up, and rickety-looking vaulted toilets. It is also a quietly attractive piece of land that straddles its namesake creek (where the fishing for trout is pretty good), with generously large, dispersed sites on either side of the smooth, dirt access road. The slightly rolling terrain is partly shaded by very mature Jeffrey and ponderosa pines, and aspens that grow alongside the creek. Its great location, just 12 miles north of Mammoth Lakes, makes Glass Creek a popular base camp for the RV set. While ranger patrols are few and far between, the presence of vacation homes at the perimeter of the property is a reassuring sign of civilization. The nearest pay phone is at the intersection with US 395, directly across the road.

BASICS

Operated By: Inyo National Forest, Mono Lake Ranger District. **Open:** Mid-May through Oct., weather permitting. **Site Assignment:** First come, first served. **Registration:** None. **Fee:** None. **Parking:** At site.

FACILITIES

Number of RV Sites: 50. **Number of Tent-Only Sites:** 0. **Hookups:** None. **Each Site:** Picnic

table, fire grate or pit. **Dump Station:** No. **Laundry:** No. **Pay Phone:** No. **Rest Rooms and Showers:** Vault toilets, no showers. **Fuel:** No. **Propane:** No. **Internal Roads:** Dirt, sand, & rocks, but negotiable. **RV Service:** No. **Market:** 12 mi. south in Mammoth Lakes. **Restaurant:** 12 mi. south in Mammoth Lakes. **General Store:** No. **Vending:** No. **Swimming:** No. **Playground:** No. **Activities:** Fishing, hiking, photography. **Nearby Attractions:** Mono Lake Tufa State Reserve in Lee Vining; Devils Postpile National Monument, Mammoth Mountain Bike Park, Mammoth Museum & outlet shopping in Mammoth Lakes. **Additional Information:** Mono County Tourism Commission, (760) 924-3699; Mammoth Lakes Visitors Bureau, (888) GO-MAMMOTH.

RESTRICTIONS

Pets: On leash. **Fires:** In fire grates or pits only. **Alcoholic Beverages:** Allowed. **Vehicle Maximum Length:** 40 ft. **Other:** 42-day stay limit.

TO GET THERE

From Mammoth Junction drive 10 mi. north on US 395, past the Caltrans Crestview Maintenance Station. Make a U-turn and head 0.5 mi. south on US 395. Turn right on Glass Creek Rd., a forest service road, and continue for 0.3 mi. to the campground access road on the right.

MAMMOTH LAKES
Twin Lakes

Twin Lakes Loop Rd., Mammoth Lakes 93546. T: (760) 924-5500; F: (760) 924-5537; www.r5.fs.fed.us/inyo.

🚐 ★★★★   ⛺ ★★★★

Beauty: ★★★★★   Site Privacy: ★★
Spaciousness: ★★★   Quiet: ★★★
Security: ★★★   Cleanliness: ★★★
Insect Control: ★★   Facilities: ★★★

To describe this camp as dramatic and pretty, peaceful and exhilarating, is to fall frustratingly short of its true splendor. The pair of lakes that inspired its name rest smack in the middle of a high Sierra canyon, jagged granite spires soaring well above the tops of the highest lodgepole pines. In spring, snow melt courses into Twin Falls, making for a spectacular cascade, visible from the campground. The very best site, with a prime panorama of the lakes, has been taken by the host. But there are many other agreeable options among the three zones that make up this park-like setting. Forget about the area by the entrance; those sites are too exposed to passing traffic. Better by far are the spots just across the bridge that divides the two lakes: 23, 25, 26, and 28 are small but enjoy their own private lake-front; 31, 33, 36, and 39, at the base of a steep hill, are fairly roomy, and detached from their neighbors; 62 and 70 are tucked into a thicket and blessed with a stunning view of the craggy canyon. The upper loop, in a more mountainous setting away from the lakes, is the roomiest; even the interior sites seem well separated. Given the elevation of 8,600 feet, you'll want to pack, along with a fishing rod, some heavy-weight fleece as a precaution against windy evenings.

BASICS

Operated By: Rocky Mountain Recreation Company, concessionaire. **Open:** June through Oct., weather permitting. **Site Assignment:** First come, first served. **Registration:** At entrance kiosk. **Fee:** $14, cash or check. **Parking:** At site.

FACILITIES

Number of RV Sites: 95. **Number of Tent-Only Sites:** 0. **Hookups:** None. **Each Site:** Picnic table, fire grate, barbecue grill. **Dump Station:** Yes. **Laundry:** No. **Pay Phone:** Yes. **Rest Rooms and Showers:** Yes. **Fuel:** No. **Propane:** No. **Internal Roads:** Paved. **RV Service:** No. **Market:** 4 mi. northeast in Mammoth Lakes. **Restaurant:** 4 mi. northeast in Mammoth Lakes. **General Store:** Yes. **Vending:** No. **Swimming:** No. **Playground:** No. **Other:** Some wheelchair-accessible facilities, boat launch. **Activities:** Fishing, horseback riding, hiking, boat rentals. **Nearby Attractions:** Mono Lake Tufa State Reserve in Lee Vining; Devils Postpile National Monument, Mammoth Mountain Bike Park, Mammoth Museum & outlet shopping in Mammoth Lakes. **Additional Information:** Mono County Tourism Commission, (760) 924-3699; Mammoth Lakes Visitors Bureau, (888) GO-MAMMOTH.

RESTRICTIONS

Pets: On leash. **Fires:** In fire grates only. **Alcoholic Beverages:** Allowed. **Vehicle Maximum Length:** 46 ft. **Other:** 7-day stay limit.

TO GET THERE

From Mammoth Junction on US 395 head west on Hwy. 203, leading into Mammoth Lakes'

Main St., and continue 4 mi. to where Main St. becomes Lake Mary Rd. Proceed straight ahead for 2.3 mi., then turn right onto Twin Lakes Loop Rd. The campground is 0.5 mi. ahead.

MARKLEEVILLE
Grover Hot Springs State Park

Hot Springs Rd., Markleeville 96120. T: (530) 694-2248 or reservations (800) 444-7275; F: (530) 694-2502; www.cal-parks.ca.gov or www.grover@gbis.com or www.reserveamerica.com.

🚐 ★★★★	🅰 ★★★★
Beauty: ★★★★★	Site Privacy: ★★★
Spaciousness: ★★★★	Quiet: ★★★★
Security: ★★★	Cleanliness: ★★★
Insect Control: ★★★	Facilities: ★★

The mineral springs of Grover Hot Springs remain a constant 102° year-round, making its hot and cool pools a major therapeutic attraction. There is more to this state park, though, than the chance to bathe oneself in simmering water. Like miles of hiking and riding trails, as well as cross-country skiing in winter. First and foremost, though, is its strikingly beautiful campground, set at 5,900 feet of altitude, with a series of corrugated Sierra peaks contributing an Arcadian quality to its forested, creekside location. The undefiled, natural look of this gorgeous preserve is furthered by its undulating terrain being well-salted with granite boulders, juniper, incense cedar and Jeffrey and lodgepole pines. Sites, covered with grass and pine needles, are generally shady, generously large and fairly well separated, though several lie on uneven turf. The most private are 11, tucked behind boulders, and 22, by a row of Jeffrey pines and a grassy meadow; 58, 66–68, and 73–75 are also worth shooting for. The pools close for maintenance the last two weeks of Sept., and shut down during thunderstorms, which occur regularly throughout July and Aug.

BASICS

Operated By: California Dept. of Parks & Recreation. **Open:** All year. **Site Assignment:** Reservations recommended; V, MC, D. **Registration:** At entrance booth. **Fee:** $12, cash or CA check. **Parking:** At site.

FACILITIES

Number of RV Sites: 76. **Number of Tent-Only Sites:** 0. **Hookups:** None. **Each Site:** Picnic table, fire grate, bearproof box. **Dump Station:** No. **Laundry:** In tubs. **Pay Phone:** Yes. **Rest Rooms and Showers:** Yes. **Fuel:** No. **Propane:** No. **Internal Roads:** Paved. **RV Service:** No. **Market:** 3.6 mi. east in Markleeville. **Restaurant:** 3.6 mi. east in Markleeville. **General Store:** No. **Vending:** No. **Swimming:** In hot springs pool. **Playground:** No. **Other:** Some wheelchair-accessible facilities. **Activities:** Hiking, fishing, bicycling, taking the "cure." **Nearby Attractions:** Alpine County Museum in Markleeville; Lake Tahoe & Lake Tahoe Historical Museum in South Lake Tahoe. **Additional Information:** Alpine County Chamber of Commerce, (530) 694-2475.

RESTRICTIONS

Pets: On 6 ft. leash. **Fires:** In fire grates only. **Alcoholic Beverages:** Allowed at site. **Vehicle Maximum Length:** 27 ft. **Other:** 14-day stay limit from May 15 to the first week in Sept., 30-day stay limit for the rest of the year; no firearms; no wood gathering.

TO GET THERE

From Markleeville on Hwy. 89 turn west on Hot Springs Rd. and drive 3.6 mi. The well-signed state park entrance is on the right.

MARKLEEVILLE
Indian Creek

Airport Rd., Markleeville 96120. T: (775) 885-6000; www.nv.blm.gov/carson/information.html.

🚐 ★★★★	🛖 ★★★★
Beauty: ★★★★	Site Privacy: ★★★
Spaciousness: ★★★	Quiet: ★★★★
Security: ★★★	Cleanliness: ★★★★
Insect Control: ★★★	Facilities: ★★

Indian Creek is easily reached along a well-signed, smoothly paved roadway, a rare double-treat for a Bureau of Land Management property. Then, when you pull into camp—the trifecta!—as this is as sweet as it gets for BLM land. It's a beautiful lakeside campground, backed up against the Sierra range, with its two loops enhanced by mature stands of piñon, ponderosa, and Jeffrey pines, as well as a few boulders and such high desert shrubs as salt bush and brittle bush. The first loop, which features walk-in sites for tents, offers the better vantage over Indian Creek Reservoir, where white pelicans were noisily cavorting our last time through. Birding is no less rewarding at the second circuit, which faces the lake on one side and a grassy marsh on another. The optimum sites there are 44, 48, and 49. The ground slopes gently toward the water, but most units are level, distributed well apart and surprisingly clean; even the sandy tent pads are raked by a conscientious host. Situated on the west side of the reservoir, Indian Creek is pleasantly illuminated by morning light, when it is almost too pretty for words.

BASICS

Operated By: Bureau of Land Management, Carson City Field Office. **Open:** First weekend in May through last weekend in Sept. **Site Assignment:** First come, first served. **Registration:** At entrance kiosk. **Fee:** $8–$10, cash or check. **Parking:** At site or in parking lot for walk-ins.

FACILITIES

Number of RV Sites: 19. **Number of Tent-Only Sites:** 10. **Hookups:** None. **Each Site:** Picnic table, makeshift fire ring, barbecue grill, bearproof box. **Dump Station:** Yes. **Laundry:** No. **Pay Phone:** No. **Rest Rooms and Showers:** Yes. **Fuel:** No. **Propane:** No. **Internal Roads:** Paved. **RV Service:** No. **Market:** 6.5 mi. south in Markleeville. **Restaurant:** 6.5 mi. south in Markleeville. **General Store:** No. **Vending:** No. **Swimming:** No. **Playground:** No. **Other:** Boat ramp. **Activities:** Fishing, hiking, birding, horseback riding, sailing, mountain biking. **Nearby Attractions:** Alpine County Museum in Markleeville; Lake Tahoe & Lake Tahoe Historical Museum in South Lake Tahoe. **Additional Information:** Alpine County Chamber of Commerce, (530) 694-2475.

RESTRICTIONS

Pets: On leash. **Fires:** In fire rings only. **Alcoholic Beverages:** Allowed. **Vehicle Maximum Length:** 30 ft. **Other:** 14-day stay limit.

TO GET THERE

From Markleeville drive 2.5 mi. north on Hwy. 89. Turn right onto Airport Rd. and continue for 4 mi., then make a left into the campground.

MCCLOUD

Fowlers Campground

FR 39N28, McCloud 96057. T: (530) 964-2184; F: (530) 964-2938; www.r5.fs.fed.us/shasta trinity.

🚐 ★★★　　　　　🔺 ★★★★

Beauty: ★★★★　　　　Site Privacy: ★★★
Spaciousness: ★★★　　Quiet: ★★★★
Security: ★★★　　　　Cleanliness: ★★★
Insect Control: ★★★　Facilities: ★★

You are barreling along on Hwy. 89 bound toward McCloud, with a fishing rod in the back of your vehicle and a kayak strapped to its roof. Where do you pull over for some R&R? Fowlers Campground is one of the better options in the area. The McCloud River flows right behind this clean, well-maintained national forest–operated property. Brown trout inhabit the river and rainbow trout are regularly stocked from this point clear down to Lake McCloud. A small put-in for kayaks and canoes is just past the photogenic series of cascades by the day-use picnic area, 0.5 miles beyond camp along the dirt road. The campground's double loop threads by level sites that are situated reasonably well apart and decently shielded by a densely forested mix of incense cedar, manzanita, and various conifers. The tree-to-tree carpet of pine needles is speckled with pumice rocks, which enhances the natural beauty of this wheelchair-accessible camp.

BASICS

Operated By: Shasta-Trinity National Forest, McCloud Ranger District. **Open:** May 1–Oct. 31. **Site Assignment:** First come, first served. **Registration:** At entrance kiosk. **Fee:** $12, cash or check. **Parking:** At site.

FACILITIES

Number of RV Sites: 38. **Number of Tent-Only Sites:** 0. **Hookups:** None. **Each Site:** Picnic table, fire grate. **Dump Station:** No. **Laundry:** No. **Pay Phone:** No. **Rest Rooms and Showers:** Vault toilets, no showers. **Fuel:** No. **Propane:** No. **Internal Roads:** Paved, narrow. **RV Service:** No. **Market:** 6 mi. west in McCloud. **Restaurant:** 6 mi. west in McCloud. **General Store:** No. **Vending:** No. **Swimming:** At the base of Middle & Lower Falls. **Playground:** No. **Other:** Some wheelchair-accessible facilities, small boat launch. **Activities:** Fishing, hiking, kayaking. **Nearby Attractions:** McCloud River Falls & Shasta Sunset Dinner Train; Mount Shasta Ski Park, Mount Shasta Hatchery, & Sisson Museum in Mount Shasta; Lake Siskiyou. **Additional Information:** Mount Shasta Chamber of Commerce & Visitors Bureau, (530) 926-4865 or (800) 926-4865; McCloud Chamber of Commerce, (530) 964-3113.

RESTRICTIONS

Pets: On leash. **Fires:** In fire grates only. **Alcoholic Beverages:** Allowed. **Vehicle Maximum Length:** 30 ft. **Other:** 14-day stay limit.

TO GET THERE

From Mount Shasta drive 2 mi. south on I-5. Head east on Hwy. 89 and drive 16 mi., past the town of McCloud, and turn right at the campground sign. Continue for 0.6 mi. and bear left at the fork. The campground is straight ahead.

MECCA

Salton Sea State Recreation Area, Headquarters Campground

100–225 State Park Rd., North Shore 92254. T: (760) 393-3052; F: (760) 393-2466; www.saltonsea.statepark.org.

🚐 ★★★　　　　　🔺 ★★★

Beauty: ★★★　　　　Site Privacy: ★★★
Spaciousness: ★★★　　Quiet: ★★★
Security: ★★★　　　　Cleanliness: ★★★
Insect Control: ★★　　Facilities: ★★★

The attraction here is the Salton Sea, a vast lake that lies 227 feet below sea level and is 25 percent saltier than the Pacific Ocean. The palm-fringed body of water is a Mecca of sorts to boaters and fishermen, as well as birders drawn by hopes of sighting some of the great range of migratory fowl that wing through between late fall and early spring. The mildest weather is from Jan. through Mar., a time that coincides with free ranger-led kayak tours of the lake (call ahead to make reservations). Of the state-run campgrounds in the area, Mecca Beach gives tenters the best beach access, but only has six spots with hookups. Headquarters, on the other hand, has the better fishing. It consists of two loops; one with 15 full-hookup sites facing the water across a paved, level parking area, the other with more space and privacy among desert ironwood trees, brittle bush, and desert scrub. A visitor center, located between the loops, has a short film strip on the lake and some interesting exhibits. This would be a delightfully peaceful bivouac if not for the occasional rattling of trains along the tracks by the park road. When the winds blow from the west side of the lake, that sweet briny air that is so reminiscent of the seaside can change in the twitch of a nose to such a strong stench of sulphur you may think you're camping next to a match factory.

BASICS

Operated By: California Dept. of Parks & Recreation. **Open:** All year. **Site Assignment:** Reservations accepted w/ V, MC, D, but not for primitive sites. **Registration:** At entrance booth. **Fee:** $10–$14, cash or CA check. **Parking:** At site.

FACILITIES

Number of RV Sites: 50. **Number of Tent-Only Sites:** 0. **Hookups:** Water, electric (30 amps). **Each Site:** Picnic table, barbecue grill, some w/ a ramada. **Dump Station:** Yes. **Laundry:** No. **Pay Phone:** Yes. **Rest Rooms and Showers:** Yes. **Fuel:** No. **Propane:** No. **Internal Roads:** Paved. **RV Service:** No. **Market:** 11 mi. north in Mecca. **Restaurant:** 11 mi. north in Mecca. **General Store:** No. **Vending:** No. **Swimming:** In Salton Sea. **Playground:** Yes. **Other:** Some wheelchair-accessible facilities. **Activities:** Fishing, boating, hiking, birding, horseshoe pit. **Nearby Attractions:** Joshua Tree National Park, San Andreas Trail, Wister Mud Pots. **Additional Information:** Coachella Chamber of Commerce, (760) 398-8089.

RESTRICTIONS

Pets: On 6 ft. leash. **Fires:** No ground fires. **Alcoholic Beverages:** Allowed at site. **Vehicle Maximum Length:** 32 ft. **Other:** 30-day stay limit; no firearms; no wood gathering.

TO GET THERE

Take Hwy. 111 south from Mecca, drive 12 mi. and turn right into the state recreation area.

MIDDLETOWN

Beaver Creek RV Park & Campground

14417 Bottle Rock Rd., Cobb Mountain 95426. T: (707) 928-4322 or reservations (800) 307-CAMP; F: (707) 928-5341; www.campbeavercreek.com.

🚐 ★★★★   ⛺ ★★

Beauty: ★★★	Site Privacy: ★★
Spaciousness: ★★	Quiet: ★★★
Security: ★★★★	Cleanliness: ★★★
Insect Control: ★★★	Facilities: ★★★★★

This is not a campground where you are likely to feel comfortable sitting in an easy chair watching the clouds drift by. Not in the summer, anyway, when a smorgasbord of activities and distractions keeps the place humming. The family-oriented entertainment ranges from such stalwarts as fishing, kayaking, softball, and basketball, to crafts and games, campfire programs, karaoke, and bingo. Bring the "bug juice" and you will have the complete summer camp experience. The flat grassy camping meadow, tucked below an attractive array of hills, is open, rather crowded, and lacking in shade. The most desirable site is 11, set back under a large oak and pine, right by the creek. There are also clean cabins for rent by the small boat pond. Beaver Creek recently changed its name from Yogi Bear's Jellystone Park Camp Resort, a sure indicator of the declining fortune of the cartoon character and his pal, Booboo. Although open year-round, upkeep tends to slide in the off-season.

BASICS

Operated By: Beaver Creek RV Park & Campground. **Open:** All year. **Site Assignment:** Reservations accepted w/ V, MC, D, AE. **Registration:** At office. **Fee:** $19–$24, cash or V, MC, AE, D. **Parking:** At site.

FACILITIES

Number of RV Sites: 97. **Number of Tent-Only Sites:** 14. **Hookups:** Water, electric (30, 50 amps), sewer. **Each Site:** Picnic table, fire grate. **Dump Station:** Yes. **Laundry:** Yes. **Pay Phone:** Yes. **Rest Rooms and Showers:** Yes. **Fuel:** No. **Propane:** Yes. **Internal Roads:** Dirt & gravel, good condition. **RV Service:** No. **Market:** 12 mi. south in Middletown. **Restaurant:** 12 mi. south in Middletown. **General Store:** Yes. **Vending:** Yes. **Swimming:** In small pool. **Playground:** Yes. **Other:** Some wheelchair-accessible facilities, rec hall, trout creek. **Activities:** Fishing, hiking, birding, shuffleboard, soccer, softball, kayak & paddleboat rentals. **Nearby Attractions:** Clear Lake Queen, Outrageous Waters Water Park & Fun Center, & Anderson Marsh State Historic Park in Clearlake. **Additional Information:** Lake County Marketing Program/Visitor Information Center, (707) 263-9544 or (800) 525-3743; Clearlake Chamber of Commerce, (707) 994-3600.

RESTRICTIONS

Pets: On leash. **Fires:** In fire grates only. **Alcoholic Beverages:** Allowed. **Vehicle Maximum Length:** None. **Other:** 180-day stay limit; no wood gathering.

TO GET THERE

From Middletown on Hwy. 29 take Hwy. 175 north for 8.7 mi. Turn left on Bottle Rock Rd. and drive 3.4 mi. to the park entrance on the left.

MILL CREEK
Hole-in-the-Ground

FR 28NO6, Mill Creek 96061. T: (530) 258-2141; F: (530) 258-5194; www.r5.fs.fed.us/lassen.

🚐 ★★★   ▲ ★★★★

Beauty: ★★★★   Site Privacy: ★★★
Spaciousness: ★★★   Quiet: ★★★★
Security: ★   Cleanliness: ★★★
Insect Control: ★★★   Facilities: ★

In spite of its name, this camp is far more than just a "hole-in-the-ground." In fact, the contrast to Elam, a few miles to the southeast, couldn't be more striking. While both consist of sites sprinkled along short camp lanes that are flanked by gurgling streams, the ones here are roomy, well-separated, and thickly populated with ponderosa pines and Douglas firs. Privacy is further enhanced by the remoteness of the setting, some three miles down a gravel washboard off of Hwy. 172, about 14 miles from the south entrance to Lassen Volcanic National Park. Amazingly, while Elam is often packed to the gills with rod-slinging campers, you may find Hole-in-the-Ground occupied by only a small handful of visitors, if at all. The reason for that is fishing here in Mill Creek is limited to catch-and-release, with barbless hooks. With an elevation of 4,300 feet, snowfall can block access to this park-like campground from mid-Oct. through May. The rusty, old-fashioned water pump is a good incentive to bring plenty of drinking water.

BASICS

Operated By: CSU Chico Research Foundation, concessionaire, & Lassen National Forest, Almanor Ranger District. **Open:** May through Oct., weather permitting. **Site Assignment:** First come, first served. **Registration:** At entrance kiosk. **Fee:** $11, cash or check. **Parking:** At site.

FACILITIES

Number of RV Sites: 13. **Number of Tent-Only Sites:** 0. **Hookups:** None. **Each Site:** Picnic table, fire grate or makeshift stone ring, some old-fashioned camp stoves. **Dump Station:** No. **Laundry:** No. **Pay Phone:** No. **Rest Rooms and Showers:** Vault toilets, no showers. **Fuel:** No. **Propane:** No. **Internal Roads:** Packed dirt & coarse gravel. **RV Service:** No. **Market:** 4 mi. north in Mineral. **Restaurant:** 4 mi. north in Mineral. **General Store:** No. **Vending:** No. **Swimming:** No. **Playground:** No. **Activities:** Fishing, kayaking, hiking. **Nearby Attractions:** Westwood Museum & Paul Bunyan & Babe the Blue Ox Statues; Lassen National Scenic Byway (Hwys. 89-44-36); Lassen Volcanic National Park; Lake Almanor. **Additional Information:** Chester–Lake Almanor Chamber of Commerce, (530) 258-2426 or (800) 350-4838.

RESTRICTIONS

Pets: On leash. **Fires:** In fire grates or rings only. **Alcoholic Beverages:** Allowed. **Vehicle Maximum Length:** 25 ft., trailers not recommended. **Other:** 14-day stay limit.

TO GET THERE

From Chester on Hwy. 36 drive 23 mi. west to the junction w/ Hwy. 172. Turn left and continue for 3.6 mi., then turn left onto FR 28N06 (campground is signposted). After 2.8 mi. take another left onto the access road. The campground is 0.6 mi. ahead. A few sudden rises in the road surface may cause problems for trailers and oversize RVs.

MODESTO
Modesto Reservoir Regional Park

Reservoir Rd. 18143, Waterford 95386. T: (209) 874-9540; F: (209) 874-4513; www.co.stanislaus.ca.us.

🚐 ★★★★   ▲ ★★

Beauty: ★★★★	Site Privacy: ★★
Spaciousness: ★★	Quiet: ★★★
Security: ★★★	Cleanliness: ★★★
Insect Control: ★★	Facilities: ★★★★

Summer seems to last for six or seven months in this steamy stretch of California's Central Valley. That's a major reason why Modesto Reservoir is so popular for much of the year; its cool, shimmering water brings relief from temperatures that frequently top 100°. Even on busy weekends, you are apt to find spots available in the sparsely shaded, full-hookup parking meadow. Far better are the smaller slots that are lined up one against another following the amoeba-like contours of the reservoir's wandering shoreline. What those lack in privacy they more than gain in shade from eucalyptus, plane trees, pines, and juniper. Their tent-side access to the lake is an added bonus. The many small islands that dot the surface of the water not only bless it with pleasing aesthetics, but also serve as safe havens for a variety of bird life, including pelicans, Canada geese, blue herons, bald eagles, red tail hawks, pheasants, and burrowing owls. An undeveloped section on the opposite side of the lake allows for more privacy, but lacks tables, fire rings, and potable water.

BASICS
Operated By: Stanislaus County Parks Dept. **Open:** All year. **Site Assignment:** First come, first served. **Registration:** At entrance kiosk. **Fee:** $12–$16, cash, CA check or V, MC; $2 per night extra for 3-day holiday weekends. **Parking:** At site.

FACILITIES
Number of RV Sites: 186. **Number of Tent-Only Sites:** Undesignated sites. **Hookups:** Water, electric (20, 30 amps), sewer. **Each Site:** Picnic table, fire grate, barbecue grill. **Dump Station:** Yes. **Laundry:** No. **Pay Phone:** Yes. **Rest Rooms and Showers:** Yes. **Fuel:** No. **Propane:** No. **Internal Roads:** Paved. **RV Service:** No. **Market:** 7 mi.

west in Waterford. **Restaurant:** 7 mi. west in Waterford. **General Store:** Yes. **Vending:** No. **Swimming:** In Modesto Reservoir. **Playground:** No. **Other:** Some wheelchair-accessible facilities, boat ramp, marina, beach, archery range. **Activities:** Fishing, boat rentals, waterskiing,. **Nearby Attractions:** McHenry Mansion & museums in Modesto; Turlock Lake State Recreation Area in La Grange. **Additional Information:** Modesto CVB, (209) 571-6480 or (800) 266-4282.

RESTRICTIONS
Pets: Not allowed. **Fires:** In fire grates only. **Alcoholic Beverages:** Allowed at site. **Vehicle Maximum Length:** None. **Other:** 14-day stay limit; MBTE-free fuel only; no fuel containers; no firearms; no wood gathering.

TO GET THERE
From Modesto drive 13 mi. east on Hwy. 132/ Yosemite Blvd. Turn left on Reservoir Rd. and continue 0.5 mi. to the park entrance.

MOJAVE
Red Rock Canyon State Park, Ricardo Campground

Hwy. 14, Cantil 93519. T: (661) 942-0662; F: (661) 940-7327; www.cal-parks.ca.gov.

🚐 ★★★★   ▲ ★★★★

Beauty: ★★★★★	Site Privacy: ★★★
Spaciousness: ★★★★	Quiet: ★★★
Security: ★★★	Cleanliness: ★★★★
Insect Control: ★★★★	Facilities: ★

White House Cliffs is a fabulous fairyland canyon of melting sandstone and fluted folds, where cliff swallows nest and great horned owls occasionally perch during their nocturnal vigils. This feast for the eyes, a part of the El Paso Mountain range, serves as host to Ricardo Campground, right at its base, and has been a featured backdrop in more than 130 movies. Coarse sand-surfaced sites are backed up against the eroded nooks and alcoves of the canyon, gaining, in addition to a touch of privacy from their neighbors, a solid shield from the afternoon sun. From this primitive setting one can look across the valley floor, an arid landscape that is enlivened by creosote bushes, Joshua trees, and rabbit brush, to the headlights of distant autos humming along on Hwy. 14, while still enjoying a brilliantly starry sky. Indeed, the star-gazing here is so exceptional that star charts have been posted by the latrines and kiosk. A visitor center and the remains of an 1890s mining operation are in the vicinity. The nearest pay phone is 14 miles south by the Cantil post office.

BASICS

Operated By: California Dept. of Parks & Recreation. **Open:** All year. **Site Assignment:** First come, first served. **Registration:** At entrance booth. **Fee:** $8, cash or CA check. **Parking:** At site.

FACILITIES

Number of RV Sites: 50. **Number of Tent-Only Sites:** 0. **Hookups:** None. **Each Site:** Picnic table, fire grate. **Dump Station:** Yes. **Laundry:** No. **Pay Phone:** No. **Rest Rooms and Showers:** Pit toilets, no showers. **Fuel:** No. **Propane:** No. **Internal Roads:** Gravel, good condition. **RV Service:** No. **Market:** 35 mi. northeast in Ridgecrest. **Restaurant:** 25 mi. southwest in Mojave. **General Store:** No. **Vending:** No. **Swimming:** No. **Playground:** No. **Other:** Some wheelchair-accessible facilities, visitor center. **Activities:** Hiking, driving tour, photography, birding, stargazing, ranger-led activities. **Nearby Attractions:** Trona Pinnacles; Fossil Falls; Last Chance Canyon & Maturango Museum in Ridgecrest; Desert Tortoise Natural Area in California City. **Additional Information:** Mojave Chamber of Commerce, (661) 824-2481; Ridgecrest Area CVB, (760) 375-8202 or (800) 847-4830.

RESTRICTIONS

Pets: On 6 ft. leash. **Fires:** In fire grates only. **Alcoholic Beverages:** Allowed at site. **Vehicle Maximum Length:** 30 ft. **Other:** 14-day stay limit; no firearms.

TO GET THERE

From Mojave on Hwy. 14 drive 24 mi. northeast to the park entrance on the left. The campground is 1 mi. ahead.

MOJAVE NATIONAL PRESERVE
Hole-in-the-Wall

Black Canyon Rd., Mojave National Preserve 92311. T: (760) 255-8801; www.nps.gov/moja.

🚐 ★★★   ▲ ★★★★

Beauty: ★★★★   Site Privacy: ★★★
Spaciousness: ★★★   Quiet: ★★★★
Security: ★★★   Cleanliness: ★★★★
Insect Control: ★★★★   Facilities: ★★★

If you chanced to visit this campground when the Mojave National Preserve was first created in 1994, there was a very good likelihood that you had the entire grounds to yourself. Times have changed as word has spread about the subtle beauty of this area, and now you will probably have neighbors. Unless, of course, you make the mistake of visiting this piece of desert in summer when it becomes a sweltering inferno without a single shade tree to be found in the camp's single loop. But at an elevation of 4,400 feet, Hole-in-the-Wall can be pretty comfortable in both autumn and spring, even if late afternoon winds often require the donning of jackets and hats for warmth. And while the yucca plants and pencil chollas don't provide much in the way of screening, sites, with both pull-through and back-in parking, are roomy, well spaced apart, and attractively positioned just below a rough looking canyon. The sunset view of the surrounding mountains is an added plus, as is the Rings Trail hike, with its trailhead half a mile to the south.

BASICS

Operated By: National Park Service. **Open:** All year. **Site Assignment:** First come, first served. **Registration:** At entrance kiosk. **Fee:** $12, cash or check. **Parking:** At site.

FACILITIES

Number of RV Sites: 35. **Number of Tent-Only Sites:** 2. **Hookups:** None. **Each Site:** Picnic table, fire ring. **Dump Station:** Yes. **Laundry:** No. **Pay Phone:** Yes, at Hole-in-the Wall Visitor Center, 0.5 mi south. **Rest Rooms and Showers:** Vaulted toilets, no showers. **Fuel:** No. **Propane:** No. **Internal Roads:** Dirt, in good condition. **RV Service:** No. **Market:** 60 mi. west in Baker. **Restaurant:** 60 mi. west in Baker. **General Store:** No.

Vending: No. **Swimming:** No. **Playground:** No. **Other:** Some wheelchair accessible sites. **Activities:** Hiking, bicycling, horseback riding. **Nearby Attractions:** Mitchell Caverns, Desert Museum, Kelso Dunes, Teutonia Peak. **Additional Information:** Mojave Desert Information Center, (760) 733-4040.

RESTRICTIONS

Pets: On 6 ft. leash; not allowed on trails. **Fires:** In fire rings only. **Alcoholic Beverages:** Allowed at site. **Vehicle Maximum Length:** None. **Other:** 14-day stay limit; no loaded firearms.

TO GET THERE

Exit I-40 at Essex Rd., drive 10 mi. north and turn right on Black Canyon Rd. Drive 10.3 mi. and turn left into campground. Or: Exit I-15 at Cima Rd. and drive south for 22 mi. Turn left on Cedar Canyon Rd. and after 6 mi. turn right on Black Canyon Rd. Proceed for 9.5 mi. to the campground on the right.

MONO CITY
Lundy Canyon Campground

Lundy Lake Rd., Mono City 93541. T: (760) 932-5252 or (760) 932-5231; F: (760) 932-5458.

🚐 ★★★★	▲ ★★★★
Beauty: ★★★★	Site Privacy: ★★★★
Spaciousness: ★★★★	Quiet: ★★
Security: ★★	Cleanliness: ★★
Insect Control: ★★★	Facilities: ★

Lundy Canyon, a county park, is one of the better bargains around, especially with the explosion of price hikes at the concession-run national forest options. There is a subtle, understated beauty to this scruffy glen, where Lundy Creek discreetly trickles through and the Sierras tower above. Level, largely grassy sites, which range in size from shoe-boxes to palatial, are spread out over several access points along Lundy Lake Rd. Skip the first 15 or so, as many later choices are endowed with superior privacy and a more generous amount of space. Excellent screening between spots is derived from thickets of aspen, as well as juniper and high desert chaparral. This diamond-in-the-rough, at 7,800 feet elevation, lacks potable water, but the county has recently installed new tables and fire grates in several sites; new vaulted toilets are reportedly on the way. A boat ramp, boat rental,s and groceries are available at Lundy Lake Resort, just up the road.

BASICS

Operated By: Mono County Building & Parks Dept. **Open:** May through Oct., weather permitting. **Site Assignment:** First come, first served. **Registration:** At entrance kiosk, pay at site 37. **Fee:** $7, cash or CA check. **Parking:** At site.

FACILITIES

Number of RV Sites: 54. **Number of Tent-Only Sites:** 0. **Hookups:** None. **Each Site:** Picnic table, fire grate. **Dump Station:** No. **Laundry:** No. **Pay Phone:** No. **Rest Rooms and Showers:** Pit & vault toilets, no showers. **Fuel:** No. **Propane:** No. **Internal Roads:** Gravel & dirt, decent condition. **RV Service:** No. **Market:** 10 mi. southeast in Lee Vining. **Restaurant:** 10 mi. southeast in Lee Vining. **General Store:** No. **Vending:** No. **Swimming:** No. **Playground:** No. **Other:** Some wheelchair-accessible facilities. **Activities:** Fishing, hiking, boating. **Nearby Attractions:** Mono Lake Tufa State Reserve in Lee Vining; Lundy Lake; Bodie State Historic Park in Bridgeport. **Additional Information:** Mono County Tourism Commission, (760) 924-3699; Lee Vining Chamber of Commerce, (760) 647-6629.

RESTRICTIONS

Pets: On 10 ft. leash. **Fires:** In fire grates only. **Alcoholic Beverages:** Allowed at site. **Vehicle Maximum Length:** 24 ft. **Other:** No stay limit.

TO GET THERE

From Lee Vining drive 7 mi. north on US 395. Turn left on Lundy Lake Rd. and continue for 2.5 mi. to the campground entrance on the left. Lundy Lake Rd. offers several access points.

MORGAN HILL
Henry W. Coe State Park, Headquarters Campground

East Dunne Ave., Morgan Hill 95038. T: (408) 779-2728 or reservations (800) 444-7275; www.coepark.parks.ca.gov or www.cal-parks.ca.gov or www.reserveamerica.com.

🚐 ★★★   ⛺ ★★★★

Beauty: ★★★★★   Site Privacy: ★★
Spaciousness: ★★   Quiet: ★★★★
Security: ★★★   Cleanliness: ★★
Insect Control: ★★★   Facilities: ★★

Much of the 135 square miles that compose Henry Coe State Park are devoted to hiking trails, making the largest state park in northern California one of the better places for backpacking. You won't need to strap a 50-pound sack to your back to appreciate the beauty of this area, though, an RV or a tent will do nicely, too. Headquarters Campground, at 2,600 feet elevation, is located on the edge of a steep hillside, a few dozen yards from the well-maintained ranch buildings that date from when the Coe family resided here half a century ago (one of those structures now houses a visitor center). This sloping terrain limits both sites (several of which are on unlevel turf) and parking slips to very confined space. Even the old-style outhouses—which look as if they, too, date from the Coe era—seem smaller than a telephone booth. Happily, the extraordinary views across the hills toward distant mountains are more than expansive enough to compensate. In springtime the hilltop meadows erupt in an array of wildflowers.

BASICS
Operated By: California Dept. of Parks & Recreation. **Open:** All year. **Site Assignment:** Reservations accepted w/ V, MC, D. **Registration:** At visitor center. **Fee:** $7, cash or CA check. **Parking:** At site.

FACILITIES
Number of RV Sites: 20. **Number of Tent-Only Sites:** 0. **Hookups:** None. **Each Site:** Picnic table, fire ring, ramada or shade tree. **Dump Station:** No. **Laundry:** No. **Pay Phone:** Yes. **Rest Rooms and Showers:** Vault toilets, no showers. **Fuel:** No. **Propane:** No. **Internal Roads:** Paved. **RV Service:** No. **Market:** 13 mi. west in Morgan Hill. **Restaurant:** 13 mi. west in Morgan Hill. **General Store:** No. **Vending:** No. **Swimming:** No. **Playground:** No. **Other:** Old farmhouse buildings, nature center. **Activities:** Hiking, mountain biking, fishing, stargazing, horseback riding. **Nearby Attractions:** Mission San Juan Bautista, San Jose museums, zoo, & parks. **Additional Information:** Morgan Hill Chamber of Commerce, (408) 779-9444.

RESTRICTIONS
Pets: On 6 ft. leash. **Fires:** In fire rings only. **Alcoholic Beverages:** Allowed at site. **Vehicle Maximum Length:** 22 ft. **Other:** 14-day stay limit; no firearms; no wood gathering.

TO GET THERE
In Morgan Hill on US 101 take the East Dunne Ave. Exit. Drive for 13 mi. along the windy, narrow, ascending road straight to the park entrance. Use a pull-out along the way to absorb the magnificent valley views.

MORRO BAY
Montaña de Oro State Park

Pecho Valley Rd., Los Osos 93402. T: (805) 528-0513; www.cal-parks.ca.gov or www.reserveamerica.com.

🚐 ★★★   ⛺ ★★★★

Beauty: ★★★★   Site Privacy: ★★
Spaciousness: ★★★   Quiet: ★★★★
Security: ★★★   Cleanliness: ★★★★
Insect Control: ★★★   Facilities: ★

In many respects this is a very ordinary campground, with adequate elbow room in the grass and dirt sites but little privacy. Facilities are minimal, and even the camp's immediate setting, with a few Bishop pines punctuating the green confines of the narrow canyon, is just a notch or two above average in pulchritude. Give the park a chance, though—all 8,000 acres of it—and what you will find is a spectacular coastal wilderness that rivals the Big Sur area in its unspoiled beauty. The drive into Montaña de Oro threads past dense groves of aromatic eucalyptus, with eye-popping views of the dune-draped shore and Morro Rock out in the bay. Tall stands of cottonwood, oak, maple, willow, and box elder thrive elsewhere. Add to that miles of pristine beaches, highland bluffs and miscellaneous meadows, and you have a nature-lover's nirvana. For sun bathers there is Spooner's Cove, a romantic patch of sand and tide pools, just below the campground off the road. The vast array of wildflowers scattered over the hills in late spring is a heaven-scent sight.

BASICS

Operated By: California Dept. of Parks & Recreation. **Open:** All year. **Site Assignment:** Reservations accepted w/V, MC, D. **Registration:** At entrance kiosk. **Fee:** $12, cash or CA check. **Parking:** At site.

FACILITIES

Number of RV Sites: 50. **Number of Tent-Only Sites:** 4. **Hookups:** None. **Each Site:** Picnic table, fire grate, food storage box. **Dump Station:** No. **Laundry:** No. **Pay Phone:** Yes. **Rest Rooms and Showers:** Vault toilets, no showers. **Fuel:** No. **Propane:** No. **Internal Roads:** Paved. **RV Service:** No. **Market:** 5 mi. northeast in Los Osos. **Restaurant:** 5 mi. northeast in Los Osos. **General Store:** No. **Vending:** No. **Swimming:** In Pacific Ocean. **Playground:** No. **Activities:** Hiking, birding, bicycling, horseback riding, tidepooling, fishing, nature programs. **Nearby Attractions:** Mission San Luis Obispo; Morro Bay State Beach & Museum of Natural History. **Additional Information:** Los Osos/Baywood Park Chamber of Commerce, (805) 528-4884.

RESTRICTIONS

Pets: On 6 ft. leash. **Fires:** In fire grates only. **Alcoholic Beverages:** Allowed at site. **Vehicle Maximum Length:** 27 ft. **Other:** 14-day stay limit; no firearms; no wood gathering.

TO GET THERE

From San Luis Obispo head 3 mi. south on US 101 and exit at Los Osos Valley Rd. Drive 11.7 mi. west, then bear left on Pecho Valley Rd. The park entrance is 1 mi. ahead and the campground is to the left after that.

MOUNT SHASTA
KOA Mount Shasta

900 North Mount Shasta Blvd., Mount Shasta 96067. T: (530) 926-4029 or reservations (800) 562-3617; www.koa.com.

🚐 ★★★★   ⛺ ★★

Beauty: ★★★	Site Privacy: ★★
Spaciousness: ★★	Quiet: ★★★
Security: ★★★★	Cleanliness: ★★★★
Insect Control: ★★★	Facilities: ★★★★★

Admit it, you've always wondered what it was like to camp at a KOA. Well, stop your wondering and get your butane-burner over to this campground. As you might expect, the facilities are top-notch, ranging from a small pool (summer season) and cabin rentals to a game room, volleyball, basketball, and even a horse corral. With snow-capped Mt. Shasta towering over the downtown property, you can imagine that you are roughing it while flipping burgers by the barbecue grill. Sites are crowded into two environments, open meadow and sparsely forested. The latter is composed mostly of pines, with support from cottonwoods, cedars, maples, and manzanita. The resulting shade and screening make that area preferable, especially for tent campers, but the narrow, meandering lanes are not recommended for big rigs. The meadow, on the other hand, while exposed to both sun and neighbors, has the virtue of pull-through parking.

BASICS

Operated By: KOA Kampgrounds. **Open:** All year. **Site Assignment:** Reservations accepted w/V, MC, D. **Registration:** At entrance office. **Fee:** $19–$26, cash or V, MC, D. **Parking:** At site.

FACILITIES

Number of RV Sites: 40. **Number of Tent-Only Sites:** 68. **Hookups:** Water, electric (30, 50 amps), sewer, Internet. **Each Site:** Half-size picnic table, fire grate, some sites have a barbecue grill. **Dump Station:** Yes. **Laundry:** Yes. **Pay Phone:** Yes. **Rest Rooms and Showers:** Yes. **Fuel:** No. **Propane:** Yes. **Internal Roads:** Paved & forest floor. **RV Service:** Yes, mobile. **Market:** 1 mi. south in Mount Shasta. **Restaurant:** 1 mi. south in Mount Shasta. **General Store:** Yes. **Vending:** Yes. **Swimming:** In small pool seasonally. **Playground:** Yes. **Other:**

Some wheelchair-accessible facilities, game room, movie rentals. **Activities:** Horseshoe pit, volleyball, basketball, shuffleboard, nearby hiking, rafting, & fishing. **Nearby Attractions:** Lake Siskiyou; Mount Shasta Ski Park, Mount Shasta Hatchery & Sisson Museum; downtown Dunsmuir; Castle Crags State Park in Castella. **Additional Information:** Mount Shasta Chamber of Commerce & Visitors Bureau, (530) 926-4865 or (800) 926-4865; Dunsmuir Chamber of Commerce, (530) 235-2177.

RESTRICTIONS

Pets: On leash. **Fires:** In fire grates only; no wood fires allowed. **Alcoholic Beverages:** Allowed. **Vehicle Maximum Length:** 85 ft. **Other:** No fireworks.

TO GET THERE

On I-5 take the central Mount Shasta Exit and drive 0.5 mi. into town on West Lake St. At the stoplight turn left on North Mount Shasta Blvd. and proceed for 0.6 mi. Turn right on East Hinkley Blvd. and drive 1 block to the campground entrance on the left.

NAPA

Putah Creek Resort

7600 Knoxville Rd., Napa 94558. T: (707) 966-2116 or (707) 966-2368; F: (707) 966-0593; www.napavalleyonline.com/directory/wsparks.html.

🚐 ★★★★   ▲ ★★

Beauty: ★★★	Site Privacy: ★★
Spaciousness: ★★	Quiet: ★★★
Security: ★★★★	Cleanliness: ★★★
Insect Control: ★★★	Facilities: ★★★★★

Like every story, there are two sides to Putah Creek Resort. As in lakeside and creekside. The main compound overlooks lovely Lake Berryessa, a glimmering body of water that was created by the Bureau of Land Reclamation back in the 1950s. Yuccas and palms, knob cone pines and oaks, oleanders and pollarded hibiscus lend an appealing dash of beauty to a camp so developed it even has motel rooms and a restaurant-bar. Partial hookups are available near the boat launch, painfully close to the bar's open-air patio and within easy earshot of the motorboats and jet skis that often zip by. Across the road is the creek camp, in a greener, more serene setting. It is also endowed with a boat launch, and though many sites are too close to each other for camping comfort, a healthy majority overlook the water. Of the latter, 21–28 offer RVers a fine lateral view of the creek, while 3–8t put tent campers at the shore's edge. One negative to the creek area is that upkeep of restrooms is sometimes neglected. Both zones are fenced and protected by gate house entrance booths.

BASICS

Operated By: Putah Creek Resort. **Open:** All year. **Site Assignment:** Reservations accepted w/ V, MC, AE. **Registration:** At entrance gate or in store. **Fee:** $21–$26, cash or V, MC, AE. **Parking:** At site.

FACILITIES

Number of RV Sites: 255. **Number of Tent-Only Sites:** 0. **Hookups:** Water, electric (30, 50 amps), sewer. **Each Site:** Picnic table, barbecue grill. **Dump Station:** Yes. **Laundry:** Yes. **Pay Phone:** Yes. **Rest Rooms and Showers:** Yes. **Fuel:** Yes. **Propane:** Yes. **Internal Roads:** Paved. **RV Service:** No. **Market:** 27 mi. east in St. Helena. **Restaurant:** 27 mi. east in St. Helena. **General Store:** Yes, also deli & snack bar. **Vending:** Yes. **Swimming:** In Lake Berryessa. **Playground:** No. **Other:** Boat ramp, motel, restaurant. **Activities:** Fishing, boat rentals. **Nearby Attractions:** Bale Gristmill State Historic Park & Bothe–Napa Valley State Park in St. Helena; winery tours. **Additional Information:** Winters District Chamber of Commerce, (530) 795-2329; Napa-Sonoma Wine Country Visitor Center, (707) 624-0686 or (800) 723-0575.

RESTRICTIONS

Pets: On leash, $2. **Fires:** No. **Alcoholic Beverages:** Allowed. **Vehicle Maximum Length:** 50 ft. **Other:** 14-day stay limit from May 15–Oct. 15, 3-month stay limit in winter.

TO GET THERE

From Napa head 16 mi. north on Hwy. 121/Monticello Rd. Turn left on Hwy. 128 and drive 5 mi. Turn right on Berryessa Knoxville Rd. and continue for 13 mi. The resort entrance is on the right, just after the Pope Canyon Rd. turnoff.

NEEDLES

Needles Marina Park

100 Marina Dr., Needles 92363. T: (760) 326-2197; F: (760) 326-4125; www.needlesmarina.com.

🚐 ★★★★   ▲ ★★

Beauty: ★★★   Site Privacy: ★★
Spaciousness: ★★   Quiet: ★★
Security: ★★★   Cleanliness: ★★★★
Insect Control: ★★★   Facilities: ★★★★

Of the many campgrounds located along the Colorado River, few are quite as visually appealing as Needles Marina Park, where palm trees blend seamlessly with eucalyptus, mulberry with mesquite, and flowering oleanders lend a splash of color to the desert scene. Add to that a swimming pool and lagoon, a small sandy beach by the river, a boat ramp and marina, a hot tub, cabin rentals, and even a rec room equipped with billiard tables and dart boards, and you've got the recipe for one fine vacation spot. All of which is not exactly a well kept secret, as is easily observed in winter when the campground seems more crowded than the Santa Monica Freeway at rush hour. Even though loops are dispersed in clusters and many sites feature pull-through parking, space is definitely on the small side, and the hard-packed pebbly dirt is inhospitable to comfortable tenting. Sites 162–166, overlooking the lagoon, are the best screened for privacy.

BASICS

Operated By: Needles Marina Park. **Open:** All year. **Site Assignment:** Reservations accepted w/ V, MC. **Registration:** At office in store. **Fee:** $26–$28, cash or V, MC. **Parking:** At sites.

FACILITIES

Number of RV Sites: 194. **Number of Tent-Only Sites:** 0. **Hookups:** Water, electric (30, 50 amps), sewer, Internet. **Each Site:** Picnic table, barbecue grill. **Dump Station:** Yes. **Laundry:** Yes. **Pay Phone:** Yes. **Rest Rooms and Showers:** Yes. **Fuel:** No. **Propane:** No. **Internal Roads:** Paved. **RV Service:** No. **Market:** 1 mi. south in Needles. **Restaurant:** 1 mi. south in Needles. **General Store:** Yes. **Vending:** Yes. **Swimming:** In pool & lagoon. **Playground:** Yes. **Other:** Boat ramp & boat slips, marina, rec room, spa. **Activities:** Fishing, pool tables, dart board, waterskiing, Needles

Municipal Golf Course. **Nearby Attractions:** London Bridge, Mitchell Caverns, Lake Havasu, Providence Mountains State Recreation Area. **Additional Information:** Needles Area Chamber of Commerce, (760) 326-2050.

RESTRICTIONS

Pets: On leash. **Fires:** In barbecue grills only. **Alcoholic Beverages:** Allowed. **Vehicle Maximum Length:** None. **Other:** No washing of vehices; no motorcycle riding; no ATVs.

TO GET THERE

From Needles drive 0.8 mi. north on Needles Hwy. Bear right as it turns into River Rd. Take a left on Marina Dr. and continue 0.1 mi. to the park entrance on the left side.

NICE

Holiday Harbor RV Park and Marina

3605 Lakeshore Blvd., Nice 95464. T: (707) 274-1136; www.sojourner2000.com/clc/hh; jsbartz@pacific.net.

🚐 ★★★   ▲ n/a

Beauty: ★★★   Site Privacy: ★★
Spaciousness: ★★   Quiet: ★★
Security: ★★★   Cleanliness: ★★★
Insect Control: ★★★   Facilities: ★★★★

Holiday Harbor is at the northern end of Clear Lake, California's second largest freshwater lake and one of the top places for bass fishing in the entire country, according to reputable angling organizations. This is more of a marina than a campground, with comparable gravel-surfaced sites encircling the boat slips at the center of the property. There are a few sycamores and junipers on the lot, and though situated in a residential neighborhood, within easy walking distance of the commercial district of Nice, a wooden fence at the perimeter lends a degree of protective privacy to the lot. A county-owned stretch of beach abuts Holiday Harbor and sunsets viewed from its pier are heart-stoppers. This is one of the few places in which you can sleep within eye-shot of your boat, but if you are not hauling one there really is not much point in staying here. Tent camping is not permitted.

BASICS

Operated By: Holiday Harbor RV Park & Marina.
Open: All year. **Site Assignment:** Reservations accepted w/ V, MC. **Registration:** At office. **Fee:** $18–$20 plus 9% local tax, cash, CA check or V, MC. **Parking:** At site.

FACILITIES

Number of RV Sites: 34. **Number of Tent-Only Sites:** 0. **Hookups:** Water, electric (20, 30 amps), sewer, Internet. **Each Site:** Half-size picnic table, garden lantern. **Dump Station:** Yes. **Laundry:** Yes. **Pay Phone:** Yes. **Rest Rooms and Showers:** Yes. **Fuel:** No. **Propane:** No. **Internal Roads:** Gravel, good condition. **RV Service:** No. **Market:** Within 0.5 mi. in Nice. **Restaurant:** Within 0.5 mi. in Nice. **General Store:** No. **Vending:** Yes. **Swimming:** At swim beach on Clear Lake. **Playground:** No. **Other:** Marina, boat ramp. **Activities:** Fishing, boating, waterskiing, hiking, bicycling, birding. **Nearby Attractions:** Lake County Museum in Lakeport; Clear Lake State Park in Kelseyville. **Additional Information:** Lakeport Chamber of Commerce, (707) 263-5092; Lake County Marketing Program/Visitor Information Center, (707) 263-9544 or (800) 525-3743.

RESTRICTIONS

Pets: On 6 ft. leash. **Fires:** No. **Alcoholic Beverages:** Allowed. **Vehicle Maximum Length:** None. **Other:** No stay limit; no tents.

TO GET THERE

From the town of Nice on Hwy. 20 at the north end of Clear Lake, turn left on Howard St. Drive 1 block, then turn left again onto Lakeshore Blvd. The campground entrance is 1 block away on the right.

O'BRIEN

Nelson Point

Conflict Point Rd., O'Brien 96070. T: (530) 275-1587 or reservations (800) 444-6777; www.r5.fs.fed.us/shastatrinity or www.reserveusa.com.

🚐 ★★★	🏕 ★★★★
Beauty: ★★★★	Site Privacy: ★★★★
Spaciousness: ★★	Quiet: ★★
Security: ★	Cleanliness: ★★
Insect Control: ★	Facilities: ★

Nelson Point is a cozy property that rests on a grassy hill just above one rippling arm of Shasta Lake, a little more than 20 miles north of Redding. It is a convenient hop just off I-5, and that is also its major drawback: you may wake up in the middle of the night to the sound of traffic and think for a moment you're in a highway rest area. Oaks and pines hover over the dirt-surfaced sites, which are also spaced well apart along the meandering camp lane. While most spots enjoy water views, number 5, a walk-in of some 20 steps, is tops in spaciousness and occupies a small promontory that is blessed with a 180-degree panorama of the lake. More private is 7, though it lies close to the road, and 6, too, is tucked away from its neighbors. The apalling amount of broken glass, food debris, bottle caps, and even bullet shells littering the ground indicates that the concessionaire operating this diamond-in-the-rough for the forest service must do more to maintain the property than simply emptying the cash box. An elevation of just 1,000 feet makes for very comfortable evenings early and late in the year.

BASICS

Operated By: Shasta Recreation Company, concessionnaire. **Open:** Apr. through Sept. **Site Assignment:** Reservations accepted w/ V, MC, D for groups & limited number of sites. **Registration:** At entrance kiosk. **Fee:** $8, cash or check. **Parking:** At site.

FACILITIES

Number of RV Sites: 8. **Number of Tent-Only Sites:** 0. **Hookups:** None. **Each Site:** Picnic table, fire grate, some sites have stone fire ring. **Dump Station:** No. **Laundry:** No. **Pay Phone:** No. **Rest Rooms and Showers:** Vault toilets, no showers. **Fuel:** No. **Propane:** No. **Internal Roads:** Paved. **RV Service:** No. **Market:** 4 mi. north in Lakehead. **Restaurant:** 14 mi. south in Shasta Lake. **General Store:** No. **Vending:** No. **Swimming:** In Shasta Lake inlet. **Playground:** No. **Activities:** Fishing, boating, waterskiing. **Nearby Attractions:** Carter House Natural Science Museum, Turtle Bay Museums & Arboretum, Waterworks Park in Redding; Shasta Lake, Caverns, & Dam; Shasta State Historic Park; Whiskeytown National Recreation Area. **Additional Information:** Redding CVB, (530) 225-4100.

RESTRICTIONS

Pets: On 6 ft. leash. **Fires:** In fire grates only. **Alcoholic Beverages:** Allowed. **Vehicle Maximum Length:** 16 ft. **Other:** 14-day stay limit.

TO GET THERE

From Redding drive 22 mi. north on I-5 and exit at Salt Creek Rd./Gilman Rd. Turn left and drive 1 block, then veer right onto Salt Creek Rd. After 0.3 mi. hang a left onto Conflict Point Rd. (opposite the highway underpass). The campground is 0.3 mi. ahead on the left.

OAKLAND
Anthony Chabot Regional Park

9999 Redwood Rd., Oakland 94619. T: (510) 562-2267; www.ebparks.org.

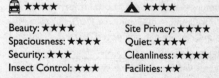 ★★★★   ▲ ★★★

Beauty: ★★★★   Site Privacy: ★★
Spaciousness: ★★★   Quiet: ★★★★
Security: ★★★   Cleanliness: ★★★
Insect Control: ★★   Facilities: ★★★

This wooded, pastoral setting is an oasis of calm and beauty only a few minutes drive from the urban bustle of Oakland and Berkeley. Five small loops are spread over a hilltop that is abundantly populated with fragrant eucalyptus trees—contrary to what may be implied by the name of the access lane, Redwood Rd.—and a few sycamores. Some of the slim, exposed sites enjoy vistas of Lake Chabot, while others overlook a fertile pasture where goats often graze. Best of the latter are 10–12 in the hookup area. The most private of the drive-to sites is number 69 but ardent tenters should consider the even more secluded walk-ins in the direction of the water. In addition to several hiking trails there is a 12-mile bicycling path that is very popular with the thin tire set. The lake, which covers 315 acres, is stocked with fish on a regular basis. Security is good, with ranger patrols and a gate that is locked nightly at 10 p.m.

BASICS

Operated By: East Bay Regional Park District. **Open:** All year. **Site Assignment:** Reservations recommended; V, MC, D. **Registration:** At entrance booth. **Fee:** $15–$20, cash or V, MC, D. **Parking:** At site.

FACILITIES

Number of RV Sites: 65. **Number of Tent-Only Sites:** 10. **Hookups:** Water, electric (30 amps), sewer. **Each Site:** Picnic table, fire grate. **Dump Station:** Yes. **Laundry:** No. **Pay Phone:**

Yes. **Rest Rooms and Showers:** Yes. **Fuel:** No. **Propane:** No. **Internal Roads:** Paved. **RV Service:** No. **Market:** 17 mi. west in Oakland. **Restaurant:** 17 mi. west in Oakland. **General Store:** No. **Vending:** No. **Swimming:** No. **Playground:** No. **Other:** Some wheelchair-accessible facilities, boat launch, marina, shooting range. **Activities:** Hiking, fishing, bicycling, horseback riding, kayaking, canoeing. **Nearby Attractions:** Berkeley Botanical Garden & museums; Oakland museums, zoo, Dunsmuir House & Gardens Historic Estate, Chabot Space & Science Center, Jack London Square & more. **Additional Information:** Oakland CVB, (510) 839-5924.

RESTRICTIONS

Pets: On 6 ft. leash; $1 fee. **Fires:** In fire grates only. **Alcoholic Beverages:** Allowed at site, beer & wine only. **Vehicle Maximum Length:** 39 ft. **Other:** 15-day stay limit; no loaded firearms; no wood gathering.

TO GET THERE

From Oakland on I-580 drive 5.5 mi. east. Exit on Hwy. 13 north and after 1 mi. turn right onto Redwood Rd. Continue for 7.8 mi. to the park entrance on the right. The campground is 2 mi. ahead.

ORICK
Prairie Creek Redwoods State Park, Elk Prairie Campground

Newton B. Drury Scenic Pkwy., Orick 95555. T: (707) 464-6101 ext. 5301 or 5064 or reservations (800) 444-7275; www.cal-parks.ca.gov or www.reserveamerica.com.

    ★★★★   ▲ ★★★★

Beauty: ★★★★   Site Privacy: ★★★★
Spaciousness: ★★★★   Quiet: ★★★★
Security: ★★★   Cleanliness: ★★★★
Insect Control: ★★★   Facilities: ★★

Tall as they are, it is easy to overlook the redwood trees when you visit this delightful park. That is largely due to the presence of a good-sized herd of photogenic Roosevelt elk, which can usually be observed grazing in the open grassland near the park's entrance along US 101, as well as down by the shore close to the primitive Gold Bluff Beach campground. The latter is in a beautiful location, between the ocean and 100-foot-high bluffs, but to reach it you will have to navigate six miles along a dirt minefield of potholes, a stress test for your nerves as well as your vehicle's axles. Prairie Creek's other campground, Elk Prairie, is inland from the bluffs and far easier to reach. Its single meadow loop—favored by RVs—is prime elk-viewing territory, and its wooded double loop allows for shade, space, and privacy. Curiously, there are few redwoods present, but an abundance of other conifers as well as maples and moss-encrusted alders contribute to a lush, rain forest atmosphere. The largest, most private sites are those nearest to the creek, where the gently gurgling water will serenade you to sleep at night.

BASICS

Operated By: California Dept. of Parks & Recreation. **Open:** All year. **Site Assignment:** Reservations recommended; V, MC, D. **Registration:** At entrance booth. **Fee:** $12, cash or CA check. **Parking:** At site.

FACILITIES

Number of RV Sites: 75. **Number of Tent-Only Sites:** 0. **Hookups:** None. **Each Site:** Picnic table, fire grate, food storage box. **Dump Station:** Yes. **Laundry:** No. **Pay Phone:** Yes. **Rest Rooms and Showers:** Yes. **Fuel:** No. **Propane:** No. **Internal Roads:** Paved, narrow, & winding. **RV Service:** No. **Market:** 4 mi. south in Orick. **Restaurant:** 4 mi. south in Orick. **General Store:** No. **Vending:** No. **Swimming:** No. **Playground:** No. **Other:** Some wheelchair-accessible facilities, visitor center. **Activities:** Hiking, bicycling, wildlife viewing, photography, beachcombing. **Nearby Attractions:** Humboldt Lagoons State Park & Redwood National & State Parks in Orick; Trees of Mystery in Klamath. **Additional Information:** Orick Chamber of Commerce, (707) 488-2885; Klamath Chamber of Commerce, (707) 482-7165.

RESTRICTIONS

Pets: On 6 ft. leash. **Fires:** In fire grates only. **Alcoholic Beverages:** Allowed at site. **Vehicle Maximum Length:** 27 ft. **Other:** 14-day stay limit from May 1–Sept. 30; no firearms; no wood gathering; no mushroom-plucking.

TO GET THERE

From Crescent City drive 37 mi. south on US 101. Exit and turn right on the Newton B. Drury Scenic Pkwy. Continue for 1.2 mi. to the park entrance on the left.

ORLAND
Buckhorn

Buckhorn Rd., Orland 95963. T: (530) 865-4781 or reservations (877) 444-6777 or marina (530) 865-2665; F: (530) 865-5283; www.spk.usace.army.mil/cespk-co/lakes/blackbutte.html or www.reserveusa.com; blackbutte-info@spk.usace.army.mil.

🚐 ★★★★	▲ ★★★★
Beauty: ★★★★	Site Privacy: ★★
Spaciousness: ★★★	Quiet: ★★★
Security: ★★★★	Cleanliness: ★★★
Insect Control: ★★★	Facilities: ★★★★

Black Butte Lake may seem like a mirage at first glance, its blue-green surface shimmering in the middle of sun-baked brown hills, with black-mauve volcanic rocks crowning the scene. Go ahead and pinch yourself, it's really there. It is also, as one of the largest lakes in the region, a hugely popular summertime recreation area that attracts anyone with a boat for miles around. Buckhorn is one of two campgrounds on this US Army Corps of Engineers domain, 12 miles west of Orland and I-5. Several loops cling to the undulating contours of the hillside abutting the lake, which results in a high percentage of lake-view sites. A sprinkling of oaks shed adequate shade, and screening and space are average. While all types of watercrafts are permitted, the stiff breezes that often sweep across the lake make sailing especially rewarding. Black Butte Lake is one of the better locations for crappie fishing in northern California.

BASICS

Operated By: US Army Corps of Engineers. **Open:** All year. **Site Assignment:** Reservations accepted w/ MC, V, D. **Registration:** At entrance booth. **Fee:** $14 from Mar. 1–Sept. 30, $10 the rest of the year; cash or check. **Parking:** At site.

FACILITIES

Number of RV Sites: 87. **Number of Tent-Only Sites:** 5. **Hookups:** None. **Each Site:** Picnic table, fire grate, barbecue grill. **Dump Station:** Yes. **Laundry:** No. **Pay Phone:** Yes. **Rest Rooms and Showers:** Flush & portable toilets, no showers. **Fuel:** No. **Propane:** Yes. **Internal Roads:** Paved. **RV Service:** No. **Market:** 12 mi. east in Orland. **Restaurant:** 12 mi. east in Orland. **General**

Store: Yes, at marina. **Vending:** No. **Swimming:** In Black Butte Lake. **Playground:** Yes. **Other:** Some wheelchair-accessible facilities, boat launch, marina. **Activities:** Fishing, hiking, sailing, windsurfing, boat rentals. **Nearby Attractions:** Tejama County Park in Corning; Chico museums & Bidwell Mansion State Historic Park; outlet shopping in Anderson; William B. Ide Adobe State Historic Park near Red Bluff. **Additional Information:** Corning District Chamber of Commerce, (530) 824-5550; Chico Chamber of Commerce & Visitor Bureau, (530) 891-5556 or (800) 852-8570.

RESTRICTIONS

Pets: On leash. **Fires:** In fire grates only. **Alcoholic Beverages:** Allowed. **Vehicle Maximum Length:** 35 ft. **Other:** 14-day stay limit.

TO GET THERE

In Orland on I-5 take the Black Butte Lake Exit. Head west on Rd. 200/Newville Rd. for 12 mi. Turn left on Buckhorn Rd. and continue straight to the campground.

OROVILLE

Lake Oroville State Recreation Area, Bidwell Canyon Campground

Arroyo Dr., Oroville 95966. T: (530) 538-2219 or (530) 538-2200 or reservations (800) 444-7275; www.cal-parks.ca.gov or www.norcal.parks.state. ca.us or www.reserveamerica.com.

🚐 ★★★★   ⛺ ★★

Beauty: ★★★	Site Privacy: ★★
Spaciousness: ★★	Quiet: ★★★
Security: ★★★	Cleanliness: ★★★
Insect Control: ★★★	Facilities: ★★★★

When Lake Oroville is full it is a beautiful sight. Unfortunately, its level depends both on winter snow melt and how much it has been drawn down during the summer. Management tries to keep the water near capacity at least through the fourth of July holiday, when the recreation area overflows with campers, but Mother Nature does not always cooperate. Not that campsites are affected either way, since few are endowed with water views. Of the two double circuits, Loop I (numbers 1–39) is the grassier, with limited space between pine- and live oak–shaded sites. The crowding is no better in Loop II (40–75), where the live oaks are complemented by madrone and manzanita. Two of the better sites for privacy are 31 and 44, but overall the constricted layout of this facility makes it more suitable for RV campers than tenters. The exceptions are the remote boat-in sites, assuming there is water available to provide access.

BASICS

Operated By: California Dept. of Parks & Recreation. **Open:** All year. **Site Assignment:** Reservations accepted w/V, MC, D. **Registration:** At entrance booth. **Fee:** $16, cash or CA check. **Parking:** At site.

FACILITIES

Number of RV Sites: 75. **Number of Tent-Only Sites:** 0. **Hookups:** Water, electric (20, 30 amps), sewer. **Each Site:** Picnic table, fire grate. **Dump Station:** No. **Laundry:** No. **Pay Phone:** Yes. **Rest Rooms and Showers:** Yes. **Fuel:** No. **Propane:** Yes. **Internal Roads:** Paved. **RV Service:** No. **Market:** 10 mi. west in Oroville. **Restaurant:** 10 mi. west in Oroville. **General Store:** Yes, w/ snack bar at marina. **Vending:** No. **Swimming:** In Lake Oroville. **Playground:** No. **Other:** Some wheelchair-accessible facilities, 7-lane boat ramp, marina. **Activities:** Fishing, waterskiing, hiking, windsurfing, horseback riding, boat rentals. **Nearby Attractions:** Oroville Dam, Chinese Temple & Garden, Pioneer Museum, Freeman Bicycle Trail; Gold Nuggett Museum in Paradise. **Additional Information:** Oroville Area Chamber of Commerce, (530) 538-2542 or (800) 655-GOLD.

RESTRICTIONS

Pets: On 6 ft. leash. **Fires:** In fire grates only. **Alcoholic Beverages:** Allowed at site. **Vehicle Maximum Length:** 40 ft. **Other:** 30-day stay limit; no firearms; no wood gathering.

TO GET THERE

From Oroville drive 7 mi. east on Hwy. 162. Turn left on Kelly Ridge Rd. and continue for 1.6 mi. to Arroyo Dr. Turn right and proceed to the park entrance 0.5 mi. ahead.

PALO ALTO
Butano State Park

1500 Cloverdale Rd., Pescadero 94060. T: (650) 879-2040 or reservations (800) 444-7275; www.cal-parks.ca.gov or www.reserveamerica.com.

🚐 ★★★   ▲ ★★★★

Beauty: ★★★★	Site Privacy: ★★★★
Spaciousness: ★★★★	Quiet: ★★★
Security: ★★★★	Cleanliness: ★★★★
Insect Control: ★★★	Facilities: ★★

You've heard the expression "good things come in small packages"? That is certainly true of this beautiful park, another in the fine constellation of coast redwood preserves that are located above Santa Cruz and to the east of San Jose. The drive to Butano is easier than the others, along a marginally wider road without quite as many mountainous turns. Sites, too, are roomier and scattered farther apart than those at Portola Redwoods State Park a few miles away. Direct sunlight onto the double loop is largely blocked by the magnificent stands of Sequoia sempervirens, which are so dominant that only a few tan oaks have been able to lay down roots. Tenters will enjoy the privacy of the many recessed walk-in sites, and of the drive-to options, 6 is level and very roomy, and 9, tucked behind a fallen giant, is quite private. We encountered quails, rabbits ,and a doe and its tiny fawn on our last visit; they were attracted to the grounds by a small creek that runs through camp.

BASICS

Operated By: California Dept. of Parks & Recreation. **Open:** All year. **Site Assignment:** Reservations accepted w/ V, MC, D. **Registration:** At entrance booth. **Fee:** $12, cash or CA check. **Parking:** At site.

FACILITIES

Number of RV Sites: 21. **Number of Tent-Only Sites:** 17. **Hookups:** None. **Each Site:** Picnic table, fire grate, food storage box. **Dump Station:** No. **Laundry:** No. **Pay Phone:** Yes. **Rest Rooms and Showers:** Flush & pit toilets, no showers. **Fuel:** No. **Propane:** No. **Internal Roads:** Paved. **RV Service:** No. **Market:** 24 mi. north in Half Moon Bay. **Restaurant:** 24 mi. north in Half Moon Bay. **General Store:** No. **Vending:**

No. **Swimming:** No. **Playground:** No. **Other:** Some wheelchair-accessible facilities, visitor center. **Activities:** Hiking, birding, exploring redwood forests. **Nearby Attractions:** Pigeon Point Lighthouse & downtown Half Moon Bay; Montara & Gray Whale Cove State Beaches; several redwood forests. **Additional Information:** Half Moon Bay Coastside Chamber of Commerce & Visitors Bureau, (650) 726-8380.

RESTRICTIONS

Pets: On 6 ft. leash. **Fires:** In fire grates only. **Alcoholic Beverages:** Allowed at site. **Vehicle Maximum Length:** 27 ft. **Other:** 14-day stay limit; no firearms; no wood gathering.

TO GET THERE

From the junction of Hwy. 1 and Hwy. 92 in Half Moon Bay, drive 17 mi. south on Hwy. 1. Turn left on Pescadero Rd., drive 2.7 mi. and turn right on Cloverdale Rd. The park entrance is 4.5 mi. ahead on the left.

PASADENA
Monte Cristo

12371 North Little Tujunga Canyon Rd., San Fernando 91342. T: (818) 899-1900; F: (818) 896-6727; www.r5.fs.fed.us/angeles.

🚐 ★★★   ▲ ★★★

Beauty: ★★★	Site Privacy: ★★★
Spaciousness: ★★★	Quiet: ★★★
Security: ★★	Cleanliness: ★★
Insect Control: ★★★★	Facilities: ★

To reach Monte Cristo you will have to drive 20 miles north of La Cañada along steep, windy roads, with the stretch on CR N3 showcasing highly dramatic craggy peaks. There is no let down at the campground, either, which is tucked under sycamores and oaks in a mountain knoll (3,600 feet elevation) deep in the Angeles National Forest. Agaves and pines round out a setting that is often overrun with family groups, especially on weekends. And no wonder, given that deep sites, surfaced with a mix of grass and dirt, are planted well apart along the camp's figure-8 loop, which is bisected by a small creek. Those spots are largely comparable, though we prefer the ones at the far end of the camp's entrance because that area picks up less road noise.

As is typical of many national forest properties, security and maintenance are lax, with the result that litter is often to be found in the fire grates.

BASICS

Operated By: Angeles National Forest, Los Angeles River Ranger District. **Open:** All year, weather permitting. **Site Assignment:** First come, first served. **Registration:** At entrance kiosk. **Fee:** $8, cash or check. **Parking:** At site.

FACILITIES

Number of RV Sites: 19. **Number of Tent-Only Sites:** 0. **Hookups:** None. **Each Site:** Picnic table, fire grate. **Dump Station:** No. **Laundry:** No. **Pay Phone:** No. **Rest Rooms and Showers:** Vault toilets, no showers. **Fuel:** No. **Propane:** No. **Internal Roads:** Paved. **RV Service:** No. **Market:** 20 mi. south in La Cañada. **Restaurant:** 20 mi. south in La Cañada. **General Store:** No. **Vending:** No. **Swimming:** No. **Playground:** No. **Other:** Some wheelchair-accessible facilities. **Activities:** Hiking, wading in creek. **Nearby Attractions:** Six Flags Magic Mountain, downtown Pasadena, Hollywood's theme parks. **Additional Information:** La Cañada Flintridge Chamber of Commerce, (818) 790-4289.

RESTRICTIONS

Pets: On leash. **Fires:** In fire grates only. **Alcoholic Beverages:** Allowed. **Vehicle Maximum Length:** 30 ft. **Other:** 14-day stay limit.

TO GET THERE

From I-210 in La Cañada/Flintridge head north on Hwy. 2. After 9 mi. turn left onto CR N3, direction Palmdale. Drive 10 mi. and turn right into the campground.

PINECREST
Pinecrest

Pinecrest Lake Rd., Pinecrest 95364. T: (209) 965-3434 or reservations (877) 444-6777; F: (209) 965-3372; www.r5.fs.fed.us/stanislaus or www.reserveusa.com.

🚐 ★★★★   ▲ ★★★

Beauty: ★★★★	Site Privacy: ★★★
Spaciousness: ★★★	Quiet: ★★
Security: ★★	Cleanliness: ★★
Insect Control: ★★★	Facilities: ★★★

There is more than merely the aura of a resort town to Pinecrest, it actually delivers the goods.

Activities range from hiking and bicycling to fishing, swimming, and boating; amenities include an expansive picnic area near the water, a marina, and, across the street, a post office, restaurant and general store stocked with everything from fresh produce to liquor to hardware. The huge campground, which is 30 miles east of Sonora, is handsomely framed by its high altitude (5,600 feet) Sierra Nevada locale, rubbing up against the clear blue Pinecrest Lake, with pine and granite studded hills all around. Even Shrangi-la had its downside, however, and Pinecrest is no different. Sites of grass and pine needles pinch a bit as space is at a premium over the camp's multiple series of loops. That constricted feeling is accentuated by the presence of private vacation cabins off to one side of the property, which also detract from the rustic atmosphere. Nonetheless, privacy is not bad, as thick groves of cedars, ponderosa, and lodgepole pines, as well as a widespread debris field of glacial erratics, contribute a degree of screening. The grungy, pitted restrooms are in urgent need of renovation.

BASICS

Operated By: Dodge Ridge Corp., concessionaire. **Open:** May through Oct., weather permitting. **Site Assignment:** Reservations required from May 15 to Sept. 5; V, MC, D, AE. **Registration:** At entrance booth. **Fee:** $16, cash or check. **Parking:** At site.

FACILITIES

Number of RV Sites: 200. **Number of Tent-Only Sites:** 0. **Hookups:** None. **Each Site:** Picnic table, fire grate. **Dump Station:** No. **Laundry:** No. **Pay Phone:** Yes. **Rest Rooms and Showers:** Yes. **Fuel:** No. **Propane:** No. **Internal Roads:** Paved. **RV Service:** No. **Market:** Across the street is a large, well-stocked general store. **Restaurant:** Across the street. **General Store:** Yes. **Vending:** No. **Swimming:** In Pinecrest Lake. **Playground:** No. **Other:** Limited wheelchair-accessible facilities, boat ramp, marina. **Activities:** Hiking, fishing, boat rentals, bicycling. **Nearby Attractions:** Tuolumne County Museum & History Center in Sonora; Yosemite National Park; Ahwahnee Whitewater Rafting in Columbia. **Additional Information:** Yosemite Area Traveler Information, (209) 723-3153; Tuolumne County Visitors Bureau, (209) 533-4420 or (800) 446-1333.

RESTRICTIONS

Pets: On leash. **Fires:** In fire grates only. **Alcoholic Beverages:** Allowed. **Vehicle Maximum Length:** 22 ft. **Other:** 14-day stay limit.

TO GET THERE

From Sonora drive 28 mi. east on Hwy. 108. Turn right at the sign for Pinecrest Lake and continue for 0.7 mi. to the campground entrance on the right.

PISMO BEACH
Pismo State Beach, North Beach Campground

Hwy. 1, Pismo Beach 93445. T: (805) 489-2684; www.cal-parks.ca.gov or www.reserveamerica.com.

🚐 ★★★   ▲ ★★★★

Beauty: ★★★★	Site Privacy: ★★★
Spaciousness: ★★★	Quiet: ★★★
Security: ★★★	Cleanliness: ★★★
Insect Control: ★★	Facilities: ★★

Sand and surf, in a nutshell, are two attributes that make this a central coast standout, one of the prettier stretches of beach in the area. Add to that the wintertime presence of tens of thousands of monarch butterflies, drawn to the park by its towering eucalyptus trees, and it's clear why swarms of tourists descend on the camp like ants to a picnic throughout the summer and most weekends the rest of the year. Located just off of Hwy. 1, one mile south of town, North Beach is separated from the water by a high series of dunes. These obstruct views of the ocean, but also buffer the campground from its blustery breezes. Grassy sites are level and of average size, with Monterey pines and flowering bottle brush enhancing the modest screening provided by the fragrant eucalyptus. Unlike Oceano, two miles to the south, North Beach does not allow day use, meaning that campers enjoy their piece of shore without the added crush of daytrippers. This is also the prettier of the two camps, but its lack of hookups means that if you need electricity Oceano is the place to be.

BASICS

Operated By: California Dept. of Parks & Recreation. **Open:** All year. **Site Assignment:** Reservations accepted w/ V, MC, D. **Registration:** At entrance booth. **Fee:** $12, cash or CA check. **Parking:** At site.

FACILITIES

Number of RV Sites: 103. **Number of Tent-Only Sites:** 0. **Hookups:** None. **Each Site:** Picnic table, fire grate, food storage box. **Dump Station:** Yes. **Laundry:** No. **Pay Phone:** Yes. **Rest Rooms and Showers:** Yes. **Fuel:** No. **Propane:** No. **Internal Roads:** Paved. **RV Service:** No. **Market:** 1 mi. north in Pismo Beach. **Restaurant:** 1 mi. north in Pismo Beach. **General Store:** No. **Vending:** Yes. **Swimming:** In Pacific Ocean, if you can tolerate it. **Playground:** No. **Other:** Some wheelchair-accessible facilities. **Activities:** Fishing, surfing, clamming, horseback riding, hiking, golf. **Nearby Attractions:** Wineries; San Luis Obispo mission & musems; Oceano Dunes State Vehicular Recreation Area. **Additional Information:** Pismo Beach Chamber of Commerce, (805) 773-4382; San Luis Obispo County Visitors & Conference Bureau, (800) 634-1414 or (805) 541-8000.

RESTRICTIONS

Pets: On 6 ft. leash. **Fires:** In fire grates only. **Alcoholic Beverages:** Allowed at site. **Vehicle Maximum Length:** 36 ft. **Other:** 7-day stay limit from Apr. 1–Oct. 29; no firearms; no wood gathering.

TO GET THERE

In Pismo Beach on US 101 take the Pismo Beach State Park Exit. Drive 2.8 mi. west (toward the ocean) on East Grand Ave. and turn right on Hwy. 1. After 0.8 mi. turn left into the campground.

POLLOCK PINES
Ice House

FR 32, Pollock Pines 95726. T: (530) 644-2349 or reservations (877) 444-6777; F: (530) 647-5405; www.r5.fs.fed.us/eldorado or www.reserveusa.com.

🚐 ★★★★   ▲ ★★★★

Beauty: ★★★★	Site Privacy: ★★★
Spaciousness: ★★★	Quiet: ★★★★
Security: ★★★	Cleanliness: ★★★
Insect Control: ★★★	Facilities: ★★

The concession that operates Ice House delivers primitive camping conditions for its nightly fee of $15, which seems appalling at first blush. Don't let price-gouging deter you, though, from coming to this beautiful, rough-cut campground. Its wild, unspoiled appearance is an idiosyncratic reminder of the relative youth and vitality of the Sierra Nevada range, and a bit reminiscent of Grover Hot Springs State Park, at Markleeville. Ice House reflects two sorts of environments, from the reservoir below its two undulating loops to the lofty, snow-dusted mountain peaks high above. Sites of dirt and pine needles are grouped closely together, but are well-buffered by an abundance of enormous boulders and concentrations of ponderosa and Jeffrey pines, incense cedar, and manzanita. The latter appears in especially thick concentrations in the second circuit, which also holds more of the quirkily engaging sites. With an elevation of 5,436 feet, roads in this area can be snow-covered from late Oct. until mid-May.

BASICS

Operated By: American Land & Leisure, concessionaire. **Open:** Mid-May to mid-Oct., weather permitting. **Site Assignment:** Reservations accepted w/ V, MC, D. **Registration:** At entrance kiosk. **Fee:** $15, cash or check; $30 for double site. **Parking:** At site.

FACILITIES

Number of RV Sites: 66. **Number of Tent-Only Sites:** 17. **Hookups:** None. **Each Site:** Picnic table, fire grate, barbecue grill. **Dump Station:** Yes. **Laundry:** No. **Pay Phone:** No. **Rest Rooms and Showers:** Vault toilets, no showers. **Fuel:** No. **Propane:** No. **Internal Roads:** Paved but bumpy, windy & narrow. **RV Service:** No. **Market:** 21 mi. southwest in Pollock Pines. **Restaurant:** 21 mi. southwest in Pollock Pines. **General Store:** No. **Vending:** No. **Swimming:** In Ice House Reservoir. **Playground:** No. **Other:** Some wheelchair-accessible facilities, boat ramp. **Activities:** Fishing, hiking, boating, bicycling, boulder scrambling. **Nearby Attractions:** Fountain-Tallman Museum in Placerville; El Dorado National Forest in Camino; Sly Park Recreation Area in Pollock Pines. **Additional Information:** El Dorado County Visitors Authority, (530) 642-8029 or (887) 588-4FUN; Pollock Pines–Camino Chamber of Commerce, (530) 644-3970 or (530) 644-2498.

RESTRICTIONS

Pets: On leash. **Fires:** In fire grates only. **Alcoholic Beverages:** Allowed. **Vehicle Maximum Length:** 22 ft. **Other:** 14-day stay limit.

TO GET THERE

From Placerville drive 20 mi. east on US 50. Turn north (left) on Ice House Rd. and continue for 11 mi. to FR 32. Hang a right, direction Ice House Reservoir, and proceed for 1.2 mi. to the campground entrance.

POLLOCK PINES

Peninsula Recreation Area, Sunset Camp and Fashoda Camp

Ice House Rd., Pollock Pines 95726. T: (530) 644-2349 or reservations (877) 444-6777; F: (530) 647-5405; www.r5.fs.fed.us/eldorado or www.reserveusa.com.

🚐 ★★★	🏕 ★★★
Beauty: ★★★★	Site Privacy: ★★★
Spaciousness: ★★★	Quiet: ★★★★
Security: ★★★	Cleanliness: ★★★
Insect Control: ★★★	Facilities: ★★

When we first saw the overnight fee for this Eldorado National Forest camp our eyes bugged out from sticker shock. Fifteen dollars seems pretty pricy for a primitive place that doesn't have showers, flush toilets, or even cold-water sinks. The charm of this handsome lakeside forest, though, can easily put one in a forgiving mood. For one thing, the campground, which is divided into Sunset and Fashoda units, occupies a densely treed peninsula that juts out into and rises above Union Valley Reservoir. The woodsy and watery setting is majestically framed by a surrounding series of jagged Sierra peaks. An odor of vanilla often permeates the air, emanating from the many stands of Jeffrey pine. Fair-sized sites are mostly level; the walk-ins at Fashoda are shady and fairly private, while Sunset's slots are screened by fallen trees and large stumps. The lake is best for boating and fishing from spring through early summer, before it gets drawn down too much. Mushroom-picking is a popular pastime in these woods.

BASICS

Operated By: American Land & Leisure, concessionaire. **Open:** Late May through Sept., weather permitting. **Site Assignment:** Reservations accepted w/ V, MC, D. **Registration:** Every loop has a kiosk for payment. **Fee:** $15, cash or check;

$30 for double site. **Parking:** At site or designated lot for walk-ins.

FACILITIES

Number of RV Sites: 131. **Number of Tent-Only Sites:** 30. **Hookups:** None. **Each Site:** Picnic table, fire grate, barbecue grill. **Dump Station:** Yes. **Laundry:** No. **Pay Phone:** No. **Rest Rooms and Showers:** Vault toilets, no showers. **Fuel:** No. **Propane:** No. **Internal Roads:** Paved but narrow, bumpy, & windy. **RV Service:** No. **Market:** 25 mi. southwest in Pollock Pines. **Restaurant:** 25 mi. southwest in Pollock Pines. **General Store:** No. **Vending:** No. **Swimming:** In Union Valley Reservoir. **Playground:** No. **Other:** Some wheelchair-accessible facilities, boat ramp, beach. **Activities:** Fishing, hiking, boating, mushroom-plucking. **Nearby Attractions:** Fountain-Tallman Museum in Placerville; El Dorado National Forest in Camino; Sly Park Recreation Area in Pollock Pines. **Additional Information:** El Dorado County Visitors Authority, (530) 642-8029 or (887) 588-4FUN; Pollock Pines–Camino Chamber of Commerce, (530) 644-3970 or (530) 644-2498.

RESTRICTIONS

Pets: On leash. **Fires:** In fire grates only. **Alcoholic Beverages:** Allowed. **Vehicle Maximum Length:** 22 ft. **Other:** 14-day stay limit.

TO GET THERE

From Placerville drive 20 mi. east on US 50. Turn north (left) on Ice House Rd. and continue for 15.2 mi. to the Peninsula Creek Recreation Area turnoff. Turn left and proceed for another mi. to the campground entrance.

POMONA

East Shore RV Park

Puddingstone Lake, 1440 Camperview Rd., San Dimas 91773. T: (909) 599-8355; F: (909) 592-7481; www.holidayguide.com/camp-usa/california/eastshorervpark; esrv@pacbell.net.

🚐 ★★★★	▲ ★★
Beauty: ★★	Site Privacy: ★★
Spaciousness: ★★★	Quiet: ★★★
Security: ★★★★	Cleanliness: ★★★
Insect Control: ★★★	Facilities: ★★★★★

When you arrive at East Shore RV Park you will be handed map of the property, which is a good thing as without it you can forget about navigating your way through its maze of loops. Located just 30 miles east of downtown Los Angeles, above the shores of Puddingstone Lake and within the Frank Bonelli Regional Park, not only is this place attractively landscaped, with undulating meadows accented by such trees as alder, eucalyptus, sycamore, magnolia, and a range of conifers, but it is well endowed with a whole host of facilities. You want boating or fishing? You've got it. Looking to play some golf? No problem. Need to hook up to the Internet? That's a "can-do," too. And security is tighter than a martinet's collar, with both an entrance booth check point and regular ranger patrols. That sites tend to be wedged rather snugly together only really impacts tenters. And for them East Shore has set aside a "wilderness area" meadow, a dubious amenity with undesignated sites on ground so curvaceous as to be unusable by RVs. Two small knocks on this outfit are the occasional buzz of airplanes using the neighboring county airport and restrooms that should be equipped with real mirrors instead of the shatterproof stainless steel more commonly seen in cut-rate national forest properties.

BASICS

Operated By: East Shore RV Park, Phyllis Cook. **Open:** All year. **Site Assignment:** Reservations accepted w/ MC, V, D. **Registration:** At office. **Fee:** $24–$29. **Parking:** At site.

FACILITIES

Number of RV Sites: 518. **Number of Tent-Only Sites:** 25. **Hookups:** Water, electric (20, 30, 50 amps), sewer, cable TV, Internet. **Each Site:** Picnic table, fire grate. **Dump Station:** Yes. **Laundry:** Yes. **Pay Phone:** Yes. **Rest Rooms and Showers:** Yes. **Fuel:** No. **Propane:** Yes. **Internal Roads:** Paved. **RV Service:** No. **Market:** 3 mi. north in San Dimas. **Restaurant:** 3 mi. north in San Dimas. **General Store:** Yes. **Vending:** Yes. **Swimming:** 2 pools. **Playground:** Yes. **Other:** Some wheelchair-accessible facilities. **Activities:** Fishing, boating, waterskiing, hiking, bicycling, volleyball, horseshoe pit, horseback riding rentals, golf. **Nearby Attractions:** Disneyland, Six Flags Magic Mountain, Riverside & its museums, gardens, & historic buildings. **Additional Information:** Pomona Chamber of Commerce, (909) 622-1256.

RESTRICTIONS

Pets: On leash, $2 fee. **Fires:** In fire grates only. **Alcoholic Beverages:** Allowed. **Vehicle Maxi-**

mum Length: 45 ft. **Other:** 7-day stay limit for tents, no stay limit for RVs.

To Get There

From I-10 at Pomona, take Exit 44A/Fairplex Dr. Proceed north for 0.7 mi. and turn left on Via Verde. After 0.5 mi., at the stop sign, turn right on Campers View. The park is straight ahead.

POMONA
Prado Regional Park

16700 Euclid Ave., Chino 91710. T: (909) 597-4260; F: (909) 393-8428; www.co.san-bernardino.ca.us/parks/prado.htm.

🚐 ★★★★   ⛺ ★★★

Beauty: ★★★★	Site Privacy: ★★★
Spaciousness: ★★★★	Quiet: ★★★★
Security: ★★★★	Cleanliness: ★★★
Insect Control: ★★	Facilities: ★★★★

This attractive park is just 35 miles east of downtown Los Angeles, and yet to look at its verdant grounds you might think you were in the middle of farm country. That impression is accentuated by the presence of a neighboring ranch that pens cattle up near one of Prado's two loops. The pitiful sight of so many beasts herded together in a small parcel of muddy, denuded soil is outdone only by the powerful reek of ammonia emanating from their direction, a one-two sensory punch that could convert the most committed of meat eaters to vegetarianism. You won't have much to beef about though if you bring your fishing rod to Prado, as the lake is well stocked w/ trout in winter and catfish in summer. Grassy sites are exposed but roomy, set under young sycamores, eucalyptus, and pines. Aim for any of 7–75, as they are not only among the shadier, but also out of view of the bovine stalag. Of the great number of amenities here, one of the more unusual is an area set aside on the lake for radio-controlled model boats.

BASICS

Operated By: San Bernardino County, Regional Parks Dept. **Open:** All year. **Site Assignment:** Reservations accepted w/ V, MC, D. **Registration:** At entrance booth. **Fee:** $15, cash, check or V, MC, D. **Parking:** At site.

FACILITIES

Number of RV Sites: 75. **Number of Tent-Only Sites:** 0. **Hookups:** Water, electric (50 amps), sewer. **Each Site:** Picnic table, fire ring. **Dump Station:** Yes. **Laundry:** Yes. **Pay Phone:** Yes. **Rest Rooms and Showers:** Yes. **Fuel:** No. **Propane:** No. **Internal Roads:** Paved. **RV Service:** No. **Market:** 8 mi. south in Corona. **Restaurant:** 8 mi. south in Corona. **General Store:** No. **Vending:** No. **Swimming:** No. **Playground:** Yes. **Other:** Some wheelchair-accessible facilities, boat ramp. **Activities:** Fishing, horseback riding rentals, soccer field, boat rentals, golf. **Nearby Attractions:** Disneyland, Six Flags Magic Mountain, Riverside & its museums, gardens, & historic buildings. **Additional Information:** San Bernardino County, Regional Parks Dept., (909) 38-PARKS.

RESTRICTIONS

Pets: On leash no longer than 6 ft., $1 fee. **Fires:** In fire rings only. **Alcoholic Beverages:** Allowed at site. **Vehicle Maximum Length:** 60 ft. **Other:** 14-day stay limit; no loaded firearms; no wood gathering.

To Get There

In Pomona exit Hwy. 60 on Euclid Ave./Hwy. 83 and head south for 0.6 mi. Turn left at the sign for the regional park.

PORTERVILLE
Tule Recreation Area

Hwy. 190, Porterville 93258. T: (559) 784-0215 or reservations (877) 444-6777; F: (559) 784-5469; www.spk.usace.army.mil/cespk-co/lakes/success.html or www.reserveusa.com.

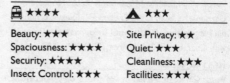

🚐 ★★★★   ⛺ ★★★

Beauty: ★★★	Site Privacy: ★★
Spaciousness: ★★★★	Quiet: ★★★
Security: ★★★★	Cleanliness: ★★★
Insect Control: ★★★	Facilities: ★★★

Sun-scorched buttes rise above the multi-pronged lake that serves as a focal point to this recreation area. How people cooled off here before the US Army Corps of Engineers created Lake Success in 1961 is anybody's guess. With plenty of iced-down beer, perhaps, and that might still be considered an essential ingredient to any summertime visit. There is a scattered presence of such trees as oak, eucalyptus, buttonwood, oleander, juniper, and various conifers throughout the double-looped campground, but shade remains scarcer than candy in a dentist's office. In a facility that appears to put function ahead of aesthetics, ramadas would be a welcome addition to the sites. But hey!, the extra exposure to the blazing sun is just one more excuse to jump in the water. Not convinced? Then try to land 26, 29, 30, or 41, some of the few, the proud, the shaded. Located just off Hwy. 190, nine miles east of Porterville, the campground is subject to traffic noise. Unfortunately, an above average amount of bottles, 'butts, and plastic pollute the grounds.

BASICS

Operated By: US Army Corps of Engineers. **Open:** All year. **Site Assignment:** Reservations recommended; V, MC, D. **Registration:** At office at the end of the driveway. **Fee:** $16–$21, cash or check. **Parking:** At site.

FACILITIES

Number of RV Sites: 104. **Number of Tent-Only Sites:** 0. **Hookups:** Water, electric (30 amps). **Each Site:** Picnic table, fire grate, barbecue grill, lantern pole. **Dump Station:** Yes. **Laundry:** No. **Pay Phone:** Yes. **Rest Rooms and Showers:** Yes. **Fuel:** No. **Propane:** No. **Internal Roads:** Paved. **RV Service:** No. **Market:** 9 mi. west in Porterville. **Restaurant:** 9 mi. west in Porterville. **General Store:** Yes. **Vending:** Yes. **Swimming:** In Lake Success. **Playground:** Yes. **Other:** Some wheelchair-accessible facilities, two boat ramps, marina. **Activities:** Fishing, boat rentals, sailing, waterskiing, hiking, horseback riding. **Nearby Attractions:** Porterville Historical Museum & Zauld House & Gardens; Kaweah Oaks Preserve in Exeter; California Hot Springs. **Additional Information:** Porterville Chamber of Commerce, (559) 784-7503.

RESTRICTIONS

Pets: On leash. **Fires:** In fire grates only. **Alcoholic Beverages:** Allowed. **Vehicle Maximum Length:** 30 ft. **Other:** 14-day stay limit.

TO GET THERE

From Porterville drive 9 mi. east on Hwy. 190 to Lake Success. The campground entrance is on the left.

PORTOLA

Grasshopper Flat

Beckwourth-Taylorsville Rd., Beckwourth 96129. T: (530) 836-2575 or reservations (877) 444-6777; F: (530) 836-0493; www.r5.fs.fed.us/plumas or www.reserveamerica.com.

🚗 ★★★★   ⛺ ★★★★

Beauty: ★★★★	Site Privacy: ★★★
Spaciousness: ★★★	Quiet: ★★★
Security: ★★★	Cleanliness: ★★★★
Insect Control: ★★★	Facilities: ★★

If you are not towing a boat to this delightful lakeside facility you will probably be in the minority. A simple fishing rod will do, though pole-less nature lovers should find the natural beauty of the setting gratifying enough. No sites verge on Lake Davis, but many of them offer excellent pine-filtered vistas of the water and short trails make access to the shore as easy as putting a night crawler on a hook. The tidy campground's three loops wind through medium-size Jeffrey and ponderosa pines. As a result, this facility, at 5,785 feet of altitude, is carpeted with pine needles and cones. There is a respectable amount of space between most sites, and the presence of both double units and pull-through parking simplifies the maneuvering of larger vehicles and trailers. A dump station is located on the opposite side of the street, two-tenths of a mile south of camp, and the Grizzly store, two miles south across the dam, has basic supplies and pay showers.

BASICS

Operated By: UST Wilderness Management Corp, concessionaire. **Open:** May through Oct. **Site Assignment:** Reservations accepted w/ V, MC, D for a limited number of sites. **Registration:** At entrance kiosk. **Fee:** $13, cash or check. **Parking:** At site.

FACILITIES

Number of RV Sites: 70. **Number of Tent-Only Sites:** 0. **Hookups:** None. **Each Site:** Picnic table, fire grate. **Dump Station:** No. **Laundry:** No. **Pay Phone:** Yes. **Rest Rooms and Showers:** Flush toilets, no showers. **Fuel:** No. **Propane:** No. **Internal Roads:** Paved. **RV Service:** No. **Market:** 8 mi. south in Portola. **Restaurant:** 8 mi. south in Portola. **General Store:** No. **Vending:** No.

Swimming: In Frenchman Lake. **Playground:** No. **Other:** Boat launch 1 mi. north. **Activities:** Fishing, boating, hiking. **Nearby Attractions:** Portola Railroad Museum; Lakes Basin Recreation Area & Plumas-Eureka State Park in Graegle; Plumas County Museum in Quincy; Plumas National Forest. **Additional Information:** Plumas County Visitors Bureau, (530) 283-6345 or (800) 326-2247.

RESTRICTIONS

Pets: On leash. **Fires:** In fire grates only. **Alcoholic Beverages:** Allowed. **Vehicle Maximum Length:** 32 ft. **Other:** 14-day stay limit.

TO GET THERE

From downtown Portola head north on West St. and follow the sign for Lake Davis Recreation Area. West St. becomes Lake Davis Rd. Drive 7.7 mi. to the stop sign across the dam and turn left onto Beckwourth-Taylorsville Rd. The campground is 0.5 mi. ahead on the left.

PORTOLA
Spring Creek

Frenchman Lake Rd., Chilcoot 96105. T: (530) 836-2575 or reservations (877) 444-6777; F: (530) 836-0493; www.r5.fs.fed.us/plumas or www.reserveusa.com.

🚐 ★★★★   ⛺ ★★★★

Beauty: ★★★★   Site Privacy: ★★★
Spaciousness: ★★★★   Quiet: ★★★
Security: ★★★   Cleanliness: ★★★★
Insect Control: ★★★   Facilities: ★★

Spring Creek is a splendid oasis of pines and salt-bush, and a smattering of aspen, standing in contrast to the refreshing blue-green waters of Frenchman Lake, just below the campground. This arid, mountain-fringed, high desert domain sits on a hillside that is handsomely studded with volcanic rocks and tufa outcroppings. There is little screening between the level, pine needle–carpeted sites, but they are decently spaced apart, with many—even on the upper tier of the double loop—enjoying great pine-filtered views of the lake. While sites on average are rather spacious, the central positioning of fire rings and tables may pose problems for campers with large tents. Despite the rock-rimmed shore, access to the lake for boating and fishing is as easy as capsizing a canoe, with a boat ramp located at Frenchman Campground, just up the road. Of the reservable spots, the best for space, privacy and water view are 30, 32, and 35. The concession that operates this Plumas National Forest facility offers double-size sites for twice the price of singles, and small bundles of firewood for $6, indications that inflation is making a comeback.

BASICS

Operated By: UST Wilderness Management Corp., concessionaire. **Open:** May through Oct., weather permitting. **Site Assignment:** Reservations accepted w/V, MC, D. **Registration:** At entrance kiosk. **Fee:** $13, cash or check, $26 for double site. **Parking:** At site.

FACILITIES

Number of RV Sites: 35. **Number of Tent-Only Sites:** 0. **Hookups:** None. **Each Site:** Picnic table, fire grate. **Dump Station:** No. **Laundry:** No. **Pay Phone:** No. **Rest Rooms and Showers:** Vault toilets, no showers. **Fuel:** No. **Propane:** No. **Internal Roads:** Paved. **RV Service:** No. **Market:** 10 mi. south in Chilcoot. **Restaurant:** 10 mi. south in Chilcoot. **General Store:** No. **Vending:** No. **Swimming:** In Lake Davis. **Playground:** No. **Other:** Some wheelchair-accessible facilities. **Activities:** Fishing, boating, birding, hiking. **Nearby Attractions:** Frenchman Lake; Portola Railroad Museum; Lakes Basin Recreation Area in Graegle; Plumas National Forest; Plumas-Eureka State Park near Graegle. **Additional Information:** Plumas County Visitors Bureau, (530) 283-6345 or (800) 326-2247.

RESTRICTIONS

Pets: On leash. **Fires:** In fire grates only. **Alcoholic Beverages:** Allowed. **Vehicle Maximum Length:** 55 ft. **Other:** 14-day stay limit; no wood gathering.

TO GET THERE

From Portola on Hwy. 70 drive 17 mi. to Chilcoot and turn left on Frenchman Lake Rd. Continue for 8.6 mi., bear right and cross the dam. Proceed for 1.2 mi. and turn left into the campground.

QUAKING ASPEN/CAMP NELSON

Quaking Aspen

Western Divide Hwy., Quaking Aspen/Camp Nelson 93208. T: (559) 539-2607 or reservations (877) 444-6777; www.r5.fs.fed.us/sequoia or www.reserveusa.com.

🚐 ★★★	▲ ★★★
Beauty: ★★★★	Site Privacy: ★★★
Spaciousness: ★★★	Quiet: ★★★★
Security: ★★★	Cleanliness: ★★★
Insect Control: ★★★	Facilities: ★

In most respects Quaking Aspen is a very average, unextraordinary campground. Yet its position, at 7,000 feet elevation in the heart of Giant Sequoia National Monument's southern unit, makes it an ideal base for day hikes into the area's redwood groves. There is a grassy meadow on one side of this pretty, peaceful, hillside camp, and Freeman Creek flows nearby. Fair-sized sites of dirt and pine needles are set reasonably far apart around the double loop, and shaded by an abundance of lodgepole pines—but curiously few aspens. Units 12, 19, 21, and 29 are among the more recessed and shady, and 23 and 24 the more private ones in the meadow area. Tenters may want to consider Belknap (no trailers or RVs allowed), nine miles west on Hwy. 190, where they can strike camp under the protective aura of redwood trees. Telephone, gasoline, propane, and a general store are available two miles south at Ponderosa Lodge.

BASICS

Operated By: California Land Management, concessionaire. **Open:** Mid-Apr. to mid-Nov., weather permitting. **Site Assignment:** Reservations accepted w/ V, MC, D. **Registration:** At entrance kiosk. **Fee:** $14, cash or check. **Parking:** At site or in designated area.

FACILITIES

Number of RV Sites: 32. **Number of Tent-Only Sites:** 0. **Hookups:** None. **Each Site:** Picnic table, fire grate. **Dump Station:** No. **Laundry:** No. **Pay Phone:** No. **Rest Rooms and Showers:** Vault toilets, no showers. **Fuel:** No. **Propane:** No. **Internal Roads:** Paved. **RV Service:** No. **Market:** 40 mi. west in Porterville. **Restaurant:** 25 mi. west in Springville. **General Store:** No. **Vending:** No. **Swimming:** No. **Playground:** No. **Other:** Some

wheelchair-accessible facilities. **Activities:** Hiking, fishing, horseback riding. **Nearby Attractions:** Sequoia National Forest; Porterville Historical Museum & Zauld House & Gardens; California Hot Springs. **Additional Information:** Springville Chamber of Commerce, (559) 539-2312; Porterville Chamber of Commerce, (559) 784-7503.

RESTRICTIONS

Pets: On leash. **Fires:** In fire grates only. **Alcoholic Beverages:** Allowed. **Vehicle Maximum Length:** 24 ft. **Other:** 14-day stay limit.

TO GET THERE

From Porterville drive 40 mi. east on Hwy. 190 (which becomes the Western Divide Hwy.). The campground entrance is on the right.

REDDING

Antlers RV Park and Campground

20682 Antler Rd., Lakehead 96051. T: (530) 238-2322 or reservations (800) 642-6849; www.antlersrv.com.

🚐 ★★★★★	▲ ★★★★
Beauty: ★★★★	Site Privacy: ★★★★
Spaciousness: ★★★★	Quiet: ★★★
Security: ★★★	Cleanliness: ★★★★
Insect Control: ★★★	Facilities: ★★★★

During a recent winter, snow and rain combined with gale-force winds to topple dozens of trees in Antlers RV Park. A lesser property would have been left scarred for years to come by such decimation. Not Antlers. The trunks and limbs were carved up and hauled away, and the campground continues to be a standout beauty. Its lovely perch above the iridescent Shasta Lake offers campers a balance of sun and shade among an abundance of such trees as oak, pine, cedar, and manzanita. Most sites are level, grassy, and surprisingly spacious for an RV-oriented campground. Even those with full hookups have plenty of elbow-room, with 108 one of the best in that class. In the ever-popular lake-view area, A 38 and A 39, decked with ramadas as well as shade trees, are the prime slots. Tent campers, too, will find more than enough space to spread their canvas, with the forested loops, where mossy boulders accentuate the natural look, providing the most privacy. Although Antlers is a mere two miles from I-5, surprisingly little road noise reaches it.

BASICS

Operated By: Antlers RV Park & Campground. **Open:** All year. **Site Assignment:** Reservations accepted w/ V, MC. **Registration:** At office. **Fee:** $12–$27.50, cash or V, MC. **Parking:** At site.

FACILITIES

Number of RV Sites: 70. **Number of Tent-Only Sites:** 37. **Hookups:** Water, electric (30, 50 amps), sewer, Internet. **Each Site:** Picnic table, fire grate, food storage box. **Dump Station:** No. **Laundry:** Yes. **Pay Phone:** Yes. **Rest Rooms and Showers:** Yes. **Fuel:** No. **Propane:** Yes. **Internal Roads:** Paved & gravel. **RV Service:** No. **Market:** 2 mi. north in Lakehead. **Restaurant:** 18 mi. south in Shasta Lake. **General Store:** Yes, open from Memorial Day to Labor Day, w/ snack bar. **Vending:** No. **Swimming:** Pool. **Playground:** Yes. **Other:** Some wheelchair-accessible facilities, marina, game room, video rentals. **Activities:** Fishing, boat rentals, waterskiing, hiking, horseshoe pit, ping pong, volleyball, basketball. **Nearby Attractions:** Carter House Natural Science Museum, Turtle Bay Museums & Arboretum, Waterworks Park in Redding; Shasta Lake, Caverns & Dam; Shasta State Historic Park; Whiskeytown National Recreation Area. **Additional Information:** Redding CVB, (530) 225-4100.

RESTRICTIONS

Pets: On leash, $3 fee. **Fires:** In fire grates only. **Alcoholic Beverages:** Allowed. **Vehicle Maximum Length:** 40 ft. **Other:** 14-day stay limit in summer; no wood gathering.

TO GET THERE

From Redding drive 26 mi. north on I-5 and exit at Lakeshore/Antlers Rd. Turn right and drive 1 block, then turn right again on Antlers Rd. Continue for 1.5 mi. to the campground entrance straight ahead.

RIDGECREST
Fossil Falls

Cinder Rd., Little Lake 93542. T: (760) 384-5400; www.ca.blm.gov/caso/index.html.

🚐 ★★★★	🅰 ★★★★
Beauty: ★★★★	Site Privacy: ★★★★
Spaciousness: ★★★★	Quiet: ★★★
Security: ★	Cleanliness: ★★★★
Insect Control: ★★★★	Facilities: ★

Heading north toward Lone Pine along US 395, a sign points the way to Fossil Falls, a geological site and campground. The falls in question are not fossilized, but rather a fantastic flow of hardened basaltic lava, spewed out of the eastern Coso Mountain range during a massive eruption 440,000 years ago. This little-known campground lies in a volcanic debris field in the arid Rose Valley, between the green-dappled Sierra Nevadas to the west, China Lake naval base to the east, and a red cinder peak marking its north side. The sublime beauty of this desolate place is not universally appreciated, especially as the grounds are exposed to an unyielding sun and periodic high winds. There are no shade trees here, just low-lying desert scrub across the mildly undulating terrain. Level cinder-based sites, spread well apart over three loops, are among the largest we've come across, and they take advantage of volcanic tufts, spires and mounds as privacy screening. Though this Bureau of Land Management facility lacks potable water and trash pick-up, the absence of ramadas is the most sorely-felt omission. Gasoline and a pay phone are available three miles south at Little Lake.

BASICS

Operated By: Bureau of Land Management, Ridgecrest Field Office. **Open:** All year. **Site Assignment:** First come, first served. **Registration:** At entrance kiosk. **Fee:** $6, cash or check. **Parking:** At site.

FACILITIES

Number of RV Sites: 5. **Number of Tent-Only Sites:** 6. **Hookups:** None. **Each Site:** Picnic table, fire grate. **Dump Station:** No. **Laundry:** No. **Pay Phone:** No. **Rest Rooms and Showers:** Vault toilets, no showers. **Fuel:** No. **Propane:** No. **Internal Roads:** Cinder gravel, wide, & bumpy. **RV Service:** No. **Market:** 31 mi. south in Ridgecrest. **Restaurant:** 21 mi. south in Inyokern. **General Store:** No. **Vending:** No. **Swimming:** No. **Playground:** No. **Other:** Limited wheelchair-accessible facilities, Fossil Falls geological site. **Activities:** Hiking, birding, stargazing, rock scrambling, philosophical ruminating. **Nearby Attractions:** Trona Pinnacles; Last Chance Canyon & Maturango Museum/Death Valley Tourist Center in Ridgecrest; Death Valley National Park. **Additional Information:** Ridgecrest Area CVB, (760) 375-8202 or (800) 847-4830.

RESTRICTIONS

Pets: On leash. **Fires:** In fire grates only. **Alcoholic Beverages:** Allowed. **Vehicle Maximum Length:** 30 ft. **Other:** 14-day stay limit.

TO GET THERE

From Ridgecrest drive 14 mi. west on Hwy. 178. Turn right on Hwy. 14/US 395. Continue 15 mi. and turn right at the sign for Fossil Falls. Proceed for 0.5 mi. and turn right again. The campground is 0.5 mi. ahead on the left.

RIVERSIDE

Lake Perris State Recreation Area, Luiseño Campground

17801 Lake Perris Dr., Perris 92571. T: (909) 940-5603; www.cal-parks.ca.gov or www.reserveamerica.com.

🚐 ★★★★   🏕 ★★★★

Beauty: ★★★★	Site Privacy: ★★★★
Spaciousness: ★★★★	Quiet: ★★★
Security: ★★★★	Cleanliness: ★★★
Insect Control: ★★	Facilities: ★★★★

If time weighs heavily on your hands during your stay at Lake Perris you will only have yourself to blame. That's because this recreation area has a little bit of something for everyone, from fishing and boating (rentals available at the marina), hiking, biking and horseback riding trails, and an Native American museum (open Wednesdays and weekends), to a pair of swimming beaches and a waterslide (summer season only). It is a pretty park, too, with lush grassy turf sloping gently toward the water and rocky hills coloring the horizon. Sites are open but spacious, many shaded by conifers, eucalyptus and pepper trees. That shade is essential, as summer temperatures typically hit 110 degrees, scorching the grass brown and sending everyone with a swimsuit into the water. The weather is milder in the spring, when a fabulous explosion of wildflowers makes this place a must-see. Boating to Alessandro Island for a romantic picnic is considered by many to be a Lake Perris rite-of-passage.

BASICS

Operated By: California Dept. of Parks & Recreation. **Open:** All year. **Site Assignment:** Reservations accepted w/ V, MC, D. **Registration:** At entrance booth. **Fee:** $8–$14, cash or CA check. **Parking:** At site.

FACILITIES

Number of RV Sites: 254. **Number of Tent-Only Sites:** 177. **Hookups:** Water, electric (30, 50 amps). **Each Site:** Picnic table, fire grate. **Dump Station:** Yes. **Laundry:** No. **Pay Phone:** Yes. **Rest Rooms and Showers:** Yes. **Fuel:** No. **Propane:** No. **Internal Roads:** Paved. **RV Service:** No. **Market:** 5 mi. south in Perris. **Restaurant:** 5 mi. south in Perris. **General Store:** Yes. **Vending:** No. **Swimming:** In Lake Perris. **Playground:** Yes. **Other:** Some wheelchair-accessible facilities, boat ramp, coffee shop. **Activities:** Fishing, bicycling, hiking, horseback riding, horseshoe pit, surfing, boat rentals, golf. **Nearby Attractions:** Perris Valley Historical Museum & Orange Empire Railway Museum; Riverside & its museums, gardens & historic buildings. **Additional Information:** Perris Valley Chamber of Commerce, (909) 657-3555.

RESTRICTIONS

Pets: On 6 ft. leash. **Fires:** In fire grates only. **Alcoholic Beverages:** Allowed at site. **Vehicle Maximum Length:** 34 ft. **Other:** 14-day stay limit from June 1–Sept. 30, 30-day stay limit for the rest of the year; no firearms; no wood gathering.

TO GET THERE

From Riverside follow I-215/Hwy. 60 east. When the 2 roads split remain on Hwy. 60 for another 4.6 mi. Exit on Moreno Beach Dr. and continue south for 3.5 mi. Turn left on Via del Lago. The park entrance is just 1 mi. ahead.

SACRAMENTO

Folsom Lake State Recreation Area, Beal's Point Campground

7806 Folsom-Auburn Rd., Folsom 95630. T: (916) 988-0205 or reservations (800) 444-7275 or marina (916) 933-1300; F: (916) 988-9062; www.cal-parks.ca.gov or www.reserveamerica.com.

🚐 ★★★★   🏕 ★★★★

Beauty: ★★★★	Site Privacy: ★★★
Spaciousness: ★★★★	Quiet: ★★★
Security: ★★★★	Cleanliness: ★★★
Insect Control: ★★★	Facilities: ★★★

Beal's Point is just 20 miles from Sacramento, a convenient proximity that explains why camping reservations are essential between May and mid-Sept. Once you get over the shock of so many people—and the absence of lake vistas from the campground—you'll be in for a treat. That's because this is a splendid woodland habitat that offers a little bit of something for everyone. At the top of that list are grassy campsites that are roomy, recessed, and shaded by conifers, blue and live oaks, and buttonwood trees. The many walk-ins make tenting here especially pleasant, though RVers do well with any of 16–38, which are level and shady. The lake features 75 miles of shoreline when it is full, and there are hiking, riding, and biking trails in the surrounding foothills. The marina offers both wet and dry slips (the latter when the water drops below 435 feet), as well as a snack bar, marine supplies and fuel. Full hookups are coming in 2002—er, make that 2003. Or maybe 2004. . . .

BASICS

Operated By: California Dept. of Parks & Recreation. **Open:** All year. **Site Assignment:** Reservations recommended; V, MC, D. **Registration:** At entrance booth. **Fee:** $12, cash or CA check. **Parking:** At site.

FACILITIES

Number of RV Sites: 31. **Number of Tent-Only Sites:** 18. **Hookups:** None. **Each Site:** Picnic table, fire grate. **Dump Station:** Yes. **Laundry:** No. **Pay Phone:** Yes. **Rest Rooms and Showers:** Yes. **Fuel:** No. **Propane:** No. **Internal Roads:** Paved. **RV Service:** No. **Market:** 3 mi. south in Folsom. **Restaurant:** 3 mi. south in Folsom. **General Store:** No. **Vending:** No. **Swimming:** In Folsom Lake. **Playground:** No. **Other:** Some wheelchair-accessible facilities, 4-lane boat ramp, marina, beach, snackbar in summer. **Activities:** Fishing, boat rentals, horseback riding, hiking, bicycling. **Nearby Attractions:** Folsom City Zoo, Dam, Powerhouse, museums, historic downtown, & outlet shopping; Sacramento Zoo, museums, Esquire Imax Theatre, & state parks. **Additional Information:** Folsom Chamber of Commerce & Visitors Center, (916) 985-2698; Sacramento CVB, (916) 264-7777 or (800) 292-2334.

RESTRICTIONS

Pets: On 6 ft. leash. **Fires:** In fire grates only. **Alcoholic Beverages:** Allowed at site. **Vehicle Maximum Length:** 31 ft. **Other:** 7-day stay limit from May 18 to Sept. 30, 30-day stay limit for the rest of the year; no firearms; no wood gathering.

TO GET THERE

From Sacramento drive 15 mi. east on US 50 and take Folsom Blvd. Exit. Head north on Folsom Blvd. (which becomes Folsom-Auburn Rd.). After 6.3 mi. turn right into the park.

SAN BERNARDINO
Camp Switzerland

24558 Lake Dr., Crestline 92325. T: (909) 338-2731.

🚐 ★★★   ⛺ ★★

Beauty: ★★★   Site Privacy: ★★
Spaciousness: ★★   Quiet: ★★★
Security: ★★★★★   Cleanliness: ★★★
Insect Control: ★★   Facilities: ★★

If you have ever wondered what campgrounds were like in the old days, wonder no longer: Camp Switzerland may be just what you are looking for. Established in 1939, this forested facility looks like something of a relic, but it is also a classic, with boulders and pines, cedars and locust trees in harmony with sites that are packed tightly along a steeply descending lane. The most private of those are at the lowest tier, but if your rig is longer than 22 feet forget about trying to maneuver it down there. The campground lies at 4,500 feet altitude at the north end of Lake Gregory in the San Bernardino Mountains, where it is not uncommon to find snow on the ground well into Apr. Though the property lacks a view of the water, the attractive lakeside town of Crestline is within modest yodeling distance a few minutes walk away.

BASICS

Operated By: Camp Switzerland, Earl & Bernie Silva, managers. **Open:** All year. **Site Assignment:** Reservations accepted w/ V, MC, D. **Registration:** At entrance office. **Fee:** $19–$23, cash, check or V, MC, D. **Parking:** At site.

FACILITIES

Number of RV Sites: 30. **Number of Tent-Only Sites:** 10. **Hookups:** Water, electric (15, 30 amps), sewer. **Each Site:** Picnic table in most sites. **Dump Station:** Yes. **Laundry:** No. **Pay Phone:** No. **Rest Rooms and Showers:** Yes. **Fuel:** No. **Propane:** Yes. **Internal Roads:** Paved. **RV Service: No. **Market:** 1 mi. west in Crestline. **Restaurant:** 1 mi. west in Crestline. **General Store:** No. **Vending:** No. **Swimming:** In Lake Gregory. **Playground:** No. **Activities:** Fishing & boating on Lake Gregory, hiking. **Nearby Attractions:** Lake Gregory, Silverwood Lake, Lake Arrowhead, Big Bear Lake. **Additional Information:** Crestline Chamber of Commerce, (909) 338-2706.

RESTRICTIONS

Pets: On leash, $3. **Fires:** No ground fires. **Alcoholic Beverages:** Allowed. **Vehicle Maximum Length:** 25 ft. **Other:** 29-day stay limit.

TO GET THERE

From San Bernardino drive twelve mi. north on Hwy. 18. Exit left on Hwy. 138. Drive 1 mi. north, then turn right onto Lake Dr.; Camp Switzerland is 3 mi. ahead on the left.

SAN BERNARDINO
Silverwood Lake State Recreation Area, Mesa Campground

14651 Cedar Cir., Hesperia 92345. T: (760) 389-2303 or (800) 444-7275; www.cal-parks.ca.gov or www.reserveamerica.com.

🚐 ★★★   🏕 ★★★

Beauty: ★★★★	Site Privacy: ★★★★
Spaciousness: ★★★	Quiet: ★★
Security: ★★	Cleanliness: ★★★
Insect Control: ★★	Facilities: ★★★

Mesa Campground offers something for everyone, from private, well-screened sites situated among thick stands of manzanita, oak, and ponderosa pines, to a network of bike paths and hiking trails. And don't overlook Silverwood Lake, below the campground, which serves triple duty among swimmers, boaters and fishermen. No wonder then that reservations are advisable, especially for weekends, from late spring through Sept. At a distance of less than 30 miles from San Bernardino, Mesa is close enough to Los Angeles to be hugely popular as a getaway destination and yet far enough out that it occasionally has problems with black bears raiding its dumpsters. You are more likely to hear, though, distant sounds of planes, trains, and automobiles, and, alas, your neighbors, as enforcement of quiet hours tends to be lax. Fortunately, sites are well dispersed through a series of eight loops, with numbers 101–106 appealingly shady and both 76 and 86 a little more secluded than the rest. The only site with a water view is 16, but gusty evening breezes make that a mixed blessing.

BASICS

Operated By: California Dept. of Parks & Recreation. **Open:** All year. **Site Assignment:** Reservations recommended; V, MC, D. **Registration:** At entrance booth. **Fee:** $8, cash or CA check. **Parking:** At site.

FACILITIES

Number of RV Sites: 136. **Number of Tent-Only Sites:** 7. **Hookups:** None. **Each Site:** Picnic table, fire grate, barbecue grill. **Dump Station:** Yes. **Laundry:** No. **Pay Phone:** Yes. **Rest Rooms and Showers:** Yes. **Fuel:** No. **Propane:** No. **Internal Roads:** Paved. **RV Service:** No. **Market:** 9 mi. south in Crestline. **Restaurant:** 9 mi. south in Crestline. **General Store:** Yes, at the marina. **Vending:** No. **Swimming:** In Silverwood Lake. **Playground:** No. **Other:** Some wheelchair-accessible facilities, boat launch, marina. **Activities:** Hiking, fishing, bicycling, boat rentals, horseshoe pit, birding. **Nearby Attractions:** Pacific Crest Trail, California Theater of Performing Arts in San Bernardino. **Additional Information:** San Bernardino CVB, (909) 889-3980 or (800) 867-8366.

RESTRICTIONS

Pets: On 6 ft. leash. **Fires:** In fire grates only. **Alcoholic Beverages:** Allowed at site. **Vehicle Maximum Length:** None. **Other:** 14-day stay limit in summer, 30-day stay limit in winter; no firearms; no wood gathering.

TO GET THERE

From San Bernardino drive 17 mi. north on I-215/I-15. Take the Silverwood Lake Exit onto Rte. 138 and drive 11 mi. Turn left into the campground.

SAN BERNARDINO
Yucaipa Regional Park

33900 Oak Glen Rd., Yucaipa 92399. T: (909) 790-3127; F: (909) 790-3121; www.co.san-bernardino.ca.us/parks.

🚐 ★★★★   ▲ ★★★★

Beauty: ★★★★   Site Privacy: ★★
Spaciousness: ★★★★   Quiet: ★★★
Security: ★★★★★   Cleanliness: ★★★★
Insect Control: ★★   Facilities: ★★★

There is quite a lot to like about Yucaipa Regional Park, from its easy-to-find suburban location just five miles off of I-10, to the lushly manicured grounds that include three ponds stocked with trout and catfish and a one acre swimming lagoon. Add to this a sandy beach and a pair of 350-foot waterslides, pull-through parking large enough to handle most of the larger RVs, and a separate area for tents complete with soft, sandy pads, and you have the makings for good family fun. Security is tight, with a gate that typically closes at 9 p.m., and there are five hosts in residence throughout the year. Critics may carp that the handsome mix of trees does not do much to shade sites, but at least they don't obscure the fine view of the San Bernardino Mountains, either. One thing to watch: a city park development going up at the campground's periphery threatens to become an eyesore.

BASICS

Operated By: San Bernardino County Regional Parks Dept. **Open:** All year. **Site Assignment:** Reservations accepted w/ V, MC, D. **Registration:** At entrance booth. **Fee:** $11–$18, cash, check or V, MC, D. **Parking:** At site.

FACILITIES

Number of RV Sites: 26. **Number of Tent-Only Sites:** 8. **Hookups:** Water, electric (30 amps). **Each Site:** Picnic table, barbecue grill. **Dump Station:** Yes. **Laundry:** No. **Pay Phone:** Yes. **Rest Rooms and Showers:** Yes. **Fuel:** No. **Propane:** No. **Internal Roads:** Paved. **RV Service:** No. **Market:** 5 mi. south in Yucaipa. **Restaurant:** 5 mi. south in Yucaipa. **General Store:** Yes. **Vending:** Yes. **Swimming:** In lake. **Playground:** Yes. **Other:** Wheelchair-accessible facilities, snack-bar. **Activities:** Fishing, horseshoe pit, pedal boat rentals. **Nearby Attractions:** Asistencia Misión de San Gabriel, Historical Glass Museum, both in Redlands. **Additional Information:** San Bernardino County Regional Parks, (909) 38-PARKS.

RESTRICTIONS

Pets: On 10 ft. leash. **Fires:** Yes (In grills only). **Alcoholic Beverages:** Allowed at site. **Vehicle Maximum Length:** None. **Other:** 14-day stay limit; no firearms.

TO GET THERE

From San Bernardino follow I-10 east for 15 mi. to the Yucaipa Exit. Drive 2.8 mi. east on Yucaipa Blvd., turn left on Oak Glen Rd. and proceed for 2 mi. to the campground on the left.

SAN CLEMENTE
San Clemente State Beach

3030 Avenida del Presidente, San Clemente 92672. T: (949) 492-3156 or (949) 492-0802; www.cal-parks.ca.gov or www.reserveamerica.com.

🚐 ★★★★   ▲ ★★★

Beauty: ★★★   Site Privacy: ★★★
Spaciousness: ★★★   Quiet: ★★
Security: ★★★★   Cleanliness: ★★★★
Insect Control: ★★★★   Facilities: ★★★

San Clemente seems to be in a constant state of renewal. A few years ago a tent loop was renovated, about a year later it was the picnic area's turn for a face lift, and recently the electrical hookups were upgraded. Now if only some vegetation could be planted in the RV hookup loop to provide buffers between its crowded slots. Until that happens, your best bet is to steer toward the two loops that lack hookups; marginally more spacious and with a bit of screening, sites there are also positioned on grass instead of the dirt surface of the RV lot. Especially roomy are 83 and 85, both of which overlook the beach and cliffs. Monterey pines, eucalyptus, and flowering ceanothus are scattered throughout the park, lending an attractive look to the domain. Less appealing is the occasional use of prison labor for landscaping.

BASICS

Operated By: California Dept. of Parks & Recreation. **Open:** All year. **Site Assignment:** Reservations recommended; V, MC, D. **Registration:** At entrance booth. **Fee:** $12–$18, cash or CA check. **Parking:** At site.

FACILITIES

Number of RV Sites: 160. **Number of Tent-Only Sites:** 0. **Hookups:** Water, electric (30 amps), sewer. **Each Site:** Picnic table, fire grate; non-hookup sites have ramada, barbecue grill, spigot. **Dump Station:** Yes. **Laundry:** No. **Pay Phone:** Yes. **Rest Rooms and Showers:** Yes. **Fuel:** No. **Propane:** No. **Internal Roads:** Paved. **RV Service:** No. **Market:** 2 mi. north in San Clemente. **Restaurant:** 2 mi. north in San Clemente. **General Store:** No. **Vending:** No. **Swimming:** In Pacific Ocean, less than 0.5 mi. **Playground:** No. **Other:** Some wheelchair-accessible facilities. **Activities:** Surfing, swimming, bicycling, 2 mi. of hiking trails. **Nearby Attractions:** San Clemente, Dana Point, Mission San Juan Capistrano. **Additional Information:** San Clemente Chamber of Commerce, (949) 492-1131.

RESTRICTIONS

Pets: On 6 ft. leash. **Fires:** In fire grates only. **Alcoholic Beverages:** Allowed at site. **Vehicle Maximum Length:** 30 ft. **Other:** 7-day stay limit; no firearms; no wood gathering.

TO GET THERE

In San Clemente exit I-5 on Avenida Calafia and proceed for 0.2 mi. Turn left (west) into the park.

SAN CLEMENTE
San Onofre State Beach, San Mateo Campground

830 Cristianitos Rd., San Clemente 92672. T: (949) 361-2531; www.cal-parks.ca.gov or www.reserveamerica.com.

 ★★★★   ▲ ★★★

Beauty: ★★★	Site Privacy: ★★★
Spaciousness: ★★★	Quiet: ★★★
Security: ★★★	Cleanliness: ★★★
Insect Control: ★★★	Facilities: ★★★

San Onofre State Beach is composed of two campgrounds, the Bluff Area by the beach and San Mateo, one mile inland off of I-5. Forget about privacy at the Bluff Area, where sites are lined up one after another on a tiny stretch of turf alongside the parking area. Tranquility is another lost cause: trains hurtle along tracks just 100 feet from camp, basically paralleling its linear layout, and a few yards beyond an interstate highway reverberates to the continuous roar of traffic.

Then there is the multitude of college-age campers that descends on the park from mid-spring through early Sept., filling it with the off-key melodies of their raucous partying and straining facilities beyond the capacity of the maintenance staff. Sites at San Mateo, by contrast, while not large, are at least scattered over three loops and enjoy decent privacy. The atmosphere is calmer—dare we say more sedate?—and setting more lush, though fine views of the coastal hills are somewhat offset by opposing vistas of power lines and produce fields. Both camps suffer from occasional helicopter overflights from neighboring Camp Pendleton. The best time to visit is from early spring through mid-summer, while the grass in the sites is still soft and green. Your San Mateo receipt covers the day-use fee at the Bluff Area beach.

BASICS

Operated By: California Dept. of Parks & Recreation. **Open:** All year. **Site Assignment:** Reservations recommended; V, MC, D. **Registration:** At entrance booth. **Fee:** $12–$18, cash or CA check, good for day use at San Onofre State Beach Bluffs Area. **Parking:** At site.

FACILITIES

Number of RV Sites: 157. **Number of Tent-Only Sites:** 0. **Hookups:** Water, electric (30 amps). **Each Site:** Picnic table, fire grate. **Dump Station:** Yes. **Laundry:** No. **Pay Phone:** Yes. **Rest Rooms and Showers:** Yes. **Fuel:** No. **Propane:** No. **Internal Roads:** Paved. **RV Service:** No. **Market:** 2 mi. north in San Clemente. **Restaurant:** 2 mi. north in San Clemente. **General Store:** No. **Vending:** No. **Swimming:** In Pacific Ocean, 1.1 mi. **Playground:** No. **Other:** Some wheelchair-accessible facilities. **Activities:** Surfing, bicycling, nature trails, skate boarding, helicopter spotting. **Nearby Attractions:** San Clemente, Dana Point, Mission San Juan Capistrano. **Additional Information:** San Clemente Chamber of Commerce, (949) 492-1131.

RESTRICTIONS

Pets: On 6 ft. leash. **Fires:** In fire grates only. **Alcoholic Beverages:** Allowed at site. **Vehicle Maximum Length:** 36 ft. **Other:** 14-day stay limit from Memorial Day through Labor Day.

TO GET THERE

From I-5 in San Clemente take the Cristianitos Rd. Exit and proceed inland for 1 mi. Turn right into the campground, which lacks adequate signposting.

SAN DIEGO
Lake Morena County Park, South Shore Campground

2550 Lake Morena Dr., Lake Morena Village 91906. T: (619) 565-3600; www.co.san-diego.ca.us/parks.

🚐 ★★★★   ⛺ ★★★

Beauty: ★★★★   Site Privacy: ★★★
Spaciousness: ★★★   Quiet: ★★★★
Security: ★★★   Cleanliness: ★★★
Insect Control: ★★   Facilities: ★★★

Lake Morena Reservoir is home to some of the better bass and trout fishing in the area, with the record for the former weighing in at a whopping 19 pounds, 3 ounces. But even when the water has been drawn down to the size of a pond, typically by late July or early Aug., there is still plenty to do here, from biking and hiking the nature trails to hooking up to the Pacific Crest Trail, which cuts through the park. Granite-spiked hills surround the domain, with the campground's grassy, fairly tightly concentrated sites well shaded by thick-limbed live oaks, incense cedars, and Jeffrey and Coulter pines. Best for spaciousness and lake view—at least when water levels are high—are sites 81 and 85, with 6–14 good fall-back options. And though restrooms are a bit shabby looking, they are kept reasonably clean. Dogs are supposed to be kept on leashes, but enforcement is lax. Tent campers looking for more space and privacy may want to stake out a spot at the North Shore primitive area.

BASICS

Operated By: County of San Diego, Dept. of Parks & Recreation. **Open:** All year. **Site Assignment:** Reservations accepted w/ V, MC, D. **Registration:** At entrance booth or ranger office. **Fee:** $12–$16, cash or V, MC, D. **Parking:** At site.

FACILITIES

Number of RV Sites: 86. **Number of Tent-Only Sites:** 0. **Hookups:** Water, electric (20, 30 amps). **Each Site:** Picnic table, fire grate. **Dump Station:** Yes. **Laundry:** No. **Pay Phone:** Yes. **Rest Rooms and Showers:** Yes. **Fuel:** No. **Propane:** No. **Internal Roads:** Mostly paved. **RV Service:**

No. **Market:** 1 mi. south in Lake Morena Village. **Restaurant:** 1 mi. south in Lake Morena Village. **General Store:** No. **Vending:** Yes. **Swimming:** No. **Playground:** No. **Other:** Some wheelchair-accessible facilities, boat launch. **Activities:** Fishing, bicycling, hiking, campfire programs, boat rentals. **Nearby Attractions:** Coral Canyon OHV Area, Pacific Crest Trail, only 8 mi. from the Mexican border, historic Campo. **Additional Information:** County of San Diego, Dept. of Parks & Recreation, (858) 694-3049.

RESTRICTIONS

Pets: On 6 ft. leash. **Fires:** In fire grates only. **Alcoholic Beverages:** Allowed at site, not exceeding 40 proof. **Vehicle Maximum Length:** 45 ft. **Other:** 14-day stay limit; no firearms; no wood gathering.

TO GET THERE

From San Diego head east on I-8 for 54 mi. Exit on Buckman Springs Rd. and continue south for 5.5 mi. Turn right on Oak Dr. and proceed for 1.5 mi. Turn right again on Lake Morena Dr. The park is 0.5 mi. ahead.

SAN FRANCISCO
Candlestick RV Park

650 Gilman Ave., San Francisco 94124. T: (415) 822-2299 or (800) 888-CAMP; F: (415) 822-7638; www.gocampingamerica.com/candlestick; candlestickrv@msn.com.

🚐 ★★★★   ⛺ ★

Beauty: ★★★   Site Privacy: ★
Spaciousness: ★   Quiet: ★★
Security: ★★★★   Cleanliness: ★★★★
Insect Control: ★★★★   Facilities: ★★★★

Short of setting up camp in Golden Gate Park, it is hard to imagine bivouacking much closer to San Francisco than in Candlestick RV Park. This facility is located directly across the street from 3Com Stadium, nee Candlestick Park, just five miles south of downtown. While its parking lot layout and the chain link security fence that encompasses the compound are not very appealing, management has done an admirable job of sewing a variety of exotic plants and trees around the perimeter. As usual for this sort of property, parking slots seem crowded together on the asphalt with no screening and negligible shade. A narrow strip of grass has been set aside for tenters but it seems to get more traffic from dogs, despite a rule that mandates dog-walking outside the fence. The washrooms, on the other hand, tend to be immaculate. Just down the street is Candlestick Point State Recreation Area, with a bike trail, picnic area, and Bay access via a boat ramp. Also nearby, alas, is the airport, with loud flyovers common enough to make you wish your RV had double-pane glass. A shuttle service is available to ferry campers to downtown San Francisco.

BASICS

Operated By: Candlestick RV Park. **Open:** All year. **Site Assignment:** Reservations recommended; V, MC, AE. **Registration:** At entrance office. **Fee:** $46–$49, cash or V, MC, AE. **Parking:** At site.

FACILITIES

Number of RV Sites: 165. **Number of Tent-Only Sites:** 12. **Hookups:** Water, electric (30, 50 amps), sewer, Internet. **Each Site:** Picnic table in some sites. **Dump Station:** No. **Laundry:** Yes. **Pay Phone:** Yes. **Rest Rooms and Showers:** Yes. **Fuel:** No. **Propane:** Yes. **Internal Roads:** Paved. **RV Service:** No. **Market:** 5 mi. north in San Francisco. **Restaurant:** 5 mi. north in San Francisco. **General Store:** Yes. **Vending:** Yes. **Swimming:** No. **Playground:** No. **Other:** Some wheelchair-accessible facilities, game room, free video tapes. **Activities:** Touring San Francisco, hiking the Bay shoreline, surfing. **Nearby Attractions:** Candlestick Point State Recreation Area; museums, Ghirardelli Square, Fisherman's Wharf, zoo, aquarium, Golden Gate Park, & much more in San Francisco. **Additional Information:** San Francisco CVB, (415) 391-2000.

RESTRICTIONS

Pets: On leash, must be under 20 pounds. **Fires:** No. **Alcoholic Beverages:** Allowed. **Vehicle Maximum Length:** 45 ft. **Other:** 29-day stay limit; no generators.

TO GET THERE

From San Francisco drive south on US 101 to the 3Com Stadium Exit. Drive around the stadium, about 1 mi., to gate 4. The park entrance is directly opposite to that, to the right.

SAN FRANCISCO
Pacific Park RV Resort

700 Palmetto Ave., Pacifica 94044. T: (800) 992-0554 or (650) 355-7093; F: (650) 355-7102; www.sanfranciscorv.com; frontdesk@sanfranciscorv.com.

🚐 ★★★★   ⛺ n/a

Beauty: ★★★	Site Privacy: ★
Spaciousness: ★	Quiet: ★★
Security: ★★★★	Cleanliness: ★★★★
Insect Control: ★★★★	Facilities: ★★★★★

Pacific Park RV Resort is conveniently located just ten miles south of San Francisco, right off of Hwy. 1 in Pacifica. It is loaded with amenities, from cable television and Internet connections to a small swimming pool and Jacuzzi, from a horseshoe pit to a video game room. The Pacific Ocean abuts the lot, filling the air with a pleasant brininess, and a very short trail leads down to the sandy beach. The view across the busy road is not bad, either, highlighted by a wavy series of grass-covered hills. The bad news is the parking slots are wedged one against another, and there are no shade trees, no privacy, and no tents allowed. The best bet is to set up as far to the western edge of the grounds as possible, where an unobstructed view of the sun setting into the water is a killer, and the crashing surf is almost loud enough to drown out the noise of incessant air and auto traffic. A shuttle service is available to ferry campers to downtown San Francisco.

BASICS

Operated By: Pacific Park RV Resort; Carol Motl, manager. **Open:** All year. **Site Assignment:** Reservations recommended; V, MC. **Registration:** At entrance office. **Fee:** $38–$69 plus 10% local tax, cash or V, MC. **Parking:** At site.

FACILITIES

Number of RV Sites: 250. **Number of Tent-Only Sites:** 0. **Hookups:** Water, electric (30, 50 amps), sewer, cable TV, Internet. **Each Site:** Communal picnic table. **Dump Station:** Yes. **Laundry:** Yes. **Pay Phone:** Yes. **Rest Rooms and Showers:** Yes. **Fuel:** No. **Propane:** Yes. **Internal Roads:** Paved. **RV Service:** No. **Market:** 1 mi. away in Pacifica. **Restaurant:** 1 mi. away in Pacifica. **General Store:** Yes. **Vending:** Yes. **Swimming:** In small heated pool. **Playground:** No. **Other:** Some wheelchair-accessible facilities, spa, game room. **Activities:** Sunning, surfing, beachcombing, horseshoe pit, touring San Francisco. **Nearby Attractions:** Candlestick Point State Recreation Area; museums, Ghirardelli Square, Fisherman's Wharf, zoo, aquarium, Golden Gate Park, & much more in San Francisco; Montara & Gray Whale Cove State Beaches. **Additional Information:** San Francisco CVB, (415) 391-2000.

RESTRICTIONS

Pets: On leash, must be under 20 pounds. **Fires:** No. **Alcoholic Beverages:** Allowed. **Vehicle Maximum Length:** 60 ft. **Other:** No stay limit; no generators.

TO GET THERE

From San Francisco drive 8 mi. south on Hwy. 1 to Pacifica. Exit on Manor Dr. and continue straight through the stop sign. Manor Dr. becomes Palmetto Ave. The resort entrance is 0.5 mi. ahead on the right.

SAN JUAN CAPISTRANO
Ronald W. Caspers Wilderness Park

Ortega Hwy. 33401, San Juan Capistrano 92675. T: (949) 728-0235; F: (949) 728-0346; www.coparks.com/caspers.

🚐 ★★★	🏕 ★★★
Beauty: ★★★★	Site Privacy: ★★★
Spaciousness: ★★★	Quiet: ★★★
Security: ★★★★	Cleanliness: ★★
Insect Control: ★★	Facilities: ★★★

Caspers Wilderness Park does not allow pets on the property for the same reason that minors must be accompanied by an adult: concern about mountain lions following a fatal attack 18 years ago. These restrictions have a positive side-effect, endowing the property with a greater degree of quietude than similar establishments elsewhere. Just eight miles inland from San Juan Capistrano and I-5, among the ranch lands and the rolling foothills of the Cleveland National Forest, Caspers occupies a transitional zone, with vegetation ranging from open grassy meadows fringed with prickly pear cacti and agaves, to sycamores and live oak. Most of the sites are rather close to each other, with about half in open grassland and the remainder appealingly sheltered under the high canopy of aged oaks. In spring there is just enough water flowing through the campside creek to generate a tremendous insect population. So either bring plenty of repellant or aim to bivouac from mid-summer on, when biting bugs should no longer be a problem. There are some fine hiking and riding trails in Caspers, as well as a separate horse camp.

BASICS

Operated By: City of Orange Public Facilities. **Open:** All year. **Site Assignment:** First come, first served. **Registration:** At entrance booth. **Fee:** $12, cash or CA check. **Parking:** At site.

FACILITIES

Number of RV Sites: 52. **Number of Tent-Only Sites:** 0. **Hookups:** None. **Each Site:** Picnic table, fire grate, barbecue grill. **Dump Station:** Yes. **Laundry:** No. **Pay Phone:** Yes. **Rest Rooms and Showers:** Yes. **Fuel:** No. **Propane:** No. **Internal Roads:** Paved & gravel. **RV Service:** No. **Market:** 8 mi. southwest in San Juan Capistrano. **Restaurant:** 8 mi. southwest in San Juan Capistrano. **General Store:** No. **Vending:** No. **Swimming:** No. **Playground:** No. **Other:** Some wheelchair-accessible facilities. **Activities:** 35 mi. of hiking trails, horseback riding, mountain biking, stargazing. **Nearby Attractions:** Mission San Juan Capistrano, Dana Point. **Additional Information:** San Juan Capistrano Chamber of Commerce, (949) 493-4700.

RESTRICTIONS

Pets: Not allowed. **Fires:** In fire grates only. **Alcoholic Beverages:** Not allowed. **Vehicle Maximum Length:** 44 ft. **Other:** 14-day stay limit; no firearms.

TO GET THERE

From I-5 in San Juan Capistrano take Hwy. 74/Ortega Hwy. east and drive 8 mi. Turn left into the park.

SAN RAFAEL

Samuel P. Taylor State Park

Sir Francis Drake Blvd., Lagunitas 94938. T: (415) 488-9897 or reservations (800) 444-7275; F: (415) 488-4315; www.cal-parks.ca.gov or www.reserveamerica.com.

🚐 ★★★   ⛺ ★★★

Beauty: ★★★★   Site Privacy: ★★★
Spaciousness: ★★★   Quiet: ★★★
Security: ★★★   Cleanliness: ★★★★
Insect Control: ★★   Facilities: ★★

In 1854 Samuel Taylor stumbled into a redwood grove here and was so enchanted by the sight that he promptly purchased 100 acres of land and set up a paper mill. Present-day visitors to this dark, densely forested park may wish that he had exercised less discretion in his timber harvesting to allow more sunshine to penetrate. No matter, it remains an appealing woodland of intermingled second-growth redwoods, tan oaks, madrones, laurels, and Douglas firs. The compact campground is tightly woven through two loops, with small dirt-surfaced sites rather crowded together. Although the preserve is open to RVs and even has six pull-through spots, narrow cornering and limited parking space make it more practical for tenting. Yet even the nylon roof set may find most sites a bit shy of elbow room. Of the two circuits, there is slightly more space and privacy in Orchard Hill (numbers 25–60). If you plan on coming between May and Oct., you will need to reserve far ahead.

BASICS

Operated By: California Dept. of Parks & Recreation. **Open:** All year. **Site Assignment:** Reservations accepted w/V, MC, D. **Registration:** At entrance booth. **Fee:** $12, cash or CA check. **Parking:** At site or adjacent to it.

FACILITIES

Number of RV Sites: 50. **Number of Tent-Only Sites:** 11. **Hookups:** None. **Each Site:** Picnic table, fire grates, food storage box. **Dump Station:** No. **Laundry:** No. **Pay Phone:** Yes. **Rest Rooms and Showers:** Yes. **Fuel:** No. **Propane:** No. **Internal Roads:** Paved, narrow, & windy. **RV Service:** No. **Market:** 2 mi. southeast in Lagunitas. **Restau-**rant: 2 mi. southeast in Lagunitas. **General Store:** No. **Vending:** No. **Swimming:** No. **Playground:** No. **Other:** Some wheelchair-accessible facilities. **Activities:** Hiking, mountain biking, horseback riding. **Nearby Attractions:** Mission San Rafael Archangel, Marin County Frank Lloyd Wright Civic Center & China Camp State Park in San Rafael; Muir Woods National Monument & Mount Tamalpais State Park in Mill Valley. **Additional Information:** San Rafael Chamber of Commerce, (415) 454-4163; Mill Valley Chamber of Commerce, (415) 388-9700.

RESTRICTIONS

Pets: On leash no longer than 6 ft., not allowed on trails. **Fires:** In fire grates only. **Alcoholic Beverages:** Allowed at site. **Vehicle Maximum Length:** 28 ft. **Other:** 7-day stay limit from Apr. 1–Oct. 31; no firearms; no wood gathering.

TO GET THERE

From San Rafael take I-580 south to the Sir Francis Drake Blvd. Exit. Head west for 17 mi. The park entrance is on the left.

SAN SIMEON

San Simeon State Park, San Simeon Creek Campground

San Simeon Creek Rd., San Simeon 93452. T: (805) 927-2035 or (805) 927-2020 or reservations (800) 444-7275; www.cal-parks.ca.gov or www.reserveamerica.com.

🚐 ★★★   ⛺ ★★★

Beauty: ★★★   Site Privacy: ★★★
Spaciousness: ★★★   Quiet: ★★
Security: ★★★   Cleanliness: ★★★★
Insect Control: ★★★   Facilities: ★★★

The two campgrounds in this state preserve are very average in nearly every respect. San Simeon Creek is the more developed, with lavatories equipped with showers, water fill-up and dump stations for RVs, and good size Monterey pines sprinkled along its five paved loops. One of those circuits, adjacent to a noisy highway overpass, is reserved for tents. That awkward position makes the more primitive Washburn, up the hill along the park road, a more peaceful option for sleeping in nylon shelters. The cinder surface to Washburn's twin loops is smooth and the vaulted toilets well-maintained. In both camps sites are level and grassy, but in need of more shade trees. The high use this rather ordinary park receives throughout the year has little to do with the neighboring beach (which, like the campgrounds themselves, is often cloaked in fog). Rather, it is the location of the magnificent Hearst Castle just five miles north on Hwy. 1 that makes this the ideal overnight spot either before or after visits to the mansion. Just remember to book your tours at (800) 444-4445 well in advance.

BASICS

Operated By: California Dept. of Parks & Recreation. **Open:** All year. **Site Assignment:** Reservations accepted w/ V, MC, D. **Registration:** At entrance booth. **Fee:** $12, cash or CA check. **Parking:** At site.

FACILITIES

Number of RV Sites: 115. **Number of Tent-Only Sites:** 19. **Hookups:** None. **Each Site:** Picnic table, fire grate. **Dump Station:** Yes. **Laundry:** No. **Pay Phone:** Yes. **Rest Rooms and Showers:** Yes. **Fuel:** No. **Propane:** No. **Internal Roads:** Paved. **RV Service:** No. **Market:** 2 mi. south in Cambria. **Restaurant:** 1 mi. north in San Simeon Acres. **General Store:** No. **Vending:** No. **Swimming:** In Pacific Ocean. **Playground:** No. **Other:** Some wheelchair-accessible facilities. **Activities:** Hiking, fishing, birding, horseshoe pit, campfire programs. **Nearby Attractions:** Hearst Castle & National Geographic Theater, wineries around Paso Robles. **Additional Information:** San Simeon Chamber of Commerce, (805) 927-3500.

RESTRICTIONS

Pets: On 6 ft. leash; not allowed on trails. **Fires:** In fire grates only, not allowed on the beach. **Alcoholic Beverages:** Allowed at site. **Vehicle Maximum Length:** 40 ft. **Other:** 10-day stay limit from Memorial Day through Labor Day; no firearms; no wood gathering.

TO GET THERE

From San Simeon on Hwy. 1 take the Hearst Castle' Exit and drive 4.7 mi. south. Turn left on San Simeon Creek Rd., then right into the well sign-posted park.

SANTA BARBARA
Cachuma Lake Recreation Area

HC 58, Hwy. 154, Santa Barbara 93105. T: (805) 686-5054; F: (805) 686-5075; www.cachuma.com or www.sbparks.org.

🚐 ★★★★   ▲ ★★★

Beauty: ★★★★	Site Privacy: ★★★
Spaciousness: ★★★	Quiet: ★★★
Security: ★★★★	Cleanliness: ★★★★
Insect Control: ★★	Facilities: ★★★★★

Confusion is an understandable state of mind for first-time visitors to Cachuma Lake. For one thing, this is a huge campground, with more than 500 mostly level, grassy sites dispersed through an intricate maze of loops. For another, though the recreation area is less than 20 miles from Santa Barbara, the large shimmering body of water is surrounded by the relatively undeveloped Santa Ynez and San Rafael Mountains, giving the impression that you are much farther out than you really are. There will be no roughing it here, though, because Cachuma has just about every possible amenity necessary to comfortable camping (and a good deal that probably aren't), including a snack bar and on-site gas station, and rentals of various size boats, bikes, golf clubs, and even yurts. The large domain is semi-forested with mature sycamores, oaks, manzanita, and holly, and if most sites lack privacy, at least a good percentage overlook the water. At an elevation of only 800 feet, weather at this park is pleasant throughout the year. Be sure to check out the excellent nature center (open weekends) for its Native American exhibits and to make reservations for naturalist-led wildlife cruises.

BASICS

Operated By: Santa Barbara County Parks. **Open:** All year. **Site Assignment:** Reservations accepted w/ V, MC, D. **Registration:** At entrance booth. **Fee:** $16–$22, cash or CA check. **Parking:** At site.

FACILITIES

Number of RV Sites: 573. **Number of Tent-Only Sites:** 0. **Hookups:** Water, electric (20, 30 amps), sewer. **Each Site:** Picnic table, fire ring (not in full hookup sites). **Dump Station:** Yes. **Laundry:** Yes. **Pay Phone:** Yes. **Rest Rooms and Showers:**

Yes. **Fuel:** Yes. **Propane:** Yes. **Internal Roads:** Paved. **RV Service:** No. **Market:** 10 mi. west in Santa Ynez. **Restaurant:** In campground or 10 mi. west in Santa Ynez. **General Store:** Yes. **Vending:** No. **Swimming:** Pool, $1 per hour. **Playground:** Yes. **Other:** Some wheelchair-accessible facilities, marina, boat launch, family fun center, nature center. **Activities:** Fishing, hiking, horseshoe pit, boat & bicycle rentals, mini-golf, volleyball, horseback riding, wildlife cruises. **Nearby Attractions:** Solvang & its mission & museums; Chumash Painted Cave State Historic Park; Santa Barbara & its mission, museums, historic buildings, zoo, Stearns Wharf, & Botanic Garden. **Additional Information:** Santa Barbara Region Chamber of Commerce, (805) 965-3023.

RESTRICTIONS

Pets: On 6 ft. leash; proof of rabies vaccination required; $2 fee. **Fires:** In fire rings only. **Alcoholic Beverages:** Allowed at site. **Vehicle Maximum Length:** None. **Other:** 14-day stay limit from Apr. 1–Sept. 14, 90-day limit the rest of the year.

TO GET THERE

In Santa Barbara exit US 101 on Hwy. 154 and drive 18 mi. north to the park entrance on the right.

SANTA BARBARA
Carpinteria State Beach

5361 6th St., Carpinteria 93013. T: (805) 684-2811 or reservations (805) 968-3294; www.cal-parks.ca.gov or www.reserveamerica.com.

🚐 ★★★   ⛺ ★★

Beauty: ★★★   Site Privacy: ★★
Spaciousness: ★★   Quiet: ★★
Security: ★★★   Cleanliness: ★★★
Insect Control: ★★★   Facilities: ★★★

The bad news about this state-run property is that many sites border the park road and some industrial buildings, and if you happen to occupy one of those near the railroad tracks you may confuse a passing freight train with an earthquake. The good news? Never mind the distant off-shore oil platforms, a fair number of sites enjoy stunning views of the ocean, and the crashing surf nearby will drown out most of the noise emanating from your neighbors. The campground, which features an attractive balance of palm trees, eucalyptus, conifers, and sycamores,

is broken into four separate sections, with Santa Cruz, Santa Rosa, and San Miguel providing beach access, while the shady Anacapa is situated away from the water. Not so coincidentally, the latter is the quietest, least crowded area in which to camp, while the former three loops feature sandy sites that are packed together like sardines in a can. The beach at Carpinteria, which is just one mile from Hwy. 101, 12 miles south of Santa Barbara, is also open to day-use and picnicking, and a large grassy meadow near it is excellent for kites and frisbee.

BASICS

Operated By: California Dept. of Parks & Recreation. **Open:** All year. **Site Assignment:** Reservations recommended; V, MC, D. **Registration:** At entrance booth. **Fee:** $12–$18, cash, CA check or V, MC, D. **Parking:** At site.

FACILITIES

Number of RV Sites: 261. **Number of Tent-Only Sites:** 1. **Hookups:** Water, electric (30 amps), sewer. **Each Site:** Picnic table, fire grate. **Dump Station:** Yes. **Laundry:** No. **Pay Phone:** Yes. **Rest Rooms and Showers:** Yes. **Fuel:** No. **Propane:** No. **Internal Roads:** Paved. **RV Service:** No. **Market:** 1 mi. north in Carpinteria. **Restaurant:** 1 mi. north in Carpinteria. **General Store:** No. **Vending:** No. **Swimming:** In Pacific Ocean. **Playground:** Yes. **Other:** Some wheelchair-accessible facilities. **Activities:** Surfing, tide pool exploring, seal watching, volleyball. **Nearby Attractions:** Mission San Buenaventura, historic Ventura, Mission Santa Barbara, Santa Barbara & its museums, historic buildings, zoo, Stearns Wharf, Botanic Garden, historic Ventura. **Additional Information:** Santa Barbara Region Chamber of Commerce, (805) 965-3023.

RESTRICTIONS

Pets: On 6 ft. leash. **Fires:** In fire grates only, not on the beach. **Alcoholic Beverages:** Allowed at site. **Vehicle Maximum Length:** 35 ft. **Other:** 7-day stay limit from June 1–Oct. 15; no firearms; no wood gathering.

TO GET THERE

From Santa Barbara drive 12 mi. southeast on US 101 and exit on Casitas Pass. Follow Casitas Pass Rd. to the right for 0.2 mi., then turn right on Carpinteria Ave. After 1 block turn left onto Palm St. Continue for 0.4 mi. straight into the campground.

SANTA BARBARA
El Capitan State Beach

10 Refugio Beach Rd., Goleta 93117. T: (805) 968-1033; www.cal-parks.ca.gov or www.reserveamerica.com.

🚐 ★★★★   ⛺ ★★★★

Beauty: ★★★★   Site Privacy: ★★★
Spaciousness: ★★★   Quiet: ★★★
Security: ★★★   Cleanliness: ★★★★
Insect Control: ★★★   Facilities: ★★★

El Capitan is not your typical beach campground. Though its four loops are set amidst a series of coastal bluffs, there is more of grass and dirt than sand in the surprisingly roomy, agreeably private sites. And aside from the time you spend on the beach, you won't need a parasol: much of the domain, which is just off Hwy. 101, 17 miles northwest of Santa Barbara, lies within a lush forest of live oak, with a few eucalyptus, sycamores, and pines tossed in for good measure. Tent campers looking for a water view should try for sites 75, 76, 78, and 80 in the third loop; RVers desiring the same will do well with 110, 111, 114, and 116 in the fourth and highest loop. The first circuit (sites 1–31), on the other hand, is one to avoid, lying nearest the railroad tracks and with no view of the ocean. This is one of the prettier beach campgrounds we've seen, with the terrain particularly green and delightful in spring.

BASICS

Operated By: California Dept. of Parks & Recreation. **Open:** All year. **Site Assignment:** Reservations recommended; V, MC, D. **Registration:** At entrance booth. **Fee:** $12, cash or CA check. **Parking:** At site.

FACILITIES

Number of RV Sites: 142. **Number of Tent-Only Sites:** 0. **Hookups:** None. **Each Site:** Picnic table, fire ring. **Dump Station:** Yes. **Laundry:** No. **Pay Phone:** Yes. **Rest Rooms and Showers:** Yes. **Fuel:** No. **Propane:** Yes. **Internal Roads:** Paved. **RV Service:** No. **Market:** 13 mi. east in Goleta. **Restaurant:** 13 mi. east in Goleta. **General Store:** Yes. **Vending:** No. **Swimming:** In Pacific Ocean. **Playground:** No. **Other:** Some wheelchair-accessible facilities. **Activities:** Fishing, hiking, bicycling, boogie board rentals. **Nearby Attractions:** Santa Barbara & its museums, historic buildings, zoo, Stearns Wharf, Botanic Garden, Mission Santa Barbara, Goleta South Coast Railroad Museum. **Additional Information:** Goleta Valley Chamber of Commerce, (805) 967-4618.

RESTRICTIONS

Pets: On 6 ft. leash. **Fires:** In fire rings only. **Alcoholic Beverages:** Allowed at site. **Vehicle Maximum Length:** 30 ft. **Other:** 14-day stay limit from June 1–Sept. 30; no firearms; no wood gathering.

TO GET THERE

From Santa Barbara drive 17 mi. west on US 101 and exit on El Capitan State Beach. Turn left (west) and proceed for 0.3 mi., under the railroad trestle, straight into the campground.

SANTA BARBARA
Gaviota State Park

Hwy. 101, Goleta 93117. T: (805) 968-1033; www.cal-parks.ca.gov.

🚐 ★★★   ⛺ ★★★

Beauty: ★★★★   Site Privacy: ★★
Spaciousness: ★★   Quiet: ★★
Security: ★★★   Cleanliness: ★★★
Insect Control: ★★★   Facilities: ★★

Gaviota was completely renovated recently after flooding buried one loop in mud and stripped out the sod in the other. Aside from the mature eucalyptus trees at the edge of the dusty, drab-looking campground, the few saplings here have only recently been planted; it will be ten or more years before they mature into shade trees—if they survive. Yet this park, which lies just off Hwy. 101, 30 miles northwest of Santa Barbara, is thrillingly set between a steep series of scenic bluffs and an unspoiled beach. To reach the shore you must walk beneath a century-old railroad trestle (more of a curiosity than noise nuisance) elevated some 75 feet off the ground. The pier by the water is fine for fishing and is equipped with a hoist for launching boats. A hot spring is located in the hills above Gaviota. The strong coastal breezes funneling through camp most afternoons and evenings make the packing of a jacket or sweater advisable.

BASICS

Operated By: California Dept. of Parks & Recreation. **Open:** All year. **Site Assignment:** First come, first served. **Registration:** At entrance booth. **Fee:** $10, cash or CA check. **Parking:** At site.

FACILITIES

Number of RV Sites: 52. **Number of Tent-Only Sites:** 0. **Hookups:** None. **Each Site:** Picnic table, fire grate. **Dump Station:** No. **Laundry:** No. **Pay Phone:** Yes. **Rest Rooms and Showers:** Yes. **Fuel:** No. **Propane:** No. **Internal Roads:** Paved. **RV Service:** No. **Market:** 11 mi. north in Buëllton. **Restaurant:** 11 mi. north in Buëllton. **General Store:** Yes (summer only). **Vending:** No. **Swimming:** In Pacific Ocean. **Playground:** No. **Other:** Some wheelchair-accessible facilities. **Activities:** Fishing, hiking, surfing, horseback riding. **Nearby Attractions:** Mission Santa Inés & museums in Solvang, La Purísima Mission State Historic Park in Lompoc, Santa Barbara & its museums, historic buildings, zoo, Stearns Wharf, Botanic Garden. **Additional Information:** Goleta Valley Chamber of Commerce, (805) 967-4618.

RESTRICTIONS

Pets: On 6 ft. leash. **Fires:** In fire grates only. **Alcoholic Beverages:** Allowed at site. **Vehicle Maximum Length:** 27 ft. **Other:** 14-day stay limit; no firearms; no wood gathering.

TO GET THERE

From Santa Barbara drive 30 mi. west on US 101 and take the Gaviota State Beach Exit to the left. Continue straight for 5 mi. to the park entrance.

SANTA CRUZ

Big Basin Redwoods State Park

21600 Big Basin Way, Boulder Creek 95006. T: (831) 338-8860 or reservations (800) 444-7275; F: (831) 338-8863; www.bigbasin.org or www.cal-parks.ca.gov or www.reserveamerica.com.

🚐 ★★★★   ⛺ ★★★★

Beauty: ★★★★★   Site Privacy: ★★★
Spaciousness: ★★★   Quiet: ★★
Security: ★★★   Cleanliness: ★★★★
Insect Control: ★★★   Facilities: ★★★

Unlike the nearby Henry Cowell Redwoods State Park, Big Basin puts campers right in the center of a dramatic redwood forest. A fair amount of sunlight filters through the dense cluster of giants—which dwarf the tan oaks and hemlocks among them—and an abundance of mossy rocks

and fallen trees decorate the thick blanket of pine needles layered on the ground. Average-size sites offer minimal privacy but their distribution over three separate campgrounds helps to reduce incidental noise. The more spacious and private spots are in the hilly Huckleberry loop, which also has tent cabins. Big Basin was established 100 years ago as California's first state park. Of its more than 80 miles of trails, the Berry Creek Falls hike (9.5 miles round trip), which threads past a superb series of redwoods to a pretty waterfall, should be atop your to-do list. Although just 24 miles northwest of Santa Cruz, the road into the park, Hwy. 236, is very slow and windy.

BASICS

Operated By: California Dept. of Parks & Recreation. **Open:** All year. **Site Assignment:** Reservations recommended; V, MC, D. **Registration:** At park headquarters. **Fee:** $12, cash or CA check. **Parking:** At site.

FACILITIES

Number of RV Sites: 39. **Number of Tent-Only Sites:** 108. **Hookups:** None. **Each Site:** Picnic table, fire grate, food storage box. **Dump Station:** Yes. **Laundry:** Yes. **Pay Phone:** Yes. **Rest Rooms and Showers:** Yes. **Fuel:** No. **Propane:** Yes. **Internal Roads:** Paved, some potholes. **RV Service:** No. **Market:** 9.5 mi. southeast in Boulder Creek. **Restaurant:** 9.5 mi. southeast in Boulder Creek. **General Store:** Yes. **Vending:** No. **Swimming:** No. **Playground:** No. **Other:** Some wheelchair-accessible facilities. **Activities:** Hiking, photography, exploring redwood forests. **Nearby Attractions:** Mission Santa Clara de Asis & various museums in Santa Clara; Hakone Japanese Gardens & Saso Herb Gardens in Saratoga; state beaches along the coast. **Additional Information:** Santa Clara CVB, (408) 224-9660 or (800) 272-6822; Saratoga Chamber of Commerce, (408) 867-0753.

RESTRICTIONS

Pets: On 6 ft. leash. **Fires:** In fire grates only. **Alcoholic Beverages:** Allowed at site. **Vehicle Maximum Length:** 27 ft. **Other:** 30-day stay limit; no firearms; no wood gathering.

TO GET THERE

From Santa Cruz drive 13.3 mi. north on Hwy. 9 to Boulder Creek. Turn left (west) on Hwy. 236 and continue for 8 mi. to the park entrance. The park headquarters are 1 mi. down the road.

SANTA ROSA
Spring Lake Regional Park

5585 Newanga Ave., Santa Rosa 95403. T: (707) 539-8092 or reservations (707) 565-2267; F: (707) 538-8038; www.sonoma-county.org/parks.

🚐 ★★★　　　🏕 ★★★

Beauty: ★★★★　　　Site Privacy: ★★★
Spaciousness: ★★★　Quiet: ★★★
Security: ★★★　　　Cleanliness: ★★★
Insect Control: ★★★　Facilities: ★★★

Spring Lake is a small body of water encircled by rolling hills of mature oaks, pines, and bay trees. It is a calm retreat just a few minutes from the heart of suburban Santa Rosa. As such, it is hardly a well-kept secret and you are liable to have company here at almost any time of year. No problem, the grass-covered sites are large enough for you to comfortably spread out your gear, and decently spaced apart around a tree-dotted meadow. Lichen-speckled rocks are scattered across the turf, adding to the natural feel of this agreeable camp. Some sites are impacted by a gentle slope toward the water, and none are graced with a view of the lake. Still, there is a good amount of fine slots, with 28 and 30, at the loop's periphery, ideal for RVers desiring privacy. Five, 26, and 27 are equipped with pull-through parking. Tent campers who don't mind being some distance from their cars should grab 12 or 14, which are secluded and give access to the lake. Note that from Oct. first through Apr. the campground is only open on weekends and holidays.

BASICS

Operated By: County of Sonoma, Regional Parks Dept. **Open:** Every day from May 1–Sept. 30; weekends & holidays only from Oct. 1–Apr. 30. **Site Assignment:** Reservations accepted w/ V, MC. **Registration:** At entrance office. **Fee:** $16, cash or CA check. **Parking:** At site.

FACILITIES

Number of RV Sites: 27. **Number of Tent-Only Sites:** 4. **Hookups:** None. **Each Site:** Picnic table, fire grate, food storage box. **Dump Station:** Yes. **Laundry:** No. **Pay Phone:** Yes. **Rest Rooms and Showers:** Yes. **Fuel:** No. **Propane:** No. **Internal Roads:** Paved. **RV Service:** No. **Market:** 2 mi. west in Santa Rosa. **Restaurant:** 2 mi. west in

Santa Rosa. **General Store:** No. **Vending:** No. **Swimming:** In swimming lagoon. **Playground:** No. **Other:** Some wheelchair-accessible facilities, boat ramp, fishing pier, visitor center. **Activities:** Hiking, bicycling, horseback riding, windsurfing, canoe & paddle boat rentals. **Nearby Attractions:** Santa Rosa museums & Luther Burbank Home & Gardens; San Francisco Solano Mission & winery tours in Sonoma. **Additional Information:** Santa Rosa CVB, (800) 404-ROSE; Sonoma County Tourism Program, (800) 5-SONOMA or (707) 565-5383.

RESTRICTIONS

Pets: On 6 ft. leash; rabies certificate required; $1 fee. **Fires:** In fire grates only. **Alcoholic Beverages:** Allowed at site. **Vehicle Maximum Length:** 40 ft. **Other:** 10-day stay limit; no firearms; no wood gathering.

TO GET THERE

From Santa Rosa on US 101 take Hwy. 12 east. After 1.25 mi. exit onto Hoen Frontage Rd. which will turn into Hoen Ave. After 1.5 mi. turn left on Newanga Ave., which veers sharply to the right. The park entrance is 0.6 mi. ahead.

SANTEE
Santee Lakes Regional Park & Campground

9040 Carlton Oaks Dr., Santee 92071. T: (619) 596-3141; F: (619) 449-4694; www.padredam.org/santee.html.

🚐 ★★★★　　　🏕 ★★

Beauty: ★★★　　　Site Privacy: ★★★
Spaciousness: ★★★　Quiet: ★★★
Security: ★★★★★　Cleanliness: ★★★★
Insect Control: ★★　　Facilities: ★★★★★

For comfort in camping, Santee Lakes merits an enthusiastic "thumbs up." From tight security to remarkably clean restrooms, from a heated pool to modem hookup in the office, RV camping does not get much better than this. California sycamores, eucalyptus, and palm trees hover over the lush, grassy grounds, which also encompass a series of seven lakes—ponds, really. One of those is dotted with tiny islands and has been set aside for canoeing and pedal boats. Two others are stocked with fish, and the great number of waterfront sites means that fishermen can camp where the action is. Still, despite respectable screening and level terrain, tent camping purists are likely to find the slots a bit too close together. Their best option—short of decamping altogether—is the remote and barren-looking Cottonwood loop (only open weekends), where an absence of such amenities as shade, screening, and barbecue grills guarantees a high level of solitude. An added plus for this park is its close proximity to a San Diego trolley stop.

BASICS

Operated By: Padre Dam Municipal Water District. **Open:** All year. **Site Assignment:** Reservations accepted w/ V, MC, D. **Registration:** At entrance booth. **Fee:** $18–$35, cash or V, MC, D. **Parking:** At site.

FACILITIES

Number of RV Sites: 224. **Number of Tent-Only Sites:** 0. **Hookups:** Water, electric (20, 30, 50 amps), sewer, Internet. **Each Site:** Picnic table, barbecue grill. **Dump Station:** Yes. **Laundry:** Yes. **Pay Phone:** Yes. **Rest Rooms and Showers:** Yes. **Fuel:** No. **Propane:** Yes. **Internal Roads:** Paved. **RV Service:** No. **Market:** 3 mi. east in Santee. **Restaurant:** 3 mi. east in Santee. **General Store:** Yes. **Vending:** Yes. **Swimming:** In heated pool. **Playground:** Yes. **Other:** Some wheelchair-accessible facilities. **Activities:** Fishing, bicycling, horseshoe pit, volleyball, canoe & pedal boat rentals. **Nearby Attractions:** San Diego & its waterfront, museums, zoo, historic district. **Additional Information:** San Diego CVB, (619) 232-3101.

RESTRICTIONS

Pets: On leash; not allowed in day-use area; $1 fee. **Fires:** No. **Alcoholic Beverages:** Allowed. **Vehicle Maximum Length:** 45 ft. **Other:** 14-day stay limit.

TO GET THERE

From Hwy. 67 in Santee exit at Woodside/Santee. Woodside changes into Mission Gorge. Drive 2 mi. on Mission Gorge, turn right onto Carlton Hills Blvd. and after 0.5 mi. turn left onto Carlton Oaks. The campground is 0.4 mi. ahead on the right.

SEQUOIA NATIONAL PARK
Potwisha

Generals Hwy., Sequoia National Park 93262. T: (559) 565-3341; www.nps.gov/seki.

🚐 ★★★★　　　　▲ ★★★

Beauty: ★★★★	Site Privacy: ★★★
Spaciousness: ★★★	Quiet: ★★★
Security: ★★★	Cleanliness: ★★★★
Insect Control: ★★	Facilities: ★★

Potwisha is named for the Native Americans who once roamed these parts. It is four miles north of Sequoia National Park's south entrance station, 12 miles from the Giant Forest grove of impossibly large redwood trees. Situated at 2,100 feet elevation, Potwisha enjoys an understated beauty, especially in spring when buttercups and other wildflowers decorate its tall green grass, the buckeye trees are ablaze with white blossoms, and the steeply sloping hills are ripe with flowering yucca. There is an authentically natural flavor to this campground, in contrast to the mega-sized Lodgepole, a camper-corral in the heart of the park. Several sites are equipped with pull-through parking, and those along the lower loop, nearer the river, are the more private. Number 18 is all by itself next to a large boulder; 21, 22, and 24, above the river, are roomy and shaded by oaks. Regular bear sightings make using the metal storage lockers a necessity. A highly scenic trail along the Marble Fork leads out of camp by site 17. The road from Potwisha to the Giant Forest and Lodgepole, an uphill, serpentine, white-knuckle drive, ascends 4,500 feet and is not recommended for vehicles over 22 feet in length.

BASICS

Operated By: National Park Service. **Open:** All year. **Site Assignment:** First come, first served. **Registration:** At entrance kiosk. **Fee:** $14, cash or check (in addition to the park entrance fee). **Parking:** At site.

FACILITIES

Number of RV Sites: 42. **Number of Tent-Only Sites:** 0. **Hookups:** None. **Each Site:** Picnic table, fire grate, bearproof box. **Dump Station:** Yes. **Laundry:** No. **Pay Phone:** Yes. **Rest Rooms and Showers:** Flush toilets, no showers. **Fuel:** No. **Propane:** No. **Internal Roads:** Paved. **RV Ser-**

vice: No. **Market:** 10 mi. southwest in Three Rivers. **Restaurant:** 10 mi. southwest in Three Rivers. **General Store:** No. **Vending:** No. **Swimming:** No. **Playground:** No. **Other:** Some wheelchair-accessible facilities. **Activities:** Hiking, wildlife viewing, white-water rafting on Kaweah River. **Nearby Attractions:** Kings Canyon National Park; Tulare County Museum in Visalia; Kaweah Oaks Preserve in Exeter; Kaweah Lake. **Additional Information:** Visalia Chamber of Commerce & Visitors Bureau, (559) 734-5876; Three Rivers–Lemoncove Business Assoc., (550) 561-0410.

RESTRICTIONS

Pets: On 6 ft. leash; not allowed on trails. **Fires:** In fire grates only. **Alcoholic Beverages:** Allowed at site. **Vehicle Maximum Length:** 32 ft. **Other:** 14-day stay limit; no loaded firearms; no food in vehicles.

TO GET THERE

From Visalia drive 37 mi. east on Hwy. 198 to the park's Ash Mountain entrance station. Continue 4 mi. north on Generals Hwy. The well-signed campground entrance is on the left.

SHELTER COVE
Tolkan

Kings Peak Rd., Shelter Cove 95589. T: (707) 986-7731 or (707) 825-2300; F: (707) 825-2301; www.ca.blm.gov/arcata/campground.html.

★★★	▲ ★★★★
Beauty: ★★★★	Site Privacy: ★★★
Spaciousness: ★★★★★	Quiet: ★★★★
Security: ★	Cleanliness: ★★★★
Insect Control: ★★★★	Facilities: ★

The Bureau of Land Management has begun an ambitious campaign to revamp many of its long-neglected properties. Nowhere is that more apparent than at this hidden gem, cloaked within the overgrown heart of the rugged King Range National Conservation Area high above the Lost Coast, about ten miles inland from Shelter Cove (the last three are a dirt washboard). After the recent refurbishing, Tolkan now features royally spacious, gravel and dirt sites equipped with new tables, fire grates, and back-in parking slots large enough to handle the most colossal of motor homes. The units have been distributed so far

apart that it is hard to go wrong with any, but the most isolated, and largest, is number seven, handsomely ensconced under a massive pine tree. An old-fashioned water tower rests on four stilts in the center of the single loop, partially screened by the varied conifers, manzanita, tan oak, madrone, and ceanothus that grow so abundantly throughout this mountainous ridge.

BASICS

Operated By: Bureau of Land Management, Arcata Field Office. **Open:** All year. **Site Assignment:** First come, first served. **Registration:** At entrance kiosk. **Fee:** $8, cash or check. **Parking:** At site.

FACILITIES

Number of RV Sites: 9. **Number of Tent-Only Sites:** 0. **Hookups:** None. **Each Site:** Picnic table, fire grate. **Dump Station:** No. **Laundry:** No. **Pay Phone:** No. **Rest Rooms and Showers:** Vault toilets, no showers. **Fuel:** No. **Propane:** No. **Internal Roads:** Gravel & dirt, decent condition. **RV Service:** No. **Market:** 18.3 mi. east in Redway. **Restaurant:** 3.7 mi. west in Shelter Cove. **General Store:** No. **Vending:** No. **Swimming:** No. **Playground:** No. **Other:** Some wheelchair-accessible facilities. **Activities:** Hiking, mushroom-plucking (permit required). **Nearby Attractions:** Richardson Grove State Park in Garberville; Smithe Redwoods State Reserve & Standish Hickey State Recreation Area in Leggett; Ave. of the Giants north of Garberville; Humboldt Redwoods State Park in Weott. **Additional Information:** Shelter Cove Information Bureau, (707) 923-1830; Garberville-Redway Area Chamber of Commerce, (707) 923-2613.

RESTRICTIONS

Pets: On leash. **Fires:** In fire grates only. **Alcoholic Beverages:** Allowed. **Vehicle Maximum Length:** 22 ft. **Other:** 14-day stay limit.

TO GET THERE

Exit US 101 at Garberville and drive through the downtown, turning left on Redwood Rd. at the sign for the King Range National Conservation Area. After 2.6 mi. turn left on Briceland Rd. which becomes the meandering and steep Shelter Cove Rd. Drive 18.3 mi. and turn right on Kings Peak Rd. Continue for 3.8 mi. to the well-marked campground on the right.

SIERRA CITY
Wild Plum

Wild Plum Rd., Sierra City 96125. T: (530) 288-3231 or (530) 993-1410; F: (530) 288-0727; www.r5.fs.fed.us/tahoe.

🚐 ★★★　　　🏕 ★★★★

Beauty: ★★★★	Site Privacy: ★★★
Spaciousness: ★★★	Quiet: ★★★★
Security: ★★★★	Cleanliness: ★★★
Insect Control: ★★★	Facilities: ★

Gadzooks! What has this book steered me to, a construction zone? may be the first words you voice when, after maneuvering down the bad camp road, you arrive at an expansive mound of river stones. Persevere; the campground, right alongside the musical, rollicking Haypress Creek (which flows into the Yuba River), is a delight and well worth your initial discomfort. Of the three separate loops to this mountainous pine forest, the middle one climbs uphill to the best sites for views of the water as well as neighboring ridge-tops. The most spacious is 32, but 33–36 also overlook the creek. On the lower tracks, 7 is set well back in a corner location and 19 is tucked behind an embankment. While the ground throughout the property is rather rocky, most dirt- and pine needle–surfaced sites have enough smooth, level ground for the staking of a tent. Parking, too, is ample for medium-size RVs and trailers. Wild Plum, which rests at 4,400 feet elevation, is often over-run by youthful kayakers, especially on summer weekends. If you find it full, there is also a fair amount of secluded sites at the less-popular Loganville Campground, 1.5 miles west of Sierra City.

BASICS

Operated By: High Sierra Campground Management, concessionaire. **Open:** May through Oct. **Site Assignment:** First come, first served. **Registration:** At entrance kiosk. **Fee:** $13, cash or check. **Parking:** At site.

FACILITIES

Number of RV Sites: 47. **Number of Tent-Only Sites:** 0. **Hookups:** None. **Each Site:** Picnic table, fire grate, some equipped w/ bearproof box. **Dump Station:** No. **Laundry:** No. **Pay Phone:** No. **Rest Rooms and Showers:** Vault toilets, no showers. **Fuel:** No. **Propane:** No. **Internal**

Roads: Paved, bumpy. **RV Service:** No. **Market:** 2 mi. west in Sierra City. **Restaurant:** 2 mi. west in Sierra City. **General Store:** No. **Vending:** No. **Swimming:** No. **Playground:** No. **Activities:** Hiking, kayaking, fishing, gold panning. **Nearby Attractions:** Kentucky Mine, Stampmill & Museum in Sierra City; Empire Mine State Historic Park in Grass Valley; Malakoff Diggins State Historic Park in Nevada City; Downieville Foundry/Museum, Gallows, & County Museum; Tahoe National Forest. **Additional Information:** Grass Valley–Nevada County Chamber of Commerce, (530) 273-4667; Sierra County Chamber of Commerce, (530) 862-0308 or (800) 200-4949.

RESTRICTIONS

Pets: On leash. **Fires:** In fire grates only. **Alcoholic Beverages:** Allowed. **Vehicle Maximum Length:** 22 ft. **Other:** 14-day stay limit.

TO GET THERE

From Grass Valley drive about 55 mi. north on Hwy. 49 to Sierra City. Continue for 0.5 mi. and turn right on Wild Plum Rd. Cross a narrow bridge and follow the gravel road for 1.5 mi. over another bridge into the campground.

SONORA
Boulder Flat

Hwy. 108, Dardanelle 95314. T: (209) 965-3434; F: (209) 965-3372; www.r5.fs.fed.us/stanislaus.

🚐 ★★★★　　　🏕 ★★★

Beauty: ★★★★	Site Privacy: ★★★
Spaciousness: ★★★	Quiet: ★★★
Security: ★★★	Cleanliness: ★★
Insect Control: ★★★★	Facilities: ★★

Of the great number of national forest campgrounds along Hwy. 108, Boulder Flat is perhaps the most appropriately-named, given its granite-strewn appearance. It is also arguably one of the prettier facilities, reflecting something of a wild, high Sierra Nevada ambiance. A spiny alpine ridge flanks one side of camp, the Stanislaus River purls by another, while a series of pointy peaks hover over the scene. Grass and dirt sites, punctuated by several stands of enormous red-bark cedars, are larger and more dispersed than at nearby Brighton Flat, and less barren-looking and exposed than those at Eureka Valley (though the latter also features an impressive array of boulders, and has the river sluicing past on two sides). It is true that Boulder Flat picks up auto noise from the Sonora Pass, but the same might be said of all the other campgrounds along this stretch of road. The town of Sonora is 50 miles west, and Dardanelle, where you will find a telephone and general store, two miles east.

BASICS

Operated By: Dodge Ridge Corp., concessionaire. **Open:** May through Sept., weather permitting. **Site Assignment:** First come, first served. **Registration:** At entrance kiosk. **Fee:** $13, cash or check. **Parking:** At site.

FACILITIES

Number of RV Sites: 20. **Number of Tent-Only Sites:** 0. **Hookups:** None. **Each Site:** Picnic table, fire grate. **Dump Station:** No. **Laundry:** No. **Pay Phone:** No. **Rest Rooms and Showers:** Vault toilets, no showers. **Fuel:** No. **Propane:** No. **Internal Roads:** Paved. **RV Service:** No. **Market:** 36 mi. southwest in Twain Harte. **Restaurant:** 36 mi. southwest in Twain Harte. **General Store:** No. **Vending:** No. **Swimming:** No. **Playground:** No. **Activities:** Fishing, hiking. **Nearby Attractions:** Tuolumne County Museum & History Center in Sonora; Pinecrest Lake; Sonora Pass. **Additional Information:** Tuolumne County Visitors Bureau, (209) 533-4420 or (800) 446-1333.

RESTRICTIONS

Pets: On leash. **Fires:** In fire grates only. **Alcoholic Beverages:** Allowed. **Vehicle Maximum Length:** 22 ft. **Other:** 14-day stay limit.

TO GET THERE

From Sonora drive 49 mi. east on Hwy. 108. The campground entrance is on the left, just beyond Clark Fork Rd.

SOUTH LAKE TAHOE

D. L. Bliss State Park

Hwy. 89, West Shore Lake Tahoe, Tahoma 96142. T: (530) 525-7277 or (530) 525-7232 or reservations (800) 444-7275; www.cal-parks.ca.gov or www.reserveamerica.com.

🚐 ★★★   🔺 ★★★

Beauty: ★★★★   Site Privacy: ★★
Spaciousness: ★★★   Quiet: ★★★
Security: ★★★   Cleanliness: ★★★
Insect Control: ★★★   Facilities: ★★

D. L. Bliss was a pioneering lumberman, banker, and railroad owner whose family donated 744 acres of this land to the state park system in 1929. More than 70 years later, the campground retains an appealingly rustic look. That it lacks the "Hooverville" feel of so many other facilities its size may be chalked up to its pleasingly chaotic Sierra Nevada setting. Huge granite boulders vie for space with incense cedars, lodgepole, and Jeffrey pines across a steep hillside that ends at a sandy beach and picnic area on the shore of Lake Tahoe. Roomy sites are tightly clustered over a series of loops, but they don't seem crowded, due to a degree of buffering provided by the boulders. For the most space and best views of the indigo water, try for the loop with sites 141–168, which also has a number of pull-through parking slots. Make time for hiking the Rubicon trail (four-and-a-half miles, one way), which offers stellar views of the lake and a chance to see osprey nesting in the tall trees. It ends at Vikingsholm Mansion (worth a visit), at scenic Emerald Bay. The shorter Balancing Rock nature trail (half a mile long) winds through the forest to a precariously positioned granite boulder.

BASICS

Operated By: California Dept. of Parks & Recreation. **Open:** Late May to mid-Sept., weather permitting. **Site Assignment:** Reservations recommended; V, MC, D. **Registration:** At entrance booth. **Fee:** $12, cash or CA check. **Parking:** At site.

FACILITIES

Number of RV Sites: 168. **Number of Tent-Only Sites:** 0. **Hookups:** None. **Each Site:** Picnic table, fire grate, bearproof box, some sites have barbecue grill. **Dump Station:** Yes. **Laundry:** No. **Pay Phone:** Yes. **Rest Rooms and Showers:** Yes. **Fuel:** No. **Propane:** No. **Internal Roads:** Paved. **RV Service:** No. **Market:** 11 mi. south in South Lake Tahoe. **Restaurant:** 11 mi. south in South Lake Tahoe. **General Store:** No. **Vending:** No. **Swimming:** In Lake Tahoe. **Playground:** No. **Other:** Beach. **Activities:** Hiking, fishing, birding. **Nearby Attractions:** Emerald Bay State Park & Vikingsholm Mansion in Tahoma; Lake Tahoe Historical Museum in South Lake Tahoe. **Additional Information:** South Lake Tahoe Chamber of Commerce, (530) 541-5255.

RESTRICTIONS

Pets: On 6 ft. leash. **Fires:** In fire grates only. **Alcoholic Beverages:** Allowed at site. **Vehicle Maximum Length:** 18 ft. **Other:** 14-day stay limit; no firearms; no wood gathering.

TO GET THERE

From South Lake Tahoe, at the junction of US 50 and Hwy. 89, follow Hwy. 89 north for 11.4 mi. to the entrance of the state park on the right. After making that turn, the campground is straight ahead.

SPRINGVILLE
Wishon

Camp Wishon Rd./CR 208, Springville 93265. T: (559) 539-2607 or reservations (877) 444-6777; www.r5.fs.fed.us/sequoia or www.reserveusa.com.

🚐 ★★★	🛖 ★★★★
Beauty: ★★★★	Site Privacy: ★★★
Spaciousness: ★★★	Quiet: ★★★★
Security: ★★★★	Cleanliness: ★★★
Insect Control: ★★	Facilities: ★★

Wishon, at 4,000 feet elevation, is not for the tidy at heart. It's a sprawling campground that overlaps a congested tangle of trees and rocks. The boulder-larded landscape adds convincingly to the mountainous feel here, and to the difficulty in walking through the domain after dark. The unspoiled allure of this primitive, peaceful setting is accentuated by craggy Sierra ridges that seem to brush the sky overhead. Middle Fork of the North Tule River cuts the camp in half, with the more appealing sites across the small bridge, where aged, spidery-limbed oaks bestow the gift of shade. Additional shelter and screening are provided by ponderosa pines, madrone, manzanita, and cedar. Sites 20, 21, and 28, tucked behind boulders, are the most private. This national forest campground is in the southern unit of the new Giant Sequoia National Monument, making it a great base for exploring trails in the area. The host's residence is adjacent to the property.

BASICS

Operated By: California Land Management, concessionaire. **Open:** All year, weather permitting. **Site Assignment:** Reservations accepted w/ V, MC, D. **Registration:** At entrance kiosk. **Fee:** $14, cash or check; $28 for double site. **Parking:** At site.

FACILITIES

Number of RV Sites: 35. **Number of Tent-Only Sites:** 0. **Hookups:** None. **Each Site:** Picnic table, fire grate, barbecue grill. **Dump Station:** No. **Laundry:** No. **Pay Phone:** Yes. **Rest Rooms and Showers:** Vault toilets, no showers. **Fuel:** No. **Propane:** No. **Internal Roads:** Paved. **RV Service:** No. **Market:** 28 mi. west in Porterville. **Restaurant:** 13 mi. west in Springville. **General Store:** No. **Vending:** No. **Swimming:** No. **Playground:** No. **Activities:** Hiking, fishing. **Nearby Attractions:** Sequoia National Forest; Porterville Historical Museum & Zauld House & Gardens; California Hot Springs. **Additional Information:** Springville Chamber of Commerce, (559) 539-2312; Porterville Chamber of Commerce, (559) 784-7503.

RESTRICTIONS

Pets: On leash. **Fires:** In fire grates only. **Alcoholic Beverages:** Allowed. **Vehicle Maximum Length:** 24 ft. **Other:** 14-day stay limit.

TO GET THERE

From Porterville drive 24 mi. east on Hwy. 190 to Camp Wishon Rd. Turn left and proceed 4 mi. to the campground entrance on the right.

ST. HELENA
Bothe-Napa Valley State Park

3801 St. Helena Hwy. (Hwy. 29), Calistoga 94515. T: (707) 942-4574 or reservations (800) 444-7275; www.cal-parks.ca.gov or www.reserveamerica.com.

🚐 ★★★	🛖 ★★★★
Beauty: ★★★★	Site Privacy: ★★★★
Spaciousness: ★★★	Quiet: ★★★
Security: ★★★	Cleanliness: ★★★
Insect Control: ★	Facilities: ★★

The Wappo Indians used to call this part of the valley home until being displaced by white settlers in the middle of the nineteenth century. In honor of its first inhabitants the park maintains a small "Native American garden" of herbs and vegetables the Wappos are believed to have cultivated. Indigenous plants are featured in a more natural setting around the campground, its lollipop loop being abundantly furnished with a variety of conifers and oaks, toyon, bay, madrone, manzanita, and poison oak. Most campers gravitate to the top of the cul-de-sac near the latrines. The more private sites, though, are 1–9 at the front end of the drive, and their gravel parking slips are long enough to accommodate almost any size RV. One of the better trails in Bothe-Napa leads to volcanic ash cliffs atop Upper Ritchey Canyon. And for unusual amenities in a state park, how about the swimming pool, open from Memorial Day through Labor Day? That sure beats wading in the stream that trickles by one side of camp, spawning hordes of mosquitoes in the spring.

BASICS

Operated By: California Dept. of Parks & Recreation. **Open:** All year. **Site Assignment:** Reservations accepted w/ V, MC, D. **Registration:** At kiosk opposite site 11. **Fee:** $12, cash or CA check. **Parking:** At site.

FACILITIES

Number of RV Sites: 40. **Number of Tent-Only Sites:** 9. **Hookups:** None. **Each Site:** Picnic table, fire grate, food storage box. **Dump Station:** No. **Laundry:** No. **Pay Phone:** Yes. **Rest Rooms and Showers:** Yes. **Fuel:** No. **Propane:** No. **Internal Roads:** Paved. **RV Service:** No. **Market:** 3 mi. north in Calistoga. **Restaurant:** 3 mi. north in Calistoga. **General Store:** No. **Vending:** No. **Swimming:** In pool seasonally. **Playground:** No. **Other:** Some wheelchair-accessible facilities, visitor center. **Activities:** Hiking, bicycling, horseback riding, birding, interpretive programs, horseshoe pit. **Nearby Attractions:** Luther Burbank Home & Gardens, Annadel State Park & museums in Santa Rosa; winery tours. **Additional Information:** Santa Rosa CVB, (800) 404-ROSE; Napa-Sonoma Wine Country Visitor Center, (707) 642-0686 or (800) 723-0575.

RESTRICTIONS

Pets: On 6 ft. leash. **Fires:** In fire grates only. **Alcoholic Beverages:** Allowed at site. **Vehicle Maximum Length:** 31 ft. **Other:** 14-day stay limit; no firearms; no wood gathering.

TO GET THERE

From St. Helena follow Hwy. 29 north for 4.5 mi. The well-marked park entrance is on the left, beyond Bale Grist Mill State Park.

STOCKTON

New Hogan Lake, Acorn West and Acorn East Campgrounds

2713 Hogan Dam Rd., Valley Springs 95252. T: (209) 772-1343 or reservations (877) 444-6777 or marina (209) 772-1462; F: (209) 772-9352; www.spk.usace.army.mil/cespk-co/lakes/ newhogan.html or www.reserveusa.com; newhogan-info@spk.usace.army.mil.

🚐 ★★★★   ⛺ ★★★

Beauty: ★★★★   Site Privacy: ★★
Spaciousness: ★★★   Quiet: ★★
Security: ★★★★   Cleanliness: ★★
Insect Control: ★★★   Facilities: ★★★★

The US Army Corps of Engineers created this reservoir in 1964 and continues to manage it. Which is not to suggest that you'll be rousted out of your sleeping bag by reveille at 0500 hours. It's more likely that the roar of motorboats will get you up, as this is a popular—though seldom full—boating and fishing spot. The only overt reminders that this is army land is the presence of uniformed volunteers at the entrance booths. In a sense that's a shame, since the oak-fringed, grassy meadows of the three camp loops, which slope water-ward, could tolerate more thorough litter control. On weekend nights, too, excessive noise, including barking, wandering dogs, can be severe enough to make you want to call in the MPs. Yet sites are well dispersed, if somewhat open, and many are shaded by toyon, pines, and oaks. There are also 30 boat-in spots available (first come, first served) from May through Sept. Oak Knoll, the primitive overflow area, costs $6 less per night and offers a few decently private, lake view sites.

BASICS

Operated By: US Army Corps of Engineers. **Open:** All year. **Site Assignment:** Reservations for 70% of the sites accepted w/ V, MC, D. **Registration:** At entrance booth. **Fee:** $16, cash or check. **Parking:** At site.

FACILITIES

Number of RV Sites: 127. **Number of Tent-Only Sites:** 0. **Hookups:** None. **Each Site:** Picnic table, fire grate, lantern pole. **Dump Station:** Yes.

Laundry: No. **Pay Phone:** Yes. **Rest Rooms and Showers:** Yes. **Fuel:** No. **Propane:** No. **Internal Roads:** Paved. **RV Service:** No. **Market:** 3 mi. northwest in Valley Springs. **Restaurant:** 3 mi. northwest in Valley Springs. **General Store:** No. **Vending:** No. **Swimming:** In New Hogan Lake. **Playground:** No. **Other:** Some wheelchair-accessible facilities, boat ramp, marina. **Activities:** Fishing, boat rentals, hiking, birding, horseback riding, mountain biking, cussing out your noisy neighbors. **Nearby Attractions:** Calaveras County Historical Society & Museum Complex in San Andreas; Amador County Museum in Jackson; planetarium & museums in Stockton. **Additional Information:** Calaveras County Visitors Bureau, (209) 736-0049.

RESTRICTIONS

Pets: On leash. **Fires:** In fire grates only. **Alcoholic Beverages:** Allowed. **Vehicle Maximum Length:** None. **Other:** 14-day stay limit.

TO GET THERE

From Stockton on Hwy. 99 drive 30 mi. east to Hogan Dam Rd. Turn right and continue for 1 mi. to the well-signed campground access road on the left. The campground entrance is 0.8 mi. from there.

SUSANVILLE

Bogard

FR 31N21, Susanville 96130. T: (530) 257-4188; F: (530) 257-4150; www.r5.fs.fed.us/lassen.

🚐 ★★★   ⛺ ★★★★

Beauty: ★★★   Site Privacy: ★★★
Spaciousness: ★★★★   Quiet: ★★★
Security: ★★   Cleanliness: ★★★
Insect Control: ★★★   Facilities: ★

Searching for a peaceful camp where you are more likely to hear birds chirping and the tapping of woodpeckers than another camper's voice? Then Bogard is just the place. Its single loop winds through a mountainous—though level—pine and alder forest, with rocks, pine needle, and grass coloring the floor of sites. That there are so few of the latter is refreshing, considering how easily another dozen could be shoe-horned into such a sizable piece of turf. Of the many good spots, the very best for privacy are 4, 6, 7, 10, and

11. We prefer Bogard as a base camp to Butte Creek, also a Lassen National Forest campground, even though the second is closer to the Butte Lake section of Lassen National Park. Bogard is used less often by hunters and has thus suffered less wear and tear during the off-season. There is no trash pick-up, and the rustic pump delivers rusty water, so plan to pack-in drinking water and pack-out your rubbish. Surprisingly, the back-in parking slots are paved.

BASICS

Operated By: CSU Chico Research Foundation, concessionaire. **Open:** May through Oct., weather permitting. **Site Assignment:** First come, first served. **Registration:** At entrance kiosk. **Fee:** $10, cash or check. **Parking:** At site.

FACILITIES

Number of RV Sites: 13. **Number of Tent-Only Sites:** 0. **Hookups:** None. **Each Site:** Picnic table, fire grate. **Dump Station:** No. **Laundry:** No. **Pay Phone:** No. **Rest Rooms and Showers:** Vault toilets, no showers. **Fuel:** No. **Propane:** No. **Internal Roads:** Paved. **RV Service:** No. **Market:** 28 mi. east in Susanville. **Restaurant:** 28 mi. east in Susanville. **General Store:** No. **Vending:** No. **Swimming:** No. **Playground:** No. **Activities:** Hiking, fishing, wildlife viewing. **Nearby Attractions:** Bizz Johnson National Recreation Trail; Railroad Depot & Lassen Historical Museum in Susanville; Lassen Volcanic National Park; Eagle Lake Recreation Area. **Additional Information:** Lassen County Chamber of Commerce, (530) 257-4323.

RESTRICTIONS

Pets: On leash. **Fires:** In fire grates only. **Alcoholic Beverages:** Allowed. **Vehicle Maximum Length:** 28 ft. **Other:** 14-day stay limit.

TO GET THERE

From Susanville drive 6 mi. west on Hwy. 36. Bear right on Hwy. 44 and continue for 20 mi., then turn left on FR 31N26 (a dirt washboard immediately after the rest area sign). Proceed for 1.6 mi. and take a right on FR 31N21. The campground is 0.5 mi. ahead.

SUSANVILLE
Goumaz

FR 30N03, Susanville 96130. T: (530) 257-4188; F: (530) 252-5803; www.r5.fs.fed.us/lassen.

⏚ ★★★★   ⛺ ★★★★

Beauty: ★★★★
Spaciousness: ★★★
Security: ★
Insect Control: ★

Site Privacy: ★★★
Quiet: ★★★★
Cleanliness: ★★★
Facilities: ★

Aside from a new-ish vaulted toilet, which is shared with hikers doing the Bizz Johnson "rails to trails" path that runs by the camp, this place has nada for facilities. If you can do without the other comforts, though, you'll have it made in the glade. Goumaz, at 5,200 feet elevation, is a thinly-forested, delightfully pretty, alpine campground in a level, sunny spot right alongside the Susan River. There is plenty of elbow room between the five sites, and four of those abut the water. Thus, it is hard to go wrong with any of these units, though number 2 enjoys a commanding view of a bend in the river and 4, which has pull-through parking (as does 1), is just 15 feet from a melodic cascade. Pine trees and grassy meadows contribute to a peaceful atmosphere that is marred only occasionally by the buzzing of a passing military jet. Biting flies can be a nuisance from mid-spring through early summer, so bring repellant. Susanville lies less than 20 miles to the east.

BASICS
Operated By: CSU Chico Research Foundation, concessionaire, & Lassen National Forest, Eagle Lake Ranger District. **Open:** May through Oct., weather permitting. **Site Assignment:** First come, first served. **Registration:** At entrance kiosk. **Fee:** $8, cash or check. **Parking:** At site.

FACILITIES
Number of RV Sites: 5. **Number of Tent-Only Sites:** 0. **Hookups:** None. **Each Site:** Picnic table, fire grate. **Dump Station:** No. **Laundry:** No. **Pay Phone:** No. **Rest Rooms and Showers:** Vault toilets, no showers. **Fuel:** No. **Propane:** No. **Internal Roads:** Packed dirt & volcanic cinder, decent condition. **RV Service:** No. **Market:** 16 mi. east in Susanville. **Restaurant:** 16 mi. east in Susanville. **General Store:** No. **Vending:** No. **Swimming:** No. **Playground:** No. **Activities:**

Hiking, bicycling, horseback riding, birding. **Nearby Attractions:** Lassen National Scenic Byway (Highways 89/44/36); Lassen Volcanic National Park; Bizz Johnson National Recreation Trail & Lassen Historical Museum in Susanville; Lake Almanor. **Additional Information:** Lassen County Chamber of Commerce, (530) 257-4323.

RESTRICTIONS
Pets: On leash. **Fires:** In fire grates only. **Alcoholic Beverages:** Allowed. **Vehicle Maximum Length:** 30 ft. **Other:** 14-day stay limit.

TO GET THERE
From Susanville drive 6 mi. west on Hwy. 36. Turn right on Hwy. 44 and continue for 7.1 mi. Turn left on FR 30N03/Goumaz Rd. The campground is 3.4 mi. ahead on the right.

SUSANVILLE
Merrill

Eagle Lake Rd., Susanville 96130. T: (530) 257-4188 or reservations (877) 444-6777; F: (530) 252-5803; www.r5.fs.fed.us/lassen or www.reserveusa.com.

⏚ ★★★★   ⛺ ★★★★

Beauty: ★★★★
Spaciousness: ★★★
Security: ★★★★
Insect Control: ★★★

Site Privacy: ★★★
Quiet: ★★★
Cleanliness: ★★★
Facilities: ★★

The deep blue Eagle Lake is California's second largest natural body of water, a magnificent mountain lake that is ringed by ponderosa, Jeffrey and white pines, with low-slung peaks nuzzling the horizon. The beauty of the scene more than compensates for the shocking impression made by the clear-cutting of national forest land along the drive to Eagle Summit, a process that appears to be turning large patches of forest into mountain heath. Sites at Merrill are evenly distributed over six loops and are either grassy or covered in pine needles, and partially shaded by pines. Many of those lie just 100 feet from the water, with 164 and 180 the most isolated. Also worth reserving are 167, 169, 171, 172, 174, 176, and 178. Security is above average for a national forest camp, with two separate hosts patrolling the domain. Also vigilant in summer are omnipresent game wardens, something to remember if you intend to fish. Showers, pay phones, fuel, groceries, and laundry machines are available at the marina, three miles away.

BASICS

Operated By: CSU Chico Research Foundation, concessionaire, & Lassen National Forest, Eagle Lake Ranger District. **Open:** May through Oct., weather permitting. **Site Assignment:** Reservations accepted w/ V, MC, D for Aspen & Pine loops. **Registration:** At entrance kiosk. **Fee:** $14–$16, cash or check. **Parking:** At site.

FACILITIES

Number of RV Sites: 180. **Number of Tent-Only Sites:** 0. **Hookups:** None, but planned. **Each Site:** Picnic table, fire grate. **Dump Station:** Yes. **Laundry:** No. **Pay Phone:** No. **Rest Rooms and Showers:** Flush toilets, no showers. **Fuel:** No. **Propane:** No. **Internal Roads:** Paved. **RV Service:** No. **Market:** 14 mi. north in Spaulding. **Restaurant:** 14 mi. north in Spaulding. **General Store:** No. **Vending:** No. **Swimming:** In Eagle Lake. **Playground:** No. **Other:** Some wheelchair-accessible facilities, boat ramp, marina. **Activities:** Fishing, waterskiing, canoeing, bicycling. **Nearby Attractions:** Bizz Johnson National Recreation Trail; Railroad Depot & Lassen Historical Museum in Susanville; Lassen Volcanic National Park. **Additional Information:** Lassen County Chamber of Commerce, (530) 257-4323.

RESTRICTIONS

Pets: On leash. **Fires:** In fire grates only. **Alcoholic Beverages:** Allowed. **Vehicle Maximum Length:** 45 ft. **Other:** 14-day stay limit except in one loop w/ a 30-day stay limit.

TO GET THERE

From Susanville drive 4 mi. west on Hwy. 36. Turn right on Eagle Lake Rd./CR A1 and continue for 13.7 mi. to Gallatin Rd. Take a right and proceed for 1 mi. to the campground entrance on the right. The marina is 1 mi. farther.

TAHOMA
Meeks Bay

Hwy. 89, West Shore Lake Tahoe, Meeks Bay 96142. T: (530) 573-2674 or (530) 583-3642; F: (530) 573-2693; www.r5.fs.fed.us/ltbmu or www.reserveusa.com.

🚐 ★★★   ⛺ ★★

Beauty: ★★★★	Site Privacy: ★★
Spaciousness: ★★★	Quiet: ★★
Security: ★★★	Cleanliness: ★★★
Insect Control: ★★★	Facilities: ★★

If your idea of a restful vacation spot is a quiet place to pitch your tent or park your camper, don't even think about stopping at Meeks Bay. Just 11 miles south of Tahoe City, this national forest camp is hunkered up against a bend in Hwy. 89 as it follows the contours of Lake Tahoe, subjecting it to the roar of an ongoing stream of traffic. If, on the other hand, beach time is what makes you tick, drive on in and sink your toes into the soft sandy stretch of shore here at the heart of the scenically gorgeous Meeks Bay. Soak up the rays and enjoy the hazy view of Nevada and its mountains across the lake. Or get out on the water via the boat ramp at the resort next door. As for the attractive campground, at 6,300 feet elevation, its level, sandy, and grassy sites are dispersed around a convoluted series of loops. Though they are rather exposed, many are shaded by mature Jeffrey pines, with smaller conifers, some manzanita, and young incense cedars adding to the beauty of the scene. The Meeks Bay trailhead leads into the Desolation Wilderness, across the road.

BASICS

Operated By: California Land Management, concessionaire. **Open:** Mid-May to end Sept. **Site Assignment:** Reservations recommended; V, MC, D. **Registration:** At entrance kiosk. **Fee:** $14, cash or check. **Parking:** At site.

FACILITIES

Number of RV Sites: 40. **Number of Tent-Only Sites:** 0. **Hookups:** None. **Each Site:** Picnic table, fire ring, barbecue grill. **Dump Station:** No. **Laundry:** No. **Pay Phone:** Yes. **Rest Rooms and Showers:** Flush toilets, no showers. **Fuel:** No.

Propane: No. **Internal Roads:** Paved. **RV Service:** No. **Market:** 4 mi. north in Homewood. **Restaurant:** 2 mi. north in Tahoma. **General Store:** Yes. **Vending:** No. **Swimming:** In Lake Tahoe. **Playground:** No. **Other:** Beach. **Activities:** Fishing, boating, bicycle rentals, counting the passing cars. **Nearby Attractions:** Gatekeeper's Museum/Marion Steinbach Indian Basket Museum & Watson Cabin Museum in Tahoe City; Emerald Bay State Park & Vikingsholm Mansion in Tahoma. **Additional Information:** South Lake Tahoe Chamber of Commerce, (530) 541-5255.

RESTRICTIONS

Pets: On 6 ft. leash; not allowed on beach. **Fires:** In fire rings only. **Alcoholic Beverages:** Allowed at site. **Vehicle Maximum Length:** 20 ft. **Other:** 14-day stay limit.

TO GET THERE

From Tahoe City drive 11.2 mi. south on Hwy. 89. The campground entrance is on the left, right after Meeks Bay RV Resort & Marina.

TAHOMA

Sugar Pine Point State Park, General Creek Campground

Hwy. 89, West Shore Lake Tahoe 7360, Tahoma 96142. T: (530) 525-7982 or (530) 525-7232 or reservations (800) 444-7275; www.cal-parks.ca.gov or www.reserveamerica.com.

🚐 ★★★	🅰 ★★★
Beauty: ★★★★	Site Privacy: ★★★
Spaciousness: ★★★	Quiet: ★★★
Security: ★★★	Cleanliness: ★★★
Insect Control: ★★★	Facilities: ★★★

So close to Lake Tahoe, and yet so far. That, in a phrase, sums up one of the more frustrating aspects of this otherwise fine state park. General Creek Campground, at an altitude of 6,250 feet, consists of several loops that wind through a level pine forest that is uphill and across the street from the lake, but offers no views of the water. There is decent screening between sites, which is fortunate, given how closely they are clustered. The circuit with units 126–175 features the most dispersed spots, while that containing 76–125 runs a close second. This is the only state park in the area to stay open all year, a boon to cross-country skiers and hardy, hot-blooded campers. Spring, though, is one of the better times to come, before the roads are clogged by tourists, and while the snow plants and manzanita are in bloom. The Hellman-Ehrman Mansion, an opulent, pine-paneled summer home built a century ago, is open for tours from July through Labor Day.

BASICS

Operated By: California Dept. of Parks & Recreation. **Open:** All year. **Site Assignment:** Reservations recommended; V, MC, D. **Registration:** At entrance booth. **Fee:** $12, cash or CA check. **Parking:** At site.

FACILITIES

Number of RV Sites: 175. **Number of Tent-Only Sites:** 0. **Hookups:** None. **Each Site:** Picnic table, fire ring, bearproof box, most sites have barbecue grill. **Dump Station:** Yes. **Laundry:** No. **Pay Phone:** Yes. **Rest Rooms and Showers:** Yes, showers closed in winter. **Fuel:** No. **Propane:** No. **Internal Roads:** Paved. **RV Service:** No. **Market:** 3 mi. north in Homewood. **Restaurant:** 1 mi. north in Tahoma. **General Store:** No. **Vending:** No. **Swimming:** In Lake Tahoe. **Playground:** No. **Other:** Lighthouse, beach, Nature Center, Hellman-Ehrman Mansion. **Activities:** Hiking, fishing, bicycle rentals, birding, cross-country skiing. **Nearby Attractions:** Gatekeeper's Museum/Marion Steinbach Indian Basket Museum & Watson Cabin Museum in Tahoe City; Emerald Bay State Park & Vikingsholm Mansion in Tahoma. **Additional Information:** South Lake Tahoe Chamber of Commerce, (530) 541-5255.

RESTRICTIONS

Pets: On 6 ft. leash. **Fires:** In fire rings only. **Alcoholic Beverages:** Allowed at site. **Vehicle Maximum Length:** 32 ft. **Other:** 14-day stay limit from June 15 to Sept. 30, 30-day stay limit for the rest of the year; no firearms; no wood gathering.

TO GET THERE

From Tahoe City drive 9.7 mi. south on Hwy. 89, past Tahoma. The campground entrance is on the right.

TEMECULA

Lake Skinner Recreation Area

37701 Warren Rd., Winchester 92596. T: (909) 926-1541 or reservations (800) 234-7275; www.riversidecountyparks.org.

🚐 ★★★★   ▲ ★★

Beauty: ★★★   Site Privacy: ★★
Spaciousness: ★★★   Quiet: ★★★★
Security: ★★★★   Cleanliness: ★★
Insect Control: ★★★   Facilities: ★★★★★

Forget the hiking and equestrian trails at Lake Skinner and its proximity to nearly a dozen wineries. There is really only one reason to visit this huge campground, and that reason is spelled f-i-s-h-i–n-g. The lake is stocked weekly from Nov. through May, making it one of the better fishing spots in southern California for trout, bass, bluegill, catfish, and crappie. Serious anglers will appreciate the lake-wide speed limit of ten miles per hour and may want to plan their trips around the derbies held for catfish in Aug. and trout in Nov., when cash prizes are awarded. Keep in mind, though, that boats must be at least ten feet long and canoes and kayaks are not permitted on the water. Of the campground itself, there are three large loops spread over grassy meadows, with few of the average-looking sites endowed with a lake view. Shade, too, is scarce, despite the scattered presence of sycamores and pepper trees. B and C loops offer sites that appear marginally less crowded together than those in loop A.

BASICS

Operated By: Riverside County Regional Park. **Open:** All year. **Site Assignment:** Reservations accepted w/ V, MC, D. **Registration:** At entrance booth. **Fee:** $15–$18, cash or CA check. **Parking:** At site.

FACILITIES

Number of RV Sites: 300. **Number of Tent-Only Sites:** 0. **Hookups:** Water, electric (30, 50 amps), sewer. **Each Site:** Picnic table, fire grate. **Dump Station:** Yes. **Laundry:** Yes. **Pay Phone:** Yes. **Rest Rooms and Showers:** Yes. **Fuel:** Yes, for boats. **Propane:** Yes. **Internal Roads:** Paved. **RV Service:** No. **Market:** 8 mi. southwest in Temecula. **Restaurant:** 8 mi. southwest in Temecula. **General Store:** Yes. **Vending:** Yes. **Swimming:** In pool seasonally. **Playground:** Yes. **Other:** Some wheelchair-accessible facilities, two boat ramps. **Activities:** Fishing, hiking, horseback riding, horseshoe pit, volleyball, boat rentals. **Nearby Attractions:** Numerous wineries, Palomar Mountain Observatory. **Additional Information:** Temecula Valley Chamber of Commerce (909) 676-5090.

RESTRICTIONS

Pets: On 6 ft. leash; $2. **Fires:** In fire grates only. **Alcoholic Beverages:** Allowed at site. **Vehicle Maximum Length:** 45 ft. **Other:** 14-day stay limit; no firearms.

TO GET THERE

From I-15 in Temecula take Rancho California Rd. Exit and head east for 9.5 mi. Turn right on Warren Rd. Campground entrance is straight ahead.

TRINIDAD

Patrick's Point State Park

4150 Patrick's Point Dr., Trinidad 95570. T: (707) 677-3570 or reservations (800) 444-7275; www.cal-parks.ca.gov or www.reserveamerica.com; ncrdppsp@humboldt1.com.

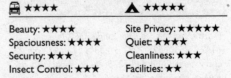

🚐 ★★★★   ▲ ★★★★★

Beauty: ★★★★   Site Privacy: ★★★★★
Spaciousness: ★★★★   Quiet: ★★★★
Security: ★★★   Cleanliness: ★★★
Insect Control: ★★★   Facilities: ★★

Visitors to this breathtakingly beautiful state park are in for a special treat. We're not referring to Sumeg, its reconstructed Yurok Indian village. Nor to the thriving tide pools and pretty beach. Beyond the chance of seeing passing whales from towering, pine-shrouded bluffs, Patrick's Point has an ace up its figurative sleeve: its campground is one of the finest in the entire state park system. There is a wild, untamed atmosphere to the domain, with the rock-studded undergrowth thick with ferns and moss. Three detached loop areas feature sites that are uncommonly spacious and well-screened, a generous allowance of space that grants campers a refreshing dignity of privacy. Those in the shady Abalone circuit (from 16–85) are the roomiest, while Agate's (86 –97) enjoy more sun exposure and have stunning views of the surf. The RV section, admittedly, is typically tight, but its ocean vistas are a balancing amelioration. Cabin and yurt rentals are also available.

BASICS

Operated By: California Dept. of Parks & Recreation. **Open:** All year. **Site Assignment:** Reservations recommended; V, MC, D. **Registration:** At entrance booth. **Fee:** $12, cash or CA check. **Parking:** At site.

FACILITIES

Number of RV Sites: 124. **Number of Tent-Only Sites:** 0. **Hookups:** None. **Each Site:** Picnic table, fire grate, food storage box. **Dump Station:** No. **Laundry:** No. **Pay Phone:** Yes. **Rest Rooms and Showers:** Yes. **Fuel:** No. **Propane:** No. **Internal Roads:** Paved. **RV Service:** No. **Market:** 6.5 mi. south in Trinidad. **Restaurant:** 6.5 mi. south in Trinidad. **General Store:** No. **Vending:** No. **Swimming:** No. **Playground:** No. **Other:** Some wheelchair-accessible facilities. **Activities:** Hiking, fishing, whale-watching, agate hunting, tidepooling. **Nearby Attractions:** Trinidad State Beach, museums, Memorial Lighthouse & Aquarium in Trinidad; Sumeg Village; Fort Humboldt State Historic Park, Humboldt Bay Harbor Cruise & Maritime Museum, Romano Gabriel Wooden Sculpture Garden, Carson Mansion, Main St., zoo, & more in Eureka. **Additional Information:** Trinidad Chamber of Commerce, (707) 677-1610; Greater Eureka Chamber of Commerce, (707) 442-3738.

RESTRICTIONS

Pets: On 6 ft. leash. **Fires:** In fire grates only. **Alcoholic Beverages:** Allowed at site. **Vehicle Maximum Length:** 31 ft. **Other:** 14-day stay limit from May 1–Sept. 30; no firearms; no wood gathering.

TO GET THERE

From Eureka drive 28 mi. north on US 101 and take the Patrick's Point State Park Exit. Drive 0.4 mi. west on Patrick's Point Dr. to the park entrance on the right.

TRUCKEE
Logger

Stampede Valley Rd., Boca 96161. T: (530) 587-3558 or (530) 544-0426 or reservations (877) 444-6777; F: (530) 587-6914; www.r5.fs.fed.us/tahoe or www.reserveusa.com.

🚐 ★★★★   ⛺ ★★★

Beauty: ★★★★   Site Privacy: ★★
Spaciousness: ★★★   Quiet: ★★★

Security: ★★★   Cleanliness: ★★★
Insect Control: ★★★   Facilities: ★★

Campers who make a practice of shying away from oversize properties with numerous loops may want to make an exception for Logger, which is so vast it has west and east entrances. In spite of its inauspicious name, there is an abundance of ponderosa pines across its hillside perch, above the south shore of the deep blue Stampede Reservoir. Sage-colored salt bush and other low-lying shrubs don't add much to the minimal screening between dirt- and pine needle–surfaced sites, but in general space and shade are above average for such a crowded campground. One of the more private sites is 22, and 39 is well-shaded, with a water view; two of the larger pull-through slots are 32, also with a lake view, and 37. Other fine options include 25, 79, 83, and 84. Logger, which is less than 20 miles from Truckee, is at an elevation of 5,949 feet, making a coat or sweater essential apparel, even in summer. Stampede Reservoir is a popular fishing spot for Kokanee salmon, so don't forget your rod. Seasonal drawdowns, however, can leave the lake disappointingly low by late summer.

BASICS

Operated By: California Land Management, concessionaire. **Open:** May 15 to Sept. 30, weather permitting. **Site Assignment:** Reservations accepted w/ V, MC, D. **Registration:** At entrance booth. **Fee:** $13, cash or check. **Parking:** At site.

FACILITIES

Number of RV Sites: 252. **Number of Tent-Only Sites:** 0. **Hookups:** None. **Each Site:** Picnic table, fire grate, barbecue grill. **Dump Station:** Yes. **Laundry:** No. **Pay Phone:** No. **Rest Rooms and Showers:** Vault toilets, no showers. **Fuel:** No. **Propane:** No. **Internal Roads:** Paved. **RV Service:** No. **Market:** 11 mi. south in Boca. **Restaurant:** 18 mi. south in Truckee. **General Store:** No. **Vending:** No. **Swimming:** In Stampede Reservoir. **Playground:** No. **Other:** Some wheelchair-accessible facilities, boat ramp. **Activities:** Fishing, boating, waterskiing, hiking, meeting your neighbors. **Nearby Attractions:** Boreal Mountain Ski Resort, Donner Memorial State Park, Western Skisport Museum, & historic downtown in Truckee; Lake Tahoe. **Additional Information:** Truckee Donner Chamber of Commerce & Visitors Center, (530) 587-2757.

RESTRICTIONS

Pets: On leash. **Fires:** In fire grates only. **Alcoholic Beverages:** Allowed. **Vehicle Maximum Length:** 32 ft. **Other:** 14-day stay limit.

TO GET THERE

From Truckee drive 7 mi. east on I-80. Take the Boca/Stampede-Hirschdale Rd. Exit and proceed north for 8.7 mi., past the Boca Reservoir. Turn left onto CR S261 and drive 2 mi. to the campground entrance on the right.

TWENTYNINE PALMS

Cottonwood

74485 National Park Dr., Twentynine Palms 92277. T: (760) 367-5525; F: (760) 367-5583; www.nps.gov/jotr.

🚐 ★★★   ⛺ ★★★

Beauty: ★★★	Site Privacy: ★★
Spaciousness: ★★	Quiet: ★★
Security: ★★★	Cleanliness: ★★★★
Insect Control: ★★★★	Facilities: ★★

This is a neat looking camp located near the southern entrance to Joshua Tree National Park, just seven miles north of I-10. It is a long drive from here to the park's concentration of granite boulders, which are looked upon almost as totemic objects by amateur climbers, and the celebrated stands of Joshua trees that thrive at higher altitudes. Thus, this facility is usually the last to fill, even on weekends. It is popular nonetheless among RVers, partly because this is one of the few campgrounds in Joshua Tree to provide potable water, and pull-up parking is the norm throughout the two loops. Despite the sites being rather small and closely situated, most are pretty well screened by a mix of mesquite, jojoba, cholla cacti, and other desert scrub. The trail to Mastodon Peak starts in the campground, and that to Lost Palms Oasis is nearby. The nearest telephone is 12 miles east on I-10 at Chiriaco Summit.

BASICS

Operated By: National Park Service. **Open:** All year. **Site Assignment:** First come, first served. **Registration:** At entrance kiosk. **Fee:** $10, cash only. **Parking:** At site.

FACILITIES

Number of RV Sites: 62. **Number of Tent-Only Sites:** 0. **Hookups:** None. **Each Site:** Picnic table, fire grate. **Dump Station:** Yes. **Laundry:** No. **Pay Phone:** No. **Rest Rooms and Showers:** Flush toilets, no showers. **Fuel:** No. **Propane:** No. **Internal Roads:** Paved. **RV Service:** No. **Market:** 12 mi. east in Chiriaco Summit. **Restaurant:** 12 mi. east in Chiriaco Summit. **General Store:** No. **Vending:** No. **Swimming:** No. **Playground:** No. **Other:** Very limited wheelchair-accessible facilities. **Activities:** Hiking, mountain climbing, bicycling, horseback riding, ranger-led programs. **Nearby Attractions:** Salton Sea National Wildlife Refuge. **Additional Information:** Twentynine Palms Chamber of Commerce & Visitors Bureau, (760) 367-3445.

RESTRICTIONS

Pets: On 6 ft. leash; not allowed on trails. **Fires:** In fire rings only. **Alcoholic Beverages:** Allowed at site. **Vehicle Maximum Length:** 27 ft. **Other:** 14-day stay limit from Oct. through May; no firearms; no wood gathering.

TO GET THERE

From the I-10 Exit for Joshua Tree National Park drive 7 mi. north. Turn right at the sign and proceed 0.7 mi. to the campground on the left.

TWENTYNINE PALMS

Hidden Valley

Park Blvd., Twentynine Palms 92277. T: (760) 367-5525; F: (760) 367-5583; www.nps.gov/jotr.

🚐 ★★   ⛺ ★★★★

Beauty: ★★★★★	Site Privacy: ★★★★
Spaciousness: ★★★	Quiet: ★★★
Security: ★★	Cleanliness: ★★★★
Insect Control: ★★★★	Facilities: ★

Hidden Valley is fairly typical of the decidedly primitive campgrounds in Joshua Tree National Park. There is no telephone, no water, and the only shade comes from the oversize boulders that decorate much of the park. It is those boulders, composed of tan-colored monzo-granite, that lend Joshua Tree much of its visual appeal. Unfortunately, because monzo-granite is enticingly easy to scale, campground boulders attract amateur climbers at all hours of the day (and occasionally night), something privacy-seekers should keep in mind when selecting their site. The sandy sites here are fairly spacious and decently far apart, with creosote bushes, Joshua trees, and rabbit brush complementing the rocky terrain. Spring, when wildflowers pop up all over the desert, is our preferred time to visit this area, with autumn and the milder temperatures it brings running a close second. Daytime temperatures are mild from late Oct. through Mar., but nights can be downright icy. Outside of summer months, when the desert heat is blistering, campgrounds fill up most weekends. Beware of beggar coyotes prowling the grounds.

BASICS

Operated By: National Park Service. **Open:** All year. **Site Assignment:** First come, first served. **Registration:** At entrance kiosk. **Fee:** None. **Parking:** At site.

FACILITIES

Number of RV Sites: 39. **Number of Tent-Only Sites:** 0. **Hookups:** None. **Each Site:** Picnic table, fire ring. **Dump Station:** No. **Laundry:** No. **Pay Phone:** No, only an emergency phone. **Rest Rooms and Showers:** Vault toilets, no showers. **Fuel:** No. **Propane:** No. **Internal Roads:** Paved, but 1 loop is a sandy washboard. **RV Service:** No. **Market:** 15 mi. north in Joshua Tree. **Restaurant:** 15 mi. north in Joshua Tree. **General Store:** No. **Vending:** No. **Swimming:** No. **Playground:** No. **Other:** Very limited wheelchair-accessible facilities. **Activities:** Hiking, rock climbing, bicycling, horseback riding, ranger-led programs. **Nearby Attractions:** Old Shoolhouse Museum in Twentynine Palms, Hi-Desert Nature Museum in Yucca Valley. **Additional Information:** Twentynine Palms Chamber of Commerce & Visitors Bureau, (760) 367-3445.

RESTRICTIONS

Pets: On 6 ft. leash; not allowed on trails. **Fires:** In fire rings only. **Alcoholic Beverages:** Allowed at site. **Vehicle Maximum Length:** 27 ft. **Other:** 14-day stay limit from Oct. through May; no firearms; no wood gathering.

TO GET THERE

From the town of Joshua Tree on Hwy. 62 turn south on Park Blvd. After 14 mi. turn left into the campground.

UKIAH
Ky-en

1160 Lake Mendocino Dr., Ukiah 95482. T: (707) 462-7581 or reservations (877) 444-6777; F: (707) 462-3372; www.spn.usace.army.mil/mendocino.html or www.reserveusa.com.

🚐 ★★★   ⛺ ★★★

Beauty: ★★★★	Site Privacy: ★★★
Spaciousness: ★★	Quiet: ★★★
Security: ★★★★	Cleanliness: ★★
Insect Control: ★★★	Facilities: ★★★

You do not need to have a fishing rod or boat to enjoy Lake Mendocino, but it will certainly add to your pleasure. This green gleaming body of water receives quite a lot of use, with most of that falling between Memorial Day and Labor Day. Ky-en (also rendered Kyen) is typical of the three campgrounds here (a fourth, Miti, is a boat-in camp), nestled against a sloping hillside between Hwy. 20 and the lake. The most popular sites abut the shore, with 75, 82, and 103 the most private. The screening and shade are far better, though, up the hill where the loops snake through such varied vegetation as juniper, pine trees, oak, toyon, manzanita, and flowering ceanothus. Best of that section are 18 and 22 (both with pull-through parking), and 15, 16, 26, and 42. Security is good, with regular ranger patrols and entrance gates that are locked between 10:30 p.m. and 7:30 a.m. Rest rooms, though, could use a face-lift, and the grounds are disturbingly littered with bottles and cans.

BASICS

Operated By: US Army Corps of Engineers. **Open:** All year. **Site Assignment:** Reservations accepted w/ V, MC, D, AE. **Registration:** At entrance booth. **Fee:** $16–$18, cash or check. **Parking:** At site.

FACILITIES

Number of RV Sites: 103. **Number of Tent-Only Sites:** 0. **Hookups:** None. **Each Site:** Picnic table, fire grate, lantern holder. **Dump Station:** Yes. **Laundry:** No. **Pay Phone:** Yes. **Rest Rooms and Showers:** Yes. **Fuel:** No. **Propane:** No. **Internal Roads:** Paved & narrow. **RV Service:** No. **Market:** 1 mi. east in Calpella. **Restaurant:** 1 mi. east in Calpella. **General Store:** Yes, in summer.

Vending: No. **Swimming:** In Lake Mendocino.
Playground: Yes. **Other:** Some wheelchair-accessible facilities, 6-lane boat ramp, visitor center. **Activities:** Fishing, waterskiing, sailing, boat rentals, hiking, disc golf. **Nearby Attractions:** Ukiah museums & Cow Mountain Recreation Area; Mendocino County Museum & Roots of Motive Power/Antique Steam Logging Equipment in Willits; Skunk Train from Willits to Fort Bragg. **Additional Information:** Greater Ukiah Chamber of Commerce, (707) 462-4705.

RESTRICTIONS

Pets: On 6 ft. leash. **Fires:** In fire grates only. **Alcoholic Beverages:** Allowed. **Vehicle Maximum Length:** 35 ft. **Other:** 14-day stay limit.

TO GET THERE

Drive 6 mi. north of Ukiah on US 101. Turn east on Hwy. 20 and after 2.3 mi. turn right on Marina Drive Rd. The campground is 0.3 mi. ahead.

UPPER LAKE
Pogie Point

Hull Mountain Rd., Potter Valley 95469. T: (916) 386-5164; www.r5.fs.fed.us/mendocino.

🚐 ★★★   ▲ ★★★

Beauty: ★★★★   Site Privacy: ★★★
Spaciousness: ★★   Quiet: ★★★
Security: ★★★   Cleanliness: ★★★
Insect Control: ★★   Facilities: ★★

Forget the jokes about "doughboy" campers and "poppin' fresh" fish: Lake Pillsbury is one pretty haven for boating, fishing, hiking, or just lazing around. There are four campgrounds in this region of the Mendocino National Forest, with Oak Flat, two miles up the road, offering better lake access than Pogie Point. The former, though, is a primitive facility and there is some truth to the waggish suggestion that this status owes more to the people it attracts than its limited amenities. Pogie Point is marginally better in the creature comforts department (though its latrines could use more regular maintenance), but leagues ahead in aesthetics. It rests above a tiny cove that is ideal for launching canoes and kayaks. The grounds are thinly forested with tan

oak, moss-covered pines, madrone trees, and oversize manzanita. Sites along its double loop range from uncomfortably small and exposed to reasonably roomy and recessed. Elk, black-tailed deer, and wild turkey frequent these parts.

BASICS

Operated By: Pacific Gas & Electric. **Open:** All year, weather permitting. **Site Assignment:** First come, first served. **Registration:** At entrance kiosk. **Fee:** $12, cash or check. **Parking:** At site.

FACILITIES

Number of RV Sites: 45. **Number of Tent-Only Sites:** 0. **Hookups:** None. **Each Site:** Picnic table, fire grate. **Dump Station:** No. **Laundry:** No. **Pay Phone:** No. **Rest Rooms and Showers:** Vault toilets, no showers. **Fuel:** No. **Propane:** No. **Internal Roads:** Paved. **RV Service:** No. **Market:** 19 mi. west in Potter Valley. **Restaurant:** 19 mi. west in Potter Valley. **General Store:** No. **Vending:** No. **Swimming:** In Lake Pillsbury. **Playground:** No. **Other:** Some wheelchair-accessible facilities, small boat launch. **Activities:** Fishing, hiking, horseback riding, mountain biking, windsurfing, boating. **Nearby Attractions:** Lakeport County Museum & Clear Lake in Lakeport. **Additional Information:** Lake County Marketing Program/Visitor Information Center, (707) 263-9544 or (800) 525-3743; Mendocino National Forest, Upper Lake Ranger District, (707) 275-2361.

RESTRICTIONS

Pets: On leash, $1 fee. **Fires:** In fire grates only. **Alcoholic Beverages:** Allowed. **Vehicle Maximum Length:** 40 ft. **Other:** 14-day stay limit.

TO GET THERE

From Hwy. 20 in Upper Lake head north on Mendenhall Ave., which becomes Elk Mountain Rd./FR M1. After 17 mi. the scenic road turns to graded dirt, then pavement again after another 9 mi. From that point, the campground access is 5.5 mi. ahead on the right.

VISALIA

Lake Kaweah Recreation Area, Horse Creek Campground

Hwy. 198, Lemoncove 93244. T: (550) 597-2301 or reservations (877) 444-6777 or marina (559) 597-2526; F: (559) 597-2468; www.spk.usace.army.mil/cespk-co/lakes/kaweah.html or www.reserveusa.com.

🚐 ★★★★   ⛺ ★★★

Beauty: ★★★★   Site Privacy: ★★
Spaciousness: ★★★   Quiet: ★★★
Security: ★★★★   Cleanliness: ★★★
Insect Control: ★★   Facilities: ★★★

Lake Kaweah is a refreshing body of water that provides welcome relief in a part of the state where summer starts early and runs late. Its level was so high last spring that several of Horse Creek's sites were underwater. Nonetheless it remains a popular weekend retreat for area families, and for good reason: you can soak yourself in Kaweah's cool waters while the campgrounds in Sequoia and Kings Canyon National Parks are still under snow. Nestled in the Sierra foothills at an elevation of 694 feet, Horse Creek's environment is framed by the boulder-streaked, grassy ridges that hover over it. Nearer at hand, sites are plentifully shaded by oak, sycamore, buckeye, and cottonwood trees. An elongated loop, with three spur circuits, puts a great number of grass and dirt sites right at the edge of the lake. Privacy-seekers, though, should look toward higher ground, where numbers 4 and 5 are roomy, set back from the camp lane and enjoy a premium vantage of the water. The marina at Lemon Hill has propane and basic supplies.

BASICS

Operated By: US Army Corps of Engineers. **Open:** All year. **Site Assignment:** Reservations recommended; V, MC, D, AE. **Registration:** At entrance booth. **Fee:** $16, cash or check. **Parking:** At site.

FACILITIES

Number of RV Sites: 80. **Number of Tent-Only Sites:** 0. **Hookups:** None. **Each Site:** Picnic table, fire grate, lantern pole. **Dump Station:** Yes. **Laundry:** No. **Pay Phone:** Yes. **Rest Rooms and Showers:** Yes. **Fuel:** No. **Propane:** No. **Internal**

Roads: Paved & occasionally flooded. **RV Service:** No. **Market:** 8 mi. east in Three Rivers. **Restaurant:** 8 mi. east in Three Rivers. **General Store:** No. **Vending:** No. **Swimming:** In Lake Kaweah. **Playground:** Yes. **Other:** Some wheelchair-accessible facilities, boat ramp. **Activities:** Fishing, boat rentals, waterskiing, hiking, whitewater rafting on the Kaweah River, bailing out your tent. **Nearby Attractions:** Sequoia & Kings Canyon National Parks; Tulare County Museum in Visalia; Kaweah Oaks Preserve in Exeter. **Additional Information:** Visalia Chamber of Commerce & Visitors Bureau, (559) 734-5876; Three Rivers–Lemoncove Business Assoc., (550) 561-0410.

RESTRICTIONS

Pets: On leash. **Fires:** In fire grates only. **Alcoholic Beverages:** Allowed. **Vehicle Maximum Length:** 45 ft. **Other:** 14-day stay limit.

TO GET THERE

From Visalia drive 24 mi. east on Hwy. 198 to Lake Kaweah's south shore. The well-signed campground entrance is on the left.

WALNUT CREEK

Mount Diablo State Park

96 Mitchell Canyon Rd., Clayton 94517. T: (925) 837-2525 or reservations (800) 444-7275; www.mdia.org or www.cal-parks.ca.gov or www.reserveamerica.com.

🚐 ★★   ⛺ ★★★★

Beauty: ★★★★   Site Privacy: ★★★
Spaciousness: ★★   Quiet: ★★★★
Security: ★★★   Cleanliness: ★★★
Insect Control: ★★★   Facilities: ★★

The rolling grass-covered hills that make up this highly scenic park are dappled with live oak, knob cone pines, and juniper. If the extraordinary valley views don't take your breath away, you had better check your pulse! Or come back in spring, when an explosion of wildflowers should stimulate even the most colorblind of campers. There are three campgrounds here set at different altitudes, with the no-reservations Junction the least appealing. We prefer the Juniper loop (3,000 feet elevation) because, in a park where sites run toward petite, its are the larger and better screened. Additionally, many are blessed with outstanding westward vistas. Prime among many fine choices is number 20, detached from its neighbors and nursed by a superannuated, overhanging tree. In summer months when the heat intensifies, the cool, shady Live Oak loop (1,450 feet elevation) is the sounder choice. As the risk of wildfires escalates in summer, the park may close. Plan to call ahead, therefore, from June through Sept.

BASICS

Operated By: California Dept. of Parks & Recreation. **Open:** All year, but may close in summer due to extreme fire danger—call ahead. **Site Assignment:** Reservations recommended; V, MC, D. **Registration:** At entrance kiosk. **Fee:** $12, cash or CA check. **Parking:** At site.

FACILITIES

Number of RV Sites: 64. **Number of Tent-Only Sites:** 0. **Hookups:** None. **Each Site:** Picnic table, fire grate, food storage box in some sites. **Dump Station:** No. **Laundry:** No. **Pay Phone:** Yes. **Rest Rooms and Showers:** Yes. **Fuel:** No. **Propane:** No. **Internal Roads:** Paved & windy. **RV Service:** No. **Market:** 10 mi. north in Livermore. **Restaurant:** 10 mi. north in Livermore. **General Store:** No. **Vending:** No. **Swimming:** No. **Playground:** No. **Other:** Some wheelchair-accessible facilities, visitor center, observation deck, Summit Museum. **Activities:** Hiking, horseback riding, star gazing, mountain biking, rock climbing. **Nearby Attractions:** Berkeley Botanical Garden & museums; Dunsmuir House & Gardens Historic Estate, Chabot Space & Science Center, Jack London Square, museums, zoo, & more in Oakland. **Additional Information:** Walnut Creek Chamber of Commerce, (925) 934-2007.

RESTRICTIONS

Pets: On 6 ft. leash. **Fires:** In fire grates only; restrictions are in effect when wildfire risk is extreme. **Alcoholic Beverages:** Not allowed. **Vehicle Maximum Length:** 20 ft. **Other:** 30-day stay limit; no firearms; no wood gathering.

TO GET THERE

From I-680 at Walnut Creek take the North Main St. Exit. Head east (toward downtown) to Ygnacio Valley Rd. Follow that for 2.1 mi. to the traffic light and turn right on Walnut Ave., which turns into North Gate Rd. Proceed to park entrance booth; Junction campground is 6.7 mi. beyond that.

WATSONVILLE
Sunset State Beach

201 Sunset Beach Rd., Watsonville 95076. T: (831) 763-7062 or reservations (800) 444-7275; www.cal-parks.ca.gov or www.reserveamerica.com.

🚐 ★★★★　　　　▲ ★★★★

Beauty: ★★★★　　　Site Privacy: ★★★
Spaciousness: ★★★　　Quiet: ★★★★
Security: ★★★　　　　Cleanliness: ★★★★
Insect Control: ★★★　　Facilities: ★★

Too often beach-side campgrounds are a compromise in comfort, especially in the southern part of the state. Sites are compact, they are laid out in a parking lot, there's no view of the water, trains thunder by at regular intervals. Sunset State Beach, located just 15 miles south of Santa Cruz, avoids most of those pitfalls, presenting campers with a stellar setting in the process. Plenty of shade is provided by the Monterey pines and eucalyptus trees that thrive throughout the property's three loops, yet sun-worshippers will appreciate that there is also an abundance of open space. Level sites are grassy, surprisingly roomy, and buffered from ocean breezes by a series of high sand dunes. Arguably, the most appealing loop is South Camp, with 26 particularly private and 25 offering a decent ocean view. The sandy beach is stunningly gorgeous, though slightly marred by the presence of a cookie-cutter housing development at its south end. Surf fishing here is reportedly very good. If you value tranquility don't even think about arriving on weekends from Easter through Labor Day.

BASICS

Operated By: California Dept. of Parks & Recreation. **Open:** All year. **Site Assignment:** Reservations recommended; V, MC, D. **Registration:** At entrance booth. **Fee:** $12, cash or CA check. **Parking:** At site.

FACILITIES

Number of RV Sites: 90. **Number of Tent-Only Sites:** 0. **Hookups:** None. **Each Site:** Picnic table, fire grate, food storage box. **Dump Station:** No. **Laundry:** No. **Pay Phone:** Yes. **Rest Rooms and Showers:** Yes. **Fuel:** No. **Propane:** No. **Internal Roads:** Paved. **RV Service:** No. **Market:** 3 mi. northeast in Watsonville. **Restaurant:** 3 mi. northeast in Watsonville. **General Store:** No.

Vending: No. **Swimming:** In Pacific Ocean. **Playground:** No. **Other:** Some wheelchair-accessible facilities. **Activities:** Fishing, surfing, beachcombing, hiking, hang gliding. **Nearby Attractions:** Mission San Juan Bautista; John Steinbeck House & Library in Salinas; outlet shopping in Gilroy; Monterey peninsula. **Additional Information:** Castroville Chamber of Commerce, (831) 633-6545.

RESTRICTIONS

Pets: On 6 ft. leash. **Fires:** In fire grates only. **Alcoholic Beverages:** Allowed at site, not on the beach. **Vehicle Maximum Length:** 31 ft. **Other:** 7-day stay limit from Apr. 1–Oct. 31; no wood gathering.

TO GET THERE

From Hwy. 1 near Watsonville take the Riverside Dr. Exit and head toward the ocean. Turn right after 1 block onto Lee Rd., then a quick left onto West Beach St. Proceed for 1.5 mi. to San Andreas Rd., where you should hang a right. In 2.1 mi. steer left onto Sunset Beach Rd. and follow it into the park.

WEAVERVILLE
Tannery Gulch

CR 172, Weaverville 96093. T: (530) 623-2121 or reservations (877) 444-6777; F: (530) 623-6010; www.r5.fs.fed.us/shastatrinity or www.reserveusa.com.

🚐 ★★★★	🛖 ★★★
Beauty: ★★★★	Site Privacy: ★★
Spaciousness: ★★★	Quiet: ★★★★
Security: ★★★	Cleanliness: ★★★★
Insect Control: ★★★	Facilities: ★★

Gold was discovered in the Trinity River in 1848. The rush that followed left its mark on this entire region, from hillsides washed away with hydraulic pumps to the colorful names attached to various locales. Tannery Gulch is an example of the second, and fortunately in its beautiful pine-forested perch above the jade-green Trinity Lake there is little evidence of the first. A few oaks and dogwoods are sprinkled among the tall conifers, and while the forest is fairly dense, a good deal of sunlight radiates through the canopy. As in any hilly area, some sites lack level ground. Most, though, are fine,

being above average in spaciousness and distributed reasonably far apart over the property's five loops. Among the better choices for space and their partial views of the lake are 33, 34, 35, 40, 41, and 42. Most people come here for the water sports, but hikers (and horse riding enthusiasts) won't have to sit idly by watching the moss grow: there are many outstanding trails immediately to the north in the Trinity Alps Wilderness. Weaverville is 12 miles south along Hwy. 3.

BASICS

Operated By: Hodge Management, concessionaire. **Open:** May through Sept. **Site Assignment:** Reservations accepted w/ V, MC, D for most sites; First come, first served for sites 50 through 62. **Registration:** At entrance kiosk. **Fee:** $12–$18, cash or check. **Parking:** At site.

FACILITIES

Number of RV Sites: 83. **Number of Tent-Only Sites:** 0. **Hookups:** None. **Each Site:** Picnic table, fire grate. **Dump Station:** No. **Laundry:** No. **Pay Phone:** No. **Rest Rooms and Showers:** Flush & vault toilets, no showers. **Fuel:** No. **Propane:** No. **Internal Roads:** Paved. **RV Service:** No. **Market:** 13 mi. south in Weaverville. **Restaurant:** 13 mi. south in Weaverville. **General Store:** No. **Vending:** No. **Swimming:** In Trinity Lake. **Playground:** No. **Other:** Limited wheelchair-accessible facilities, seasonal boat ramp. **Activities:** Fishing, hiking, boating, waterskiing. **Nearby Attractions:** Weaverville museums, National Historic District, & Joss House State Historic Park; Historic Trinity River Bridge in Lewiston. **Additional Information:** Weaverville Chamber of Commerce, (530) 623-3840; Trinity County Chamber of Commerce, (530) 623-6101 or (800) 487-4648.

RESTRICTIONS

Pets: On leash. **Fires:** In fire grates only. **Alcoholic Beverages:** Allowed. **Vehicle Maximum Length:** 40 ft. **Other:** 14-day stay limit.

TO GET THERE

Exit Hwy. 299 in Weaverville onto Hwy. 3, northward direction. After 12 mi. turn right on CR 172. The campground entrance is 1.25 mi. ahead.

WHISKEYTOWN

Whiskeytown National Recreation Area, Oak Bottom Campground

Hwy. 299, Whiskeytown 96095. T: (530) 359-2027 or (530) 242-3400 or reservations (800) 365-CAMP; F: (530) 246-5154; www.nps.gov/whis.

🚐 ★★   ⛺ ★★★

Beauty: ★★★★   Site Privacy: ★★
Spaciousness: ★★   Quiet: ★★★
Security: ★★★   Cleanliness: ★★★
Insect Control: ★★★   Facilities: ★★★★

Some jokingly refer to this campground as "Rock Bottom," but you will probably not be laughing if you roll in hauling a motor home. That is because the area designated for RVs, right by the boat launch, is a paved parking lot with no shade trees or privacy. At least it is near the water, a good thing since you'll want to spend most of your time swimming or boating in summer, when it is so hot in these parts you could fry a trout on the blistering pavement. Tent campers fare far better with grassy walk-in sites situated on an oak and pine-shaded knoll overlooking Whiskeytown Lake. A number of those are just a few steps from the park loop, but there is less litter and more privacy as you walk farther toward the lake. On average, the walk-ins are surprisingly level, and though many are wedged closely together, they are decently buffered by manzanita, madrone, and ceanothus. The concession that operates this National Park Service property, which is located 13 miles west of Redding along Hwy. 299, needs to devote more attention to the dilapidated restrooms and neglected grounds. Note that from Apr. 20, 2002, personal watercrafts (e.g. jet skis) will no longer be permitted on Whiskeytown Lake.

BASICS

Operated By: Ken Smith, concessionaire. **Open:** All year. **Site Assignment:** Reservations recommended; V, MC, D. **Registration:** At campground store. **Fee:** $7–$18, cash, check or V, MC, D. **Parking:** At site or designated area for walk-ins.

FACILITIES

Number of RV Sites: 22. **Number of Tent-Only Sites:** 102. **Hookups:** None. **Each Site:** Picnic table, fire grate, bearproof box. **Dump Station:** Yes. **Laundry:** No. **Pay Phone:** Yes. **Rest Rooms and Showers:** Yes. **Fuel:** No. **Propane:** No. **Internal Roads:** Paved. **RV Service:** No. **Market:** 13 mi. east in Redding. **Restaurant:** 13 mi. east in Redding. **General Store:** Yes, in summer; also snack bar. **Vending:** Yes. **Swimming:** In Whiskeytown Lake at swim beach. **Playground:** No. **Other:** Some wheelchair-accessible facilities, boat ramp, marina. **Activities:** Hiking, bicycling, boat rentals, sailing, windsurfing, fishing. **Nearby Attractions:** Carter House Natural Science Museum, Turtle Bay Museums & Arboretum, Waterworks Park in Redding; Shasta Lake & Dam, Shasta State Historic Park. **Additional Information:** Redding CVB, (530) 225-4100.

RESTRICTIONS

Pets: On 6 ft. leash. **Fires:** In fire grates only. **Alcoholic Beverages:** Allowed at site. **Vehicle Maximum Length:** 35 ft. **Other:** 14-day stay limit from May 15–Sept. 14, 30-day limit the rest of the year.

TO GET THERE

From Redding drive 13 mi. west on Hwy. 299. Turn left at the sign for the campground.

WILLITS

Hidden Valley Campground

29801 North U.South 101, Willits 95490. T: (707) 459-2521; F: (707) 459-3396; www.rvdestinations.com/hiddenvalley; hvcgd@jps.net.

🚐 ★★★   ⛺ ★★

Beauty: ★★★   Site Privacy: ★★
Spaciousness: ★★   Quiet: ★★
Security: ★★★   Cleanliness: ★★★
Insect Control: ★★   Facilities: ★★★

There are campgrounds worth building a vacation around, little islands of paradise one would willingly drive hours to reach. Places where the passing of time is happily marked in days, even weeks, and when the moment finally arrives—all too soon, alas—to decamp, sighs of resignation involuntarily rise up from one's chest. Then there are the in-transit campgrounds, those we use while on our way to someplace else. Hidden Valley falls into the second category. It is a pleasant, average-looking camp, conveniently located just off of US 101 about midway between Eureka and

San Francisco, six miles north of Willits. Its single lane leads gently uphill from the entrance and several long-term RVs, past pines, oaks, locusts, and bay trees. The most private and quiet of the somewhat closely grouped sites are 42 and 43, ensconced at the far end of the acreage. Other grass- and dirt-based sites worth reserving include 23, 25, 26, and 28. The security gate is closed between 8:30 p.m. and 6:30 a.m.

BASICS

Operated By: Hidden Valley Campground, Ed & Carol Rotramel, owners. **Open:** All year. **Site Assignment:** Reservations accepted w/ V, MC. **Registration:** At entrance office. **Fee:** $17–$21, cash or V, MC. **Parking:** At site.

FACILITIES

Number of RV Sites: 50. Number of Tent-Only Sites: 0. Hookups: Water, electric (30 amps), sewer, cable TV, Internet. **Each Site:** Half-size picnic table, fire grate. **Dump Station:** Yes. **Laundry:** Yes. **Pay Phone:** Yes. **Rest Rooms and Showers:** Yes. **Fuel:** No. **Propane:** No. **Internal Roads:** Paved & gravel, good condition. **RV Service:** No. **Market:** 6.5 mi. south in Willits. **Restaurant:** 6.5 mi. south in Willits. **General Store:** No. **Vending:** Yes. **Swimming:** No. **Playground:** No. **Other:** Some wheelchair-accessible facilities. **Activities:** Hiking, horseshoe pit, ping pong, basketball. **Nearby Attractions:** Skunk Train from Willits to Fort Bragg; Ukiah museums & Cow Mountain Recreation Area; Mendocino County Museum & Roots of Motive Power/Antique Steam Logging Equipment in Willits. **Additional Information:** Willits Chamber of Commerce, (707) 459-7910.

RESTRICTIONS

Pets: On leash; rabies certificate required. **Fires:** In fire grates only. **Alcoholic Beverages:** Allowed. **Vehicle Maximum Length:** 40 ft. **Other:** No stay limit; no wood gathering.

TO GET THERE

From Willits on US 101 drive 6.5 mi. north. The well-marked campground entrance is on the right side of the road.

WOFFORD HEIGHTS
Tillie Creek

Hwy. 155, Wofford Heights 93285. T: (760) 379-5646 or reservations (877) 444-6777; F: (760) 379-8597; www.r5.fs.fed.us/sequoia or www.reserveusa.com.

🚐 ★★★★   ▲ ★★★

Beauty: ★★★★	Site Privacy: ★★★
Spaciousness: ★★	Quiet: ★★★
Security: ★★★	Cleanliness: ★★★
Insect Control: ★★★	Facilities: ★★★

Isabella Lake is a Mecca of sorts for windsurfing, waterskiing, and year-round fishing. Cottonwoods skirt its meandering shoreline, whereas oak trees and pines populate the higher ground, especially around Tillie Creek, on the lake's western rim. The rocky locale, in the foothills of the Sierra Nevadas, is attractively wild, in a sun-baked area of wavy brown hills. There is plenty of shade throughout most of the multiple loops, with the exception of sites nearest the water, which are uncomfortably exposed. Across the domain, units are so shallow and small that tent campers will find it challenging to use the fire ring without singing their nylon. There are some larger-size spots available in the type three and four categories, but none may be reserved by specific number. Thus, you have no guarantee of getting a shady site, or even a lake view. A distressing amount of broken glass litters an otherwise tidy camp. Basic supplies and laundry machines are available in Wofford Heights.

BASICS

Operated By: California Land Management, concessionaire. **Open:** All year. **Site Assignment:** Reservations accepted w/ V, MC, D. **Registration:** With campground host. **Fee:** $14, cash or check. **Parking:** At site.

FACILITIES

Number of RV Sites: 155. Number of Tent-Only Sites: 0. Hookups: None. **Each Site:** Picnic table, fire grate, barbecue grill. **Dump Station:** Yes. **Laundry:** No. **Pay Phone:** Yes. **Rest Rooms and Showers:** Yes. **Fuel:** No. **Propane:** No. **Internal Roads:** Paved. **RV Service:** No. **Market:** 6.5 mi. south in Lake Isabella. **Restaurant:** 6.5 mi. south in Lake Isabella. **General Store:** No. **Vending:** No. **Swimming:** In Lake Isabella. **Playground:** Yes.

Other: Some wheelchair-accessible facilities.
Activities: Fishing, hiking, boating, waterskiing.
Nearby Attractions: Sequoia National Forest;
California Hot Springs; Greenhorn Mountain Park in
Alta Sierra. **Additional Information:** Kern
County Board of Trade, (661) 861-2367 or (800)
500-KERN.

RESTRICTIONS

Pets: On leash. **Fires:** In fire grates only. **Alcoholic
Beverages:** Allowed. **Vehicle Maximum
Length:** 45 ft. **Other:** 14-day stay limit.

TO GET THERE

From Wofford Heights drive 1 mi. south on
Hwy. 155. Turn left at the campground sign;
the entrance is just ahead.

YOSEMITE NATIONAL PARK
North Pines

Southside Dr., Yosemite Valley, Yosemite National
Park 95389. T: (209) 372-0265 or reservations (800)
436-7275; F: (209) 372-0371; www.nps.gov/yose or
www.reservations.nps.gov.

🚐 ★★★★   🛖 ★★★

Beauty: ★★★★	Site Privacy: ★★
Spaciousness: ★★★	Quiet: ★★
Security: ★★★★	Cleanliness: ★★★
Insect Control: ★★	Facilities: ★★★

Given a choice, it is best to see Yosemite Valley in
late spring, when its many waterfalls are at their
peak and the dogwoods are in bloom. You'll be
joining thousands of others then, so make your
campground reservations well in advance. There
are three campgrounds situated near each other,
and which you end up at may come down to the
one with available space. If possible, aim for
North Pines, which is superior for its views of the
granite environs and its thrilling position at the
confluence of the Merced River and Tenaya
Creek. Like the neighboring camps, this is a fam-
ily-friendly atmosphere that makes a great launching point for a number of excellent hikes. Level
sites are, alas, packed rather closely together, and
the many stands of lodgepole pine and oak provide only minimal screening. Best for privacy and
access to the river are 136, 502, 503, 504, and
506. Do pay attention to the bear warnings, use
the metal food lockers, and keep a whistle—or
other noise maker—handy after dark. The nearest
gas station is at Crane Flat, just outside the valley.

BASICS

Operated By: National Park Service. **Open:** Apr.
through Sept., weather permitting. **Site Assign-
ment:** Reservations required; V, MC. **Registration:**
At reservation office. **Fee:** $18, cash, check or V,
MC (in addition to the park entrance fee). **Parking:**
At site.

FACILITIES

Number of RV Sites: 81. **Number of Tent-
Only Sites:** 0. **Hookups:** None. **Each Site:** Picnic
table, fire ring, barbecue grill, bearproof box. **Dump
Station:** Yes. **Laundry:** Yes. **Pay Phone:** Yes. **Rest
Rooms and Showers:** Yes. **Fuel:** No. **Propane:**
No. **Internal Roads:** Paved. **RV Service:** No.
Market: In Yosemite Valley. **Restaurant:** In
Yosemite Valley. **General Store:** Yes. **Vending:** No.
Swimming: At Ahwahnee Lodge & Curry Village.
Playground: No. **Other:** Visitor center, several
stores, post office. **Activities:** Hiking, fishing, horse
& bicycle rentals, mountaineering classes, free art
classes, rafting, ranger-led activities, bear-spotting.
Nearby Attractions: El Capitan, waterfalls,
LeConte Memorial Lodge, sightseeing tours,
museum & gallery in Yosemite Valley. **Additional
Information:** Yosemite Public Information Office,
(209) 372-0200.

RESTRICTIONS

Pets: On 6 ft. leash; not allowed on trails. **Fires:** In
fire rings only, from May 1 to Oct. 15, 5–10 p.m. only.
Alcoholic Beverages: Allowed at site. **Vehicle
Maximum Length:** 40 ft. **Other:** 14-day stay limit;
no firearms; no fireworks; no metal detectors; no
food in vehicles (bear habitat); no wood gathering.

TO GET THERE

On entering the park from the west via Hwy.
120, follow the signs first to Yosemite Valley,
then to Curry Village. Proceed straight ahead,
past Lower and Upper Pines, drive over Clarks
Bridge and turn left into the campground.

YOSEMITE NATIONAL PARK
Tuolumne Meadows

Tioga Rd./Hwy. 120, Yosemite National Park 95389.
T: (209) 372-0265 or reservations (800) 436-7275;
F: (209) 372-0371; www.nps.gov/yose or
www.reservations.nps.gov.

🚐 ★★★★   ▲ ★★★★

Beauty: ★★★★	Site Privacy: ★★
Spaciousness: ★★★	Quiet: ★★
Security: ★★★★	Cleanliness: ★★★★
Insect Control: ★	Facilities: ★★★

Summer doesn't last long in Yosemite National Park's high country, which translates to a short season for Tuolumne Meadows Campground, elevation 8,600 feet. Perhaps it's that scarcity of available time that lends an extra frisson to the delights of being in this glacier-wracked wilderness camp, which is only 20 miles west of Lee Vining. It is surprisingly attractive, given its enormous dimensions. Young lodgepole pines rise up off ubiquitous slanting slabs of granite and poke past giant boulders, while the fresh, clear Tuolumne River twists and bends, churning noisily by the campground. In late spring, and after heavy rainfalls, the river brims to the very edge of sites, verging on overflowing the campground. Of this camp's two sections, the A loops run closer to the river and offers vistas of Lembert Dome. Best for views, river access or privacy are A 50, 51, 52, 55, 63, 65, 66, 67, 71, 74, and 89. Sites in the B area are in a more forested setting, recessed from the road and a touch roomier. We find the $18 fee outrageous, given the austere facilities, but if you don't take the site, someone else will. The Tioga Rd. closes in winter, depending on snowfall; call ahead if traveling in late fall or early spring.

BASICS
Operated By: National Park Service. **Open:** July through Sept., weather permitting. **Site Assignment:** Half by advanced reservations, half by same-day reservations; V, MC. **Registration:** At entrance kiosk. **Fee:** $18, cash, check or V, MC (in addition to the park entrance fee). **Parking:** At site.

FACILITIES
Number of RV Sites: 304. **Number of Tent-Only Sites:** 25. **Hookups:** None. **Each Site:** Picnic table, fire ring, barbecue grill, bearproof box.

Dump Station: Yes. **Laundry:** No. **Pay Phone:** Yes. **Rest Rooms and Showers:** Yes. **Fuel:** Yes. **Propane:** Yes. **Internal Roads:** Partly paved, partly dirt, but decent. **RV Service:** No. **Market:** 20 mi. east in Lee Vining. **Restaurant:** In Tuolumne Meadows. **General Store:** Yes. **Vending:** No. **Swimming:** No. **Playground:** No. **Other:** Visitor center, bookstore, sport shop, post office. **Activities:** Hiking, fishing, horse rentals, mountaineering classes, ranger-led activities. **Nearby Attractions:** Mono Lake Tufa State Reserve in Lee Vining; Bodie State Historic Park in Bridgeport. **Additional Information:** Yosemite Public Information Office, (209) 372-0200.

RESTRICTIONS
Pets: On 6 ft. leash; not allowed on trails. **Fires:** In fire rings only. **Alcoholic Beverages:** Allowed at site. **Vehicle Maximum Length:** 35 ft. **Other:** 14-day stay limit; no firearms; no fireworks; no food in vehicles (bear habitat).

TO GET THERE
Just south of Lee Vining on US 395 head west on Hwy. 120. Drive 20 mi., past the Yosemite National Park entrance, to the campground on the left.

YOSEMITE NATIONAL PARK
Wawona

Wawona Rd./Hwy. 41, Yosemite National Park 95389. T: (209) 372-0265 or reservations (800) 436-7275; F: (209) 372-0371; www.nps.gov/yose or www.reservations.nps.gov.

🚐 ★★★★   ▲ ★★★

Beauty: ★★★★	Site Privacy: ★★
Spaciousness: ★★★	Quiet: ★★★
Security: ★★★★	Cleanliness: ★★★
Insect Control: ★★	Facilities: ★★★

Sitting in a camp chair, gazing over the South Fork Merced River as the afternoon sun radiates through the oaks, cedars, and cinnamon-barked ponderosa pines onto the enormous boulders protruding from the hilly domain, you may well feel a part of Eden. Go ahead and look for snakes, though bears are more likely nighttime visitors. Wawona, 21 miles north of Oakhurst, near Yosemite's southern entrance, is one of the national park's prettier, more sedate campgrounds. It is also one of the more spacious, as its series of loops are elongated alongside the Merced, rather than being concentrated one against another. As a result of that thoughtful layout, dirt- and grass-covered sites seem less jammed together, and a high number are favored with waterfront locations. Highly recommended are 34 and 37, and to a lesser extent, 51–53; while tent campers should consider such prime river sites as walk-ins 1–4. Away from the water, 42 and 44 are among the more private. The nearby Mariposa Grove trail leads into a forest of numerous spectacular sequoia trees, as well as many other impressive conifers.

BASICS

Operated By: National Park Service. **Open:** All Year. **Site Assignment:** Reservations required May–Sept.; V, MC; first come, first served Oct.–Apr. **Registration:** At entrance kiosk. **Fee:** $18, cash, check or V, MC (in addition to the park entrance fee). **Parking:** At site.

FACILITIES

Number of RV Sites: 89. **Number of Tent-Only Sites:** 4. **Hookups:** None. **Each Site:** Picnic table, fire ring, barbecue grill, bearproof box. **Dump Station:** Yes. **Laundry:** No. **Pay Phone:** No. **Rest Rooms and Showers:** Flush toilets, no showers. **Fuel:** No. **Propane:** No. **Internal Roads:** Paved, many potholes. **RV Service:** No. **Market:** 20 mi. east in Lee Vining. **Restaurant:** 1.25 mi. south in the Wawona Hotel. **General Store:** Yes. **Vending:** No. **Swimming:** In South Fork Merced River. **Playground:** No. **Other:** Some wheelchair-accessible facilities, hotel, golf course, bookstore. **Activities:** Hiking, fishing, horse rentals. **Nearby Attractions:** Mariposa Grove of giant redwoods; Yosemite Mountain Sugarpine Railroad in Fish Camp; Yosemite Valley & its attractions. **Additional Information:** Yosemite Sierra Visitors Bureau, (559) 683-5697.

RESTRICTIONS

Pets: On 6 ft. leash; not allowed on trails. **Fires:** In fire rings only. **Alcoholic Beverages:** Allowed at site. **Vehicle Maximum Length:** 35 ft. **Other:** 7-day stay limit; no firearms; no fireworks; no food in vehicles (bear habitat).

TO GET THERE

From Oakhurst drive 15 mi. north on Hwy. 41 to the Yosemite National Park entrance station. Continue for 6 mi. to the campground on the left.

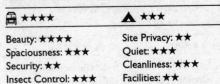

YREKA
Tree of Heaven

Hwy. 96, Yreka 96097. T: (530) 468-5351; F: (530) 468-1290; www.r5.fs.fed.us/klamath.

★★★★   ★★★

Beauty: ★★★★	Site Privacy: ★★
Spaciousness: ★★★	Quiet: ★★★
Security: ★★	Cleanliness: ★★★
Insect Control: ★★★	Facilities: ★★

Tree of Heaven is the common name for *Ailantus altissima*, a non-native tree that grows in this small campground, which lies just eight miles west of I-5. The forest service has thoughtfully installed a sign informing visitors that *Ailantus altissima* were "planted by early settlers for soil conservation and resistance to air pollution." That they were a fast-growing source of shade is a more likely reason miners settled on them, something campers can be glad of, too. Pines, junipers, and maples round out the shady mix of trees here, with grassy, level sites evenly spaced out along a single loop. The grounds and limited facilities show none of the neglect so ubiquitous to forest service campgrounds elsewhere. On the contrary, scrupulous manicuring may leave some campers feeling that the "wilderness" has been snipped right out of the domain. The frothy waters of the Klamath River, which is popular for its rafting opportunities, churn right alongside the property. A fish-cleaning station is located next to the river.

BASICS

Operated By: Klamath National Forest, Scott River Ranger District. **Open:** All year; no water in winter. **Site Assignment:** Reservations accepted w/ V, MC. **Registration:** At central kiosk. **Fee:** $10, cash or check. **Parking:** At site.

FACILITIES

Number of RV Sites: 21. **Number of Tent-Only Sites:** 0. **Hookups:** None. **Each Site:** Picnic table, fire grate, barbecue grill. **Dump Station:** Yes. **Laundry:** No. **Pay Phone:** No. **Rest Rooms and Showers:** Vault toilets, no showers. **Fuel:** No. **Propane:** No. **Internal Roads:** Paved. **RV Service:** No. **Market:** 12 mi. east in Yreka. **Restaurant:** 12 mi. east in Yreka. **General Store:** No. **Vending:** No. **Swimming:** In Klamath River. **Play-**

ground: No. **Other:** Some wheelchair-accessible facilities, small boat ramp. **Activities:** Fishing, hiking, rafting, kayaking, canoeing. **Nearby Attractions:** Klamath National Forest; Yreka National Historic District, Western Railroad, Siskiyou County Courthouse & Museum in Yreka. **Additional Information:** Siskiyou County Visitors Bureau, (530) 926-3850; Yreka Chamber of Commerce, (530) 842-1649.

RESTRICTIONS

Pets: On leash. **Fires:** In fire grates only. **Alcoholic Beverages:** Allowed. **Vehicle Maximum Length:** 34 ft. **Other:** 14-day stay limit.

TO GET THERE

From Yreka drive 8 mi. north on Hwy. 263. Turn west (left) on Hwy. 96 and continue for 4 mi. to the campground entrance on the left.

Nevada

Nevada is much more than just Las Vegas, though the state has no shortage of casino RV parks combining parking-lot camping and hookups with buffets, entertainment, and gaming. Within an hour of Las Vegas, nature lovers can begin experiencing another Nevada, where livestock and wild burros wander across roads and ancient Native American petroglyphs hide among red rock formations that hold their own with the best in the American West.

High mountains and high deserts present winter sports opportunities, the best known being around **Lake Tahoe** and **Carson City.** High elevations also mean summer opportunities to escape the searing desert heat outside the air-conditioned casinos, though weekend reservations are needed to edge out locals fleeing Las Vegas for the cool juniper and pine forests of **Spring Mountain National** and **Lee Canyon Recreation Areas.**

Nevada has 200 isolated mountain ranges snaking north and south among its equally numerous desert valleys. Small government campgrounds and attractive lakes and reservoirs present summer recreation and winter possibilities like helicopter skiing and ice fishing. There are numerous amenities and hookups in cities like **Fallon, Hawthorne, Winnemucca, Ely,** and **Elko.** But the best of the northern and central mountain ranges are the province of self-sufficient campers seeking out the more primitive campgrounds to experience nature in all its raw ruggedness and isolated beauty.

The folded, rippled, uplifted, and otherwise intriguingly contorted and colorfully banded sedimentary and metamorphic mountain ranges are more than just geologic curiosities. Indeed, camping in Nevada is often a history lesson in the Old West, particularly the boom-and-bust economics of mining. A pathetic failure of a gold miner named Mark Twain turned it into literary gold in "Roughing It." Though Nevada's many working mines produce everything from gypsum and copper to silver and gold, there is a widespread legacy of old gold, silver, mercury, and tungsten mines and ghost towns near places as far-flung as **Beatty, Tonopah, Gabbs, Ely, Elko, Pioche,** and **Carson City.**

Nevada is also a state with incredible manmade lakes like **Lakes Mead** and **Mohave** south of Las Vegas, which are popular for fishing, houseboats, and water sports. Natural lakes in the middle of the desert are not a mirage. **Walker Lake** is a still-shrinking remnant of ancient Lake Lahontan, which once filled Nevada's desert valleys and left ancient Native Americans living along a shoreline that is now mountaintops.

The following facilities accept payment in checks or cash only:

Bailey's Hot Springs, Beatty

Berlin Ichthyosaur State Park, Gabbs

Boulder Beach, Boulder City

Callville Bay, Lake Mead National Recreation Area

Cathedral Gorge State Park, Panaca

Cave Lake State Park, Ely

Cottonwood Cove, Cottonwood Cove

Davis Creek Regional Park, Carson City

Echo Bay RV Park, Lake Mead National Recreation Area

Echo Canyon State Park, Pioche

Fort Churchill State Historic Park, Silver Springs

Hilltop Campground, Spring Mountain National Recreation Area

Katherine Campground, Boulder City

Kyle Canyon & Fletcher View Campgrounds, Spring Mountain National Recreation Area

Las Vegas Bay Campground, Henderson

Lower & Upper Lehman Creek Campgrounds, Great Basin National Park

McWilliams & Dolomite Campgrounds, Lee Canyon Recreation Area

Sportsman's Beach Recreation Site, Walker Lake

Spring Valley State Park, Ursine

13 Mile Campground, Red Rock Canyon National Conservation Area

Valley of Fire State Park, Overton

Ward Mountain Campground, Ely

Washoe Lake State Park, Carson City

The following facilities feature 50 sites or fewer:

Bailey's Hot Springs, Beatty

Berlin Ichthyosaur State Park, Gabbs

Fort Churchill State Historic Park, Silver Springs

Kyle Canyon & Fletcher View Campgrounds, Spring Mountain National Recreation Area

Lower & Upper Lehman Creek Campgrounds, Great Basin National Park

Quik-Pik Mini Mart & Campground, Rachel

The Station House, Tonopah

AMARGOSA VALLEY

Longstreet Inn, Casino, RV Park & Golf Club

HCR 70 Box 559, Amargosa Valley 89020. T: (702) 372-1777; F: (702) 372-1280; www.longstreetinn.com.

🚐 ★★★   ⛺ ★★

Beauty: ★★★   Site Privacy: ★★★★
Spaciousness: ★★★★   Quiet: ★★★★
Security: ★★★★   Cleanliness: ★★★★★
Insect Control: ★★★★   Facilities: ★★★★★

An isolated stopping post for those crossing Death Valley Junction, Longstreet is far enough from Beatty's RV parks on US 95 to provide relative solitude. The 25-foot-wide spaces are meant to accommodate anything on the road, and snag Furnace Creek traffic. The gravel RV park with its few scraggly trees looks out over a small golf course towards Death Valley's Funeral Mountains. Sharp eyes can detect the ridge where the old Tidewater & Tonopah Railroad ran. The casino, with its pool and large freeform rock firewater reservoir (often mistaken for the pool), acts as a protective backdrop and is the source of all amenities here. Nearby Ash Meadows National Wildlife Refuge, designated a "Wetland of International Importance," contains "fossil water," an endangered pup fish, and 24 plant and animals found nowhere else in the world. There are no tables or grills (fire hazard), and tent campers need air mattresses.

BASICS

Operated By: Longstreet Inn, Casino, RV Park & Golf Club. **Open:** All year. **Site Assignment:** First come, first served. **Registration:** At hotel front desk in casino. **Fee:** $16 (VISA, MC, AE, D, DC, CB). **Parking:** At site.

FACILITIES

Number of RV Sites: 52. **Number of Tent-Only Sites:** 0. **Hookups:** Electric (50 amp), water, sewer, cable TV, phone (16 sites). **Each Site:** Varies. **Dump Station:** Yes. **Laundry:** Yes. **Pay Phone:** Yes. **Rest Rooms and Showers:** Yes. **Fuel:** No. **Propane:** No. **Internal Roads:** Gravel, dusty but good. **RV Service:** No. **Market:** In casino.

Restaurant: In casino. **General Store:** Yes. **Vending:** Yes. **Swimming:** In hotel pool. **Playground:** No. **Other:** 9-hole par-28 golf course, jacuzzi. **Activities:** Gambling. **Nearby Attractions:** Death Valley, Ash Meadows National Wildlife Refuge. **Additional Information:** Ash Meadows NWR, (775) 372-5435.

RESTRICTIONS

Pets: On leash under owner's control. **Fires:** No. **Alcoholic Beverages:** Allowed. **Vehicle Maximum Length:** 75 ft.

TO GET THERE

From junction of US Hwy. 95 at Lathrop Wells, go 7 mi. south on NV Hwy. 373.

BEATTY

Bailey's Hot Springs

U. South Hwy. 95, Beatty 89003. T: (775) 553-2395.

🚐 ★★★   ⛺ ★★★

Beauty: ★★★   Site Privacy: ★★★★
Spaciousness: ★★★★   Quiet: ★★★★
Security: ★★★   Cleanliness: ★★★
Insect Control: ★★★   Facilities: ★★

One of five RV parks in Beatty, Bailey's is the only campground with hot springs (available for day-use visitors), though it is also furthest from the casinos and markets. Beatty's RV parks are all along the highway, but traffic is relatively light at night. Tent campers on the lawns here are protected by reeds and can fall asleep to the sound of running creek water (which irrigates local farms). The campground is shady, breezy, and friendly. Most here are regulars and word-of-mouth customers stopping for a night or two of hot-spring use, coming and going from Death Valley. The adjacent corral houses the owner's breeding horses, and the view across the highway is BLM land (OK to hike) and Death Valley mountain ranges. Only weekly customers get sewer hookups because of the high water table from the spring and the underground Amargosa River.

BASICS

Operated By: Sharon Patton. **Open:** All year. **Site Assignment:** First come, first served. **Registration:** In office (an RV). **Fee:** $12. **Parking:** At site.

FACILITIES

Number of RV Sites: 14. **Number of Tent-Only Sites:** Undesignated sites. **Hookups:** Electric (30 amp), water. **Each Site:** Varies. **Dump Station:** No. **Laundry:** No. **Pay Phone:** Yes. **Rest Rooms and Showers:** Yes. **Fuel:** No. **Propane:** No. **Internal Roads:** Gravel, good. **RV Service:** No. **Market:** Beatty, 5 mi. **Restaurant:** Beatty, 5 mi. **General Store:** No. **Vending:** No. **Swimming:** Hot springs. **Playground:** No. **Other:** Central picnic area w/ BBQ. **Activities:** Soaking in hot springs. **Nearby Attractions:** Death Valley, Rhyolite ghost town, Amargosa Valley, Goldfield. **Additional Information:** Beatty Chamber of Commerce, (775) 553-2424.

RESTRICTIONS

Pets: On leash under owner's control. **Fires:** Yes (in fire ring only). **Alcoholic Beverages:** Allowed. **Vehicle Maximum Length:** 30 ft. **Other:** High water table limits sewage discharge.

TO GET THERE

Go 5 mi. north of Beatty on US Hwy. 95.

BOULDER CITY
Boulder Beach

601 Nevada Hwy., Boulder City 89005. T: (702) 293-8907; F: (702) 293-8936; www.nps.gov/lame/home.html.

🚐 ★★★   ⛺ ★★★

Beauty: ★★★★★	Site Privacy: ★★★★
Spaciousness: ★★★	Quiet: ★★★★★
Security: ★★★	Cleanliness: ★★★★★
Insect Control: ★★★★	Facilities: ★★

Boulder Beach shares the same scenic Lake Mead desert landscape as Las Vegas Bay, which is seven miles to the north along the Lakeshore Scenic Drive. The park's Alan Bible Visitor Center is nine miles southwest and Hoover Dam is five miles southeast, making this an especially good choice for first-time visitors getting acquainted with the area. Unlike Las Vegas Bay, there is swimming here. South of Hoover Dam the waters flow through Black Canyon, a prime bighorn sheep viewing area, and become Lake Mohave. Another 20 miles south on US Hwy. 93 (a route leading to the South Rim of the Grand Canyon) is Willow Beach, a 1,500-year-old Native American trading site known for petro-glyphs and fine fishing. Those wanting Boulder Beach with hookups can check into the adjacent Lakeshore Trailer Village (See Appendix), which has 80 "transient" spaces with cable TV among the 215 mobile homes.

BASICS

Operated By: National Park Service. **Open:** All year. **Site Assignment:** First come, first served. **Registration:** Self-pay entrance fee station. **Fee:** $10. **Parking:** At site.

FACILITIES

Number of RV Sites: 142. **Number of Tent-Only Sites:** 0. **Hookups:** None. **Each Site:** Table, grill. **Dump Station:** Yes. **Laundry:** Yes. **Pay Phone:** Yes. **Rest Rooms and Showers:** Yes (shower fee at trailer village). **Fuel:** No (boat fuel only). **Propane:** No. **Internal Roads:** Paved, good. **RV Service:** No. **Market:** Boulder City, 6 mi. **Restaurant:** Boulder City, 6 mi. **General Store:** Yes. **Vending:** Yes. **Swimming:** In lake at own risk. **Playground:** No. **Other:** Partial handicap access, motel, boat launch. **Activities:** Boating, fishing. **Nearby Attractions:** Lake Mead, Las Vegas, Henderson, Hoover Dam. **Additional Information:** Lakeshore Trailer Village, (702) 293-2540; Lake Mead Resort, (800) 752-9669, (702) 293-3484; Lake Mead Cruises, (702) 293-6180.

RESTRICTIONS

Pets: On leash under owner's control. **Fires:** Yes. **Alcoholic Beverages:** Allowed. **Vehicle Maximum Length:** 30 ft. **Other:** 30-day max. stay.

TO GET THERE

From Boulder City, go 6 mi. northeast on NV Hwy. 166 (Lakeshore Rd.).

BOULDER CITY
Katherine Campground

601 Nevada Hwy., Boulder City 89005. T: (520) 754-3272 (Katherine Camp) or (702) 293-8906 (Alan Bible Visitors Center); www.nps.gov/lame/home.html.

🚐 ★★★★   ⛺ ★★★★

Beauty: ★★★★	Site Privacy: ★★★★
Spaciousness: ★★★★	Quiet: ★★★★
Security: ★★★★	Cleanliness: ★★★★
Insect Control: ★★★	Facilities: ★★★★

About five miles north of Bullhead City and Laughlin's casinos, in the Lake Mead National

Recreation Area, Katherine is divided into five smaller campgrounds with solar power, paved roads, and gravel sites separated by oleanders, eucalyptus, and palms. Though the Park Service does not provide hookups, a private concessionaire (Lake Mojave Resort and Marina) offers sites with hookups ($18; register at motel), along with a trailer village, motel, marina, houseboat rentals, restaurant, and lounge. A favorite of Californians, on a recent three-day holiday weekend Katherine was overrun by 44,000 visitors. A warning to the wise: those who didn't snag a campsite on the Thursday prior to the holiday were backed up in a two-hour line of cars, only to be turned away. But when the crowds abate, Katherine offers enough true desert relaxation and water to make the rest of the world seem like memories from a distant planet.

BASICS

Operated By: National Park Service (also separate Lake Mojave Resort & Marina concession). **Open:** All year. **Site Assignment:** First come, first served; no reservations (except groups). **Registration:** At entrance kiosk. **Fee:** $10 ($5 w/ Golden Age & Golden Access passes; cash only). **Parking:** At site.

FACILITIES

Number of RV Sites: 173. **Number of Tent-Only Sites:** 0. **Hookups:** None (private Lake Mojave Resort & Marina concession offers sites w/ hookups). **Each Site:** Table, grill. **Dump Station:** Yes. **Laundry:** Yes. **Pay Phone:** Yes. **Rest Rooms and Showers:** Yes. **Fuel:** Yes. **Propane:** Yes. **Internal Roads:** Paved, in good condition. **RV Service:** Limited; better in Bullhead City or Laughlin. **Market:** Yes. **Restaurant:** Yes. **General Store:** Yes. **Vending:** Yes. **Swimming:** No. **Playground:** No. **Activities:** House boat rentals, full marina, fishing. **Nearby Attractions:** Laughlin casinos & outlet shopping. **Additional Information:** Lake Mohave Resort & Marina, (520) 754-3245 or (800) 752-9669.

RESTRICTIONS

Pets: Must be kept on 6-ft. leash and not left alone. **Fires:** Yes (in grills only). **Alcoholic Beverages:** In designated areas. **Vehicle Maximum Length:** 25 ft. **Other:** 30-day stay limit, NRA entry fee must also be paid.

TO GET THERE

From junction of Hwy. 95 and Hwy. 68, north of Bullhead City, go west 0.25 mi. on Hwy. 68, then north 3 mi. on Katherine Rd.

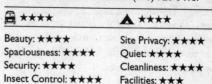

CALIENTE
Young's RV Park

P.O. Box 84, Caliente 89008. T: (775) 726-3418.

🚐 ★★★★   ⛺ ★★★★

Beauty: ★★★★	Site Privacy: ★★★★
Spaciousness: ★★★★	Quiet: ★★★★
Security: ★★★★	Cleanliness: ★★★★
Insect Control: ★★★★	Facilities: ★★★

For travelers between Las Vegas and Great Basin National Park on US Hwy. 93, Young's is the only intermediate stop with full hookups. Young's is also a popular stopping place for migrating snowbirds, who like the poplar, cottonwood, and elm trees, as well as the grass strips between the three gravel rows. Tent campers share a large grassy area with a few tables. The campground can be a bit tricky to locate, as the sign for the dirt turnoff road on the southwest edge of Caliente says "Young's" in tiny black letters easily missed. Look instead for the big blue letters saying "RV Park" above the large red arrow to spot the turnoff. About half the park's business comes from the sign whose tiny white letters advertise full hookups and showers. Except for the Union Pacific train rumbling through at night, it is fairly quiet because highway traffic slows to 25 mph entering town.

BASICS

Operated By: Chad & Brenda Young. **Open:** All year. **Site Assignment:** First come, first served. **Registration:** In office. **Fee:** $13.50. **Parking:** At site.

FACILITIES

Number of RV Sites: 27. **Number of Tent-Only Sites:** Undesignated sites. **Hookups:** Electric (20, 30 amp), water, sewer. **Each Site:** Table. **Dump Station:** Yes. **Laundry:** Yes. **Pay Phone:** Yes. **Rest Rooms and Showers:** Yes. **Fuel:** No. **Propane:** No. **Internal Roads:** Gravel, good. **RV Service:** No. **Market:** Caliente. **Restaurant:** Caliente. **General Store:** No. **Vending:** No. **Swimming:** No. **Playground:** No. **Activities:** Historic buildings tour. **Nearby Attractions:** Several state parks, Pioche Boot Hill Cemetery, Caliente train depot. **Additional Information:** Caliente Chamber of Commerce, (775) 726-3129; Nevada Division of State Parks Regional Visitors Center, (775) 728-4460.

RESTRICTIONS

Pets: On leash under owner's control. **Fires:** Yes. **Alcoholic Beverages:** Allowed. **Vehicle Maximum Length:** 60 ft.

TO GET THERE

From US Hwy. 93 near the bridge at the southwest outskirts of Caliente, turn down the gravel road running between the BLM building and the Lincoln County shops.

CARSON CITY
Davis Creek Regional Park

25 Davis Creek Rd., Carson City 89704. T: (775) 849-1825.

🚐 ★★★★	▲ ★★★★
Beauty: ★★★★	Site Privacy: ★★★★
Spaciousness: ★★★★	Quiet: ★★★
Security: ★★★	Cleanliness: ★★★★
Insect Control: ★★★	Facilities: ★★

An attractive area where pine forests meet sagebrush desert on the eastern slope of the Sierra Nevada Mountains in the Washoe Valley north of Carson City, Davis Creek Regional Park features a picnic area surrounding a three-acre pond. The pond, used for ice skating in winter, was once an ice source for Virginia City. The park, once part of the 4,000-acre Winters Ranch known for its racetrack and horse breeding in the early 1900s, has separate North and South Campgrounds for tents and RVs that can be reserved by groups. Granite boulders line the perimeter, tall ponderosa pines provide shade and whiffs of vanilla scent, and pine needles carpet the campground. The Ophir Creek Trail leads from the campground through steep canyons, mountain creeks, and boulder fields to Price Lake and Tahoe Meadows. Reno's gaming and entertainment is only 21 miles away.

BASICS

Operated By: Washoe County Parks & Recreation Dept. **Open:** All year. **Site Assignment:** First come, first served; group reservations. **Registration:** Self-pay fee station. **Fee:** $11 (cash or check only). **Parking:** At site.

FACILITIES

Number of RV Sites: 19. **Number of Tent-Only Sites:** 44. **Hookups:** None. **Each Site:**

Table, fire ring. **Dump Station:** Yes. **Laundry:** No. **Pay Phone:** Yes. **Rest Rooms and Showers:** Yes. **Fuel:** No. **Propane:** No. **Internal Roads:** Paved, excellent. **RV Service:** No. **Market:** Carson City, 12 mi. **Restaurant:** Carson City, 12 mi. **General Store:** No. **Vending:** No. **Swimming:** Pool at Bowers Mansion Regional Park, 1 mi. **Playground:** No. **Other:** Wheelchair-accessible site, amphitheather, pond. **Activities:** Horseback riding, fishing, boating, ice skating. **Nearby Attractions:** Bowers Mansion, Lake Tahoe. **Additional Information:** Carson Valley Chamber of Commerce & Visitors Authority, (800) 727-7677, www.carsonvalleynv.org.

RESTRICTIONS

Pets: On leash under owner's control. **Fires:** Yes (only in fire pits, no fires when danger is high in summer). **Alcoholic Beverages:** Allowed. **Vehicle Maximum Length:** 30 ft. **Other:** No firearms or patio torches, food must be locked from bears, no amplified music.

TO GET THERE

Go 12 mi. north from Carson City on US 395 and 0.5 mi. southwest on Old US Hwy. 395.

CARSON CITY
Washoe Lake State Park

4855 East Lake Blvd., Carson City 89704. T: (775) 687-4319; F: (775) 684-8053; www.state.nv.us/stparks.

🚐 ★★★★	▲ ★★★★
Beauty: ★★★★	Site Privacy: ★★★★★
Spaciousness: ★★★★	Quiet: ★★★★
Security: ★★★★	Cleanliness: ★★★★
Insect Control: ★★★★	Facilities: ★★★

Six-foot tall sagebrush teeming with quail and sand dunes stand between the two campground loops and Washoe Lake, while the backdrop is forested mountains in one direction and low rocky hills that turn golden in summer in the other. Loop B (sites 25–49) is at a slightly higher elevation than Loop A (sites 1–24) and has more glimpses of the lake over the sand dunes. A few tables are sheltered, but the mostly small trees have yet to grow tall enough to provide much shade. Site 37 is wheelchair accessible and one of the few sites with a tall cottonwood tree for shade and a good lake view. The lake's willows and cattails were used for basketry by the Washo Indians thousands of years ago, and provide good migratory bird-watching habitat today. Carson City is 5 miles south and Reno only 18 miles to the north.

BASICS

Operated By: Nevada State Parks. **Open:** All year. **Site Assignment:** First come, first served; group area requires reservations. **Registration:** Self-pay fee station. **Fee:** $10 (cash or check only). **Parking:** At site.

FACILITIES

Number of RV Sites: 47. **Number of Tent-Only Sites:** 2. **Hookups:** None. **Each Site:** Table, fire ring. **Dump Station:** Yes. **Laundry:** No. **Pay Phone:** Yes. **Rest Rooms and Showers:** Yes. **Fuel:** No. **Propane:** No. **Internal Roads:** Paved, excellent. **RV Service:** No. **Market:** Carson City, 6 mi. **Restaurant:** Carson City, 6 mi. **General Store:** No. **Vending:** No. **Swimming:** Lake. **Playground:** No. **Other:** Boat launch, windsocks, equestrian & wildlife viewing areas, day-use picnic tables & grills. **Activities:** Hang gliding, fishing, hunting, boating, bird-watching, golf. **Nearby Attractions:** Virginia City, historic areas, museums. **Additional Information:** Carson City Chamber of Commerce, (775) 882-1565, www.carsoncitychamber.com.

RESTRICTIONS

Pets: On leash at all times (except in wetlands during hunting season). **Fires:** Yes (in grills only, no wood collection, firewood sold). **Alcoholic Beverages:** Allowed. **Vehicle Maximum Length:** 45 ft. **Other:** 7-day limit per 30-day period.

TO GET THERE

From US Hwy. 395 exit 42 north of Carson City, go 2 mi. east on East Lake Blvd.

COTTONWOOD COVE
Cottonwood Cove

P.O. Box 123, Searchlight 89046. T: (702) 293-8907; F: (702) 293-8936; www.nps.gov/lame/home.html.

🚐 ★★★★	⛺ ★★★★★
Beauty: ★★★★★	Site Privacy: ★★★★★
Spaciousness: ★★★★	Quiet: ★★★★★
Security: ★★★★★	Cleanliness: ★★★★★
Insect Control: ★★★	Facilities: ★★★★★

Like Katherine near Bullhead City, AZ, Cottonwood Cove is a very popular Lake Mohave destination that begins filling up on Thursday for long weekends. At peak times consider instead a reservation at the Forever Resorts (call (800) 255-5561; www.foreverresorts.com) trailer village (30, 50 amp hookups) and camp out amongst the mobile homes. Tent campers will like having a whole loop area of their own, an unusual arrangement in the Lake Mead National Recreation Area. The gray desert beauty and solitude of the location should provide solace against holiday crowds. The ranger station has a cactus garden with several cholla species and a good display of area history, ranging from local railroad spikes to minerals. It is only 14 miles (west) to Searchlight and a roadside casino with 10-cent coffee. Like the rest of the Lake Mead National Recreation Area, Lake Mohave life revolves around the water and boating.

BASICS

Operated By: National Park Service. **Open:** All year. **Site Assignment:** First come, first served. **Registration:** Self-pay entrance fee station. **Fee:** $10. **Parking:** At site.

FACILITIES

Number of RV Sites: 100. **Number of Tent-Only Sites:** 45. **Hookups:** None. **Each Site:** Table, fire pit. **Dump Station:** Yes. **Laundry:** Yes. **Pay Phone:** Yes. **Rest Rooms and Showers:** Yes. **Fuel:** Yes. **Propane:** Yes. **Internal Roads:** Paved, good. **RV Service:** No. **Market:** At marina. **Restaurant:** At marina. **General Store:** Yes. **Vending:** Yes. **Swimming:** In lake at own risk. **Playground:** No. **Other:** Boat launch, motel. **Activities:** Boating, canoeing, fishing. **Nearby Attractions:** Laughlin. **Additional Information:** Cottonwood Cove Marina & Resort, (702) 297-1464, www.foreverresorts.com.

RESTRICTIONS

Pets: On leash under owner's control. **Fires:** Yes. **Alcoholic Beverages:** Allowed in moderation; problems will result in arrest. **Vehicle Maximum Length:** 30 ft. **Other:** No loaded firearms, no fireworks, no disturbing plants or rocks or archaeological features.

TO GET THERE

Take NV Hwy. 164 between Laughlin and Las Vegas, and at Searchlight go east for 14 mi. on Cottonwood Cove Rd.

ELKO

Valley View RV Park

6000 East Idaho St. (Hwy. 40 East), Elko 89801. T:
(775) 753-9200.

🚐 ★★★   ⛺ ★★★

Beauty: ★★★	Site Privacy: ★★★
Spaciousness: ★★★★	Quiet: ★★★
Security: ★★★★	Cleanliness: ★★★★
Insect Control: ★★★★	Facilities: ★★★★

Just down the road from the Hilton and the bare
gravel Double Dice RV Park, Valley View at least
offers some attractive patches of grass, a friendly
family feel, and the best campsite prices in town.
The word of mouth here is good, and repeat customers stop by regularly for three to five days.
Families settling in for longer stays let their kids
pick up the school bus at the bus stop in front.
The owners are amiable, and Valley View seems
like a friendly little town where people have the
time to stop and chat. There is some noise from
the highway being nearby, but the trees provide
an offset and a snack bar should soon be in operation to lessen the need for trips into town. All in
all, a pleasant alternative to Nevada's prevalent
casino RV parking lots and about as good as they
come in this remote area.

BASICS

Operated By: Elaine Poirier. **Open:** All year. **Site
Assignment:** First come, first served. **Registration:** Office. **Fee:** $9 tent; $15 RV (V, MC). **Parking:** At site.

FACILITIES

Number of RV Sites: 100. **Number of Tent-
Only Sites:** Undesignated sites. **Hookups:** Electric
(30, 50 amp), water, sewer, phone (modem), cable
TV. **Each Site:** Grills & tables in tent area only.
Dump Station: Yes. **Laundry:** Yes. **Pay Phone:**
Yes. **Rest Rooms and Showers:** Yes. **Fuel:** No.
Propane: No. **Internal Roads:** Paved, good. **RV
Service:** No. **Market:** Elko, 3 mi. **Restaurant:**
Elko, 1 mi. **General Store:** No. **Vending:** Yes.
Swimming: At park in town. **Playground:** Yes.
Other: Mail delivery, school-bus pickup, dog walk.
Activities: Fishing, hunting, biking, golf, baseball,
bird-watching. **Nearby Attractions:** Ruby Moun-
tains, Lamoille Canyon, Jarbridge Wilderness, ghost
towns. **Additional Information:** Elko Chamber of

Commerce, (775) 738-7135, www.elko-nevada.com.

RESTRICTIONS

Pets: On leash and/or contained at all times. **Fires:**
Yes. **Alcoholic Beverages:** Allowed. **Vehicle
Maximum Length:** 55 ft. **Other:** Children must
have adult supervision at all times.

TO GET THERE

From US I-80 Exit 303, go 3 mi. east on Idaho
St. (Hwy. 40).

ELY

Cave Lake State Park

P.O. Box 761, Ely 89301. T: (775) 728-4467;
www.state.nv.us/stparks.

🚐 ★★   ⛺ ★★★★

Beauty: ★★★★	Site Privacy: ★★★★
Spaciousness: ★★★	Quiet: ★★★★★
Security: ★★★★	Cleanliness: ★★★★
Insect Control: ★★★	Facilities: ★★

The road to Elk Flat and Lake View Campgrounds in Cave Lake State Park is lined with
typical Great Basin big sagebrush and rabbitbrush, but the campgrounds are heavily wooded
with pinyon pines and junipers. The surrounding Humboldt-Toiyabe National Forest is a
prime elk habitat with scenic upthrusts, narrow
canyons, and shallow caves. Elk Flat (16 sites) is
newer and more spacious, but closes with the
snows and cold weather between mid-October
and early May. Lake View remains open year-
round for ice fishing, ice skating, and other winter sports, but you need to bring your own water
then and without 4WD there is a risk of being
stuck a day or two waiting for the snow plows.
Large vehicles may need to camp at the roadside
turnouts (which are overflow areas and trailheads
for streams with native brown trout), as the tight
campground turns have trapped large RVs
(necessitating towing).

BASICS

Operated By: Nevada State Parks. **Open:** All year.
Site Assignment: First come, first served. **Registration:** Self-pay fee station. **Fee:** $12 (cash or
check only). **Parking:** At site.

FACILITIES

Number of RV Sites: 34. **Number of Tent-
Only Sites:** 0. **Hookups:** None. **Each Site:** Table,

grill, fire pit. **Dump Station:** Yes. **Laundry:** No. **Pay Phone:** No. **Rest Rooms and Showers:** Yes. **Fuel:** No. **Propane:** No. **Internal Roads:** Gravel, good. **RV Service:** No. **Market:** Ely, 14 mi. **Restaurant:** Ely, 14 mi. **General Store:** No. **Vending:** No. **Swimming:** Lake. **Playground:** No. **Other:** Boat ramp, 1 wheelchair-accessible site. **Activities:** Winter sports, fishing, crawdading, boating, horseback riding. **Nearby Attractions:** Ward Charcoal Ovens, Great Basin National Park, Ely museum, historic railroad. **Additional Information:** Ely Ranger District, (702) 289-3031, www.fs.fed.us; White Pine County Chamber of Commerce, (702) 289-8877.

RESTRICTIONS

Pets: On leash. **Fires:** Yes. **Alcoholic Beverages:** Allowed. **Vehicle Maximum Length:** 24 ft. **Other:** 5 trout limit, 5 mph (flat wake) motorized boat speed limit, no snowmobiles, after 10 p.m. children under 18 years must be under the supervision of a parent or legal guardian.

TO GET THERE

From Ely, go 8 mi. south on US Hwy. 93 and 7 mi. east on NV Hwy. 486 (Success Summit Rd.).

ELY
Ward Mountain Campground

350 8th St., P.O. Box 539, Ely 89301. T: (702) 289-3031; www.fs.fed.us.

🚐 ★★★★   ⛺ ★★★★★

Beauty: ★★★★★
Spaciousness: ★★★★
Security: ★★★★
Insect Control: ★★★
Site Privacy: ★★★★★
Quiet: ★★★★
Cleanliness: ★★★★
Facilities: ★★

When the hunger for open space is strong enough that Ely's rustic KOA and Valley View (no relation to the one in Elko) RV Parks and even the free promo hookups at the Holiday Inn casino will no longer do, Ward Mountain's large, wide (site 29 is 38-feet wide and 126-feet long) spaces deep in the pines and junipers may be the perfect remedy. Large RVs have their own private loop (sites 22–29) with a huge parking area near the South Trailhead. Two loops with smaller sites are on either side of the RV loop. Though Ward Mountain is popular for group picnics, it rarely reaches 50% occupancy (usually at Ely special event).

Typically, a half dozen campers a night share the three loops, which are on the German and Swiss tourist routes for doing the national parks between San Francisco and Denver.

BASICS

Operated By: Humboldt-Toiyabe National Forests Ely Ranger District. **Open:** All year. **Site Assignment:** First come, first served; day-use picnic area reservations. **Registration:** Self-pay fee station. **Fee:** $4 (cash or check only). **Parking:** At site.

FACILITIES

Number of RV Sites: 29. **Number of Tent-Only Sites:** 0. **Hookups:** None. **Each Site:** Table, grill, fire ring. **Dump Station:** No. **Laundry:** No. **Pay Phone:** No. **Rest Rooms and Showers:** No showers, pit toilets. **Fuel:** No. **Propane:** No. **Internal Roads:** Gravel, well maintained. **RV Service:** No. **Market:** Ely, 6 mi. **Restaurant:** Ely, 6 mi. **General Store:** No. **Vending:** No. **Swimming:** No. **Playground:** Yes (baseball field). **Other:** Amphitheater. **Activities:** Baseball. **Nearby Attractions:** Ward Charcoal Ovens, Cave Lake State Park, Great Basin National Park, museum, historic railroad. **Additional Information:** White Pine County Chamber of Commerce, (702) 289-8877.

RESTRICTIONS

Pets: On leash under owner's control. **Fires:** Yes. **Alcoholic Beverages:** Allowed. **Vehicle Maximum Length:** 126 ft. **Other:** 14-day limit, no saddle or pack animals, no water Oct. 16–May 20.

TO GET THERE

From Ely, go 6 mi. southwest on US Hwy. 6 and 1 mi. on gravel road (FR 10439) turnoff.

GABBS
Berlin Ichthyosaur State Park

HC Box 61200, Austin 89310. T: (775) 964-2440; F: (775) 964-2012; www.state.nv.us/stparks.

🚐 ★★★   ⛺ ★★★★

Beauty: ★★★★
Spaciousness: ★★★
Security: ★★★★
Insect Control: ★★★
Site Privacy: ★★★★★
Quiet: ★★★★★
Cleanliness: ★★★★
Facilities: ★★★

An unusual combination of ghost town and aquatic dinosaur fossil site, Berlin Ichthyosaur State Park is relatively remote, even by Nevada standards. Nevada mining towns have a history of boom and bust, with miners carting off the scarce wood and moving to the next site when the ore plays out. What makes Berlin unique is the intact nature of the town. Summer weekends the rangers even run some of the old mining equipment. The ichthyosaur fossils were first exposed by erosion, not miners, and the 50-foot-long specimens in the fossil shelter are among the world's largest. The campsites pose a back-in challenge for trailers, but each site is very private and screened from the others by tall junipers and pines. Seven miles to the north along a gravel road, the historic mercury-mining town of Ione clings to life with a few prospectors, a bar, and several RV sites with hookups.

BASICS

Operated By: Nevada State Parks. **Open:** All year. **Site Assignment:** First come, first served; group reservations required. **Registration:** Self-pay fee station. **Fee:** $3–$7 ($7 April 1–Oct. 31; $3 Nov. 1–Mar. 30; cash or check only). **Parking:** At site.

FACILITIES

Number of RV Sites: 14. **Number of Tent-Only Sites:** 0. **Hookups:** None. **Each Site:** Sheltered table, grill, fire ring. **Dump Station:** Yes. **Laundry:** No. **Pay Phone:** No. **Rest Rooms and Showers:** No showers. **Fuel:** No. **Propane:** No. **Internal Roads:** Gravel, good. **RV Service:** No. **Market:** Tonopah, 77 mi. **Restaurant:** Gabbs, 23 mi. **General Store:** No. **Vending:** No. **Swimming:** No. **Playground:** No. **Other:** Drinking water (mid-Apr.–Oct.). **Activities:** Fossil, mine- & ghost-town exploration. **Nearby Attractions:** Ghost towns. **Additional Information:** Ione Mercantile (RV hookups), (775) 847-0571.

RESTRICTIONS

Pets: On leash. **Fires:** Yes (in designated fire containers or commercial stoves/fireplaces only). **Alcoholic Beverages:** Allowed. **Vehicle Maximum Length:** 25 ft. **Other:** No horses without permit, no metal detectors, no loaded firearms, no wood gathering.

TO GET THERE

From Gabbs, go 23 mi. east on NV Hwy. 844 (last 4 mi. are gravel).

GREAT BASIN NATIONAL PARK
Lower & Upper Lehman Creek Campgrounds

100 Great Basin National Park, Baker 89311. T: (775) 234-7331; www.nps.gov/grba/; grbainterpretation@nps.gov.

🚐 ★★★★   ⛺ ★★★★★

Beauty: ★★★★★   Site Privacy: ★★★★★
Spaciousness: ★★★★   Quiet: ★★★★★
Security: ★★★★   Cleanliness: ★★★★
Insect Control: ★★★   Facilities: ★

One of the eight least visited National Parks in the nation, Great Basin's four campgrounds usually fill up only on weekends and holidays like Memorial Day, Labor Day, 4th of July, and Utah Pioneer Days (July). Lower Lehman campsites offer ample privacy where the desert sagebrush, greasewood, and rabbitbrush give way to evergreen pines and aspens in this vast park that includes alpine meadows, cool streams, Lehman Caves, and nineteenth-century mining remnants like Osceola Ditch. Lower Lehman Creek (six pull-through sites) and sites 1–8 of Upper Lehman Creek are best for RVs and trailers. Upper Lehman has tent-only sites, and the road narrows too much for all but the smallest trailers on the secluded loop with sites 17–24. Wheeler Peak Campground, further up a steep (8%) grade) scenic road, is not recommended for long vehicles. However, four miles of sagebrush-lined dirt road lead to Baker Campground, which has seven pull-through sites.

BASICS

Operated By: National Park Service. **Open:** All year. **Site Assignment:** First come, first served. **Registration:** Self-pay fee station. **Fee:** $10 (cash or check only). **Parking:** At site.

FACILITIES

Number of RV Sites: 25. **Number of Tent-Only Sites:** 9. **Hookups:** None. **Each Site:** Table, fire ring. **Dump Station:** Yes. **Laundry:** No. **Pay Phone:** Yes (Visitor Center). **Rest Rooms and Showers:** No showers. **Fuel:** No. **Propane:** No. **Internal Roads:** Paved, rough w/ ruts, pot holes. **RV Service:** No. **Market:** Baker, 5 mi. **Restau-**

rant: Baker, 5 mi. (Park cafe has limited hours). **General Store:** No. **Vending:** No. **Swimming:** No. **Playground:** No. **Other:** Ranger-led summer programs. **Activities:** Cave tours, horseback riding. **Nearby Attractions:** Baker Archaeological Site, Johnson Lake Mining District. **Additional Information:** White Pine Chamber of Commerce, (775) 289-8877; Great Basin Assoc., (775) 234-7270.

RESTRICTIONS

Pets: On leash under owner's physical control at all times. **Fires:** Yes (only in metal fire rings, no collecting of firewood, which is sold 24 hours in Baker). **Alcoholic Beverages:** Allowed. **Vehicle Maximum Length:** 35 ft. **Other:** No fireworks.

TO GET THERE

From junction of NV Hwys. 487 & 488 in Baker, go 5 mi. west on NV Hwy. 488.

HENDERSON
Las Vegas Bay Campground

601 Nevada Hwy., Boulder City 89005. T: (702) 293-8907; F: (702) 293-8936; www.nps.gov/lame/home.html.

🚐 ★★★   ⛺ ★★★

Beauty: ★★★   Site Privacy: ★★★
Spaciousness: ★★★   Quiet: ★★★
Security: ★★★   Cleanliness: ★★★★★
Insect Control: ★★★★   Facilities: ★★

A small, very relaxing campground, Las Vegas Bay combines Lake Mead water recreation with nearness to the Henderson and Las Vegas casino strips. The 650-slip marina does not rent houseboats or allow swimming, but many campsites have marina or lake views. Landscaping is the Lake Mead National Recreation Area standard of palms, oleanders, and eucalyptus. The gray desert backdrop is greened up some by the creosote bush desert wash plant community of rabbit brush, brittle brush, and mesquite. One loop houses both tents and RVs, so a steady hum of diesel generators can often be heard until the quiet hours, 10 p.m. to 6 a.m. There are plenty of picnic tables to make this part of a day trip from Las Vegas, possibly stopping off at the Ethel M chocolate factory and cactus garden en route to Hoover Dam.

However, even picnic table use requires the same $5 entry fee and $10 charge as overnight camping.

BASICS

Operated By: National Park Service. **Open:** All year. **Site Assignment:** First come, first served. **Registration:** Self-pay entrance fee station. **Fee:** $10. **Parking:** At site.

FACILITIES

Number of RV Sites: 86. **Number of Tent-Only Sites:** 0. **Hookups:** None. **Each Site:** Table, grill. **Dump Station:** Yes. **Laundry:** No. **Pay Phone:** Yes. **Rest Rooms and Showers:** Yes. **Fuel:** No (boat fuel only). **Propane:** No. **Internal Roads:** Paved, good. **RV Service:** No. **Market:** Henderson, 8 mi. **Restaurant:** At marina. **General Store:** Yes. **Vending:** No. **Swimming:** No. **Playground:** No. **Other:** Boat ramp, marina, partial handicap access. **Activities:** Fishing, boating. **Nearby Attractions:** Lake Mead, Las Vegas, Henderson, Hoover Dam. **Additional Information:** Las Vegas Bay Marina, (702) 565-9111.

RESTRICTIONS

Pets: On leash under owner's control. **Fires:** Yes. **Alcoholic Beverages:** Allowed. **Vehicle Maximum Length:** Not specified. **Other:** 30-day max. stay.

TO GET THERE

From Henderson, go 9 mi. northeast on NV Hwy. 146.

LAKE MEAD NATIONAL RECREATION AREA
Callville Bay

601 Nevada Hwy., Boulder City 89005. T: (702) 293-8906; www.nps.gov/lame/home.html.

🚐 ★★★   ⛺ ★★★

Beauty: ★★★★   Site Privacy: ★★★
Spaciousness: ★★★   Quiet: ★★★★
Security: ★★★★   Cleanliness: ★★★★
Insect Control: ★★★   Facilities: ★★★★

A 589-slip boating and water recreation site on the huge desert lake created when Hoover Dam was built, Callville Bay offers access to Lake Mead and proximity to Las Vegas Territory casinos. Low desert foothills surround the campsites, which are jammed close together and separated from each other by tall poisonous oleanders (watch young kids closely). The nearby marina offers ample facilities and rentals for water fun. RV hookups can be found across the street at Callville Bay Resort (operated by Forever Resorts; (800) 255-5561), which caters to mobile-home residents. A word of warning: Though near the lake, the area is still desert, and summer temperatures in locked vehicles can reach 130° F in 30 minutes. So, don't leave pets in locked vehicles. For more impressive desert scenery and red rocks, continue east on NV Hwy. 167 towards Echo Bay or head inland to Valley of Fire State Park.

BASICS

Operated By: National Park Service. **Open:** All year. **Site Assignment:** First come, first served. **Registration:** Self-pay station at entrance. **Fee:** $10 ($5 Golden Age/Access). **Parking:** At site.

FACILITIES

Number of RV Sites: 80. **Number of Tent-Only Sites:** 0. **Hookups:** None. **Each Site:** Sheltered table, grill. **Dump Station:** Yes. **Laundry:** Yes. **Pay Phone:** Yes. **Rest Rooms and Showers:** Yes. **Fuel:** Yes. **Propane:** Yes. **Internal Roads:** Paved, good condition. **RV Service:** No. **Market:** At nearby marina. **Restaurant:** At nearby marina. **General Store:** No. **Vending:** Yes. **Swimming:** In lake at own risk. **Playground:** No. **Other:** Boat & houseboat rentals, launch ramp, yacht club, trailer village. **Activities:** Boating, fishing. **Nearby Attractions:** Las Vegas, Hoover Dam, Lost City Museum, Valley of Fire State Park. **Additional Information:** Callville Bay Resort, (702) 565-8958 or (800) 255-5561; Alan Bible Visitor Center (NPS), (702) 293-8990.

RESTRICTIONS

Pets: On leash under handler's control. **Fires:** Grills only, no ground fires. **Alcoholic Beverages:** Allowed at site. **Vehicle Maximum Length:** Not specified. **Other:** 30-day limit, noon checkout, 8 people & 2 vehicles or 4 motorcycles per site.

TO GET THERE

From North Las Vegas go east on Lake Mead Blvd. (NV Hwy. 147) 12 mi., then northeast on NV Hwy. 167 (Northshore Scenic Dr.) for 8 mi. and south at Callville Bay turnoff for 4 mi.

LAKE MEAD NATIONAL RECREATION AREA
Echo Bay

601 Nevada Hwy., Boulder City 89005. T: (702) 293-8906; www.nps.gov/lame/home.html.

🚙 ★★★   ⛺ ★★★★★

Beauty: ★★★★   Site Privacy: ★★★★
Spaciousness: ★★★★   Quiet: ★★★★
Security: ★★★★   Cleanliness: ★★★★
Insect Control: ★★   Facilities: ★★★★

After the Overton Beach tent campground flooded out four years ago, Echo Bay became the northern-most tent campground along Lake Mead. The sites are small and best for car camping, but nearby Echo Bay RV Park has large pull-through sites. More RV sites are also available 18 miles north at Overton Beach Resort. Echo Bay is a good place to stake tents because it combines access to water fun on Lake Mead with nearness to the red-rock formations of Valley of Fire State Park. Two widely separated loops (designated upper and lower) function like separate campgrounds with their own entrances and fee stations. The lower loop has several advantages. It is closer to the marina, has taller oleanders between sites, shady cottonwood and olive trees, and a ranger station perched on a ledge overlooking the campground. The upper loop has smaller oleanders, eucalyptus, small olives, and palms.

BASICS

Operated By: National Park Service. **Open:** All year. **Site Assignment:** First come, first served. **Registration:** Self-pay entrance fee station. **Fee:** $10 ($5 Golden Age/Access). **Parking:** At site.

FACILITIES

Number of RV Sites: 155. **Number of Tent-Only Sites:** 0. **Hookups:** None. **Each Site:** Table, fire ring. **Dump Station:** Yes. **Laundry:** Yes. **Pay Phone:** Yes. **Rest Rooms and Showers:** Yes (shower fee at trailer village). **Fuel:** Yes. **Propane:** Yes. **Internal Roads:** Paved, excellent. **RV Service:** No. **Market:** At marina. **Restaurant:** At marina. **General Store:** No. **Vending:** No. **Swimming:** In lake at own risk. **Playground:** No. **Other:** Houseboat & watercraft rentals, motel. **Activities:** Boating, fishing. **Nearby Attractions:** Las Vegas, Hoover Dam, Lost City Museum (Overton), Valley of Fire State Park. **Additional Information:** Alan Bible Visitor Center (NPS), (702) 293-8990; Seven Crowns Resorts, (702) 394-4000.

RESTRICTIONS

Pets: On leash under owner's control. **Fires:** Yes (in grills only). **Alcoholic Beverages:** Allowed; disorderly conduct and/or public intoxication will result in arrest. **Vehicle Maximum Length:** Not specified. **Other:** 30-day max. stay.

TO GET THERE

From junction of NV Hwys. 147 & 167, go 32 mi. northeast on Hwy. 167 and then 5 mi. east on Echo Bay Rd.

LAKE MEAD NATIONAL RECREATION AREA
Echo Bay RV Park

HC30 Box 30, Overton 89040. T: (702) 394-4000 or (800) 752-9669 (reservations); www.sevencrown.com.

🚐 ★★★★	▲ n/a
Beauty: ★★★★	Site Privacy: ★★★★
Spaciousness: ★★★★	Quiet: ★★★★
Security: ★★★★	Cleanliness: ★★★★
Insect Control: ★★★	Facilities: ★★★★

Pleasant desert living amongst eucalyptus trees best sums up Echo Bay RV Park, which is geared for larger rigs that don't fit into the nearby Echo Bay campground. Some sites have views of Lake Mead, and the nearby marina beckons with water play rentals ranging from houseboats and fishing gear to water skiis, sea-doos, and knee boards. The sites lack tables and grills, but most people are too busy at the lake to even notice the occasional bighorn sheep wandering into the RV park for water during the day. It is harder to miss the wild burros wandering in at night. The campground is further from the water than the one at Overton Beach Marina. But Echo Bay RV Park has a rustic charm that makes Overton seem like a lakeside parking lot.

BASICS

Operated By: Seven Crowns Resorts. **Open:** All year. **Site Assignment:** First come, first served; reservations advised for peak times. **Registration:** At motel in marina. **Fee:** $12–$18 (V, MC, AE). **Parking:** At site.

FACILITIES

Number of RV Sites: 58. **Number of Tent-Only Sites:** 0. **Hookups:** Electric (30, 50 amp), water, sewer. **Each Site:** Wood posts. **Dump Station:** Yes. **Laundry:** Yes. **Pay Phone:** Yes. **Rest Rooms and Showers:** Yes. **Fuel:** Yes. **Propane:** Yes. **Internal Roads:** Paved, weathered. **RV Service:** No. **Market:** At Echo Bay Marina. **Restaurant:** At Echo Bay Marina. **General Store:** No. **Vending:** Yes. **Swimming:** In lake at own risk. **Playground:** No. **Other:** Houseboat, watercraft & water sport rentals, moorage slips, dry storage, motel, airstrip. **Activities:** Boating, fishing. **Nearby Attractions:** Las Vegas, Lost City Museum (Overton), Roger Springs, Valley of Fire State Park. **Additional Information:** Alan Bible Visitor Center (NPS), (702) 293-8990, www.nps.gov/lame/home.html.

RESTRICTIONS

Pets: On leash under owner's control. **Fires:** Yes. **Alcoholic Beverages:** Allowed. **Vehicle Maximum Length:** 45 ft.

TO GET THERE

From junction of NV Hwys. 147 & 167, go 32 mi. northeast on Hwy. 167 and then 5 mi. east on Echo Bay Rd.

LAKE TAHOE
Zephyr Cove RV Park & Campground

760 Hwy. 50, Zephyr Cove 89448. T: (775) 589-4981; F: (775) 588-9627; www.tahoedixie2.com; zcr-campground@aramark.com.

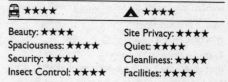

🚐 ★★★★	▲ ★★★★
Beauty: ★★★★	Site Privacy: ★★★★
Spaciousness: ★★★★	Quiet: ★★★★
Security: ★★★★	Cleanliness: ★★★★
Insect Control: ★★★★	Facilities: ★★★★

A National Forest Service campground that stretches far back from the trolley stop fronting US Hwy. 50, Zephyr Cove's coveted boulder-strewn, walk-in tent sites must keep foodstuffs locked from black bears that roam across the street from beaches and water recreation. Pull-through sites book up quickly and are closest to the highway, which means more road noise and lake views. There are also good lake views from the 47 walk-in tent sites, especially 45–53, but 32–43 and 54–57 are more secluded among the campground's tall ponderosa pine trees. The drive-in tent sites, 1–10, and RV sites like 117–120 are also attractively situated among the tall ponderosa pines and boulders. Weekends, particularly in summer, the campground books solid and reservations are a necessity. Besides Lake Tahoe's casinos, Zephyr Cove Resort has beaches, an operational Mississippi River Paddleboat, the M.S. Dixie II, stables with horses, and a restaurant across the street from the campground.

BASICS

Operated By: Aramark. **Open:** All year. **Site Assignment:** First come, first served; reservations advised. **Registration:** Office/trailer at entrance. **Fee:** $32 RV, $22 tent (V, MC, AE). **Parking:** At site; parking areas for walk-in tent sites.

FACILITIES

Number of RV Sites: 94. **Number of Tent-Only Sites:** 57. **Hookups:** Electric (30, 50 amp), water, sewer, cable TV, phone (modem, unlimited Internet access). **Each Site:** Table, fire pit. **Dump Station:** Yes. **Laundry:** Yes. **Pay Phone:** Yes. **Rest Rooms and Showers:** Yes. **Fuel:** No. **Propane:** No. **Internal Roads:** Paved, good. **RV Service:** No. **Market:** Stateline, 2 mi. **Restaurant:** Across street. **General Store:** Yes. **Vending:** Yes. **Swimming:** Lake. **Playground:** No. **Other:** Cabins, lodge accommodations, stables, marina, Mississippi River paddleboat. **Activities:** Boating, fishing, horseback riding, winter sports, gambling. **Nearby Attractions:** Incline Village ski slopes. **Additional Information:** Forest Service (Lake Tahoe), www.r5.fs.fed.us/ltbmu; Lake Tahoe Visitors Authority, (530) 544-5050. www.virtualtahoe.com.

RESTRICTIONS

Pets: On leash under owner's control. **Fires:** Yes (no higher than 1 ft. above fire ring or after 11 p.m., $50 fine for ground fires, firewood for sale). **Alcoholic Beverages:** Allowed. **Vehicle Maximum Length:** No limit. **Other:** No kegs, loud music, or generators.

TO GET THERE

At the Zephyr Cove stoplight on US Hwy. 50.

LAS VEGAS
Silverton Hotel Casino RV Park

3333 Blue Diamond Rd., Las Vegas 89139. T: (702) 263-7777 or (800) 588-7711; F: (702) 897-4208; www.silvertoncasino.com.

🚐 ★★★★   ⛺ n/a

Beauty: ★★★	Site Privacy: ★★★
Spaciousness: ★★★★	Quiet: ★★★
Security: ★★★★★	Cleanliness: ★★★★
Insect Control: ★★★★	Facilities: ★★★★★

With a sizeable pine tree, tan gravel, and a small wood fence separating each site, Silverton is one of the most pleasant Las Vegas casino RV parks. Indeed, it is proof that sites can be squeezed close together without resembling a parking lot. The casino itself has Old West charm and a friendly, laid-back feel more like rural Nevada than modern Las Vegas. The restaurant has timber and leather chairs and cafeteria-style buffets at prices reminiscent of the Strip of long ago, plus a 10% senior discount and sugar-free deserts for the health conscious. The 45-foot back-in and 70-foot pull-through sites are far enough from the highway that only the loudest of trucks plying the I-15 are bothersome. Shuttle buses run to the Tropicana on the Strip and to the factory outlet stores from this island of sanity just southwest of the international airport.

BASICS

Operated By: Silverton Hotel Casino RV Park. **Open:** All year. **Site Assignment:** First come, first served; reservations accepted. **Registration:** Office. **Fee:** $17–$23 (V, MC, AE, D, DC). **Parking:** At site.

FACILITIES

Number of RV Sites: 460. **Number of Tent-Only Sites:** 0. **Hookups:** Electric (30, 50 amp), water, sewer, cable TV, phone (modem). **Each Site:** Table, grill, 12-ft. wide concrete pad. **Dump Station:** Yes. **Laundry:** Yes. **Pay Phone:** Yes. **Rest Rooms and Showers:** Yes. **Fuel:** No. **Propane:** Yes. **Internal Roads:** Paved, excellent. **RV Service:** No. **Market:** Las Vegas, 3 mi. **Restaurant:** Casino, adjacent. **General Store:** Yes. **Vending:** Yes. **Swimming:** Pool. **Playground:** No. **Other:** Whirlpool, horseshoes, pet area, airport shuttle, free USA Today newspaper. **Activities:** Horseback riding, golf, gun range. **Nearby Attractions:** Red Rock Canyon, Death Valley. **Additional Information:** Las Vegas Convention & Visitors Authority, (702) 892-0711, www.lasvegas24hours.com.

RESTRICTIONS

Pets: On leash under owner's control (cannot be left alone at night). **Fires:** Yes (in charcoal containers or hibachis only, no open fires). **Alcoholic Beverages:** Allowed. **Vehicle Maximum Length:** 70 ft. **Other:** No skateboards, drugs or generator use.

TO GET THERE

From US I-15, go west 0.25 mi. on NV Hwy. 160 (Blue Diamond Rd.).

LAUGHLIN

Riverside RV Park

P.O. Box 500, Laughlin 89029. T: (800) 227-3849 or (702) 298-2535.

🚐 ★★★	🏕 n/a
Beauty: ★★★	Site Privacy: ★★★★
Spaciousness: ★★★★	Quiet: ★★★★
Security: ★★★★	Cleanliness: ★★★★
Insect Control: ★★★	Facilities: ★★★★

Across the street from Don Laughlin's Riverside Resort Hotel and Casino, at the north edge of Casino Dr., across the river from Bullhead City, AZ, is a nicely terraced alternative to the informal camping prevalent in casino parking lots here. The terraces add a sense of privacy and a view, but are too unstable for walking or child's play. However, children can use two swimming pools and play the latest coin games in the casino kids arcade. Cable TV, phone, and modem hookups are among the other comforts. Besides casino entertainment, outlet stores and a bank are next door. Sellouts are the rule when special events come to town, so reservations are advised three weeks in advance (no cancellation penalties). Bullhead City across the river also has several conventional RV parks to choose from, albeit sans casinos, and there are more isolated casino RV parks north and south of here (See appendix).

BASICS

Operated By: Don Laughlin's Riverside Resort Hotel & Casino. **Open:** All year. **Site Assignment:** First come, first served; reservations highly recom-

mended. **Registration:** At office. **Fee:** $17 (V, MC, AE, D). **Parking:** At site.

FACILITIES

Number of RV Sites: 740. **Number of Tent-Only Sites:** 0. **Hookups:** Electric (30, 50 amps), cable TV, phone. **Each Site:** Varies. **Dump Station:** Yes. **Laundry:** Yes. **Pay Phone:** Yes. **Rest Rooms and Showers:** Yes. **Fuel:** Nearby. **Propane:** Yes. **Internal Roads:** Paved, excellent condition. **RV Service:** No. **Market:** Next door. **Restaurant:** Yes (across street, at casino). **General Store:** No. **Vending:** Yes. **Swimming:** Yes. **Playground:** No. **Other:** Boat ramp, casino shuttles. **Activities:** Casino has bowling, movies, auto museum, Kids Kastle. **Nearby Attractions:** Casinos, outlet stores, river boating, fishing. **Additional Information:** Laughlin Visitor Center, (702) 298-3321 or (800) 4-LAUGHLIN

RESTRICTIONS

Pets: 2 per rig; must be kept attended on leash. **Fires:** In approved containers only. **Alcoholic Beverages:** Nevada state law prevails. **Vehicle Maximum Length:** Not specified (tries to accommodate, 20-ft. width most common). **Other:** Firearms & firecrackers prohibited.

TO GET THERE

From Laughlin Civic Drive and Colorado River bridge, go 0.25 mi. south on Casino Dr.

LEE CANYON RECREATION AREA

McWilliams & Dolomite Campgrounds

HCR 38, P.O. Box 451, Las Vegas 89124. T: (702) 872-0156 or (800) 328-6226 or (877) 444-6777 (Reserve America or reservations only); F: (702) 872-0018; www.thousandtrails.com.

🚐 ★★★★	🏕 ★★★★
Beauty: ★★★★	Site Privacy: ★★★★★
Spaciousness: ★★★★	Quiet: ★★★★★
Security: ★★★★	Cleanliness: ★★★★★
Insect Control: ★★★★	Facilities: ★

When summer temperatures are hitting 110° F in Las Vegas, the locals are fleeing to their reserved sites here under the tall ponderosa pines for long, cool (7–85° F) three-day mountain weekends. In winter this Humboldt Toiyabe

National Forest area is a bustling ski and snowboard resort. At McWilliams, 1–9 are double sites reservable for families (240 days in advance); loop sites 26–40 are reservable single sites; sites 10–25 on a long hilly straightaway are first-come first-serve. Both McWilliams and Dolomite Campgrounds are exceptionally well maintained by Thousand Trails Inc. under a special use permit granted by the Humboldt Toiyabe National Forest. A totally separate entity, National Recreation Reservation Service, handles phone and Internet (www.reserveusa.com) reservations. For tent site reservations, request McWilliams, which has only a few 34-foot sites. Big vehicles do best at adjacent Dolomite (20 reservable sites), which accommodates 40-foot vehicles.

BASICS

Operated By: Thousand Trails Inc. **Open:** May–Sept. (weather permitting). **Site Assignment:** First come, first served; weekend, holiday reservations advised. **Registration:** Self-pay entrance fee station. **Fee:** $13 ($20 double sites; $30 triple sites). **Parking:** At site.

FACILITIES

Number of RV Sites: 70. **Number of Tent-Only Sites:** 0. **Hookups:** None. **Each Site:** Table, fire ring, grill. **Dump Station:** Yes. **Laundry:** No. **Pay Phone:** Yes. **Rest Rooms and Showers:** No showers. **Fuel:** No. **Propane:** No. **Internal Roads:** Paved, good condition. **RV Service:** No. **Market:** Las Vegas, 35 mi. **Restaurant:** Kyle Canyon, 15 mi. **General Store:** No. **Vending:** No. **Swimming:** No. **Playground:** No. **Other:** Double & triple sites, helicopter pad, large picnic areas nearby. **Activities:** Boating, skiing, winter sports. **Nearby Attractions:** Las Vegas, Mt. Charleston trails, Lee Canyon Ski & Snowboard Resort. **Additional Information:** Humboldt Toiyabe National Forest, (702) 873-8800, www.fs.fed.us.htnf.

RESTRICTIONS

Pets: On leash at all times. **Fires:** Yes (firewood sold). **Alcoholic Beverages:** Allowed (provided no boisterous behavior). **Vehicle Maximum Length:** 34 ft. (McWilliams), 40 ft. (Dolomite). **Other:** $5 per extra vehicle at family sites, no tree chopping.

TO GET THERE

From US Hwy. 95 20 mi. north of Las Vegas, go west 15 mi. on NV Hwy. 156 (Lee Canyon Rd.).

OVERTON

Overton Beach Marina

HCR 30, Box 7, Overton 89040. T: (702) 394-4040; F: (702) 394-4124; www.overtonbeachmarina.com.

🚐 ★★★★   ⛺ n/a

Beauty: ★★★★   Site Privacy: ★★★★
Spaciousness: ★★★★   Quiet: ★★★★
Security: ★★★★   Cleanliness: ★★★★
Insect Control: ★★★   Facilities: ★★★★

Well run by a National Park Service concessionaire inside Lake Mead National Recreation Area, the Overton Beach Marina RV park is a boater's paradise. The campground itself is down a short road (dirt and paved patches alternate) separated by a quarter mile stretch of swimming beach and a boat launch from the busy Marina, where there is a store, gas station, fish cleaner, restaurant, lounge, motel, and ranger station. The middle of the three rows of RV sites accommodates the largest vehicles. Each site is attractively separated by a low wooden fence and has its own cottonwood tree. Many sites also enjoy at least a partial lake view. Most sites also have room to park a trailer with a boat. Indeed, life here centers around the lake and lovely marina. It is hard to go wrong here, but best to call ahead and reserve a site.

BASICS

Operated By: Overton Beach Marina. **Open:** All year. **Site Assignment:** First come, first served; reservations accepted. **Registration:** Inside Marina store. **Fee:** $18 (V, MC). **Parking:** At site.

FACILITIES

Number of RV Sites: 41. **Number of Tent-Only Sites:** 0. **Hookups:** Electric, water, sewer. **Each Site:** Table, grill, cottonwood tree, low wood fence. **Dump Station:** Yes. **Laundry:** Yes. **Pay Phone:** Yes. **Rest Rooms and Showers:** Yes. **Fuel:** Yes. **Propane:** No. **Internal Roads:** Pavement, worn in spots. **RV Service:** No. **Market:** Overton, 8 mi. **Restaurant:** At Marina. **General Store:** Yes. **Vending:** Yes. **Swimming:** In lake at own risk. **Playground:** No. **Other:** House boat,

boat & slip rentals, launch ramp, fish cleaner, motel, boat storage. **Activities:** boating, fishing. **Nearby Attractions:** Lost City Museum, Valley of Fire State Park. **Additional Information:** Alan Bible Visitor Center (NPS), (702) 293-8990.

RESTRICTIONS

Pets: On leash under handler's control. **Fires:** Grills only. **Alcoholic Beverages:** Allowed. **Vehicle Maximum Length:** 65 ft.

TO GET THERE

From junction of NV Hwys. 167 & 169, go 4 mi. south on Overton Beach Rd.

OVERTON
Valley of Fire State Park

P.O. Box 515, Overton 89040. T: (702) 397-2621; F: (702) 397-2088; www.state.nv.us/stparks.

🚐 ★★	▲ ★★★★★
Beauty: ★★★★★	Site Privacy: ★★★★★
Spaciousness: ★★★	Quiet: ★★★★★
Security: ★★★★	Cleanliness: ★★★★
Insect Control: ★★★	Facilities: ★★

Nevada's first state park, Valley of Fire, began with 1930s CCC sandstone cabins and now has two campgrounds, Atlatl Rock and Arch Rock, scenically hidden amongst twisted, weathered, and black-stained orange-and-red sandstone formations. Atlatl Rock Campground has a shower building, a loop with 19 campsites (one is wheelchair accessible) and a smaller loop with three more isolated walk-in sites for those craving more wilderness. One Atlatl Rock site is big enough for anything on the road, but most are car camping size. Arch Rock Campground is even more secluded amongst the eroded red rocks, and its sites accommodate Tiogas, but nothing much larger. Camping among the red sandstone formations with birds, jack rabbits, and other desert wildlife (shake the boots for scorpions) is a real Nevada wilderness experience, with rock art and red rocks changing color with the sun's movement.

BASICS

Operated By: Nevada State Parks. **Open:** All year. **Site Assignment:** First come, first served; reservations required for group areas. **Registration:** Self-pay fee station at campground. **Fee:** $12 (cash

or check). **Parking:** At site (48); nearby for 3 walk-in sites.

FACILITIES

Number of RV Sites: 48. **Number of Tent-Only Sites:** 3. **Hookups:** None. **Each Site:** Table, grill or fire ring, tent pad. **Dump Station:** Yes. **Laundry:** No. **Pay Phone:** Yes. **Rest Rooms and Showers:** Yes. **Fuel:** No. **Propane:** No. **Internal Roads:** Gravel, good condition. **RV Service:** No. **Market:** Overton. **Restaurant:** Overton Beach Marina. **General Store:** No. **Vending:** No. **Swimming:** No. **Playground:** No. **Other:** Shelter over tables at many sites. **Activities:** Picnic areas. **Nearby Attractions:** Lake Mead National Recreation Area, Lost City Museum. **Additional Information:** Overton Chamber of Commerce, (702) 397-2193.

RESTRICTIONS

Pets: On leash under handler's control. **Fires:** Yes (only in grills, fire rings). **Alcoholic Beverages:** No public intoxication. **Vehicle Maximum Length:** (see description). **Other:** 2 vehicles & 8 persons per site, disturbing human artifacts or nature is a criminal offense.

TO GET THERE

Exit I-15 at NV Hwy. 169 (Exit 75), and go 18 mi. east.

PANACA
Cathedral Gorge State Park

P.O. Box 176, Panaca 89042. T: (775) 728-4460; F: (775) 728-4469; www.state.nv.us/stparks.

🚐 ★★★★	▲ ★★★★
Beauty: ★★★★	Site Privacy: ★★★★
Spaciousness: ★★★★	Quiet: ★★★★
Security: ★★★★	Cleanliness: ★★★★
Insect Control: ★★★	Facilities: ★★

Though mostly an overnight stop because the turnoff is right off US Hwy. 93, Cathedral Gorge is beautifully surrounded by white, tan, and buff colored eroding clay and siltstone cliffs and spires from a million-year-old lakebed known as the Panaca Formation. The badland cliffs are fronted by desert scrub loaded with black-tailed jackrabbits and the occasional rattler. Snowbirds on their spring and fall migration journeys often stop here, and if their timing is lucky snag one of the two large pull-through sites (the other 20 sites are mostly 24–30 feet). With Russian olive trees providing shade, this is actually a very relaxing stop and far enough from the highway that noise is not a factor. Advantages to overnighters include being nearer to historic towns (Caliente, Pioche, Panaca) and the main highway (US 93) than either Echo Canyon or Spring Valley State Parks, which require roundtrips down NV Hwy. 322.

BASICS

Operated By: Nevada State Parks. **Open:** All year. **Site Assignment:** First come, first served; group site reservation only. **Registration:** Self-pay entrance fee station. **Fee:** $12. **Parking:** At site.

FACILITIES

Number of RV Sites: 22. **Number of Tent-Only Sites:** 0. **Hookups:** None. **Each Site:** Sheltered table, grill. **Dump Station:** Yes. **Laundry:** No. **Pay Phone:** Yes. **Rest Rooms and Showers:** Yes. **Fuel:** No. **Propane:** No. **Internal Roads:** Gravel, good. **RV Service:** No. **Market:** Panaca, 2 mi. **Restaurant:** Panaca, 2 mi. **General Store:** No. **Vending:** No. **Swimming:** No. **Playground:** No. **Other:** Wheelchair accessible. **Activities:** Bird-watching. **Nearby Attractions:** Bullionville Cemetery, Caliente, Pioche, Echo Canyon, Spring Valley. **Additional Information:** Panaca District Ranger, (775) 728-4467.

RESTRICTIONS

Pets: On leash under owner's control. **Fires:** Yes (bring own firewood). **Alcoholic Beverages:** Allowed (if quiet & not drunk). **Vehicle Maximum Length:** 40 ft. **Other:** No guns.

TO GET THERE

Go 2 mi. north of Panaca to park turnoff.

PIOCHE
Echo Canyon State Park

Star Rte. Box 295, Pioche 89043. T: (775) 962-5103; www.state.nv.us/stparks.

🚐 ★★	⛺ ★★★★★
Beauty: ★★★★★	Site Privacy: ★★★★★
Spaciousness: ★★	Quiet: ★★★★
Security: ★★★★	Cleanliness: ★★★★
Insect Control: ★★	Facilities: ★

Hot summers and cool winters prevail at this high-desert park 12 miles east of the Nevada-Utah border. The campground itself is just across the road from earthen Echo Dam, where the reservoir is a mix of cold and warm waters favorable to largemouth bass, rainbow and brown trout, and white crappie. A drive across the dusty earthen dam leads to group campsites, some less developed near the water's edge and one with a restroom perched atop a windy hill surveying surrounding alfalfa farms. Individual campsites on the opposite side of the road from the reservoir offer plenty of privacy in the shade of pines, Russian olives, cottonwood, and sage. There is only one 40-foot pull-through site, making this more a secluded retreat for tent campers. RVs over 32 feet will find more spots continuing east through Ursine to Spring Valley State Park.

BASICS

Operated By: Nevada State Parks. **Open:** All year. **Site Assignment:** First come, first served; group area may be reserved. **Registration:** Self-pay entrance fee station. **Fee:** $8. **Parking:** At site.

FACILITIES

Number of RV Sites: 34. **Number of Tent-Only Sites:** 0. **Hookups:** None. **Each Site:** Sheltered table, grill, fire ring. **Dump Station:** Yes. **Laundry:** No. **Pay Phone:** Yes. **Rest Rooms and Showers:** No showers. **Fuel:** No. **Propane:** No. **Internal Roads:** Gravel, slippery. **RV Service:** No. **Market:** Pioche, 12 mi. **Restaurant:** Pioche, 12 mi. **General Store:** No. **Vending:** No. **Swimming:** In reservoir at own risk. **Playground:** No. **Other:** Boat launch, fish cleaning station, picnic tables. **Activities:** Boating, fishing, bird-watching. **Nearby Attractions:** Spring Valley State Park, Pioche Boot Hill Cemetery. **Additional Information:** Pioche Chamber of Commerce, (775) 962-5544.

RESTRICTIONS

Pets: On leash under owner's control. **Fires:** Yes (firewood sold). **Alcoholic Beverages:** Allowed. **Vehicle Maximum Length:** 40 ft. **Other:** 14-day max. stay, occasional winter snow.

TO GET THERE

From Pioche, go 4 mi. east on NV Hwy. 322 and then 8 mi. east on NV Hwy. 323.

RACHEL
Quik-Pik Mini Mart & Campground

HCR 61 Box 23, Rachel 89001. T: (775) 729-2529.

🚐 ★★★　　　　　　　Ⓐ ★★★

Beauty: ★★★　　　　　Site Privacy: ★★★★
Spaciousness: ★★★★　　Quiet: ★★★★
Security: ★★★★　　　　Cleanliness: ★★★★
Insect Control: ★★★★　　Facilities: ★★

The only stopping place on the Extraterrestrial Highway (NV Hwy. 375), so named because it leads the world in UFO sightings, the 22-year-old town of Rachel is a major motorcycle stopping place, as heading west the next gas is 110 miles away in Tonopah. Rachel's 3,000 acres of high-protein alfalfa trucked to California dairies are overshadowed by its proximity to Area 51. ET buffs believe that the US government's super-secret weapons development center around usually dry Groom Lake houses the remains of space aliens from the 1947 Roswell, NM, crash. The lady and her son running the store, gas station, and RV park are skeptics, but they'll sell you alien T-shirts and souvenirs to take home. The trailer park itself has 22 spots filled by permanent residents. The 10 available spaces across from the Rachel Senior Center Thrift Store are gravel with a bit of desert brush.

BASICS
Operated By: Fay Day. **Open:** All year. **Site Assignment:** First come, first served. **Registration:** At Quik-Pik Mini Mart. **Fee:** $12. **Parking:** At site.

FACILITIES
Number of RV Sites: 10. **Number of Tent-Only Sites:** 0. **Hookups:** Electric (20, 30 amp), water, sewer. **Each Site:** Gravel. **Dump Station:** Yes. **Laundry:** Yes. **Pay Phone:** Yes. **Rest Rooms and Showers:** Yes. **Fuel:** Yes. **Propane:** Yes. **Internal Roads:** Gravel, good. **RV Service:** No. **Market:** At Mini Mart (limited; Tonopah, 110 mi.). **Restaurant:** In Rachel. **General Store:** Yes. **Vending:** No. **Swimming:** No. **Playground:** No. **Activities:** UFO-watching. **Nearby Attractions:** Area 51. **Additional Information:** Little A'Le Inn, (702) 729-2515.

RESTRICTIONS
Pets: On leash under owner's control. **Fires:** No. **Alcoholic Beverages:** Allowed. **Vehicle Maximum Length:** Any size.

TO GET THERE
From triple junction of US Hwy. 93 and NV Hwys. 318 & 375, go west 36 mi. on NV Hwy. 375.

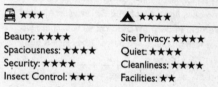

RED ROCK CANYON NATIONAL CONSERVATION AREA
13 Mile Campground

HCR 33 Box 5500, Las Vegas 89124. T: (702) 363-1921; www.redrockcanyon.blm.gov.

🚐 ★★★　　　　　　　Ⓐ ★★★★

Beauty: ★★★★　　　　Site Privacy: ★★★★
Spaciousness: ★★★★　　Quiet: ★★★★
Security: ★★★★　　　　Cleanliness: ★★★★
Insect Control: ★★★　　　Facilities: ★★

Watch for wildlife when driving Blue Diamond Road between Las Vegas and Red Rock Canyon, as cottontail rabbits, wild horses, and burros dart onto the highway in this National Conservation Area that is so incongruously close to the glitzy Vegas strip. During the sizzling summer months only about 25% of 13 Mile Campground's loops are open. Nevertheless, people come here to camp in the cool evening hours and leave to do their hiking by 6 a.m., before the desert temperatures once again soar. Tent campers will appreciate the 25 walk-in sites and the level gray gravel pads widely dispersed among the low desert scrub, though red-rock views are lacking. The Visitor Center has vending machines, a botanical display, and excellent exhibits explaining the shallow sea origins of nearby gypsum mines and how the area's stunning red rocks formed from 180-million-year-old iron oxide-tinged sand dunes.

BASICS
Operated By: BLM. **Open:** All year. **Site Assignment:** First come, first served; 5 group sites require advance reservation. **Registration:** Self-pay fee station. **Fee:** $10 (cash or check only). **Parking:** At site; parking area for walk-in sites.

FACILITIES

Number of RV Sites: 70. **Number of Tent-Only Sites:** 25. **Hookups:** None. **Each Site:** Table, grill, fire ring. **Dump Station:** No. **Laundry:** No. **Pay Phone:** No. **Rest Rooms and Showers:** No showers. **Fuel:** No. **Propane:** No. **Internal Roads:** Gravel, good. **RV Service:** No. **Market:** Las Vegas, 17 mi. **Restaurant:** Bonnie Springs, 7 mi. **General Store:** No. **Vending:** No. **Swimming:** No. **Playground:** No. **Other:** Visitor Center, gift shop. **Activities:** Horseback riding, biking, rock climbing. **Nearby Attractions:** Las Vegas casinos. **Additional Information:** Friends of Red Rock Canyon, (702) 255-8743.

RESTRICTIONS

Pets: On leash under owner's control. **Fires:** Yes (no open fires). **Alcoholic Beverages:** Allowed. **Vehicle Maximum Length:** 40 ft. **Other:** Do not feed or touch wild burros (they kick & bite).

TO GET THERE

From Las Vegas go 20 mi. west on NV Hwy. 159 (Blue Diamond Rd.).

SILVER SPRINGS

Fort Churchill State Historic Park

US Hwy. 50, Silver Springs 89429. T: (775) 577-2345; www.state.nv.us/stparks.

🚐 ★★★	⛺ ★★★★
Beauty: ★★★★	Site Privacy: ★★★★
Spaciousness: ★★★★	Quiet: ★★★★
Security: ★★★★	Cleanliness: ★★★★
Insect Control: ★★★★	Facilities: ★★★

After three white male kidnappers were killed and their outpost burned by local American Indians to free two of their girls held hostage, a volunteer group of white settlers declared all-out war and were routed near Pyramid Lake in 1860. Government troops were called in from California and Fort Churchill was constructed to guard the Pony Express and serve as a base for anti–American Indian expeditions. Fort Churchill was abandoned in 1869, and all that remains now are some old adobe ruins that can be explored, a cemetery, some relics, and an interpretive center. A scenic trail network connecting up with Lahontan State Recreation Area is an on-going state project. The campground at Fort Churchill, which is reached via a gravel road crossing a one-lane wood bridge, has large cottonwood trees shading widely dispersed campsites with good views of the surrounding low rolling hills and cattle grazing in pastures.

BASICS

Operated By: Nevada State Parks. **Open:** All year. **Site Assignment:** First come, first served; group reservation required. **Registration:** Self-pay fee station. **Fee:** $7 (cash or check only). **Parking:** At site.

FACILITIES

Number of RV Sites: 20. **Number of Tent-Only Sites:** 0. **Hookups:** None. **Each Site:** Table, fire ring. **Dump Station:** Yes. **Laundry:** No. **Pay Phone:** Yes. **Rest Rooms and Showers:** No showers. **Fuel:** No. **Propane:** No. **Internal Roads:** Gravel, good. **RV Service:** No. **Market:** Lahontan, 5 mi. **Restaurant:** Silver Springs, 9 mi. **General Store:** No. **Vending:** Yes. **Swimming:** No. **Playground:** No. **Other:** Museum, cemetery, wheelchair-accessible site. **Activities:** Boating, water sports, horseback riding, bird-watching, hunting. **Nearby Attractions:** Virginia City, Carson City, Reno. **Additional Information:** Lyon County Information Center, (775) 463-2246, www.tele-net.net/lyontour.

RESTRICTIONS

Pets: On leash. **Fires:** Yes (only in fire rings, bring own firewood or approved stove). **Alcoholic Beverages:** Allowed. **Vehicle Maximum Length:** 30 ft. **Other:** Do not climb on the ruins, 14-day stay limit.

TO GET THERE

From junction of US Hwys. 50 & Alt 95, go 8 mi. south on Alt 95 and 1 mi. west on Old Fort Churchill Rd.

SILVER SPRINGS

Lahontan State Recreation Area/ Silver Springs Beach

16799 Lahontan Dam, Fallon 89406. T: (775) 577-2226 or (775) 867-3500; www.state.nv.us/stparks.

🚐 ★★★　　　　　▲ ★★★★

Beauty: ★★★★
Spaciousness: ★★★★
Security: ★★★★
Insect Control: ★★★

Site Privacy: ★★★★
Quiet: ★★★★
Cleanliness: ★★★★
Facilities: ★★★

A 17-mile-long reservoir with 69 miles of shoreline, Lahontan State Recreation Area offers unlimited beach camping on the sand right up to the water's edge, and a small number of designated sites shaded by tall cottonwood trees. Beach 7 has designated campsites, some with lake views and a few large enough to accommodate any vehicle on the road. Large diesel trucks have camped here, and there is no limit on what can be driven onto the beaches. However, the undesignated beach camping sites have no facilities other than restrooms, not even shade. Just beyond Beach 7 the pavement ends and a sign says "Where the pavement ends and the fun begins," which is where a vendor offers horse rides across Lahontan's varied terrain. Additional designated campsites are available about 25 miles northeast on the Carson River near Lahontan Dam and the park headquarters in Fallon.

BASICS

Operated By: Nevada State Parks. **Open:** All year. **Site Assignment:** First come, first served. **Registration:** Entrance kiosk. **Fee:** $8 (V, MC). **Parking:** At site.

FACILITIES

Number of RV Sites: 29. **Number of Tent-Only Sites:** 0. **Hookups:** None. **Each Site:** Table, fire ring. **Dump Station:** Yes. **Laundry:** No. **Pay Phone:** Yes. **Rest Rooms and Showers:** Yes. **Fuel:** No. **Propane:** No. **Internal Roads:** Paved, excellent. **RV Service:** No. **Market:** Lahontan, 1 mi. **Restaurant:** Silver Springs, 5 mi. **General Store:** No. **Vending:** No. **Swimming:** Lake. **Playground:** No. **Other:** Boat launch, horseback ride vendor, wheelchair-accessible site. **Activities:** Boating, water sports, bird watching. **Nearby Attrac-**

tions: Virginia City, Carson City, Reno. **Additional Information:** Lahontan Trails (horse rides), (775) 577-4696.

RESTRICTIONS

Pets: On leash. **Fires:** Yes. **Alcoholic Beverages:** Allowed. **Vehicle Maximum Length:** No limit. **Other:** No ATVs.

TO GET THERE

From junction of US Hwys. 50 & Alt 95, go 4 mi south on US Hwy. Alt 95 and 1.5 mi. east on Fir St.

SPRING MOUNTAIN NATIONAL RECREATION AREA

Hilltop Campground

HCR 38, P.O. Box 451, Las Vegas 89124. T: (702) 872-0156 or (800) 328-6226 or (877) 444-6777 (Reserve America or reservations only); F: (702) 872-0018; www.thousandtrails.com.

🚐 ★　　　　　▲ ★★★★

Beauty: ★★★★★
Spaciousness: ★★
Security: ★★★★
Insect Control: ★★★★

Site Privacy: ★★★★★
Quiet: ★★★★★
Cleanliness: ★★★★
Facilities: ★

Midway between Lee Canyon and Kyle Canyon on a twisting mountain highway with gnarled bristlecone pines and spectacular views into distant canyons, Hilltop Campground is the most remote area campground and the only one with showers (coin-operated; often inoperative). The entrance from NV Hwy. 158 forks, with one road leading to Spring Mountain Youth Camp Correctional Facility and the adjacent Hilltop Exit sporting a warning sign for the tire shredders that will ruin the day of those entering the wrong way. Like Lee Canyon, 60% of the sites among the gnarled hillside pines here are reserved in advance on hot Vegas weekends. Sites have either forest views or views deep into the valleys below. Reserve sites 9–11,13,14, and 16–18 for the best valley views (not for those afraid of heights). Sites 25–30 (no reservations) are among the most private looking into the forest. Nearby Mahogany Grove has two group sites.

BASICS

Operated By: Thousand Trails Inc. **Open:** May 15– Oct. 15 (weather permitting). **Site Assignment:** First come, first served. **Registration:** Self-pay entrance fee station. **Fee:** $13 ($20 double sites; $30 triple sites). **Parking:** At site.

FACILITIES

Number of RV Sites: 35. **Number of Tent-Only Sites:** 0. **Hookups:** None. **Each Site:** Table, grill, fire ring. **Dump Station:** No. **Laundry:** No. **Pay Phone:** No. **Rest Rooms and Showers:** Yes. **Fuel:** No. **Propane:** No. **Internal Roads:** Paved, excellent condition. **RV Service:** No. **Market:** Las Vegas, 35 mi. **Restaurant:** Kyle Canyon, 6 mi. **General Store:** No. **Vending:** No. **Swimming:** No. **Playground:** No. **Other:** Tire shredders at exit. **Activities:** Archery range. **Nearby Attractions:** Mt. Charleston, Lee Canyon, Las Vegas. **Additional Information:** Humboldt Toiyabe National Forest, (702) 873-8800, www.fs.fed.us.htnf; Spring Mountains Assoc., (702) 896-7213.

RESTRICTIONS

Pets: On leash under owner's control. **Fires:** Yes. **Alcoholic Beverages:** Allowed. **Vehicle Maximum Length:** 25 ft. **Other:** No fireworks.

TO GET THERE

From junction of US Hwy. 95 & NV Hwy. 157 north of Las Vegas, go 17 mi. west on Hwy. 157 and then 6 mi. northwest on NV Hwy. 158.

SPRING MOUNTAIN NATIONAL RECREATION AREA
Kyle Canyon & Fletcher View Campgrounds

HCR 38, P.O. Box 451, Las Vegas 89124. T: (702) 872-0156 or (800) 328-6226 or (877) 444-6777 (Reserve America or reservations only); F: (702) 872-0018; www.thousandtrails.com.

🚐 ★★★★   ▲ ★★★★

Beauty: ★★★★   Site Privacy: ★★★★★
Spaciousness: ★★★★   Quiet: ★★★★
Security: ★★★★   Cleanliness: ★★★★
Insect Control: ★★★   Facilities: ★

Nestled alongside a dry creek bed with shady oaks and ponderosa pines, Kyle Canyon and Fletcher View Campgrounds are closer to Las Vegas than Hilltop, Dolomite, and McWilliams Campgrounds. All five campgrounds attract the same weekenders seeking to beat the Vegas summer heat by fleeing to the mountains. The dozen Fletcher View sites are very spread out, relatively spacious (most can squeeze in 36–40-foot vehicles) and cannot be reserved in advance. In contrast, 10 of the 25 Kyle Canyon sites, which are closer together, can be reserved, and often are booked up well in advance (beginning Friday night) on summer weekends. Picnics are also popular, and the Visitors Centers has hiking. Less than a mile down the road is Kyle Canyon RV Camp, which lacks toilets but can hold 15 self-contained vehicles as an overflow area or be reserved as a group area.

BASICS

Operated By: Thousand Trails Inc. **Open:** May–Sept. (weather permitting). **Site Assignment:** First come, first served; 60% of sites reservable. **Registration:** Self-pay entrance fee station. **Fee:** $13. **Parking:** At site.

FACILITIES

Number of RV Sites: 37. **Number of Tent-Only Sites:** 0. **Hookups:** None. **Each Site:** Table, grill, fire ring. **Dump Station:** No. **Laundry:** No. **Pay Phone:** Yes. **Rest Rooms and Showers:** No showers. **Fuel:** No. **Propane:** No. **Internal Roads:** Gravel, good. **RV Service:** No. **Market:** Las Vegas, 23 mi. **Restaurant:** Kyle Canyon. **General Store:** No. **Vending:** No. **Swimming:** No. **Playground:** No. **Other:** Wheelchair-accessible sites, hotel, picnic area. **Activities:** Hiking, winter sports. **Nearby Attractions:** Lee Canyon Ski Area, Mt. Charleston, Las Vegas. **Additional Information:** Humboldt Toiyabe National Forest, (702) 873-8800, www.fs.fed.us.htnf; Spring Mountains Assoc., (702) 896-7213.

RESTRICTIONS

Pets: On leash under owner's control. **Fires:** Yes. **Alcoholic Beverages:** Allowed. **Vehicle Maximum Length:** 36 ft.

TO GET THERE

From junction of US Hwy. 95 & NV Hwy. 157 north of Las Vegas, go 18 mi. west on Hwy. 157.

TONOPAH
The Station House

P.O. Box 1351, 1100 Erie St., Tonopah 89049. T: (775) 482-9777.

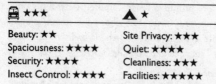

🚐 ★★★　　　　　　　▲ ★

Beauty: ★★	Site Privacy: ★★★
Spaciousness: ★★★★	Quiet: ★★★★
Security: ★★★★	Cleanliness: ★★★
Insect Control: ★★★★	Facilities: ★★★★★

Halfway between Las Vegas and Reno, Tonopah is a boom-and-bust mining town (the copper mine is currently going bust and buildings are getting boarded up) best known for its Air Force testing range where the F-117A Blackhawk stealth fighter was secretly test flown on moonless nights. The Station House is a friendly small town Old West casino complex where the back of the small rear parking lot has back-in spaces with hookups. There is some competition from the Bang Club Casino down the street, where the sign on the adjacent gravel lot invites self-contained RVs and trucks to park for free. But with the exception of the funky Twister trailer park, these are the only hookups in town and for 93 miles. In winter people even pitch their tents on the asphalt, plug in their heaters and use the facilities. The casino's Old West facade helps mitigate the asphalt ambiance.

BASICS

Operated By: The Station House. **Open:** All year. **Site Assignment:** First come, first served; reservations advised for special-event weekends. **Registration:** At hotel desk inside casino. **Fee:** $16.08 (V, MC, AE, D, DC). **Parking:** At site.

FACILITIES

Number of RV Sites: 18. **Number of Tent-Only Sites:** 0. **Hookups:** Electric (20, 30 amp), water, sewer. **Each Site:** Blacktop space. **Dump Station:** Yes. **Laundry:** Yes. **Pay Phone:** Yes. **Rest Rooms and Showers:** Yes. **Fuel:** Yes (nearby). **Propane:** No. **Internal Roads:** Paved, good. **RV Service:** No. **Market:** On the property. **Restaurant:** In casino. **General Store:** Yes. **Vending:** Yes. **Swimming:** No. **Playground:** Yes. **Other:** 24-hour casino, slot machine museum, clothing store, wheelchair accessible. **Activities:** Gambling, video arcade for kids, Tues.–Sun. live band, Monday night

big-screen footbal. **Nearby Attractions:** Tonopah Historic Mining Park, Central Nevada Museum. **Additional Information:** Tonopah Chamber of Commerce, (775) 482-3859.

RESTRICTIONS

Pets: On leash under owner's control; not allowed in hotel. **Fires:** No. **Alcoholic Beverages:** Allowed. **Vehicle Maximum Length:** 44 ft. **Other:** All spots are back-in.

TO GET THERE

Go 0.25 mi. south on US Hwy. 95 from the junction of US Hwys. 95 & 6.

URSINE
Spring Valley State Park

Star Rte. Box 201, Pioche 89043. T: (775) 962-5102; www.state.nv.us/stparks.

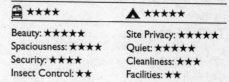

🚐 ★★★★　　　　　　▲ ★★★★★

Beauty: ★★★★★	Site Privacy: ★★★★★
Spaciousness: ★★★★	Quiet: ★★★★★
Security: ★★★★	Cleanliness: ★★★
Insect Control: ★★	Facilities: ★★

Horsethief Gulch Campground is the most developed of Spring Valley State Park's two campgrounds, with 36 sites just west of Eagle Valley Reservoir where paved NV Hwy. 322 ends after winding through several miles of tall gray spires reminiscent of Great Basin National Park to the north. Two miles north of Horsethief Gulch via a dirt road is the primitive six-site Ranch Campground (tables, grills, restroom). Many RVs skip the park fees altogether and park on nearby BLM land (a big turnout loop just before the paved road ends), mooching free showers at the park while swimming, fishing, and boating at the reservoir. The upper loop at Horsethief Gulch has a large pull-through site and is particularly private thanks to many large junipers (a source of rot resistant wood in NV's early days) growing amongst the singleleaf pinons (edible nuts), big sagebrush (state flower), and rubber rabbitbrush (winter jackrabbit food).

BASICS

Operated By: Nevada State Parks. **Open:** All year. **Site Assignment:** First come, first served; group site reservations. **Registration:** Self-pay entrance fee station. **Fee:** $12. **Parking:** At site.

FACILITIES

Number of RV Sites: 42. **Number of Tent-Only Sites:** 0. **Hookups:** None. **Each Site:** Sheltered table, grill, fire ring. **Dump Station:** Yes. **Laundry:** No. **Pay Phone:** Yes. **Rest Rooms and Showers:** Yes. **Fuel:** No. **Propane:** No. **Internal Roads:** Gravel, good. **RV Service:** No. **Market:** Pioche, 18 mi. **Restaurant:** Pioche, 18 mi. **General Store:** No. **Vending:** No. **Swimming:** In reservoir at own risk. **Playground:** No. **Other:** Boat launch, fish cleaning station, 2 wheelchair-accessible sites. **Activities:** Boating, fishing. **Nearby Attractions:** Pioche, Echo Canyon, Cathedral Gorge. **Additional Information:** Pioche Chamber of Commerce, (775) 962-5544.

RESTRICTIONS

Pets: On leash under owner's control. **Fires:** Yes. **Alcoholic Beverages:** Allowed. **Vehicle Maximum Length:** 40 ft. **Other:** Firewood collection prohibited.

TO GET THERE

From Pioche, go 18 mi. northeast on NV Hwy. 322 through the town of Ursine until the paved road ends.

WALKER LAKE

Sportsman's Beach Recreation Site

1535 Hot Springs Rd., Suite 330, Carson City 89706. T: (775) 885-6000; www.blm.gov.

🚐 ★★★	🏕 ★★★
Beauty: ★★★★★	Site Privacy: ★★★★
Spaciousness: ★★★★	Quiet: ★★★
Security: ★★	Cleanliness: ★★★
Insect Control: ★★★	Facilities: ★★

One of Nevada's few natural desert freshwater lakes, Walker Lake's wave-cut shoreline has been steadily shrinking for several thousand years since the climate began warming at the end of the last Ice Age. Closest to the roadside at Sportsman's Beach are 16 lake-view campsites with sheltered tables on cement pads. Switchbacks wend down to campsites even closer to the lake. The cluster of campsites numbered 17–21 just above the boat ramp have the most vehicle parking, and small stake-like signs documenting lake water levels indicate that this area was underwater in the 1940s. Sites 22–32 have narrow circular pull-through areas capable of accommodating boats and narrow vehicles well over 30 feet in length. More primitive beach camping (restrooms only; bring your own tables, chairs and stoves) is available less than a mile north via badly rutted roads at Tamarack and 20 Mile Beaches.

BASICS

Operated By: BLM. **Open:** All year. **Site Assignment:** First come, first served. **Registration:** Self-pay fee station. **Fee:** $4–$6 ($4 primitive sites; $6 developed sites; cash or check only). **Parking:** At site.

FACILITIES

Number of RV Sites: 34. **Number of Tent-Only Sites:** 0. **Hookups:** None. **Each Site:** Sheltered table, fire ring. **Dump Station:** Yes. **Laundry:** No. **Pay Phone:** No. **Rest Rooms and Showers:** No showers. **Fuel:** No. **Propane:** No. **Internal Roads:** Paved road needing patching turns to gravel. **RV Service:** No. **Market:** Hawthorne, 12.5 mi. south. **Restaurant:** Paiute reservation truck stop, 5 mi. north. **General Store:** No. **Vending:** No. **Swimming:** In lake at own risk. **Playground:** No. **Other:** Boat ramp. **Activities:** Boating, fishing, bird-watching. **Nearby Attractions:** Ghost towns. **Additional Information:** Mineral County Chamber of Commerce, (775) 945-5896.

RESTRICTIONS

Pets: On leash. **Fires:** Yes (only in fire ring). **Alcoholic Beverages:** Allowed. **Vehicle Maximum Length:** 28 ft. **Other:** 14 day limit.

TO GET THERE

From Hawthorne, go 12.5 mi. north on US Hwy. 95.

WINNEMUCCA

Hi-Desert RV Park

5575 East Winnemucca Blvd., Winnemucca 89455. T: (775) 623-4513 or (800) 699-3959; F: (775) 625-4329; www.hi-desertrv.com; Camp@hi-desertrv.com.

🚐 ★★★★   ⛺ ★★★★

Beauty: ★★★★   Site Privacy: ★★★★
Spaciousness: ★★★★   Quiet: ★★★★
Security: ★★★★   Cleanliness: ★★★★
Insect Control: ★★★★   Facilities: ★★★★

Winnemucca is a good stopping place between Reno and Salt Lake City or Boise, and Hi-Desert is an attractive alternative to the casino parking lots. Poplar and walnut trees provide shade, grassy strips separate each site, and attractive white-bulb fixtures sit atop black lamp poles. The highway is nearby, but the rustling of tree leaves in the wind helps muffle the occasional motorcycle or truck at this well-maintained park. The tent area is grass, and conveniently located near the store and pool. The gift shop has an interesting selection of knives sheathed in python, alligator, and rattlesnake skin cases, plus gambling machines to satisfy casino urges. Heading east there is not another good RV park until Elko, as Battle Mountain has been suffering from low gold prices and the miners living in the RV Parks there have moved on.

BASICS

Operated By: Connie Sasser. **Open:** All year. **Site Assignment:** First come, first served; reservations advised May–Aug. **Registration:** Office. **Fee:** $16 tent; $22.50 RV (V, MC, AE, D. **Parking:** At site.

FACILITIES

Number of RV Sites: 137. **Number of Tent-Only Sites:** 11. **Hookups:** Electric (20, 30, 50 amp), water, sewer, cable TV. **Each Site:** Table. **Dump Station:** Yes. **Laundry:** Yes. **Pay Phone:** Yes. **Rest Rooms and Showers:** Yes. **Fuel:** No. **Propane:** Yes. **Internal Roads:** Paved, good. **RV Service:** No. **Market:** Winnemucca, 2 mi. **Restaurant:** Winnemucca, 0.3 mi. **General Store:** Yes. **Vending:** Yes. **Swimming:** Pool. **Playground:** Yes. **Other:** Grills in tent area, dog walk, free shuttle to town, whirlpool, tetherball, volleyball, horseshoes. **Activities:** Golf, bowling, gambling, hunting, fishing, biking. **Nearby Attractions:** Buckaroo Hall of Fame, Paradise Valley. **Additional Information:** Winnemucca Convention Center, (775) 623-5071, (800) 962-2638, www.winnemucca.com.

RESTRICTIONS

Pets: On leash under owner's control. **Fires:** Yes (no open fires, only in grills). **Alcoholic Beverages:** Allowed. **Vehicle Maximum Length:** 61 ft. **Other:** Children must be under adult supervision & in campsites by 10 p.m.

TO GET THERE

From US I-80, take Exit 180 west 0.8 mi.

Utah

Utah is a land of high deserts, sagebrush, mountains, mesas, canyons, weathered red-orange Navajo sandstone formations, ancient Native American rock art and ruins, internationally famous national parks, lesser-known but no less interesting state parks, Olympic ski slopes, river rafting, and enough lakes and reservoirs to make boating and fishing part of the campground experience. Southeast Utah is one of the more popular destinations, being home to **Monument Valley, Natural Bridges** and **Hovenweep National Monuments, Arches** and **Canyonlands National Parks,** the **Halls Crossing** and **Bullfrog Marina** portions of **Lake Powell,** and river rafting on the **Colorado, San Juan,** and **Green Rivers.**

River rafting, mountain biking, backpacking, and four-wheel drive and jeep explorations are popular ways of getting beyond the campground for better views of the desert washes, slickrock benches, canyons, flattop mesas, buttes, eroded spires, hoodoos, entrenched meanders, and balanced rocks beyond pavement's end. Indeed, campgrounds barely scratch the surface of **Grand-Staircase Escalante National Monument's** 1.7 million acres. But make adequate preparations and take sensible precautions, as this is a land of summer flash floods, rattlesnakes, and long distances between gas stations and fresh water.

Zion and **Bryce Canyon National Parks** in southwestern Utah are among the most popular national parks in the United States, though the red sandstone monoliths and pioneer fruit orchards of **Capitol Reef** are also spectacular. Don't overlook the sometimes spectacular scenery of lesser-known campgrounds like **Cedar Breaks National Monument,** which is like a smaller, higher-elevation version of Bryce Canyon's multi-colored sandstone amphitheaters. Similarly, little-known **Kodachrome Basin, Coral Pink Sand Dunes,** and **Goblin Valley State Parks** are among the many geologically spectacular Utah State Park camping experiences.

Utah's many lakes and reservoirs are popular with locals for boating and fishing, and summer and holiday weekends fill to capacity. But weekdays and before Memorial Day and after Labor Day it is often possible to find some solitude. Near Salt Lake City are many campground escapes, including **Antelope Island State Park** in the middle of the Great Salt Lake and **Wasatch Mountain State Park** closer to the Olympic winter sports venues. Call ahead to the parks and get reservations where available or plan to arrive early ahead of the crowds. Also, take advantage of the many excellent commercial campgrounds just outside the park boundaries.

The following facilities accept payment in checks or cash only:

Antelope Island State Park, Syracuse

Bullfrog Resort & Marina Campground/ RV Park, Lake Powell

Calf Creek Campground, Escalante

Cedar Canyon Campground, Cedar City

Dead Horse Point State Park, Moab

Devil's Canyon, Blanding

Devil's Garden Campground, Arches National Park

Duck Creek Campground, Cedar City

Escalante State Park, Escalante

Fruita Campground, Torrey

Goosenecks State Park, Mexican Hat

Green River State Park, Green River

Halls Crossing RV Park/Campground, Lake Powell

Hovenweep Campground, Hovenweep National Monument

Kodachrome Basin State Park, Cannonville

Minersville State Park, Beaver

Mitten View Campground, Monument Valley

Natural Bridges, Natural Bridges National Monument

North Campground, Bryce Canyon

Oasis Campground, Yuba State Park

Point Supreme Campground, Cedar Breaks National Monument

Ponderosa Grove Recreation Site, Kanab

Quail Creek State Park, St. George

Red Canyon Campground, Bryce Canyon

Red Cliffs Recreation Site, Leeds

Rendezvous Beach, Bear Lake State Park

Snow Canyon State Park, St. George

South & Watchman Campgrounds, Zion National Park

Squaw Flat Campground, Canyonlands National Park Needles District

Sunset Campground, Bryce Canyon

Virgin River Canyon Recreation Area, Littlefield

Virgin River Canyon Recreation Area, Littlefield

White Bridge Campground, Panguitch Lake

Willow Flat Campground, Canyonlands National Park Island in the Sky District

The following facilities feature 50 sites or fewer:

Calf Creek Campground, Escalante

Cedar Canyon Campground, Cedar City

Goosenecks State Park, Mexican Hat

Natural Bridges, Natural Bridges National Monument

Oasis Campground, Yuba State Park

Ponderosa Grove Recreation Site, Kanab

Red Cliffs Recreation Site, Leeds

Willow Flat Campground, Canyonlands National Park Island in the Sky District

ARCHES NATIONAL PARK
Devil's Garden Campground

P.O. Box 907, Moab 84532. T: (435) 719-2299; www.nps.gov/arch.

🚐 ★★★★   ⛺ ★★★★★

Beauty: ★★★★★   Site Privacy: ★★★★★
Spaciousness: ★★★★   Quiet: ★★★★
Security: ★★★★   Cleanliness: ★★★★★
Insect Control: ★★★   Facilities: ★★

Arches National Park, where disabled Civil War veteran John Wesley Wolfe and son Fred once lived a solitary log-cabin life, grazing cattle and sheep, now gets a million visitors a year. But Devil's Garden is like paradise to self-sufficient campers eschewing the showers, shops, and amenities of Moab to show up early in the morning and snag a campsite among the sandstone fins and balanced rocks. Park parking spaces become maddeningly scarce on busy holiday weekends, but campground denizens have solar powered restrooms and their own trailheads to Broken Arch and Sand Dune Arch. Many campsites have 50-foot-long pads, though most are 12-foot-wide back-ins (some 25-foot-long sites are 20-feet wide) tucked in amongst Navajo sandstone formations and flanked with junipers, pines, and desert scrub. This is as close as it gets outside the backcountry to having a private vista of this 2,000-arch park.

BASICS

Operated By: National Park Service. **Open:** All year. **Site Assignment:** First come, first served; group site reservations. **Registration:** Self-pay fee station. **Fee:** $10 (cash or check only). **Parking:** At site.

FACILITIES

Number of RV Sites: 50. **Number of Tent-Only Sites:** 0. **Hookups:** None. **Each Site:** Table, grill. **Dump Station:** No. **Laundry:** No. **Pay Phone:** Yes. **Rest Rooms and Showers:** No showers. **Fuel:** No. **Propane:** No. **Internal Roads:** Paved, good. **RV Service:** No. **Market:** Moab, 23 mi. **Restaurant:** Moab, 23 mi. **General Store:** No. **Vending:** No. **Swimming:** No. **Playground:** No. **Other:** Amphitheater, 1 wheelchair-accessible site. **Activities:** Evening ranger programs. **Nearby Attractions:** Canyonlands,

Moab. **Additional Information:** Canyonlands Natural History Assoc., (435) 259-6003, www.cnha.org; Grand County Travel Council, (800) 635-MOAB.

RESTRICTIONS

Pets: On leash under owner's control. **Fires:** Yes (in grills only, no collecting firewood). **Alcoholic Beverages:** Allowed. **Vehicle Maximum Length:** 50 ft. **Other:** 7-day max. stay, no feeding wildlife.

TO GET THERE

From Moab go 5 mi. north on US Hwy. 191, then follow park entrance road 18 mi. north.

BEAR LAKE STATE PARK
Rendezvous Beach

P.O. Box 184, Garden City 84028. T: (435) 946-3343 or (800) 322-3770 (reservations); www.nr.state.ut.us/www1/bear.htm; nrdpr.brsp@state.ut.us.

🚐 ★★★★★   ⛺ ★★★★

Beauty: ★★★★   Site Privacy: ★★★★
Spaciousness: ★★★★   Quiet: ★★★★
Security: ★★★★   Cleanliness: ★★★★
Insect Control: ★★★   Facilities: ★★★

A 28,000 year old earthquake-created freshwater lake with warm summer waters (60–70° F June–July) and 120 miles of groomed snowmobile trails in winter, Bear Lake is ringed with camping sites (mostly primitive) on both the Utah and Idaho sides. But Rendezvous Beach contains the best collection of developed campgrounds. Odd-numbered (except 29) Willow Campground tent sites are beachfront, and even-numbered sites are in deep vegetation on the opposite side of what is essentially a paved vehicle parking lot. Cottonwood Campground tent sites 5–42 are beachfront. Birch Campground has 60 50-amp sites, with 16, 18, 27, 28, 30, 38, 39, 48, 49, and 51 being the beachfront best. At Big Creek, an older (20, 30 amp) RV campground, sites 15–33 and 35–38 are beachfront. RV sites are quieter than tent sites, which get group party action on weekends and holidays, when those without reservations get shunted to more primitive and rockier East Side beaches (only South Eden has drinking water: 14 reservable sites; $7).

BASICS

Operated By: Utah State Parks & Recreation. **Open:** All year (no water or sewer after Nov., but electricity stays on in winter). **Site Assignment:** First come, first served; reservations highly recommended Memorial Day to Labor Day. **Registration:** Entrance kiosk (rangers collect fees in winter). **Fee:** $15 tent; $19 RV ($6.25 reservation fee). **Parking:** At site.

FACILITIES

Number of RV Sites: 106. **Number of Tent-Only Sites:** 75. **Hookups:** Electric (20, 30, 50 amp), water, sewer. **Each Site:** Table, fire ring. **Dump Station:** Yes. **Laundry:** No. **Pay Phone:** Yes. **Rest Rooms and Showers:** Yes. **Fuel:** No. **Propane:** No. **Internal Roads:** Paved, excellent. **RV Service:** No. **Market:** Logan, 50 mi. **Restaurant:** Garden City, 6 mi. **General Store:** No. **Vending:** Yes. **Swimming:** Lake. **Playground:** No. **Other:** Birch sites have sheltered table on cement pad, marina, boat & slip rentals. **Activities:** ATV (surrounding national forest), fishing, boating, water sports, winter sports. **Nearby Attractions:** Logan, Ogden. **Additional Information:** Rich County, (435) 793-2415.

RESTRICTIONS

Pets: On leash under owner's control. **Fires:** Yes. **Alcoholic Beverages:** Allowed. **Vehicle Maximum Length:** No limits. **Other:** Gates close 10 p.m. to 6 a.m. in summer.

TO GET THERE

From Laketown, go 2 mi. north on UT Hwy. 30.

BEAVER
Minersville State Park

P.O. Box 1531, Beaver 84713. T: (435) 438-5472; www.nr.state.ut.us.

🚐 ★★★★	⛺ ★★★★★
Beauty: ★★★★	Site Privacy: ★★★
Spaciousness: ★★★	Quiet: ★★★★★
Security: ★★★★	Cleanliness: ★★★★
Insect Control: ★★★★	Facilities: ★★

Known for trophy rainbow and cutthroat trout that fatten up on crayfish and shrimp, Minersville is also popular for its hookups. But the lake, which holds water for downstream irrigation and freezes in cold weather, has a limit of one 20-inch trout that must be caught using only artificial lures and flies. Bicyclists from around the world brave strong winds to stop at this jewel in the sagebrush desert for the gravel campsites backed by grass strips. Tent pad users can tap into the 20-amp outlets (30-amp outlets are kept for RVs). Rock hounds hunt top-grade obsidian, chalcedony, and agates in the surrounding region. Bird-watchers flock for waterfowl like white-faced ibis, great blue herons, white pelicans, western grebes, and double-crested cormorants. Cottonwood, willow, elm, mulberry, and Russian olive trees provide shade. There are also three narrow (12 feet) wheelchair-accessible sites and a large gravel overflow area.

BASICS

Operated By: Utah State Parks & Recreation. **Open:** All year (Apr.–Nov. 1 full services, depending upon weather). **Site Assignment:** First come, first served. **Registration:** Self-pay fee station. **Fee:** $14 (cash or check only). **Parking:** At site.

FACILITIES

Number of RV Sites: 29. **Number of Tent-Only Sites:** 0. **Hookups:** Electric (20, 30 amp), water. **Each Site:** Sheltered table, grill. **Dump Station:** Yes. **Laundry:** No. **Pay Phone:** Yes. **Rest Rooms and Showers:** Yes. **Fuel:** No. **Propane:** No. **Internal Roads:** Gravel, good. **RV Service:** No. **Market:** Beaver, 12 mi. **Restaurant:** Beaver, 12 mi. **General Store:** No. **Vending:** No. **Swimming:** In lake at own risk. **Playground:** No. **Other:** Boat ramp, horseshoes, volleyball, air compressor, 3 wheelchair-accessible sites. **Activities:** Boating, water sports, fishing, biking, bird-watching, rock hounding, golf. **Nearby Attractions:** Fishlake National Forest. **Additional Information:** Beaver County Travel Council, (435) 438-2975.

RESTRICTIONS

Pets: On leash (keep out of grass). **Fires:** Yes (in grills only, firewood available). **Alcoholic Beverages:** Allowed. **Vehicle Maximum Length:** 40 ft. **Other:** No boats inside campground, Jan. 1–May 28 no fishing (certain years).

TO GET THERE

From Beaver go 12 mi. southwest on UT Hwy. 21.

BEAVER

United Beaver Campground

P.O. Box 1060, Beaver 84713. T: (435) 438-2808.

🚐 ★★★★   ⛺ ★★★

Beauty: ★★★★	Site Privacy: ★★★
Spaciousness: ★★★★	Quiet: ★★★★
Security: ★★★★	Cleanliness: ★★★★
Insect Control: ★★★★	Facilities: ★★★★

Situated at the gateway to Fishlake National Forest, which has a number of small high-elevation (5,900 to 9,300 feet) summer campgrounds, United Beaver is top-notch, one of the few area campgrounds open year-round with long level pull-through sites and hookups. United Beaver is also a good stopping place on the way to Great Basin National Park in Nevada, Salt Lake City, and southern destinations like the Grand Canyon and Las Vegas. Beaver is a relaxed and friendly travel stop (e.g. RV repair facilities) with two Mexican restaurants, including Kan-Kun just opposite the campground. There are grass strips between RV sites at this campground conveniently located near a highway exit at the south end of town. United Beaver is relatively quiet, with the wind blowing in the trees and chirping birds being louder than the highway. All in all, United Beaver is a friendly place where people are on a first-name basis and helpfulness prevails.

BASICS

Operated By: Mary (would not give last name). **Open:** All year. **Site Assignment:** First come, first served. **Registration:** Office. **Fee:** $10.50–$13 tent, $15–$18 RV. **Parking:** At site.

FACILITIES

Number of RV Sites: 90. **Number of Tent-Only Sites:** Undesignated sites. **Hookups:** Electric (20, 30, 50), water, sewer. **Each Site:** Table, grill. **Dump Station:** Yes. **Laundry:** Yes. **Pay Phone:** Yes. **Rest Rooms and Showers:** Yes. **Fuel:** No. **Propane:** Yes. **Internal Roads:** Gravel, good. **RV Service:** No. **Market:** Beaver, 1 mi. **Restaurant:** Beaver, across road. **General Store:** Yes. **Vending:** Yes. **Swimming:** Pool. **Playground:** Yes. **Other:** Game room, dog run, horseshoes, Dutch oven pit in tent area. **Activities:** Golf, horseshoes, volleyball, fishing, boating, hunting, skiing, winter sports. **Nearby Attractions:** Cedar Breaks, Bryce, Paiute ATV Trail. **Additional Information:** Cedar City

Ranger District, (435) 865-3200; Beaver County Travel Council, (435) 438-2975, (800) 280-2975.

RESTRICTIONS

Pets: On leash. **Fires:** Yes. **Alcoholic Beverages:** Allowed. **Vehicle Maximum Length:** 70 ft. **Other:** No parking or carpets on grass.

TO GET THERE

From US I-15 get off at Exit 109.

BLANDING

Devil's Canyon

c/o Monticello Ranger District, 496 East Central, P.O. Box 820, Monticello 84535. T: (435) 587-2041 or (877) 446-6777 (reservations).

🚐 ★★   ⛺ ★★★★★

Beauty: ★★★★★	Site Privacy: ★★★★★
Spaciousness: ★★★	Quiet: ★★★★
Security: ★★★★	Cleanliness: ★★★★★
Insect Control: ★★★	Facilities: ★

Located in the Manti-Lasal National Forest, Devil's Canyon is a US Forest Service campground operated under permit by a private concessionaire, United Land Management (P.O. Box 970099, Orem, UT 84097). Reservations are usually not necessary, but may be a good idea during peak seasons, particularly when special events come to the area and all the campgrounds in Moab, Green River, and the surrounding environs book full. If hookups and all the amenities are a prerequisite, the numerous commercial roadside RV campgrounds between Mexican Hat and Green River are a better choice. But if the feeling of camping in the forest is paramount, then Devil's Canyon offers self-sufficient campers a good location for exploring Hovenweep, Natural Bridges, the Needles District of Canyonlands, and even Arches. Sites 9 and 10 are best for big RVs. For the most seclusion and privacy among the tall junipers and ponderosa pines choose sites 1–7.

BASICS

Operated By: United Land Management. **Open:** May–Oct. **Site Assignment:** First come, first served; reservations accepted. **Registration:** Self-pay fee station. **Fee:** $10 (cash or check only). **Parking:** At site.

FACILITIES

Number of RV Sites: 33. **Number of Tent-Only Sites:** 0. **Hookups:** None. **Each Site:** Table, fire pit. **Dump Station:** No. **Laundry:** No. **Pay Phone:** No. **Rest Rooms and Showers:** No showers. **Fuel:** No. **Propane:** No. **Internal Roads:** Paved, rutted. **RV Service:** No. **Market:** Blanding, 10 mi. **Restaurant:** Blanding, 10 mi. **General Store:** No. **Vending:** No. **Swimming:** No. **Playground:** No. **Activities:** Hiking trails. **Nearby Attractions:** Natural Bridges, Hovenweep, Canyonlands. **Additional Information:** San Juan County Visitor Services, (435) 587-3235, (800) 574-4386.

RESTRICTIONS

Pets: On leash. **Fires:** Yes. **Alcoholic Beverages:** Allowed. **Vehicle Maximum Length:** 35 ft. **Other:** Protect food from bears, no fireworks.

TO GET THERE

From Blanding go 9.5 mi. northeast on US Hwy. 191.

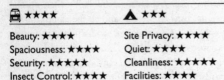

BLUFF
Cadillac Ranch RV Park

Hwy. 191, P.O. Box 157, Bluff 84512. T: (435) 672-2262 or (800) 538-6195; F: (435) 672-2417; www.bluffutah.org; ranch@sanjuan.net.

🚐 ★★★★	⛺ ★★★
Beauty: ★★★★	Site Privacy: ★★★★
Spaciousness: ★★★★	Quiet: ★★★★
Security: ★★★★★	Cleanliness: ★★★★★
Insect Control: ★★★★	Facilities: ★★★★

A good overnight stopping place south of Moab and north of Monument Valley and Kayenta, AZ, Bluff and Cadillac Ranch also make a good base for exploring this part of southeastern Utah. Cadillac Ranch is a homey little campground with 30-foot-wide RV spaces where deer and wild turkey wander in and out on their own schedules. The atmosphere is friendly, and TV antennas pick up six channels. In the evening people sit and talk while having a drink on the office verandah overlooking the pond. The pond is available for free fishing (bass, bluegill, catfish, trout) and paddle boating, or just watching aquatic waterfowl like ducks, geese, ibis, cranes, and blue herons. The tent sites are especially attractive, being on the opposite side of the pond

from the RVs, though sometimes Europeans pack their tents tightly on the lawns around the office when the official tent sites are all taken.

BASICS

Operated By: Rayma Percell. **Open:** All year. **Site Assignment:** First come, first served. **Registration:** Office. **Fee:** $16 (V, MC, D). **Parking:** At site.

FACILITIES

Number of RV Sites: 20. **Number of Tent-Only Sites:** 10. **Hookups:** Electric (30, 50 amp), water, sewer, phone (modem). **Each Site:** Table, grill. **Dump Station:** Yes. **Laundry:** No. **Pay Phone:** Yes. **Rest Rooms and Showers:** Yes. **Fuel:** No. **Propane:** No. **Internal Roads:** Gravel, good. **RV Service:** No. **Market:** Bluff, less than 1 mi. **Restaurant:** Bluff, less than 1 mi. **General Store:** No. **Vending:** Yes. **Swimming:** Pool. **Playground:** No. **Other:** Paddleboats. **Activities:** Horseback riding, horseshoes, volleyball, pond fishing. **Nearby Attractions:** Valley of the Gods, Monument Valley, Natural Bridges, Hovenweep, Lake Powell. **Additional Information:** San Juan County Visitor Services, (435) 587-3235, (800) 574-4386.

RESTRICTIONS

Pets: On leash under owner's control. **Fires:** Yes (firewood supplied gratis). **Alcoholic Beverages:** Allowed. **Vehicle Maximum Length:** 40 ft. **Other:** Don't let children throw or roll rocks.

TO GET THERE

On US Hwy. 191 in town.

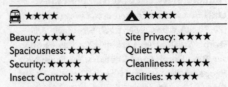

BRYCE CANYON
Bryce Canyon Pines

P.O. Box 43, Hwy. 12, Bryce 84764. T: (800) 892-7923 or (801) 834-5441; F: (801) 834-5330.

🚐 ★★★★	⛺ ★★★★
Beauty: ★★★★	Site Privacy: ★★★★
Spaciousness: ★★★★	Quiet: ★★★★
Security: ★★★★	Cleanliness: ★★★★
Insect Control: ★★★★	Facilities: ★★★★

A convenient campground for excursions into Bryce National Park (just six miles away) and Red Canyon, Bryce Canyon Pines has ample amenities and is nicely setback from the highway. The campground itself is intimate, like being in a small pine forest bisected by gravel roads. Little patches of meadow between campsites add to the rustic feel. Occasional power outages from the area's high winds are a nuisance that comes with the territory. A heated pool (at the motel, but available to campers), a restaurant, gas pumps (fill up when the power grid is working, because they are electronic) and a well-stocked store with a pool table add up to ample comforts without the crush of the crowds and tour buses at the nearby national park. In short, being outside of Bryce and away from the summer crowds is a good reason to put down here for the night.

BASICS

Operated By: Kenny & Randy Miller. **Open:** April 1–Oct. 31. **Site Assignment:** First come, first served; reservations accepted. **Registration:** In store. **Fee:** $16 tent, $22 RV (V, MC, AE, D). **Parking:** At site.

FACILITIES

Number of RV Sites: 24. **Number of Tent-Only Sites:** 15. **Hookups:** Electric (30 amp), water, sewer, phone (modem, Internet access). **Each Site:** Table. **Dump Station:** Yes. **Laundry:** Yes. **Pay Phone:** Yes. **Rest Rooms and Showers:** Yes. **Fuel:** Yes. **Propane:** No. **Internal Roads:** Gravel, good condition. **RV Service:** No. **Market:** Part of country store. **Restaurant:** At motel. **General Store:** Yes. **Vending:** Yes. **Swimming:** Heated pool in motel. **Playground:** No. **Other:** Portable grills on request. **Activities:** Horseback riding, horseshoes, game room (TV, pool table). **Nearby Attractions:** Red Canyon, Bryce. **Additional Information:** Bryce Canyon National Park, (435) 834-5322.

RESTRICTIONS

Pets: Small pets on leash. **Fires:** Yes (firewood sold). **Alcoholic Beverages:** Allowed. **Vehicle Maximum Length:** Not limited. **Other:** 11 a.m. checkout.

TO GET THERE

Go 4 mi. west on UT Hwy. 12 from the UT Hwy. 63 junction.

BRYCE CANYON
North Campground

P.O. Box 170001, Bryce Canyon 84717. T: (435) 834-5322/4801; www.nps.gov/brca.

🚐 ★★★   ⛺ ★★★★★

Beauty: ★★★★	Site Privacy: ★★★★
Spaciousness: ★★★★	Quiet: ★★★★
Security: ★★★★	Cleanliness: ★★★★
Insect Control: ★★★	Facilities: ★★

North Campground is in a ponderosa pine forest with pink cliffs and hoodoos at 8,000 feet elevation, where winter comes early and spring late. The primitive feel is reinforced by placement of facilities like showers a short walk outside the campground. Campsites are spread out on a tiered hillside in four loops, all of which fill up on summer weekends. Loop A is lowest, and Loop D is highest in elevation and most private. Loops A and B nearest the entrance allow only vehicles 20 feet and longer, and hum with the noise of generators from 8 a.m. to 8 p.m. Loop C bans generators. Loop D bans generators and vehicles over 20 feet, making it a haven for tent campers. The site is windy, but the cool breezes are welcomed in summer. Though the tendency is to seek shady sites, summer tent campers should opt for sunny sites so tents can dry off from thunderstorms.

BASICS

Operated By: National Park Service. **Open:** All year (Loop A only). **Site Assignment:** First come, first served. **Registration:** Self-pay entrance fee station. **Fee:** $10. **Parking:** At site.

FACILITIES

Number of RV Sites: 107. **Number of Tent-Only Sites:** 0. **Hookups:** None. **Each Site:** Table, fire pit. **Dump Station:** Yes. **Laundry:** No. **Pay Phone:** Yes. **Rest Rooms and Showers:** Yes. **Fuel:** No. **Propane:** No. **Internal Roads:** Paved, rough in spots. **RV Service:** No. **Market:** At Ruby's. **Restaurant:** At Ruby's or lodge, within 2 mi. **General Store:** No. **Vending:** No. **Swimming:** No. **Playground:** No. **Activities:** Horseback riding, ranger interpretative programs. **Nearby Attractions:** Kodachrome Basin, Red Canyon. **Additional Information:** National Park Service, www.nps.gov/brca.

RESTRICTIONS

Pets: On leash; not allowed outside campgrounds, parking lots. **Fires:** Yes. **Alcoholic Beverages:** Allowed. **Vehicle Maximum Length:** No limits, but over 40 ft. is hard to maneuver. **Other:** 15 mph speed limit enforced in campground.

TO GET THERE

Turnoff from Hwy. 63 just past Bryce Canyon National Park Visitor Center.

BRYCE CANYON
Red Canyon Campground

P.O. Box 80, Panguitch 84759. T: (435) 676-8815.

🚐 ★★★★   ⛺ ★★★★★

Beauty: ★★★★★	Site Privacy: ★★★★★
Spaciousness: ★★★★★	Quiet: ★★★★
Security: ★★★★	Cleanliness: ★★★★
Insect Control: ★★★	Facilities: ★★

This National Forest Service campground, nestled among tall pines and breathtaking red-spired sandstone hills within ten miles of Bryce, is run by a Mom and Pop concessionaire, High Country Recreation, which has been among the region's best over the past two decades. Red Canyon Campground is just a few thousand yards east of the Dixie National Forest Visitor Center, which has soda machines, a pay phone, and the short Pink Ledges Nature Walk trailhead. Campsites, some big enough for 3–4 vehicles, are on alternating sides of the road on uphill and downhill loops, with lots of sage, junipers, and pine trees offering an extra measure of privacy. Unlike Kings Creek (See appendix), which opens later in the season and gets people coming in for a week with four-wheel-drive vehicles, Red Canyon tends to be an overnight stop, though there are good trails from which a horse can be ridden into Bryce.

BASICS

Operated By: High Country Recreation. **Open:** April 15-Oct. 25 (weather permitting). **Site Assignment:** First come, first served. **Registration:** Self-pay entrance fee station. **Fee:** $10. **Parking:** At site.

FACILITIES

Number of RV Sites: 39. **Number of Tent-Only Sites:** 0. **Hookups:** None. **Each Site:** Table, grill. **Dump Station:** Yes. **Laundry:** No. **Pay Phone:** Yes. **Rest Rooms and Showers:** Yes. **Fuel:** No. **Propane:** No. **Internal Roads:** Gravel, excellent condition. **RV Service:** No. **Market:** Mile marker 10 on Hwy. 12 at Bryce Canyon Pines. **Restaurant:** Mile marker 10 on Hwy. 12 at Bryce Canyon Pines. **General Store:** No. **Vending:** Yes. **Swimming:** No. **Playground:** Yes. **Other:** asphalt bike trail. **Activities:** Horseback riding. **Nearby Attractions:** Red Canyon, Bryce, Kodachrome Basin, Escalante. **Additional Information:** Powell Ranger District, (435) 676-8815.

RESTRICTIONS

Pets: On leash under owner's control. **Fires:** Yes. **Alcoholic Beverages:** Allowed. **Vehicle Maximum Length:** 45 ft. **Other:** 14-day limit.

TO GET THERE

From junction of US Hwy. 89 & UT Hwy. 12, go 10 mi. east on Hwy. 12.

BRYCE CANYON
Ruby's RV Park & Campground

P.O. Box 22, Hwy. U-63, Bryce 84764. T: (435) 834-5301 (Apr.–Oct.) or (435) 834-5341 (Nov.–Mar.) or (800) 468-8600; F: (435) 834-5481; www.rubysinn.com; blainea@rubysinn.com.

🚐 ★★★★★   ⛺ ★★★★★

Beauty: ★★★★	Site Privacy: ★★★★
Spaciousness: ★★★★★	Quiet: ★★★★
Security: ★★★★	Cleanliness: ★★★★
Insect Control: ★★★	Facilities: ★★★★★

Just a mile north of the Park entrance, Ruby's is part of a tourist complex that includes an excellent buffet (good value; friendly staff) packed with tour buses at peak hours. The Ruby family first settled on a ranch here in 1916, seven years before Bryce became a national monument, and has been doing an excellent job in tourism ever since, now handling 1.7 million visits per year. Full hookup sites are closest to the highway, just behind the RV-park office. Electric and water sites are hidden from the tourist hordes at a lower elevation in a more rustic world of their own, with many pine trees and little depressions between sites containing bits of meadow greenery. Many of these back sites share water views with the large expanse of meadow (no designated sites) reserved for tents. Though Bryce seems hectic, with long lines of cars looking for parking in summer, Ruby's is as good as commercial camping gets.

BASICS

Operated By: The Ruby family, Shauna & Blaine. **Open:** April 1–Oct. 31. **Site Assignment:** First come, first served; reservations recommended. **Registration:** At office. **Fee:** $15 tent, $22–$25 RV (V, MC, AE, D, DC). **Parking:** At site.

FACILITIES

Number of RV Sites: 118. **Number of Tent-Only Sites:** 100. **Hookups:** Electric (20, 30, 50 amp), water, sewer. **Each Site:** Table. **Dump Station:** Yes. **Laundry:** Yes. **Pay Phone:** Yes. **Rest Rooms and Showers:** Yes. **Fuel:** Yes. **Propane:** Yes. **Internal Roads:** Gravel, good condition. **RV Service:** Yes. **Market:** Yes. **Restaurant:** Yes. **General Store:** Yes. **Vending:** Yes. **Swimming:** Pool. **Playground:** No. **Other:** ATM machine, business center, bus wash, car rentals, film processing, tram stop. **Activities:** ATV, helicopter & horseback rides, mountain biking, petting farm, gold panning, rodeo, country music dinners, cross-country skiing. **Nearby Attractions:** Bryce Canyon National Park. **Additional Information:** Bryce Canyon National Park, (435) 834-5322.

RESTRICTIONS

Pets: On leash at all times. **Fires:** Yes (charcoal). **Alcoholic Beverages:** Allowed. **Vehicle Maximum Length:** No limit. **Other:** 1 p.m. checkout.

TO GET THERE

On UT Hwy. 63, 1 mi. north of park entrance.

BRYCE CANYON

Sunset Campground

P.O. Box 170001, Bryce Canyon 84717. T: (435) 834-5322/4801; www.nps.gov/brca.

🚐 ★★★★   ▲ ★★★★★

Beauty: ★★★★   Site Privacy: ★★★★
Spaciousness: ★★★★   Quiet: ★★★★
Security: ★★★★   Cleanliness: ★★★★
Insect Control: ★★★   Facilities: ★★

Sunset is usually the last park campground opening in the spring, after the snowfall has melted and camper demand has filled up North Campground's loops. Sunset has an isolated ponderosa

pine forest feel, being furthest from Visitor Center crowds and a mile from amenities such as showers. No tents are allowed on loop A, whose widely dispersed sites are set aside for RVs and their noisy generators. The smaller and more intimate Loops B and C accommodate tents and ban generators and vehicles over 20 feet. Wheelchair accessibility, including at the group site, is another plus. Mule deer grazing under the shade of ponderosa pines are a common sight. Overall, Sunset is worthwhile because it puts some distance between campers and the park crowds, though the tradeoff is hiking, driving, or riding the new park shuttles to showers and other facilities.

BASICS

Operated By: National Park Service. **Open:** Spring–fall (exact dates depend on weather). **Site Assignment:** First come, first served; group site requires reservation. **Registration:** Self-pay entrance fee station. **Fee:** $10. **Parking:** At site.

FACILITIES

Number of RV Sites: 80. **Number of Tent-Only Sites:** 0. **Hookups:** None. **Each Site:** Table, fire ring. **Dump Station:** Yes. **Laundry:** No. **Pay Phone:** Yes. **Rest Rooms and Showers:** Yes (showers 1 mi. away). **Fuel:** No. **Propane:** No. **Internal Roads:** Paved, weathered. **RV Service:** No. **Market:** At Ruby's, 2 mi. north. **Restaurant:** At lodge, 1 mi. north. **General Store:** Yes (1 mi. away). **Vending:** No. **Swimming:** No. **Playground:** No. **Activities:** Horseback riding, ranger interpretative programs. **Nearby Attractions:** Kodachrome Basin, Red Canyon, Escalante, Cedar Breaks. **Additional Information:** National Park Service, www.nps.gov/brca.

RESTRICTIONS

Pets: On leash under owner's control; not allowed on trails. **Fires:** Yes (in grills only). **Alcoholic Beverages:** Allowed. **Vehicle Maximum Length:** No limit. **Other:** 14 day limit, no firewood gathering, don't feed squirrels or chipmunks.

TO GET THERE

From Visitor Center, go two mi. south on Hwy. 63.

CANNONVILLE

Cannonville/Bryce Valley KOA

P.O. Box 22, Cannonville 84718. T: (435) 679-8988 or (888) 562-4710 (reservations only); www.grand staircasekoa.com; bvkoa@color-country.net.

🚐 ★★★★★   ⛺ ★★★★★

Beauty: ★★★★   Site Privacy: ★★★★
Spaciousness: ★★★★   Quiet: ★★★★
Security: ★★★★   Cleanliness: ★★★★
Insect Control: ★★★   Facilities: ★★★★

One of the more attractive campgrounds, public or private, this relatively new KOA (opened May 2000) integrated an old apple orchard into its front RV sites. There is a separate tent-site loop, but a dirt road leading behind the hills has even more isolated campsites that are real wilderness with good sand pads for tents. These sites are invisible from the highway and nestled among scenic red sandstone badlands, with native high-desert pinyon pine, juniper, and desert scrub. Cannonville is a town of 131 people, so campground vistas facing away from the main highway tend to be mostly banded sandstone hills and pastoral irrigated ranches, though a gas station, restaurant, and motel are only a block away. All in all, not a bad base from which to explore Bryce Canyon National Park and Kodachrome Basin State Park.

BASICS

Operated By: John Holland. **Open:** All year (pool etc. seasonal). **Site Assignment:** First come, first served; reservations accepted. **Registration:** At office. **Fee:** $17 tent, $26 RV. **Parking:** At site.

FACILITIES

Number of RV Sites: 50. **Number of Tent-Only Sites:** 25. **Hookups:** Electric (50 amp), water, sewer. **Each Site:** Table, fire ring. **Dump Station:** Yes. **Laundry:** Yes. **Pay Phone:** Yes. **Rest Rooms and Showers:** Yes. **Fuel:** No. **Propane:** Yes. **Internal Roads:** Gravel, good. **RV Service:** No. **Market:** In Cannonville. **Restaurant:** In Cannonville. **General Store:** Yes. **Vending:** Yes. **Swimming:** Heated outdoor pool. **Playground:** Yes. **Other:** Covered pavillion w/ kitchen, some grills, game room, dataports. **Activities:** Biking, horseback riding, fishing, rockhounding. **Nearby Attractions:** Bryce, Kodachrome Basin, Escalante, Boulder Mountain lakes. **Additional Information:**

Escalante Interagency Office, (435) 826-5499.

RESTRICTIONS

Pets: On leash under owner's control at all times. **Fires:** Yes (firewood sold). **Alcoholic Beverages:** At site only. **Vehicle Maximum Length:** No limit. **Other:** No digging holes, disturbing ground cover, chopping vegetation, or placing doormats on grass, no firearms or fireworks, 11 a.m. checkout.

TO GET THERE

15 mi. east of Bryce at junction of UT Hwy. 12 and Red Rock Rd. in Cannonville.

CANNONVILLE

Kodachrome Basin State Park

P.O. Box 238, Cannonville 84718. T: (435) 679-8562 or (800) 322-3770 (group reservations only); F: (435) 679-8542.

🚐 ★★★★   ⛺ ★★★★★

Beauty: ★★★★★   Site Privacy: ★★★★
Spaciousness: ★★★★   Quiet: ★★★★
Security: ★★★★   Cleanliness: ★★★★
Insect Control: ★★★★   Facilities: ★★★

Named after the film, Kodachrome Basin State Park is noted for its colorful sandstone spires resembling huge chimneys. The campground is surrounded by colorful banded sandstone hills, sand pipes, and hoodoos. Big gnarly-barked junipers add privacy to the sites. There is even a wheelchair-accessible site with a raised wood tent platform with ramps. The general store, which also rents cabins, is a bit eccentric and liable to close on a whim on a busy Saturday. This is one of the few places where you are encouraged to feed an animal, namely the chukars, an introduced bird that resembles a partridge and needs help making it through the harsh winters. Dirt roads and trails lead to rock formations, coves, and colorful geyser remnants (e.g. chimneys) where the play of light changes the colors through a moody array of whites, grays, reds, and oranges. Add in the proximity to Bryce and Escalante, and this makes a fine stopping place.

BASICS

Operated By: Utah State Parks. **Open:** All year. **Site Assignment:** First come, first served; reservations for 4 group sites. **Registration:** Self-pay station. **Fee:** $13 vehicle. **Parking:** At site.

FACILITIES

Number of RV Sites: 27. **Number of Tent-Only Sites:** 0. **Hookups:** None. **Each Site:** Table, grill on cement pad. **Dump Station:** Yes. **Laundry:** No. **Pay Phone:** Yes. **Rest Rooms and Showers:** Yes. **Fuel:** No. **Propane:** No. **Internal Roads:** Pavement, excellent condition. **RV Service:** No. **Market:** 14 mi. in Tropic. **Restaurant:** 9 mi. in Cannonville. **General Store:** Yes. **Vending:** Yes. **Swimming:** No. **Playground:** No. **Other:** Wheelchair-accessible site. **Activities:** Horseback riding, mountain biking. **Nearby Attractions:** Bryce, Escalante, Cottonwood Canyon, Grosvenor Arch. **Additional Information:** Escalante Interagency Office, (435) 826-5499.

RESTRICTIONS

Pets: On leash under owner's control at all times. **Fires:** Yes. **Alcoholic Beverages:** Allowed. **Vehicle Maximum Length:** 30 ft. **Other:** 14-day max. stay, no guns, bows, slingshots, or fireworks, no firewood collecting, ATVs must remain on trailers while in park, no climbing on rocks.

TO GET THERE

From junction of UT Hwy. 12 in Cannonville, go 9 mi. southeast on Cottonwood Canyon Rd.

CANYONLANDS NATIONAL PARK, ISLAND IN THE SKY DISTRICT
Willow Flat Campground

2282 South West Resource Blvd., Moab 84532.
T: (435) 259-4712 or (435) 719-2313;
www.nps.gov/cany.

🚐 ★★★   ⛺ ★★★★

Beauty: ★★★★★	Site Privacy: ★★★★★
Spaciousness: ★★★	Quiet: ★★★★
Security: ★★★★	Cleanliness: ★★★★★
Insect Control: ★★	Facilities: ★

Set amidst flattop mesas and buttes that have eroded into spires, Willow Flat is a place of isolation and beauty for self-sufficient campers. It is best to pickup firewood and water in Moab before coming here, as the Visitors Center has only a limited number of gallon water jugs for sale. The dozen campsites are spread out along a curve for maximum privacy. Though voices tend to carry in the Canyonlands, generator noise is limited to two hours in the morning and 4–8 p.m. The longest site length is an 80-foot pull-through, but it is only 11 feet wide. There is a 50-foot-long pull-through that is 16-feet wide, and among the 33- and 35-foot-long sites are 19, 24, and 25-foot widths. Checkout time is 10 a.m., and arrival an hour or two before that is the best way to snag a space.

BASICS

Operated By: National Park Service. **Open:** All year. **Site Assignment:** First come, first served. **Registration:** Self-pay fee station. **Fee:** $5 (cash or check only). **Parking:** At site.

FACILITIES

Number of RV Sites: 12. **Number of Tent-Only Sites:** 0. **Hookups:** None. **Each Site:** Table, fire grate. **Dump Station:** No. **Laundry:** No. **Pay Phone:** Yes. **Rest Rooms and Showers:** No showers. **Fuel:** No. **Propane:** No. **Internal Roads:** Gravel, bumpy in spots. **RV Service:** No. **Market:** Moab, 46 mi. **Restaurant:** Moab, 46 mi. **General Store:** No. **Vending:** No. **Swimming:** No. **Playground:** No. **Other:** Visitor center. **Activities:** Evening campfire programs (seasonal). **Nearby Attractions:** Arches National Park, Dead Horse Point State Park, Moab. **Additional Information:** Canyonlands Natural History Assoc., (435) 259-6003, www.cnha.org.

RESTRICTIONS

Pets: On leash. **Fires:** Yes (in fire grates only, no wood gathering). **Alcoholic Beverages:** Allowed. **Vehicle Maximum Length:** 80 ft. **Other:** 14-day max. stay.

TO GET THERE

From US Hwy. 191 10 mi. north of Moab go 36 mi. southwest on UT Hwy. 313.

CANYONLANDS NATIONAL PARK, NEEDLES DISTRICT
Squaw Flat Campground

2282 South West Resource Blvd., Moab 84532. T: (435) 259-4711 or 259-7164; www.nps.gov/cany.

🚐 ★★★★　　　　▲ ★★★★★

Beauty: ★★★★★　　Site Privacy: ★★★★★
Spaciousness: ★★★★★　Quiet: ★★★★★
Security: ★★★★★　　Cleanliness: ★★★★★
Insect Control: ★★★　　Facilities: ★★

Make sure the gas tank is full and that you have enough water and firewood for the duration before turning onto UT Hwy. 211 en route to the Needles District of Canyonlands National Park. There is a small private campground catering to RVs (no hookups; $15) with gas, propane, showers, and a store with haphazard hours just outside the park boundary at Needles Outpost (call (435) 979-4007), but Squaw Flat Campground demands self-sufficiency. In return Squaw Flat offers relatively large sites, each tucked into its own little sandstone rock formation and far from its neighbor. Walk-in tent sites nestled among the orange sandstone rocks provide an even more primitive slot canyon feel. High clearance four-wheel-drive vehicles and technical driving skills are needed to visit the major geologic features; even mountain bikes quit moving in the deep sandy washes. Peak season (Mar.–May and mid-Sept.–Oct.), campsites are all snagged by 10 a.m.

BASICS

Operated By: National Park Service. **Open:** All year. **Site Assignment:** First come, first served; group site reservations. **Registration:** Self-pay fee station. **Fee:** $10 (cash or check only). **Parking:** At site; parking area near walk-in tent sites.

FACILITIES

Number of RV Sites: 20. **Number of Tent-Only Sites:** 6. **Hookups:** None. **Each Site:** Table, fire ring. **Dump Station:** No. **Laundry:** No. **Pay Phone:** Yes. **Rest Rooms and Showers:** No showers. **Fuel:** No. **Propane:** No. **Internal Roads:** Gravel, good. **RV Service:** No. **Market:** Monticello, 62 mi. **Restaurant:** Monticello, 62 mi. **General Store:** No. **Vending:** No. **Swimming:**

No. **Playground:** No. **Other:** Visitor center, campfire circle. **Activities:** Four-wheel driving, mountain biking. **Nearby Attractions:** Newspaper Rock, Canyon Rims Recreation Area, Chesler Park. **Additional Information:** Canyonlands Natural History Assoc., (435) 259-6003, www.cnha.org.

RESTRICTIONS

Pets: On leash & attended at all times (not allowed on hiking trails or 4WD roads, even in a vehicle). **Fires:** Yes (only in metal fire rings, no wood gathering). **Alcoholic Beverages:** Allowed. **Vehicle Maximum Length:** 116 ft. **Other:** No ATVs, 2 vehicles & 10 people per site, 10 a.m. checkout, 14-day limit.

TO GET THERE

From US Hwy. 191 14 mi. north of Monticello go 48 mi. west on UT Hwy. 211.

CEDAR BREAKS NATIONAL MONUMENT
Point Supreme Campground

2390 West Hwy. 56, Suite 11, Cedar City 84720. T: (435) 586-9451.

🚐 ★★　　　　　▲ ★★★★★

Beauty: ★★★★★　　Site Privacy: ★★★★★
Spaciousness: ★★★★　　Quiet: ★★★★
Security: ★★★★　　　Cleanliness: ★★★★
Insect Control: ★★★　　Facilities: ★★

Just south of the renowned Brian Head ski area, where lifts carry summer mountain bikers and hikers to 100 miles of alpine meadow and aspen grove trails, 10,000-foot elevation Cedar Breaks is known for its wildflower displays and its folded, uplifted, and eroded orange and white spires, arches, columns, and canyons that have been liked to a miniature version of Bryce Canyon. A large meadow with tables and grills just off the paved road marks the entrance to Point Supreme Campground. Trees provide privacy between the campsites, though there are also good meadow views. The largest sites are 11, 12, 15, and 17. Tents must be positioned at least 20 feet from the campfire grates in order to allow campground vegetation to grow back. Besides deepening the colors of the rocks from roadside overlooks, sunrise and sunset bring deer into the campground. Snow and flash floods can close access roads.

BASICS

Operated By: National Park Service. **Open:** June 15–Oct. 1. **Site Assignment:** First come, first served. **Registration:** Self-pay fee station. **Fee:** $10. **Parking:** At site.

FACILITIES

Number of RV Sites: 30. **Number of Tent-Only Sites:** 0. **Hookups:** None. **Each Site:** Table, grill. **Dump Station:** Yes. **Laundry:** No. **Pay Phone:** Yes. **Rest Rooms and Showers:** No showers. **Fuel:** No. **Propane:** No. **Internal Roads:** Gravel, good. **RV Service:** No. **Market:** Cedar City, 23 mi. **Restaurant:** Brian Head, 20 mi. **General Store:** No. **Vending:** No. **Swimming:** No. **Playground:** No. **Other:** Visitor center, amphitheater. **Activities:** Ranger programs, mountain biking. **Nearby Attractions:** Panguitch Lake, Bryce, Zion. **Additional Information:** Iron County Tourism, (800) 354-4849.

RESTRICTIONS

Pets: On leash or under physical restraint at all time. **Fires:** Yes (in grills or portable barbecues only, no wood gathering). **Alcoholic Beverages:** Allowed. **Vehicle Maximum Length:** 24 ft. **Other:** No fireworks, 2 tents per site.

TO GET THERE

From Cedar City go 18 mi. east on UT Hwy. 14 and 5 mi. north on UT Hwy. 148.

CEDAR CITY
Cedar Canyon Campground

P.O. Box 627, Cedar City 84721. T: (435) 865-3200 or (877) 444-6777 (reservations); www.fsfed.us/outernet/dixie-nf/welcome.htm.

🚐 ★★   ⛺ ★★★★

Beauty: ★★★★★	Site Privacy: ★★★★★
Spaciousness: ★★★	Quiet: ★★★★
Security: ★★★★	Cleanliness: ★★★★
Insect Control: ★★★	Facilities: ★★

Perched at 8,100-feet elevation on UT Hwy. 14, Cedar Canyon offers self-sufficient campers the best of both worlds: Cedar City's Tony Award–winning Shakespeare festival (2000 best regional theater) and the orange-and-white spires and columns of higher elevation Cedar Breaks National Monument. Cedar Canyon Campground is situated in a beautiful forest of spruce, fir, and aspen. Rocky, tree-lined Crow Creek separates the campground from the highway. Run by National Forest Service concessionaire AuDi, sites 4, 6, 7, and 17 can be reserved. For closest creek proximity select sites 2, 4, 6–8, 12, 14, or 16; site 12, one of three double sites, accommodates up to 16 people. The campground creek is not fishable, but there is a kid's fishing pond nearby at Iron County's Wood Ranch. Though water (piped in from a nearby spring) and sanitation services are shutdown after Labor Day to avoid freezing, the campground can still be used.

BASICS

Operated By: AuDi, Inc. **Open:** June 15–Sept. 6. **Site Assignment:** First come, first served; group & some individual sites (4,6,7,17) can be reserved. **Registration:** Self-pay fee station. **Fee:** $8 single site, $16 double site (cash or check only). **Parking:** At site.

FACILITIES

Number of RV Sites: 19. **Number of Tent-Only Sites:** 0. **Hookups:** None. **Each Site:** Table, fire ring. **Dump Station:** No. **Laundry:** No. **Pay Phone:** No. **Rest Rooms and Showers:** No showers. **Fuel:** No. **Propane:** No. **Internal Roads:** Paved, excellent. **RV Service:** No. **Market:** Cedar City, 14 mi. **Restaurant:** Cedar City, 14 mi. **General Store:** No. **Vending:** No. **Swimming:** No. **Playground:** No. **Activities:** Biking, horseback riding. **Nearby Attractions:** Cedar Breaks National Monument, Virgin River Rim Trail, Brian Head, Zion. **Additional Information:** Iron County Tourism, (800) 354-4849.

RESTRICTIONS

Pets: On leash & always attended. **Fires:** Yes (in fire rings, stoves only). **Alcoholic Beverages:** Allowed. **Vehicle Maximum Length:** 24 ft. **Other:** 14-day limit, lock food away from bears.

TO GET THERE

From Cedar City go 14 mi. east on UT Hwy. 14.

CEDAR CITY
Duck Creek Campground

P.O. Box 627, Cedar City 84721. T: (435) 865-3200 or (877) 444-6777 (reservations); www.fsfed.us/outernet/dixie-nf/welcome.htm.

🚐 ★★★★   ⛺ ★★★★

Beauty: ★★★★   Site Privacy: ★★★★
Spaciousness: ★★★★   Quiet: ★★★★
Security: ★★★★   Cleanliness: ★★★★
Insect Control: ★★   Facilities: ★★★

A large duck pond at 8,600-feet elevation and campsites heavily forested with tall aspens and spruce make Duck Creek's five loops an attractive, reservable alternative to driving gravel roads to reach the smaller 9,200-foot-elevation Te-Ah and Navajo Lake Campgrounds (See Appendix). National Forest Service concessionaire AuDi keeps Duck Creek in top shape, and added amenities like electric hookups are not too far-fetched a possibility in coming seasons. At Loop A, which is nearest the highway and has a very large picnic area, sites 4–13, 15, 17–20, and 24–37 are reservable. At smaller and more intimate Loop B, sites 38–40, 42, 43, and 46–48 can be reserved. Loops C, D and E are most primitive in feel, and only the Roundup and Wagon Train group areas can be reserved in these loops. Nearby Duck Creek Village provides many of the amenities missing at the campground.

BASICS
Operated By: AuDi Inc. **Open:** June 15–Sept. 6. **Site Assignment:** First come, first served; group & some individual sites reservable. **Registration:** Self-pay entrance fee station. **Fee:** $10 single sites, $18 double sites (cash or check only). **Parking:** At site.

FACILITIES
Number of RV Sites: 96. **Number of Tent-Only Sites:** 0. **Hookups:** None. **Each Site:** Table, fire ring. **Dump Station:** Yes. **Laundry:** No. **Pay Phone:** Yes. **Rest Rooms and Showers:** No showers. **Fuel:** No. **Propane:** No. **Internal Roads:** Gravel, good. **RV Service:** No. **Market:** Cedar City, 30 mi. **Restaurant:** Duck Creek Village, 2 mi. **General Store:** No. **Vending:** No. **Swimming:** No. **Playground:** No. **Other:** Amphitheater, picnic area, boat ramp. **Activities:** Boating, fishing, horseback riding. **Nearby Attrac-**

tions: Cedar Breaks, Navajo Lake, Brian Head, Bryce, Zion. **Additional Information:** Iron County Tourism, (800) 354-4849.

RESTRICTIONS
Pets: On leash (pets not recommended; plague warning). **Fires:** Yes (firewood sold). **Alcoholic Beverages:** Allowed. **Vehicle Maximum Length:** 35 ft. **Other:** No fireworks.

TO GET THERE
From Cedar City go 30 mi. east on UT Hwy. 14.

ESCALANTE
Broken Bow RV Camp

495 West Main St., P.O. Box 505, Escalante 84726. T: (888) 241-8785 or (435) 826-4959.

🚐 ★★★★   ⛺ ★★★

Beauty: ★★★   Site Privacy: ★★★
Spaciousness: ★★★   Quiet: ★★★
Security: ★★★★   Cleanliness: ★★★★
Insect Control: ★★★★   Facilities: ★★★

A small family operation on Escalante's Main Street that is easy to miss, being fronted by a handpainted wooden sign of Broken Bow Arch (the owner's favorite place) surrounded by old rusted equipment, a funky rock shop, and a tall plastic sign with the previous owner's "SSS" name adding to the obfuscation. But the Moqui Motel and Nature Sounds Drum Factory are just across the street. Though a bit hidden, the RV park is well maintained. A new pine building has pine toilet stalls, showers, and a new laundry room. A large sloping grassy strip along a fence is set aside for tents, and there is a group or extended tent area. Between the tent areas are two gravel rows of RV sites, with small grassy strips between the sites. Nothing fancy here, but the popular Cowboy Blues restaurant and the whole town are within a few block radius, making this a convenient stopping place.

BASICS
Operated By: Catherine Barnes. **Open:** All year. **Site Assignment:** First come, first served. **Registration:** Office trailer. **Fee:** $11 tent, $25–$29 RV. **Parking:** At site.

FACILITIES
Number of RV Sites: 28. **Number of Tent-Only Sites:** 20. **Hookups:** Electric (30, 50 amp),

water, sewer. **Each Site:** Table, grill. **Dump Station:** Yes. **Laundry:** Yes. **Pay Phone:** Yes. **Rest Rooms and Showers:** Yes. **Fuel:** No. **Propane:** No. **Internal Roads:** Gravel, good. **RV Service:** No. **Market:** Escalante, two blocks distant. **Restaurant:** Escalante, across the street. **General Store:** No. **Vending:** No. **Swimming:** No. **Playground:** No. **Other:** Modem access, rock shop. **Activities:** Fishing, water sports, horseback riding. **Nearby Attractions:** Grand Staircase-Escalante National Monument, Anasazi Indian Village State Park, Boulder Mountain lakes, Bryce. **Additional Information:** Escalante Interagency Office, (435) 826-5499.

RESTRICTIONS

Pets: Yes. **Fires:** Yes. **Alcoholic Beverages:** Allowed. **Vehicle Maximum Length:** 49 ft.

TO GET THERE

At the corner of Main & 500 W St. in Escalante, where UT Hwy. 12 becomes Main St.

ESCALANTE
Calf Creek Campground

P.O. Box 225, Escalante 84726. T: (435) 826-5400; www.utso.ut.blm.gov.

🚙 ★   ⛺ ★★★★★

Beauty: ★★★★★   Site Privacy: ★★★★★
Spaciousness: ★★★★★   Quiet: ★★★★★
Security: ★★★★   Cleanliness: ★★★★
Insect Control: ★★   Facilities: ★

The natural beauty of being surrounded by Escalante sandstone cliffs and the nearness of popular trailheads makes Calf Creek Campground so popular that it fills to capacity almost every night. People turned away the night before show up early the next morning to grab the coveted spots. Fortunately, a campground host acts as traffic cop, as the small parking area fills up with day hikers and big rigs can have trouble maneuvering to turn around and exit. The campsites are coveted because they are widely dispersed on alternating sides of the road on both sides of a creek cutting through the campground. Dense vegetation scraping big vehicles on the narrow road adds extra privacy. However, many of the sites are not level, and high water or flash floods can make creek crossings and site access impossible. Long sleeves and long pants are advised, as biting deer flies breed in the creek.

BASICS

Operated By: BLM. **Open:** All year. **Site Assignment:** First come, first served. **Registration:** Self-pay entrance fee station. **Fee:** $7 (exact cash or check). **Parking:** At site.

FACILITIES

Number of RV Sites: 10. **Number of Tent-Only Sites:** 3. **Hookups:** None. **Each Site:** Cement table, fire pit. **Dump Station:** No. **Laundry:** No. **Pay Phone:** No. **Rest Rooms and Showers:** No showers. **Fuel:** No. **Propane:** No. **Internal Roads:** Narrow in spots, w/ creek crossings. **RV Service:** No. **Market:** Escalante, 16 mi. **Restaurant:** Kiva Coffeehouse, 1 mi. **General Store:** No. **Vending:** No. **Swimming:** No. **Playground:** No. **Activities:** Fishing, water sports, horseback riding. **Nearby Attractions:** Lower Calf Creek Falls, Boynton Arch, Escalante Natural Bridge, Anasazi Indian Village State Park, Boulder Mountains, Burr Trail, Capitol Reef. **Additional Information:** Escalante Interagency Office, (435) 826-5499.

RESTRICTIONS

Pets: On leash. **Fires:** Yes. **Alcoholic Beverages:** Allowed. **Vehicle Maximum Length:** 25 ft. **Other:** 14-day limit, no firearms, fireworks, horses, or pack animals.

TO GET THERE

16 mi. east of Escalante, on UT Hwy. 12.

ESCALANTE
Escalante State Park

710 North Reservoir Rd., Escalante 84726. T: (435) 826-4466 or (800) 322-3770.

🚙 ★★   ⛺ ★★★★★

Beauty: ★★★★★   Site Privacy: ★★★★★
Spaciousness: ★★★   Quiet: ★★★★
Security: ★★★★   Cleanliness: ★★★★
Insect Control: ★★   Facilities: ★★★

Escalante State Park stretches along the shoreline of Wide Hollow Reservoir, which supplies Escalante with its irrigation water. The Aquarius Plateau and views of red rocks add to the rugged charm of the campground, which is a short distance back from the water and slightly buffered from day users. Aside from water activities like boating and fishing for bluegill and rainbow trout, there is a popular one-mile petrified-forest trail and an array of aquatic birds ranging from loons and cormorants to spotted sandpipers and marbled godwits. The mixture of flat dirt and grassy sites, some with junipers and shade canopies and others under tall cottonwood trees, works best for tents and small vehicles. Gnats and deer flies are an occasional nuisance, but the area is still very popular with day users. All in all, a pleasant place to spend the day, or even have a picnic lunch if just passing through.

BASICS

Operated By: Utah State Parks. **Open:** All year. **Site Assignment:** First come, first served; reservations (one night only; up to 16 weeks in advance of checkout date for individuals; 11 months for group site). **Registration:** Visitor Center (if open); otherwise self-pay fee station. **Fee:** $13. **Parking:** At site.

FACILITIES

Number of RV Sites: 22. **Number of Tent-Only Sites:** 0. **Hookups:** None. **Each Site:** Table, bench, grill on cement pad. **Dump Station:** Yes. **Laundry:** No. **Pay Phone:** Yes. **Rest Rooms and Showers:** Yes. **Fuel:** No. **Propane:** No. **Internal Roads:** Paved, excellent. **RV Service:** No. **Market:** Escalante, 2 mi. **Restaurant:** Escalante, 2 mi. **General Store:** No. **Vending:** Yes. **Swimming:** In lake. **Playground:** No. **Other:** Boat ramp, canoe rentals, shade canopies at some sites. **Activities:** Boating, waterskiing, lake fishing, aquatic bird-watching, petrified forest. **Nearby Attractions:** Grand Staircase-Escalante National Monument, Anasazi Indian Village State Park, Boulder Mountain lakes & forest, Calf Creek, Bryce. **Additional Information:** Escalante Interagency Office, (435) 826-5499.

RESTRICTIONS

Pets: On leash. **Fires:** Yes (firewood sold). **Alcoholic Beverages:** Allowed. **Vehicle Maximum Length:** 30 ft. **Other:** 14-day max. stay.

TO GET THERE

1 mi. west of Escalante on UT Hwy. 12, then 1 mi. north on Wide Hollow Rd.

FILLMORE

Fillmore KOA

410 West 900 South, Fillmore 84631. T: (435) 743-4420 or (800) 562-1516; www.koa.com. fillmorekoa@xmission.com.

🚐 ★★★★   ⛺ ★★★★

Beauty: ★★★★★   Site Privacy: ★★★★
Spaciousness: ★★★★   Quiet: ★★★★
Security: ★★★★   Cleanliness: ★★★★★
Insect Control: ★★★   Facilities: ★★★★

Named after Millard Fillmore, a U.S. President friendly to persecuted Mormons, and briefly Utah's state capital in the 1850s, Fillmore is now the sleepy anchor for surrounding alfalfa and cattle ranches. It is easy to whiz by the I-15 Fillmore Exit without stopping at the Territorial Statehouse State Park Museum or the Fillmore KOA, a grassy poplar-shaded little gem of a campground in a windy area away from the highway. The office and general store are inside a log cabin, and the pool looks like stone (actually Gunite™ and white paint). Geology buffs should consult the host, a survivor of Mt. St. Helen's who can wax on about the geothermal ice caves, lava flows to the west, and differences in age and type between Utah and Pacific Northwest volcanoes. The town has a new golf course, and with a little luck the mini-golf course at the KOA may get finished.

BASICS

Operated By: Ann & Dick Flones. **Open:** All year (limited services Dec. 15–Mar. 1; sometimes closed by snow). **Site Assignment:** First come, first served. **Registration:** Office. **Fee:** $15–$17 tent, $18–$22 RV (V, MC, AE, D). **Parking:** At site.

FACILITIES

Number of RV Sites: 49. **Number of Tent-Only Sites:** 7. **Hookups:** Electric (30, 50 amp), water, sewer. **Each Site:** Table. **Dump Station:** Yes. **Laundry:** Yes. **Pay Phone:** Yes. **Rest Rooms and Showers:** Yes. **Fuel:** No. **Propane:** Yes. **Internal Roads:** Gravel, good. **RV Service:** No. **Market:** Fillmore, 1 mi. **Restaurant:** Fillmore, 1 mi. **General Store:** Yes. **Vending:** Yes. **Swimming:** Pool. **Playground:** Yes (also volleyball, tetherball, game room). **Other:** Tent sites have grass pads, electric, water, sheltered tables, grills, fire rings; 5 cabins. **Activities:**

Fishing, boating, hunting, golf. **Nearby Attractions:** Paiute ATV Trail, Cove Fort. **Additional Information:** Fillmore Area Chamber of Commerce, (435) 743-6121.

RESTRICTIONS

Pets: On leash. **Fires:** Yes. **Alcoholic Beverages:** Allowed. **Vehicle Maximum Length:** 90 ft.

TO GET THERE

From US I-15 Exit163 go 0.25 mi. north on business loop and 0.5 mi. east on 900 South.

GLENDALE
Bryce/Zion KOA

P.O. Box 189, Glendale 84729. T: (435) 648-2490 or (800) 562-8635 (reservations); www.koa.com.

🚐 ★★★   ▲ ★★★

Beauty: ★★★★   Site Privacy: ★★★★
Spaciousness: ★★★★   Quiet: ★★★
Security: ★★★★   Cleanliness: ★★★★
Insect Control: ★★★★   Facilities: ★★★★

Though alongside a grade in US Hwy. 89 with tour-bus and truck engine noise, the strategic location merits careful consideration, as it is only 25 miles to Coral Pink Sand Dunes State Park, 30 miles to Zion, 35 miles to Cedar Breaks, and 45 miles to Bryce. A horse pasture and spring-fed pond border one side, and Bryce-like orange sandstone spires on the surrounding hills add a park-like ambiance. The grassy sites and gravel roads of Bryce/Zion KOA add to the impression of pastoral tranquility. Buffalo Bistro next door is known area-wide for its buffalo burgers, fruit cobblers, and rabbit-rattlesnake sausage served with spicy mustard, having been almost an east Zion institution before relocating here. The group tent sites, dog walk, car wash, and horse and hiking trails are added bonuses. Though there are some poplar trees, not every site has shade. Nevertheless, overall this is a superior stopping place.

BASICS

Operated By: Ellen Lamb. **Open:** May 1–Sept. 30. **Site Assignment:** First come, first served; reservations. **Registration:** Office. **Fee:** $17 tent, $20–$22 RV (V, MC, AE, D). **Parking:** At site.

FACILITIES

Number of RV Sites: 62. **Number of Tent-Only Sites:** 20. **Hookups:** Electric (20, 30 amp),

water, sewer. **Each Site:** Table, grill. **Dump Station:** Yes. **Laundry:** Yes. **Pay Phone:** Yes. **Rest Rooms and Showers:** Yes. **Fuel:** No. **Propane:** No. **Internal Roads:** Gravel, good condition. **RV Service:** No. **Market:** 5 mi. south in Glendale. **Restaurant:** Adjacent to Buffalo Bistro. **General Store:** Yes. **Vending:** Yes. **Swimming:** Pool. **Playground:** Yes. **Other:** Modem connection. **Activities:** Fishing, horseback riding. **Nearby Attractions:** Bryce, Zion, Cedar Breaks, Escalante. **Additional Information:** Kane County Office of Tourism, 78 S. 100 East, Kanab, UT 84741; (435) 644-5033; (800) 733-5263; kanetrav@kaneutah.com; www.kaneutah.com.

RESTRICTIONS

Pets: On leash under owner's control. **Fires:** Yes (firewood sold). **Alcoholic Beverages:** Allowed. **Vehicle Maximum Length:** 35 ft.

TO GET THERE

5 mi. north of Glendale on US Hwy. 89.

GREEN RIVER
Green River KOA

P.O. Box 14, Green River 84525. T: (435) 564-3651 or (800) 562-3649 (reservations); www.koa.com.

🚐 ★★★★   ▲ ★★★

Beauty: ★★★★   Site Privacy: ★★★★
Spaciousness: ★★★★   Quiet: ★★★★
Security: ★★★★   Cleanliness: ★★★★
Insect Control: ★★   Facilities: ★★★★

Literally across the street from Green River State Park, this KOA came into existence to handle the state park's overflow, adding hookups and louder proximity to the train. Overflow camping is what Green River is about much of the time, though, being half way between Las Vegas and Denver, it attracts its fair share of the traffic plying I-70. During summer, particularly special-event weekends, Arches, Canyonlands, and Moab can fill up, leaving campers to choose between heading south towards Monticello or north towards Green River. Green River is actually closer to the Canyonlands and Arches entrances, and is a peaceful little truck-stop town compared to bustling Moab. Campers could do worse than holing up in the big grassy sites here, and might even be pleasantly surprised by the excellent River History Museum, which doubles as a Visitor Center.

BASICS

Operated By: KOA franchisee. **Open:** Apr. 1–Sept. 30. **Site Assignment:** First come, first served; reservations accepted. **Registration:** At office. **Fee:** $17 tent, $19–$21 RV (V, MC, AE, D). **Parking:** At site.

FACILITIES

Number of RV Sites: 77. **Number of Tent-Only Sites:** 30. **Hookups:** Electric (30 amp), water, sewer, cable TV. **Each Site:** Table, grill. **Dump Station:** Yes. **Laundry:** Yes. **Pay Phone:** Yes. **Rest Rooms and Showers:** Yes. **Fuel:** No. **Propane:** No. **Internal Roads:** Gravel, good. **RV Service:** No. **Market:** Green River, 1 mi. **Restaurant:** Green River. **General Store:** Yes. **Vending:** Yes. **Swimming:** Heated pool. **Playground:** Yes. **Other:** Dog walk. **Activities:** Fishing, rockhounding, golf. **Nearby Attractions:** John Wesley Powell River History Museum, Canyonlands, Dead Horse State Park, Goblin Valley State Park, Arches, Moab. **Additional Information:** Emery County Travel Bureau, (888) 564-3600, www.emerycounty.com.

RESTRICTIONS

Pets: On leash under owner's control. **Fires:** Yes (charcoal only in grills). **Alcoholic Beverages:** Allowed. **Vehicle Maximum Length:** 105 ft. **Other:** No generator use, 11 a.m. checkout.

TO GET THERE

From US I-70, take Green River Main St. Exit, turn south on Green River Blvd. for 0.5 mi.

GREEN RIVER
Green River State Park

P.O. Box 637, Green River 84525. T: (435) 564-3633 or (800) 322-3770 (reservations).

🚐 ★★★★	⛺ ★★★★★
Beauty: ★★★★	Site Privacy: ★★★★★
Spaciousness: ★★★★★	Quiet: ★★★★
Security: ★★★★★	Cleanliness: ★★★★★
Insect Control: ★★	Facilities: ★★★

Muskrats, beavers, ibises, egrets, and herons share Green River State Park with golfers, campers, picnickers, boaters, rafters, and river runners. This well-run park is near the center of town, the river museum, and restaurants, but it feels away from it all, except for the pesky summer gnats (bird food) and the train that rumbles by the river. Large pull-through sites can handle the biggest rigs and are shaded by cottonwoods, willows, and Russian olive trees full of chirping birds. During summer the grass is watered at 10 a.m., and everything needs to be sealed up or put away to avoid a soaking. Tents need to be moved at least every other day anyway, to avoid killing the grass. Though hookups are lacking, this is the premier campground in Green River, and it is less than an hour from Arches.

BASICS

Operated By: Utah State Parks. **Open:** All year. **Site Assignment:** First come, first served; all but 10 sites can be reserved (3–110 days in advance). **Registration:** Entrance kiosk. **Fee:** $12. **Parking:** At site.

FACILITIES

Number of RV Sites: 42. **Number of Tent-Only Sites:** 0. **Hookups:** None. **Each Site:** Table on cement pad, grill or fire pit. **Dump Station:** Yes. **Laundry:** No. **Pay Phone:** Yes. **Rest Rooms and Showers:** Yes. **Fuel:** No. **Propane:** No. **Internal Roads:** Paved, some ruts. **RV Service:** No. **Market:** In Green River. **Restaurant:** In Green River. **General Store:** No. **Vending:** No. **Swimming:** No. **Playground:** No. **Other:** 9-hole golf course, boat ramp & dock, vehicle storage, amphitheater, wheelchair-accessible restroom. **Activities:** River float trips, Memorial Day Friendship Cruise to Moab, Sept. Melon Days. **Nearby Attractions:** John Wesley Powell River History Museum, Canyonlands, Dead Horse State Park, Goblin Valley State Park, Arches, Moab. **Additional Information:** Emery County Travel Bureau, (888) 564-3600, www.emerycounty.com.

RESTRICTIONS

Pets: On leash under owner's control. **Fires:** Yes. **Alcoholic Beverages:** Allowed at site, but not to the point of public intoxication. **Vehicle Maximum Length:** No limit. **Other:** 14-day limit, tents must be moved every other day.

TO GET THERE

From US I-70 Exit 162, go west on Main St., turn south on Green River Blvd.

GREEN RIVER
Shady Acres RV Park & Campground

P.O. Box 598, Green River 84525. T: (800) 537-8674 or (435) 564-8838; F: (435) 564-8838; www.shadyacresrv.com; shadya@etv.net.

🚐 ★★★★★   ⛺ ★★★★

Beauty: ★★★★   Site Privacy: ★★★★
Spaciousness: ★★★★★   Quiet: ★★★★
Security: ★★★★   Cleanliness: ★★★★
Insect Control: ★★   Facilities: ★★★★★

On the opposite side of the muddy brown Green River from United Campground and a block across the street from the truck scales and the 24-hour West Winds Restaurant (hearty trucker meals), Shady Acres shields itself from Main Street with cottonwood trees. But everything is here, including cable TV, groceries, a gas station with a submarine sandwich franchise, and RV repairs. The gravel campsites are well back from Main Street, and the cottonwood trees blowing in the wind make more noise than the steady parade of slow trucks exiting I-70. The basketball and volleyball courts among the swings and horseshoes add a touch of resort ambiance. This well-run family operation has almost zero tolerance for offensive language, and the county sheriff takes care of intoxicated trouble-makers. With the Powell River History Museum down the street and the state park nearby, the range of amenities here may tip the scales for some.

BASICS

Operated By: Private family. **Open:** All year. **Site Assignment:** First come, first served; reservations recommended for long holiday weekends. **Registration:** At office. **Fee:** $10–$13 tent, $17–$22 RV (V, MC, AE, D). **Parking:** At site.

FACILITIES

Number of RV Sites: 97. **Number of Tent-Only Sites:** 14. **Hookups:** Electric (50 amp), water, sewer, cable TV. **Each Site:** Table, grill. **Dump Station:** Yes. **Laundry:** Yes. **Pay Phone:** Yes. **Rest Rooms and Showers:** Yes. **Fuel:** Yes. **Propane:** No. **Internal Roads:** Gravely pavement, good condition. **RV Service:** No. **Market:** Nearby. **Restaurant:** Across the street. **General Store:** Yes. **Vending:** Yes. **Swimming:** Pool. **Playground:** Yes. **Other:** Dog walk, wheelchair-accessible sites,

Internet connection in office, car/RV wash. **Activities:** Golf. **Nearby Attractions:** Crystal Geyser, Black Dragon Pictograph, Goblin Valley, Arches, Canyonlands. **Additional Information:** Emery County Travel Bureau, (888) 564-3600, www.emerycounty.com.

RESTRICTIONS

Pets: On leash. **Fires:** Yes. **Alcoholic Beverages:** Intoxication is not tolerated. **Vehicle Maximum Length:** 100 ft. **Other:** No foul language, no changing of oil or mechanical repairs in the park.

TO GET THERE

From US I-70, exit Green River at Main St., go to 350 E. Main St.

GREEN RIVER
United Campground

P.O. Box 143, Green River 84525. T: (435) 564-8195.

🚐 ★★★★   ⛺ ★★★★

Beauty: ★★★★   Site Privacy: ★★★★
Spaciousness: ★★★★★   Quiet: ★★★
Security: ★★★★★   Cleanliness: ★★★★★
Insect Control: ★★   Facilities: ★★★★

One of the better I-70 halfway stops between Las Vegas and Denver, United is also a good overflow site for Moab, Arches, and Canyonlands (within 45 miles) on holidays like Easter. Tucked well-back from Main Street behind the Motel 6 and adjacent to an alfalfa field, the campground is a collection of large grassy sites shaded by tall trees and bisected by a gravel roadway and parking. The Tamarisk Restaurant at the Best Western next door is one of Green River's best, with seating overlooking the river bridge and colonies of swifts swooping down to catch insects (bug repellent is a good summer precaution). Across the street is the John Wesley Powell River History Museum building, which also houses a gallery and visitors center. Overall, the location is very convenient for parking and walking once settled in, and a good base for exploring the surrounding area.

BASICS

Operated By: Charles & Linda Burrage. **Open:** All year. **Site Assignment:** First come, first served; reservations recommended holiday weekends. **Registration:** At office. **Fee:** $14.50 tent, $19.50 RV. (V, MC, AE, D). **Parking:** At site.

FACILITIES

Number of RV Sites: 65. **Number of Tent-Only Sites:** 14. **Hookups:** Electric (20, 30, 50 amp), water, sewer, cable TV. **Each Site:** Table. **Dump Station:** Yes. **Laundry:** Yes. **Pay Phone:** Yes. **Rest Rooms and Showers:** Yes. **Fuel:** No. **Propane:** Yes. **Internal Roads:** Gravel, excellent. **RV Service:** No. **Market:** 2 blocks. **Restaurant:** Next door. **General Store:** Yes. **Vending:** No. **Swimming:** Pool. **Playground:** Yes. **Other:** Portable grill on request, modem hookup in office. **Activities:** Boating, river rafting. **Nearby Attractions:** Arches, Canyonlands, Capitol Reef, Goblin Valley State Park. **Additional Information:** Emery County Travel Bureau, (888) 564-3600, www.emerycounty.com.

RESTRICTIONS

Pets: On leash under owner's control. **Fires:** Yes. **Alcoholic Beverages:** Allowed. **Vehicle Maximum Length:** Over 100 ft. **Other:** 11 a.m. checkout.

TO GET THERE

Exit I-70 at Main Street in Green River, enter via driveway between Motel 6 and Best Western.

HANKSVILLE

Goblin Valley State Park

P.O. Box 637, Green River 84525. T: (435) 564-3633 or (800) 322-3770 (reservations).

🚐 ★★★★   ⛺ ★★★★★

Beauty: ★★★★★	Site Privacy: ★★★★★
Spaciousness: ★★★★★	Quiet: ★★★★★
Security: ★★★★	Cleanliness: ★★★★
Insect Control: ★★★	Facilities: ★★

The intriguing chocolate-colored goblins giving this park its name result from uneven wind and rain erosion of sandstone layers of varying hardness in this remote area once frequented by uranium miners and ancient Native Americans. The San Rafael Reef, which has steep canyons hidden inside its sawtooth swells, is also part of the Jurassic and Triassic sandstone and siltstone scenery left behind by an ancient sea in what is now the Green River Desert. The campground itself is a half loop backed by orange-and-white sandstone walls with hoodoos, spires, and a hilltop oil well

pumping away next to solar panels. The restroom and hot showers are also powered by solar arrays. There is little shade from the midday sun. On hot summer days the sandstone walls surrounding the spacious campground sites radiate extra heat. But the goblins, reefs, badlands, balanced rocks, spires, and hoodoos make a colorful geologic adventure for self-sufficient campers.

BASICS

Operated By: Utah State Parks. **Open:** All year. **Site Assignment:** First come, first served; 14 sites can be reserved (up to 16 weeks in advance of checkout date for individuals; up to 11 months in advance for group site). **Registration:** Self-pay entrance fee station. **Fee:** $12. **Parking:** At site.

FACILITIES

Number of RV Sites: 21. **Number of Tent-Only Sites:** 0. **Hookups:** None. **Each Site:** Table, grill. **Dump Station:** Yes. **Laundry:** No. **Pay Phone:** No. **Rest Rooms and Showers:** Yes. **Fuel:** No. **Propane:** No. **Internal Roads:** Paved, good condition. **RV Service:** No. **Market:** Hanksville, 32 mi.; Green River, 35 mi. **Restaurant:** Hanksville, 32 mi.; Green River, 35 mi. **General Store:** No. **Vending:** No. **Swimming:** No. **Playground:** No. **Other:** Covered picnic pavilion at observation point, wheelchair-accessible rest room. **Activities:** Geologic exploration. **Nearby Attractions:** Capitol Reef, Canyonlands. **Additional Information:** Emery County Travel Bureau, (888) 564-3600, www.emerycounty.com.

RESTRICTIONS

Pets: On leash under owner's control. **Fires:** Yes. **Alcoholic Beverages:** Allowed. **Vehicle Maximum Length:** No limit. **Other:** No ground fires, 14-day limit.

TO GET THERE

Go 20 mi. north from Hanksville on UT Hwy. 24, at milepost 137 turn west onto Temple Mountain Road for 5 mi., then at intersection go 7 mi. south on graded dirt county road.

HANKSVILLE

Red Rock Restaurant and Campground

Box 55, Hanksville 84734. T: (435) 542-3235;
www.hanksville.com; redrock@hanksville.com.

🚐 ★★★★   ⛺ ★★★

Beauty: ★★★   Site Privacy: ★★
Spaciousness: ★★   Quiet: ★★★★
Security: ★★★★   Cleanliness: ★★★★
Insect Control: ★★★★   Facilities: ★★★★

With gas stations, RV repair, a post office, and other amenities within blocks, this friendly restaurant with a well-maintained campground in back makes a good stopping point en route to Capitol Reef, Bullfrog Marina on Lake Powell, or Canyonlands. The restaurant has everything from steaks to beer and wine, which is handy, as there are no grills. Just behind the restaurant is a grassy area for tent camping that will suffice for a night. Three gravel rows for RVs extend further back, with a small tree between each site and a fence separating the property from an irrigated field at the rear. Though more an overnight stop, the location does lend itself to day trips to Goblin Valley State Park, Capitol Reef, and an adventurous dirt-road excursion (not to be attempted when rain threatens) heading north to Green River via the San Rafael Desert.

BASICS

Operated By: Elliot & Layne Arnoldson. **Open:** Mar. 15–Nov. 1. **Site Assignment:** First come, first served; reservations accepted. **Registration:** In restaurant. **Fee:** $10 tent, $16 RV (V, MC, D). **Parking:** At site.

FACILITIES

Number of RV Sites: 60. **Number of Tent-Only Sites:** 60. **Hookups:** Electric (30, 50 amp), water, sewer. **Each Site:** Table. **Dump Station:** Yes. **Laundry:** Yes. **Pay Phone:** Yes. **Rest Rooms and Showers:** Yes. **Fuel:** No. **Propane:** No. **Internal Roads:** Gravel, good condition. **RV Service:** No. **Market:** 1.5 blocks away. **Restaurant:** On site. **General Store:** No. **Vending:** Yes. **Swimming:** No. **Playground:** No. **Activities:** Geologic exploration. **Nearby Attractions:** Goblin Valley State Park, Capitol Reef, Canyonlands, Hite Marina, Natural Bridges. **Additional Information:** Emery County Travel Bureau, (888) 564-3600, www.emerycounty.com.

RESTRICTIONS

Pets: On leash. **Fires:** Yes. **Alcoholic Beverages:** Allowed. **Vehicle Maximum Length:** Unlimited in circle area.

TO GET THERE

Go 200 ft. west on Hwy. 24 from junction of Utah Hwys 24 & 95.

HATCH

Riverside Motel & RV Park

P.O. Box 521, Hatch 84735. T: (435) 735-4223 or (800) 824-5651; F: (435) 735-4220; brycecanyoncountry.com/accommodations/hatch; riversid@color-country.net.

🚐 ★★★   ⛺ ★★★

Beauty: ★★★★   Site Privacy: ★★★★
Spaciousness: ★★★★   Quiet: ★★★★
Security: ★★★★   Cleanliness: ★★★★
Insect Control: ★★★   Facilities: ★★★★

Strategically situated on the banks of the Sevier River just south of the Bryce Junction (where UT Hwy. 12 intersects US Hwy. 89), Riverside is a magnet for tour buses. The campground is isolated in a small valley behind an office/gift shop, motel, and restaurant and is bordered by the river on two sides. The seven designated tent sides are along the river, separated from the RVs by a large grass playing field that doubles as a tour bus group tent site. International groups, ranging from musicians to teens, like the river and distant Red Canyon mountain backdrops, as well as the group pavilion. But the campground quiets down after 10 p.m., and an occasional truck and the raging wind are about the extent of the noise most nights. The 18-foot wide pull-through sites, network TV reception, and convenient location make this a good RV stop.

BASICS

Operated By: Cordell & Julie Peters/Brent & Kathy Parkinson. **Open:** Mar. 1–Nov. 1. **Site Assignment:** First come, first served; reservations accepted. **Registration:** Office inside store. **Fee:** $13 tent, $17–$20 RV (V, MC). **Parking:** At site.

FACILITIES

Number of RV Sites: 47. **Number of Tent-Only Sites:** Undesignated sites. **Hookups:** Electric (20, 30, 50 amp), water, sewer. **Each Site:** Table, grill. **Dump Station:** Yes. **Laundry:** Yes. **Pay Phone:** Yes. **Rest Rooms and Showers:** Yes. **Fuel:** No. **Propane:** Yes. **Internal Roads:** Gravel, good. **RV Service:** No. **Market:** Panguitch, 8 mi. **Restaurant:** On site. **General Store:** Yes. **Vending:** Yes. **Swimming:** In river. **Playground:** Yes. **Other:** Horseshoe pit, basketball court, motel. **Activities:** Fishing. **Nearby Attractions:** Panguitch Lake, Red Canyon, Cedar Breaks, Bryce, Zion. **Additional Information:** Garfield County Travel Council, (800) 444-6689; Bryce Canyon National Park Headquarters, (435) 834-5322.

RESTRICTIONS

Pets: On leash under owner's control. **Fires:** Yes. **Alcoholic Beverages:** Allowed. **Vehicle Maximum Length:** Over 45 ft.

TO GET THERE

From junction w/ UT Hwy. 12, go 2 mi. south on US Hwy. 89.

HOVENWEEP NATIONAL MONUMENT
Hovenweep Campground

McElmo Rte., Cortez 81321. T: (970) 562-4282; www.nps.gov/hove.

🚐 ★★	⛺ ★★★★
Beauty: ★★★★	Site Privacy: ★★★★
Spaciousness: ★★	Quiet: ★★★★
Security: ★★★★	Cleanliness: ★★★★★
Insect Control: ★★★	Facilities: ★★

Designed in the 1960s for tent and car camping when there was little need for pull-through sites, Hovenweep has narrow roads and tight cornering. Self-sufficiency is the watchword here, as there are sand pads for tents and some sheltered tables but neither dump stations nor showers. Only two sites are adequate for larger vehicles, but small vehicles and tent campers will do well in the small sites separated by tall junipers alive with twittering birds. High-axle or four-wheel drive vehicles are needed to reach archaeological sites like Holly, Horseshoe, and Hackberry Ruins. But regular hiking trails dotted with creamy cliff roses lead to other archaeological sites, such as Hovenweep Castle, the tall canyon-bottom Square Tower, and the double-walled Cajon sun house built near a spring at the head of a canyon. During winter, the trails get slippery from snow and ice and become dangerous near cliffs.

BASICS

Operated By: National Park Service. **Open:** All year. **Site Assignment:** First come, first served. **Registration:** Self-pay fee station. **Fee:** $10 (cash or check only). **Parking:** At site.

FACILITIES

Number of RV Sites: 31. **Number of Tent-Only Sites:** 0. **Hookups:** None. **Each Site:** Table, grill. **Dump Station:** No. **Laundry:** No. **Pay Phone:** No. **Rest Rooms and Showers:** No showers. **Fuel:** No. **Propane:** No. **Internal Roads:** Gravel, good. **RV Service:** No. **Market:** Bluff, 40 mi. **Restaurant:** Bluff, 40 mi. **General Store:** No. **Vending:** No. **Swimming:** No. **Playground:** No. **Other:** Visitor center, amphitheater, Anasazi crop garden, ranger program (summer weekends). **Activities:** Mountain biking. **Nearby Attractions:** Monument Valley, Canyonlands, Natural Bridges. **Additional Information:** Edge of the Cedars State Park, (435) 678-2238.

RESTRICTIONS

Pets: On leash (allowed on trails w/ short leashes). **Fires:** Yes (in fire grates only, no wood collection, must bring own wood or charcoal). **Alcoholic Beverages:** Allowed. **Vehicle Maximum Length:** 25 ft. **Other:** Collection of artifacts is illegal, 2 tents or 6 people per site.

TO GET THERE

From Bluff go 30 mi. east on US Hwy. 262 and then 10 mi. northeast at Aneth.

HURRICANE
Brentwood RV Resort

150 North 3700 West, Hurricane 84737. T: (435) 635-2320 or (800) 447-2239.

🚐 ★★★★	⛺ ★★
Beauty: ★★★★	Site Privacy: ★★★★
Spaciousness: ★★★★	Quiet: ★★★★
Security: ★★★★	Cleanliness: ★★★★
Insect Control: ★★★	Facilities: ★★★★

Hurricane is located between St. George and Zion National Park and makes a good shopping place for those wanting to purchase food, hardware, and other supplies. There are many fine campground options between St. George and Zion, but Brentwood boasts a convenient roadside location, wide spaces for slide-outs, and amenities like bowling and billiards. Tent campers have a grassy area near the playground and tennis courts with mulberries and other trees still too small to provide much shade. The shadiest part of the tent area has four spaces right up against the tennis courts. Canyons RV Resort and Willowind RV Park (see Appendix) are grassier, smaller, and further back from the road. Nearby Quail Creek State Park is probably the better place for a boating weekend. If Zion National Park is the destination, then Zion River Resort in Virgin, Zion Canyon Campground in Springdale, and the two National Park Service campgrounds should be considered.

BASICS

Operated By: Brentwood Resort. **Open:** All year. **Site Assignment:** First come, first served; reservations accepted. **Registration:** Office. **Fee:** $12 tent, $19 RV (V, MC, AE, D). **Parking:** At site.

FACILITIES

Number of RV Sites: 187. **Number of Tent-Only Sites:** Undesignated sites. **Hookups:** Electric (30, 50 amp), water, sewer, cable TV. **Each Site:** Table. **Dump Station:** Yes. **Laundry:** Yes. **Pay Phone:** Yes. **Rest Rooms and Showers:** Yes. **Fuel:** No. **Propane:** No. **Internal Roads:** Paved, good. **RV Service:** No. **Market:** Hurricane, 1 mi. **Restaurant:** Hurricane, 1 mi. **General Store:** No. **Vending:** Yes. **Swimming:** Pool. **Playground:** Yes. **Other:** Bowling, billiards, tennis, some grills. **Activities:** Golf, horseshoes, shuffleboard, boating, fishing. **Nearby Attractions:** Quail Creek State Park, Zion. **Additional Information:** Washington County Travel Bureau, (435) 634-5747, (800) 869-6635.

RESTRICTIONS

Pets: On leash under owner's control. **Fires:** Yes. **Alcoholic Beverages:** Allowed. **Vehicle Maximum Length:** 60 ft. **Other:** Children under 18 must be under parental supervision.

TO GET THERE

From US I-15 8 mi. north of St. George go east 5 mi. on UT Hwy. 9.

KANAB

Coral Pink Sand Dunes State Park

P.O. Box 95, Kanab 84741. T: (435) 648-2800 or (800) 322-3770; F: (435) 648-2801; www.parks.state.ut.us.

🚐 ★★★★　　　　Ⓐ ★★★★

Beauty: ★★★★★	Site Privacy: ★★★★★
Spaciousness: ★★★★★	Quiet: ★★★★
Security: ★★★★★	Cleanliness: ★★★★
Insect Control: ★★★	Facilities: ★★

Beautiful orange-sand dunes dotted with ponderosa pine trees and six-foot-tall dune grasses support both off-highway vehicle activity and scientific study areas with the unique Coral Pink Sand Dunes tiger beetle and Welsh milkweed. Coral Pink Sand Dunes State Park is also very popular with student groups, who come to learn about dune life from wood walkways protecting the dunes. Campsites are especially spacious, with parking loops accommodating extra long vehicles (e.g. 75–148 feet) or multiple smaller vehicles. Tall junipers growing out of the orange sand screen campsites from each other, and bicyclists pedal the paved roads. At 6,000 feet elevation, the park gets snow for winter activities. Hiking trails offer views of Zion, the Grand Canyon's North Rim, and ancient Native American pictographs. Reservations are advised at this popular park, and can be made 11 months in advance by groups or up to 16 weeks in advance of checkout date (a minimum of three days in advance of arrival) by individuals.

BASICS

Operated By: Utah State Parks. **Open:** All year. **Site Assignment:** First come, first served; group reservations; specific sites can be reserved one night at a time. **Registration:** Entrance kiosk. **Fee:** $13 per vehicle (V, MC, Utah checks). **Parking:** Loops at site.

FACILITIES

Number of RV Sites: 22. **Number of Tent-Only Sites:** 0. **Hookups:** Water, electric (30 amp). **Each Site:** Table, grill. **Dump Station:** Yes. **Laundry:** No. **Pay Phone:** Yes. **Rest Rooms and Showers:** Yes. **Fuel:** No. **Propane:** No. **Internal Roads:** Paved, good condition. **RV Service:** No. **Market:** 22 mi. northwest in Kanab. **Restaurant:** 22 mi. northwest in Kanab. **General Store:** No.

Vending: No. **Swimming:** No. **Playground:** No. **Other:** ADA accessible wood walkways over sand dunes, off-highway access to dunes. **Activities:** Off-highway vehicle riding, biking, snow mobiling, snow tubing. **Nearby Attractions:** Pipe Springs National Monument, Kanab, Escalante Staircase National Monument, Zion, Grand Canyon North Rim. **Additional Information:** Kane County Office of Tourism, 78 S. 100 East, Kanab, UT 84741; (435) 644-5033; (800) 733-5263; kanetrav@kaneutah.com; www.kaneutah.com.

RESTRICTIONS

Pets: On leash, never unattended. **Fires:** Yes (firewood sold). **Alcoholic Beverages:** Allowed. **Vehicle Maximum Length:** 148 ft. **Other:** 14-day limit, no wood gathering, no fireworks.

TO GET THERE

Go 13 mi. north from Kanab on US Hwy. 89, then southwest on Hancock Rd. to Sand Dunes Rd. for 11 mi.

KANAB
Ponderosa Grove Recreation Site

318 North 1st E, Kanab 84721.T: (435) 644-2672 or (801) 539-4002; www.utso.ut.blm.gov.

🚐 ★★   ▲ ★★★

Beauty: ★★★★	Site Privacy: ★★★★
Spaciousness: ★★★	Quiet: ★★★★
Security: ★★★	Cleanliness: ★★★★
Insect Control: ★★★★	Facilities: ★

Along with the tall grass and sand "Meadow," a big open field with pine cones where camping is free, Ponderosa Grove Recreation Site also acts as an overflow for the often full Coral Pink Sand Dunes State Park. Tall ponderosa pines and junipers give a forested feel to this 6,500-foot-elevation high-desert BLM campground. Though a primitive experience with off-road vehicle access to the rolling orange-sand dunes, Ponderosa Grove offers disabled access. Two large group sites on small loops accommodate ten vehicles each. Showers are available for a fee at Coral Pink Sand Dunes State Park. For good food, head 16 miles to Mt. Carmel Junction and the excellent honey butter scones at the Golden Hills Restaurant, or 15 miles to the many restaurants, stores, and full-hookup RV parks (see Appendix) of Kanab, where the visitor center is lined with posters of movies filmed in the area, which western film-buffs call "Little Hollywood."

BASICS

Operated By: BLM. **Open:** April 1–Oct. 31. **Site Assignment:** First come, first served. **Registration:** Self-pay entrance fee station. **Fee:** $5. **Parking:** At site.

FACILITIES

Number of RV Sites: 9. **Number of Tent-Only Sites:** 0. **Hookups:** None. **Each Site:** Table & grills on cement pads. **Dump Station:** No. **Laundry:** No. **Pay Phone:** No. **Rest Rooms and Showers:** No shower. **Fuel:** No. **Propane:** No. **Internal Roads:** Dirt road, good condition. **RV Service:** No. **Market:** Kanab. **Restaurant:** Kanab or Mt. Carmel Junction. **General Store:** No. **Vending:** No. **Swimming:** No. **Playground:** No. **Other:** Disabled access. **Activities:** Off-highway vehicle riding. **Nearby Attractions:** Pipe Springs & Escalante Staircase National Monuments, Zion, Grand Canyon North Rim. **Additional Information:** Coral Pink Sand Dunes State Park, (435) 648-2800; Kane County Office of Tourism, 78 S. 100 East, Kanab, UT 84741; (435) 644-5033; (800) 733-5263; kanetrav@kaneutah.com; www.kaneutah.com.

RESTRICTIONS

Pets: On leash under owner's control. **Fires:** Yes. **Alcoholic Beverages:** Allowed. **Vehicle Maximum Length:** 24 ft. **Other:** 14-day max. stay.

TO GET THERE

Go 7 mi. north from Kanab on US Hwy. 89, then 7 mi. southwest on Hancock Rd.

LAKE POWELL
Bullfrog Resort & Marina Campground/RV Park

P.O. Box 56909, Phoenix 85079.T: (435) 684-7000; F: (435) 684-2319; www.visitlakepowell.com.

🚐 ★★★★   ▲ ★★★★

Beauty: ★★★★★	Site Privacy: ★★★★
Spaciousness: ★★★★	Quiet: ★★★★
Security: ★★★★	Cleanliness: ★★★★
Insect Control: ★★	Facilities: ★★★★★

Bullfrog Resort & Marina in Glen Canyon National Recreation Area includes the Painted

Hills RV Park and Bullfrog Campground. Both are operated by Aramark Parks & Resorts, an authorized National Park Service concessionaire. The year-round RV Park has full hookups and is attractively nestled among tall conifers and low yellowish sandstone hills. The RV Park does not allow tents. Tent camping is allowed only at the seasonal Campground, which is also open to RV vehicles; sites 1–21 on Loop A have the best lake views. Tent campers must go to the village store and shell out additional money ($2) to take a shower, whereas the RV Park has showers. But it is the boating, fishing, and water sports, not campground amenities, that is the attraction here. Indeed, many locals skip the two pricey campgrounds in favor of primitive camping on the beaches (no designated sites) lining the shores of Lake Powell.

BASICS

Operated By: Aramark Parks & Resorts. **Open:** All year (for RVs; tents Mar.–Oct. only). **Site Assignment:** First come, first served; reservations accepted. **Registration:** Self-pay fee station (Campground); Lodge (RV Park). **Fee:** $16–$27 (cash only; US currency, no checks). **Parking:** At site.

FACILITIES

Number of RV Sites: 110. **Number of Tent-Only Sites:** 0. **Hookups:** Electric (20, 30 amp), water, sewer. **Each Site:** Table, grill. **Dump Station:** Yes. **Laundry:** Yes. **Pay Phone:** Yes. **Rest Rooms and Showers:** Yes. **Fuel:** No. **Propane:** Yes. **Internal Roads:** Paved & gravel, good. **RV Service:** No. **Market:** Blanding, 84 mi. **Restaurant:** Bullfrog Marina. **General Store:** Yes. **Vending:** Yes. **Swimming:** Lake. **Playground:** No. **Other:** Ferry, boat rental, motel. **Activities:** Boating, fishing, water sports. **Nearby Attractions:** Natural Bridges. **Additional Information:** National Park Service, (435) 684-7400; Lake Powell Ferry, (435) 684-3000; Glen Canyon Natural History Assoc., www.pagelakepowell.org.

RESTRICTIONS

Pets: On leash & under control at all times. **Fires:** Yes (in grills only, no ground fires). **Alcoholic Beverages:** Allowed. **Vehicle Maximum Length:** 35 ft. **Other:** No fireworks or loaded firearms.

TO GET THERE

From junction of UT Hwys 95 & 276 south of Hanksville, go 46 mi. south on UT Hwy. 276.

LAKE POWELL
Halls Crossing RV Park/ Campground

P.O. Box 56909, Phoenix 85079. T: (435) 684-7000; F: (435) 684-2319; www.visitlakepowell.com.

🚐 ★★★   ⛺ ★★★

Beauty: ★★★★   Site Privacy: ★★★★
Spaciousness: ★★★   Quiet: ★★★★
Security: ★★★★   Cleanliness: ★★★★
Insect Control: ★★   Facilities: ★★★★

A National Park Service concessionaire, Aramark Parks & Resorts, operates two camping areas on the Halls Crossing side of Lake Powell in the Glen Canyon National Recreation Area. Halls Crossing is most easily reached by highway from Blanding to the east, though a ferry (hours vary seasonally and are limited, ending well before nightfall) links Halls Crossing with Bullfrog Marina to the north. The gravel RV Park sites are attractively nestled in an oasis of trees providing shade and a buffer from the surrounding high-desert sagebrush and scrub. Tents are not allowed in Halls Crossing RV Park, which has full hookups. But Halls Crossing Campground, which lacks hookups, is open to both tents and self-sufficient RVs and trailers. The Campground has trees shading the tents from the hot summer sun, and good lake views looking down from an elevation across sagebrush-studded orange sands.

BASICS

Operated By: Aramark Parks & Resorts. **Open:** All year (for RVs; tents Apr.–Oct. only). **Site Assignment:** First come, first served; reservations accepted. **Registration:** Self-pay fee station. **Fee:** $18–$28 (cash only; US currency, no checks). **Parking:** At site.

FACILITIES

Number of RV Sites: 97. **Number of Tent-Only Sites:** 0. **Hookups:** Electric (20, 30 amp), water, sewer. **Each Site:** Table, grill. **Dump Station:** Yes. **Laundry:** Yes. **Pay Phone:** Yes. **Rest Rooms and Showers:** Yes. **Fuel:** No. **Propane:** Yes. **Internal Roads:** Paved, good. **RV Service:** No. **Market:** Blanding, 84 mi. **Restaurant:** Bullfrog Marina. **General Store:** Yes. **Vending:** Yes. **Swimming:** Lake. **Playground:** No. **Other:** Ferry, boat rental. **Activities:** Boating, fishing, water sports.

Nearby Attractions: Natural Bridges. **Additional Information:** National Park Service, (435) 684-7400; Lake Powell Ferry, (435) 684-3000; Glen Canyon Natural History Assoc., www.pagelakepowell.org.

RESTRICTIONS

Pets: On leash (not allowed on marina or archaeological sites). **Fires:** Yes (in grills only, no ground fires). **Alcoholic Beverages:** Allowed (but not when driving a boat). **Vehicle Maximum Length:** 35 ft. **Other:** No fireworks or loaded firearms.

TO GET THERE

From junction of UT Hwys 95 & 276 west of Blanding, go 42 mi. west on UT Hwy. 276.

LEEDS
Red Cliffs Recreation Site

225 North Bluff, St. George 84770. T: (435) 688-3246; www.utso.ut.blm.gov.

🚐 ★★   ▲ ★★★★

Beauty: ★★★★★   Site Privacy: ★★★★★
Spaciousness: ★★   Quiet: ★★★★
Security: ★★★★   Cleanliness: ★★★★
Insect Control: ★★★   Facilities: ★

The frontage road ducks under an 11.5-foot-high tunnel under US I-15 and crosses seasonal Quail Creek on the way to Red Cliffs. But self-sufficient campers (bring your own water, as the park water is not safe for drinking) are rewarded with three trails leading through the scenic red sandstone to Anasazi ruins, an old silver-mining area and red-cliff views. The Silver Reef is particularly unusual, as the silver ore fueling an 1880s mining boom was embedded in sandstone. Though campsite 1 is large enough to accommodate any vehicle on the road, most sites are relatively small and big rigs would find maneuvering difficult, even if they squeezed through the narrow underpass tunnel. The picnic area is alongside a creek, with tall cottonwood trees providing shade and a wheelchair ramp. Winters are mild, with nighttime lows above 20° F, and snow rare. Summer temperatures can soar above 100° F.

BASICS

Operated By: BLM. **Open:** All year. **Site Assignment:** First come, first served. **Registration:** Self-pay entrance fee station. **Fee:** $8 (cash or check only). **Parking:** At site.

FACILITIES

Number of RV Sites: 16. **Number of Tent-Only Sites:** 0. **Hookups:** None. **Each Site:** Table, grill. **Dump Station:** Yes. **Laundry:** No. **Pay Phone:** No. **Rest Rooms and Showers:** No showers. **Fuel:** No. **Propane:** No. **Internal Roads:** Paved, adequately maintained. **RV Service:** No. **Market:** St. George, 15 mi. **Restaurant:** St. George, 15 mi. **General Store:** No. **Vending:** No. **Swimming:** No. **Playground:** No. **Other:** Picnic area. **Activities:** Golf, boating, fishing. **Nearby Attractions:** Quail Creek State Park, Zion, Cedar Breaks, Brian Head. **Additional Information:** Washington County Travel Bureau, (435) 634-5747, (800) 869-6635.

RESTRICTIONS

Pets: On leash under owner's control. **Fires:** Yes (limited when high fire danger). **Alcoholic Beverages:** Allowed (at site; not allowed on trail). **Vehicle Maximum Length:** 24 ft. **Other:** Gate closed 10 p.m. to 6 a.m., no off-road vehicles or firearms.

TO GET THERE

From St. George take US I-15 north to Exit 22 and go south on frontage road under tunnel to BLM Rd.

LEEDS
Zion West RV Park

175 South Valley Rd., P.O. Box 460721, Leeds 84746. T: (435) 879-2854.

🚐 ★★★★   ▲ ★★★★

Beauty: ★★★★   Site Privacy: ★★★★
Spaciousness: ★★★★   Quiet: ★★★★
Security: ★★★★   Cleanliness: ★★★★
Insect Control: ★★★★   Facilities: ★★★★

Carved out of an alfalfa field belonging to the farmer next door, Zion West is still relatively new and the trees do not provide as much shade as is found at the Leeds RV Park & Motel next door. At 3,200 feet there is rarely snow, but Brian Head ski area is about an hour away, making this such a popular destination that the RV park is booked full from October to May. Indeed, many snowbirds book their October reservations when leaving in May. Tent campers have a large grassy area with tables without designated sites, as well as another area when more space is needed. Leeds RV parks make a good alternative to the roadside RV parks in nearby St. George, as they are farther back from the road. But the tradeoff for additional quietness is being further from the urban amenities of St. George.

BASICS

Operated By: Jim & Gloria Parnell. **Open:** All year. **Site Assignment:** First come, first served; reservations advised Oct.-May. **Registration:** Office. **Fee:** $12 tent, $15 RV (cash or check only). **Parking:** At site.

FACILITIES

Number of RV Sites: 30. **Number of Tent-Only Sites:** 12. **Hookups:** Electric (30, 50 amp), water, sewer. **Each Site:** Table. **Dump Station:** Yes. **Laundry:** Yes. **Pay Phone:** Yes. **Rest Rooms and Showers:** Yes. **Fuel:** No. **Propane:** No. **Internal Roads:** Paved, good. **RV Service:** No. **Market:** St. George, 11 mi. **Restaurant:** St. George, 11 mi. **General Store:** No. **Vending:** Yes. **Swimming:** No. **Playground:** No. **Other:** Dog walk. **Activities:** Rock climbing, biking, golf, horseback riding. **Nearby Attractions:** Zion, Quail Creek, Cedar Breaks, Brian Head. **Additional Information:** Washington County Travel Bureau, (435) 634-5747, (800) 869-6635.

RESTRICTIONS

Pets: On leash (noisy pets not tolerated). **Fires:** Yes. **Alcoholic Beverages:** Allowed. **Vehicle Maximum Length:** 45 ft.

TO GET THERE

From St. George take US I-15 11 mi. north to Exit 22, then go 0.5 mi. north on frontage road and south a block on Mulberry Lane.

LITTLEFIELD

Virgin River Canyon Recreation Area

390 North 3050 East, St. George 84770. T: (435) 688-3246.

🚐 ★★	🏕 ★★★
Beauty: ★★★★★	Site Privacy: ★★★★
Spaciousness: ★★★★	Quiet: ★★★★
Security: ★★★★	Cleanliness: ★★★★
Insect Control: ★★★	Facilities: ★

Situated in the remote northwest corner of Arizona where US I-15 crosses from Nevada into Utah, Virgin River is popular among international rock climbers and job hunters who can't decide between Mesquite, Nevada, and St. George, Utah.

Big rigs and groups can fill up the campground in spring, fall, or winter. But in summer, when temperatures top 110° F in the shade, a handful of campers typically have the three loops to themselves. Except for the clusters of four sites around the restroom with wheelchair accessibility, the sites are relatively far apart. Some truck noise can be heard from the highway, but the scenic green, orange, yellow, and white sandstone hills of the Paiute Wilderness and Beaver Dam Mountains are a visual delight. It is an easy hike to the Virgin River, cell phones work, and the area's 100 bighorn sheep occasionally make an appearance.

BASICS

Operated By: BLM. **Open:** All year. **Site Assignment:** First come, first served; group reservations. **Registration:** Self-pay fee station. **Fee:** $8 (cash or check only). **Parking:** At site.

FACILITIES

Number of RV Sites: 71. **Number of Tent-Only Sites:** 0. **Hookups:** None. **Each Site:** Table, charcoal pit. **Dump Station:** No (gray water dump). **Laundry:** No. **Pay Phone:** No. **Rest Rooms and Showers:** No showers. **Fuel:** No. **Propane:** No. **Internal Roads:** Paved, gravelly. **RV Service:** No. **Market:** Mesquite, NV, or St. George, UT, 18 mi. **Restaurant:** Mesquite, NV, or St. George, UT, 18 mi. **General Store:** No. **Vending:** No. **Swimming:** No. **Playground:** No. **Other:** Sheltered tables, wheelchair-accessible sites. **Activities:** Rock climbing, horseback riding. **Nearby Attractions:** Nevada casinos, Utah Mormon monuments. **Additional Information:** Washington County Travel Bureau, (435) 634-5747, (800) 869-6635.

RESTRICTIONS

Pets: On leash (horses must be kept outside campground). **Fires:** Yes (in grills only, no ground fires, LPG, or big petroleum stoves). **Alcoholic Beverages:** Allowed. **Vehicle Maximum Length:** 45 ft. **Other:** Smoking only in barren areas at least 3 ft. in diameter, gate closes 9 p.m.–6 a.m.

TO GET THERE

Go 18 mi. south from St. George, UT, or 18 mi. north from Mesquite, NV, on US I-15 to the Cedar Pockets Exit.

MANTI

Palisade State Park

2200 Palisade Rd., P.O. Box 650070, Sterling 84655. T: (835) 835-7275 or (800) 322-3770; www.nr.state.ut.us.

🚐 ★★★★ ⛺ ★★★★

Beauty: ★★★★ Site Privacy: ★★★★
Spaciousness: ★★★★ Quiet: ★★★★
Security: ★★★★ Cleanliness: ★★★★
Insect Control: ★★ Facilities: ★★★★

Started in the 1860s by rancher Daniel Funk, who built the original reservoir (Funk's Lake) and a dance pavilion at what became a popular resort in the horse-and-buggy days, Palisade State Park now boasts a golf course with a clubhouse and PGA pro a short walk from the North Campground, which has the largest pull-through sites. The South Campground, furthest from the golf course and nearest the sandy beach, has a group pavilion and tent area. Eleven double sites are spread out among the South, North, and East Campgrounds. Developers are trying to sell homes and commercial spaces on the two miles of Palisades Road leading into the park. But for now this remains a sleepy backwater campground (use peaks on summer weekends) with lake-view campsites (50–53 are best), non-motorized boating, cutthroat and rainbow trout, and ice fishing and ice skating during the winter.

BASICS

Operated By: Utah State Parks & Recreation. **Open:** All year. **Site Assignment:** First come, first served; reservations for individuals (120 days in advance) & groups (1 year in advance). **Registration:** Entry kiosk (sporadically open) or self-pay fee station (the usual). **Fee:** $13 (V, MC if entry kiosk open; otherwise cash or check only). **Parking:** At site.

FACILITIES

Number of RV Sites: 53. **Number of Tent-Only Sites:** 0. **Hookups:** None. **Each Site:** Table, grill. **Dump Station:** Yes. **Laundry:** No. **Pay Phone:** Yes. **Rest Rooms and Showers:** Yes. **Fuel:** No. **Propane:** No. **Internal Roads:** Paved, excellent. **RV Service:** No. **Market:** Manti, 7 mi. **Restaurant:** Manti, 7 mi. **General Store:** Yes. **Vending:** Yes. **Swimming:** Lake (swimmer's itch,

schistosomiasis warning). **Playground:** No. **Other:** Boat ramp, canoe & paddleboat rental, golf course (18 hole, par 72) & clubhouse w/ pro, amphitheater, extensive picnic areas. **Activities:** Golf, fishing, non-motorized boating, winter sports. **Nearby Attractions:** Manti Temple, national forest. **Additional Information:** Sanpete County Heritage Council, (435) 283-4321, (800) 281-4346, www.sanpete.com.

RESTRICTIONS

Pets: On leash under owner's control (kept off beach & out of water). **Fires:** Yes (in grills or metal containers 6 inches off ground). **Alcoholic Beverages:** Allowed (but not mixed w/ boating). **Vehicle Maximum Length:** 40 ft. **Other:** No diving from rocks, no hanging or tying things to trees, personal flotation devices must be worn on boats, firearms must be unloaded & locked away.

TO GET THERE

Go 6 mi. south of Manti on US Hwy. 89 and 2 mi. east on Palisades Rd.

MEXICAN HAT

Goosenecks State Park

c/o Edge of Cedars State Park Museum, 660 West 400 North, Blanding 84511. T: (435) 678-2238; www.nr.state.ut.us.

🚐 ★★ ⛺ ★★

Beauty: ★★★★★ Site Privacy: ★★★★
Spaciousness: ★★★ Quiet: ★★★★
Security: ★★★★ Cleanliness: ★★★★★
Insect Control: ★★★★ Facilities: ★

The view looking 1,000 feet down into the Goosenecks of the San Juan River is often photographed for geology textbooks as a classic case of an entrenched meander. Basically, tectonic plate collisions have uplifted 300-million-year-old rocks and allowed a meandering river to create a meandering river canyon. RVs must bring their own water and brace for very strong winds and summer thunderstorms when camping out at 5,000-feet elevation along the edge of the scenic overlook. Parking is pretty much anywhere in open areas with views of the wide expanse stretching south into Monument Valley. Dust devils along the road are not uncommon, and signs warn off large vehicles towing other vehicles. Indeed, unimproved roads with sharp curves and steep grades will keep big rigs from going further north on UT Hwy. 261 to explore the Valley of the Gods, whose rock formations are like a Monument Valley in miniature.

BASICS

Operated By: Utah State Parks & Recreation. **Open:** All year. **Site Assignment:** First come, first served. **Registration:** Self-pay entrance fee station. **Fee:** None. **Parking:** At site.

FACILITIES

Number of RV Sites: 8. Number of Tent-Only Sites: 0. Hookups: None. **Each Site:** Table. **Dump Station:** Yes. **Laundry:** No. **Pay Phone:** No. **Rest Rooms and Showers:** No showers. **Fuel:** No. **Propane:** No. **Internal Roads:** Gravel, good. **RV Service:** No. **Market:** Bluff, 27 mi. **Restaurant:** Mexican Hat, 8 mi. **General Store:** No. **Vending:** No. **Swimming:** No. **Playground:** No. **Other:** Pavilion at overlook w/ sheltered table & grill. **Activities:** Picnicking, biking, off-road vehicles. **Nearby Attractions:** Edge of Cedars State Park Museum, Valley of the Gods, Monument Valley, Hovenweep, Natural Bridges. **Additional Information:** San Juan County Visitor Services, (435) 587-3235, (800) 574-4386.

RESTRICTIONS

Pets: On leash. **Fires:** Yes (in grills). **Alcoholic Beverages:** Allowed. **Vehicle Maximum Length:** No limit.

TO GET THERE

From Mexican Hat go 3 mi. northwest on US Hwy. 163, 1 mi. north on UT Hwy. 261 and 4 mi. west on UT Hwy. 316.

MIDWAY

Wasatch Mountain State Park

P.O. Box 10, Midway 84049. T: (435) 654-1791 or (800) 322-3770 (reservations); www.nr.state.ut.us.

🚐 ★★★★★   ⛺ ★★★★★

Beauty: ★★★★★	Site Privacy: ★★★★★
Spaciousness: ★★★★★	Quiet: ★★★★
Security: ★★★★	Cleanliness: ★★★★
Insect Control: ★★★	Facilities: ★★★

Three different campgrounds with 72 holes of golf and secluded oak thickets within an hour of Salt Lake City make Wasatch Mountain so desirable that anyone without a weekend reservation is usually turned away. Park City's Olympic ski lifts and the Olympic biathlon park at Soldier Hollow are nearby, as are state parks at Jordenelle, and Deer Creek Reservoirs for water recreation. Two Wasatch Mountain campgrounds have hookups, and one loop is set aside for tents. Mahogany Campground is popular for its pull-through sites (1, 3, 5, 21, 23, 25, 27); sites 15–26 have great views across Heber Valley. Cottonwood Campground RV sites 36–47 are coveted for their tall cottonwood trees providing shade all day. Tent camping is restricted to Oak Hollow Campground's 40 sites, many enclosed in oak canopies. Children can use the playground and fish in a pond near the Visitor Center, which has a display explaining the hot springs underlying the area.

BASICS

Operated By: Utah State Parks & Recreation. **Open:** Early Apr.–until snow closes (no reservations taken after Oct. 15). **Site Assignment:** First come, first served (for available sites); reservations necessary weekends (starting Friday) from Memorial Day to Labor Day. **Registration:** Entry kiosk. **Fee:** $14–$16 (V, MC; $6.25 site reservation fee). **Parking:** At site.

FACILITIES

Number of RV Sites: 106. Number of Tent-Only Sites: 0. Hookups: Electric (20, 30, 50 amp), water, sewer. **Each Site:** Table, grill or fire ring. **Dump Station:** Yes. **Laundry:** No. **Pay Phone:** Yes. **Rest Rooms and Showers:** Yes. **Fuel:** No. **Propane:** No. **Internal Roads:** Paved, cracks patched. **RV Service:** No. **Market:** Midway, 5 mi. **Restaurant:** Midway, 0.5 mi. **General Store:** No. **Vending:** No. **Swimming:** Homestead Resort, 2 mi. **Playground:** Yes (at Visitor Center). **Other:** 72 holes of golf, ice for sale, pavilions, amphitheater. **Activities:** Golf, horseback riding, fishing, boating. **Nearby Attractions:** Park City, Soldier Hollow, Timpanogos Cave National Monument, historic railway, reservoirs. **Additional Information:** Heber Valley Chamber of Commerce, (435) 654-3666, www.hebervalleycc.org.

RESTRICTIONS

Pets: On leash under owner's control. **Fires:** Yes (grill or fire pit only, firewood sold, no fires when extreme summer danger). **Alcoholic Beverages:**

Allowed. **Vehicle Maximum Length:** 75 ft.
Other: 10 p.m.–8 a.m. gate locked, no fireworks.

To Get There

From junction of UT Hwy. 113 and Main St. in Midway, go 6 mi. north on Pine Canyon Rd.

MOAB

Arch View Camp Park

P.O. Box 1406, Canyonlands Campground 84532. T: (435) 259-7854 or (800) 813-6622; www.moab.net/archview; archview@lasal.net.

🚐 ★★★★   ▲ ★★★

Beauty: ★★★★   Site Privacy: ★★★★
Spaciousness: ★★★★   Quiet: ★★★
Security: ★★★★   Cleanliness: ★★★★
Insect Control: ★★★   Facilities: ★★★★

Well-positioned at the Canyonlands National Park and Dead Horse Point State Park junction (UT Hwy. 313) and just five miles north of the Arches National Park entrance, Arch View seems isolated in the countryside, surrounded by red sandstone hills. But the Moab action is only nine miles to the south. The office and general-store building was originally built as a TV movie set for "Riders of the Purple Sage," and the area is popular with film crews. There are good views of Mt. Peale and the North and South Windows in Arches National Park. Cottonwood trees between gravel RV sites and cottontail rabbits scampering into the surrounding desert scrub add to the rural ambiance, though the campground is not free from highway noise. Tent sites are shaded by tall cottonwood trees and are predominately grass, though there is some dirt. About the only amenity missing is a restaurant.

Basics

Operated By: Mitch White. **Open:** Mar.–Jan. **Site Assignment:** First come, first served; reservations recommended peak seasons & holidays. **Registration:** Office. **Fee:** $17–$20 (V, MC, AE, D, DC). **Parking:** At site.

Facilities

Number of RV Sites: 60. **Number of Tent-Only Sites:** 28. **Hookups:** Electric (20, 30, 50 amp), water, sewer, cable TV, phone (modem). **Each Site:** Table, grill. **Dump Station:** Yes. **Laundry:**

Yes. **Pay Phone:** Yes. **Rest Rooms and Showers:** Yes. **Fuel:** Yes. **Propane:** Yes. **Internal Roads:** Gravel, good. **RV Service:** No. **Market:** Moab, 9 mi. **Restaurant:** Moab, 9 mi. **General Store:** Yes. **Vending:** Yes. **Swimming:** Pool. **Playground:** Yes. **Other:** Cabins. **Activities:** Horseback riding, golf, biking, fishing, boating, rafting. **Nearby Attractions:** Arches, Canyonlands, Dead Horse Point. **Additional Information:** Grand County Travel Council, (800) 635-MOAB, Canyonlands Natural History Assoc., (435) 259-6003, www.cnha.org.

Restrictions

Pets: On leash, quiet, & under owner's control at all times. **Fires:** Yes (at community fire site only, firewood sold). **Alcoholic Beverages:** Allowed. **Vehicle Maximum Length:** 50 ft. **Other:** No dirt bike, ATV riding, or firearms.

To Get There

From Moab go 9 mi. north on US Hwy. 191.

MOAB

Canyonlands Campground

555 South Main St., Moab 84532. T: (435) 259-6848 or (800) 522-6848; F: (435) 259-6848; www.moab utah.com/canyonlands/RV.html; cancamp@lasal.net.

🚐 ★★★★   ▲ ★★★★

Beauty: ★★★   Site Privacy: ★★★
Spaciousness: ★★★   Quiet: ★★★
Security: ★★★★★   Cleanliness: ★★★★★
Insect Control: ★★★   Facilities: ★★★★★

In the center of Moab, within walking distance of bakeries with cappuccino, microbreweries, galleries, and shops, Canyonlands has tall cottonwood trees and level shaded pull-through spaces with cement pads. RV spaces in rows 5–8 can also be used for tents, and there are also two separate dirt areas for tents. The best tent sites in row G have sheltered tables. A footbridge across Pack Creek leads to 15 more secluded walk-in tent sites sharing a common sheltered eating area. Though in the center of town, Canyonlands is surprisingly quiet late at night, with less truck noise than the KOA outside of town, because speeds slow to 25 miles per hour downtown and there is no need for truckers to use noisy engine brakes. Thus, Moab's oldest campground remains very popular, and reservations are a must on holiday weekends and from June on, when Canyonlands fills up every night.

BASICS

Operated By: Paul & Aggie Evans. **Open:** All year. **Site Assignment:** First come, first served; reservations recommended peak times. **Registration:** Office. **Fee:** $16–$23 (V, MC, AE, D). **Parking:** At site; separate parking for walk-in tent sites.

FACILITIES

Number of RV Sites: 105. **Number of Tent-Only Sites:** 28. **Hookups:** Electric (30, 50 amp), water, sewer, cable TV, phone (modem). **Each Site:** Table, grill. **Dump Station:** Yes. **Laundry:** Yes. **Pay Phone:** Yes. **Rest Rooms and Showers:** Yes. **Fuel:** Yes. **Propane:** No. **Internal Roads:** Gravel, good. **RV Service:** No. **Market:** Moab, 1 block. **Restaurant:** Moab, less than 1 block. **General Store:** Yes. **Vending:** Yes. **Swimming:** Pool. **Playground:** No. **Other:** Pavilion, pet walk, horseshoes, cabins. **Activities:** Biking, boating, rafting, fishing, golf, jeep touring. **Nearby Attractions:** Arches, Canyonlands. **Additional Information:** Grand County Travel Council, (800) 635-MOAB.

RESTRICTIONS

Pets: On leash & not left unattended. **Fires:** Yes. **Alcoholic Beverages:** Allowed. **Vehicle Maximum Length:** 45 ft. **Other:** No hammocks allowed.

TO GET THERE

From Main (US Hwy. 191) & Center Sts. in downtown Moab, go 5 blocks south on Main St. and enter next to Amoco Station.

MOAB

Dead Horse Point State Park

P.O. Box 609, Moab 84532. T: (435) 259-2614 or (800) 322-3770 (reservations).

🚐 ★★★★   ⛺ ★★★★

Beauty: ★★★★★	Site Privacy: ★★★★
Spaciousness: ★★★★★	Quiet: ★★★★
Security: ★★★★★	Cleanliness: ★★★★★
Insect Control: ★★★	Facilities: ★★

Named after a wild mustang corral where horses died of thirst, Dead Horse Point Overlook offers a marvelous view (80–100 miles most clear days) across deep sandstone mesas and a gooseneck in the Colorado River where the silence is so complete that a lone motorized raft can be clearly heard far below. Water is scarce on this high plateau, as it has to be trucked in from Moab, so bring your own or buy it by the gallon (limited) from the Visitor Center. The campground loop has tall pinyon pines and Utah junipers separating spacious orange-sand sites, the smallest accommodating a 40-foot rig. If the crowds in Arches and Moab get too much, this is a good place to come for quiet, though noises can really travel through the campground. At the very least, this is a scenic stop en route to Canyonlands Island in the Sky District.

BASICS

Operated By: Utah State Parks. **Open:** All year. **Site Assignment:** First come, first served; reservations accepted (required for group site). **Registration:** At park entrance. **Fee:** $13. **Parking:** At site.

FACILITIES

Number of RV Sites: 21. **Number of Tent-Only Sites:** 0. **Hookups:** None. **Each Site:** Sheltered table, charcoal grill, sand tent pad. **Dump Station:** Yes. **Laundry:** No. **Pay Phone:** Yes. **Rest Rooms and Showers:** No showers. **Fuel:** No. **Propane:** No. **Internal Roads:** Paved, good condition. **RV Service:** No. **Market:** Moab, 32 mi. **Restaurant:** Moab, 32 mi. **General Store:** No. **Vending:** Yes. **Swimming:** No. **Playground:** No. **Other:** One wheelchair-accessible site. **Activities:** Evening ranger programs in amphitheater (May–Sept.). **Nearby Attractions:** Canyonlands, Arches, Moab. **Additional Information:** Canyonlands Natural History Assoc., (435) 259-6003, www.cnha.org; Grand County Travel Council, (800) 635-MOAB.

RESTRICTIONS

Pets: On 6-ft. leash under owner's control. **Fires:** Charcoal only in grills, no ground or wood fires. **Alcoholic Beverages:** Allowed. **Vehicle Maximum Length:** 105 ft. **Other:** 8 people & 2 vehicles per site, no firearms, fireworks, or harassing wildlife.

TO GET THERE

Go 11 mi. northwest from Moab on US Hwy. 191, then 23 mi. southwest on UT Hwy. 313.

MOAB
Moab KOA

3225 South Hwy. 191, Moab 84532. T: (435) 259-6682 or (800) 562-0372; www.moab-utah.com/koa; koa@lasal.net.

🚐 ★★★★   ▲ ★★★

Beauty: ★★★   Site Privacy: ★★★
Spaciousness: ★★★   Quiet: ★★★
Security: ★★★★★   Cleanliness: ★★★★★
Insect Control: ★★★★   Facilities: ★★★★★

Surrounded by farms, mountains, and sagebrush-covered desert land, the Moab KOA has what appears to be an idyllic location. The gravel sites and abundance of trees reinforce the rural feel of the open countryside and surrounding mountains. There are two playgrounds, mini-golf, a pool, and more than enough amenities to make this a worthwhile base for exploring the territory both north and south of Moab. Besides, all the shops, galleries, restaurants, and microbreweries of Moab are only four miles down the road. The only drawback for those who are light sleepers is that the campground is situated alongside a steep highway grade where truckers use their noisy engine brakes late at night. But other than that, it is hard to find fault with this clean, well-maintained campground and its hardworking and helpful hosts.

BASICS

Operated By: Bob & Lila Ott. **Open:** Mar.–Oct. **Site Assignment:** First come, first served; reservations accepted. **Registration:** Office. **Fee:** $20–$27 (V, MC, AE, D). **Parking:** At site.

FACILITIES

Number of RV Sites: 73. **Number of Tent-Only Sites:** 52. **Hookups:** Electric (30, 50 amp), water, sewer, cable TV, phone (modem). **Each Site:** Table, grill. **Dump Station:** Yes. **Laundry:** Yes. **Pay Phone:** Yes. **Rest Rooms and Showers:** Yes. **Fuel:** No. **Propane:** Yes. **Internal Roads:** Gravel, good. **RV Service:** No. **Market:** Moab, 4 mi. **Restaurant:** Moab, 4 mi. **General Store:** Yes. **Vending:** Yes. **Swimming:** Pool. **Playground:** Yes. **Other:** Game room, mini-golf, dog walk, cabins. **Activities:** Boating, rafting, horseback riding, golf, rock climbing, biking, jeep touring. **Nearby Attractions:** Arches, Canyonlands, Newspaper Rock. **Additional Information:** Grand County Travel Council, (800) 635-MOAB.

RESTRICTIONS

Pets: On leash & attended by owner at all times (not allowed in playground or store area). **Fires:** Yes (only charcoal fires in grills). **Alcoholic Beverages:** Allowed (at site only). **Vehicle Maximum Length:** 70 ft. **Other:** No wasting water or running generators, children must be under adult supervision.

TO GET THERE

From Moab go 4 mi. south on US Hwy. 191.

MOAB
Moab Rim Campark

1900 South Hwy. 191, Moab 84532. T: (435) 259-5002 or (888) 599-6622; F: (435) 259-5002; www.moab-utah.com/moabrimcampark.html; moabrim@moab-utah.com.

🚐 ★★★   ▲ ★★

Beauty: ★★★★   Site Privacy: ★★★
Spaciousness: ★★★   Quiet: ★★★
Security: ★★★★   Cleanliness: ★★★★★
Insect Control: ★★★★   Facilities: ★★★

Fronted by vineyards that provide a bit of a highway noise buffer and remind of the new wine industry here, Moab Rim is attractively situated part way up a hillside across the street from the Crazy Horse Saloon. Only ten RV sites have full hookups, while nine have electric and water. Moab Rim is one of the few commercial campgrounds with more tent sites than RV sites. Fire pits are located at designated locations rather than at every site, in expectation than many travelers will partake of Moab's many restaurants and microbreweries instead of cooking for themselves after a hard day of hiking or sightseeing. In any case, the fire-pit areas are excellent locations for sitting in the evening, as they offer excellent vistas of Moab and the surrounding mountains. All in all, a good stop for those preferring a small, intimate, almost boutique type of campground.

BASICS

Operated By: Jim & Sue Farrell. **Open:** Mar. 1–Nov. 30. **Site Assignment:** First come, first served; reservations recommended on weekends. **Registration:** Office. **Fee:** $15–$22 (V, MC). **Parking:** At site.

FACILITIES

Number of RV Sites: 22. **Number of Tent-Only Sites:** 30. **Hookups:** Electric (30, 50 amp), water, sewer. **Each Site:** Table. **Dump Station:** Yes. **Laundry:** No. **Pay Phone:** Yes. **Rest Rooms and Showers:** Yes. **Fuel:** No. **Propane:** No. **Internal Roads:** Gravel, good. **RV Service:** No. **Market:** Moab, 2 mi. **Restaurant:** Moab, 2 mi. **General Store:** Yes. **Vending:** Yes. **Swimming:** No. **Playground:** No. **Other:** Cabins, fire pits at designated locations. **Activities:** Boating, rafting, horseback riding, golf, biking. **Nearby Attractions:** Arches, Canyonlands, Newspaper Rock. **Additional Information:** Grand County Travel Council, (800) 635-MOAB.

RESTRICTIONS

Pets: On leash under owner's control. **Fires:** Yes. **Alcoholic Beverages:** Allowed. **Vehicle Maximum Length:** 35 ft. **Other:** No dishwashing in restroom sinks.

TO GET THERE

From downtown Moab, go 2 mi. south on US Hwy. 191.

MOAB
Portal RV Park & Fishery

1261 North Hwy. 191, Moab 84532. T: (435) 259-6108 or (800) 574-2028; F: (435) 259-7931; www.portalrvpark.com; camp@portalrvpark.com.

🚐 ★★★★	⛺ ★★★★
Beauty: ★★★★	Site Privacy: ★★★
Spaciousness: ★★★★	Quiet: ★★★★
Security: ★★★★	Cleanliness: ★★★★★
Insect Control: ★★★★	Facilities: ★★★★

Just south of the Colorado River Bridge and the bend in US Hwy. 191 north of Moab, Portal is positioned behind a pasture well back from the main highway, which means less noise than at the roadside Spanish Trail RV Park next door. However, Portal is only five years old and its cottonwood trees do not provide the lush shady environment found at Spanish Trail. But Portal does have fishing ponds, optional hookups to a private well with mountain spring water, trails to view birds and wildlife, horses and geese next door, and good La Sal Mountain views. Tent campers will like the grassy sheltered sites, and two group areas hold 25 tents each. Thus, Portal makes an excellent base for exploring Canyonlands and Arches National Parks and Moab. The small friendly campground is usually booked full peak season (Mar.–May) and holidays, when reservations are always recommended in Moab.

BASICS

Operated By: Kent & Ann Oldham. **Open:** All year. **Site Assignment:** First come, first served; reservations recommended. **Registration:** Self-pay entrance fee station. **Fee:** $17–$25 (V, MC). **Parking:** At site.

FACILITIES

Number of RV Sites: 36. **Number of Tent-Only Sites:** 10. **Hookups:** Electric (30, 50 amp), water, sewer, cable TV, phone (modem). **Each Site:** Table, grill. **Dump Station:** Yes. **Laundry:** Yes. **Pay Phone:** Yes. **Rest Rooms and Showers:** Yes. **Fuel:** No. **Propane:** No. **Internal Roads:** Gravel, good. **RV Service:** No. **Market:** Moab, 2 mi. **Restaurant:** Moab, 2 mi. **General Store:** Yes. **Vending:** Yes. **Swimming:** No. **Playground:** No. **Other:** Pavilion, picnic areas, dog walk, fishing ponds, cabins. **Activities:** Horseback riding, biking, boating, rafting, golf. **Nearby Attractions:** Arches, Canyonlands. **Additional Information:** Canyonlands Natural History Assoc., (435) 259-6003, www.cnha.org; Grand County Travel Council, (800) 635-MOAB.

RESTRICTIONS

Pets: On leash under owner's control. **Fires:** Yes (only in tent site fire rings, no fires at RV sites). **Alcoholic Beverages:** Allowed (must be confined to site; no rowdiness or drunkness). **Vehicle Maximum Length:** 60 ft. **Other:** No firearms or fireworks, no dirt bike or ATV riding.

TO GET THERE

Go 2 mi. north of Moab on US Hwy. 191.

MONUMENT VALLEY
Goulding's Monument Valley Campground

Box 360001, Monument Valley 84536. T: (435) 727-3235; F: (435) 727-3344; www.gouldings.com; gouldings@gouldings.com.

🚐 ★★★★   ⛺ ★★★★

Beauty: ★★★★   Site Privacy: ★★
Spaciousness: ★★★   Quiet: ★★★★
Security: ★★★★★   Cleanliness: ★★★★
Insect Control: ★★★★   Facilities: ★★★★★

Long the premier establishment in Monument Valley and headquarters for film-makers such as John Ford, whose film "Stagecoach" with John Wayne turned the area into a popular movie and TV commercial locale, Goulding's has successfully extended its quality franchise from trading post to lodge to campground. With an indoor swimming pool and nearby gas station, grocery store, restaurant, and air strip, Goulding's red-dirt campground is a compact oasis surrounded by imposing red rock sandstone formations. The only real activity here, besides touring Goulding's Trading Post Museum, watching a multimedia presentation, and visiting the tribal visitor center, is touring Monument Valley itself. While private vehicles are allowed down some of the dirt roads, half- and full-day (and longer) jeep and horseback riding tours are a popular alternative. There are obligatory stops at Navajo hogans to watch women weave, photograph Navajos (a gratuity is expected) in their finery on horseback, and view the area's geology and petroglyphs.

BASICS
Operated By: Goulding's Lodge & Trading Post. **Open:** Mar. 15–Nov. 1. **Site Assignment:** First come, first served. **Registration:** Office in convenience store. **Fee:** $15 tent, $24 RV (V, MC, AE, D, DC). **Parking:** At site.

FACILITIES
Number of RV Sites: 66. **Number of Tent-Only Sites:** 45. **Hookups:** Electric (20, 30 amp), water, sewer, cable TV, phone (modem). **Each Site:** Table, grill. **Dump Station:** Yes. **Laundry:** Yes. **Pay Phone:** Yes. **Rest Rooms and Showers:** Yes. **Fuel:** Yes. **Propane:** Yes. **Internal Roads:** Paved,

good. **RV Service:** No. **Market:** Monument Valley, 1 mi. **Restaurant:** Monument Valley, 1 mi. **General Store:** Yes. **Vending:** Yes. **Swimming:** Indoor pool. **Playground:** Yes. **Other:** Free shuttle to lodge, air strip. **Activities:** Navajo Tribal Park tours, horseback riding. **Nearby Attractions:** Navajo Tribal Park. **Additional Information:** Monument Valley Visitors Center, (435) 727-3287; Black's Hiking & Jeep Tours, (435) 739-4226, (800) 749-4226.

RESTRICTIONS
Pets: On leash at all times (not allowed in restrooms, store, laundry, or undeveloped areas). **Fires:** Yes. **Alcoholic Beverages:** Allowed. **Vehicle Maximum Length:** 36 ft. **Other:** "Do onto others as you would have them do onto you."

TO GET THERE
From US Hwy. 163 0.5 mi. north of UT–AZ border, go 2.5 mi. west on Monument Valley Rd.

MONUMENT VALLEY
Mitten View Campground

P.O. Box 360289, Monument Valley 84536. T: (435) 727-3287 or (435) 727-3353.

🚐 ★★★★   ⛺ ★★★★★

Beauty: ★★★★★   Site Privacy: ★★★★
Spaciousness: ★★★★   Quiet: ★★★★
Security: ★★★★   Cleanliness: ★★★★
Insect Control: ★★★★   Facilities: ★★★

Surrounded by sandstone mesas and a panorama of red plateaus, buttes, pinnacles, and talus piles, Mitten View Campground is one of the best places to wake up to the morning light and watch the sunsets turn the sagebrush-studded land into a palette of reds, browns, and oranges. Mitten View is adjacent to the Monument Valley Visitors Center, where payment is made to drive the 17 miles of dirt road open to the public. The road is rough, and many visitor's opt for a guided tour by jeep to save the wear and tear on their vehicles and learn from the Navajo guides. Fortunately the campground has sheltered tables, as the few short junipers and desert scrub provide little shade. Indeed, tents can become virtual hothouses in hot weather. But the small tent sites ringing the perimeter have better views of the 30,000-acre Monument Valley than the larger interior pull-through sites.

BASICS

Operated By: Navajo Parks & Recreation Bureau. **Open:** All year. **Site Assignment:** First come, first served; reservations advised May–Sept. **Registration:** Self-pay fee station. **Fee:** $10 (cash or check only). **Parking:** At site.

FACILITIES

Number of RV Sites: 52. **Number of Tent-Only Sites:** 44. **Hookups:** None. **Each Site:** Sheltered table, grill. **Dump Station:** Yes. **Laundry:** No. **Pay Phone:** No. **Rest Rooms and Showers:** Yes. **Fuel:** No. **Propane:** No. **Internal Roads:** Gravel, good. **RV Service:** No. **Market:** Goulding's, 4 mi. **Restaurant:** Goulding's, 4 mi. **General Store:** No. **Vending:** No. **Swimming:** No. **Playground:** No. **Other:** Visitor Center nearby. **Activities:** Monument Valley tours, horseback riding. **Nearby Attractions:** Goulding's Trading Post. **Additional Information:** Monument Valley Visitors Center, (435) 727-3287; Black's Hiking & Jeep Tours, (435) 739-4226, (800) 749-4226.

RESTRICTIONS

Pets: On leash. **Fires:** Yes. **Alcoholic Beverages:** Prohibited on tribal lands. **Vehicle Maximum Length:** 36 ft. **Other:** No rock climbing.

TO GET THERE

Follow US Hwy. 163 to Monument Valley Visitors Center.

NATURAL BRIDGES NATIONAL MONUMENT
Natural Bridges

Box 1, Lake Powell 84533. T: (435) 692-1234; F: (435) 692-1111; www.nps.gov/nabr.

🚐 ★★   ▲ ★★★★★

Beauty: ★★★★★   Site Privacy: ★★★★★
Spaciousness: ★★   Quiet: ★★★★★
Security: ★★★★   Cleanliness: ★★★★★
Insect Control: ★★★   Facilities: ★

Established as a National Monument by President Theodore Roosevelt in 1908, Natural Bridges lies at 6,000-feet elevation in a high desert where rabbitbrush and sage meet a forest of pinyon pine and Utah juniper. Formed by stream erosion, the natural bridges continue to erode and will eventually disappear. The small campground is busiest on Saturdays, but most days even mid-afternoon arrivals snag a campsite. When the campground is full, campers are shunted to a large BLM overflow area six miles away, which also accommodates vehicles longer than Natural Bridges's 26-feet limit. The flat orange-sand tent pads are good, though amenities outside the Visitor Center are few. For campgrounds with more amenities, head to Blanding or go 55 miles west to Halls Crossing or Bullfrog Marina on Lake Powell. In winter the campground stays open, but the one-way nine-mile loop drive to the natural bridge overlooks and trailheads is closed.

BASICS

Operated By: National Park Service. **Open:** All year. **Site Assignment:** First come, first served. **Registration:** Self-pay fee station. **Fee:** $10 (cash or check only). **Parking:** At site.

FACILITIES

Number of RV Sites: 13. **Number of Tent-Only Sites:** 0. **Hookups:** None. **Each Site:** Table, grill, fire ring. **Dump Station:** Yes. **Laundry:** No. **Pay Phone:** No. **Rest Rooms and Showers:** No showers. **Fuel:** No. **Propane:** No. **Internal Roads:** Paved, good. **RV Service:** No. **Market:** Blanding, 42 mi. **Restaurant:** Fry Canyon, 20 mi. **General Store:** No. **Vending:** No. **Swimming:** No. **Playground:** No. **Other:** Visitor center, amphitheater. **Activities:** Boating, evening ranger programs. **Nearby Attractions:** Bullfrog Marina/Lake Powell, Goosenecks State Park. **Additional Information:** Canyonlands Natural History Assoc., (435) 259-6003, www.cnha.org.

RESTRICTIONS

Pets: On leash (not allowed on trails). **Fires:** Yes (in grills only, no fires allowed in dry years when high fire danger). **Alcoholic Beverages:** Allowed. **Vehicle Maximum Length:** 26 ft. **Other:** 1 vehicle & 8 people per site.

TO GET THERE

From US Hwy. 191 4 mi. south of Blanding go 32 mi. west on UT Hwy. 95 and 6 mi. west on UT Hwy. 275.

NEPHI

Nephi KOA/ Horseshoe Bar Ranch

Salt Creek Canyon, P.O. Box 309, Nephi 84648. T:
(435) 623-0811.

🚐 ★★★★   ⛺ ★★★★

Beauty: ★★★★★   Site Privacy: ★★★★
Spaciousness: ★★★★   Quiet: ★★★★★
Security: ★★★★   Cleanliness: ★★★★★
Insect Control: ★★★   Facilities: ★★★★

Situated on a 700-acre cattle ranch established in
1882 by the owner's grandfather, Heber B.
Ockey, a Mormon pioneer who survived "Indian
problems" and tough times, the over three-
decade-old Nephi KOA is isolated in a canyon
adjacent to a relatively quiet, scenic highway several miles from town. The friendly ambiance and
canyon solitude bring repeat business from those
stumbling upon the place for the first time as an
overnight stop. Two creeks running through the
ranch offer trout fishing possibilities, and nearby
Mt. Nebo offers trails and a scenic drive. But
there is no real destination draw for this off-the-
beaten-track bit of wilderness, which is a good
stopping place for relaxation. Nephi itself is an
agricultural hub with a decent Mexican restaurant, some drive-ins, cafes, gas stations, and
stores serving the surrounding farming community. Good signs from the center of town provide
campground directions, but first-time around
make the approach in daylight.

BASICS

Operated By: Jim & Carolyn Ockey. **Open:**
May–Oct. **Site Assignment:** First come, first
served; reservations accepted. **Registration:** Self-
pay entrance fee station. **Fee:** $17–$23 (V, MC, D).
Parking: At site.

FACILITIES

Number of RV Sites: 62. **Number of Tent-
Only Sites:** 20. **Hookups:** Electric (20, 30 amp),
water, sewer. **Each Site:** Table. **Dump Station:**
Yes. **Laundry:** Yes. **Pay Phone:** Yes. **Rest Rooms
and Showers:** Yes. **Fuel:** No. **Propane:** No.
Internal Roads: Paved, excellent. **RV Service:**
No. **Market:** Nephi, 5 mi. **Restaurant:** Nephi, 5
mi. **General Store:** Yes. **Vending:** Yes. **Swimming:** Pool. **Playground:** Yes. **Other:** 7 cabins,
fenced dog walk, game room, fish pond, sports field.

Activities: Fishing, horseback riding. **Nearby
Attractions:** National Forests. **Additional Information:** Nephi/Juab County Chamber of Commerce, (435) 623-2411.

RESTRICTIONS

Pets: On leash under owner's control. **Fires:** Yes.
Alcoholic Beverages: Allowed (provided not
excessive). **Vehicle Maximum Length:** 55 ft.
Other: No motor bike riding.

TO GET THERE

From US I-15 Exit 225 at Nephi, go west 6 mi.
on UT Hwy. 132.

PANGUITCH

Panguitch Big Fish KOA

P.O. Box 384, Panguitch 84759. T: (435) 676-2225 or
(800) 562-1625; zionkoa@color-country.net.

🚐 ★★★★   ⛺ ★★★★

Beauty: ★★★★   Site Privacy: ★★★★
Spaciousness: ★★★★   Quiet: ★★★★
Security: ★★★★★   Cleanliness: ★★★★
Insect Control: ★★★   Facilities: ★★★★

A very well-maintained campground with plenty
of shade trees and grass, Panguitch Big Fish KOA
feels very rural, with distant mountains and
neighboring pastures where horse and sheep
graze only five blocks from town. The tent sites
are grassy, and the afternoon breeze welcome in
summer. Over half the clientele is European,
drawn to this location because it is quiet and off
the main drag, as well as near town and equidis-
tant between important park destinations. To the
west, Panguitch Lake and Cedar Breaks are less
than an hour away. To the east, Bryce Canyon
and Kodachrome Basin are similarly near, making this a good central location for area exploration, though not as wilderness in feel as the
Red Canyon or Cannonville KOA campgrounds. Overall, this is a safe choice, reliable
and well run, with ample activities (e.g. video
games, pool, badminton net) for kids.

BASICS

Operated By: Gregg & Jo Green. **Open:** Apr.
15–Oct. 15. **Site Assignment:** First come, first
served; reservations accepted. **Registration:** At
office. **Fee:** $19–$21 tent, $23–$26 RV (V, MC, AE,
D). **Parking:** At site.

FACILITIES

Number of RV Sites: 45. **Number of Tent-Only Sites:** 14. **Hookups:** Electric (50 amp), water, sewer. **Each Site:** Table, grill. **Dump Station:** Yes. **Laundry:** Yes. **Pay Phone:** Yes. **Rest Rooms and Showers:** Yes. **Fuel:** No. **Propane:** No. **Internal Roads:** Gravel, good condition. **RV Service:** No. **Market:** In Panguitch, 5 blocks north. **Restaurant:** In Panguitch. **General Store:** Yes. **Vending:** Yes. **Swimming:** Pool. **Playground:** Yes. **Other:** Game room, Internet access, pet walk. **Activities:** Wildlife museum in town. **Nearby Attractions:** Panguitch Lake, Cedar Breaks, Red Canyon, Bryce. **Additional Information:** Garfield County Travel Council, (800) 444-6689.

RESTRICTIONS

Pets: On leash under owner's control. **Fires:** Yes (firewood sold). **Alcoholic Beverages:** Allowed. **Vehicle Maximum Length:** 65 ft. **Other:** No running of generators, noon checkout.

TO GET THERE

From US 89 in Panguitch at intersection of Main and Center Sts., go 5 blocks south on Main St.

PANGUITCH
Red Canyon RV Park

P.O. Box 717, Panguitch 84759. T: (435) 676-2690; F: (435) 676-2765; www.redcanyon.net or www.onpages.com/thestore.

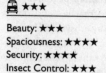

🚐 ★★★   ⛺ ★★

Beauty: ★★★	Site Privacy: ★★★
Spaciousness: ★★★★	Quiet: ★★★
Security: ★★★★	Cleanliness: ★★★★
Insect Control: ★★★	Facilities: ★★★

Red Canyon RV Park (not to be confused with the US Forest Service Red Canyon Campground) is on a relatively isolated stretch of UT Hwy. 12, just 16 miles from Bryce and 7 miles from Panguitch. The compact, well-run RV park, whose clientele is mostly seniors, has a few large pull-through sites among two short rows of RV sites. The grassy tent area is almost close enough to the highway to double as a roadside shoulder. But this is a good base camp to park the RV while biking area trails or taking a jeep or four-wheel-drive vehicle into Red Canyon. Coyote, elk, deer, cottontail, and jackrabbits visit the RV park, and red-headed woodpeckers peck away at the trees, adding a sense of wilderness to what would otherwise be a roadside stop. All in all, not a bad alternative for Red Canyon explorers and national park visitors when the campgrounds closer to Bryce fill up.

BASICS

Operated By: Arthur & Wenda Mae Tebbs. **Open:** April 1–Oct. 31 (weather permitting). **Site Assignment:** First come, first served. **Registration:** At office. **Fee:** $10 tent, $18 RV (V, MC, D). **Parking:** At site.

FACILITIES

Number of RV Sites: 40. **Number of Tent-Only Sites:** 20. **Hookups:** Water, electric (20, 30, 50 amp), sewer. **Each Site:** Table, shade canopy, grill. **Dump Station:** Yes. **Laundry:** No. **Pay Phone:** Yes. **Rest Rooms and Showers:** Yes. **Fuel:** Yes. **Propane:** No. **Internal Roads:** Gravel, excellent. **RV Service:** No. **Market:** 7 mi. northwest in Panguitch. **Restaurant:** 7 mi. northwest in Panguitch. **General Store:** Yes. **Vending:** Yes. **Swimming:** No. **Playground:** No. **Other:** Native American crafts store, rock shop, dog walk area. **Activities:** Jeep tours, bike trails. **Nearby Attractions:** Bryce, Lake Panguitch, Red Canyon. **Additional Information:** Powell Ranger District, (435) 676-8815.

RESTRICTIONS

Pets: On leash under owner's control. **Fires:** Yes. **Alcoholic Beverages:** Allowed. **Vehicle Maximum Length:** 60 ft.

TO GET THERE

Go 16 mi. west on UT Hwy. 12 from Bryce Canyon; or 1 mi. east on Hwy. 12 from the junction w/ US Hwy. 89.

PANGUITCH LAKE
Bear Paw Lakeview Resort

P.O. Box 397, 905 South Hwy. 143, Panguitch Lake 84759. T: (435) 676-2650 or (888) 553-8439; www.BearPawFishingResort.com; bearpaw@color-country.net.

🚐 ★★★   ⛺ n/a

Beauty: ★★★★   Site Privacy: ★★★★
Spaciousness: ★★★   Quiet: ★★★★
Security: ★★★★   Cleanliness: ★★★★
Insect Control: ★★   Facilities: ★★★

Located in Dixie National Forest near an area of massive lava flows, Bear Paw Lakeview Resort is a mixture of cabins and RV sites on a hillside dotted with pine trees and sage. A rustic pine wood general store and small cafe anchor the steeply sloping hillside. A 40-foot walk crossing UT Hwy. 143 leads to Panguitch Lake's rainbow, cutthroat, brook, and brown trout (worms, tackle, and fishing licenses for sale at the general store). Ironically, the Resort's small roadside cafe serves up almost everything but lake trout, claiming Utah state law allows restaurants to serve only USDA-inspected trout from fish farms. Kids and pets do well here, but space is limited and reservations are recommended. Indeed, the 32 RV sites up the road at Rustic Lodge & RV Park, which is under the same ownership, are booked up year after year in advance by the same people, many of whom have even built their own private fenced-in decks.

BASICS
Operated By: Laura & Glenn Adams. **Open:** First week in May–Oct. 31. **Site Assignment:** First come, first served; reservations (one night; refundable one week prior to arrival). **Registration:** In store. **Fee:** $19 (V, MC, AE, D). **Parking:** At site.

FACILITIES
Number of RV Sites: 17. **Number of Tent-Only Sites:** 0. **Hookups:** Electric (20, 30 amp), water, sewer. **Each Site:** Table, fire ring. **Dump Station:** Yes. **Laundry:** Yes. **Pay Phone:** Yes. **Rest Rooms and Showers:** Yes. **Fuel:** No. **Propane:** No. **Internal Roads:** Graded gravel, on slope. **RV Service:** No. **Market:** 15 mi. in Panguitch. **Restaurant:** Resort cafe serves 3 meals. **General Store:** Yes. **Vending:** Yes. **Swimming:** In lake. **Playground:** Yes. **Other:** Boat launch, horse-riding, boat slip, boat & mountain-bike rentals. **Activities:**

Trout fishing in lake & creeks. **Nearby Attractions:** Cedar Breaks, Bryce, Brian Head Ski Resort. **Additional Information:** Dixie National Forest, (435) 865-3200, www.fs.fed.us/dxnf.

RESTRICTIONS
Pets: On leash under owner's control. **Fires:** Yes. **Alcoholic Beverages:** Allowed. **Vehicle Maximum Length:** 34 ft.

TO GET THERE
17 mi. west of Panguitch or 12 mi. east of Cedar Breaks on UT Hwy. 143.

PANGUITCH LAKE
White Bridge Campground

P.O. Box 80, Panguitch Lake 84759. T: (877) 444-6777.

🚐 ★★★   ⛺ ★★★★

Beauty: ★★★★★   Site Privacy: ★★★★
Spaciousness: ★★★★   Quiet: ★★★★★
Security: ★★★★   Cleanliness: ★★★★
Insect Control: ★★   Facilities: ★

At 7,900-feet elevation, this Dixie National Forest campground nestled among hillsides covered with gray-green desert scrub opens and closes based on local snowfall dates. Campsites are widely dispersed on alternating sides of a good gravel road. Panguitch Creek flows through White Bridge, adding a bucolic burbling backdrop. However, for the entomophobic, Utah's lake and creek ecosystems may be too much nature. Periodic hatches of mayflies and other flying insects signify a healthy ecosystem (and are not sprayed in the National Forest), and fatten the trout, lizards, birds, and other wildlife for the tough winter ahead (and were a high-protein food source gathered by ancient Native Americans). The only warm-weather alternative for those who would rather appreciate the landscape without any nuisance or DEET (insect repellent) is to stick to drier desert areas. Seasoned campers already accustomed to watching out for the region's legendary rattlers and scorpions, will find Utah's lake and creek campgrounds a pleasant base for boating, trout fishing, horseback riding, and exploring nearby national parks.

BASICS
Operated By: Aud & Di Campground Services (US Forest Service concessionaire). **Open:**

May–first snow (Sept. or Oct.). **Site Assignment:** First come, first served; 11 sites can be reserved. **Registration:** Self-pay fee station at entrance. **Fee:** $10. **Parking:** At site.

FACILITIES

Number of RV Sites: 24. **Number of Tent-Only Sites:** 5. **Hookups:** None. **Each Site:** Table, grills. **Dump Station:** Yes. **Laundry:** No. **Pay Phone:** No. **Rest Rooms and Showers:** No showers. **Fuel:** No. **Propane:** No. **Internal Roads:** Gravel, good condition. **RV Service:** No. **Market:** 10 mi. northeast in Panguitch. **Restaurant:** 4 mi. west at Panguitch Lake. **General Store:** No. **Vending:** No. **Swimming:** In lake. **Playground:** No. **Activities:** Fishing. **Nearby Attractions:** Panguitch Lake, Cedar Breaks, Bryce. **Additional Information:** Dixie National Forest, (435) 865-3200, www.fs.fed.us/dxnf.

RESTRICTIONS

Pets: On leash. **Fires:** Yes. **Alcoholic Beverages:** Allowed. **Vehicle Maximum Length:** 32 ft. **Other:** No fireworks or firearms, noon checkout, 14-day limit.

TO GET THERE

Go 10 mi. southwest of Panguitch on UT Hwy. 143 or 4 mi. east from Panguitch Lake.

SALINA

Butch Cassidy Campground

1100 South State St., Salina 84654. T: (435) 529-7400 or (800) 551-6842.

🚐 ★★★   ⛺ ★★

Beauty: ★★★★	Site Privacy: ★★★★
Spaciousness: ★★★★	Quiet: ★★★
Security: ★★★★	Cleanliness: ★★★★
Insect Control: ★★★	Facilities: ★★★★

A rural crossroads for coal, salt, and gypsum (wallboard) mining traffic, Salina is a rustic overnight stop on the long trek across Utah on I-70. Tent camping is on the grass under trees alongside the highway or in quieter back-in RV sites. The RV sites, including 26 pull-throughs, are elevated on a hillside with less highway noise. Mobile homes are on a terrace above the RVs. Trees and grass provide pleasant visuals, but the real attraction is Mom's Cafe at the corner of Main and State Streets (US Hwy. 89). Mom sits

at a desk under a clock above the salad bar surveying the restaurant, and prides herself on some remarkably good road food. For breakfast try the Mad House Cafe on Main Street, where ceramics and children's art decorate the walls, and portions are large enough for a hungry trucker and a famished farmer to split (or just order blueberry pancakes at a buck apiece).

BASICS

Operated By: Lee, Danielle & Mich Crysel. **Open:** All year. **Site Assignment:** First come, first served; reservations accepted. **Registration:** Office. **Fee:** $12 tents, $15–$20 RV (V, MC). **Parking:** At site.

FACILITIES

Number of RV Sites: 38. **Number of Tent-Only Sites:** 20. **Hookups:** Electric (20, 30, 50 amp), water, sewer. **Each Site:** Table. **Dump Station:** Yes. **Laundry:** Yes. **Pay Phone:** Yes. **Rest Rooms and Showers:** Yes. **Fuel:** No. **Propane:** No. **Internal Roads:** Gravel, good. **RV Service:** No. **Market:** Salina, 1 mi. **Restaurant:** Across the street. **General Store:** Yes. **Vending:** Yes. **Swimming:** Pool. **Playground:** Yes. **Other:** Tent & back-in sites have grills. **Activities:** ATVs, fishing. **Nearby Attractions:** Fish Lake. **Additional Information:** Fish Lake National Forest, (435) 896-9233.

RESTRICTIONS

Pets: On leash at all times. **Fires:** Yes (in designated fire pits or grills). **Alcoholic Beverages:** Allowed. **Vehicle Maximum Length:** 60 ft. **Other:** No fireworks, no clothes lines.

TO GET THERE

From US I-70 Exit 54, go north 0.5 mi. on State St. (US Hwy. 89).

SPRINGDALE

Zion Canyon Campground

479 Zion Park Blvd., Springdale 84767. T: (435) 772-3237; www.zioncanyoncampground.com.

🚐 ★★★★   ⛺ ★★★★

Beauty: ★★★★	Site Privacy: ★★★★
Spaciousness: ★★★★	Quiet: ★★★★
Security: ★★★★	Cleanliness: ★★★★
Insect Control: ★★★	Facilities: ★★★★

The Zion National Park shuttle bus stops in front and the Virgin River is the back border of

Zion Canyon Campground, a bustling little village run by the same family for the past three decades. A popular pizza restaurant next door to the office and store has outdoor tables bordering UT Hwy. 14 and the campground's front entrance. The showers here are very popular with campers staying at the two campgrounds inside Zion National Park. Indeed, Zion Canyon is held in such high regard that National Park overflow is sent here. While not as rustic as the National Park campgrounds, the views of Zion's sandstone mountains are still good. The campground also has plenty of trees and a pond. RV sites B20 and B21 are open-ended and can accommodate any RV currently on the road. There are also numerous grassy sites with dirt perimeters close to the river.

BASICS

Operated By: Dave & Stew Ferber. **Open:** All year. **Site Assignment:** First come, first served. **Registration:** Office. **Fee:** $16–$20 (V, MC). **Parking:** At site.

FACILITIES

Number of RV Sites: 120. **Number of Tent-Only Sites:** 100. **Hookups:** Electric (30, 50 amp), water, sewer, cable TV. **Each Site:** Table, grill. **Dump Station:** Yes. **Laundry:** Yes. **Pay Phone:** Yes. **Rest Rooms and Showers:** Yes. **Fuel:** No. **Propane:** No. **Internal Roads:** Gravel, good. **RV Service:** No. **Market:** Springdale, 1 mi. **Restaurant:** On premises. **General Store:** Yes. **Vending:** Yes. **Swimming:** Pool, river. **Playground:** Yes. **Other:** Game room, pavilion. **Activities:** Biking, horseback riding. **Nearby Attractions:** Zion National Park. **Additional Information:** Washington County Travel Bureau, (435) 634-5747, (800) 869-6635.

RESTRICTIONS

Pets: On leash (in RV area; no pets in tent area). **Fires:** Yes. **Alcoholic Beverages:** Allowed. **Vehicle Maximum Length:** No limit.

TO GET THERE

Go 0.5 mi. south of Zion National Park south entrance on UT Hwy. 9.

ST. GEORGE

Quail Creek State Park

P.O. Box 1943, St. George 84771. T: (435) 879-2378 or (800) 322-3770 (reservations); www.nr.state.ut.us.

🚐 ★★★★	🔺 ★★★★
Beauty: ★★★★	Site Privacy: ★★★★
Spaciousness: ★★★★	Quiet: ★★★★
Security: ★★★★	Cleanliness: ★★★★
Insect Control: ★★	Facilities: ★★

Hundred-foot-deep warm blue waters and a red sandstone cliff backdrop only 15 miles northeast of St. George make 3,300-foot-elevation Quail Creek Reservoir one of Utah's most popular summer water playgrounds. The 600 acre reservoir was created in 1990 by damming Quail Creek for hydroelectric power below the lower slopes of the Pine Mountains and filling the basin behind the 202-foot-tall dam with Virgin River water. Most of the namesake quail have been hunted out of the area. But the small hillside campground and its large curving pull-through and flat tent sites command good views across waters crowded with boaters and water skiers. Sheltered picnic tables overlooking the reservoir also make this a popular day-trip party destination. Though a jaunt to Hurricane is needed for amenities, a campsite here can also be a base for exploring the Red Cliffs and Silver Reef near Leeds, as well as Zion National Park.

BASICS

Operated By: Utah State Parks & Recreation. **Open:** All year. **Site Assignment:** First come, first served; reservations advised peak times. **Registration:** Entrance kiosk. **Fee:** $10 (cash or check). **Parking:** At site.

FACILITIES

Number of RV Sites: 23. **Number of Tent-Only Sites:** 0. **Hookups:** None. **Each Site:** Sheltered table on cement pad, grill. **Dump Station:** Yes. **Laundry:** No. **Pay Phone:** No. **Rest Rooms and Showers:** No showers. **Fuel:** No. **Propane:** No. **Internal Roads:** Paved, good. **RV Service:** No. **Market:** St. George, 14 mi. **Restaurant:** St. George, 14 mi. **General Store:** No. **Vending:** No. **Swimming:** Lake. **Playground:** No. **Other:** Boat launch, fish cleaning station, 3 wheelchair-accessible sites. **Activities:** Boating, fishing. **Nearby Attractions:** Zion National Park. **Additional Information:** Washington County Travel & Convention Bureau, (435) 634-5747, (800) 869-6635.

RESTRICTIONS

Pets: On leash under owner's control. **Fires:** Yes. **Alcoholic Beverages:** Allowed. **Vehicle Maximum Length:** No limit. **Other:** 3-day limit without reservations.

TO GET THERE

From St. George go north on US I-15 to Exit 16, and then 3 mi. east on UT Hwy. 9.

ST. GEORGE

Snow Canyon State Park

1002 Snow Canyon Dr., Ivins 84738. T: (435) 628-2255 or (800) 322-3770 (reservations); parks.state.ut.us.

🚐 ★★★★   ⛺ ★★★★

Beauty: ★★★★★
Spaciousness: ★★★★
Security: ★★★★
Insect Control: ★★
Site Privacy: ★★★★
Quiet: ★★★★★
Cleanliness: ★★★★
Facilities: ★★★

Located west of Leeds among 170-million-year-old eroding red-orange sandstone mountains and white hills in the Red Cliffs Desert Reserve, Snow Canyon was chanced upon by cowboys searching for lost cattle and named after early pioneers Erastus and Lorenzo Snow. Also popular for day trips, as picnic areas as well as 25 campsites in the two loops are reservable, Snow Canyon's geologic riches include recent lava flows, deep caves, steep canyons, soft red and petrified sand dunes, and Anasazi petroglyphs. Wildlife ranges from ringtail cats to giant desert hairy scorpions (shake boots upside down in the morning before wearing). The paved sites (1–14, 3–8, and 11–14 reservable) with electric hookups at the front of the campground have sheltered tables, but their 15-foot width is too narrow for big rigs with sliders and tip-outs. A smattering of trees and desert scrub separates the other more primitive campsites.

BASICS

Operated By: Utah State Parks & Recreation. **Open:** All year. **Site Assignment:** First come, first served; some sites can be reserved (120 days in advance). **Registration:** Self-pay fee station. **Fee:**

$13–$15 (cash or check only). **Parking:** At site.

FACILITIES

Number of RV Sites: 35. **Number of Tent-Only Sites:** 0. **Hookups:** Electric (30 amp), water. **Each Site:** Table, grill. **Dump Station:** Yes. **Laundry:** No. **Pay Phone:** Yes. **Rest Rooms and Showers:** Yes. **Fuel:** No. **Propane:** No. **Internal Roads:** Paved, excellent. **RV Service:** No. **Market:** St. George, 10 mi. **Restaurant:** St. George, 10 mi. **General Store:** No. **Vending:** Yes. **Swimming:** No. **Playground:** No. **Other:** Picnic area, basketball court in group area, cactus/native-plant garden. **Activities:** Biking, horseback riding. **Nearby Attractions:** Zion National Park. **Additional Information:** Washington County Travel & Convention Bureau, (435) 634-5747, (800) 869-6635.

RESTRICTIONS

Pets: On leash (not allowed on trail). **Fires:** Yes (in grills only, no fires June 1–Sept. 15, firewood available). **Alcoholic Beverages:** Allowed. **Vehicle Maximum Length:** 60 ft. **Other:** No climbing on rocks behind campground.

TO GET THERE

From St. George go 10 mi. north on UT Hwy. 18.

SYRACUSE

Antelope Island State Park

4528 West 1700 South, Syracuse 84075. T: (801) 773-2941 or (800) 322-3770; www.nr.state.ut.us.

🚐 ★★★★   ⛺ ★★★★

Beauty: ★★★★★
Spaciousness: ★★★★
Security: ★★★★★
Insect Control: ★★★
Site Privacy: ★★★★★
Quiet: ★★★★★
Cleanliness: ★★★★
Facilities: ★★★

An 8-mile-long two-lane causeway with swooping birds diving down and scaring drivers crosses the Great Salt Lake on the drive from the Antelope Island entrance kiosk to Bridger Bay Campground. Though the area is a popular day-use park with many migratory waterfowl and secluded turnouts and beaches for picnics, campers must bring their own water (or use the Visitor Center faucets and soft drink vending machines). Wildlife, including introduced bison and re-introduced antelope, have it better, as this largest of the 10 Great Salt Lake islands has 40 springs. The primitive campsites are widely dispersed and attractively situated among the rocky grasslands and sagebrush coming down from the hills overlooking the lake. Campsites are booked up well in advance for weekends, particularly prime vacation holidays, and visitors without reservations are frequently turned away. The sites are long and narrow, and very wide or long vehicles should call the park before coming.

BASICS

Operated By: Utah State Parks & Recreation. **Open:** All year. **Site Assignment:** First come, first served; reservations (120 days in advance for individuals, 1 year for groups, an absolute necessity holidays, weekends). **Registration:** Entrance kiosk. **Fee:** $10 ($6.25 reservation fee; cash or check). **Parking:** At site.

FACILITIES

Number of RV Sites: 26. **Number of Tent-Only Sites:** 0. **Hookups:** None. **Each Site:** Table, fire ring w/ grill. **Dump Station:** Yes. **Laundry:** No. **Pay Phone:** No. **Rest Rooms and Showers:** Yes. **Fuel:** No. **Propane:** No. **Internal Roads:** Gravel, good. **RV Service:** No. **Market:** Syracuse, 12 mi. **Restaurant:** Buffalo Point, 2 mi. (limited hours; outdoor tables). **General Store:** No. **Vending:** No. **Swimming:** Lake. **Playground:** No. **Other:** Visitor Center, gift shop, marina, horse concessions, ranger programs. **Activities:** Biking, horseback riding, bird-watching. **Nearby Attractions:** Farmington Bay Waterfowl Management Area. **Additional Information:** Davis County Tourism, (801) 451-3286, www.co.davis.ut.us/discoverdavis; Farmington Bay Waterfowl Area, (801) 451-7386.

RESTRICTIONS

Pets: On leash (not allowed on beach). **Fires:** Yes (charcoal in fire rings or gas stoves when fire danger is low, absolutely no fires when grasslands are dry in summer). **Alcoholic Beverages:** Allowed. **Vehicle Maximum Length:** 50 ft. **Other:** Horses not allowed in campground.

TO GET THERE

From US I-15 Exit 335 18 mi. north of Salt Lake City, go 14 mi. west on UT Hwy. 127.

TORREY
Fruita Campground

HC 70 Box 16, Torrey 84775. T: (435) 425-3791; www.nps.gov/care; interpretation@nps.gov.

🚐 ★★★★ ▲ ★★★★

Beauty: ★★★★   Site Privacy: ★★★★
Spaciousness: ★★★   Quiet: ★★★★
Security: ★★★★   Cleanliness: ★★★★
Insect Control: ★★   Facilities: ★★

Fruita Campground is named for the surrounding historic orchards, where cherries, peaches, and other fruit can be picked in season. As the only developed campground within Capitol Reef National Park, campsites in Fruita are coveted and the campground often fills by early afternoon. Fruita is laid out alongside the Fremont River (so be prepared with bug repellent during warm months) and is noted for its many large shade trees and grassy tent sites. The three loops resemble a dense little village, with Loop C having the largest RV sites. Tent campers wanting a more primitive camping experience (no water provided) in the park may wish to head to the campgrounds at Cedar Mesa (5 no-fee tent sites; but navigating the dirt road is not advised during wet weather) or Cathedral Valley (6 no-fee sites; road conditions also a wet-weather concern). For hookups and amenities, head to Torrey.

BASICS

Operated By: National Park Service. **Open:** All year. **Site Assignment:** First come, first served; reservations taken only for group site. **Registration:** Self-pay entrance fee station. **Fee:** $10 (half price for Golden Age or Golden Access; cash or check only). **Parking:** At site.

FACILITIES

Number of RV Sites: 70. **Number of Tent-Only Sites:** 0. **Hookups:** None. **Each Site:** Table, grill. **Dump Station:** Yes. **Laundry:** No. **Pay Phone:** Yes. **Rest Rooms and Showers:** No showers. **Fuel:** No. **Propane:** No. **Internal Roads:** Paved, good condition. **RV Service:** No. **Market:** In Torrey, 16 mi. west. **Restaurant:** In Torrey, 16 mi. west. **General Store:** No. **Vending:** No. **Swimming:** No. **Playground:** No. **Activities:** None. **Nearby Attractions:** Capitol Reef,

Escalante, Goblin Valley State Park. **Additional Information:** Capitol Reef Country, (800) 858-7951, (435) 425-3365, www.capitolreef.org; Wayne County Travel Council, (800) 858-7159.

RESTRICTIONS

Pets: On leash under owner's control. **Fires:** Yes. **Alcoholic Beverages:** Allowed if over 18 years old. **Vehicle Maximum Length:** 30 ft. **Other:** Do not feed or approach wildlife, 14-day limit Apr. 1–Nov. 30, 30-day limit Dec. 1–Mar. 31.

TO GET THERE

11 mi. east of Torrey on UT Hwy. 24, then 1 mi. south on scenic road past Visitor Center.

TORREY

Thousand Lakes RV Park

P.O. Box 750070, Torrey 84775. T: (800) 355-8995 or (435) 425-3500; www.thousandlakesrvpark.com.

🚐 ★★★★	🏕 ★★★★
Beauty: ★★★★★	Site Privacy: ★★★★
Spaciousness: ★★★★	Quiet: ★★★★
Security: ★★★★	Cleanliness: ★★★★★
Insect Control: ★★★★	Facilities: ★★★★

Tall cottonwood trees and grass between the gravel sites lend a pleasant pastoral feel to Thousand Lakes RV Park, which boasts an exceptionally good gift shop and is within a mile of such Torrey institutions as Cafe Diablo, the Capitol Reef Inn & Cafe, and Robber's Roost Books & Beverages. Week nights from May to early October, Thousand Lakes serves up a western cookout complete with Dutch oven potatoes, cowboy beans, buttermilk scones, and entrees ranging from ribeye steak to vegetarian. With everything from horseshoes, a playground for the kids, a dog walk, and nearby espressos, guests sometimes forget that they came here for the national park and the incomparable sunrise and sunset light on the chiseled sandstone cliffs that define Capitol Reef. The combination of hookups and nearby restaurants and amenities brings a fair amount of repeat business and makes this a pleasant base camp for commuting to Capitol Reef National Park.

BASICS

Operated By: John & Vally Reilly. **Open:** April 1–Oct. 31. **Site Assignment:** First come, first served; reservations accepted. **Registration:** In office. **Fee:** $12.50 tent, $15.50–$18.50 RV (V, MC, AE). **Parking:** At site.

FACILITIES

Number of RV Sites: 58. **Number of Tent-Only Sites:** 9. **Hookups:** Electric (30, 50 amp), water, sewer. **Each Site:** Table, grill. **Dump Station:** Yes. **Laundry:** Yes. **Pay Phone:** Yes. **Rest Rooms and Showers:** Yes. **Fuel:** No. **Propane:** No. **Internal Roads:** Gravel, good condition. **RV Service:** No. **Market:** In Torrey, 1 mi. east. **Restaurant:** Within 0.25 mi. **General Store:** Yes. **Vending:** No. **Swimming:** Heated pool. **Playground:** Yes. **Other:** Modem hookup in store, 4WD rentals, hair care. **Activities:** Western cookouts. **Nearby Attractions:** Capitol Reef, Boulder Mountain lakes, Escalante. **Additional Information:** Capitol Reef Country, (800) 858-7951, (435) 425-3365, www.capitolreef. org; Wayne County Travel Council, (800) 858-7159.

RESTRICTIONS

Pets: On leash under owner's control. **Fires:** Yes. **Alcoholic Beverages:** Allowed. **Vehicle Maximum Length:** 70 ft.

TO GET THERE

On UT Hwy. 24, 2 mi. west of junction w/ UT Hwy. 12.

TORREY

Wonderland RV Park

Jct. of Hwys. 12 & 24, Torrey 84775. T: (435) 425-3775 or (800) 458-0216; F: (435) 425-3212; www.capitolreefwonderland.com; wonderland@color-country.net.

🚐 ★★★★	🏕 ★★★★
Beauty: ★★★★	Site Privacy: ★★★★
Spaciousness: ★★★★	Quiet: ★★★★
Security: ★★★★	Cleanliness: ★★★★★
Insect Control: ★★★★	Facilities: ★★★★

Though situated at a key highway junction with a Days Inn and two gas stations with mini-marts and a Subway franchise, Wonderland RV Park looks out on a scenic vista of pasture and high desert that merges into the distant mountains. Tent sites are along a grassy strip protected by a windbreak fence. The highway gets little truck traffic, though the coyotes can howl up a storm. Almost all the amenities are here or very nearby, including use of the motel pool and restaurant, which are atop an adjacent hill. This family-run enterprise, which includes the gas station, minimart, and motel, also has Malfunction Junction for arranging 4WD and fishing tours with guides who have exclusive access to 25 miles of private streams on the Fremont River and Boulder Creek, which is another way to see the backcountry. All in all, well situated for exploring Torrey and Capitol Reef and even the Boulder Mountains or Escalante.

BASICS

Operated By: Raymond & Diane Potter. **Open:** Mar.–Nov. (or until first freeze). **Site Assignment:** First come, first served; reservations advised after June 1. **Registration:** At office or in Texaco mini-mart. **Fee:** $15 tent, $18 RV (V, MC, AE, D, DC). **Parking:** At site.

FACILITIES

Number of RV Sites: 33. **Number of Tent-Only Sites:** 12. **Hookups:** Electric (20, 30, 50 amp), water, sewer, cable TV. **Each Site:** Table, fire pit. **Dump Station:** Yes. **Laundry:** Yes. **Pay Phone:** Yes. **Rest Rooms and Showers:** Yes. **Fuel:** Yes. **Propane:** Yes. **Internal Roads:** Gravel, good. **RV Service:** No. **Market:** Texaco mini-mart. **Restaurant:** Several within 1 mi. **General Store:** Yes. **Vending:** Yes. **Swimming:** At Wonderland Inn (motel) pool. **Playground:** No. **Other:** 13 sites have phone (modem) hookup, RV/car wash. **Activities:** 4WD & fishing tours. **Nearby Attractions:** Capitol Reef, Boulder Mountains, Escalante. **Additional Information:** Capitol Reef Country, (800) 858-7951, (435) 425-3365, www.capitolreef.org; Wayne County Travel Council, (800) 858-7159.

RESTRICTIONS

Pets: On leash. **Fires:** Yes. **Alcoholic Beverages:** Allowed. **Vehicle Maximum Length:** 72 ft.

TO GET THERE

At the junction of Utah Hwys 12 & 24, enter across the street from Texaco station.

VIRGIN

Zion River Resort RV Park & Campground

730 East Hwy. 9, P.O. Box 790219, Virgin 84779. T: (435) 635-8594 or (800) 838-8594; F: (435) 635-3934; www.zionriverresort.com; info@zrr.com.

🚐 ★★★★   ▲ ★★★

Beauty: ★★★★   Site Privacy: ★★★★
Spaciousness: ★★★★   Quiet: ★★★
Security: ★★★★   Cleanliness: ★★★★★
Insect Control: ★★★   Facilities: ★★★★

With spacious pull-through sites able to handle double sliders, Zion River Resort is the place for big rigs. Even though winter night temperatures drop a few degrees below freezing, snowbirds flock here from November to March for the Zion mountain views through the surrounding trees. A well-stocked office store adds convenience, and there are enough amenities, including coin-operated video games, a pool table, and big-screen TV to keep children occupied. Tent sites 123–131 are alongside the Virgin River, while sites 118–122 are roadside. The RV sites closest to the cotton-wood tree–lined Virgin River Walk are back-ins numbered 48–73 and 88–99. Budget campers will probably want to go elsewhere, as the fine facilities do not come cheap. Others will prefer camping inside Zion National Park itself, sacrificing amenities for a forested setting and closeness to park sites. Only Zion Canyon Campground in Springdale, just outside the Zion National Park entrance, offers comparable amenities.

BASICS

Operated By: Robert, Todd & Ron Smith. **Open:** All year. **Site Assignment:** First come, first served; reservations accepted. **Registration:** Office. **Fee:** $20 tent, $29–$32 RV (V, MC, AE, D). **Parking:** At site.

FACILITIES

Number of RV Sites: 112. **Number of Tent-Only Sites:** 14. **Hookups:** Electric (30, 50 amp), water, sewer, phone (modem). **Each Site:** Table, grill. **Dump Station:** Yes. **Laundry:** No. **Pay Phone:** No. **Rest Rooms and Showers:** Yes. **Fuel:** No. **Propane:** Yes. **Internal Roads:** Paved, excellent. **RV**

Service: No. **Market:** Hurricane, 9 mi. **Restaurant:** Hurricane, 9 mi. **General Store:** Yes. **Vending:** Yes. **Swimming:** Pool. **Playground:** Yes. **Other:** Cabins, teepees, whirlpool, volleyball, badminton, pet exercise area. **Activities:** Biking, horseback riding, golf, river tubing, ATV rides. **Nearby Attractions:** Zion National Park. **Additional Information:** Washington County Travel Bureau, (435) 634-5747, (800) 869-6635.

RESTRICTIONS

Pets: On leash (not allowed w/ tents). **Fires:** Yes (charcoal or wood in fire rings only). **Alcoholic Beverages:** Allowed. **Vehicle Maximum Length:** 70 ft. **Other:** No firearms, fireworks or RV storage.

TO GET THERE

From US I-15 8 mi. north of St. George go east 18 mi. on UT Hwy. 9.

WILLARD

Willard Bay State Park

900 West 650 North Box A, Willard 84340. T: (801) 734-9494 or (801) 322-3770 or (800) 322-3770; www.nr.state.ut.us.

🚐 ★★★★	🅰 ★★★★
Beauty: ★★★★	Site Privacy: ★★★★
Spaciousness: ★★★★	Quiet: ★★★
Security: ★★★★	Cleanliness: ★★★★
Insect Control: ★★★★	Facilities: ★★★

About a dozen miles north of Ogden and 35 miles north of Salt Lake City, Willard Bay has a more primitive tree-shaded grassy South Marina camping area favored by fishermen in the South Recreation Area (US I-15 Exit 354) and two more developed campgrounds five miles north in the North Recreation Area (US I-15 Exit 360). In the North, Cottonwood Campground has hookups, gray soil, and cottonwood trees for shade; sites 1–3, 10, 17, and 19–23 get the most highway noise. Willow Creek Campground lacks hookups but has a creek running through the campground, a pond, and sites tucked away in deep arbors of vegetation resembling coastal rainforest more than the arid grasslands and sage surrounding this Great Salt Lake floodplain. Willow Creek sites 10–35 have the best water views; sites 3–9 are nearest the pond. The bird

refuge is a big attraction, and traffic picks up in January when the bald eagles start arriving.

BASICS

Operated By: Utah State Parks & Recreation. **Open:** All year. **Site Assignment:** First come, first served; reservations (120 days in advance; highly recommended weekends, holidays). **Registration:** At entry kiosk. **Fee:** $10–$16 (cash or check only). **Parking:** At site.

FACILITIES

Number of RV Sites: 97. **Number of Tent-Only Sites:** 0. **Hookups:** Electric (30 amp), water, sewer (Cotton Campground only). **Each Site:** Table, grill or fire ring. **Dump Station:** Yes. **Laundry:** No. **Pay Phone:** No. **Rest Rooms and Showers:** Yes. **Fuel:** No. **Propane:** No. **Internal Roads:** Paved, excellent condition. **RV Service:** No. **Market:** Ogden, 12 mi. **Restaurant:** Willard, 1 mi. **General Store:** No. **Vending:** No. **Swimming:** Beach. **Playground:** No. **Other:** 3 boat launch ramps. **Activities:** Fishing, bird-watching. **Nearby Attractions:** Great Salt Lake. **Additional Information:** Golden Spike Empire, (801) 627-8288, www.ogdencvb.org.

RESTRICTIONS

Pets: On leash under owner's control (not allowed in public buildings). **Fires:** Yes (in fire pits & grills only). **Alcoholic Beverages:** Allowed (if over 21 years). **Vehicle Maximum Length:** 53 ft. **Other:** Off-highway vehicles & firearms prohibited.

TO GET THERE

From US I-15 follow signs from Exit 360 into north campgrounds; take Exit 354 for more primitive south campground.

YUBA STATE PARK

Oasis Campground

P.O. Box 159, Levan 84639. T: (435) 758-2611 or (800) 322-3770 (reservations); F: (435) 758-2489; www.nr.state.ut.us.

🚐 ★★★★	🅰 ★★★★★
Beauty: ★★★★★	Site Privacy: ★★★★
Spaciousness: ★★★★★	Quiet: ★★★★
Security: ★★★★	Cleanliness: ★★★★
Insect Control: ★★★	Facilities: ★★★

Warm (70–75° F) summer waters keep the small Oasis Campground fronting the rock-strewn sandy shores of Yuba Reservoir full most weekends and holidays during the school-vacation season. But on weekdays after the holiday crunch it is not unusual for a lone boater or two to have the whole 22-mile long, 80-foot deep lake as a private playground. Bait machines near the fish cleaning area dispense night crawlers and leeches to tempt walleye, northern pike, channel catfish, and yellow perch. Half the campground sites are over 60-feet long and the landscaping of green grass, sagebrush, cottonwood, and other trees makes this a real oasis from the seemingly distant (five miles) interstate highway for road-weary travelers. On the opposite side of the lake, Eagle View Campground's primitive boat-access-only sites 1,2,3,5,7,13, and 17 alongside a sandy day-use beach can be reserved with boat docks (sites 3 and 7 are wheelchair accessible).

BASICS

Operated By: Utah State Parks & Recreation. **Open:** All year. **Site Assignment:** First come, first served; reservations recommended weekends, holidays. **Registration:** Entrance kiosk. **Fee:** $14 (cash or check; $8 for Eagle View Campground). **Parking:** At site.

FACILITIES

Number of RV Sites: 20. **Number of Tent-Only Sites:** 0. **Hookups:** None. **Each Site:** Table on cement pad, grill, fire ring. **Dump Station:** Yes. **Laundry:** No. **Pay Phone:** Yes. **Rest Rooms and Showers:** Yes. **Fuel:** No. **Propane:** No. **Internal Roads:** Paved, excellent. **RV Service:** No. **Market:** Nephi, 25 mi. **Restaurant:** Nephi, 25 mi. **General Store:** No. **Vending:** Yes. **Swimming:** Lake. **Playground:** No. **Other:** Boat ramp, beaches. **Activities:** Fishing, water sports. **Nearby Attractions:** Mormon Temple (Manti), Territorial Statehouse (Fillmore). **Additional Information:** Nephi/Juab County Chamber of Commerce, (435) 623-2411.

RESTRICTIONS

Pets: On leash under owner's control. **Fires:** Yes. **Alcoholic Beverages:** Allowed. **Vehicle Maximum Length:** 87 ft. **Other:** Turn in tagged walleyes for research use.

TO GET THERE

From US I-15 Exit 202 near Mills, go 5 mi. south on reservoir perimeter road.

ZION NATIONAL PARK
Mukuntuweep RV Park & Campground

P.O. Box 193, Orderville 84758. T: (435) 648-2154; F: (435) 648-2829; www.xpressweb.com/zionpark; zionpark@xpressweb.com.

🚐 ★★★   ⛺ ★★★

Beauty: ★★★★   Site Privacy: ★★★★
Spaciousness: ★★★★   Quiet: ★★★★
Security: ★★★★   Cleanliness: ★★★★
Insect Control: ★★★★   Facilities: ★★★★

Mukuntuweep, the Paiute word for sacred cliffs, was the pre-Mormon name for the Zion National Park area. Mukuntuweep RV Park & Campground actually borders the park's eastern boundary, and the majestic rock-cliffs characteristic of Zion provide a scenic backdrop. Besides being the closest RV park to Zion, Mukuntuweep is somewhat of a refuge from the national park campground hustle and bustle, though it is right off the state highway. A gravel loop with pull-through sites (up to 40-feet wide) circles like a wagon train around an inner cluster of RVs near the entrance. Cottonwoods in the RV area are just getting to the size where they provide noticeable shade. Tenters have two gravel roads to choose from, and are out of sight of the RVs, with grass and junipers adding a more rugged wilderness feel. With ample amenities and diligent management living on site, Mukuntuweep makes a good base for exploring the park.

BASICS

Operated By: Frank Baca. **Open:** All year. **Site Assignment:** First come, first served; reservations available. **Registration:** Office. **Fee:** $15 tent, $19 RV. **Parking:** At site.

FACILITIES

Number of RV Sites: 30. **Number of Tent-Only Sites:** 110. **Hookups:** Water, electric (20, 30 amp), sewer. **Each Site:** Table, grill. **Dump Station:** Yes. **Laundry:** Yes. **Pay Phone:** Yes. **Rest Rooms and Showers:** Yes. **Fuel:** Yes. **Propane:** No. **Internal Roads:** Gravel, good. **RV Service:** No (limited repairs). **Market:** Yes. **Restaurant:** Yes. **General Store:** Yes. **Vending:** Yes. **Swimming:** No. **Playground:** No. **Other:** Mountain bike rentals, horseback riding, video arcade w/ pool table, handicap accessible. **Activities:** Stream fishing, golf. **Nearby Attractions:** Zion, Bryce. **Additional Information:** Kane County Office of Tourism, 78 S. 100 East, Kanab, UT 84741; (435) 644-5033; (800) 733-5263; kanetrav@kaneutah.com; www.kaneutah.com.

RESTRICTIONS

Pets: On leash, cleaned up after, kept out of buildings. **Fires:** Yes (firewood sold). **Alcoholic Beverages:** Allowed. **Vehicle Maximum Length:** 70 ft. **Other:** 11 a.m. checkout.

TO GET THERE

On Utah State Hwy. 9, go 0.25 mi. east from east entrance to Zion national Park; or from junction of Hwy. 9 and US Hwy. 89 at Mt. Carmel Junction, go 13 mi. west.

ZION NATIONAL PARK
South & Watchman Campgrounds

P.O. Box 1099, Springdale 84767. T: (435) 772-3256; www.nps.gov/zion.

RV ★★★★ Tent ★★★★★

Beauty: ★★★★★	Site Privacy: ★★★★
Spaciousness: ★★★★	Quiet: ★★★★
Security: ★★★★★	Cleanliness: ★★★★
Insect Control: ★★★★	Facilities: ★★★

Two Zion National Park campgrounds, South and Watchman, can handle RVs. But only Watchman Campground's Loop A and B have electric hookups (73 are 30 amp, two are 50 amp); Loop B has five 40-foot sites, but most are 35–36 feet. Tunnels on roads leading into the park will not accommodate vehicles over 50-feet long, and big rigs need special escort vehicles ($10). South Campground's two loops have a 24-foot length limit and tight turns difficult for large wider-bodied RVs. Watchman Loops C and D are for tent camping. Loop D's 36 sites are most coveted, being right up against scenic Mount Watchman. South Campground has three wheelchair-accessible sites (103, 114, 115) and 69 tent-only sites, including seven walk-in sites along the river. Watchman fills via reservation many days from Easter to Halloween, while South fills by 2:30 p.m. on a first-come-first-served basis.

BASICS

Operated By: National Park Service. **Open:** All year (Watchman); Apr.–Oct. 15 (South). **Site Assignment:** First come, first served (South); reservations (Watchman; Easter-Halloween). **Registration:** Entry kiosk; self-pay fee station. **Fee:** $16 (cash or check only). **Parking:** At site; parking area for South Campground's 7 walk-in sites.

FACILITIES

Number of RV Sites: 346. **Number of Tent-Only Sites:** 7. **Hookups:** Electric (30, 50 amp). **Each Site:** Table, fire pit. **Dump Station:** Yes. **Laundry:** No. **Pay Phone:** Yes. **Rest Rooms and Showers:** No showers. **Fuel:** No. **Propane:** No. **Internal Roads:** Paved, some bumps. **RV Service:** No. **Market:** Springdale, 1 mi. **Restaurant:** Springdale, 1 mi. **General Store:** No. **Vending:** No. **Swimming:** No. **Playground:** No. **Other:** Visitor center, amphitheater, 3 wheelchair-accessible sites. **Activities:** Fishing, ranger programs. **Nearby Attractions:** Bryce. **Additional Information:** Washington County Travel Bureau, (435) 634-5747, (800) 869-6635.

RESTRICTIONS

Pets: On leash. **Fires:** Yes (in fire pit only, no wood gathering). **Alcoholic Beverages:** Allowed (at site only; zero tolerance for drinking & driving and marijuana). **Vehicle Maximum Length:** 40 ft.

TO GET THERE

Go 0.5 mi. north of Springdale on UT Hwy. 14 to Zion National Park entrance.

Supplemental Directory of Campgrounds

Aguila

Fairhaven RV Park, 52227 West Hwy. US 60 P.O. (P.O. Box 38), 85320. T: (520) 685-2412. RV/tent: 55. $15–$16. Hookups: electric (30 amp), water, sewer.

Ajo

Ajo Heights RV Park, 2000 North Hwy. 85, 85321. T: (520) 387-6796. rose@ajorvparks.com. RV/tent: 40. $20. Hookups: electric (30, 50 amp), water, sewer, cable TV, phone.

Belly Acres RV Park, 2050 North Hwy. 85, 85321. T: (520) 387-6062. del-sur@tabletoptelephone. com. RV/tent: 55. $16. Hookups: electric (30 amp), water, sewer, cable TV.

La Siesta Motel & RV Resort, 2561 North Ajo-Gila Bend Hwy., 85321. T: (520) 387-6569. RV/tent: 29. $18–$20. Hookups: electric (30 amp), water, sewer, cable TV.

Shadow Ridge RV Resort, 431 North 2nd Ave., 85321. T: (520) 387-6569. F: (520) 387-5055. RV/tent: 125. $20. Hookups: electric (30, 50 amp), water, sewer, cable TV.

Apache Junction

Apache Skies Mobile Home Park, 102 South Ironwood, 85219. T: (480) 982-6916 or (800) 625-7264. F: (480) 982-5735. RV/tent: 38. $25. Hookups: water, electric (20, 30, 50 amp), sewer, phone (modem).

Arizonian Travel Trailer Resort, 15976 East Hwy. 60, 85219. T: (520) 463-2585. RV/tent: 75. $24. Hookups: water, electric (30, 50 amp), sewer.

Budget RV Park, Old West Hwy., 85219. T: (480) 982-5856. RV/tent: 175. $20. Hookups: water, electric (30, 50 amp), sewer.

Countryside Travel Trailer Resort, Idaho Rd., 85219. T: (480) 982-1537. RV/tent: 560. $29. Hookups: electric (30, 50 amp), water, sewer, phone.

Dana's Trailer Ranch, Apache Trail, 85219. T: (480) 986-1471. RV/tent: 60. $20. Hookups: water, electric (20, 30 amp), sewer, phone.

Gold Canyon RV Resort, 7151 East Hwy. 60, 85219. T: (480) 982-5800 or (877) 465-3266. RV/tent: 754. $32. Hookups: electric (30, 50 amp), water, sewer.

Golden Sun RV Resort, 999 West Broadway, 85220. T: (480) 983-3760. RV/tent: 330. $25. Hookups: electric (30, 50 amp), water, sewer, phone.

La Hacienda RV Resort, 1797 West 28th Ave., 85220. T: (480) 982-2808. www.hacienda-RV.com. information@hacienda-RV.com. RV/tent: 280. $30. Hookups: electric (30, 50 amp), water, sewer, cable TV, phone (modem).

Rock Shadows RV Resort, 600 South Idaho Rd., 85219. T: (480) 982-0450. rockrv1@aol.com. RV/tent: 683. $29. Hookups: electric (30, 50 amp), water, sewer, phone.

Sunrise RV Resort, 1403 West Broadway, 85220. T: (480) 983-2500 or (877) 633-3133. RV/tent: 483. $27. Hookups: electric (30, 50 amp), water, sewer.

Superstition Lookout RV Resort, 1371 East Fourth Ave., 85219. T: (480) 982-2008. RV/tent: 192. $31. Hookups: electric (30, 50 amp), water, sewer, phone.

Superstition Sunrise RV Resort, 702 South Meridian Dr., 85220. T: (480) 986-8404 or (800) 624-7027. supersun01@aol.com. RV/tent: 1119. $35. Hookups: electric (30, 50 amp), water, sewer, cable TV, phone (modem).

VIP RV Resort, 401 South Ironwood Dr., 85220. T: (480) 983-0847. RV/tent: 128. $19. Hookups: water, electric (20, 30, 50 amp), sewer, phone (modem).

Weaver's Needle Travel Trailer Resort, 250 South Tomahawk Rd., 85219. T: (480) 982-3683. RV/tent: 400. $29. Hookups: water, electric (20, 30, 50 amp), sewer, phone (modem).

ARIZONA (continued)

Arizona City

Quail Run RV Resort, 14010 South Amado Blvd., 85223. T: (520) 466-6000 or (800) 301-8114. RV/tent: 324. $22–$25. Hookups: electric (20, 30, 50 amp), water, sewer, phone (modem).

Benson

Benson I-10 RV Park, 840 North Ocotillo, 85602. T: (520) 586-4262. RV/tent: 88. $12.50–$20.50. Hookups: electric (30, 50 amp), water, sewer.

Benson KOA, 180 Four Feathers Ln., 85602. T: (520) 586-9815. F: (520) 586-3977. www.koakamp-grounds.com/where/az/3133.html. djsunkular@theriver.com. RV/tent: 107. $19–$23.50. Hookups: electric (20, 30, 50 amp), water, sewer, cable TV, phone (modem).

Butterfield RV Resort, 251 South Ocotillo Ave., 85602. T: (520) 507-6161. RV/tent: 173. $29. Hookups: electric (30, 50 amp), water, sewer, cable TV, phone (modem).

Pato Blanco Lakes RV Park, 635 East Pearl St., 85602. T: (520) 586-8966 or (800) 229-9368. www.patoblanco.com. patoblancolakes@the river.com. RV/tent: 103. $18. Hookups: electric (20, 30, 50 amp), water, sewer, cable TV, phone (modem).

Quarter Horse RV Park, 800 West 4th St., 85602. T: (520) 586-3371 or (800) 527-5025. qhrvpark@ theriver.com. RV/tent: 50. $16. Hookups: electric (20, 30, 50 amp), water, sewer, cable TV, phone (modem)

Red Barn Campground, Campground Rd., 85602. T: (520) 586-2035. RV/tent: 49. $13. Hookups: electric (30 amp), water, sewer.

San Pedro Territory 55+ Mobile Home & RV Resort, 1110 South Hwy. 80 Box 1, 85602. T: (520) 586-9546 or (877) 235-9100. RV/tent: 169. $17. Hookups: electric (20, 30, 50 amp), water, sewer.

Bisbee

San Jose Lodge & RV Park, 1002 Naco Hwy., 85603. T: (520) 432-5761. F: (520) 432-4302. www.san joselodge.com. info@sanjoselodge.com. RV/tent: 50. $14. Hookups: electric, water, sewer, cable TV.

Brenda

Desert Gold RV Park, 46628 East Hwy. 60, 85348. T: (520) 927-7800 or (800) 927-2101. www.g7inc. org. RV/tent: 425. $20. Hookups: water, electric (30, 50 amp), sewer, modem, cable TV.

Buckeye

Destiny Phoenix RV Resort, 416 North Citrus Rd., 85326. T: (888) 667-2454. www.destinyrv.com.

RV/tent: 284. $30–$37. Hookups: water, electric (20, 30, 50 amp), sewer, phone (modem).

Leaf Verde RV Park, 1500 South Apache Rd., 85326. T: (623) 386-3132. leafrv@aol.com. RV/tent: 400. $20. Hookups: electric (30, 50 amp), water, sewer, cable TV, phone (modem).

Bullhead City

Blackstone RV Park, 3299 Boundary Cone Rd., 86426. T: (520) 768-3303. www.bullheadcityaz. com/blackstonervpark. blackstonervpark@ yahoo.com. RV/tent: 136. $15. Hookups: water, electric (20, 30, 50 amp), sewer, phone (modem).

Ridgeview RV Resort, 775 Bullhead Parkway, 86429. T: (520) 754-2595 or (800) 392-8560. ridgerv@ ctaz.com. RV/tent: 302. $18. Hookups: water, electric (30, 50 amp), sewer, phone (modem), cable TV.

River City RV Park, 2225 Merrill Ave., 86442. T: (520) 754-2121. RV/tent: 134. $16. Hookups: water, electric (30, 50 amp), sewer.

Silver Creek RV Park, 1515 Gold Rush Rd., 86442. T: (520) 763-2444. RV/tent: 140. $15. Hookups: none.

Snowbird RV Resort, 1600 Joy Ln., 86426. T: (520) 768-7141. F: (520) 768-7145. RV/tent: 135. $16. Hookups: water, electric (30, 50 amp), sewer, phone (modem).

Casa Grande

Campground Buena Tierra, 1995 South Cox Rd., 85222. T: (520) 836-3500 or (888) 520-8360. RV/tent: 266. $14–$19. Hookups: water, electric (20, 30, 50 amp), sewer.

Fiesta Grande, 1511 East Florence Blvd., 85222. T: (520) 426-7000 or (888) 934-3782. RV/tent: 767. $26. Hookups: electric (30, 50 amp), water, sewer, phone (modem).

Foothills West RV Resort, 19501 West Hopi Dr., 85222. T: (520) 836-2531. F: (520) 836-0471. www.foothillswest.com. veli@c2i2.com. RV/tent: 180. $22. Hookups: electric (30, 50 amp), water, sewer, phone (modem).

Leisure Valley RV Resort, 9985 North Pinal Ave., 85222. T: (520) 836-9449 or (800) 993-9449. RV/tent: 125. $20. Hookups: water, electric (20, 30, 50 amp), sewer.

Palm Creek Golf and RV Resort, 1110 North Henness Rd., 85222. T: (800) 421-7004. www.palm creekgolf.com. RV/tent: 1089. $28. Hookups: electric (30, 50 amp), water, sewer, cable TV, phone (modem).

ARIZONA (continued)

Casa Grande (continued)

Sundance 1 RV Resort, 1920 North Thornton Rd., 85222. T: (520) 426-9662 or (888) 332-5335. sundance@c2i2.com. RV/tent: 711. $20. Hookups: electric (30, 50 amp), water, sewer.

Val Vista Winter Village RV Resort, 16680 West Val Vista Rd., 85222. T: (520) 836-7800 or (877) 836-7801. F: (520) 836-2638. RV/tent: 345. $25. Hookups: water, electric (20, 30, 50 amp), sewer, phone (modem).

Chloride

Chloride Western RV Park, 5123 Tennessee Ave., P.O. Box 498, 86431. T: (520) 565-4492. RV/tent: 93. $7–$13. Hookups: water, electric (30, 50 amp), sewer.

Shep's RV Park, 9827 2nd St., 86431. T: (877) 565-4251. jmcn1122@aol.com. RV/tent: 7. $10–$15. Hookups: water, electric, sewer.

Dateland

The Oasis at Aztec Hills, P.O. Box 324, 85333. T: (520) 454-2229. RV/tent: 37. $19. Hookups: electric (30, 50 amp), water, sewer, phone (modem).

Dewey

Orchard RV Ranch, 11250 East Hwy. 69, 86327. T: (520) 772-8266 or (800) 352-6305. F: (480) 924-2044. RV/tent: 315. $24–$26. Hookups: water, electric (20, 30, 50 amp), sewer, phone (modem), cable TV.

Ehrenberg

Ehrenberg/Colorado River KOA, 50238 Ehrenberg-Parker Hwy., 85334. T: (520) 923-7213 or (800) 562-8651. RV/tent: 169. $20–$33. Hookups: electric (20, 30, 50 amp), water, sewer.

Flagstaff

Flagstaff KOA, 5803 North Hwy. 89, 86004. T: (520) 526-9926 or (800) KOA-FLAG. F: (520) 527-8356. jsatkoaflag@aol.com. RV/tent: 150. $20–$26. Hookups: water, electric (20, 30 amp), sewer, phone (modem).

J&H RV Park, 7901 North Hwy. 89, 86004. T: (520) 526-1829 or (800) 243-5264 or (623) 879-3215 (winter). F: (623) 879-3215 (winter). j&h@flagstaffrvparks.com. RV/tent: 64. $24–$30. Hookups: water, electric (20, 30, 50 amp), sewer, phone (modem).

Woody Mountain Campground & RV Park, 2727 West Rte. 66, 86001. T: (520) 774-7727 or (800) 732-7986. F: (520) 773-9882. woodymtnrvpark @webtv.net. RV/tent: 146. $17–$23. Hookups: water, electric (20, 30 amp), sewer, phone (modem).

Florence

Desert Gardens RV Park, P.O. Box 1186, 85232. T: (520) 868-3800 or (800) 868-1018. RV/tent: 84. $10–$18. Hookups: water, electric (20, 30, 50 amp), sewer, phone (modem).

Globe

Gila County RV Park & Batting Range, 300 South Pine St., 85501. T: (800) 436-8083. RV/tent: 24. $13–$16. Hookups: water, electric (30, 50 amp), sewer, modem, cable TV.

Gold Canyon

Canyon Vistas RV Resort, 6601 East Hwy. 60, 85219. T: (480) 288-8844. F: (480) 648-5590. www.cal-am.com. reservations@cal-am.com. RV/tent: 637. $20–$30. Hookups: electric (30, 50 amp), water, sewer, cable TV, phone (modem).

Golden Valley

Adobe RV Park, 4950 Apache Way, 86413. T: (520) 565-3010. RV/tent: 75. $16. Hookups: electric (20, 30, 50 amp), water, sewer.

Grand Canyon

Desert View, P.O. Box 129, 86023. T: (520) 638-7888. RV/tent: 50. $10. Hookups: none.

Grand Canyon Camper Village, Box 490, 86023. T: (520) 638-2887. RV/tent: 300. $15–$25. Hookups: water, electric (20, 30 amp), sewer, phone (modem).

Ten-X, FR7302C, 86023. T: (520) 638-2443. RV/tent: 70. $10. Hookups: none.

Happy Jack

Happy Jack Lodge & RV Resort, P.O. Box 19569, 86024. T: (520) 477-2805 or (800) 430-0385. RV/tent: 73. $21. Hookups: water, electric (20, 30, 50 amp), sewer.

Hereford

Lakeview Campground, 5990 South Hwy. 92, 85615. T: (520) 378-0311. www.fs.fed.us/r3/coronado. RV/tent: 65. $10. Hookups: none.

Huachuca City

Mountain View RV Park, Post 309, Hwy. 90, 85616. T: (520) 456-2860 or (800) 772-4103. RV/tent: 100. $17. Hookups: electric (30, 50 amp), water, sewer, cable TV, phone (modem).

ARIZONA (continued)

Huachuca City (continued)

Tombstone Territories RV Park, 2111 East Hwy. 82, 85616. T: (520) 457-2584 or (877) 316-6714. F: (520) 457-2584. TTRVPARK@yahoo.com. RV/tent: 102. $23. Hookups: electric (20, 30, 50 amp), water, sewer, phone (modem).

Kingman

A Quality Star RV Park, 3131 McDonald Ave., 86401. T: (520) 753-2277. F: (520) 753-4142. RV/tent: 49. $14–$18. Hookups: water, electric (20, 30 amp), sewer, phone (modem), cable TV.

Blake RV Ranch, I-40 & Blake Ranch Rd., 86401. T: (520) 565-3010 or (800) 270-1332. RV/tent: 58. $17. Hookups: electric (20, 30, 50 amp), water, sewer.

Hualapai Mountain Park, P.O. Box 7000, 86402. T: (520) 757-3859. RV/tent: 75. $9–$16. Hookups: electric (30 amp), water, sewer.

Zuni Village RV, 2840 Airway Ave., 86401. T: (520) 692-6202. RV/tent: 84. $17. Hookups: electric (20, 30, 50 amp), water, sewer.

Lake Havasu City

Beachcomber RV Resort, 601 Beachcomber Blvd., 86403. T: (520) 855-2322. F: (520) 855-3707. RV/tent: 50. $28–$33. Hookups: water, electric (30 amp), sewer, phone (modem), cable TV.

Cattail Cove State Park, P.O. Box 1990, 86405. T: (520) 855-1223. F: (520) 855-1730. RV/tent: 101. $8–$16. Hookups: Electric (30 amp), water.

Crazy Horse Campgrounds, 1534 Beachcomber Blvd., 86403. T: (520) 855-4033. www.crazyhorse-campgrounds.com. RV/tent: 777. $24–$38. Hookups: electric (20, 30, 50 amp), water, sewer, cable TV, phone.

London Bridge RV Park, 3405 London Bridge Rd., 86405. T: (520) 764-3700. RV/tent: 56. $25. Hookups: water, electric (20, 30 amp), sewer.

Marana

A Bar A RV Park, 9015 West Tangerine Rd., 85653. T: (520) 682-4333. F: (520) 682-4332. abaraaz@netscape.com. RV/tent: 85. $19. Hookups: electric (20, 30, 50 amp), water, sewer, phone (modem).

Valley of the Sun RV Mobile Home Park, 13377 North Sandario Rd., 85653. T: (520) 682-3434. RV/tent: 65. $20. Hookups: electric (30, 50 amp), water, sewer, phone (modem).

McNeal

Double Adobe Campground, 5057 West Double Adobe Rd., 85617. T: (520) 364-4000 or (800) 694-4242. www.theriver.com/doubleadobe. doubleadobe@theriver.com. RV/tent: 70. $10–

$14. Hookups: electric (30 amp), water, sewer, cable TV.

Mesa

The Resort, 1101 South Ellsworth Rd., 85208. T: (480) 986-8404. RV/tent: 792. $30. Hookups: electric (30, 50 amp), water, sewer, cable TV, phone (modem).

Apache Wells RV Resort, 2656 North 56th St., 85215. T: (480) 832-4324. RV/tent: 320. $34. Hookups: electric (30, 50 amp), water, sewer, phone (modem).

Canyon Lake Marina, P.O. Box 5800, 26 North Mac-Donald, 85211. T: (602) 467-2511 or (602) 379-6446. RV/tent: 115. $10. Hookups: none.

Fiesta RV Resort, 3811 East University Dr., 85205. T: (480) 832-6490 or (877) 506-0071. RV/tent: 336. $28. Hookups: water, electric (20, 50 amp), sewer, phone (modem).

Good Life RV Resort, 3403 East Main St., 85213. T: (480) 832-4990 or (800) 999-4990. RV/tent: 1184. $32. Hookups: electric (30, 50 amp), water, sewer, phone (modem).

Greenfield Village RV Resort, 111 South Greenfield Rd., 85206. T: (480) 832-4990 or (800) 999-4990. RV/tent: 1184. $35. Hookups: electric (30, 50 amp), water, sewer.

Las Palmas Grand, 2550 South Ellsworth Rd., 85212. T: (480) 380-3000 or (800) 982-2250. RV/tent: 63. $30. Hookups: electric (20, 30, 50 amp), water.

Mesa Regal RV Resort, 4700 East Main, 85205. T: (480) 830-2821 or (800) 845-4752. RV/tent: 2005. $35. Hookups: electric (30, 50 amp), water, sewer, phone (modem).

Orangewood Shadows RV Resort, 3165 East University, 85213. T: (480) 832-9080 or (800) 826-0909. RV/tent: 474. $31. Hookups: electric (30, 50 amp), water, sewer.

Palm Gardens Mobile Home/RV Community, 2929 East Main St., 85213. T: (480) 832-0290. RV/tent: 115. $35. Hookups: electric (30, 50 amp), water, sewer, phone (modem).

Paradise Palms Resort, 1608 East Main St., 85203. T: (480) 964-3552. RV/tent: 25. $16. Hookups: electric (30 amp), water, sewer, phone (modem).

Park Place RV Resort, 306 South Recker Rd., 85206. T: (480) 830-1080. RV/tent: 288. $16. Hookups: electric (30, 50 amp), water, sewer.

Silveridge RV Resort, 8265 East Southern, 85208. T: (480) 373-7000. F: (480) 373-7647. www.silveridge.com. RV/tent: 687. $30. Hookups: electric (30, 50 amp), water, sewer, cable TV, phone (modem).

ARIZONA (continued)

Mesa (continued)

Sun Life RV Resort, 5055 East University, 85205. T: (480) 981-9500. RV/tent: 761. $25. Hookups: electric (30, 50 amp), water, sewer, phone (modem).

Tortilla, P.O. Box 5800, 26 North MacDonald, 85211.T: (602) 467-2511 or (602) 379-6446. RV/tent: 77. $8. Hookups: water.

Towerpoint RV Resort, 4860 East Main, 85205. T: (480) 832-4996. www.towerpointresort.com. RV/tent: 1115. $30. Hookups: water, electric (20, 30, 50 amp), sewer, phone (modem).

Trailer Village, 3020 East Main St., 85213.T: (480) 832-1770 or (877) 924-6709. RV/tent: 1800. $16–$32. Hookups: water, electric (20, 30, 50 amp), sewer, phone (modem).

Trailing Ranch, 8730 East Apache Trail, 85208. T: (480) 984-0592:(800) 625-7266. F: (480) 984-2592. RV/tent: 55. $25. Hookups: electric (30, 50 amp), water, sewer, phone (modem).

Val Vista Village RV Resort, 233 North Val Vista Dr., 85213.T: (480) 832-2547. RV/tent: 1016. $30. Hookups: electric (30, 50 amp), water, sewer, phone (modem).

Valle de Oro RV Resort, 1452 South Ellsworth, 85208.T: (480) 984-1146:(800) 626-6686. www.valledeloro.com. RV/tent: 1802. $35. Hookups: electric (30, 50 amp), water, sewer, phone (modem).

Venture Out, 5001 East Main St., 85205.T: (480) 832-0200. RV/tent: 1749. $20–$30. Hookups: electric (30, 50 amp), water, sewer.

View Point RV & Golf Resort, 8700 East University, 85207.T: (480) 373-8700. RV/tent: 1784. $35. Hookups: electric (30, 50 amp), water, sewer, cable TV, phone (modem).

Mormon Lake

Mormon Lake Lodge RV Park and Campground, P.O. Box 38102, Main St., 86038.T: (520) 354-2227. www.foreverresorts.com. scott.gold@ inetmail.att.net. RV/tent: 86. $8–$24. Hookups: water, electric (20, 30, 50 amp), sewer, phone (modem).

Naco

Turquoise Valley Golf Course & RV Park, P.O. Box 727, 85620.T: (520) 432-3091. www.turquoise valley.com. golfer@turquoisevalley.com. RV/tent: 100. $15. Hookups: electric (30, 50 amp), water, sewer, cable TV, phone (modem).

Overgaard

Elk Pines RV Resort, P.O. Box 422, 2256 East Hwy. 260, 85933.T: (520) 535-3833. elkpines@pinenet.

com. RV/tent: 68. $21. Hookups: water, electric (20, 30, 50 amp), sewer, phone (modem).

Page

Page-Lake Powell Campground, 849 South Coppermine Rd., 86040.T: (928) 645-3374. F: (928) 645-2588. campground.page-lakepowell.com. RV/tent: 133. $17–$26. Hookups: water, electric (20, 30, 50 amp), sewer, modem, cable TV.

Parker

Fox's Pierpoint Landing, 6350 Riverside Dr., 85344. T: (520) 667-3444. F: (520) 667-4100. RV/tent: 70. $20–$25. Hookups: electric (20, 30, 50 amp), water, sewer.

Tony's Road Runner RV Park, 7000 Riverside Dr., 85344.T: (520) 667-4252. F: (520) 667-3293. www.roadrunnerfloating.com. RV/tent: 35. $27–$30. Hookups: electric (20, 30 amp), water, sewer, phone (modem), cable TV.

Peoria

Pleasant Harbor RV Resort, 8708 West Harbor Blvd., 85382.T: (800) 475-3272 or (602) 269-0077. F: (602) 269-0838. www.pleasantharbor.com. mwd@pleasantharbor.com. RV/tent: 200. $25–$32. Hookups: water, electric (20, 30, 50 amp), sewer, phone (modem).

Quality Inn RV Park, Grand Ave., 85382.T: (800) 572-9295. RV/tent: 72. $26. Hookups: water, electric (20, 30 amp), sewer.

Sundial Mobil & RV Park, 75th Ave., 85382.T: (623) 979-1921. RV/tent: 102. $16. Hookups: water, electric (30, 50 amp), sewer.

Phoenix

Desert Shadows Travel Trailer Resort, 19203 North 29th Ave., 85027.T: (623) 869-8178 or (800) 595-7290. RV/tent: 638. $25. Hookups: water, electric (30, 50 amp), sewer.

Desert's Edge RV Park, 22623 North Black Canyon Hwy., 85027.T: (623) 587-0940. F: (623) 587-0029. RV/tent: 250. $22. Hookups: water, electric (30, 50 amp), sewer, phone (modem).

Prescott

Point of Rocks Campground, 3025 North Hwy. 89, 86301.T: (520) 445-9018. www.northlink.com/ ~rhorsely. RV/tent: 96. $18. Hookups: water, electric (20, 30 amp), sewer.

Willow Lake RV & Camping Park, 1617 Heritage Park Rd., 86301.T: (520) 445-6311 or (800) 940-2845. RV/tent: 200. $20. Hookups: water, electric (20, 30, 50 amp), sewer, phone (modem), cable TV.

ARIZONA (continued)

Quartzsite

88 Shades RV Park, 575 West Main St., 85346. T: (520) 927-6336 or (800) 457-4392. RV/tent: 250. $18–$22. Hookups: electric (30 amp), water, sewer.

B-10 Campground, P.O. Box 4613, 85359. T: (520) 927-4393. RV/tent: 174. $16–$23. Hookups: electric (30, 50 amp), water, sewer.

Desert Gardens, P.O. Box 619, 85346. T: (520) 927-6361. RV/tent: 270. $18. Hookups: electric (20, 30, 50 amp), water, sewer, phone (modem).

Holiday Palms RV Park, P.O. Box 4800, 85346. T: (520) 927-5666. RV/tent: 254. $18–$22. Hookups: electric (20, 30 amp), water, sewer.

Queen Valley

Encore RV Park, 50 West Oro Viejo Dr., 85219. T: (877) 337-2757. F: (520) 463-2331. www.rvon thego.com. RV/tent: 210. $18–$24. Hookups: water, electric (30, 50 amp), sewer, phone (modem).

Roosevelt

Apache Lake Resort, Hwy. 88, HCO 2 Box 4800, 85545. T: (602) 467-2511 or (520) 467-3200. RV/tent: 12. $2. Hookups: yes (unspecified).

Safford

Roper Lake State Park, Rte 2 Box 712, 85546. T: (520) 428-6760. RV/tent: 71. $4–$15. Hookups: none.

Sahuarita

Rancho Resort RV Park, 1300 West Sahuarita Rd., 85629. T: (888) 363-8616 or (520) 399-3900. www.ranchoresort.com. info@ranchoresort.com. RV/tent: 100. $19–$30. Hookups: water, electric, sewer, cable TV, phone.

Salome

Desert Palms Golf & RV Resort, 39258 Harquahala Rd., 85348. T: (520) 859-2000. F: (520) 859-2001. desertpalmssp@netscape.net. RV/tent: 750. $18. Hookups: electric (30, 50 amp), water, sewer.

Tomahawk RV Park, I-10 & Exit 45 at Vicksburg Rd., P.O. Box A4, 85348. T: (520) 859-3843 or (800) 925-2407. RV/tent: 95. $19. Hookups: electric (20, 30, 50 amp), water, sewer.

Sedona

Rancho Sedona RV Park, 135 Bear Wallow Ln., 86336. T: (520) 282-7255 or (888) 641-4261. www.ranchosedona.com. ranchosedona@kachina. net. RV/tent: 84. $27. Hookups: water, electric (30, 50 amp), sewer, modem, cable TV.

Show Low

K-Bar RV Park, 300 North 15th Ave., 85901. T: (520) 537-2886. RV/tent: 92. $20. Hookups: electric (20, 30, 50 amp), water, sewer, cable TV, phone (modem).

Waltner's RV Park, 4800 South 28th St., 85901. T: (520) 537-4611. RV/tent: 145. $25. Hookups: electric (30 amp), water, sewer, cable TV, phone (modem).

Sierra Vista

Pueblo del Sol RV Resort, 3400 Resort Dr., 85650. T: (520) 378-0282 or (888) 551-1432. www.pds rvresort.com. pdsrv@C2I2.com. RV/tent: 135. $19–$27. Hookups: water, electric (30, 50 amp), sewer, cable TV, phone (modem).

St. David

Holy Trinity Monastery/Monte Cassino RV Park, P.O. Box 298, Hwy. 80-303, 85630. T: (520) 720-4016. F: (520) 720-4202. RV/tent: 23. $13. Hookups: water, electric (20, 30 amp), sewer.

Sun City

Paradise RV Resort, 10950 West Union Hills Dr., 85373. T: (623) 977-0344 or (800) 847-2280. RV/tent: 950. $35. Hookups: electric (30, 50 amp), water, sewer, cable TV, phone (modem).

Surprise

Donorma RV Park, 15637 Norma Ln., 85374. T: (623) 583-8195. F: (623) 583-0649. RV/tent: 66. $23. Hookups: water, electric (20, 30, 50 amp), sewer, phone (modem).

Sunflower Resort, 16501 North El Mirage Rd., 85374. T: (623) 583-0100 or (800) 627-8637. F: (623) 583-2007. Sunflowr@doitnow.com. RV/tent: 1156. $24–$32. Hookups: electric (30, 50 amp), water, sewer, cable TV, phone (modem).

Tempe

Apache Palms RV Park, 1836 East Apache Blvd., 85281. T: (480) 966-7399. apacheplms@aol.com. RV/tent: 75. $19–$29. Hookups: electric (20, 30, 50 amp), water, sewer, cable TV, phone (modem).

Tombstone

Stampede RV Park, 201 West Allen, P.O. Box 1247, 85638. T: (520) 457-3738. stampederv@desert-gold.com. RV/tent: 22. $22. Hookups: water, electric (20, 30, 50 amp), sewer, phone (modem).

Tombstone Hills RV Park & Campground, P.O. Box 99, 85638. T: (520) 457-3829. RV/tent: 86. $20. Hookups: water, electric (50 amp), sewer.

ARIZONA (continued)

Tonopah

Saddle Mountain RV Park, 3607 North 411th St., P.O. Box 146, 85354. T: (623) 386-3892. www.saddle mountain.com. RV/tent: 139. $10–$20. Hookups: electric (30, 50 amp), water, sewer, phone (modem).

Stage Stop RV Park, 2614 South Wintersberg Rd., 85354. T: (623) 386-1601. F: (623) 386-1612. RV/tent: 146. $23. Hookups: water, electric (20, 30, 50 amp), sewer, phone (modem).

Tucson

Beaudry RV Resort, 5151 South Country Club Rd., 85706. T: (520)806-8156 or (877) 806-8156. www. beaudryrvresort.com. RV/tent: 400. $30. Hookups: water, electric (50 amp), sewer, cable TV, phone (modem).

Cactus Country RV Resort, 10195 South Houghton Rd., 85747. T: (520) 574-3000 or (800) 777-8799. F: (520) 574-9004. www.arizonguide.com/cactus co. RV/tent: 263. $26. Hookups: water, electric (20, 30, 50 amp), sewer, cable TV, phone (modem).

Far Horizons Trailer Village, 555 North Pantano Rd., 85710. T: (520) 296-1234. F: (520) 733-9003. farhorizonstv@worldnet.att.net. RV/tent: 514. $26. Hookups: water, electric (30, 50 amp), sewer, phone (modem).

Justin's RV Park & WaterWorld, 3551 South San Joaquin Rd., 85735. T: (520) 883-8340 or (888) 883-8340. RV/tent: 220. $10–$18. Hookups: water, electric (30, 50 amp), sewer, phone (modem).

Miracle RV Park, 333 West Glenn St., 85705. T: (520) 624-0142 or (888) 624-0142. RV/tent: 86. $16. Hookups: water, electric (20, 30 amp), sewer, phone (modem).

Mission RV Resort, 31 West Los Reales Rd., 85735. T: (800) 444-8439. missnview@aol.com. RV/tent: 152. $28. Hookups: water, electric (30, 50 amp), sewer.

Prince of Tucson, 3501 North Freeway, 85705. T: (520) 887-3501 or (800) 955-3501. princeof tucson@worldnet.att.net. RV/tent: 212. $22. Hookups: water, electric (20, 30, 50 amp), sewer.

Rincon Country East RV Resort, 8989 East Escalante, 85730. T: (520) 886-8431. eastinfo@ rinconcountry.com. RV/tent: 460. $28. Hookups: water, electric (30, 50 amp), sewer.

Rincon Country West RV Resort, 4555 South Mission Rd., 85746. T: (520) 294-5608 or (800) 782-7275. westinfo@rinconcountry.com. RV/tent: 1100. $26–$29. Hookups: water, electric (30, 50 amp), sewer, cable TV, phone (modem).

Rose Canyon, Mile Post 17 Catalina Hwy., 85750. T: (520) 749-8700. www.azstarnet.com.public/non profit/coronado/d5home1.htm. RV/tent: 74. $7. Hookups: none.

South Forty RV Ranch, 3600 West Orange Grove Rd., 85741. T: (520) 297-2503. south40rv@the river.com. RV/tent: 229. $22–$26. Hookups: water, electric (20, 30 amp), sewer, phone (modem).

Spencer Canyon, Mile Post 22 Catalina Hwy., 85750. T: (520) 749-8700. www.azstarnet.com.public/non profit/coronado/d5home1.htm. RV/tent: 77. $7. Hookups: none.

Western Way RV Resort, 3100 South Kinney Rd., 85713. T: (520) 578-1715 or (800) 292-8616. accenth@azstarnet.com. RV/tent: 300. $15–$25. Hookups: water, electric (20, 30 amp), sewer.

Whispering Palms RV Trailer Park, 3445 North Romero Rd., 85705. T: (520) 888-2500 or (800) 266-8577. RV/tent: 103. $15–$19. Hookups: water, electric (30 amp), sewer.

Wellton

M&M RV Village, 28541 West AZ Ave., 85356. T: (520) 785-4273. F: (520) 785-9651. tsmangine@ aol.com. RV/tent: 90. $15. Hookups: water, electric (30 amp), sewer, phone (modem).

West Sedona

Lo Lo Mai Springs Outdoor Resort, P.O. Box 3169, 86340. T: (520) 634-4700. www.lolomai.com. lolo mai@sedona.net. RV/tent: 90. $23–$32. Hookups: electric (30 amp), water, sewer.

Why

Coyote Howls Campground, P.O Box 1134, US Hwy. 86, 85321. T: (520) 387-5209. coyosurf@ tabletoptelephone.com. RV/tent: 550. $8. Hookups: none.

Hickiwan Trails RV Park, South US Hwy. 86, 85321. T: (520) 362-3267. RV/tent: 95. $15. Hookups: water, electric (20, 30 amp), sewer.

Las Palmas RV Park, Hwy. 85, 85321. T: (520) 387-3300. RV/tent: 47. $15. Hookups: water, electric (20, 30 amp), sewer.

Roberts Ranch Resort, 1600 South US Hwy. 86, 85321. T: (800) 699-7983. RV/tent: 85. $6–$18. Hookups: water, electric (20, 30, 50 amp), sewer.

Wickenburg

Desert Cypress Trailer Ranch, 610 Jack Burden Rd., space No. 1, 85390. T: (520) 684-2153. RV/tent: 32. $20. Hookups: water, electric (20, 30, 50 amp), sewer, cable TV.

ARIZONA (continued)

Willcox

Fort Willcox RV Park, RR2 Box 512, 85643. T: (520) 384-4986. F: (520) 384-4986. RV/tent: 35. $10–$15. Hookups: water, electric (20, 30, 50 amp), sewer.

Grande Vista RV Park, 711 Prescott Ave. North, 85643. T: (520) 384-4002. F: (520) 384-0458. connet1@vtc.net. RV/tent: 37. $16. Hookups: water, electric (30, 50 amp), sewer, cable TV, phone (modem).

Lifestyle RV Resort, 622 North Haskell Ave., 85643. T: (520) 384-3303. F: (520) 384-0740. RV/tent: 60. $13–$21. Hookups: water, electric (30, 50 amp), sewer.

Magic Circle RV Park, 700 North Virginia Ave., 85643. T: (520) 384-3212 or (800) 333-4720. Magic1@vtc.net. RV/tent: 56. $20. Hookups: water, electric (20, 30, 50 amp), sewer, cable TV, phone (modem).

Williams

Canyon Gateway RV Park, 1060 North Grand Canyon Blvd., 86046. T: (888) 635-0329. F: (520) 635-2733. RV/tent: 101. $18. Hookups: water, electric (30, 50 amp), sewer.

Circle Pines KOA, 1000 Circle Pines Rd., 86046. T: (520) 635-2626 or (800) 562-9379. F: (520) 635-2627. CABA66@aol.com. RV/tent: 149. $18–$27. Hookups: water, electric (20, 30 amp), sewer, phone (modem).

Flinstone's Bedrock City, HCR-34 Box A, 86046. T: (520) 635-2600. F: (520) 635-2600. RV/tent: 60. $16. Hookups: electric (30 amp).

Railside RV Ranch, 877 Rodeo Rd., 86046. T: (520) 635-4077 or (888) 635-4077. www.thegrand canyon.com/railside. railside@thegrand canyon.com. RV/tent: 100. $15–$20. Hookups: water, electric (20, 30, 50 amp), sewer, modem, cable TV.

Yuma

Araby Acres Travel Trailer Park, 6649 East Hwy. 80, 85365. T: (520) 344-8666. arabyacres@aol.com. RV/tent: 338. $28. Hookups: electric (30, 50 amp), water, sewer, phone (modem).

Arizona Sands RV Park, 5510 East 32nd St., 85365. T: (520) 726-0286. azsandsrvparks@aol.com. RV/tent: 200. $20–$25. Hookups: electric (30, 50 amp), water, sewer.

Blue Sky RV Park, 10247 South Frontage Rd., 85365. T: (877) 367-5220. RV/tent: 287. $25–$40. Hookups: electric (30, 50 amp), water, sewer.

Bonita Mesa RV Resort, 9400 East North Frontage Rd., 85365. T: (520) 342-2999. RV/tent: 472. $24. Hookups: water, electric (30, 50 amp), sewer, phone (modem), cable TV.

Caravan Oasis RV Park, 10500 North East Frontage Rd., 85365. T: (520) 342-1480. RV/tent: 742. $21. Hookups: water, electric (30, 50 amp), sewer, phone (modem), cable TV.

Cocopah RV & Golf Resort, 6800 Strand Ave., 85364. T: (520) 343-9300 or (800) 537-7901. RV/tent: 806. $27. Hookups: water, electric (30, 50 amp), sewer, phone (modem), cable TV.

Desert Paradise RV Resort, 10537 South Ave. 9E, 85367. T: (520) 342-9313. dprvresort@aol.com. RV/tent: 260. $25. Hookups: water, electric (30, 50 amp), sewer, phone (modem), cable TV.

El Prado Estates RV Park, 6200 East Hwy. 95, 85365. T: (520) 726-4006. F: (602) 978-0613. RV/tent: 120. $14. Hookups: electric (30 amp), water, sewer.

Fortuna de Oro RV Resort, 13650 North Frontage Rd., 85367. T: (520) 342-5051. RV/tent: 763. $20. Hookups: water, electric (20, 30, 50 amp), sewer.

Friendly Acres Trailer Park, 2779 West Eighth St., 85364. T: (520) 783-8414. RV/tent: 280. $16. Hookups: water, electric (30 amp), sewer, phone (modem), cable TV.

Hidden Shores RV Village, Star Rte. 4 Box 40, 85365. T: (520) 783-1448. F: (520) 329-4654. RV/tent: 354. $12–$21. Hookups: water, electric (20, 30, 50 amp), sewer, phone (modem).

Las Quintas Oasis RV Park, 1442 North Frontage Rd., 85365. T: (520) 305-9005 or (877) 975-9005. RV/tent: 460. $21. Hookups: water, electric (30, 50 amp), sewer, phone (modem), cable TV.

Shangri-La RV Resort, 10498 North Frontage Rd., 85365. T: (520) 340-9123. RV/tent: 302. $21–$25. Hookups: water, electric (30, 50 amp), sewer.

Sun Vista RV Resort, 7201 East Hwy. 80, 85365. T: (520) 726-8920 or (800) 423-8382. RV/tent: 1230. $29. Hookups: water, electric (30, 50 amp), sewer, phone (modem), cable TV.

Villa Alameda RV Resort, 11451 South Ave. 5E, 85365. T: (520) 344-8081. RV/tent: 302. $23. Hookups: water, electric (30, 50 amp), sewer, phone (modem), cable TV.

West Wind RV & Golf Resort, 9797 East Frontage Rd., 85365. T: (520) 342-2992. RV/tent: 1083. $27. Hookups: water, electric (20, 30, 50 amp), sewer, phone (modem), cable TV.

Wind Have RV Park, 6580 East Hwy. 80, 85365. T: (520) 726-0284. F: (520) 726-6622. RV/tent: 135. $27. Hookups: water, electric (20, 30, 50 amp), sewer.

Yuma Mesa RV Park, 5990 East Hwy. 80, 85365. T: (520) 344-3369. RV/tent: 183. $23. Hookups: water, electric (30 amp), sewer.

CALIFORNIA

Acton

The Californian RV Resort, 1535 West Sierra Hwy., 93510. T: (888) RVRV-FUN or (661) 269-0919. www.calrv.com. RV/tent: 73. $33. Hookups: water, electric (20, 30, 50 amp), sewer, cable TV, phone.

Adin

Lower Rush Creek, County Rd. 198A, 96006. T: (530) 299-3215. F: (530) 299-8409. www.r5.fs. fed.us/modoc. RV/tent: 15. $6. Hookups: none.

Allensworth

Colonel Allensworth State Historic Park, Palmer Ave., 93219. T: (800) 444-7275 or (661) 634-3795. F: (661) 849-3433. www.reserveamerica.com. RV/tent: 15. $8. Hookups: none.

Anaheim

Anaheim Harbor RV Park, 1009 South Harbor Blvd., 92805. T: (714) 535-6495. F: (714) 535-4239. www.anaheimharborrvpark.com. RV/tent: 198. $24–$38 . Hookups: water, electric (30, 50 amp), sewer, cable TV, phone.

Anaheim Resort RV Park, 200 West Midway Dr., 92805. T: (714) 774-3860. F: (714) 774-5970. www.anaheimresortrvpark.com. RV/tent: 150. $36. Hookups: water, electric (20, 30, 50 amp), sewer, cable TV, phone.

Angels Camp

Angels Camp RV & Camping Resort, 3069 South Hwy. 49, 95222. T: (888) 398-0404 or (209) 736-0404. F: (209) 736-2849. www.gocamping america.com/angelscamp/. RV/tent: 44. $25. Hookups: water, electric (20, 30, 50 amp), sewer.

Angelus Oaks

Barton Flats, Hwy. 38, 92305. T: (877) 444-6777 or (909) 794-1123. F: (909) 794-1125. www.reserve usa.com. RV/tent: 47. $20. Hookups: none.

Heart Bar Family Camp, FR 1N02, 92305. T: (877) 444-6777 or (909) 794-1123. F: (909) 794-1125. www.reserveusa.com. RV/tent: 94. $15. Hookups: none.

San Gorgonio, Hwy. 38, 92305. T: (877) 444-6777 or (909) 794-1123. F: (909) 794-1125. www.reserve usa.com. RV/tent: 55. $20. Hookups: none.

South Fork, Hwy. 38, 92305. T: (877) 444-6777 or (909) 794-1123. F: (909) 794-1125. www.reserve usa.com. RV/tent: 24. $15. Hookups: none.

Anza

Kamp-Anza RV Resort, 41560 Terwilliger Rd., 92539. T: (909) 763-4819. www.koan.com/. RV/tent: 115. $12–$18. Hookups: water, electric (30 amp), sewer, TV, phone.

Arcadia

Santa Anita Village & RV Park, 4241 East Live Oak Ave., 91006. T: (626) 447-3878. RV/tent: 100. $25. Hookups: water, electric (30 amp), sewer, phone.

Arcata

Mad River Rapids RV Park, 3501 Janes Rd., 95521. T: (800) 822-7776 or (707) 822-7275. F: (707) 822-7286. www.madriverrv.com. RV/tent: 92. $29. Hookups: water, electric (30, 50 amp), sewer, cable TV, phone.

Auburn

Auburn KOA, 3550 KOA Way, 95602. T: (800) 562-6671 or (530) 885-0990. www.koa.com. RV/tent: 80. $25–$35. Hookups: water, electric (20, 30, 50 amp), sewer.

Bakersfield

Bakersfield Palms RV Park, 250 Fairfax Rd., 93307. T: (888) 725-6778 or (661) 366-6700. F: (661) 366-6704. www.palmsrv.com. RV/tent: 116. $20–$22. Hookups: water, electric (30, 50 amp), sewer, cable TV, phone.

Bakersfield Trav-L-Park, 8633 East Brundage Ln., 93307. T: (800) 962-4546 (CA only) or (661) 366-3550. www.bakersfieldtravelpark.com/. RV/tent: 126. $19. Hookups: water, electric (20, 30, 50 amp), sewer, cable TV, phone.

Orange Grove RV Park, 1452 South Edison Rd., 93307. T: (800) 553-7126 or (661) 366-4662. F: (661) 366-8915. www.orangegrovervpark.com/. RV/tent: 146. $22. Hookups: water, electric (50 amp), sewer, cable TV, phone.

Southland RV Park, 9901 Southland Court, 93307. T: (877) 834-4868. www.gocampingamerica.com/ southlandrvpk/. RV/tent: 91. $22. Hookups: water, electric (30, 50 amp), sewer, TV, phone.

Banning

Stagecoach RV Park, 1455 South San Gorgonio Ave., 92220. T: (909) 849-7513. F: (909) 849-7998. RV/tent: 97. $14–$19.50. Hookups: water, electric (20, 30, 50 amp), sewer, cable TV, phone.

Bard

Senator Wash Recreation Area, Senator Wash Rd., 92222. T: (520) 317-3200. F: (520) 317-3250. www.ca.blm.gov/caso/information.html. RV/tent: undesignated. $5. Hookups: none.

Squaw Lake, Senator Wash Rd., 92222. T: (520) 317-3200. F: (520) 317-3250. www.ca.blm.gov/caso/ information.html. RV/tent: 80. $5. Hookups: none.

CALIFORNIA (continued)

Barstow

Shady Lane RV Camp, 36445 Soap Mine Rd, 92311.
T: (760) 256-5332. RV/tent: 33. $19–$20.
Hookups: water, electric (20, 30 amp), sewer,
phone.

Bass Lake

Chilkoot, Beasore Rd., 93604. T: (559) 877-2218.
F: (559) 877-3108. www.r5.fs.fed.us/sierra.
RV/tent: 14. $12. Hookups: none.

Forks, County Rd. 222, 93604. T: (559) 877-2218.
F: (559) 877-3108. www.r5.fs.fed.us/sierra.
RV/tent: 31. $16. Hookups: none.

Spring Cove, County Rd. 222, 93604. T: (559) 877-
2218. F: (559) 877-3108. www.r5.fs.fed.us/sierra.
RV/tent: 65. $16. Hookups: none.

Wishon Point, County Rd. 222, 93604. T: (559) 877-
2218. F: (559) 877-3108. www.r5.fs.fed.us/sierra.
RV/tent: 47. $16. Hookups: none.

Beckwourth

Grizzly, Lake Davis Rd., 96129. T: (530) 836-2575.
F: (530) 836-0493. www.r5.fs.fed.us/plumas.
RV/tent: 55. $13. Hookups: none.

Lightning Tree, Lake Davis Rd., 96129. T: (530) 836-
2575. F: (530) 836-0493. www.r5.fs.fed.us/plumas.
RV/tent: 38. $6. Hookups: none.

Bethel Island

Lundborg Landing, 6777 Riverview Rd, 94511.
T: (925) 684-9351. F: (925) 684-9366. www.
lundborglanding.com. RV/tent: 96. $16–$20.
Hookups: water, electric (30 amp), sewer.

Big Bear Lake

Holloway's Marina & RV Park, 398 Edgemoor Rd.,
92325. T: (800) 448-5335 or (909) 866-5706.
www.bigbearboating.com/. RV/tent: 99. $25–$40.
Hookups: water, electric (20, 30, 50 amp), sewer,
cable TV.

Big Pine

Sage Flat, Glacier Lodge Rd., 93513. T: (760) 873-
2500. F: (760) 873-2563. www.r5.fs.fed.us/inyo.
RV/tent: 28. $11. Hookups: none.

Upper Sage Flat, Glacier Lodge Rd., 93513. T: (760)
873-2500. F: (760) 873-2563. www.r5.fs.fed.us/
inyo. RV/tent: 21. $11. Hookups: none.

Big Sur

Big Sur Campgrounds & Cabins, Hwy. 1, 93920.
T: (831) 667-2322. www.bigsurcalifornia.org/
camping.html. RV/tent: 81. $26–$29. Hookups:
water, electric (20, 30 amp).

Bishop

Big Trees, Hwy. 168, 93514. T: (760) 873-2500.
F: (760) 873-2563. www.r5.fs.fed.us/inyo. RV/tent:
9. $12. Hookups: none.

Bishop Park, Hwy. 168, 93514. T: (760) 873-2500.
F: (760) 873-2563. www.r5.fs.fed.us/inyo. RV/tent:
20. $12. Hookups: none.

Brown's Millpond Campground, Sawmill Rd., 93514.
T: (760) 872-6911. F: (760) 872-1373. www.the
sierraweb.com/recreation/browns/millpond.html.
RV/tent: 74. $14–$19. Hookups: water, electric (30
amp).

Brown's Owens River Campground, Benton Crossing Rd., 93514. T: (760) 920-0975 or (760) 872-
6911. F: (760) 872-1373. www.thesierraweb.
com/recreation/browns/owens.html. RV/tent: 75.
$14–$19. Hookups: water, electric (30 amp).

Brown's Town, Schober n., 93514. T: (760) 873-8522.
F: (760) 872-1373. www.thesierraweb.com/
recreation/browns/browns.html. RV/tent: 155.
$14. Hookups: water, electric (30 amp).

Creekside RV Park, South Lake Rd., 93514. T: (760)
873-4483. www.thesierraweb.com/lodging/
creekside/. RV/tent: 49. $20–$28. Hookups: water,
electric (15, 30 amp), sewer.

Forks, Hwy. 168, 93514. T: (760) 873-2500. F: (760)
873-2563. www.r5.fs.fed.us/inyo. RV/tent: 8. $12.
Hookups: none.

Four Jeffrey, South Lake Rd., 93514. T: (760) 873-
2500. F: (760) 873-2563. www.r5.fs.fed.us/inyo.
RV/tent: 106. $12. Hookups: none.

Highlands RV Park, 2275 North Sierra Hwy., 93514.
T: (760) 873-7616. RV/tent: 103. $24. Hookups:
water, electric (15, 30, 50 amp), sewer, cable TV.

Intake, Hwy. 168, 93514. T: (760) 873-2500. F: (760)
873-2563. www.r5.fs.fed.us/inyo. RV/tent: 15. $12.
Hookups: none.

North Lake, FR 8S02, 93514. T: (760) 873-2500.
F: (760) 873-2563. www.r5.fs.fed.us/inyo. RV/tent:
11. $12. Hookups: none.

Sabrina, Hwy. 168, 93514. T: (760) 873-2500. F: (760)
873-2563. www.r5.fs.fed.us/inyo. RV/tent: 18. $12.
Hookups: none.

Blythe

Coon Hollow, Wiley's Well Rd., 92225. T: (760) 251-
4800. F: (760) 251-4899. www.ca.blm.gov/caso/
information.html. RV/tent: 27. $20. Hookups: none.

Destiny's McIntyre RV Resort, 8750 East 26th Ave.,
92225. T: (760) 922-8205. www.destinyrv.com/
River2.htm. RV/tent: 161. $29–$37. Hookups:
water, electric (30 amp), sewer.

CALIFORNIA (continued)

Blythe (continued)

Destiny's Riviera RV Resort & Marina, 14100 Riviera Dr., 92225. T: (760) 922-5350. www.destinyrv.com/River2.htm. RV/tent: 268. $32–$39. Hookups: water, electric (30, 50 amp), sewer, cable TV, phone.

Wiley's Well, Wiley's Well Rd., 92225. T: (760) 251-4800. F: (760) 251-4899. www.ca.blm.gov/caso/information.html. RV/tent: 13. $20. Hookups: none.

Boca

Boca, County Rd. 73, 96161. T: (877) 444-6777 or (530) 587-3558. F: (530) 587-6914. www.r5.fs.fed.us/tahoe; www.reserveusa.com. RV/tent: 22. $10. Hookups: none.

Boca Rest Campground, County Rd. 270, 96161. T: (877) 444-6777 or (530) 587-3558. F: (530) 587-6914. www.r5.fs.fed.us/tahoe; www.reserveusa.com. RV/tent: 31. $8. Hookups: none.

Boyington Mill, County Rd. 270, 96161. T: (877) 444-6777 or (530) 587-3558. F: (530) 587-6914. www.r5.fs.fed.us/tahoe; www.reserveusa.com. RV/tent: 10. $10. Hookups: none.

Cold Creek, Hwy. 89, 96161. T: (877) 444-6777 or (530) 587-3558. F: (530) 587-6914. www.r5.fs.fed.us/tahoe; www.reserveusa.com. RV/tent: 13. $10. Hookups: none.

Lower Little Truckee, Hwy. 89, 96161. T: (877) 444-6777 or (530) 587-3558. F: (530) 587-6914. www.r5.fs.fed.us/tahoe; www.reserveusa.com. RV/tent: 15. $10. Hookups: none.

Upper Little Truckee, Hwy. 89, 96161. T: (877) 444-6777 or (530) 587-3558. F: (530) 587-6914. www.r5.fs.fed.us/tahoe; www.reserveusa.com. RV/tent: 26. $10. Hookups: none.

Bodega Bay

Bodega Bay RV Park, 2001 Hwy. 1, 94923. T: (800) 201-6864 or (707) 875-3701. F: (707) 875-9811. www.bodegabayrvpark.com. RV/tent: 72. $25–$31. Hookups: water, electric (30, 50 amp), sewer, TV.

Doran Regional Park, Hwy. 1, 94923. T: (707) 875-3540. www.sonomacounty.org. RV/tent: 134. $16. Hookups: none.

Sonoma Coast State Beach, Wrights Beach, Hwy. 1, 94923. T: (707) 875-3483 or (800) 444-7275. www.cal-parks.ca.gov; www.reserveamerica.com. RV/tent: 30. $12. Hookups: none.

Westside Regional Park, Bay Flat Rd., 94923. T: (707) 875-3540. www.sonomacounty.org. RV/tent: 47. $16. Hookups: none.

Borrego Springs

Anza-Borrego Desert State Park, Arroyo Salado Primitive Camp, County Rd. S22, 92004. T: (760) 767-5311. F: (760) 767-3427. www.cal-parks.ca.gov. RV/tent: Dispersed. $5. Hookups: none.

Anza-Borrego Desert State Park, Tamarisk Grove, Hwy. 78 and Yaqui Pass Rd., 92004. T: (760) 767-5311. F: (760) 767-3427. www.cal-parks.ca.gov. RV/tent: 27. $10. Hookups: none.

Anza-Borrego Desert State Park, Yaqui Pass Primitive Camp, Yaqui Pass Rd., 92004. T: (760) 767-5311. F: (760) 767-3427. www.cal-parks.ca.gov. RV/tent: dispersed. $5. Hookups: none.

Anza-Borrego Desert State Park, Yaqui Well Primitive Camp, Yaqui Pass Rd., 92004. T: (760) 767-5311. F: (760) 767-3427. www.cal-parks.ca.gov. RV/tent: dispersed. $5. Hookups: none.

Palm Canyon Resort RV Park, 221 Palm Canyon Dr., 92004. T: (800) 242-0044 or (760) 767-5341. F: (760) 767-4073. www.pcresort.com/. RV/tent: 132. $29. Hookups: water, electric (30 amp), sewer, cable TV, phone (long-term only).

Bradley

Lake Nacimiento Resort, 10625 Nacimiento Lake Dr., 93426. T: (800) 323-3839 or (805) 238-3256. www.nacimientoresort.com/. RV/tent: 340. $18–$30. Hookups: water, electric (30 amp), sewer.

Bridgeport

Crags, Twin Lakes Rd., 93517. T: (760) 932-7070. F: (760) 932-1299. www.r5.fs.fed.us/htnf/honecamp.htm. RV/tent: 26. $9. Hookups: none.

Lower Twin Lake, Twin Lakes Rd., 93517. T: (760) 932-7070. F: (760) 932-1299. www.r5.fs.fed.us/htnf/honecamp.htm. RV/tent: 14. $9. Hookups: none.

Paha, Twin Lakes Rd., 93517. T: (760) 932-7070. F: (760) 932-1299. www.r5.fs.fed.us/htnf/honecamp.htm. RV/tent: 22. $9. Hookups: none.

Robinson Creek, Twin Lakes Rd., 93517. T: (760) 932-7070. F: (760) 932-1299. www.r5.fs.fed.us/htnf/honecamp.htm. RV/tent: 54. $9. Hookups: none.

Bucks Lake

Grizzly Creek, Oroville-Quincy Rd./FR 33, 95971. T: (530) 283-0555. F: (530) 283-1821. www.r5.fs.fed.us/plumas. RV/tent: 8. $14. Hookups: none.

Haskins Valley, Bucks Lake Rd., 95971. T: (530) 283-0555. F: (530) 283-1821. www.r5.fs.fed.us/plumas. RV/tent: 65. $15. Hookups: none.

Lower Bucks, Bucks Lake Dam Rd./FR 33, 95971. T: (530) 283-0555. F: (530) 283-1821. www.r5.fs.fed.us/plumas. RV/tent: 6. $10. Hookups: none.

CALIFORNIA (continued)

Bucks Lake (continued)

Mill Creek, Bucks Lake Dam Rd./FR 33, 95971. T: (530) 283-0555. F: (530) 283-1821. www.r5.fs. fed.us/plumas. RV/tent: 8. $14. Hookups: none.

Sundew, Bucks Lake Dam Rd./FR 33, 95971. T: (530) 283-0555. F: (530) 283-1821. www.r5.fs.fed. us/plumas. RV/tent: 19. $13. Hookups: none.

Whitehorse, Bucks Lake Rd., 95971. T: (530) 283-0555. F: (530) 283-1821. www.r5.fs.fed.us/plumas. RV/tent: 20. $14. Hookups: none.

Buellton

Flying Flags RV Park & Campground, 180 Avenue of the Flags, 93427. T: (805) 688-3716. F: (805) 688-9245. www.flyingflags.com. RV/tent: 300. $18–$26. Hookups: water, electric (20, 30, 50 amp), sewer, TV, phone.

Camp Nelson

Belknap, Nelson Dr., 93208. T: (559)539-2607. www.r5.fs.fed.us/sequoia. RV/tent: 15. $12. Hookups: none.Nelson

Coy Flat, Coy Flat Rd., 93208. T: (559)539-2607. www.r5.fs.fed.us/sequoia. RV/tent: 20. $10. Hookups: none.

Lower Peppermint, Lloyd Meadow Rd., 93208. T: (559)539-2607. www.r5.fs.fed.us/sequoia. RV/tent: 17. $12. Hookups: none.

Camptonville

Cal-Ida, Cal-Ida Rd., 95922. T: (530) 288-3231. F: (530) 288-0727. www.r5.fs.fed.us/tahoe. RV/tent: 20. $12. Hookups: none.

Carlton, Hwy. 49, 95922. T: (530) 288-3231. F: (530) 288-0727. www.r5.fs.fed.us/tahoe. RV/tent: 21. $12. Hookups: none.

Dark Day, Dark Day Rd., 95922. T: (530) 692-3200 or (530) 288-3231. F: (530) 288-0727. www.r5.fs. fed.us/tahoe. RV/tent: 16. $14. Hookups: none.

Fiddle Creek, Hwy. 49, 95922. T: (530) 288-3231. F: (530) 288-0727. www.r5.fs.fed.us/tahoe. RV/tent: 15. $12. Hookups: none.

Indian Valley, Hwy. 49, 95922. T: (530) 288-3231. F: (530) 288-0727. www.r5.fs.fed.us/tahoe. RV/tent: 17. $12. Hookups: none.

Ramshorn, Hwy. 49, 95922. T: (530) 288-3231. F: (530) 288-0727. www.r5.fs.fed.us/tahoe. RV/tent: 16. $12. Hookups: none.

Rocky Nest, Hwy. 49, 95922. T: (530) 288-3231. F: (530) 288-0727. www.r5.fs.fed.us/tahoe. RV/tent: 10. $12. Hookups: none.

Carmel

Carmel by the River RV Park, 27680 Schulte Rd., 93923. T: (831) 624-9329. F: (831) 624-8416. RV/tent: 35. $40–$45. Hookups: water, electric (20, 30 amp), sewer, cable TV, phone.

Carrville

Eagle Creek, Hwy. 3, 96091. T: (530) 623-2121. F: (530) 623-6010. www.r5.fs.fed.us/shastatrinity. RV/tent: 17. $8. Hookups: none.

Trinity River, Hwy. 3, 96091. T: (530) 623-2121. F: (530) 623-6010. www.r5.fs.fed.us/shastatrinity. RV/tent: 7. $8. Hookups: none.

Castaic

Castaic Lake RV Park, 31540 Ridge Rte. Rd., 91384. T: (661) 257-3340 or (877) 450-3340. F: (661) 257-1077. www.gocampingamerica.com/castaic lake/. RV/tent: 103. $18–$25. Hookups: water, electric (30 amp), sewer, cable TV, phone.

Cathedral City

Palm Springs Oasis RV Resort, 36100 Date Palm Dr., 92234. T: (800) 680-0144 or (760) 328-4813. F: (760) 328-8455. RV/tent: 140. $25–$32. Hookups: water, electric (20, 30, 50 amp), sewer, cable TV, phone.

Chester

Benner Creek, Juniper Lake Rd., 96020. T: (530) 258-2141. F: (530) 258-5194. www.r5.fs.fed.us/lassen. RV/tent: 9. $9. Hookups: none.

Domingo Springs, County Rd. 311, 96020. T: (530) 258-2141. F: (530) 258-5194. www.r5.fs.fed. us/lassen. RV/tent: 18. $11. Hookups: none.

High Bridge, County Rd. 312, 96020. T: (530) 258-2141. F: (530) 258-5194. www.r5.fs.fed.us/lassen. RV/tent: 12. $11. Hookups: none.

North Shore Campground, Hwy. 36, 96020. T: (530) 258-3376. www.gocampingamerica.com/ northshorecpgrd/. RV/tent: 128. $17–$20. Hookups: water, electric (20, 30 amp), phone.

Warner Creek, County Rd. 311, 96020. T: (530) 258-2141. F: (530) 258-5194. www.r5.fs.fed.us/ lassen. RV/tent: 13. $9. Hookups: none.

Chico

Almond Tree RV Park, 3124 Esplanade, 95973. T: (530) 899-1271. F: (530) 892-0523. http://now 2000.com/rvpark/. RV/tent: 42. $24. Hookups: water, electric (30, 50 amp), sewer, TV, phone.

CALIFORNIA (continued)

Chula Vista

Chula Vista RV Resort & Marina, 460 Sandpiper Way, 91910. T: (619) 422-0111. F: (619) 422-8872. www.gocampingamerica.com/chulavista/. RV/tent: 237. $28.50–$47.50. Hookups: water, electric (30, 50 amp), sewer, TV, phone.

KOA San Diego Metropolitan, 111 North Second St., 91910. T: (800) KOA-9877 or (619) 427-3601. F: (619) 427-3622. www.sandiegokoa.com. RV/tent: 270. $26–$45. Hookups: water, electric (30, 50 amp), sewer, cable TV.

Sweetwater Regional Park-Summit Site (San Diego County Park), Summit Meadow Rd., 91910. T: (877) 565-3600 or (858) 694-3049. www.co.san diego.ca.us/cnty/cntydepts/landuse/parks/camping/sweetwater/. RV/tent: 60. $16. Hookups: water, electric (30 amp).

Cloverdale

KOA Cloverdale Camping Resort, 26460 River Rd., 95425. T: (800) 562-4042 or (707) 894-3337. www.koa.com. RV/tent: 151. $28–$42. Hookups: water, electric (30, 50 amp).

Coleville

Bootleg, US 395, 96107. T: (760) 932-7070. F: (760) 932-1299. www.r5.fs.fed.us/htnf/soncamp.htm. RV/tent: 63. $10. Hookups: none.

Chris Flat, US 395, 96107. T: (760) 932-7070. F: (760) 932-1299. www.r5.fs.fed.us/htnf/soncamp.htm. RV/tent: 15. $10. Hookups: none.

Obsidian, US 395, 96107. T: (760) 932-7070. F: (760) 932-1299. www.r5.fs.fed.us/htnf/soncamp.htm. RV/tent: 14. $5. Hookups: none.

Coloma

Coloma Resort & RV Park, 6921 Mt. Murphy Rd., 95613. T: (530) 621-2267 or (800) 238-2298. F: (530) 621-4960. www.colomaresort.com. RV/tent: 165. $26–$30. Hookups: water, electric (30 amp), sewer.

Columbia

49er RV Ranch, 23223 Italian Bar Rd., 95310. T: (209) 532-4978. F: (209) 532-4978. www.49rv.com. RV/tent: 45. $2,750. Hookups: water, electric (30 amp), sewer, cable TV.

Marble Quarry RV Park, 11551 Yankee Hill Rd., 95310. T: (209) 532-9539. F: (209) 532-8631. www.marblequarry.com. RV/tent: 87. $17–$30. Hookups: water, electric (30, 50 amp), sewer, satellite TV.

Colusa

Colusa-Sacramento River State Recreation Area, 10th St., 95932. T: (800) 444-7275 or (530) 458-4927. F: (530) 538-2200. www.reserveamerica.com. RV/tent: 14. $10. Hookups: none.

Crescent City

Bayside RV Park, Citizen Dock Rd., 95531. T: (800) 446-9482. RV/tent: 110. $15–$20. Hookups: water, electric (30 amp), sewer, phone.

Hiouchi Hamlet RV Resort, 2000 Hwy. 199, 95531. T: (707) 458-3321. F: (707) 458-4223. RV/tent: 120. $15–$25. Hookups: water, electric (20, 30, 50 amp), sewer, cable TV, phone.

KOA-Crescent City Redwoods, 4241 Hwy. 101 North, 95531. T: (800) 562-5754 or (707) 464-5744. www.koa.com. RV/tent: 94. $20–$27. Hookups: water, electric (15, 20, 30 amp), sewer, cable TV.

Sunset Harbor RV Park, 205 King St., 95531. T: (707) 464-3423. F: (707) 464-2084. RV/tent: 69. $20. Hookups: water, electric (30, 50 amp), sewer, cable TV, phone.

Village Camper Inn, 1543 Parkway Dr., 95531. T: (707) 464-3544. RV/tent: 158. $14.50–$18.50. Hookups: water, electric (20, 30, 50 amp), sewer, cable TV, phone.

Dardanelle

Baker, Hwy. 108, 95314. T: (209) 965-3434. F: (209) 965-3372. www.r5.fs.fed.us/stanislaus. RV/tent: 44. $10. Hookups: none.

Brightman Flat, Hwy. 108, 95314. T: (209) 965-3434. F: (209) 965-3372. www.r5.fs.fed.us/stanislaus. RV/tent: 33. $10. Hookups: none.

Cascade Peak, Hwy. 108, 95314. T: (209) 965-3434. F: (209) 965-3372. www.r5.fs.fed.us/stanislaus. RV/tent: 14. $5. Hookups: none.

Dardanelle, Hwy. 108, 95314. T: (209) 965-3434. F: (209) 965-3372. www.r5.fs.fed.us/stanislaus. RV/tent: 28. $14. Hookups: none.

Deadman, Kennedy Meadow Rd., 95314. T: (209) 965-3434. F: (209) 965-3372. www.r5.fs.fed.us/stanislaus. RV/tent: 17. $11. Hookups: none.

Eureka Valley, Hwy. 108, 95314. T: (209) 965-3434. F: (209) 965-3372. www.r5.fs.fed.us/stanislaus. RV/tent: 28. $12. Hookups: none.

Fence Creek, FR 6N06, 95314. T: (209) 965-3434. F: (209) 965-3372. www.r5.fs.fed.us/stanislaus. RV/tent: 34. $5. Hookups: none.

Pigeon Flat, Hwy. 108, 95314. T: (209) 965-3434. F: (209) 965-3372. www.r5.fs.fed.us/stanislaus. RV/tent: 7. $8. Hookups: none.

CALIFORNIA (continued)

Dardanelle (continued)

Sand Flat, Clark Fork Rd., 95314. T: (209) 965-3434. F: (209) 965-3372. www.r5.fs.fed.us/stanislaus. RV/tent: 68. $7. Hookups: none.

Death Valley

Stovepipe Wells, Hwy. 190, 92328. T: (800) 365-2267 or (760) 786-2331. F: (760) 786-3283. www.nps. gov/deva; reservations.nps.gov. RV/tent: 199. $10. Hookups: none.

Sunset, Hwy. 190, 92328. T: (800) 365-2267 or (760) 786-2331. F: (760) 786-3283. www.nps.gov/deva; reservations.nps.gov. RV/tent: 1000. $10. Hookups: none.

Texas Spring, Hwy. 190, 92328. T: (800) 365-2267 or (760) 786-2331. F: (760) 786-3283. www.nps. gov/deva; reservations.nps.gov. RV/tent: 92. $10. Hookups: none.

Delhi

McConnell State Recreation Area, Pepper St., 95315. T: (800) 444-7275 or (209) 394-7755. www.reserveamerica.com. RV/tent: 19. $12. Hookups: none.

Dunnigan

Campers Inn RV & Golf Resort, 2501 CR 88, 95937. T: (800) 79-GOLF-3 or (530) 724-3350. F: (530) 724-3110. www.campersinnrv.com. RV/tent: 85. $15–$21. Hookups: water, electric (30, 50 amp), sewer.

Dunsmuir

Railroad Park Resort, 100 Railroad Park Rd., 96025. T: (530) 235-9983. F: (530) 235-4470. www.rrpark. com. RV/tent: 60. $16–$24. Hookups: water, electric (20, 30 amp), sewer, cable TV.

El Cajon

Circle RV Ranch, 1835 East Main St., 92021. T: (800) 422-1835 or (619) 440-0040. F: (619) 440-8050. www.gocampingamerica.com/circlervranch/. RV/tent: 179. $27. Hookups: water, electric (30, 50 amp), sewer, TV, phone.

Oak Creek RV Resort, 15379 Oak Creek Rd., 92021. T: (619) 390-7132. F: (619) 390-7171. www.oakcreekrv.com. RV/tent: 120. $25–$29. Hookups: water, electric (30, 50 amp), sewer, cable TV, phone.

El Centro

Desert Trails RV Park & Country Club, 225 Wake Ave., 92243. T: (760) 352-7275. RV/tent: 388. $26. Hookups: water, electric (30, 50 amp), sewer, TV, phone.

Encinitas

San Elijo State Beach, US 101, 92023. T: (800) 444-7275 or (760) 753-5091. www.reserve america.com. RV/tent: 150. $12–$18. Hookups: water, electric (30 amp).

Escondido

Escondido RV Resort, 1740 Seven Oaks Rd., 92026. T: (760) 740-5000. F: (760) 740-5982. www. escondidorv.com. RV/tent: 67. $29.50–$34.50. Hookups: water, electric (20, 30, 50 amp), sewer, cable TV, phone (long term).

Essex

Providence Mountains State Recreation Area, Essex Rd., 92332. T: (760) 928-2586. F: (661) 940-7327. RV/tent: 6. $12. Hookups: none.

Etna

Mountain Village RV Park, 30 Commercial Way, 96027. T: (877) 386-2787. F: (530) 467-6402. www.etnarvp.com. RV/tent: 44. $22. Hookups: water, electric (20, 30, 50 amp), sewer, cable TV, phone.

Eureka

KOA-Eureka, 4050 Hwy. 101 North, 95503. T: (800) 562-3136 or (707) 822-4243. F: (707) 822-0126. www.koa.com. RV/tent: 156. $20–$26. Hookups: water, electric (20, 30, 50 amp), sewer, cable TV, phone.

Redwood Acres Fairground, 3750 Harris St., 95503. T: (707) 445-3037. F: (707) 445-1583. www.red woodacres.com. RV/tent: 52. $15. Hookups: water, electric (30, 50 amp), sewer.

Felton

Cotillion Gardens Recreational Vehicle Park, 300 Old Big Trees Rd., 95018. T: (831) 335-7669. RV/tent: 80. $29–$31. Hookups: water, electric (20, 30 amp), sewer, cable TV, phone.

Fort Bragg

Pomo RV Park & Campground, 17999 Tregoning Ln., 95437. T: (707) 964-3373. www.infortbragg.com/ pomo/. RV/tent: 125. $ 20–$27. Hookups: water, electric (20, 30, 50 amp), sewer, cable TV, phone.

Woodside RV Park & Campgrounds, 17900 North Hwy. 1, 95437. T: (707) 964-3684. F: (707) 964-5221. www.gocampingamerica.com/woodsiderv/. RV/tent: 104. $19–$22. Hookups: water, electric (15, 30 amp), sewer, TV, phone.

CALIFORNIA (continued)

Fouts Springs

Letts Lake, FR 17N02, 95979. T: (530) 963-3128.
F: (530) 963-3173. www.r5.fs.fed.us/mendocino.
RV/tent: 40. $8. Hookups: none.

Mill Valley, FR 17N02, 95979. T: (530) 963-3128.
F: (530) 963-3173. www.r5.fs.fed.us/mendocino.
RV/tent: 15. $5. Hookups: none.

Frazier Park

McGill, Mount Piños Hwy., 93222. T: (661) 245-3731.
F: (661) 245-1526. RV/tent: 73. $8. Hookups: none.

Mount Piños, Mount Piños Hwy., 93222. T: (661)
245-3731. F: (661) 245-1526. RV/tent: 19. $8.
Hookups: none.

Fresno

West Olive Mobile/RV Park, 3147 West Olive Ave.,
93722. T: (559) 275-0154. RV/tent: 55. $15.
Hookups: water, electric (20, 30, 50 amp), sewer,
phone.

Garbervile

Benbow Valley RV Resort & Golf Course, 7000 Benbow Dr., 95542. T: (866) BENBOWRV or (707) 923-
2777. F: (707)923-2821. www.benbowrv.com.
RV/tent: 112. $28.90–$43.50. Hookups: water,
electric (20, 30, 50 amp), sewer, cable TV, phone.

Gasquet

Smith River National Recreation Area, Big Flat, FR
15N59, 95543. T: (707) 457-3131. F: (707) 457-
3794. www.r5.fs.fed.us/sixrivers. RV/tent: 28. $8.
Hookups: none.

Smith River National Recreation Area, Grassy Flat,
US 199, 95543. T: (877) 444-6777 or (707) 457-
3131. F: (707) 457-3794. www.r5.fs.fed.us/
sixrivers; www. reserveusa.com. RV/tent: 19. $10.
Hookups: none.

Smith River National Recreation Area, Patrick
Creek, US 199, 95543. T: (877) 444-6777 or (707)
457-3131. F: (707) 457-3794. www.r5.fs.fed.us/
sixrivers; www. reserveusa.com. RV/tent: 13. $13.
Hookups: none.

Gorman

Los Alamos, Smokey Bear Rd., 93243. T: (661) 245-
3731. F: (661) 245-1526. RV/tent: 93. $10.
Hookups: none.

Groveland

Dimond "O", Evergreen Rd., 95321. T: (209) 962-
7825. F: (209) 962-6406. www.r5.fs.fed.us/
stanislaus. RV/tent: 38. $13. Hookups: none.

Lost Claim, Hwy. 120, 95321. T: (209) 962-7825.
F: (209) 962-6406. www.r5.fs.fed.us/stanislaus.
RV/tent: 10. $9. Hookups: none.

Sweetwater, Hwy. 120, 95321. T: (209) 962-7825.
F: (209) 962-6406. www.r5.fs.fed.us/stanislaus.
RV/tent: 13. $11. Hookups: none.

Thousand Trails-Yosemite Lakes, Hwy. 120, 95321.
T: (800) 533-1001. www.1000trails.com. RV/tent:
445. $25. Hookups: water, electric (20, 30, 50
amp), sewer, phone.

Yosemite Pines RV Resort, 20450 Old Hwy. 120,
95321. T: (800) 368-5386 or (209) 962-5042.
F: (209) 962-5269. www.yosemitepines.com.
RV/tent: 214. $17–$32. Hookups: water, electric
(20, 30, 50 amp), sewer, cable TV, phone.

Grover Beach

Le Sage Riviera RV Park, 319 Hwy. 1, 93433. T: (805)
489-5506. RV/tent: 82. $25–$30. Hookups: water,
electric (20, 30 amp), sewer, phone.

Gustine

San Luis Reservoir State Recreation Area, Basalt
Campground, Hwy. 152, 95322-9737. T: (800) 444-
7275 or (209) 826-1196. F: (209) 826-0284.
www.cal-parks.ca.gov; www.reserveamerica.com.
RV/tent: 79. $12. Hookups: none.

San Luis Reservoir State Recreation Area, Medeiros
Campground, Hwy. 33, 95322-9737. T: (209) 826-
1196. F: (209) 826-0284. www.cal-parks.ca.gov.
RV/tent: 350. $7. Hookups: none.

Half Moon Bay

Half Moon Bay State Beach, Kelly Ave., 94019. T:
(650) 726-8820. F: (415) 330-6300. RV/tent: 55.
$12. Hookups: none.

Hamburg

O'Neil Creek, Hwy. 96, 96086. T: (877) 444-6777 or
(530) 493-2243. F: (530) 493-1796. www.r5.fs.fed.
us/klamath. RV/tent: 18. $4. Hookups: none.

Happy Camp

Curly Jack, Curly Jack Rd., 96039. T: (530) 493-2243.
F: (530) 493-1796. www.r5.fs.fed.us/klamath.
RV/tent: 17. $10. Hookups: none.

West Branch, Indian Creek Rd., 96039. T: (530) 493-
2243. F: (530) 493-1796. www.r5.fs.fed.us/klamath.
RV/tent: 15. $4. Hookups: none.

CALIFORNIA (continued)

Hat Creek

Rancheria RV Park, 15565 Black Angus Ln., 96040.
T: (800) 346-3430 or (530) 335-7418. www.
rancheriarv.com. RV/tent: 75. $20–$22. Hookups:
water, electric (30, 50 amp), sewer, satellite TV.

Hemet

Casa del Sol RV Resort, 2750 West Acacia, 92545.
T: (909) 925-2515. www.casadelsolrvpark.com.
RV/tent: 358. $15–$23. Hookups: water, electric
(30, 50 amp), sewer, cable TV, phone.

Golden Village Palms RV Resort, 3600 West Florida
Ave., 92545. T: (800) 323-9610 or (909) 925-2518.
F: (909) 929-5672. www.goldenvillagepalms.com/.
RV/tent: 1,019. $33. Hookups: water, electric (20,
30, 50 amp), sewer, cable TV, phone.

Mountain Valley RV Park, 235 South Lyon Ave.,
92543. T: (800) 926-5593 or (909)-925-5812.
F: (909) 658-6272. www.mountainvalleyrvp.com/.
RV/tent: 170. $30. Hookups: water, electric (20, 30,
50 amp), sewer, cable TV, phone.

Hesperia

Hesperia Lake Park & Campground, Arrowhead
Lake Rd., 92345. T: (800) 521-6332 or (760) 244-
5951. www.hesperiaparks.com/pages/PG12.HTM.
RV/tent: 86. $12–$15. Hookups: water, electric (30
amp).

Hollister

Casa De Fruta RV Orchard Resort, 10031 Pacheco
Pass Hwy., 95023. T: (800) 548-3813 or (408) 842-
9316. F: (408) 842-3793. www.casadefruta.com/
orchardresort.asp. RV/tent: 301. $29–$31. Hookups: water, electric (20, 30 amp), sewer, satellite TV.

Huntington Beach

Huntington By The Sea RV Park, 21871 Newland St.,
92646. T: (714) 536-8316 or (800) 439-3486.
F: (714) 846-8874. www.gocampingamerica.com/
huntingtonbythesea/. RV/tent: 140. $24–$38. Hookups: water, electric (30 amp), sewer, cable TV,
phone.

Idyllwild

Boulder Basin, FR 4S01, 92549. T: (909) 659-2117.
F: (909) 659-2107. www.r5.fs.fed.us/san-
bernardino. RV/tent: 34. $10. Hookups: none.

Dark Canyon, FR 4S02, 92549. T: (909) 659-2117.
F: (909) 659-2107. www.r5.fs.fed.us/san-
bernardino. RV/tent: 21. $12. Hookups: none.

Fern Basin, FR 4S02, 92549. T: (909) 659-2117.
F: (909) 659-2107. www.r5.fs.fed.us/san-
bernardino. RV/tent: 22. $10. Hookups: none.

Marion Mountain, FR 4S02, 92549. T: (909) 659-
2117. F: (909) 659-2107. www.r5.fs.fed.us/san
bernardino. RV/tent: 24. $10. Hookups: none.

Mount San Jacinto State Park, Idyllwild Campground, Hwy. 243, 92549. T: (909) 659-2607;
reservations (800) 444-7275. F: (909) 659-4769.
www.sanjac.statepark.org/. RV/tent: 33. $12.
Hookups: none.

Piñon Flat, Hwy. 74, 92549. T: (909) 659-2117.
F: (909) 659-2107. www.r5.fs.fed.us/san-
bernardino. RV/tent: 18. $8. Hookups: none.

Indio

Fiesta RV Park, 46-421 Madison St., 92201. T: (760)
342-2345. F: (760) 342 - 2712. www.fiesta
rvpark.com. RV/tent: 200. $25–$35. Hookups:
water, electric (30, 50 amp), sewer, cable TV,
phone.

Jamestown

Lake Tulloch RV Campground and Marina, 14448
Tulloch Rd., 95327. T: (800) 894-2267 or (209)
881-0107. F: (209) 881-0107. www.laketulloch
campground.com. RV/tent: 130. $17.50–$27.50.
Hookups: water, electric (50 amp), sewer.

Julian

Pinezanita Trailer Ranch, 4446 Hwy. 79, 92036.
T: (760) 765-0429. F: (760) 765-2426. www.pine
zanita.com. RV/tent: 230. $18–$24. Hookups:
water, electric (20, 30 amp), sewer.

June Lake

Gull Lake, Hwy. 158, 93529. T: (760) 647-2408.
F: (760) 647-3046. www.r5.fs.fed.us/inyo. RV/tent:
11. $12. Hookups: none.

June Lake, Hwy. 158, 93529. T: (760) 647-2408. F:
(760) 647-3046. www.r5.fs.fed.us/inyo. RV/tent: 28.
$12. Hookups: none.

Oh! Ridge, Oh! Ridge Rd., 93529. T: (760) 647-2408.
F: (760) 647-3046. www.r5.fs.fed.us/inyo. RV/tent:
148. $12. Hookups: none.

Reversed Creek, Hwy. 158, 93529. T: (760) 647-
2408. F: (760) 647-3046. www.r5.fs.fed.us/inyo.
RV/tent: 17. $12. Hookups: none.

Silver Lake, Hwy. 158, 93529. T: (760) 647-2408.
F: (760) 647-3046. www.r5.fs.fed.us/inyo. RV/tent:
63. $12. Hookups: none.

Kelseyville

Edgewater Resort & RV Park, 6420 Soda Bay Rd.,
95451. T: (800) 396-6224 or (707) 279-0208.
F: (707) 279-0138. www.edgewaterresort.net.
RV/tent: 61. $25–$35. Hookups: water, electric
(20, 30 amp), sewer, cable TV, phone.

CALIFORNIA (continued)

Kernville

Camp 3, Sierra Way Rd., 93238. T: (760) 376-3781. F: (760) 376-3795. www.r5.fs.fed.us/sequoia. RV/tent: 52. $12–$14. Hookups: none.

Headquarters, Sierra Way Rd., 93238. T: (760) 376-3781. F: (760) 376-3795. www.r5.fs.fed.us/sequoia. RV/tent: 44. $12–$14. Hookups: none.

Hospital Flat, Sierra Way Rd., 93238. T: (760) 376-3781. F: (760) 376-3795. www.r5.fs.fed.us/sequoia. RV/tent: 40. $12–$14. Hookups: none.

Rivernook Campground, 14001 Sierra Way, 93238. T: (760) 376-2705. RV/tent: 269. $17–$23. Hookups: water, electric (20, 30, 50 amp), sewer, cable TV.

King City

Ciudad Del Rey, 50557 Wild Horse Rd., 93930. T: (831) 385-4827. RV/tent: 38. $25. Hookups: water, electric (20, 30, 50 amp), sewer, phone.

Kings Canyon National Park

Crystal Springs, Hwy. 180, Grant Grove Village, 93633. T: (559) 565-3341. www.nps.gov/seki. RV/tent: 67. $14. Hookups: none.

Moraine, Hwy. 180, Cedar Grove Village, 93633. T: (559) 565-3341. www.nps.gov/seki. RV/tent: 120. $14. Hookups: none.

Sentinel, Hwy. 180, Cedar Grove Village, 93633. T: (559) 565-3341. www.nps.gov/seki. RV/tent: 83. $14. Hookups: none.

Sheep Creek, Hwy. 180, Cedar Grove Village, 93633. T: (559) 565-3341. www.nps.gov/seki. RV/tent: 111. $14. Hookups: none.

Sunset, Hwy. 180, Grant Grove Village, 93633. T: (559) 565-3341. www.nps.gov/seki. RV/tent: 214. $14. Hookups: none.

Kingsburg

Riverland, 38743 West Frontage Rd., 93631. T: (559) 897-5166. www.riverlandresorts.com. RV/tent: 196. $19.95–$29.95. Hookups: water, electric (15, 30, 50 amp), sewer.

Kit Carson

Caples Lake, Hwy. 88, 95644. T: (209) 295-4251. F: (209) 295-5994. RV/tent: 35. $12. Hookups: none.

East Silver Lake, Hwy. 88, 95644. T: (877) 444-6777 or (209) 295-4251. F: (209) 295-5994. www.reserveusa.com. RV/tent: 62. $12. Hookups: none.

Kirkwood Lake, Hwy. 88, 95644. T: (209) 295-4251. F: (209) 295-5994. RV/tent: 12. $11. Hookups: none.

Woods Lake, Woods Lake Turnoff, 95644. T: (209) 295-4251. F: (209) 295-5994. RV/tent: 25. $11. Hookups: none.

Klamath

Camp Marigold Garden Cottages & RV Park, 16101 Hwy. 101 S, 95548. T: (800) 621-8513 or (707) 482-3585. www.clia.com/CampMarigold-Klamath/. RV/tent: 45. $15. Hookups: water, electric (30 amp), sewer, cable TV.

Chinook RV Resort, 17465 Hwy. 101, 95548. T: (707) 482-3511. www.rvdestinations.com/chinook/. RV/tent: 80. $18. Hookups: water, electric (30 amp), sewer, cable TV, phone.

Klamath's Camper Corral, Hwy. 101 at 169 Interchange, 95548. T: (707) 482-5741 or (800) 701-PARK. www.rvdestinations.com/campercorral/. RV/tent: 120. $14–$22.25. Hookups: water, electric (30 amp), sewer, cable TV.

Mystic Forest RV Park, 15875 US 101, 95548. T: (707) 482-4901. F: (707) 482-0704. www.rvdestinations.com/mysticforest/. RV/tent: 44. $16. Hookups: water, electric (20, 30 amp), sewer, cable TV, phone.

La Grange

Turlock Lake State Recreation Area, Lake Rd., 95329. T: (800) 444-7275 or (209) 874-2008. F: (818) 874-2611. www.reserveamerica.com. RV/tent: 66. $12. Hookups: none.

La Porte

Black Rock, County Rd. 514/Little Grass Valley Rd., 95981. T: (530) 534-6500. F: (530) 532-1210. www.r5.fs.fed.us/plumas. RV/tent: 30. $12. Hookups: none.

Little Beaver, County Rd. 514/Little Grass Valley Rd., 95981. T: (530) 534-6500. F: (530) 532-1210. www.r5.fs.fed.us/plumas. RV/tent: 120. $13–$15. Hookups: none.

Peninsula Tent, County Rd. 514/Little Grass Valley Rd., 95981. T: (530) 534-6500. F: (530) 532-1210. www.r5.fs.fed.us/plumas. RV/tent: 25. $12. Hookups: none.

Red Feather Camp, County Rd. 514/Little Grass Valley Rd., 95981. T: (530) 534-6500. F: (530) 532-1210. www.r5.fs.fed.us/plumas. RV/tent: 60. $13–$15. Hookups: none.

Running Deer, FR 22N57, 95981. T: (877) 444-6777 or (530) 534-6500. F: (530) 532-1210. www.r5.fs.fed.us/plumas; www.reserveusa.com. RV/tent: 40. $13–$15. Hookups: none.

Wyandotte, County Rd. 514/Little Grass Valley Rd., 95981. T: (530) 534-6500. F: (530) 532-1210. www.r5.fs.fed.us/plumas. RV/tent: 28. $13–$22. Hookups: none.

CALIFORNIA (continued)

Lake Elsinore

Lake Elsinore West Marina, 32700 Riverside Dr., 92530. T: (800) 328-6844 or (909) 678-1300. F: (909) 678-6377. www.gocampingamerica.com/elsinorewest/. RV/tent: 197. $27.50–$32.50. Hookups: water, electric (30, 50 amp), sewer, cable TV, phone.

Lake Isabella

Lake Isabella RV Resort, 11936 Hwy. 178, 93240. T: (800) 787-9920. F: (760) 379-2046. www.lakeisabellarv.com. RV/tent: 91. $24. Hookups: water, electric (30, 50 amp), sewer, cable TV, phone.

Lakehead

Lakeshore Villa RV Park, 20672 Lakeshore Dr., 96051. T: (800) 238-8688. F: (530) 238-8688. www.gocampingamerica.com/lakeshorevilla/. RV/tent: 92. $17.50–$19.50. Hookups: water, electric (30, 50 amp), sewer, cable TV, phone.

Shasta Lake RV Resort & Campground, 20433 Lakeshore Dr., 96051. T: (800) 374-2782 or (530) 238-8500. F: (530) 238-2083. www.shastacounty.com/shastalake/. RV/tent: 70. $16–$24. Hookups: water, electric (30 amp), sewer.

Lakeside

Rancho Los Coches RV Park, 13468 Hwy. 8 Business, 92040. T: (800) 630-0448 or (619) 443-2025. F: (619) 443-8440. www.rancholoscochesrv.com/. RV/tent: 147. $23–$35. Hookups: water, electric (30, 50 amp), sewer, cable TV, phone.

Lancaster

Saddleback Butte State Park, Ave. J, 93535. T: (661) 942-0662. F: (661) 940-7327. RV/tent: 50. $10. Hookups: none.

Lee Vining

Big Bend, Hwy. 120, 93541. T: (760) 932-5451. F: (760) 932-5458. RV/tent: 17. $11. Hookups: none.

Boulder, Hwy. 120, 93541. T: (760) 932-5451. F: (760) 932-5458. RV/tent: 32. $7. Hookups: none.

Cattle Guard, Hwy. 120, 93541. T: (760) 932-5451. F: (760) 932-5458. RV/tent: 17. $7. Hookups: none.

Junction, Saddlebag Lake Rd., 93541. T: (760) 873-2400 or (760) 647-3044. F: (760) 647-3046. www.r5.fs.fed.us/inyo. RV/tent: 13. $6. Hookups: none.

Lower Lee Vining, Hwy. 120, 93541. T: (760) 932-5451. F: (760) 932-5458. RV/tent: 74. $7. Hookups: none.

Mono Vista RV Park, US 395, 93541. T: (760) 647-6401. www.thesierraweb.com/recreation/monovista/. RV/tent: 63. $13–$23. Hookups: water, electric (20, 30, 50 amp), sewer, cable TV.

Morraine, Hwy. 120, 93541. T: (760) 932-5451. F: (760) 932-5458. RV/tent: 20. $7. Hookups: none.

Saddlebag Lake, Saddlebag Lake Rd., 93541. T: (760) 873-2400 or (760) 647-3044. F: (760) 647-3046. ww.r5.fs.fed.us/inyo. RV/tent: 20. $11. Hookups: none.

Tioga Lake, Hwy. 120, 93541. T: (760) 873-2400 or (760) 647-3044. F: (760) 647-3046. www.r5.fs.fed.us/inyo. RV/tent: 25. $11. Hookups: none.

Leggett

Redwoods River Resort & Campground, 75000 Hwy. 101, 95585. T: (707) 925-6249. F: (707) 925-6413. www.rvdestinations.com/redwoodsriver/. RV/tent: 60. $17–$26. Hookups: water, electric (20, 30, 50 amp), sewer.

Lewiston

Ackerman, Trinity Dam Blvd., 96052. T: (530) 623-2121. F: (530) 623-6010. www.r5.fs.fed.us/shastatrinity. RV/tent: 66. $10. Hookups: none.

Mary Smith, Trinity Dam Blvd., 96052. T: (530) 623-2121. F: (530) 623-6010. www.r5.fs.fed.us/shastatrinity. RV/tent: 18. $9. Hookups: none.

Tunnel Rock, Trinity Dam Blvd., 96052. T: (530) 623-2121. F: (530) 623-6010. www.r5.fs.fed.us/shastatrinity. RV/tent: 6. $5. Hookups: none.

Lodi

Tower Park Resort, 14900 West Hwy. 12, 95242. T: (209) 369-1041. F: (209) 943-5656. RV/tent: 442. $22–$26. Hookups: water, electric (20, 30 amp), sewer.

Loma Linda

Mission RV Park, Redlands Blvd., 92354. T: (909) 796-7570. www.woodalls.com. RV/tent: 79. $20. Hookups: water, electric (20, 30, 50 amp), sewer, phone.

Lone Pine

Boulder Creek RV Resort, 2550 South Hwy. 395, 93545. T: (800) 648-8965 or (760) 876-4243. www.395.com/bouldercreek/. RV/tent: 65. $24. Hookups: water, electric (30, 50 amp), sewer, cable TV, phone.

Lone Pine, Whitney Portal Rd., 93545. T: (760) 876-6200. F: (760) 876-6202. www.r5.fs.fed.us/inyo. RV/tent: 43. $10. Hookups: none.

Loomis

KOA Loomis, 3945 Taylor Rd., 95650. T: (916) 652-6737. F: (916) 652-5026. www.koa.com. RV/tent: 78. $26–$28. Hookups: water, electric (20, 30 amp), sewer.

CALIFORNIA (continued)

Lucia

Limekiln State Park, Hwy. 1, 93921. T: (877) 444-6777 or (831) 667-2403. www.reserveusa.com. RV/tent: 43. $12. Hookups: none.

Nacimiento, Nacimiento Fergusson Rd., 93921. T: (831) 385-5434. F: (831) 385-0628. www.r5.fs.fed.us/lospadres/. RV/tent: 17. $5. Hookups: none.

Plaskett Creek, Hwy. 1, 93921. T: (831) 385-5434. F: (831) 385-0628. www.r5.fs.fed.us/lospadres/. RV/tent: 43. $16. Hookups: none.

Mammoth Lakes

Agnew Meadows, Minaret Summit Rd., 93546. T: (760) 924-5500. F: (760) 924-5537. www.r5.fs.fed.us/inyo. RV/tent: 21. $12. Hookups: none.

Coldwater, Lake Mary Rd., 93546. T: (760) 924-5500. F: (760) 924-5537. www.r5.fs.fed.us/inyo. RV/tent: 78. $13. Hookups: none.

Lake George, Lake Mary Rd., 93546. T: (760) 924-5500. F: (760) 924-5537. www.r5.fs.fed.us/inyo. RV/tent: 16. $13. Hookups: none.

Lake Mary, Lake Mary Rd., 93546. T: (760) 924-5500. F: (760) 924-5537. www.r5.fs.fed.us/inyo. RV/tent: 48. $13. Hookups: none.

Mammoth Mountain RV Park, Hwy. 203, 93546. T: (760) 934-3822. F: (760) 934-1896. www.mammothweb.com/lodging/mammothrv/mammothrv.html. RV/tent: 183. $18–$28. Hookups: water, electric (30, 50 amp), sewer, cable TV.

Minaret Falls, Minaret Summit Rd., 93546. T: (760) 924-5500. F: (760) 924-5537. www.r5.fs.fed.us/inyo. RV/tent: 28. $12. Hookups: none.

New Shady Rest, Sawmill Cutoff, 93546. T: (760) 924-5500. F: (760) 924-5537. www.r5.fs.fed.us/inyo. RV/tent: 95. $12. Hookups: none.

Old Shady Rest, Sawmill Cutoff, 93546. T: (760) 924-5500. F: (760) 924-5537. www.r5.fs.fed.us/inyo. RV/tent: 51. $12. Hookups: none.

Pine City, Lake Mary Rd., 93546. T: (760) 924-5500. F: (760) 924-5537. www.r5.fs.fed.us/inyo. RV/tent: 10. $13. Hookups: none.

Pine Glen, Sawmill Cutoff, 93546. T: (760) 924-5500. F: (760) 924-5537. www.r5.fs.fed.us/inyo. RV/tent: 11. $12. Hookups: none.

Pumice Flat, Minaret Summit Rd., 93546. T: (760) 924-5500. F: (760) 924-5537. www.r5.fs.fed.us/inyo. RV/tent: 17. $12. Hookups: none.

Red's Meadow, Minaret Summit Rd., 93546. T: (760) 924-5500. F: (760) 924-5537. www.r5.fs.fed.us/inyo. RV/tent: 56. $12. Hookups: none.

Upper Soda Springs, Minaret Summit Rd., 93546. T: (760) 924-5500. F: (760) 924-5537. www.r5.fs.fed.us/inyo. RV/tent: 29. $12. Hookups: none.

Manchester

KOA Manchester Beach, 44300 Kinney Rd., 95459. T: (800) KOA-4188 or (707) 882-2375. F: (707) 882-3104. www.koa.com. RV/tent: 125. $27–$41. Hookups: water, electric (20, 30 amp), sewer, cable TV, phone.

Manchester State Park, Kinney Ln., 95468. T: (707) 937-5804. F: (707) 937-2953. RV/tent: 46. $12. Hookups: none.

Manteca

Oakwood Lake RV Campround, 874 East Woodward Ave., 95337. T: (800) 626-5253 or (209) 249-2500 ext. 308. www.oakwoodlake.com. RV/tent: 357. $19–$31. Hookups: water, electric (20, 30 amp), sewer, phone.

Marina

Marina Dunes RV Park, 3330 Dunes Dr., 93933. T: (831) 384-6914. F: (831) 384-0285. RV/tent: 75. $29.50–$39. Hookups: water, electric (20, 30 amp), sewer, cable TV, phone.

Mariposa

Mariposa Fairgrounds, 5007 Fairgrounds Rd., 95338. T: (209) 966-2432. F: (209) 966-6273. www.mariposafair.com/camping.htm. RV/tent: 350. $18. Hookups: water, electric (20, 30, 50 amp).

Markleeville

Markleeville, Hwy. 89, 96120. T: (775) 882-2766. F: (775) 884-8199. RV/tent: 10. $9. Hookups: none.

McCloud

Ah-Di-Na, Lake McCloud Rd., 96057. T: (530) 964-2184. F: (530) 964-2938. www.r5.fs.fed.us/shastatrinity. RV/tent: 16. $8. Hookups: none.

Cattle Camp, Hwy. 89, 96057. T: (530) 964-2184. F: (530) 964-2938. www.r5.fs.fed.us/shastatrinity. RV/tent: 29. $10. Hookups: none.

Meeks Bay

Kaspian, Hwy. 89, West Shore Lake Tahoe, 96142. T: (877) 444-6777 or (530) 573-2674. F: (530) 573-2693. www.r5.fs.fed.us/ltbmu; www.reserveusa.com. RV/tent: 10. $12. Hookups: none.

Mendocino

Caspar Beach RV Park, 14441 Point Cabrillo Dr., 95460. T: (707) 964-3306. F: (707) 964-0526. www.casparbeachrvpark.com. RV/tent: 118. $22–$29.50. Hookups: water, electric (30 amp), sewer, cable TV, phone.

CALIFORNIA (continued)

Mineral

Crags, Lassen Volcanic National Park, Lassen Park Rd., 96063. T: (530) 595-4444. F: (530) 595-3262. www.nps.gov/lavo. RV/tent: 45. $8. Hookups: none.

Juniper Lake, Juniper Lake Rd., 96063. T: (530) 595-4444. F: (530) 595-3262. www.nps.gov/lavo. RV/tent: 18. $10. Hookups: none.

North Summit Lake, Lassen Park Rd., 96063. T: (530) 595-4444. F: (530) 595-3262. www.nps. gov/lavo. RV/tent: 46. $14. Hookups: none.

South Summit Lake, Lassen Park Rd., 96063. T: (530) 595-4444. F: (530) 595-3262. www.nps.gov/lavo. RV/tent: 48. $12. Hookups: none.

Southwest, Lassen Park Rd., 96063. T: (530) 595-4444. F: (530) 595-3262. www.nps.gov/lavo. RV/tent: 21. $12. Hookups: none.

Volcano Country RV Park & Campground, Hwy. 36 East, 96063. T: (530) 595-3347. F: (530) 595-4452. RV/tent: 30. $16–$21. Hookups: water, electric (20, 30 amp), sewer.

Warner Valley, Warner Valley Rd., 96063. T: (530) 595-4444. F: (530) 595-3262. www.nps.gov/lavo. RV/tent: 18. $12. Hookups: none.

Mojave National Preserve

Mid Hills, Black Canyon Rd., 92311. T: (760) 255-8801. www.nps.gov/moja. RV/tent: 26. $10. Hookups: none.

Monterey

Cypress Tree Inn of Monterey, 2227 North Fremont St., 93940. T: (800) 446-8303 (CA only) or (831) 372-7586. F: (831 372-2940. www.cyprestree inn.com/rv.html. RV/tent: 25. $20–$40. Hookups: water, electric (20, 30 amp).

Morro Bay

Bay Pines Travel Trailer Park, 1502 Quintana Rd., 93442. T: (805) 772-3223. F: (805) 772-0288. www.baypinesrv.com/. RV/tent: 112. $23. Hook-ups: water, electric (30 amp), sewer, satellite TV, phone.

Morro Bay State Park, State Park Rd., 93443. T: (805) 772-7434; reservations (800) 444-7275. F: (805) 772-5760. www.reserveamerica.com. RV/tent: 125. $7. Hookups: water, electric (30 amp).

Morro Dunes RV Park, 1700 Embarcadero, 93442. T: (805) 772-2722. F: (805) 772-5319. www.rv destinations.com/morrodunes/. RV/tent: 226. $17.60–$26.40. Hookups: water, electric (15, 30 amp), sewer, cable TV, phone.

Mount Laguna

Agua Dulce, Sunrise Hwy./Laguna Mountain Rd., 91948. T: (877) 444-6777 or (619) 445-6235. F: (619) 445-1753. www.r5.fs.fed.us/cleveland. RV/tent: 5. $13. Hookups: none.

Burnt Rancheria, Sunrise Hwy./Laguna Mountain Rd., 91948. T: (877) 444-6777 or (619) 445-6235. F: (619) 445-1753. www.r5.fs.fed.us/cleveland; www.reserveusa.com. RV/tent: 109. $14. Hookups: none.

Cibbets Flat, Kitchen Creek Rd., 91948. T: (619) 445-6235. F: (619) 445-1753. www.r5.fs.fed. us/cleveland. RV/tent: 23. $10. Hookups: none.

Laguna, Sunrise Hwy./Laguna Mountain Rd., 91948. T: (877) 444-6777 or (619) 445-6235. F: (619) 445-1753. www.r5.fs.fed.us/cleveland; www. reserveusa.com. RV/tent: 103. $14. Hookups: none.

Napa

Spanish Flat Resort, 4290 Knoxville Rd., 94558. T: (707) 966-7700. F: (707) 966-7704. www. spanishflatresort.com. RV/tent: 120. $21–$26. Hookups: water, electric (50 amp).

Needles

KOA Needles, 5400 National Old Trails Hwy., 92363. T: (800) 562-3407 or (760) 326-4207. F: (460) 326-6329. www.koa.com. RV/tent: 101. $18–$26. Hookups: water, electric (30 amp), sewer, phone.

Rainbo Beach Resort, Rte. 4 Box 139 River Rd., 92363. T: (760) 326-3101. F: (760) 326-5085. www. coloradoriverinfo.com/needles/rainbobeach/. RV/tent: 64. $22. Hookups: water, electric (20, 30, 50 amp), sewer, phone.

Niland

Fountain of Youth Spa, 10249 Coachella Canal Rd., 92257. T: (888) 800-0772. F: (760) 354-1558. www.foyspa.com. RV/tent: 1000. $16–$30. Hook-ups: water, electric (50 amp), sewer, cable TV.

North Shore

Salton Sea State Recreation Area, Corvina Beach, Hwy. 111, 92254. T: (760) 393-3052. F: (760) 393-2466. www.saltonsea.statepark.org/. RV/tent: 500. $10. Hookups: none.

Recreation Area, Mecca Beach, Hwy. 111, 92254. T: (760) 393-3052. F: (760) 393-2466. www.salton sea.statepark.org/. RV/tent: 110. $10. Hookups: water, electric (30 amp).

CALIFORNIA (continued)

North Shore (continued)

Salton Sea State Recreation Area, Salt Creek Primitive Area, Hwy. 111, 92254. T: (760) 393-3052. F: (760) 393-2466. www.saltonsea.statepark.org/. RV/tent: 150. $10. Hookups: none.

Northridge

Walnut RV Park, 19130 Nordhoff St., 91324. T: (800)-868-2749. F: (818) 775- 0384. www. walnutrvpark.com. RV/tent: 114. $35. Hookups: water, electric (50 amp), sewer, cable TV, phone (long term).

Novato

Novato RV Park, 1530 Armstrong Ave., 94945. T: (800) 733-6787 or (415) 897-1271. F: (415) 897-5500. http://209.24.94.35/novatorvpark/. RV/tent: 86. $3050–$36.50. Hookups: water, electric (20, 30, 50 amp), sewer, TV, phone.

O'Brien

Antlers, Antlers Rd., 96070. T: (877) 444-6777 or (530) 275-1587. www.r5.fs.fed.us/shastatrinity; www.reserveusa.com. RV/tent: 59. $15. Hookups: none.

Gregory Creek, Gregory Creek Rd., 96070. T: (877) 444-6777 or (530) 275-1587. www.r5.fs.fed.us/shastatrinity; www.reserveusa.com. RV/tent: 18. $12. Hookups: none.

Lakeshore East, Lakeshore Dr., 96070. T: (877) 444-6777 or (530) 275-1587. www.r5.fs.fed.us/shasta trinity; www.reserveusa.com. RV/tent: 25. $15. Hookups: none.

Moore Creek, Gilman Rd., 96070. T: (877) 444-6777 or (530) 275-1587. www.r5.fs.fed.us/shastatrinity; www.reserveusa.com. RV/tent: 12. $12. Hookups: none.

Old Station

Big Pine Camp, Hwy. 89, 96071. T: (530) 336-5521. F: (530) 335-4518. www.r5.fs.fed.us/lassen. RV/tent: 19. $10. Hookups: none.

Bridge Camp, Hwy. 89, 96071. T: (530) 336-5521. F: (530) 335-4518. www.r5.fs.fed.us/lassen. RV/tent: 25. $11. Hookups: none.

Cave Camp, Hwy. 89, 96071. T: (530) 336-5521. F: (530) 335-4518. www.r5.fs.fed.us/lassen. RV/tent: 46. $13. Hookups: none.

Crater Lake, FR 32N08, 96071. T: (530) 257-4188. F: (530) 252-5803. www.r5.fs.fed.us/lassen. RV/tent: 32. $11. Hookups: none.

Hat Creek, Hwy. 89, 96071. T: (877) 444-6777 or (530) 336-5521. F: (530) 335-4518. www.r5.fs. fed.us/lassen; www.reserveusa.com. RV/tent: 73. $13. Hookups: none.

Honn, Hwy. 89, 96071. T: (530) 336-5521. F: (530) 335-4518. www.r5.fs.fed.us/lassen. RV/tent: 6. $8. Hookups: none.

Orick

Prairie Creek Redwoods State Park, Gold Bluff Beach, Newton B. Drury Scenic Parkway, 95555. T: (707) 464-6101 ext. 5301 or 5064. www.cal-parks.ca.gov. RV/tent: 25. $12. Hookups: none.

Orland

Old Orchard RV Park, 4490 County Rd. HH, 95963. T: (530) 865-5335. F: (530) 865-5335. RV/tent: 72. $12–$22. Hookups: water, electric (30, 50amp), sewer.

Orland Buttes, Newville Rd./Rd. 200, 95963-8901. T: (877) 444-6777 or (530) 865-4781. F: (530) 865-5283. www.spk.usace.army.mil/cespkco/lakes/blackbutte.html; www.reserveusa.com. RV/tent: 39. $14. Hookups: none.

Orleans

Aikens Creek West, Hwy. 96, 95556. T: (530) 626-3291. F: (530) 627-3401. www.r5.fs.fed.us/sixrivers. RV/tent: 0. $7. Hookups: none.

Dillon Creek, Hwy. 96, 95556. T: (530) 626-3291. F: (530) 627-3401. www.r5.fs.fed.us/sixrivers. RV/tent: 21. $9. Hookups: none.

E-Ne-Luck, Hwy. 96, 95556. T: (530) 626-3291. F: (530) 627-3401. www.r5.fs.fed.us/sixrivers. RV/tent: 11. $9. Hookups: none.

Fish Lake, Fish Lake Rd., 95556. T: (530) 626-3291. F: (530) 627-3401. www.r5.fs.fed.us/sixrivers. RV/tent: 24. $9. Hookups: none.

Oxnard

Evergreen RV Park, 2135 Oxnard Blvd., 93030. T: (805) 485-1936. www.caohwy.com/e/evergtrp. htm. RV/tent: 81. $30. Hookups: water, electric (30 amp), sewer.

Palmdale

Saddleback Butte State Park, Ave. J, 93551. T: (661) 942-0662. F: (661) 940-7327. RV/tent: 50. $10. Hookups: none.

Paso Robles

Wine Country RV Resort, Airport Rd., 93446. T: (805) 238-4560. RV/tent: 82. $28–$30. Hookups: water, electric (30, 50 amp), sewer.

CALIFORNIA (continued)

Petaluma

KOA San Francisco North-Petaluma, 20 Rainsville Rd., 94952. T: (800) 992-2267 or (707) 763-1492. www.sanfranciscokoa.com. RV/tent: 312. $31–$38. Hookups: water, electric (20, 30, 50 amp), sewer, cable TV, phone.

Pine Valley

Boulder Oaks, Old Hwy. 80, 91962. T: (877) 444-6777 or (619) 445-6235. F: (619) 445-1753. www.r5.fs.fed.us/cleveland; www.reserveusa.com. RV/tent: 18. $10–$12. Hookups: none.

Pismo Beach

Pismo State Beach, Oceano Campground, Pier Ave., 93445. T: (800) 444-7275 or (805) 489-2684. www.cal-parks.ca.gov; www.reserveamerica.com. RV/tent: 82. $12–$18. Hookups: water, electric (30 amp).

Pollock Pines

Jones Fork, Ice House Rd., 95726. T: (530) 644-2349. F: (530) 647-5405. www.r5.fs.fed.us/eldorado. RV/tent: 10. $5. Hookups: none.

Northwind, Ice House Rd., 95726. T: (530) 644-2349. F: (530) 647-5405. www.r5.fs.fed.us/eldorado. RV/tent: 9. $5. Hookups: none.

Silver Creek, Ice House Rd., 95726. T: (530) 644-2349. F: (530) 647-5405. www.r5.fs.fed.us/eldorado. RV/tent: 12. $6. Hookups: water, electric (20, 30, 50), phone, cable TV.

Strawberry Point, Ice House Rd., 95726. T: (530) 644-2349. F: (530) 647-5405. www.r5.fs.fed.us/eldorado. RV/tent: 10. $5. Hookups: none.

Wench Creek, Ice House Rd., 95726. T: (530) 644-2349. F: (530) 647-5405. www.r5.fs.fed.us/eldorado. RV/tent: 100. $13–$20. Hookups: none.

Wolf Creek, Union Valley Rd., 95726. T: (877) 444-6777 or (530) 644-2349. F: (530) 647-5405. www.r5.fs.fed.us/eldorado; www.reserveusa.com. RV/tent: 42. $13–$20. Hookups: none.

Yellowjacket, Union Valley Rd., 95726. T: (877) 444-6777 or (530) 644-2349. F: (530) 647-5405. www.r5.fs.fed.us/eldorado; www.reserveusa.com. RV/tent: 40. $13–$20. Hookups: none.

Pomona

KOA Pomona-Fairplex, 2200 North White Ave., 91768. T: (909) 593-8915 or (888) 562-4230. www.koa.com. RV/tent: 185. $25–$40. Hookups: water, electric (30, 50 amp), sewer, phone.

Port Hueneme

Point Mugu State Park, Big Sycamore Canyon Campground, Hwy. 1, 93043. T: (800) 444-7275 or (818) 880-0350. F: (818) 880-6165. www.reserve america.com. RV/tent: 55. $12. Hookups: none.

Point Mugu State Park, Thornhill Broome Campground, Hwy. 1, 93043. T: (800) 444-7275 or (818) 880-0350. F: (818) 880-6165. www.reserveamerica. com. RV/tent: 88. $7–$12. Hookups: none.

Porterville

Deer Creek RV Park, 10679 Main St., 93257. T: (559) 781-3337. RV/tent: 78. $18. Hookups: water, electric (20, 30, 50 amp), sewer, phone.

Portola

Sierra Springs Trailer Resort, 70099 Hwy. 70, 96122. T: (530) 836-2747. F: (530) 836-2559. www.psln. com/sstr/. RV/tent: 40. $20. Hookups: water, electric (20, 30 amp), sewer, cable TV, phone.

Pratville

Cool Springs, Butt Valley Rd., 95923. T: (916) 386-5164. www.r5.fs.fed.us/lassen. RV/tent: 30. $15. Hookups: none.

Last Chance Creek, Lake Almanor Causeway, 95923. T: (916) 386-5164. www.r5.fs.fed.us/lassen. RV/tent: 12. $13. Hookups: none.

Ponderosa Flat, Butt Valley Rd., 95923. T: (916) 386-5164. www.r5.fs.fed.us/lassen. RV/tent: 63. $15. Hookups: none.

Yellow Creek, County Rd. 307, 95923. T: (916) 386-5164. www.r5.fs.fed.us/lassen. RV/tent: 10. $13. Hookups: none.

Redding

JGW RV Park, 6612 Riverland Dr., 96002. T: (800) 469-5910 or (530) 365-7965. F: (530) 244-0420. RV/tent: 65. $25. Hookups: water, electric (20, 30, 50 amp), sewer, cable TV, phone.

Mountain Gate RV Park, 14161 Holiday Rd., 96003. T: (800) 404-6040 or (530) 275 4600. F: (530) 275-1905. www.mt-gatervpark.com/. RV/tent: 122. $23.50 . Hookups: water, electric (30, 50 amp), sewer, satellite TV, phone.

Redding RV Park, 11075 Campers Ct., 96003. T: (800) 428-2089 or (530) 241-0707. F: (530) 243-2781. www.gocampingamerica.com/redding/. RV/tent: 110. $22–$23. Hookups: water, electric (30, 50 amp), sewer, satellite TV, phone.

CALIFORNIA (continued)

Redwood City

Trailer Villa, 3401 East Bayshore Rd., 94063. T: (800) 366-7880. F: (650) 366-7948. www.gocamping america.com/trailervillarv/. RV/tent: 90. $26. Hookups: water, electric (20, 30 amp), sewer, phone.

Sacramento

Oak Haven RV Park, 2145 Auburn Blvd., 95821. T: (916) 922-0814. F: (916) 924-0814. www.go campingamerica.com/oakhavenrv/. RV/tent: 90. $19–$21. Hookups: water, electric (30, 50 amp), sewer, TV, phone.

Stillman Adult RV Park, 3880 Stillman Park Cir., 95824. T: (916) 392-2820 or (800) 570-6562. www.gocampingamerica.com/stillman/. RV/tent: 65. $29. Hookups: water, electric (20, 30, 50 amp), sewer, TV, phone.

Salinas

Laguna Seca Recreation Area, Hwy. 68, 93901. T: (831) 755-4895. www.carmelfun.com/parks. html. RV/tent: 177. $18–$22. Hookups: water, electric (20, 30 amp).

San Bernardino

KOA San Bernardino, 1707 Cable Canyon Rd., 92407. T: (800) KOA-4155 or (909) 887-4098. F: (909) 887-8499. www.koa.com. RV/tent: 153. $19–$32. Hookups: water, electric (20, 30, 50 amp), sewer, phone.

San Diego

Campland on the Bay, 2211 Pacific Beach Dr., 92109. T: (800) 4-BAY-FUN. F: (858) 581-4264. www.campland.com. RV/tent: 750. $36–$155. Hookups: water, electric (50 amp), sewer, cable TV, phone.

De Anza Harbor Resort, De Anza Dr., 92109. T: (858) 273-3211. RV/tent: 262. $20–$72. Hookups: water, electric (20, 30 amp), sewer, phone.

La Pacifica RV Park, 1010 West San Ysidro Blvd., 92109. T: (619) 428-4413. F: (619) 428-4413. www.gocampingamerica.com/lapacificarvpk/. RV/tent: 177. $20. Hookups: water, electric (30, 50 amp), sewer, phone, satellite TV.

San Fernando

Buckhorn, Hwy. 2, 91342. T: (818) 899-1900. F: (818) 896-6727. www.r5.fs.fed.us/angeles. RV/tent: 38. $12. Hookups: none.

Chilao, Hwy. 2, 91342. T: (818) 899-1900. F: (818) 896-6727. www.r5.fs.fed.us/angeles. RV/tent: 110. $12. Hookups: none.

Horse Flats, Santa Clara Divide Rd., 91342. T: (818) 899-1900. F: (818) 896-6727. www.r5.fs.fed.us /angeles. RV/tent: 25. $10. Hookups: none.

Messenger Flats, Santa Clara Divide Rd., 91342. T: (818) 899-1900. F: (818) 896-6727. www.r5.fs. fed.us/angeles. RV/tent: 10. $5. Hookups: none.

San Juan Bautista

Betabel RV Resort, 9664 Betabel Rd., 95045. T: (800) 278-7275. F: (831) 623-2028. www.betabel.com. RV/tent: 155. $30–$32. Hookups: water, electric (30, 50 amp), sewer, satellite TV, phone.

Fremont Peak State Park, San Juan Canyon Rd., 95045. T: (831) 623-4255. F: (831) 623-4612. RV/tent: 25. $7. Hookups: none.

Mission Farm RV Park, 400 San Juan-Hollister Rd., 95045. T: (831) 623-4456. www.missionfarm.com. RV/tent: 165. $25–$28. Hookups: water, electric (20, 30 amp), sewer, cable TV, phone.

San Luis Obispo

Avila Valley Hot Springs Spa & RV Resort, 250 Avila Beach Dr., 93405. T: (805) 595-2359 or (800) 332-2359 or (800) 543-2359. F: (805) 595-7914. www.rvdestinations.com/avila/. RV/tent: 100. $30–$40. Hookups: water, electric (20, 30 amp), sewer, cable TV.

San Rafael

China Camp State Park, North San Pedro Rd., 94903. T: (800) 444-7275 or (415) 456-0766. F: (415) 456-1743. www.reserveamerica.com. RV/tent: 30. $1 per person. Hookups: none.

San Simeon

San Simeon State Park, Washburn Campground, San Simeon Creek Rd., 93452. T: (800) 444-7275; (805) 927-2035 or (805) 927-2020. www.cal-parks. ca.gov; www.reserveamerica.com. RV/tent: 70. $7. Hookups: none.

Santa Barbara

Santa Barbara Sunrise RV Park, 516 South Salinas, 93103. T: (800) 345-5018 or (805) 966-9954. F: (805) 966-7950. www.gocampingamerica.com/ santabarbara/. RV/tent: 33. $35. Hookups: water, electric (20, 30 amp), sewer, cable TV, phone.

Scott Bar

Indian Scotty, Scott River Rd., 96085. T: (530) 468-5351. F: (530) 468-1290. www.r5.fs.fed.us/klamath. RV/tent: 28. $6. Hookups: none.

CALIFORNIA (continued)

Scotts Valley

Carbonero Creek RV Park, 917 Disc Dr., 95066. T: (408) 438-1288 / (800) 546-1288. F: (408) 438-2877. www.gocampingamerica.com/carbonero/. RV/tent: 104. $22–$29. Hookups: water, electric (20, 30 amp), sewer, cable TV, phone.

Sequoia National Park

Atwell Mill, Mineral King Rd., 93262. T: (559) 565-3341. www.nps.gov/seki. RV/tent: 21. $8. Hookups: none.

Buckeye Flat, Hwy. 198, 93262. T: (559) 565-3341. www.nps.gov/seki. RV/tent: 28. $14. Hookups: none.

Cold Springs, Mineral King Rd., 93262. T: (559) 565-3341. www.nps.gov/seki. RV/tent: 40. $8. Hookups: none.

Dorst, Generals Hwy., 93262. T: (559) 565-3341. www.nps.gov/seki. RV/tent: 218. $16. Hookups: none.

Lodgepole, Generals Hwy., 93262. T: (559) 565-3341. www.nps.gov/seki. RV/tent: 214. $16. Hookups: none.

South Fork, South Fork Rd., 93262. T: (559) 565-3341. www.nps.gov/seki. RV/tent: 13. $8. Hookups: none.

Shelter Cove

Horse Mountain, Kings Peak Rd., 95589. T: (707) 986-7731or (707) 825-2300. F: (707) 825-2301. www.ca.blm.gov/arcata/campground.html. RV/tent: 9. $5. Hookups: none.

Nadelos, Chemise Mountain Rd., 95589. T: (707) 986-7731 or (707) 825-2300. F: (707) 825-2301. www.ca.blm.gov/arcata/campground.html. RV/tent: 8. $8. Hookups: none.

Wailaki, Chemise Mountain Rd., 95589. T: (707) 986-7731 or (707) 825-2300. F: (707) 825-2301. www.ca.blm.gov/arcata/campground.html. RV/tent: 13. $8. Hookups: none.

Sierra City

Loganville, Hwy. 49, 96125. T: (530) 288-3231 or (530) 993-1410. F: (530) 288-0727. www.r5.fs.fed.us/tahoe. RV/tent: 20. $12. Hookups: none.

Stockton

Tiki Lagun Resort & Marina, 12988 West McDonald Rd., 95206. T: (877) 444-TIKI or (209) 941-8975. F: (209) 941-4575. www.tikimarina.com. RV/tent: 103. $25. Hookups: water, electric (30 amp), sewer, cable TV.

Susanville

Christie, County Rd. 231, 96130. T: (877) 444-6777 or (530) 257-4188. F: (530) 252-5803. www.r5.fs.fed.us/lassen; www.reserveusa.com. RV/tent: 69. $14. Hookups: none.

Mariners Resort, 509-725 Stones Rd., 96130. T: (800) 700-5253. F: (530) 825-3397. www.marinersresort.com. RV/tent: 67. $25–$30. Hookups: water, electric (30, 50 amp), sewer, satellite TV, phone.

Mountain View RV Park, 3075 Johnstonville Rd., 96130. T: (877) 686-7878. F: (530) 251-0796. RV/tent: 77. $24. Hookups: water, electric (30, 50 amp), sewer, cable TV, phone.

Tahoe City

Tahoe State Recreation Area, Hwy. 28, 96145. T: (530) 583-3074. www.reserveamerica.com. RV/tent: 38. $12. Hookups: none.

William Kent, Hwy. 89, West Shore Lake Tahoe, 96145. T: (877) 444-6777; (530) 573-2674 or (530) 583-3642. F: (530) 573-2693. www.r5.fs.fed.us/ltbmu; www.reserveusa.com. RV/tent: 95. $14. Hookups: none.

Tahoma

Emerald Bay State Park, Hwy. 89, West Shore Lake Tahoe, 96142. T: (800) 444-7275; (530) 525-7277 or (530) 525-7232. www.cal-parks.ca.gov; www.reserveamerica.com. RV/tent: 120. $12. Hookups: none.

Temecula

Indian Oaks Trailer Ranch Campground, 38120 East Benton Rd., 92593. T: (909) 302-5399. F: (909) 302-5399. www.gocampingamerica.com/indianoaks/. RV/tent: 62. $18–$25. Hookups: water, electric (20, 30 amp), sewer, phone.

Pechanga RV Resort, 45000 Pala Rd., 92592. T: (909) 587-0484 or (877) 997-8386. F: (909) 587-8204. www.pechangarvresort.com/. RV/tent: 170. $32. Hookups: water, electric (20, 30, 50 amp), sewer, cable TV, phone.

Three Rivers

Three Rivers Motel & RV Park, 43365 Sierra Dr., 93271. T: (559) 561-4413. RV/tent: 26. $14–$20. Hookups: water, electric (15, 30 amp), sewer, TV, phone.

Toms Place

Big Meadow, Rock Creek Rd., 93514. T: (760) 873-2500. F: (760) 873-2563. www.r5.fs.fed.us/inyo. RV/tent: 11. $12. Hookups: none.

CALIFORNIA (continued)

Toms Place (continued)

French Camp, Rock Creek Rd., 93514. T: (760) 873-2500. F: (760) 873-2563. www.r5.fs.fed.us/inyo. RV/tent: 86. $12. Hookups: none.

Holiday, Rock Creek Rd., 93514. T: (760) 873-2500. F: (760) 873-2563. www.r5.fs.fed.us/inyo. RV/tent: 35. $12. Hookups: none.

Iris Meadows, Rock Creek Rd., 93514. T: (760) 873-2500. F: (760) 873-2563. www.r5.fs.fed.us/inyo. RV/tent: 14. $12. Hookups: none.

Palisade, Rock Creek Rd., 93514. T: (760) 873-2500. F: (760) 873-2563. www.r5.fs.fed.us/inyo. RV/tent: 5. $12. Hookups: none.

Pine Grove, Rock Creek Rd., 93514. T: (760) 873-2500. F: (760) 873-2563. www.r5.fs.fed.us/inyo. RV/tent: 11. $12. Hookups: none.

Rock Creek Lake, Rock Creek Rd., 93514. T: (760) 873-2500. F: (760) 873-2563. www.r5.fs.fed.us/inyo. RV/tent: 28. $12. Hookups: none.

Tuff, US 395, 93514. T: (760) 873-2500. F: (760) 873-2563. www.r5.fs.fed.us/inyo. RV/tent: 34. $12. Hookups: none.

Upper Pine Grove, Rock Creek Rd., 93514. T: (760) 873-2500. F: (760) 873-2563. www.r5.fs.fed.us/inyo. RV/tent: 8. $12. Hookups: none.

Trinidad

Azalea Glen RV Park & Campground, 3883 Patricks Point Dr., 95570. T: (707) 677-3068. www.azalea glen.com. RV/tent: 42. $15–$24. Hookups: water, electric (30, 50 amp), sewer, cable TV, phone.

Truckee

Goose Meadows, Hwy. 89, 96161. T: (877) 444-6777; (530) 587-3558 or (530) 544-0426. F: (530) 587-6914. www.r5.fs.fed.us/tahoe; www.reserveamerica.com. RV/tent: 24. $10. Hookups: none.

Granite Flat, Hwy. 89, 96161. T: (877) 444-6777; (530) 587-3558 or (530) 544-0426. F: (530) 587-6914. www.r5.fs.fed.us/tahoe www.reserveamerica.com. RV/tent: 75. $12. Hookups: none.

Silver Creek, Hwy. 89, 96161. T: (877) 444-6777; (530) 587-3558 or (530) 544-0426. F: (530) 587-6914. www.r5.fs.fed.us/tahoe; www.reserveamerica.com. RV/tent: 21. $10. Hookups: none.

Tulare

Sun & Fun RV Park, 1000 East Rankin Ave., 93274. T: (559) 686-5779. www.tldirectory.com/camp grounds/sunandfun/. RV/tent: 64. $23. Hookups: water, electric (30, 50 amp), sewer, cable TV, phone.

Tulelake

A.H. Hogue, FR 49/Medicine Lake Rd., 96134. T: (530) 667-2246. F: (530) 667-8609. www.r5.fs.fed.us/modoc. RV/tent: 24. $7. Hookups: none.

Headquarters, FR 49/Medicine Lake Rd., 96134. T: (530) 667-2246. F: (530) 667-8609. www.r5.fs.fed.us/modoc. RV/tent: 9. $7. Hookups: none.

Hemlock, FR 49/Medicine Lake Rd., 96134. T: (530) 667-2246. F: (530) 667-8609. www.r5.fs.fed.us/modoc. RV/tent: 19. $7. Hookups: none.

Medicine, FR 49/Medicine Lake Rd., 96134. T: (530) 667-2246. F: (530) 667-8609. www.r5.fs.fed.us/modoc. RV/tent: 22. $7. Hookups: none.

Tuttletown

Tuttletown Recreation Area; Big Oak Campground, Glory Hole Rd., 95222. T: (209) 536-9094. F: (209) 536-9652. www.recreation.gov. RV/tent: 55. $14. Hookups: none.

Tuttletown Recreation Area; Glory Hole Campground, Glory Hole Rd., 95222. T: (209) 536-9094. F: (209) 536-9652. www.recreation.gov. RV/tent: 20. $14. Hookups: none.

Tuttletown Recreation Area; Ironhorse Campground, Glory Hole Rd., 95222. T: (209) 536-9094. F: (209) 536-9652. www.recreation.gov. RV/tent: 89. $14. Hookups: none.

Twentynine Palms

29 Palms RV and Golf Resort, 4949 Desert Knoll Ave., 92277. T: (800) 874-4548 or (760) 367-3320. www.29palmsrvgolfresort.com/. RV/tent: 197. $27. Hookups: water, electric (30, 50 amp), sewer, phone.

Black Rock Canyon, Joshua Tree National Park, Black Rock Canyon Rd., 92277-3597. T: (760) 367-5525. F: (760) 367-5583. www.nps.gov/jotr. RV/tent: 100. $10. Hookups: none.

Indian Cove, Indian Cove Rd., Joshua Tree National Park, 92277-3597. T: (760) 367-5525. F: (760) 367-5583. www.nps.gov/jotr. RV/tent: 101. $10. Hookups: none.

Ukiah

Bu-Shay, Inlet Rd., 95482-9404. T: (877) 444-6777 or (707) 462-7581. F: (707) 462-3372. www.spn.usace.army.mil/mendocino.html; www.reserve usa.com. RV/tent: 164. $16. Hookups: none.

Che-Ka-Ka, Lake Mendocino Dr., 95482-9404. T: (877) 444-6777 ot (07) 462-7581. F: (707) 462-3372. www.spn.usace.army.mil/mendocino.html; www.reserveusa.com. RV/tent: 22. $8. Hookups: none.

CALIFORNIA (continued)

Valencia

Valencia Travel Village, 27946 Henry Mayo Dr., 91384. T: (661) 257-3333. RV/tent: 460. $22–$42. Hookups: water, electric (20, 30, 50 amp), sewer, cable TV, phone.

Vallejo

Tradewinds RV Park of Vallejo, 239 Lincoln Rd. West, 94590. T: (707) 643-4000. www.gocampingamerica. com/tradewinds/. RV/tent: 78. $25. Hookups: water, electric (30, 50 amp), sewer, phone.

Ventura

Emma Wood State Beach, State Beach Rd., 93005. T: (805) 648-4807. RV/tent: 94. $12. Hookups: none.

Ventura Beach RV Resort, 800 W Main St., 93001. T: (805) 643-9137. F: (805) 643-7479. www.cao hwy.com/v/venbearv.htm. RV/tent: 168. $22–$32. Hookups: water, electric (50 amp), sewer.

Visalia

KOA Visalia-Fresno South, 7480 Ave 308, 93291. T: (800) 562-0540 or (559) 651-0544. F: (559) 651-1080. www.koa.com. RV/tent: 137. $20–$28. Hookups: water, electric (20, 30 amp), sewer, cable TV.

Watsonville

KOA SantaCruz-Monterey Bay, 1186 San Andreas Rd., 95076. T: (800) 562-7701 or (831)722-0551. F: (831)722-0989. www.koa.com. RV/tent: 230. $32–$50. Hookups: water, electric (30, 50 amp), sewer.

Weaverville

Alpine View, Gun Covington Dr., 96093. T: (877) 444-6777 or (530) 623-2121. F: (530) 623-6010. www.r5.fs.fed.us/shastatrinity; www.reserve usa.com. RV/tent: 66. $12–$18. Hookups: none.

Hayward Flat, FR 35N26Y, 96093. T: (877) 444-6777 or (530) 623-2121. F: (530) 623-6010. www.r5.fs.fed.us/shastatrinity; www.reserve usa.com. RV/tent: 97. $12–$18. Hookups: none.

Preacher Meadow, Hwy. 3, 96093. T: (877) 444-6777 or (530) 623-2121. F: (530) 623-6010. www.r5.fs.fed.us/shastatrinity; www.reserve usa.com. RV/tent: 45. $8. Hookups: none.

Sidney Gulch RV Park, Hwy. 299 West & Tinnen St., 96093. T: (530) 623-6621. RV/tent: 40. $19. Hookups: water, electric (20, 30 amp), sewer, cable TV, phone.

Stoney Point, Hwy. 3, 96093. T: (530) 623-2121. F: (530) 623-6010. www.r5.fs.fed.us/shastatrinity. RV/tent: 22. $10. Hookups: none.

Weott

Humboldt Redwoods State Park, Albee Creek Campground, Avenue of the Giants, 95571. T: (800) 444-7275; (707) 946-2409 or (707) 946-2015. F: (707) 946-2326. www.cal-parks.ca.gov; www.reserveamerica.com. RV/tent: 72. $12. Hookups: none.

Humboldt Redwoods State Park, Hidden Springs Campground, Avenue of the Giants, 95571. T: (800) 444-7275; (707) 946-2409 or (707) 946-2015. F: (707) 946-2326. www.cal-parks.ca.gov; www.reserveamerica.com. RV/tent: 154. $12. Hookups: none.

West Sacramento

KOA Sacramento-Metropolitan, 3951 Lake Rd., 95691. T: (800) KOA-2747 or (916) 371-6771. F: (916) 371-0622. www.koa.com. RV/tent: 122. $25–$33. Hookups: water, electric (20, 30 amp), sewer, cable TV, phone.

Sherwood Harbor Marina & RV Park, 35050 South River Rd., 95691. T: (916) 371-3471. F: (916) 372-0997. www.sherwoodharbor.com/rvpark.html. RV/tent: 40. $22. Hookups: water, electric (20 amp).

Westport

Westport-Union Landing State Beach, Hwy. 1, 95488. T: (707) 937-5804. F: (707) 937-2953. RV/tent: 130. $12. Hookups: none.

Winterhaven

Picacho State Recreation Area, Picacho Rd., 92283. T: (760) 393-3059. RV/tent: 58. $12. Hookups: none.

Wofford Heights

Boulder Gulch, Hwy. 155, 93285. T: (760) 379-5646. F: (760) 379-8597. www.r5.fs.fed.us/sequoia. RV/tent: 78. $14. Hookups: none.

Camp 9, Sierra Way, 93285. T: (877) 444-6777 or (760) 379-5646. F: (760) 379-8597. www.r5.fs. fed.us/sequoia. RV/tent: 109. $8. Hookups: none.

Hungry Gulch, Hwy. 155, 93285. T: (760) 379-5646. F: (760) 379-8597. www.r5.fs.fed.us/sequoia. RV/tent: 78. $14. Hookups: none.

Pioneer Point, Hwy. 155, 93285. T: (760) 379-5646. F: (760) 379-8597. www.r5.fs.fed.us/sequoia. RV/tent: 78. $14. Hookups: none.

Woodfords

Crystal Springs, Hwy. 88, 96120. T: (775) 882-2766. F: (775) 884-8199. www.r5.fed.fs.us/htnf. RV/tent: 20. $9. Hookups: none.

CALIFORNIA (continued)

Woodfords (continued)

Kit Carson, Hwy. 88, 96120. T: (775) 882-2766. F: (775) 884-8199. www.r5.fed.fs.us/htnf. RV/tent: 12. $9. Hookups: none.

Wrightwood

Lake, Big Pines Hwy., 92397. T: (661) 944-2187. F: (661) 944-4698. www.r5.fs.fed.us/angeles. RV/tent: 18. $10. Hookups: none.

Table Mountain, Table Mountain Rd., 92397. T: (661) 944-2187. F: (661) 944-4698. www.r5.fs.fed.us/angeles. RV/tent: 115. $12. Hookups: none.

Yermo

KOA Barstow-Calico, 35250 Outer Hwy. 15, 92398. T: (800) 562-0059 or (760) 254-2311. F: (760) 254-2247. www.koa.com. RV/tent: 78. $18–$26. Hookups: water, electric (20, 30, 50 amp), sewer, phone.

Yosemite National Park

Bridalveil Creek, Mineral King Rd., 95389. T: (800) 436-7275 or (209) 372-0265. F: (209) 372-0371. www.nps.gov/yose; www.reservations.nps.gov. RV/tent: 74. $14. Hookups: none.

Crane Flat, Hwy. 120, 95389. T: (800) 436-7275 or (209) 372-0265. F: (209) 372-0371. www.nps.gov/yose; www.reservations.nps.gov. RV/tent: 166. $18. Hookups: none.

Hodgdon Meadow, Hwy. 120, 95389. T: (800) 436-7275 or (209) 372-0265. F: (209) 372-0371. www.nps.gov/yose; www.reservations.nps.gov. RV/tent: 105. $18. Hookups: none.

Lower Pines, Southside Dr., Yosemite Valley, 95389. T: (800) 436-7275 or (209) 372-0265. F: (209) 372-0371. www.nps.gov/yose; www.reservations.nps.gov. RV/tent: 60. $18. Hookups: none.

Porcupine Flat, Tioga Rd./Hwy. 120, 95389. T: (800) 436-7275 or (209) 372-0265. F: (209) 372-0371. www.nps.gov/yose; www.reservations.nps.gov. RV/tent: 52. $6. Hookups: none.

Upper Pines, Southside Dr., Yosemite Valley, 95389. T: (800) 436-7275 or (209) 372-0265. F: (209) 372-0371. www.nps.gov/yose; www.reservations.nps.gov. RV/tent: 238. $18. Hookups: none.

White Wolf, White Wolf Rd., 95389. T: (800) 436-7275 or (209) 372-0265. F: (209) 372-0371. www.nps.gov/yose; www.reservations.nps.gov. RV/tent: 87. $10. Hookups: none.

Yosemite Creek, Yosemite Creek Campground Rd., 95389. T: (800) 436-7275 or (209) 372-0265. F: (209) 372-0371. www.nps.gov/yose; www.reservations.nps.gov. RV/tent: 75. $6–$8. Hookups: none.

NEVADA

Amargosa Valley

Fort Amargosa, P.O. Box 245, 89020. T: (775) 372-1178. F: (775) 372-1166. RV/tent: 98. $14. Hookups: electric (20, 30, 50 amp), water, sewer.

Austin

Austin RV Park, US Hwy. 50, 89310. T: (775) 964-1011. F: (775) 964-2601. tdw@austin.igate.com. RV/tent: 21. $10–$16. Hookups: electric (20, 30 amp), water, sewer.

Big Creek Campground, P.O. Box 130, 89310. T: (702) 964-2671. RV/tent: 6. $3. Hookups: none.

Bob Scott Campground, P.O. Box 130, 89310. T: (702) 964-2671. RV/tent: 10. $4. Hookups: none.

Baker

Baker Creek Campground, Superintendent, Great Basin National Park, 89311. T: (775) 234-7331. www.nps.gov/grba. RV/tent: 30. $10. Hookups: none.

Wheeler Creek Campground, Superintendent, Great Basin National Park, 89311. T: (775) 234-7331. www.nps.gov/grba. RV/tent: 37. $10. Hookups: none.

Whispering Elms RV Park, P.O. Box 105, 89311. T: (775) 234-7343. RV/tent: 20. $10–$16. Hookups: electric (20, 30 amp), water, sewer.

Battle Mountain

Broadway Flying J Service Center, 650 West Front, 89820. T: (775) 635-5424. F: (775) 635-0371. RV/tent: 96. $15. Hookups: electric (20, 30, 50 amp), water, sewer.

Beatty

Burro Inn, US Hwy. 95, P.O. Box 7, 89003. T: (775) 553-2225 or (800) 843-2078. F: (775) 553-2892. www.burroinn.com. RV/tent: 43. $15. Hookups: electric (20, 30, 50 amp), water, sewer.

NEVADA (continued)

Beatty (continued)

Kay's Korral RV Park, US Hwy. 95, 89003. T: (775) 553-2732. kskorral@parhump.com. RV/tent: 25. $12. Hookups: electric, water, sewer.

Rio Rancho RV Park, US Hwy. 95 North, P.O. Box 905, 89003. T: (775) 553-2238 or (800) 448-4423. RV/tent: 35. $16. Hookups: electric (30, 50 amp), water, sewer.

Space Station RV Park & Market, US Hwy. 95, P.O. Box 568, 89003. T: (775) 553-9039. RV/tent: 24. $15. Hookups: electric (30 amp), water, sewer.

Boulder City

Boulder Oaks RV Resort, 1010 Industrial Rd., 89005. T: (702) 294-4425 or (800) 478-5687(outside NV). www.aardvarkrv/boulderoaks. boulderoaksrv@yahoo.com. RV/tent: 275. $28. Hookups: electric (30, 50 amp), water, sewer, cable TV, phone (modem).

Canyon Trail RV Park, 1200 Industrial Rd., 89005. T: (702) 293-1200. F: (702) 293-1954. RV/tent: 156. $18. Hookups: electric (30, 50 amp), water, sewer.

Lakeshore Trailer Village, 268 Lakeshore Rd., 89005. T: (702) 293-2540. RV/tent: 80. $18. Hookups: electric (30 amp), water, sewer, cable TV.

Cal Nev Ari

Cal Nev Ari, US Hwy. 95, P.O. Box 430, 89039. T: (702) 297-1115. F: (702) 297-1167. RV/tent: 58. $13. Hookups: electric (20, 30, 50 amp), water, sewer, cable TV.

Caliente

Agua Caliente Trailer Park, US Hwy. 93 North, 89008. T: (775) 726-3399. F: (775) 726-3205. RV/tent: 5. $10–$15. Hookups: electric (20 amp), water, sewer.

Carson City

Camp-N-Town, 2438 North Carson St., 89706. T: (775) 883-1132 or (800) 872-1132. F: (775) 883-1123. RV/tent: 130. $20–$25. Hookups: electric (30, 50 amp), water, sewer, cable TV, phone (modem).

Comstock Country RV Resort, 5400 South Carson St., 89701. T: (775) 882-2445 or (800) NEVADA-1. F: (775) 882-1197. www.comstocknv.com. RV/tent: 166. $18–$24. Hookups: electric (20, 30, 50 amp), water, sewer, cable TV.

Crystal Springs Campground, 1536 South Carson St., 89701. T: (775) 882-2766. RV/tent: 22. $8. Hookups: none.

Indian Creek Campground, 5665 Morgan Hill Rd., 89701. T: (775) 885-6000. RV/tent: 29. $8–$10. Hookups: none.

Kit Carson Campground, 1536 South Carson St., 89701. T: (775) 882-2766. RV/tent: 12. $6. Hookups: none.

Mount Rose Campground, 1536 South Carson St., 89701. T: (775) 882-2766. RV/tent: 24. $8. Hookups: none.

Oasis RV Park, 4550 South Carson St., 89701. T: (775) 882-1375. RV/tent: 20. $10–$17. Hookups: electric (20, 30 amp), water, sewer, cable TV.

Pinon Plaza Casino Resort & RV Park, 2171 US Hwy. 50 East, 89701. T: (775) 885-9000 x-1037 or (877) 519-5567. F: (775) 888-8003. www.pinon plaza.com. RV/tent: 70. $18–$21. Hookups: electric (30, 50 amp), water, sewer, cable TV, phone (modem).

Cottonwood Cove

Cottonwood Cove Marina & Resort, P.O. Box 1000, 89046. T: (702) 297-1464. www.foreverresorts. com. RV/tent: 73. $17–$20. Hookups: electric (30, 50 amp), water, sewer.

Dayton

Dayton State Park, P.O. Box 412, 89403. T: (775) 687-4379. RV/tent: 10. $9. Hookups: none.

Denio

Royal Peacock RV Park, Virgin Valley Rd., 89404. T: (775) 941-0374 or (775) 272-3201. RV/tent: 20. $9–$16. Hookups: electric (20, 30 amp), water, sewer.

Elko

Best Western Gold Country RV Park, Inn & Casino, 2050 Idaho St., 89801. T: (775) 738-8421 or (800) 621-1332. F: (775) 738-1798. www.bestwestern nevada.com. RV/tent: 26. $20. Hookups: electric (20, 30, 50 amp), water, sewer.

Double Dice RV Park, 3730 East Idaho St., 89801. T: (775) 738-5642 or (888) 738-3423. F: (775) 753-0055. www.gocampingamerica.com/doubledice. RV/tent: 150. $20–$23. Hookups: electric (30, 50 amp), water, sewer, cable TV, phone (modem).

Dunn's Wildhorse Resort, HC 31 Box 213 (62 mi. north of Elko), 89801. T: (775) 758-6472. F: (775) 758-5400. RV/tent: 34. $9–$18. Hookups: electric (20, 30 amp), water, sewer.

Hidden Valley Guest & RV Resort, P.O. Box 1454, 89803. T: (775) 738-2347. RV/tent: 27. $10–$20. Hookups: electric (30 amp), water, sewer.

North Wildhorse Campground, 3900 East Idaho St., 89801. T: (775) 753-0200. RV/tent: 18. $6. Hookups: none.

NEVADA (continued)

Elko (continued)

Ryndon RV Park, 303-11 Ryndon, P.O. Box 1656, 89801. T: (775) 738-3448. F: (775) 738-4825. RV/tent: 54. $17–$20. Hookups: electric (30, 50 amp), water, sewer, phone (modem).

South Fork State Recreation Area, HC 30 353-8, 89801. T: (775) 744-4346. RV/tent: 25. $9. Hookups: none.

Wildhorse State Recreation Area, HC 31 Box 265 (67 mi. north of Elko), 89801. T: (775) 758-6493. RV/tent: 33. $9. Hookups: none.

Wilson Reservoir Campground, 3900 East Idaho St., 89801. T: (775) 753-0200. RV/tent: 15. $5. Hookups: none.

Ely

El Dorado Service, HC 31 Box 31020, 89301. T: (775) 237-7253. RV/tent: 14. $10–$16. Hookups: electric (30 amp), water, sewer.

Harry's Wilderness RV, No. 58 McGill Hwy., 89301. T: (775) 289-8727. RV/tent: 10. $10–$16. Hookups: electric (30 amp), water, sewer.

KOA of Ely, US Hwy. 93S, 89301. T: (775) 289-3413 or (800) 526-3413. www.elykoa.com. elykoa@netxxpress.net. RV/tent: 107. $16–$22. Hookups: electric (20, 30, 50 amp), water, sewer, cable TV, phone (modem).

Lanes Ranch Motel, HC 34 (Preston) Box 34145, 89301. T: (775) 238-5246. F: (775) 238-5248. RV/tent: 7. $8–$15. Hookups: electric (30 amp), water, sewer.

Major's Station RV Park, US Hwy. 93 & US Hwy. 50 Junction, 89301. T: (775) 591-0430. RV/tent: 7. $10. Hookups: electric (30 amp), water, sewer, phone.

Prospector Casino RV Park (Holiday Inn), US Hwy. 93, 89301. T: (775) 289-8900. F: (775) 289-4607. RV/tent: 22. $10. Hookups: electric (20, 30, 50 amp), water, sewer.

Stage Stop, HCR 33 Box 33900, 89301. T: (775) 591-0397. F: (775) 591-0401. RV/tent: 4. $10–$15. Hookups: electric (30 amp), water, sewer.

Timber Creek, 350 8th St., P.O. Box 539, 89301. T: (702) 289-3031. RV/tent: 15. $4. Hookups: none.

Valley View RV Park, No. 65 McGill Hwy., 89301. T: (775) 289-3303. RV/tent: 46. $15. Hookups: electric (20, 30, 50 amp), water, sewer, cable TV, phone (modem).

West End RV Park, No. 50 Aultman St., 89301. T: (775) 289-8900. RV/tent: 11. $10. Hookups: electric (30 amp), water, sewer.

Eureka

Eureka RV Park, P.O. Box 734, 89316. T: (775) 237-7203. RV/tent: 25. $10–$20. Hookups: electric (30 amp), water, sewer, cable TV.

Pita RV, P.O. Box 27, 89316. T: (775) 237-5281. F: (775) 237-7001. RV/tent: 11. $10–$16. Hookups: electric (30 amp), water, sewer, cable TV.

Silver Sky RV Park, P.O. Box 573, 89316. T: (775) 237-7146. RV/tent: 15. $8–$15. Hookups: electric (30 amp), water, sewer.

T/C Trailer Park, P.O. Box 176, 89316. T: (775) 237-5331. RV/tent: 14. $10–$17. Hookups: electric (30 amp), water, sewer, cable TV.

Fallon

Bonanza RV Park, 855 West Williams, 89407. T: (775) 423-6031. F: (775) 423-6282. RV/tent: 20. $12. Hookups: electric (30 amp), water, sewer.

Fallon RV Park, 5787 Reno Hwy., 89406. T: (775) 867-2332. F: (775) 867-4392. RV/tent: 64. $18–$20. Hookups: electric (30, 50 amp), water, sewer.

The Hub Totel RV Park, 4800 Reno Hwy. (US Hwy. 50), 89406. T: (775) 867-3636. RV/tent: 44. $19. Hookups: electric (20, 30 amp), water, sewer, cable TV, phone (modem).

Fernley

Desert Rose RV Park, 3285 Hwy. 50 East, 89408. T: (877) 767-3478. www.desertroserv.com. RV/tent: 112. $20–$22. Hookups: electric (30, 50 amp), water, sewer, cable TV, phone (modem).

Fernley RV Park, 550 West Main St., 89408. T: (775) 575-5222. RV/tent: 40. $21. Hookups: electric (30, 50 amp), water, sewer, cable TV, phone (modem).

Gardnerville

Topaz Lodge & Casino RV Park, 1995 US Hwy. 395 South, P.O. Box 187, 89410. T: (775) 266-3338 or (800) 962-0732. F: (775) 266-3046. www.enterit.com. RV/tent: 59. $10–$17. Hookups: electric, water, sewer, cable TV.

Goldfield

Goldfield RV Park, P.O. Box 315, 89013. T: (775) 485-3280. F: (775) 485-3279. home.earthlink.net/~siebert. RV/tent: 10. $10. Hookups: electric (30, 50 amp), water, sewer.

Hawthorne

Desert Lake Campground, US Hwy. 95 Walker Lake, P.O. Box 647, 89415. T: (775) 945-3373. RV/tent: 25. $8–$15. Hookups: electric (30 amp), water, sewer.

NEVADA (continued)

Hawthorne (continued)

Frontier RV Park, Fifth & L St., 89415. T: (775) 945-2733. RV/tent: 27. $10–$15. Hookups: electric (30, 50 amp), water, sewer.

Scotty's RV Park, 1101 5th St., 89415. T: (775) 945-2079. RV/tent: 16. $15. Hookups: electric (20, 30, 50 amp), water, sewer, cable TV.

Henderson

Desert Sands RV Park, 1940 North Boulder Hwy., 89015. T: (702) 565-1945. F: (702) 565-3534. RV/tent: 300. $15–$21. Hookups: electric (20, 30, 50 amp), water, sewer.

Jackpot

Cactus Pete's Saquaro RV Park, 1385 Hwy. 93, 89825. T: (775) 755-2321 or (800) 821-1103. www.ameristarcasinos.com/cactus_petes.asp. RV/tent: 91. $10–$14. Hookups: electric (20, 30 amp), water, sewer, cable TV, phone (modem).

Spanish Gardens RV Park, P.O. Box 390, 89825. T: (775) 755-2396 or (800) 422-8233. F: (775) 755-2630. RV/tent: 38. $14. Hookups: electric (30, 50 amp), water, sewer, cable TV.

Las Vegas

Arizona Charlie's East Hotel, Casino & RV Park, 4575 Boulder Hwy., 89121. T: (702) 951-5911 or (800) 970-7280. F: (702) 951-9211. RV/tent: 239. $18. Hookups: electric (20, 30, 50 amp), water, sewer, phone (modem).

Boulder Lakes RV Resort, 6201 Boulder Hwy., 89122. T: (702) 435-1157. F: (702) 435-1125. RV/tent: 417. $20–$25. Hookups: electric (20, 30, 50 amp), water, sewer, cable TV, phone (modem).

Castaways RV Park, 2960 Fremont St., 89104. T: (702) 383-9333 or (800) 826-2800. F: (702) 385-9163. www.showboat-lv.com. RV/tent: 84. $18–$20. Hookups: electric (20, 30, 50 amp), water, sewer, cable TV, phone (modem).

Circusland RV Park, 500 Circus Circus Dr., 89109. T: (702) 794-3757 or (800) 444-CIRCUS. F: (702) 792-2280. RV/tent: 365. $13–$24. Hookups: electric (30, 50 amp), water, sewer, phone (modem).

Destiny's Oasis Las Vegas RV Resort, 2711 Windmill Rd., 89123. T: (702) 260-2020 or (800) 566-4747. F: (702) 263-5160. www.destinyrv.com. RV/tent: 701. $20–$56. Hookups: electric (30, 50 amp), water, sewer, cable TV, phone (modem).

Hitchin' Post RV Park, 3640 Las Vegas Blvd. North, 89115. T: (702) 644-1043 or (888) 433-8402. F: (702) 644-8359. RV/tent: 196. $18. Hookups: electric (20, 30, 50 amp), water, sewer, cable TV, phone (modem).

Holiday Travel Park, 3890 South Nellis Blvd., 89121. T: (702) 451-8005. F: (702) 451-5806. RV/tent: 403. $18. Hookups: electric (30, 50 amp), water, sewer, phone (modem).

KOA Las Vegas, 4315 Boulder Hwy., 89121. T: (702) 451-5527 or (800) 562-7782. F: (702) 434-8729. RV/tent: 300. $25–$33. Hookups: electric (20, 30, 50 amp), water, sewer, phone (modem).

Nevada Palace VIP Travel Trailer Park, 5325 Boulder Hwy., 89122. T: (702) 451-0232 or (800) 634-6283. F: (702) 458-3361. www.nvpalace.com. RV/tent: 168. $14. Hookups: electric (30 amp), water, sewer.

Riviera RV Park, 2200 Palm, 89104. T: (702) 457-8700. F: (702) 457-1488. RV/tent: 135. $20. Hookups: electric (20, 30, 50 amp), water, sewer, phone (modem).

Road Runner RV Park, 4711 Boulder Hwy., 89121. T: (702) 456-4711. RV/tent: 200. $15–$20. Hookups: electric (30, 50 amp), water, sewer.

Sam's Town Boulder RV Park, 5225 Boulder Hwy., 89122. T: (702) 454-7777 or (800) 634-6371. F: (702) 456-5665. RV/tent: 291. $18. Hookups: electric (20, 30, 50 amp), water, sewer, cable TV.

Sam's Town Nellis RV Park, 4040 South Nellis Blvd., 89121. T: (702) 456-7777 or (800) 634-6371. F: (702) 456-5665. RV/tent: 207. $18. Hookups: electric (20, 30, 50 amp), water, sewer, cable TV.

Sunrise RV Park, 4445 Boulder Hwy., 89121. T: (702) 458-7275 or (800) 970-7280. F: (702) 898-7275. RV/tent: 239. $18. Hookups: electric (30, 50 amp), water, sewer, phone (modem).

Western RV Park, 1023 East Fremont, 89104. T: (702) 384-1033. RV/tent: 69. $10. Hookups: electric (20, 30, 50 amp), water, sewer.

Laughlin

Avi RV Park, P.O. Box 77011, 89028. T: (702) 535-5555. F: (702) 535-5400. RV/tent: 240. $17–$27. Hookups: electric (50 amp), water, sewer, cable TV, phone (modem).

Lovelock

Rye Patch Reservoir State Recreation Area, 2505 Rye Patch Reservoir Rd., 89419. T: (775) 538-7321. RV/tent: 44. $4–$10. Hookups: none.

Mesquite

Casablanca RV Park, 950 West Mesquite Blvd., P.O. Box 2737, 89024. T: (702) 346-7529 or (800) 459-7529. F: (702) 346-6862. www.casablanca resort.com. RV/tent: 45. $12. Hookups: electric (20, 30, 50 amp), water, sewer, cable TV.

NEVADA (continued)

Mesquite (continued)

Desert Skies RV Resort, 99 Peppermill Palms Dr., P.O. Box 3780, 89024. T: (520) 347-6000 or (800) 818-2773. F: (520) 347-6002. RV/tent: 189. $20–$24. Hookups: electric (20, 30, 50 amp), water, sewer, cable TV.

Si Redd's Oasis Resort RV Park, P.O. Box 360, 89024. T: (702) 346-5232 or (800) 21-OASIS. F: (702) 346-2746. www.oasisresort.com. RV/tent: 91. $14. Hookups: electric (20, 30, 50 amp), water, sewer, cable TV.

Virgin River RV Park, I-15 Exit 122, 89024. T: (702) 346-7777 or (800) 346-7721. F: (702) 346-7780. www.virginriver.com. RV/tent: 55. $10. Hookups: electric (20, 30 amp), water, sewer, cable TV.

Mina

Sunrise Valley RV Park LLC, US Hwy. 95, P.O. Box 345, 89422. T: (775) 573-2214. F: (775) 573-2602. www.sunrisevalley.com. RV/tent: 27. $18. Hookups: electric (30, 50 amp), water, sewer, cable TV.

Minden

Carson Valley Inn Hotel Casino RV Resort, 1627 US Hwy. 395 North, 89423. T: (775) 782-9711 or (800) 321-6983. www.cvinn.com. RV/tent: 60. $16. Hookups: electric (20, 30, 50 amp), water, sewer, cable TV, phone (modem).

Silver City RV Resort, 3165 Hwy. 395, 89423. T: (800) 997-6393. www.silvercityrvresort.com. RV/tent: 206. $20–$25. Hookups: electric (30, 50 amp), water, sewer, cable TV, phone (modem).

Overton

Robbin's Nest Mobile Village, P.O. Box 130, 479 South Moapa Dr., 89040. T: (702) 397-2364. www.robbinsnestmv.com. rnmv@robbins nestmv.com. RV/tent: 50. $14. Hookups: electric (30, 50 amp), water, sewer, phone (modem).

Pahrump

Pahrump Station RV Park, P.O. Box 38, 89041. T: (775) 727-5100. F: (775) 751-1325. RV/tent: 48. $18. Hookups: electric (20, 30, 50 amp), water, sewer, cable TV, phone (modem).

Saddle West Hotel, Casino, RV Resort, 1220 South Hwy. 160, 89048. T: (775) 727-1111 or (800) 433-3987. www.saddlewest.com. RV/tent: 80. $18. Hookups: electric (20, 30, 50 amp), water, sewer, cable TV.

Seven Palms RV Park, 101 South Linda St., 89048. T: (775) 727-6091. RV/tent: 59. $15. Hookups: electric (20, 30, 50 amp), water, sewer.

Terrible's Lakeside Casino & RV Resort, 5870 South Homestead Rd., 89048. T: (775) 751-7770 or (888) 558-LAKE. F: (775) 751-7746. www.terrible herbst.com. RV/tent: 160. $19. Hookups: electric (50 amp), water, sewer, cable TV, phone (modem).

Panaca

Beaver Dam State Park, P.O. Box 176, 89042. T: (775) 728-4467. www.state.nv.us/stparks/. RV/tent: 42. $8. Hookups: none.

Primm

Primadonna RV Village, P.O. Box 93718, 89193. T: (702) 382-1212 or (800) 386-7867. F: (702) 679-5195. www.primadonna.com. RV/tent: 197. $12–$15. Hookups: electric (30, 50 amp), water, sewer, cable TV.

Reno

Bordertown Casino RV Resort, 19575 US Hwy. 395 N, 89506. T: (775) 677-0169 or (800) 218-9339. RV/tent: 50. $15–$25. Hookups: electric (20, 30, 50 amp), water, sewer, cable TV, phone (modem).

Chism Trailer Park, 1300 West 2nd St., 89503. T: (775) 322-2281 or (800) 638-2281. F: (775) 322-6376. www.chismtrailerpark.com. RV/tent: 152. $19. Hookups: electric (20, 30, 50 amp), water, sewer, cable TV.

Keystone RV Park, 1455 West Fourth St., 89503. T: (775) 324-5000 or (800) 686-8559. RV/tent: 102. $21–$23. Hookups: electric (20, 30, 50 amp), water, sewer, cable TV, phone (modem).

KOA at the Reno Hilton, 2500 East 2nd St., 89595. T: (775) 789-2000 or (888) 562-5698. F: (775) 789-2418. RV/tent: 230. $15–$28. Hookups: electric (30, 50 amp), water, sewer, phone (modem).

Reno RV Park, 735 Mill St., 89502. T: (775) 323-3381 or (800) 445-3381. F: (775) 323-7266. RV/tent: 46. $23. Hookups: electric (30 amp), water, sewer, cable TV, phone (modem).

Shamrock RV Park, 260 Parr Blvd., 89512. T: (775) 329-5222 or (800) 322-8248. F: (775) 329-9065. RV/tent: 121. $19–$22. Hookups: electric (20, 30, 50 amp), water, sewer, cable TV, phone (modem).

Silver Sage RV Park, 2760 South Virginia St., 89502. T: (775) 829-1919. www.cris.com/~rvparks/. RV/tent: 43. $18–$22. Hookups: electric (30, 50 amp), water, sewer, cable TV, phone (modem).

Ruth

Copperpit RV Park, 5 Main St., 89319. T: (775) 289-6032. RV/tent: 17. $8–$14. Hookups: electric (20, 30 amp), water, sewer, cable TV.

NEVADA (continued)

Searchlight

Cree's, US Hwy. 164, 89046. T: (702) 297-1532. F: (702) 297-1532. RV/tent: 10. $10–$13. Hookups: electric (20, 30 amp), water, sewer, cable TV.

Smith

Walker River Resort, P.O. Box 90, 89430. T: (775) 465-2573 or (800) 465-2573. RV/tent: 130. $16–$18. Hookups: electric (30, 50 amp), water, sewer, phone (modem).

South Lake Tahoe

Nevada Beach Campground, P.O. Box 14000, 94301. T: (775) 588-5562 or (877) 444-6777. RV/tent: 54. $18–$20. Hookups: none.

Sparks

Rivers Edge RV Park, 1405 South Rock Blvd., 89431. T: (775) 358-8533 or (800) 621-4792. F: (775) 358-3168. RV/tent: 164. $21. Hookups: electric (30, 50 amp), water, sewer, phone (modem).

Victorian RV Park, 205 Nichols Blvd., 89431. T: (775) 356-6400 or (800) 955-6405. F: (775) 358-1542. RV/tent: 92. $20. Hookups: electric (20, 30, 50 amp), water, sewer.

Tonopah

Twister Inn RV Park, Ketten Rd. & US Hwy. 6, 89049. T: (775) 482-9444. RV/tent: 13. $10–$16. Hookups: electric (30 amp), water, sewer, cable TV.

Verdi

Boomtown RV Park, P.O. Box 399, 89439. T: (775) 345-8650 or (887) 626-6686. F: (775) 345-8666. www.boomtowncasinos.com. RV/tent: 203. $28. Hookups: electric (30, 50 amp), water, sewer, cable TV, phone (modem).

Gold Ranch Casino RV Park, I-80 Exit 2, 89439. T: (775) 345-6789. RV/tent: 155. $20–$30. Hookups: electric (20, 30, 50 amp), water, sewer, cable TV, phone (modem).

Virginia City

Virginia City RV Park, 355 North F St., P.O. Box 1070, 89440. T: (775) 847-0999 or (800) 889-1240. www.vcrvpark.com. RV/tent: 56. $12–$20. Hookups: electric (30, 50 amp), water, sewer, phone (modem).

Wells

Angel Creek Campground, P.O. Box 246, 89825. T: (775) 752-3357. RV/tent: 19. $7. Hookups: none.

Angel Lake Campground, P.O. Box 246, 89825. T: (775) 752-3357. RV/tent: 37. $7. Hookups: none.

Beverly Hills RV Ranch, I-80 Exit 348, 89825. T: (775) 752-3800. RV/tent: 55. $18. Hookups: electric (20, 30 amp), water, sewer, phone (modem).

Crossroads RV Park, P.O. Box 161, 89835. T: (775) 752-3012. RV/tent: 24. $16. Hookups: electric (30 amp), water, sewer.

Thomas Canyon Campground, P.O. Box 246, 89825. T: (702) 752-3357. RV/tent: 42. $6. Hookups: none.

Wendover

Stateline RV Park, P.O. Box 789, 89883. T: (775) 664-2221 or (800) 848-7300. RV/tent: 56. $17–$20. Hookups: electric (30, 50 amp), water, sewer.

Wendover KOA, 651 North Camper Dr., 89883. T: (775) 664-3221 or (800) 562-8552. F: (775) 664-3712. RV/tent: 122. $17–$28. Hookups: electric (20, 30, 50 amp), water, sewer.

Winnemucca

Model T Hotel/Casino/RV Park, 1130 West Winnemucca Blvd., 89445. T: (775) 623-2588. www.ModelT.com. RV/tent: 58. $22. Hookups: electric (30, 50 amp), water, sewer, cable TV, phone (modem).

Westerner Trailer Lodge, 800 East Fourth St., 89445. T: (775) 623-2907. RV/tent: 20. $14. Hookups: electric (30 amp), water, sewer.

Winnemucca RV Park, 5255 East Winnemucca Blvd., 89445. T: (775) 623-4458 or (877) 787-2750. wmcarvpark@the-onramp.net. RV/tent: 121. $16–$23. Hookups: electric (30, 50 amp), water, sewer, cable TV, phone (modem).

UTAH

American Fork

American Campground, 418 East 620 South, 84003.
T: (801) 756-5502. RV/tent: 52. $18–$20.
Hookups: electric (20, 30 amp), water, sewer,
phone (modem).

Antimony

Antimony Mercantile Campground, 700 North
Hwy. 22, 84712. T: (435) 624-3253. RV/tent: 24.
$10–$15. Hookups: electric (30 amp), water,
sewer.

Otter Creek RV & Marina, P.O. Box 43, 84712.
T: (435) 624-3268. RV/tent: 32. $15. Hookups:
electric (15, 30 amp), water, sewer.

Otter Creek State Park, Hwy. 22, 84712. T: (800)
441-3292. RV/tent: 30. $10–$12. Hookups: none.

Beaver

Anderson Meadow, 575 South Main, P.O. Box E,
84713. T: (435) 438-2436. RV/tent: 10. $6.
Hookups: none.

Beaver Canyon Campground, 1419 East Canyon
Rd., P.O. Box 1528, 84713. T: (435) 438-5654.
RV/tent: 105. $10–$12. Hookups: electric (20, 30
amp), water, sewer.

Kents Lake, 575 South Main, P.O. Box E, 84713.
T: (435) 438-2436. RV/tent: 38. $8. Hookups: none.

KOA Beaver, Manderfield Rd., 84713. T: (435) 438-
2924. RV/tent: 75. $16–$20. Hookups: electric (20,
30 amp), water, sewer.

Blanding

Kampark, 861 South Main St., 84511. T: (435) 678-
2770. RV/tent: 69. $11–$15. Hookups: electric (20,
30, 50 amp), water, sewer, phone (modem).

Bluff

Cottonwood RV Park, P.O. Box 6, 84512. T: (435)
672-2287. RV/tent: 41. $14–$16. Hookups: Electric
(20, 30, 50 amp), water, sewer, phone (modem).

Boulder

Boulder Exchange, 425 North Hwy. 12 Box 1418,
84716. T: (435) 335-7304. RV/tent: 6. $10–$20.
Hookups: electric (20 amp), water, sewer.

Brigham City

Brigham City/Perry South KOA, Box 579, 84302.
T: (435) 723-5503 or (800) 562-0903. RV/tent:
102. $19–$23. Hookups: electric (20, 30 amp),
water, sewer.

Crystal Hot Springs, 8215 North Hwy. 38, 84314.
T: (435) 279-8104. RV/tent: 120. $9–$19.
Hookups: electric (20, 30 amp), water, sewer.

Golden Spike RV Park, 1100 South 905 West,
84302. T: (435) 723-8858. RV/tent: 60. $13–$24.
Hookups: electric (20, 30, 50 amp), water, sewer,
cable TV, phone (modem).

Caineville

Sleepy Hollow Campground, HC 70 Box 40, 84775.
T: (435) 456-9130. RV/tent: 39. $12. Hookups:
electric (30 amp).

Cedar City

Best Western Town & Country RV Park, 200 North
Main St., 84720. T: (435) 586-9900. F: (435) 586-
1664. RV/tent: 10. $26 (includes breakfast).
Hookups: electric (20, 30, 50 amp), water, sewer,
cable TV, phone (modem).

KOA Cedar City, 1121 North Main, 84720. T: (435)
586-9872. RV/tent: 129. $18–$22. Hookups: electric (20, 30 amp), water, sewer, phone.

Navajo Lake, P.O. Box 627, 84721. T: (435) 865-
3200. www.fsfed.us/outernet/dixie-nf/welcome.
htm. RV/tent: 28. $7. Hookups: none.

Te-Ah, P.O. Box 627, 84721. T: (435) 865-3200.
www.fsfed.us/outernet/dixie-nf/welcome.htm.
RV/tent: 42. $7. Hookups: none.

Delta

Antelope Valley RV Park, 776 West Main, P.O. Box
843, 84624. T: (435) 864-1813. RV/tent: 96. $20.
Hookups: water, electric (20, 30, 50 amp), sewer.

Duchesne

Aspen Grove Campground, 85 West Main, P.O. Box
981, 84021. T: (435) 738-2482. RV/tent: 33. $6–$9.
Hookups: none.

Hades Campground, 85 West Main, P.O. Box 981,
84021. T: (435) 738-2482. RV/tent: 17. $6.
Hookups: none.

Iron Mine Campground, 85 West Main, P.O. Box
981, 84021. T: (435) 738-2482. RV/tent: 27. $6.
Hookups: none.

Miners Gulch Campground, 85 West Main, P.O. Box
981, 84021. T: (435) 738-2482. RV/tent: 5. $8.
Hookups: none.

Moon Lake Campground, 85 West Main, P.O. Box
981, 84021. T: (435) 738-2482. RV/tent: 51. $8.
Hookups: none.

South Fork Campground, 85 West Main, P.O. Box
981, 84021. T: (435) 738-2482. RV/tent: 5. $8.
Hookups: none.

Starvation State Park, P.O. Box 584, 84021. T: (435)
738-2326. RV/tent: 54. $12. Hookups: none.

Yellowpine Campground, 85 West Main, P.O. Box
981, 84021. T: (435) 738-2482. RV/tent: 29. $8.
Hookups: none.

UTAH (continued)

Escalante

Blue Spruce Campground, P.O. Box 246, 84726.
T: (435) 826-5400 or (877) 444-6777. RV/tent: 6.
$7. Hookups: none.

Moqui Motel & RV Park, 480 West Main St. Box 434,
84726. T: (435) 826-4210. RV/tent: 7. $20–$29.
Hookups: electric (20, 30 amp), water, sewer.

Pine Lake Campground, P.O. Box 246, 84726.
T: (435) 826-5600 or (877) 444-6777. RV/tent: 33.
$9. Hookups: none.

Posey Lake Campground, P.O. Box 246, 84726.
T: (435) 826-5400 or (877) 444-6777. RV/tent: 23.
$8. Hookups: none.

Farmington

Lagoon RV Park & Campground, 375 North Lagoon
Dr., 84025. T: (801) 451-8100 or (800) 748-5246.
RV/tent: 208. $18–$26. Hookups: electric (20, 30,
50 amp), water, sewer.

Fillmore

Wagons West RV Park and Campground, 545
North Main, 84631. T: (435) 743-6188. RV/tent: 50.
$20. Hookups: electric (20, 30, 50 amp), water,
sewer, cable TV, phone (modem).

Garden City

Bear Lake KOA, 485 North Bear Lake Blvd., 84028.
T: (435) 946-3454 or (800) 562-3442. F: (435)
946-3454. RV/tent: 160. $17–$26. Hookups: electric (30, 50 amp), water, sewer.

Sweetwater RV Park & Marina, Ideal Beach, South
Shore, 84028. T: (435) 946-8735. RV/tent: 19. $25.
Hookups: electric (30 amp), water, sewer.

Hanksville

Starr Spring Campground, 100 West 400 S, 84734.
T: (435) 542-3461. www.utso.ut.blm.gov. RV/tent:
12. $4. Hookups: none.

Hatch

Bryce-Zion Midway Resort, US Hwy. 89, 84735.
T: (888) 299-3531 or (435) 735-4199. F: (435)
735-4198. www.netutah.com/bzrhatch. bzm-
rhatch@juno.com. RV/tent: 20. $19. Hookups:
electric (30 amp), water, sewer.

Heber City

Currant Creek Campground, 2460 South Hwy. 40,
84032. T: (435) 654-0470. RV/tent: 99. $10.
Hookups: none.

Heber Valley RV Park Resort, 7000 North Hwy. 40,
84032. T: (435) 654-4049. F: (435) 654-5496.
RV/tent: 120. $20. Hookups: electric (20, 30, 50
amp), water, sewer.

High Country Inn & RV Park, 1000 South Main,
84032. T: (435) 654-0201 or (800) 345-9198.
RV/tent: 38. $20–$25. Hookups: electric (20, 30,
50 amp), water, sewer.

Jordenelle State Park - Hailstone Campground, SR
319, No. 515 Box 4, 84032. T: (435) 649-9540.
RV/tent: 186. $15–$17. Hookups: electric (20, 30,
50 amp), water, sewer.

Lodgepole Campground, 2460 South Hwy. 40,
84032. T: (435) 654-0470. RV/tent: 50. $7–$10.
Hookups: none.

Mill Hollow, 2460 South Hwy. 40, 84032. T: (435)
654-0470. RV/tent: 26. $7. Hookups: none.

Soldier Creek, 2460 South Hwy. 40, 84032. T: (435)
654-0470. RV/tent: 165. $10. Hookups: none.

Strawberry Bay, 2460 South Hwy. 40, 84032. T: (435)
654-0470. RV/tent: 357. $10. Hookups: none.

Huntington

Huntington State Park, P.O. Box 1343, 84528.
T: (435) 687-2491. RV/tent: 22. $13. Hookups:
none.

Millsite State Park, P.O. Box 1343, 84528. T: (435)
687-2491. RV/tent: 20. $13. Hookups: none.

Hurricane

The Canyons RV Resort, Box 331-2, 84737.
T: (435) 635-0200. RV/tent: 20. $15–$20.
Hookups: Electric (30, 50 amp), water, sewer.

Hyrum

Hyrum State Park, 405 West 300 South, 84319.
T: (435) 245-6866. RV/tent: 32. $12. Hookups: none.

Jensen

Bedrock Campground & RV Park, 9650 East 6000
South, 84035. T: (435) 781-6000 or (800) 852-
7336. RV/tent: 131. $12–$16. Hookups: electric
(20, 30, 50 amp), water, sewer.

Kamas

Beaver View Campground, 50 East Center, P.O. Box
68, 84036. T: (801) 783-4338. RV/tent: 8. $10.
Hookups: none.

Butterfly Lake Campground, 50 East Center, P.O.
Box 68, 84036. T: (801) 783-4338. RV/tent: 20. $7.
Hookups: none.

UTAH (continued)

Kamas (continued)

Christmas Meadows Campground, 50 East Center, P.O. Box 68, 84036. T: (801) 783-4338. RV/tent: 21. $10. Hookups: none.

Cobble Rest Campground, 50 East Center, P.O. Box 68, 84036. T: (801) 783-4338. RV/tent: 18. $10. Hookups: none.

Hayden Fork Campground, 50 East Center, P.O. Box 68, 84036. T: (801) 783-4338. RV/tent: 9. $10. Hookups: none.

Ledgefork Campground, 50 East Center, P.O. Box 68, 84036. T: (801) 783-4338. RV/tent: 73. $11. Hookups: none.

Lost Lake Campground, 50 East Center, P.O. Box 68, 84036. T: (801) 783-4338. RV/tent: 34. $10. Hookups: none.

Mirror Lake Campground, 50 East Center, P.O. Box 68, 84036. T: (801) 783-4338. RV/tent: 85. $11. Hookups: none.

Moose Horn Lake Campground, 50 East Center, P.O. Box 68, 84036. T: (801) 783-4338. RV/tent: 33. $9. Hookups: none.

Shady Dell Campground, 50 East Center, P.O. Box 68, 84036. T: (801) 783-4338. RV/tent: 20. $11. Hookups: none.

Shingle Creek Campground, 50 East Center, P.O. Box 68, 84036. T: (801) 783-4338. RV/tent: 21. $10. Hookups: none.

Smith and Moorehouse Campground, 50 East Center, P.O. Box 68, 84036. T: (801) 783-4338. RV/tent: 34. $13. Hookups: none.

Soapstone Campground, 50 East Center, P.O. Box 68, 84036. T: (801) 783-4338. RV/tent: 33. $11. Hookups: none.

Stillwater Campground, 50 East Center, P.O. Box 68, 84036. T: (801) 783-4338. RV/tent: 21. $10. Hookups: none.

Sulphur Campground, 50 East Center, P.O. Box 68, 84036. T: (801) 783-4338. RV/tent: 21. $10. Hookups: none.

Trial Lake Soapstone Campground, 50 East Center, P.O. Box 68, 84036. T: (801) 783-4338. RV/tent: 60. $11. Hookups: none.

Kanab

Hitchin' Post RV Park, 196 East 300 South, 84741. T: (435) 644-2142. RV/tent: 50. $12–$16. Hookups: water, electric (20, 30, 50 amp), sewer.

Kanab RV Corral, 483 South 100 East, 84741. T: (435) 644-5330 or (888) 818-5330. F: (435) 644-5464. rvcoral@xpressweb.com. RV/tent: 40. $17–$20. Hookups: water, electric (20, 30, 50 amp), sewer, phone (modem).

Kanarraville

Red Ledge RV Park & Campground, 15 North Main, 84742. T: (435) 586-9150. RV/tent: 22. $12–$19. Hookups: water, electric (30, 50 amp), sewer.

Leeds

Leeds RV Park & Motel, 97 South Valley Rd., 84746. T: (435) 673-2970. leedsrv@infowest.com. RV/tent: 59. $15. Hookups: water, electric (20, 30, 50 amp), sewer, phone (modem).

Loa

Bowery Campground, 138 South Main St., 84747. T: (801) 836-2811. RV/tent: 43. $9. Hookups: none.

Doctor Creek Campground, 138 South Main St., 84747. T: (801) 836-2811. RV/tent: 30. $9. Hookups: none.

Mackinaw Campground, 138 South Main St., 84747. T: (801) 836-2811. RV/tent: 68. $9. Hookups: none.

Piute Campground, 138 South Main St., 84747. T: (801) 836-2811. RV/tent: 48. $4. Hookups: none.

Logan

Box Elder Campground, 1500 East Hwy. 89, 84327. T: (435) 755-3620. RV/tent: 26. $6. Hookups: none.

Bridger Campground, 1500 East Hwy. 89, 84327. T: (435) 755-3620. RV/tent: 10. $9–$12. Hookups: none.

Guinavah-Malibu Campground, 1500 East Hwy. 89, 84327. T: (435) 755-3620. RV/tent: 40. $8. Hookups: none.

Lewis M. Turner Campground, 1500 East Hwy. 89, 84327. T: (435) 755-3620. RV/tent: 10. $8. Hookups: none.

Lodge Campground, 1500 East Hwy. 89, 84327. T: (435) 755-3620. RV/tent: 10. $7. Hookups: none.

LW's Phillips 66, 1936 North Main (US Hwy. 91), 84327. T: (435) 753-1025. RV/tent: 13. $15. Hookups: water, electric (20, 50 amp), sewer.

Pioneer Campground, 1500 East Hwy. 89, 84327. T: (435) 755-3620. RV/tent: 15. $6. Hookups: none.

Red Banks Campground, 1500 East Hwy. 89, 84327. T: (435) 755-3620. RV/tent: 12. $7. Hookup: none.

Riverside RV Park & Campground, 447 West 1700 South, 84327. T: (435) 245-4469. RV/tent: 14. $17–$19. Hookups: water, electric (20, 30 amp), sewer.

Spring Hollow Campground, 1500 East Hwy. 89, 84327. T: (435) 755-3620. RV/tent: 12. $8. Hookups: none.

Sunrise Campground, 1500 East Hwy. 89, 84327. T: (435) 755-3620 or (877) 444-6777. RV/tent: 27. $9–$12. Hookups: none.

UTAH (continued)

Logan (continued)

Tony Grove Lake, 1500 East Hwy. 89, 84327. T: (435) 755-3620. RV/tent: 36. $10. Hookups: none.

Traveland RV Park, 2020 South Hwy. 89-91, 84321. T: (435) 787-2060. F: (435) 787-4590. RV/tent: 52. $15–$22. Hookups: electric (20, 30, 50 amp), water, sewer.

Western Park Campground, 350 West 800 South, 84321. T: (435) 752-6424. RV/tent: 13. $17. Hookups: water, electric (20, 30 amp), sewer.

Manila

Antelope Flat Campground, P.O. Box 279, 84046. T: (801) 784-3448. RV/tent: 126. $9. Hookups: none.

Canyon Rim Campground, P.O. Box 279, 84046. T: (801) 784-3448. RV/tent: 19. $9. Hookups: none.

Deep Creek, P.O. Box 279, 84046. T: (801) 784-3448. RV/tent: 17. $9. Hookups: none.

Dripping Springs Campground, P.O. Box 279, 84046. T: (801) 784-3448. RV/tent: 25. $10. Hookups: none.

Firefighters Memorial Campground, P.O. Box 279, 84046. T: (801) 784-3448. RV/tent: 94. $11. Hookups: none.

Flaming Gorge KOA, P.O. Box 157, 84046. T: (435) 784-3184 or (800) 562-3254. RV/tent: 50. $17–$27. Hookups: electric (20, 30, 50 amp), water, sewer.

Greens Lake Campground, P.O. Box 279, 84046. T: (801) 784-3448. RV/tent: 20. $9. Hookups: none.

Lucerne Valley Campground, P.O. Box 279, 84046. T: (801) 784-3448. RV/tent: 147. $11. Hookups: none.

Mustang Ridge Campground, P.O. Box 279, 84046. T: (801) 784-3448. RV/tent: 73. $11. Hookups: none.

Skull Creek Campground, P.O. Box 279, 84046. T: (801) 784-3448. RV/tent: 17. $9. Hookups: none.

Spirit Lake Campground, P.O. Box 279, 84046. T: (801) 784-3448. RV/tent: 24. $6. Hookups: none.

Manti

Manti Campground & RV Park, 490 North 250 East, P.O. Box 126, 84642. T: (435) 835-2267. RV/tent: 71. $10–$19. Hookups: water, electric (20, 30 amp), sewer.

Mantua

Mountain Haven RV Park & Country Store, 130 North Main, 84324. T: (435) 723-1292. RV/tent: 57. $17. Hookups: electric (15 amp), water, sewer.

Midway

Deer Creek State Park, P.O. Box 257, 84049. T: (435) 654-0171. RV/tent: 35. $12. Hookups: none.

Moab

Devil's Canyon Campground, 2290 South West Resource Blvd., 84532. T: (435) 259-7155. RV/tent: 33. $6. Hookups: none.

Moab Valley RV & Campark, 1773 North Hwy. 191, 84532. T: (435) 259-4469. RV/tent: 128. $16–$24. Hookups: electric (20, 30, 50 amp), water, sewer.

O.K. RV Park & Canyonlands Stables, 3310 Spanish Valley Dr., 84532. T: (435) 259-1400. RV/tent: 45. $17–$20. Hookups: electric (20, 30, 50 amp), water, sewer.

Park Creek Campground & RV Park, Murphy Ln., 84532. T: (435) 259-2982. RV/tent: 48. $17–$20. Hookups: electric (20, 30 amp), water, sewer.

Price Canyon, 82 East Dogwood Rd., 84501. T: (435) 637-4584. RV/tent: 18. $6. Hookups: none.

Riverside Oasis RV Park, P.O. Box 412, 84532. T: (435) 259-3424. F: (435) 259-2305. www.moab:ut. com/riversideoasis. Rsoasis@lasal.net. RV/tent: 60. $20. Hookups: electric (20, 30, 50 amp), water, sewer, cable TV, phone (modem).

Slickrock Campground, 1301 1/2 North Hwy. 191, 84532. T: (435) 259-7660 or (800) 448-8873. www.slickrockcampground. RV/tent: 173. $16–$18. Hookups: electric (20, 30 amp), water, sewer, cable TV, phone (modem).

Spanish Trail RV Park & Campground, 2980 South Hwy. 191, 84532. T: (800) 787-2751. F: (435) 259-2710. RV/tent: 73. $24. Hookups: electric (20, 30, 50 amp), water, sewer, cable TV, phone (modem).

Morgan

East Canyon State Park, 5535 South Hwy. 66, 84050. T: (801) 829-6866. RV/tent: 59. $12. Hookups: none.

Mount Carmel

East Zion RV Park, Junction of US Hwy. 69 & State Hwy. 9, 84755. T: (435) 648-2326. RV/tent: 20. $15. Hookups: water, electric (30 amp), sewer.

Ogden

Anderson Cove, 507 25th St., suite 103, P.O. Box 1433, 84401. T: (801) 625-5112. RV/tent: 74. $8. Hookups: none.

Century RV Park & Campground, 1399 West 2100 South, 84401. T: (801) 731-3800. cp1399@aol. com. RV/tent: 168. $17–$23. Hookups: electric (20, 30, 50 amp), water, sewer, cable TV, phone (modem).

UTAH (continued)

Ogden (continued)

Maple Grove, 2501 Wall Ave., 84401. T: (435) 743-5721. RV/tent: 11. $5. Hookups: none.

Meadows Campground, 507 25th St., suite 103, 84401. T: (801) 625-5110. RV/tent: 26. $11. Hookups: none.

Monte Cristo Campground, 507 25th St., suite 103, 84401. T: (801) 625-5110. RV/tent: 47. $9. Hookups: none.

Oak Creek, 2501 Wall Ave., 84401. T: (435) 743-5721. RV/tent: 23. $5. Hookups: none.

Perception Park Campground, 507 25th St., suite 103, 84401. T: (801) 625-5110. RV/tent: 60. $11. Hookups: none.

Panguitch

Hitch-N-Post Campground, 420 North Main St., 84759. T: (435) 676-2436. RV/tent: 48. $15–$18. Hookups: electric (20, 30, 50 amp), water, sewer.

Kings Creek Campground, P.O. Box 80, 84759. T: (435) 676-8815. RV/tent: 38. $9. Hookups: none.

Panguitch Lake General Store, Gift Shop & RV Park, 53 West Hwy. 143, P.O. Box 688, 84759. T: (435) 676-2464. www.panguitchlake.net. RV/tent: 14. $22. Hookups: electric (20, 30 amp), water, sewer.

Panguitch Lake Resort, P.O. Box 567, 84759. T: (435) 676-2657. F: (435) 676-2000. www.panguitch lake.net. babe@colorcountry.net. RV/tent: 62. $23. Hookups: electric (20, 30 amp), water, sewer.

Paradise RV Park & Campground, 2153 North Hwy. 89, 84759. T: (435) 676-8348. F: (435) 676-8092. www.brycecanyonparadiserv.com. RV/tent: 67. $18. Hookups: electric (20, 30, 50 amp), water, sewer.

Park City

Hidden Haven Campground, 2200 Rasmussen Rd., 84098. T: (435) 649-8935 or (800) 553-8269. red-landsrvpark.com. RV/tent: 88. $15–$21. Hookups: electric (20, 30, 50 amp), water, sewer, cable TV, phone (modem).

Parowan

Sportsmen's Country RV Park & Restaurant, 492 North Main, P.O. Box 888, 84761. T: (435) 477-3714. RV/tent: 56. $10–$15. Hookups: electric (20, 30 amp), water, sewer, cable TV, phone (modem).

Peoa

Rockport State Park, 9040 North Hwy. 302, 84061. T: (435) 336-2241. RV/tent: 102. $8–$15. Hookups: electric (20, 30 amp), water, sewer.

Price

Budget Host Inn & RV Park, 145 North Carbonville Rd., 84501. T: (435) 637-2424. RV/tent: 40. $18–$20. Hookups: electric (20, 30, 50 amp), water, sewer.

Flat Canyon Campground, 599 West Price River Dr., 84501. T: (801) 637-2817. RV/tent: 12. $10. Hookups: none.

Price

Old Folks Flat Campground, 599 West Price River Dr., 84501. T: (801) 637-2817. RV/tent: 8. $10. Hookups: none.

Scofield State Park, P.O. Box 166, 84501. T: (435) 448-9449(summer) or (435) 637-2732(winter). RV/tent: 70. $11–$13. Hookups: none.

Provo

Granite Flat Campground, 88 West 100 North, 84601. T: (801) 342-5100. RV/tent: 32. $12. Hookups: none.

Hope Campground, 88 West 100 North, 84601. T: (801) 342-5100. RV/tent: 24. $6. Hookups: none.

Lakeside RV Campground, 4000 West Center, 84601. T: (801) 373-5267 or (800) 906-5267. www.lakesidervcampground.com. RV/tent: 145. $16–$21. Hookups: electric (20, 30 amp), water, sewer, phone (modem).

Little Mill Campground, 88 West 100 North, 84601. T: (801) 342-5100. RV/tent: 79. $6–$12. Hookups: none.

Mt. Timpanogos Campground, 88 West 100 North, 84601. T: (801) 342-5100. RV/tent: 27. $6–$12. Hookups: none.

Payson Lakes Campground, 88 West 100 North, 84601. T: (801) 342-5100. RV/tent: 88. $8. Hookups: none.

Provo KOA, 320 N . 2050 West, 84601. T: (801) 375-2994 or (800) 562-1894. F: (801) 375-1373. RV/tent: 95. $19–$27. Hookups: electric (20, 30 amp), water, sewer.

Timpooneke Campground, 88 West 100 North, 84601. T: (801) 342-5100. RV/tent: 32. $6–$12. Hookups: none.

Utah Lake State Park, 4400 West Center St., 84601. T: (801) 375-0731. RV/tent: 54. $11–$13. Hookups: none.

Richfield

JR Munchies Convenience Store, US Hwy. 89, 84701. T: (435) 896-9340. RV/tent: 21. $16. Hookups: electric (30, 50 amp), water, sewer.

UTAH (continued)

Richfield (continued)

KOA Richfield, 600 West 600 South, 84701.T: (435) 896-6674. RV/tent: 141. $18–$26. Hookups: electric (20, 30, 50 amp), water, sewer.

Roosevelt

Swift Creek Campground, 244 West Hwy. 40, 84066.T: (801) 722-5018. RV/tent: 13. $6. Hookups: none.

Yellowstone Campground, 244 West Hwy. 40, 84066.T: (801) 722-5018. RV/tent: 14. $6. Hookups: none.

Salina

Salina Creek RV Camp, State St., 84654.T: (435) 529-3711 or (888) 529-3711. RV/tent: 27. $16. Hookups: electric (20, 30, 50 amp), water, sewer.

Albion Basin Campground, 6944 South 300 East, 84121.T: (801) 943-1794. RV/tent: 24. $10. Hookups: none.

Big Bend Recreation Site, 324 South State St., 84145.T: (435) 259-6111. RV/tent: 22. $5. Hookups: none.

Bountiful Peak Campground, 6944 South 300 East, 84121.T: (801) 943-1794. RV/tent: 26. $10. Hookups: none.

Bridge Hollow Campground, 324 South State St., 84145.T: (435) 781-4400. RV/tent: 12. $5. Hookups: none.

Camp VIP Salt Lake City, 1400 West North Temple St., 84116.T: (801) 328-0224 or (800) 226-7752. F: (801) 355-1055. RV/tent: 413. $25–$29. Hookups: electric (20, 30, 50 amp), water, sewer, cable TV, phone (modem).

Deer Creek Campground, 324 South State St., 84145.T: (801) 539-4002. www.utso.ut.blm.gov. RV/tent: 7. $5. Hookups: none.

Oasis Campground (Little Sahara Recreation Area), 324 South State St., 84145.T: (435) 896-1551. www.utso.ut.blm.gov. RV/tent: 114. $6. Hookups: none.

Redman Campground, 6944 South 300 East, 84121. T: (801) 943-1794. RV/tent: 37. $12. Hookups: none.

Spruces Campground, 6944 South 300 East, 84121. T: (801) 943-1794. RV/tent: 86. $14. Hookups: none.

Sunset Campground, 6944 South 300 East, 84121. T: (801) 943-1794. RV/tent: 32. $10. Hookups: none.

Tanner's Flat Campground, 6944 South 300 East, 84121.T: (801) 943-1794. RV/tent: 36. $12. Hookups: none.

White Sands Campground (Little Sahara Recreation Area), 324 South State St., 84145.T: (435) 896-1551. www.utso.ut.blm.gov. RV/tent: 99. $6. Hookups: none.

Sandy

Ardell Brown's Quail Run RV Park, 9230 South State St., 84070.T: (801) 255-9300. rvpark@abrv. com. RV/tent: 69. $25. Hookups: electric (20, 30, 50 amp), water, sewer, cable TV, phone (modem).

Santa Clara

Gunlock State Park, P.O. Box 637, 84525.T: (435) 564-3633. RV/tent: 30. $8. Hookups: none.

Sevier

Fremont Indian State Park & Museum, 11550 West Clear Creek Canyon Rd., 84766.T: (435) 527-4631. RV/tent: 31. $10. Hookups: none.

Snowville

Lottie-Dell Campground, 490 West Main St Box 601, 84336.T: (435) 872-8273. RV/tent: 76. $18–$20. Hookups: electric (15, 20, 30 amp), water, sewer, phone (modem).

Springville

East Bay RV Park, 1750 West 1600 North, 84663. T: (801) 491-0700. F: (801) 491-0800. www.estbayrvpark.com. RV/tent: 230. $16–$22. Hookups: electric (20, 30, 50 amp), water, sewer, cable TV, phone (modem).

St. George

Baker Dam, 225 North Bluff, 84770.T: (435) 673-4654. RV/tent: 20. $6. Hookups: none.

McArthur's Temple View RV Resort, 975 South Main, 84770.T: (435) 673-6400 or (888) 255-2552. RV/tent: 266. $19–$27. Hookups: electric (20, 30, 50 amp), water, sewer, cable TV, phone (modem).

Redlands RV Park, 650 West Telegraph, 84770. T: (435) 673-9700 or (800) 553-8269. Redlandsrvpark.com. RV/tent: 200. $16–$22. Hookups: electric (20, 30, 50 amp), water, sewer, cable TV, phone (modem).

Settler's RV Park, 1333 East 100 South, 84790. T: (435) 628-1624 or (800) 628-2255. RV/tent: 175. $21. Hookups: electric (20, 30, 50 amp), water, sewer.

St. George RV Park & Campground, 2100 East Middleton Dr., 84770.T: (435) 673-2970. RV/tent: 135. $15–$25. Hookups: electric (20, 30 amp), water, sewer, cable TV, phone (modem).

UTAH (continued)

Teasdale

Oak Creek Campground, 138 East Main, P.O. Box 99, 84773. T: (435) 425-3702. RV/tent: 9. $10. Hookups: none.

Pleasant Creek Campground, 138 East Main, P.O. Box 99, 84773. T: (435) 425-3702. RV/tent: 19. $10. Hookups: none.

Single Tree Campground, 138 East Main, P.O. Box 99, 84773. T: (435) 425-3702 or (877) 444-6777. RV/tent: 33. $11. Hookups: none.

Ticaboo

Ticaboo Resort, Restaurant & Campground, Hwy. 276 Box 2110-T, 84533. T: (877) 842-2267. RV/tent: 22. $20–$30. Hookups: electric (30 amp), water, sewer.

Torrey

Sand Creek RV Park, Campground & Hostel, 540 Hwy. 24, P.O. Box 750276, 84775. T: (435) 425-3577 or (877) 425-3578. RV/tent: 24. $9, $15–$18. Hookups: electric (30, 50 amp), water, sewer.

Vernal

Dinosaurland KOA, 930 North Vernal Ave., 84078. T: (435) 789-2148. RV/tent: 110. $17–$22. Hookups: electric (20, 30, 50 amp), water, sewer, cable TV.

East Park, 353 N. Vernal Ave., 84078. T: (801) 789-1181. RV/tent: 21. $8. Hookups: none.

Fossil Valley RV Park, 999 West Hwy. 40, 84078. T: (435) 789-6450. RV/tent: 34. $17–$20. Hookups: electric (30, 50 amp), water, sewer.

Lodgepole Springs Campground, 353 North Vernal Ave., 84078. T: (801) 789-1181. RV/tent: 35. $8. Hookups: none.

Oaks Park, 353 N. Vernal Ave., 84078. T: (801) 789-1181. RV/tent: 11. $8. Hookups: none.

Red Fleet State Park, 8750 North Hwy. 191, 84078. T: (435) 789-4432. F: (435) 789-4475. RV/tent: 39. $10. Hookups: none.

Steinaker State Park, 4355 North Hwy. 191, 84078. T: (435) 789-4432. F: (435) 789-4475. RV/tent: 31. $10. Hookups: none.

Wellington

Mountain View RV Park, 50 South 700 East, 84542. T: (435) 637-7980. RV/tent: 24. $17. Hookups: water, electric (20, 30 amp), sewer

Index

California

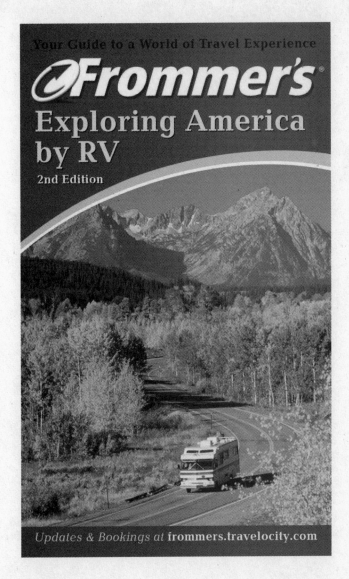